The Peoples of the Caribbean

The Peoples of the Caribbean

An Encyclopedia of Archaeology and Traditional Culture

Nicholas J. Saunders

A B C 🟢 C L I O

Santa Barbara, California   Denver, Colorado   Oxford, England

Library of Congress Cataloging-in-Publication Data
Saunders, Nicholas J.
The peoples of the Caribbean: An encyclopedia of Caribbean archaeology and traditional culture / Nicholas J. Saunders.
     p.   cm.
   Includes bibliographical references and index.
   ISBN 1-57607-701-2 (hardcover : alk. paper)—ISBN 1-57607-702-0 (e-book)
   1. Indians of the West Indies—Antiquities—Encyclopedias.   2. Indians of the West Indies—History—Encyclopedias.   3. Indians of the West Indies—Social life and customs—Encyclopedias.   4. Caribbean Area—Antiquities—Encyclopedias.   5. Caribbean Area—History—Encyclopedias.   6. Caribbean Area—Social life and customs—Encyclopedias.
I. Title.

F1619.S38   2005
972.900497'0729—dc22   2005029606

08   07   06   05   10 9 8 7 6 5 4 3 2 1

This book is also available on the World Wide Web as an e-book. Visit http://www.abc-clio.com for details.

ABC-CLIO, Inc.
130 Cremona Drive, P.O. Box 1911
Santa Barbara, California 93116-1911

This book is printed on acid-free paper.

Manufactured in the United States of America

Contents

Introduction, ix
Map of the Lesser Antilles, xxiii
Map of the Caribbean, xxiv

Accompong, 1
Aesthetic of Brilliance, 2
Agouti, 3
Agüeybana (Taíno chief), 3
Amazons, 3
Anacaona (Taíno queen), 6
Anegada (BVI), 7
Anguilla, 7
Anse Des Pères (site, St. Martin), 9
Antigua, 10
Arauquinoid (pottery), 12
Archaic Period, 13
Areíto, 16
Aruba, 17
Atajadizo, 18

Balboa, Vasco Núñez de, 21
Ball-Game, 22
Banwari Trace (site, Trinidad), 24
Barbados, 25
Barrancoid, 27
Behechio (Taíno chief), 28
Betty's Hope (site, Antigua), 29
Birds, 31
Black Legend, 32
Bonaire, 33
Breton, Father Raymond, 34

Cacao, 37
Caguana/Capá (site, Puerto Rico), 38
Caimito, El, 40

Caonabo (Taíno chief), 41
Carib Territory/Waitukubuli Karifuna
        Community (Dominica), 41
Caribs, 44
Carnival (Trinidad), 52
Casimiroid, 55
Cassava (manioc), 56
Cayman Islands, 59
Cayo (pottery), 61
Cedros (site, Trinidad), 62
Chancery Lane (site, Barbados), 62
Chichén Itzá Cenote (site, Mexico), 63
Clifton Plantation, 65
Cocoa Panyols, 65
Cohoba, 66
Columbus, Christopher, 67
Conch, 79
Coralie (site, Turks and Caicos), 80
Cozumel, 80
Creole/Creolization, 82
Crocodile, 83
Cuba, 84
Cuna, 86
Curaçao, 89

Dabajuroid, 91
Darién (Panama), 92
Disease, 93
Dogs, 95
Dominica, 96
Dominican Republic, 99

Drake Manuscript, 101
Drax Hall (site, Jamaica), 101
Dudley, Sir Robert, 104
Duhos, 104

El Dorado, 107
Elenan, 108
Encomienda, 109

Galways Plantation, 111
Garifuna (Black Caribs), 112
Gold, 114
Golden Rock (site, St. Eustatius), 115
Great Inagua Island, 116
Grenada, 117
Guacanagarí (Taíno chief), 119
Guadeloupe, 120
Guanahatabey, 122
Guarionex (Taíno chief), 124
Guayabitoid (pottery), 125

Hacienda Grande, 127
Haiti, 128
Heywoods (site, Barbados), 130
Hillcrest (site, Barbados), 131
Historical Archaeology, 131
Hope Estate (site, St. Martin), 137
Hueca, La (Puerto Rico), 138

Igneri, 141
Indian Creek (site, Antigua), 141
Indian Warner, 142

Jamaica, 145
Jolly Beach (site, Antigua), 147
Jolly John, 147

Kalinago/Kalina, 149
Key Marco (site, Florida, USA), 149
Krum Bay (site, St. Thomas), 150

La Aleta (site, Dominican Republic), 153

La Isabela (site, Dominican Republic), 154
La Navidad/En Bas Saline (site, Haiti), 157
La Sorcé (site, Vieques, Puerto Rico), 158
Landfall, Columbus's First, 159
Languages, 160
Las Casas, Bartolomé de, 162
Los Buchillones (site, Cuba), 165
Los Roques Islands (Venezuela), 166
Lovers' Retreat (site, Tobago), 167
Lucayans, 168

Maisabel (site, Puerto Rico), 171
Maize, 172
Margarita Island (Venezuela), 173
Maroons, 174
Martinique, 179
Martyr, Peter, 181
Maya, 182
Mayoid (pottery), 186
Meillacan, 186
Miskito, 187
Molasses Reef Wreck, 188
Montserrat, 189
Music, 190

Nanny Town (site, Jamaica), 197
Nelson's Dockyard (Antigua), 198
New Seville (site, Jamaica), 199
Newton Plantation (Barbados), 200
Norman Estate (site, St. Martin), 201
Nuestra Señora de Atocha, Wreck of, 202
Nuestra Señora de la Concepción, Wreck of, 203
Nuestra Señora de las Maravillas, Wreck of, 204

Obeah, 207
Orisha/Shango (Trinidad), 209
Ortoiroid, 211

Osoid, 212
Ostionoid, 212
Oviedo y Valdés, Gonzalo Fernández de, 213

Palmetto, 215
Palo Seco (site, Trinidad), 216
Pané, Father Ramón, 216
Paradise Park (site, Jamaica), 218
Pearls (gems), 218
Pearls (site, Grenada), 220
Pepper Pot, 221
Pitch Lake (site, Trinidad), 221
Port Royal (Jamaica), 223
Puerto Real (site, Haiti), 225
Puerto Rico, 227

Ralegh, Sir Walter, 231
Rastafarianism, 232
Ronquinan, 236

Saladoid, 239
Salt River (site, St. Croix), 240
Santa Rosa Carib Community (Arima, Trinidad), 241
Santería, 245
Shamanism, 248
Silver Sands (site, Barbados), 251
Sint Maarten/Saint-Martin, 252
Slavery, 253
St. Croix (USVI), 256
St. Eustatius, 258
St. John (USVI), 259

St. Kitts and Nevis, 260
St. Lucia, 262
St. Thomas (USVI), 264
St. Vincent and the Grenadines, 265
Suazey/Suazoid, 267
Sugar, 268

Taíno (Arawak), 271
Tancah (site, Mexico), 280
Tanki Flip (site, Aruba), 282
Ten Sail, Wreck of the, 283
Tobacco, 284
Tordesillas (Treaty of), 286
Tortola (BVI), 286
Toussaint L'Ouverture, 288
Trees, Spiritual Importance of, 288
Trinidad and Tobago, 290
Troumassoid, 297
Tulum (site, Mexico), 298
Turks and Caicos, 300
Turtles, 301

Underwater Archaeology, 303

Vespucci, Amerigo, 311
Vodoun, 312

Warao, 317
Water Island (USVI), 319
White-on-Red Pottery (W-O-R), 319

Zemís, 321
Zic Pottery, 325

Bibliography, 327
Index, 387
About the Author, 399

Introduction

The Caribbean is a string of islands stretching from Trinidad, in the south, northward in an arc through Puerto Rico westward to Cuba. Although every island is distinct, from the lush, forest-clad mountains of Dominica to low, flat, beachy Antigua, the region is generally divided between the smaller islands of the eastern Caribbean, the Lesser Antilles, and the larger more northerly ones, the Greater Antilles.

Geologically, the Caribbean is part of a tectonic plate that includes Central America and is creeping slowly westward at about 4 cm a year. Many Caribbean islands lie on the active boundary of this plate, and on its easternmost edge, where it confronts the North American and South American plates, the point of contact is a subduction zone that creates active volcanoes such as La Soufrière on St. Vincent and Mont Pelée on Martinique. Some areas, such as Barbados and northern Jamaica, are rising while others, such as the Bahamas and Antigua, are gently submerging. This mosaic of natural environments supports an array of fauna and flora that offered a wide variety of homes to the region's native inhabitants.

These peoples did not originate in the Caribbean but arrived from South America and possibly also Mesoamerica (probably Mexico's Yucatán region) by seagoing canoe sometime between 5,000 and 4,000 B.C. The sole exception seems to have been Trinidad, which at this time was still attached to the South American mainland. Its first human inhabitants could have walked across and later been cut off by a rise in sea level. Adapting to the endless variety of natural landscapes, the Caribbean's prehistoric peoples developed rich and varied cultures that owed much to their mainland origins yet were also finely tuned to their distinctively Caribbean surroundings.

Geographical reality imposed constraints and offered opportunities to the region's indigenous peoples. Many islands were resource poor, while others had an abundance. Some, such as Cuba and Hispaniola (modern-day Haiti and Dominican Republic), had expanses of fertile agricultural land, while others such as Antigua compensated with rich supplies of flint used by prehistoric peoples to make their tools. In such a varied region, canoe travel linked the islands, facilitated by ocean currents and the fact that most islands are visible one to another. The practical aspects of living in this extended archipelago shaped many of the essential features of indigenous life in the Caribbean.

In typical Amerindian fashion, physical landscapes were prototypes for symbolic landscapes and the kinds of sacred beings that inhabited them. Gods, spirits, and ancestral beings embodied the elemental forces of the natural world, from hurricane winds to earthquakes, from volcanic eruptions to eclipses of the sun and moon. Such forces were ever-present in the trees, birds, animals, and physical features of the Caribbean world, whether mountain peaks, coral lagoons, vents of sulfurous smoke, or the deep and dark sinkholes that are a feature of some islands.

The Caribbean was, and remains, defined by its extraordinary maritime geography—a unique physical reality that inspired Amerindian, European, and African peoples to create their own historically distinctive cultures within its varied landscapes. Today innumerable tourists journey to a paradise of palm-fringed beaches and azure seas. The archaeology and traditional cultures of the Caribbean illustrate a crucial aspect of being human—we inherit the world from Nature but then endlessly remake it in our imaginations.

First Encounter

On 3 August 1492, Christopher Columbus set sail from Palos on Spain's Atlantic coast with three ships—the *Santa Maria, Niña,* and *Pinta.* Columbus sailed west, expecting to find a shortcut to the spice-rich Orient, for which reason he had brought along a Jewish linguist who spoke Chaldean and Arabic as well as Hebrew. After a brief sojourn in the Canary Islands, the little fleet set sail again on 6 September, running before the northeast trade winds that blew westward from Africa.

At 2 A.M. on Friday, 10 October, land was sighted, and when the sun rose, Columbus waded ashore to take possession of the island for King Ferdinand and Queen Isabella of Spain. He christened it San Salvador, though he later learned that its native name was Guanahaní. Columbus noticed the shiny gold ornaments the natives wore in their noses, and though neither the Spanish nor the natives could speak each other's language, he endeavored to discover the source of the precious metal. He then made a move that established an enduring tradition of such meetings by offering glass beads in exchange for food, water, information, and local goods. Such were the first maneuvers in one of the most momentous chains of events in history.

Columbus noted the timid nature of the natives and believed that they would be easy to enslave and convert to Christianity. To illustrate his point, he abducted seven of the Amerindians to take back to Spain. On leaving San Salvador, the three Spanish ships cruised the Bahamas, hearing rumors of a gold-rich island called Cipangu. On 28 October, Columbus believed he had finally reached Cathay (China), although in fact he was off the coast of Cuba. Expeditions inland proved fruitless, and by 5 December, he was offshore of the island known to its Taíno (Arawak) inhabitants as Bohío, which he named La Española (i.e., Hispaniola—modern-day Haiti and Dominican Republic).

Disaster struck as he was sailing along Hispaniola's northern coast. The *Santa Maria* ran aground, and only the timely help of the local Taíno chief Guacanagarí enabled the Spanish to salvage their valuables from Columbus's wrecked flagship. In meetings between the two leaders, Columbus repeated his previous act of exchanging low-value European goods for Amerindian gold jewelry. Conversations, such as they were, soon came around again to the source of the precious metal, and Columbus was heartened to learn that there was a gold-rich land known as Cibao in the center of the island.

Ever the opportunist, Columbus made a virtue of necessity. His two remaining ships could not transport all his men back to Spain, and so he decided to build La Navidad, the first European settlement in the Americas. The thirty-eight men whom, of necessity, he left behind, would find and collect gold as they awaited his return. And so, on 16 January 1493, the *Niña* and *Pinta* set sail for Spain with the momentous news.

Such are the bare bones of this first encounter between Europeans and the indigenous peoples of the Americas. Yet, they conceal far more than they reveal. In the real-life experiences framed by these events lay hidden worlds of meaning that would shape the European experience of the Americas and change history for ever. Columbus's accidental discovery of the Americas was full of irony, not least of which was the intersection, overlaying, and mutual incomprehensibility of Amerindian and European worldviews. In the Caribbean itself, there was an immediate confusion of real and imagined landscapes, illustrated by Columbus's belief that he had reached the East Indies and his consequent labeling of the native peoples as "Indians"—a term still used after five hundred years.

Columbus also took with him the intellectual baggage of late-medieval Europe, much of it derived from classical antiquity, which posited the existence of strange and foreign places inhabited by equally exotic creatures such as Amazons and cannibals. These notions represented the polar opposites of European social and moral norms. Amazon societies were controlled by women, and cannibals were people whose habit of eating human flesh was the antithesis of civilized Christian behavior. Amerindians walked about naked, and, even worse, appeared to be unashamed of the fact, in defiance of biblical tradition.

Columbus, and those who traveled in his wake, heard rumors of monsters—people without heads, with only one eye, or who spent their lives carrying trees around. Ideas from medieval alchemy also came into play, such as the belief that gold was produced by warm climates. At first the Caribbean, and then Middle and South America, along with their inhabitants, were understood as definitively "other," mythical landscapes and peoples constructed in European minds into which Columbus's discoveries were forced, as if into a straitjacket.

Apart from these preconceptions and misconceptions, there were problems of translation and interpretation. Columbus quickly classified the Taíno as peaceful and the Carib as warlike. From the outset, the cultural geography of the Caribbean was drafted by Europeans in terms of docile, cooperative but simple-minded Indians and savage, warlike, and troublesome subhuman cannibals. The richly varied and endlessly fascinating complexity of Caribbean Amerindian peoples was thus reduced almost immediately to bizarre stereotypes—a typical outsider's view that is still taught in many of the region's schools.

In fact, Columbus's first voyage brought him stumbling not into a world of savagery but rather into a sophisticated universe where mythology had the force of history and where humans, animals, plants, and even the weather were endlessly connected to the powerful spirit forces of ancestors and gods.

When the Taíno of Hispaniola and Puerto Rico first met the Spanish, they recognized a powerful ally against their Carib enemies, whom they accused of eating their men and stealing their women. These accusations appeared to be supported by Columbus's subsequent experiences in Dominica and Guadeloupe, where he rescued captured Taíno women and encountered human bones hanging inside Carib houses. The Spanish misunderstood these traditional Amerindian customs of respect for the dead and humiliation of defeated enemies. These customs included the ritual display of human bones, the tasting of small strips of flesh, and the drinking of manioc beer mixed with powdered human bone.

This apparent evidence of bestial behavior clearly suited the desire of Columbus and his successors to justify continued attacks on and enslavement of the Caribs. "Carib" and "cannibal" quickly became synonymous, with the term "cannibalism" replacing the older Greek word "anthropophagy" as a universal term for the "ultimate crime" of consuming human flesh. It was another irony that the region would soon come to be known as the Caribbean.

Such were some of the complex issues that enveloped Columbus's first encounter with the native peoples of the Caribbean and that helped shape the idea of the Americas in the European imagination. But what of the people themselves? Who were they? Where did they come from? And when?

The Prehistoric Caribbean

The islands of the Caribbean offered a bewildering variety of landscapes and resources to early prehistoric peoples. The diversity of their interactions with local environments led to different kinds of lifeways, dwellings, and material culture that are often difficult for archaeologists to interpret. Once consequence has been different ways of classifying cultural remains and of trying to build an overall picture of cultural development from the scattered, fragmentary, and often ambiguous evidence.

The earliest Caribbean peoples belonged to the so-called Archaic Period and appeared around 5500 B.C. at the sites of Banwari Trace and St. John Oropuche in Trinidad, opposite the South American mainland. They were hunters, fishers, and gatherers who lived a transient existence, probably in small family groups. They did not make or use pottery but did have spears tipped with bone, roughly shaped stone tools, and manos and metates for grinding. From their archaeological remains, it appears that they gathered vast quantities of shellfish, whose empty shells they discarded onto huge heaps known today as shell middens. These sites are typically located near mangrove swamps and beaches.

The earliest evidence for the human occupation of Cuba, far to the north, dates to a slightly later time, somewhere around 4000 B.C.. Sites such as Seboruco are often rock shelters or caves, with flaked-stone tools scattered on the floor. Some sites are thought to date back even earlier, possibly to 6000 B.C. However, around 2000 B.C., these early preceramic sites become more frequent and are divided into a number of different, and not universally accepted, subdivisions of the Archaic Period. Examples include Painted Cave in Cuba, Barrera-Mordan in the Dominican Republic, and Caño Hondo and Angostura in Puerto Rico, the latter site including human burials. Some sites, such as Cayo Redondo on

Cuba, had a long life, spanning the period 2000 B.C. to A.D. 1300, and include shell middens and painted caves. On Antigua, the site of Jolly Beach flourished around 1800 B.C. as a workshop area where stone flakes were struck from the abundant local pebbles. Similarly, at Hope Estate on St. Martin, flint flakes and shell artifacts have been dated to between 2350 and 1800 B.C. On St. Thomas, the site of Krum Bay has yielded stone tools and jewelry made from bone and shell between 880 B.C. and 225 B.C.

Making archaeological sense of these early sites continues to be problematic. Some sites that lack pottery have been called preceramic and assigned to the Archaic Period rather than more accurately being called aceramic and thus potentially of a much later date. The most notorious problem has arguably been identifying the first preceramic inhabitants of Cuba. These people, called the Ciboney, lived in caves with lifeways defined by simple stone tools. They were assumed to be the ancestors of the "primitive" Guanahatabey people who occupied the same area when Europeans arrived. The thorny question remains whether the Guanahatabeys should be considered a surviving relic of the Archaic Period surrounded by more sophisticated pottery-using peoples or a creation resulting from our inability to make sense of a patchy archaeological record.

Somewhere between 500 and 200 B.C., a new and different kind of people arrived in the Caribbean. These were the pottery-using, village-dwelling Saladoid people who had left their South American homeland for Trinidad and then sailed north in seagoing canoes to colonize the Greater Antilles. Their arrival isolated, marginalized, and possibly absorbed the earlier hunter-gatherers of the Archaic Period.

The Saladoid peoples originated from the mouth of the Orinoco River in Venezuela and brought with them a settled village life, agriculture, and a shamanic religion typical of tropical rainforest societies in lowland Amazonia. They grew manioc, sweet potato, cotton, and tobacco and introduced pottery making in the form of distinctive white-on-red decorated ceramics that take their name—Saladoid—from the type-site of Saladero in Venezuela. Their stone tools were more varied and efficient than those of their predecessors, and they were able to fell larger trees and clear more extensive areas for their fields and villages.

By about A.D. 300, Saladoid peoples had spread throughout the Caribbean, and most islands probably had some variation of Saladoid culture. The sea continued to play an important role in everyday and spiritual life, as canoe travel connected the islands with each other and also with mainland South America. For the Saladoid and later periods, there is a strong argument for looking at the islands and South America as an integrated unit—an "interaction sphere" of diverse but connected peoples and landscapes rather than the separate political entities they became after Europeans arrived.

Saladoid cultures eventually developed, in different ways on different islands, into what archaeologists call the Ostionoid cultural tradition, named after the Ostiones culture on Hispaniola (ca. A.D. 500). Local developments of the Ostionoid tradition are known as Meillacan in Hispaniola, Cuba, and Jamaica; Elenan in the Leeward and Virgin Islands; and Palmetto in the Bahamas. On Hispaniola, local developments led, by around A.D. 1200, to the Chican Ostionoid culture—the name given by archaeologists to the remains of the Taíno peoples first encountered by Columbus in 1492.

The Taíno, like their Saladoid predecessors, lived a settled village life and practiced agriculture, supplementing their main food crops of manioc, maize, and sweet potatoes with guava, papaya, pineapple, and tobacco. They grew cotton from which they manufactured clothing; collected clams, oysters, and crabs; and hunted birds, snakes, manatees, and sea turtles. Their arts and crafts included body painting, earrings, nose ornaments, lip plugs, and colorful feather headdresses. Carved stone beads and ornaments known as *çibas* were worn with gold ornaments that were in fact usually the gold-copper-silver alloy known as *guanín*.

The Taíno were expert woodworkers and carved the distinctive ceremonial stools known as *duhos.* These were used by shamans *(behiques)* and chiefs (caciques) to connect them to supernatural powers and were often decorated with shell or guanín. The Taíno built large, elaborate canoes, traveling regularly between islands and maintaining a network of trade relationships. Many of their sophisticated guanín items were obtained in down-the-line maritime trade between islands from their original source in South America. Regarded as high-class items, these objects embodied supernatural power and as such were ceremonially exchanged by Taíno chiefs. It is no surprise that such valuable items were among those offered to Columbus in 1492 by Chief Guacanagarí on Hispaniola.

Taíno society was ruled by hereditary chiefs, with status inherited through the mother's line. Consequently, high-born women had great status in Taíno society. Chiefs could have as many as thirty wives, suggesting that many marriages were little more than opportunistic political alliances. This tight organization of society is reflected in the size and sophistication of Taíno villages. The larger ones could have hundreds of communal houses occupied by extended families. They were arranged around a central plaza, which was used for social and religious events such as ceremonial dances called *areítos* and ball games known as *batey.* The chief's house, or *caney,* was the largest of all and served as a council house for the community.

The religion of the Taíno was based on the shamanic tradition inherited from their Saladoid ancestors. They saw plants, animals, and landscapes as infused with spirit force derived from the ancestors and the natural world. It was the Taíno chiefs and shamans who controlled the forces of life and death through a philosophy founded on analogical symbolic reasoning. In such a spiritually animated universe, all things possessed sacred and secular importance.

The main focus of religion was the veneration of gods and spirits known as *zemís* whose supernatural powers were embodied in sacred images—that is, three-dimensional objects fashioned from stone, bone, wood, shell, clay, and cotton, sometimes in combination. Yúcahu was one of several major Taíno gods—an invisible lord of fertility and "spirit of cassava." His female counterpart was Atabey, "Mother of Waters," who was associated with rivers and the rain needed to fertilize the cassava crops. She was also responsible for women's fertility and childbirth. With these deities and others, the Taíno symbolized their intimate relationship with the natural forces that shaped the world.

This relationship was enshrined in myths that emphasized the idea of metamorphosis. Mythic hero figures had superhuman animal strength, and animals possessed human qualities. Some animals were tribal ancestors, some trees the spirits of dead chiefs. Taíno myths accounted for the origins of the world and of women and tobacco. One myth told how women were created when woodpeckers pecked a hole in strange, sexless creatures, where female sexual parts are now located.

Although the evidence for warfare in Taíno society is ambiguous, battles undoubtedly took place between different chiefdoms to resolve disputes. Nevertheless, it was the Carib peoples of the Lesser Antilles to the east and south who were the common enemy because they raided Taíno islands mainly for marriageable women. Whether or not such accusations were true, the Taíno initially saw the Spanish as powerful potential allies against the traditional foe.

The Caribs, unlike the Taíno, were late arrivals in the Caribbean. They sailed large seagoing canoes from South America perhaps around A.D. 1400 and began colonizing the Lesser Antilles, especially Dominica, Martinique, St. Vincent, and Guadeloupe. They maintained close trading relationships with their mainland cousins up to and beyond the period of European colonization.

Carib society was primarily agricultural, though not as intensive as that of the Taíno. They grew and consumed manioc, making it into cassava bread, and also ate a stew known as pepper pot. These were supplemented by sweet potatoes, yams, beans, and tobacco. Fishing was also important, and the Carib used nets, hooks, and harpoons to catch fish. They also collected shellfish and hunted sea turtles and the agouti *(Dasyprocta aguti),* which had been introduced from South America.

Carib society was less hierarchical and sophisticated than that of the Taíno. There were no major chiefs, though each village had its own headman. Wider alliances seem to have formed only during war, at which time outstanding war leaders exercised temporary authority. Carib villages were small and focused on the men's house, or *carbet,* which also served as the communal meeting place within which a special men-only language was spoken.

Carib arts and crafts were also basic when compared to those of the Taíno. Their pottery was undecorated, though basketry was highly prized, and cotton weaving was practiced to make hammocks and jewelry. Their canoes were especially valued due to the economic importance of long-distance maritime trade, which itself provided luxury items from South America such as the *caracoli,* a crescent-shaped guanín object worn as jewelry.

As with the Taíno, Carib religion followed the shamanic traditions of South America, where plants, animals, and landscapes were infused with the spirituality of ancestors and nature. There were few recognizable gods and no evidence of the elaborate zemí figures of the Taíno. Nevertheless, they made and wore figurines of stone and wood to protect against evil spirits known as *mabouya* and to decorate their war clubs and canoes. Good spirits were called *akamboue,* and each Carib was believed to have their own guardian spirit. Zoomorphic and geometric designs of these supernatural beings were carved as petroglyphs on boulders and rockfaces throughout the Carib region.

Carib culture is dramatically and endlessly misrepresented by the emphasis on cannibalism. Taíno accusations to Columbus of Carib cannibalism became a defining feature of savage behavior by indigenous Caribbean peoples. As noted before, so dominant did this image become that the terms "cannibal" and "cannibalism," themselves derived from the name "Carib," replaced the previous Greek term "anthropophagy" to describe the eating of human flesh.

Unlike the Taíno, the Caribs survived well into the European period in the Caribbean, but it was not until the seventeenth century that French missionaries in Dominica, Guadeloupe, and Martinique began to observe and record Carib cultural traditions. The most influential of these missionaries was the Dominican Father Raymond Guillaume Breton, the "Apostle to the Caribs." Carib society as we know it today is in many respects a seventeenth-century creation and is clearly entangled with European propaganda and misunderstandings, and further confused by the comparatively little archaeological research that has been carried out to date.

The prehistoric Caribbean was a region of unique cultural development and diversity— as much a mosaic of peoples and places as it was to become after the arrival of Europeans.

Conquest and Colonization

The Spanish colonization of the Greater Antilles quickly followed in the wake of Columbus's first voyage. It had dramatic effects on the cultural and physical landscapes of the region. Although poor in gold (compared with Aztec Mexico or Inca Peru), the larger islands were rich in natural resources. The land itself was often fertile, and, at least initially, indigenous human resources were plentiful.

Despite the early help extended to them, the Spanish brutally subdued the Taíno, treating them virtually as slaves in the notorious *encomienda* system, where they were forced to work the land with little food and no pay. Ravaged increasingly by diseases against which they had little or no immunity, disenfranchised from their land and traditional forms of agriculture, and embroiled in conflicts between competing European powers, the Taíno, and later the Caribs, were virtually extinguished. With them died the physical and symbolic landscapes that they and their predecessors had constructed over at least two thousand years, and which archaeologists today are painstakingly attempting to reconstruct and understand.

In the early years of conquest and colonization, the Taíno had close relationships with the Spanish. On Hispaniola, Columbus established the first European settlement in the Americas when he ordered the building of La Navidad near the village of the Taíno chief Guacaganarí. On his return, one reaction to discovering that his men had been killed and La Navidad burned was the founding of La Isabela in January 1494. It was here that important interactions between the native peoples and Europeans took place.

Columbus built a fortified house and watchtower and a church in whose cemetery archaeologists have found the remains of Europeans and the local Taínos. Disease, food shortages, and the general unpreparedness of the settlers doomed the town, however. The local Taínos, abused and mistreated, fled the area, exacerbating the food-supply situation, and in 1497 La Isabela was abandoned. The focus of Spanish administration then became Santo Domingo on the island's south coast.

There followed a long and disastrous sequence of events that saw revolts among the Spanish themselves and the continued abuse of the Taíno to such an extent that their numbers declined and they ceased to be a recognizable cultural entity. Part of this process is visible at the town of Puerto Real, established in 1503 by the Spanish governor Nicolás de Ovando as part of his attempts to pacify the Taíno. Ironically, it was established over the remains of a prehistoric Amerindian village. Working the gold and copper mines, the Taíno population began to decline, and for a time the town became the center of local slave raids to the Bahamas in search of indigenous Lucayan replacements. By 1576, Amerindians had virtually disappeared and had been replaced by some 30,000 imported African slaves.

Archaeological investigations at Puerto Real provided the opportunity to understand colonialism and the rise of Hispanic-American culture. For example, historical sources record that the Spanish took Taíno women for slaves or concubines, and archaeological evidence indicates that these women continued using (perhaps making) indigenous forms of local pottery for domestic purposes. As the town's Taíno inhabitants died out, they were replaced by African slaves who brought with them their own pottery-making traditions.

Similar events took place throughout the Caribbean during this period. On the north coast of Jamaica, the Spanish built the settlement of New Seville in 1509 next to a Taíno village. In Cuba, Puerto Rico, the Lesser Antilles, and down to Trinidad, indigenous settlements were variously destroyed, assimilated, or replaced by new towns established by the Spanish, French, English, and Dutch.

In Cuba, Columbus's first encounter in October 1492 was followed in 1511 by a vicious and bloody conquest by the Spanish conquistador Diego de Velázquez. So violent was the subjugation of the island and the treatment of its indigenous inhabitants that the chronicler and churchman Bartolomé de las Casas was moved to give up his own encomienda, petition King Ferdinand of Spain to abolish the institution, and document the atrocities in his *A Short Account of the Destruction of the Indies,* published in 1552.

In Trinidad, in the wake of Columbus's first landfall there in 1498, the Englishmen Sir Robert Dudley and Sir Walter Ralegh commented on the strange phenomenon of Pitch Lake and its value for calking their ships. In 1592, when the Spanish took formal possession of the island, it had a multiethnic Amerindian population of perhaps 50,000, but a century later only about 4,000 were left. These survivors were eventually gathered together by Capuchin missionaries in mission villages such as Mayo, where today the remains of an Amerindian village lie beneath the concrete foundations of a recently rebuilt church.

At the same time that these seemingly endless tragedies were befalling the region's indigenous peoples, the Caribbean became increasingly entangled in disputes between the competing European powers. In the Lesser Antilles especially, the local Carib peoples, sometimes with escaped African slaves, were dragged into alliances, wars, and atrocities between the French and English.

European-style settlements, albeit with a distinctive Caribbean nature, also appeared at this time and are now investigated by historical archaeologists and valued as cultural heritage and tourist attractions. On Jamaica's south coast, the town of Port Royal developed rapidly after 1655, becoming an infamous haunt of pirates and privateers. It soon became the most important English port in the Americas. It came to a dramatic end when it collapsed into the sea during an earthquake in 1692. Today, streets and houses still survive beneath the waves, and underwater archaeologists have retrieved cutlery and pewter plates from the site whose makers they have been able to identify using historical documents.

In a variety of ways, and for many different reasons, the Taíno, Carib, and other Amerindian peoples of the Island Caribbean and its adjacent mainland areas of Mesoamerica and South America suffered at the hands of Europeans. The first tragedy of the Caribbean—the extinction of its aboriginal inhabitants—was a rapid and calamitous event, especially in the Greater Antilles. Nevertheless, it was only the beginning and was soon followed by an even more momentous sequence of events that was itself produced by the virtual elimination of the Amerindians.

Slavery, Plantations, and Afro-Caribbean Culture

As the Amerindian world disappeared, another came into being—one so alien and cataclysmic that its legacy still shapes the Caribbean today. This was the world of the European plantation system—the engine that drove slavery, created a new Afro-Caribbean culture, and left an indelible mark on the archaeological record. The physical remains of this momentous era are today investigated by historical archaeology, a multidisciplinary endeavour that combines archaeological techniques, historical methods, and textual evidence. Historical archaeology is regarded by some as the archaeology of the capitalist transformation of the world.

During the sixteenth century, the labor shortage created by the collapse of the Amerindian population led to the importation of increasing numbers of African slaves, mainly from West Africa. Between 1550 and 1575, Spain's American colonies took in about 25,000 African slaves, most destined to work in the burgeoning sugar-cane industry. From the 1640s, when sugar finally took over from tobacco, slavery increased dramatically, and by the last quarter of the century, about 175,000 African slaves had been brought to the British Caribbean alone. By the end of the eighteenth century, around 80,000 slaves a year were being transported to the Americas. The relationship between slaves and plantation profits was clear: Jamaica had 300,000 slaves in 1797 and produced 100,000 tons of sugar in 1805. Despite appalling mortality rates during the Atlantic crossings, over nine million slaves were shipped to the Americas between 1551 and 1870.

Plantations were often like small towns, with the overseer's house, offices, hospital, sugar-cane-grinding mill, boiling house, and slave quarters all lying in the shadow of the estate owner's Great House. However, not all plantations were for growing sugar cane. Coffee, cacao (cocoa), tobacco, and indigo were also produced by slave workers. These different kinds of activities required different machinery and buildings, the remains of which still lie scattered across the islands of the Caribbean.

Although different kinds of plantations existed, to date it is the sugar-cane estates that have attracted most attention from historians and historical archaeologists. One aim of such investigations into the material remains of slavery is to throw light on the everyday lives, habits, and beliefs of those who were disenfranchised and least able to record their own lives in their own words. Such investigations have revealed how many influences, reactions, and compromises helped create a distinctive kind of Afro-Caribbean culture, not simply African societies transplanted intact from Africa.

African spiritualism was influenced by Christianity and the faint echoes of Taíno shamanic beliefs to produce new hybrid religions such as Vodoun (voodoo), Santería, and Obeah. Vodoun priests and Obeah sorcerers often had fearsome reputations, though the malignant aspects of their religious activities were often exaggerated due to the cruel conditions they and their fellow slaves had to endure. In many cases, they were also healers, ritual experts, and keepers and interpreters of traditional knowledge.

These new religions were in one sense a form of resistance to the white-dominated society that had enslaved them. A more dramatic reaction was running away from plantations and taking refuge in the mountains or remote areas. This act was called "marronage," and escaped slaves were known as Maroons. Throughout the Caribbean region, Maroon communities sprang up and, like Nanny Town in Jamaica, developed their own variation of culture and tradition—heavily African in character but also distinctively Caribbean. Maroon societies formed the most obvious and strident kind of resistance to slavery.

The changing lives of African slaves and free laborers have been documented at many plantations throughout the region, such as Galways Plantation on Montserrat and Betty's Hope on Antigua. The eighteenth-century sugar plantation of Drax Hall, Jamaica, has yielded a mix of historical and archaeological information.

Comparing the slave quarters and the Great House has illustrated differences in architecture and the changing use of pottery from original West African earthenware to the use of European ceramic styles and the resulting uniquely Caribbean Afro-Jamaican forms. On St. Croix, similarly, research has identified a distinctive Afro-Cruzan style of pottery that avoided European techniques and features and produced traditional African hand-molded and unglazed items. Some of these creolized pottery forms were also a subtle form of resistance, used as magical objects in Obeah rituals but unrecognizable as such by Europeans.

On Barbados, investigations have shown how the practices of slave burials at Newton Plantation changed over time, from traditional African ways of disposing of the dead to west-facing burials influenced by Christian ideas. More subtle perhaps has been the recent recognition of how slave religions such as Vodoun and Shango were incorporated into what Europeans at the time regarded as straightforward activities. Many Afro-Caribbean blacksmiths forged wrought-iron gates and fences for the white plantocracy in foundries that also served as locations for African religious activities in which iron-making was traditionally associated with supernatural powers.

It is becoming increasingly clear that between the seventeenth and nineteenth centuries, slave societies of the Caribbean were far more than master-and-slave phenomena.

The creole children of original African slaves negotiated a new sense of identity through language, religion, and material culture, thereby reaffirming their African heritage in a Caribbean context.

At the same time that the disappearance of the Taíno and the influx of Africans were changing the cultural landscape of the Greater Antilles, an unusual variation of these events was occurring on St. Vincent in the Windward Islands. During the mid-eighteenth century, African slaves arrived on the island and mingled with the local Carib peoples—the offspring of which were the so-called Black Caribs (now known as the Garifuna). The Caribs joined with the French to fight the British, but when they were defeated, the darker-skinned Black Caribs were an easy target for retribution. In 1797, they were deported across the Caribbean to the island of Roatán off Honduras in Central America in 1797.

During the nineteenth century, after slavery's eventual abolition, other peoples came to the Caribbean, often to replace the slaves who had previously served as laborers. Hindus and Sikhs from India came as indentured labor, and many subsequently decided to stay. Muslims came from the Middle East and Chinese workers from Asia. Each in their own way have shaped the cultural landscape of the Caribbean.

During the five hundred years after Columbus's first landfall, there was a population transfusion in the Caribbean. In archaeological and anthropological terms, it changed the physical appearance of the region, created new kinds of culture, transformed the political economy, and produced new layers of European and Afro-Caribbean material culture superimposed over the fragile remains of the region's earlier Amerindian peoples.

Caribbean Paradise, Tourism, and Heritage

The abolition of slavery, the decline of the plantation system, twentieth-century political developments such as the granting of independence to many islands by former colonial powers, and the inexorable rise of tourism have had a profound effect on the region.

The arrival of nonstop jet flights from North America and Europe during the 1960s initiated a new phase in the development of the Caribbean—mass tourism. For over a century, tourism to the region had been a prerogative of the rich and had had comparatively little impact on the physical and cultural landscapes of the islands. However, regular long-distance air links and, since the 1980s, an explosive increase in the number of cruise ships have combined to change the fragile landscapes of the region—sometimes out of all recognition.

Once again, ideas, attitudes, and fashions beyond the region were affecting the ways in which the Caribbean was perceived. Whereas during colonial times direct sunlight was shunned and people "covered up" for reasons of health and propriety, during the 1960s there was a trend to undress and acquire a tan, preferably on exotic palm-fringed beaches. The Caribbean was tailor-made for such changes and was marketed as the ultimate fantasy destination. Poverty and history were ignored, and the Caribbean became one of the world's most popular tourist destinations. External forces were once again reshaping and reinventing the Caribbean to accord with the visitors' own mental images of what it should be—a process little changed from that employed by Columbus five hundred years before.

The numbers of tourists involved give a dramatic indication of the effects of this new invasion. In 1994, some sixteen million tourists visited the Caribbean, more than six times the figure for 1970, and they generated US$12 billion in revenues. The growth for some islands was astonishing: stayover visitors to Anguilla increased from 1,000 in 1970 to over 43,000 in 1994, and during the same period, arrivals in the Dominican Republic grew from 63,000 to almost two million.

The growth of the multibillion-dollar cruise-ship industry is especially notable, with ever greater numbers of ever larger ships being built by the main cruise companies. At the local level, this change has created discord within the hotel trade, between developers and heritage agencies, with islands being played off against each other by multinational conglomerates. Cruise ships are now so large that they cannot dock in many harbors and are resorting to marketing their on-board services with the Caribbean as a mere tropical backdrop. Similar isolating tendencies are the "all-inclusive" hotels where visitors are hermetically sealed from the real landscapes of Jamaica or St. Lucia in favor of unlimited food, drink, and organized activities.

The ironies are many and complex. The damage and destruction of archaeological sites are crystallized in the competing needs of hotel development and local heritage. It is a commonplace that in many smaller islands, low-lying flat land is at a premium and the most important pre-Columbian Amerindian archaeological sites now lie beneath the expanding airports and runways. More serious is the lack of heritage legislation, or the weakness of its enforcement, which allows local and multinational developers to build new hotels on top of archaeological sites, both prehistoric and historic. Nevertheless, there are exceptions, such as the Mount Irvine Hotel in Tobago, which preserved an important collection of Amerindian artifacts for many years before transferring them to a specially built museum within a restored fort built originally by the British to protect the island from the French and Dutch.

Cultural tourism and ecotourism have also been increasing in recent times, especially in islands that offer niche-market wildlife, trekking, and botanical tours, such as Dominica and Trinidad. However, even these visits change the landscape simply by making these islands popular. Trinidad is unlikely to lose its appeal to specialist birdwatchers in the near future, but the visitors may, if they increase beyond a small number, make such undertakings increasingly difficult if not impossible. There is always the danger that cultural tourism may become nothing less than a cleverly packaged ragbag of miscellaneous activities.

Reclaiming the Ancestors

The Caribbean today is a very different place from when Columbus waded ashore on Guanahaní island in October 1492. Popular culture is mainly of African origin, although its dominant languages are English, French, and Spanish, with a diversity of local creole tongues. In this vibrant melting pot of peoples and pressures, hotels, cruise ships, reggae, Carnival, and poverty, there would appear to be little chance of hearing a whisper from the long-forgotten pre-Columbian past. It might seem that too many landscapes have been piled upon that first world encountered by Europeans—that the past is well and truly buried. Yet indigenous voices survive—faint and fragile, yet louder now than at any time in the last three hundred years.

On Dominica, several thousand Amerindians of Carib descent live in the Carib Territory—the Waitukubuli Karifuna Community—on the northeast of the island. They have lost their language but retained and relearned some of their ancestral skills, such as basket weaving and the traditional method of making canoes with fire and water. They have a council and chief as well as their own distinctive church.

In Trinidad, similarly, there have been stirrings of an Amerindian consciousness in the last two decades. Although little known outside the island, the Santa Rosa Carib Community of Arima is a mixed-blood community made up of the descendants of Caribs from St. Vincent, Trinidad's own Mission Amerindians, Venezuelans of mixed Amerindian-Spanish blood, and Africans. They take their tolerant and typically Trinidadian multiethnic inspiration from the Roman Catholic festival of Santa Rosa, whose statue is kept in the local church, itself built on land once occupied by an Amerindian village.

Today the Carib Community's attempts to reclaim aspects of its indigenous identity focus partly on making cassava bread by traditional Amerindian methods. The people weave cassava squeezers, build *ajoupa* houses with local materials, and collect the folklore names and knowledge of Trinidad's trees, flowers, and medicinal plants. Some of these skills have been passed down by community elders, such as the Carib Queen, and others have been transmitted by visiting indigenous groups from Guyana and Dominica. After hundreds of years during which the remnants of the island's indigenous people were marginalized and silent, they have now found a voice.

In the Caribbean today, the scattered groups of indigenous peoples in Dominica, St. Vincent, Trinidad, and Puerto Rico have forged links with their more numerous and influential cousins in Guyana, Venezuela, and Belize. Calling themselves the Caribbean Organization of Indigenous Peoples, they seek recognition as the original inhabitants of the Caribbean in order to gain formal title to land, and to reclaim, at least symbolically, the sacred landscapes of their ancestors.

The modern Caribbean is a palimpsest of astonishing contrasts that, since 1492, has been and continues to be defined by outside influences. It remains a region of vibrant cultural traditions and deep historical contradictions with a diverse archaeological heritage and endlessly varied traditional cultures.

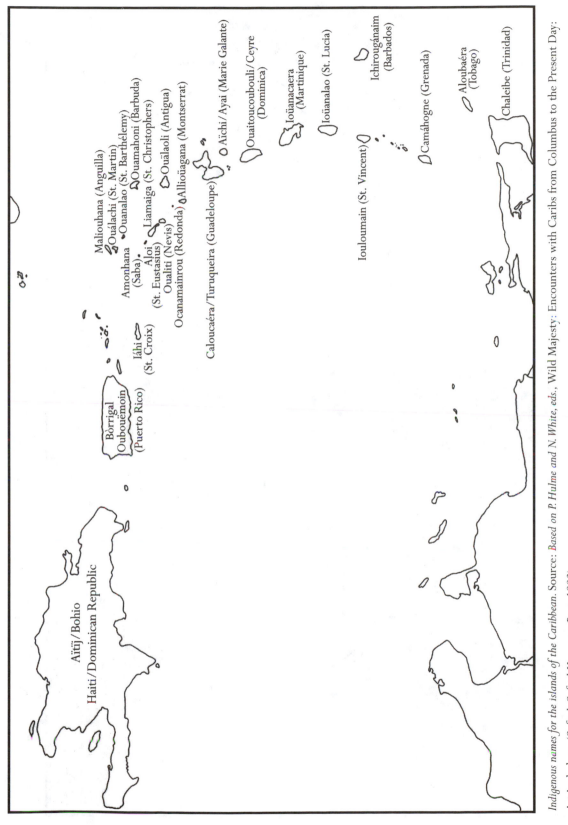

Aïtij / Bohio
Haiti / Dominican Republic

Borrigal
Oubouémoin
(Puerto Rico)

Iáhi
(St. Croix)

Maliouhana (Anguilla)
Ouálachi (St. Martin)
Amonhana •Ouanalao (St. Barthélemy)
(Saba) Ouamahoni (Barbuda)
Aloi Liamaiga (St. Christophers)
(St. Eustasius)
Oualiti (Nevis) Oualaoli (Antigua)
Ocanamainrou (Redonda) Allioüagana (Montserrat)

Caloucaéra / Turuqueira (Guadeloupe)

Aichi / Ayai (Marie Galante)

Ouaitoucoubouli / Ceyre
(Dominica)

Ioüanacaera
(Martinique)

Ioüanalao (St. Lucia)

Iouloumain (St. Vincent)

Ichirougánaim
(Barbados)

Camáhogne (Grenada)

Aloubaéra
(Tobago)

Chaleibe (Trinidad)

Indigenous names for the islands of the Caribbean. Source: *Based on P. Hulme and N. White, eds.*, Wild Majesty: Encounters with Caribs from Columbus to the Present Day: An Anthology *(Oxford: Oxford University Press, 1992).*

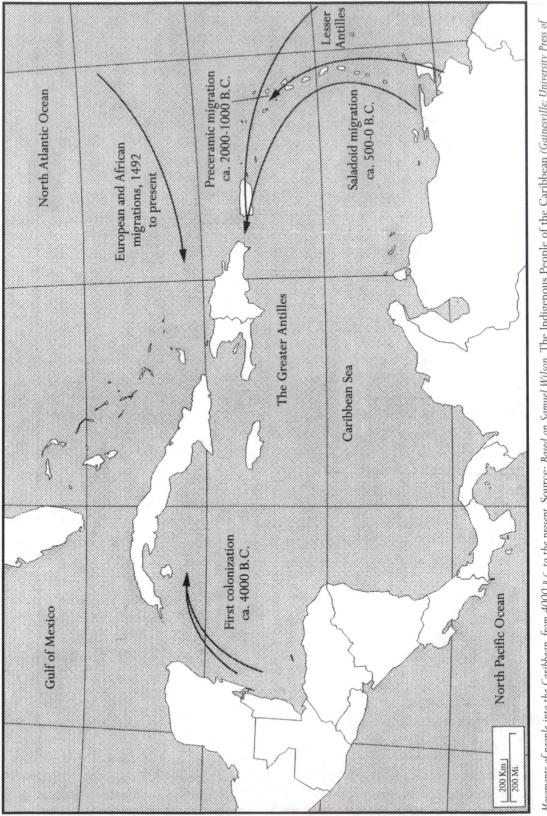

Movements of people into the Caribbean, from 4000 B.C. to the present. Source: *Based on Samuel Wilson, The Indigenous People of the Caribbean (Gainesville: University Press of Florida, 1997).*

A

Accompong

Accompong is a Maroon settlement in the remote area of central-western Jamaica known as the Cockpit Country. Today, the town is relatively new, having been moved from an earlier location known as Old Accompong Town that had been founded by the Maroon hero Cudjoe (sometimes spelled Kojo), who fought the British and signed the subsequent peace treaty.

The area around Old Accompong is a sacred landscape dotted with important sites from Maroon history such as Simon Hill (where the head of the evil Quancoo is buried), Kindah (where Maroon leaders planned their assaults on the British), and a cave known as Ambush from where they spied on their enemy. Not surprisingly, the main festival at Accompong is the annual celebration of Cudjoe's rout of an entire British regiment at Peace Cave, which led to the peace treaty that guaranteed self-government for the Maroons. The festival takes place every January, when Maroons are summoned by the *abeng* (cow horn) and gather to eat, recount folk tales, sell goods, chant, and dance, as well take part in war dances, road marches and sing treaty songs. The whole event binds the community, preserves traditions, and fosters pride in a communal identity that stresses a self-image as the Americas' first freedom fighters.

Today, there are five churches in Accompong New Town, and although under pressure from local Jamaican politics, the community retains a cohesiveness manifested even in the use of herbal medicines—an indigenous Taíno as well as African tradition. Recent archaeological investigations at Old Accompong recovered musket balls, earthenware, and glass bottles dating to the seventeenth and eighteenth centuries. Also found were West African cowrie shells that may have been part of an ornament and possibly served as currency.

See also: Jamaica; Maroons; Nanny Town (site, Jamaica)

References
Agorsah, E. K. 1994. Archaeology of Maroon Settlements in Jamaica. In K. Agorsah (ed.), *Maroon Heritage: Archaeological, Ethnographic, and Historical Perspectives,* pp. 163–187. Kingston: Canoe Press; Besson, J. 1997. Caribbean Common Tenures and Capitalism: The Accompong Maroons of Jamaica. *Plantation Society in the Americas* 4 (2–3): 201–232; Campbell, M. C. 1990. *The Maroons of Jamaica 1655–1796.* Trenton, NJ: Africa World Press Inc.; Dunham, K. 1946. *Journey to Accompong.* Westport, CT: Negro Universities Press; Wright, M. L. 1994.

Accompong Maroons of Jamaica. In E. K. Agorsah (ed.), *Maroon Heritage*, pp. 64–71. Kingston: Canoe Press.

Aesthetic of Brilliance

Throughout the Americas, native peoples inhabited a world of spirits, ancestors, and sorcery—a landscape of invisible powers that infused life-force equally in people and the things they made, as well as in animals, mountains, rivers, and natural phenomena. This was a secret world, unseen by the first European discoverers, and misunderstood by the conquistadors and adventurers who came in their wake.

Native Americans saw spirituality and the divine in the luminous glow of nature—whether sun and moon, fire and ice, the sparkle of stars, the translucence of pearls, or the iridescence of the rainbow or a butterfly's wings. Gold and silver were but two manifestations of the light that filled the universe with sacred brilliance. Colorful costumes, burnished pottery, and glittering pyramids displayed the lustrous shine prized as the epitome of incorruptible cosmic power.

Brilliant objects were "solid light" and light itself the repository of extraordinary powers, symbolizing fertilizing energy, moral order, political stability, health, and vitality. The physical world and its natural phenomena, as well as the artifacts of culture, shared in this fundamental view of existence, where shimmering surfaces embodied the essence of life. The magical qualities accorded to light were part of a deeply rooted natural philosophy and, at heart, a pan-Amerindian phenomenon.

It was this brilliant world that Columbus encountered in October 1492, bringing with him a Medieval European and Christian view of the world, characterized and driven by the commercial imperatives of secular values attached to gold, silver, and gemstones. White-skinned, dressed in shiny armor, and possessing a seemingly inexhaustible supply of base-metal trinkets, mirrors, and glass beads, Europeans were received by the indigenous inhabitants of the Caribbean and elsewhere as supernatural beings—their excess of "brilliance" indicating their god-like status. Throughout the Caribbean, native peoples saw European shiny objects as "like for like" and willingly traded gold, silver, emeralds, and pearls for bits of glass, glazed majolica, mirrors, and brass bells. Europeans, in turn, saw Amerindians as gullible and foolish, ignorant of the true worth of their traded goods.

Such encounters were based on a fatally flawed understanding of what was taking place. Blinded by lust and ignorance, Europeans often received copper and minerals instead of gold and pearls, and Amerindians soon discovered that the white man's shiny things possessed no supernatural powers. At the same time, European disease spread like wildfire, killing millions of native peoples but leaving Europeans themselves magically unscathed. For the native peoples, disease and death equated with darkness and chaos—the end of the world as they knew it. So keenly was this rupture of indigenous reality felt that many committed suicide. The consequences of European arrival for native peoples was a physical and psychological trauma that became history's most devastating holocaust.

See also: El Dorado; Gold; Pearls (gems); Shamanism

References

Oliver, J. R. 2000. Gold Symbolism among Caribbean Chiefdoms: Of Feathers, *Çibas,* and *Guanín* Power among Taíno Elites. In C. McEwan (ed.), *Pre-Columbian Gold: Technology, Style, and Iconography,* pp. 196–219. London: British Museum Press; Saunders, N. J. 1998. Stealers of Light, Traders in Brilliance: Amerindian Metaphysics in the Mirror of Conquest. *RES: Anthropology and Aesthetics* 33 (1): 225–252; Saunders, N. J. 1999. Biographies of Brilliance: Pearls, Transformations of Matter and Being, ca. A.D. 1492. *World Archaeology* 31 (2): 243–257; Saunders, N. J. 2002. The Colours of Light: Materiality and Chromatic Cultures of the Americas. In A. Jones and G. MacGregor (eds.). *Colouring the Past: The Significance of Archaeological Research.* Oxford: Berg Publishers, pp. 209–226; Whitehead, N. L. 1997. *The Discoverie* as Ethnological Text. In *Sir Walter Ralegh, The Discoverie of the Large, Rich and Bewtiful Empyre of Guiana,* pp. 60–116. (Transcribed, annotated, and introduced by N. L. Whitehead.) Manchester: Manchester University Press.

Agouti

Agoutis are tropical rainforest rodents belonging to the family *Daysproctidae* and divided into two genera and some ten species. They were not native to the Island Caribbean but introduced by the first wave of pottery-making agriculturalists from South America. Somewhere between 500 B.C. and 250 B.C. these Saladoid peoples moved into Trinidad, the Lesser Antilles, and then throughout the Caribbean, bringing with them dogs, domesticated plants, and the agouti. The size of a small rabbit, agoutis are daylight animals, live in burrows, and typically give birth twice a year.

See also: Dogs; Saladoid

Agüeybana (Taíno chief)

Agüeybana was a Taíno chief (cacique) in Puerto Rico (native Borinquén) in A.D. 1508, when a Spanish expedition under Juan Ponce de León arrived on the island. The Spanish discovered placer gold in the rivers and quickly established several settlements. Intimidated by the Higüey massacre in Hispaniola, the Borinquén Taínos initially acquiesced to Spanish demands. They were assigned to *encomiendas* and worked in hard labor, searching the river deposits for gold, growing food for the invaders, and acting as beasts of burden. Their oppression caused unrest, and Agüeybana organized a rebellion, supported by allies from St. Croix and the Virgin Islands. The uprising was short-lived, however, and Agüeybana was summarily executed.

See also: Encomienda; Puerto Rico

Amazons

As with so many European ideas brought as cultural baggage to the Americas, the myth of the Amazons originated in classical antiquity. In Greek mythology, Amazons were societies of warrior women who lived without men and waged war in the barbarian lands of Asia. They were said to slice off one breast so they could more easily use their bows and arrows

Amazon women participate in a cannibalistic feast, an image owing more to the European imagination than to reality. Engraving by Theodore de Bry (1528–1598). (Corbis)

and to keep men as slaves, using them only to procreate. The most famous Amazon was Queen Penthesileia, who was killed by Achilles in Homer's *Iliad.* In Greek art, they are commonly depicted fighting against heroes—an example of which survives on the Parthenon frieze of between 447 B.C. and 432 B.C.

In the Medieval European imagination, societies ruled by women were a defining feature of the exotic, equally as fantastic as men with dogs' heads, cannibals, and the alchemic notion of gold being produced by the heat of the sun. Such a matriarchal society represented what has been called the "radical other" for the male-dominated societies of Europe at the time. It was no surprise that in the strange and unknown lands of the Americas, early European explorers imagined Amazons as easily as they did monsters and inexhaustible golden treasures.

Amazon societies seemed to exist—or at least rumors of them were heard—throughout the Caribbean and South America. On Columbus's first voyage, he reported hearing stories from the Taíno (Arawak) of strange people and practices farther south in the Caribbean, where cannibal men had intercourse with women whose society had no men. In one story from Taíno mythology, the hero-ancestor Guayahona had taken all the women from Hispaniola to live on the island of Matinino (Martinique) without men; in one variation the women were turned into frogs. The cannibalistic Tupinamba Amerindians of Brazil insisted to Europeans that such peoples lived in their lands, thereby adding to the legend. Graphic images of Amazon women leaning on their bows and shooting their arrows at men strung up from trees were popularized in Europe by the illustrator Theodore de Bry.

The idea of American Amazons was fixed in the European imagination by the naming of one of the world's great rivers. Between 1541 and 1542, the Spanish conquistador Francisco de Orellana navigated the Amazon River from its source in the eastern Andes to its mouth on the Atlantic coast of South America. During this epic journey, the Spanish reportedly fought against a race of female warriors who wore their hair down to their feet. In tales that mixed ideas of warrior women with legends of the golden realm of El Dorado, the Amazons were said to live in great stone cities whose temples were adorned with gold and silver female idols. No men were allowed to stay in the city after nightfall, their main duty being the annual impregnation of the women. Coñori was said to be the Amazon queen. Although many contemporaries were skeptical of what they saw as fanciful notions, the name took hold and the great waterway became known as the river of the Amazons.

Amazons also feature in Sir Walter Ralegh's account of his search for El Dorado known as *The Discoverie of the Large, Rich and Bewtiful Empyre of Guiana,* published in London in 1596. Here the Amazons seem associated with the idea of the Americas' untouched and strange landscapes as female. In this belief at least, Ralegh and others might have been influenced by the widespread Amerindian notion of the earth as the sacred mother. Ralegh freely mixes European tradition with Amerindian ideas. He describes how once a year, in April, the queens of the Amazons choose and then sleep with the kings of nearby patriarchal tribes. If they conceive a son, he is returned to the father, but a daughter is kept by them and brought up as part of their society. When the daughters mature, their right breast or nipple is cut off so as to not interfere with their martial activities. Again, Ralegh's interpretation may reflect some background reality inasmuch as Europeans had noticed that some Amerindian women—such as the Taíno queen Anacaona—held high social status and wielded considerable political influence.

Whatever the truth of the matter, embedded in Ralegh's text are more complex ideas concerning the relationships between men and women in the Americas, the treatment of Amerindian women by European—especially Spanish—men, and not least, the ambiguities of Ralegh's own subject status to Queen Elizabeth I. The impetus for the English queen to conquer the lands controlled by the Spanish king, to acquire some of the warrior characteristics of the Amazons, and at the same time to remain a virgin queen are all contentious and difficult aspects of the relationships between Amazons and Europeans in Ralegh's text.

See also: Anacaona (Taíno queen); Caribs; Columbus, Christopher; El Dorado; Ralegh, Sir Walter

References

Boomert, A. 1987. Gifts of the Amazons: "Greenstone" Pendants and Beads as Items of Ceremonial Exchange in Amazonia. *Antropologia* 67: 33–54; Medina, J. T. 1988. *The Discovery of the Amazon.* New York: Dover; Whitehead, N. L. 1997. *The Discoverie* as Ethnological Text. In *Sir Walter Ralegh, The Discoverie of the Large, Rich and Bewtiful Empyre of Guiana,* pp. 60–116. (Transcribed, annotated, and introduced by N. L. Whitehead.) Manchester: Manchester University Press.

Anacaona (Taíno queen)

Anacaona was the royal sister of the Taíno lord Behechio Anacaochoa, principal chief (cacique) of the kingdom of Xaraguá in southwestern Hispaniola at the time of Columbus's arrival in 1493. She was married to Caonabo, the chief of the adjacent province of Maguana, though whether she was his highest-ranking wife or had children is not known. Her name, like her husband's, incorporates the Taíno word for gold, *caona,* and indicates high social status. Anacaona's role in the power politics of the two kingdoms and, more widely, concerning the status of Taíno women is ambiguous and unresolved.

Anacaona played a central if enigmatic role in the hospitality that the Taíno offered to the Spanish. While she appears to have presided as an equal with her brother during early discussions with the Spanish, it was during a subsequent meeting in late 1496 or early 1497 that her ambiguous status became noticeable. At this time, Bartolomé Columbus returned to Xaraguá to receive a tribute of cotton and food. He was greeted, as before, with great hospitality by Anacaona, Behechio, and thirty-two other chiefs. When a Spanish caravel anchored off the coast to take aboard the supplies, Anacaona is said to have persuaded her brother and others to accompany their Spanish guests. En route, they stopped for the night at a small village belonging to Anacaona. Here the Spanish saw a special storehouse belonging to the queen that was reportedly packed full of prestige goods made of cotton, ceremonial wooden seats (*duhos*) and many skillfully made wooden dishes, bowls, and sculptures.

Anacaona presented Bartolomé with fourteen of the beautifully carved and highly polished black-wood duho seats, as well as white cotton skirts and four large balls of spun cotton. The Spanish noted that the wood was *Lignum vitae,* and that on the island of Ganabara—modern Ile de la Gonâve—it was women who made such things. Undoubtedly, the giving of such precious gifts was part of Taíno elite exchange and power politics, and the fact that this was done at Anacaona's behest adds to the problem of understanding her status and the wider role of women in Taíno society.

When the group arrived at the coast, Anacaona refused to take to her own large and painted canoe and insisted instead on traveling in the same boat as Bartolomé Columbus. Both Anacaona and Behechio appear to have been duly impressed by the size and maneuverability of the Spanish ship and especially by the firing of its lombard guns.

Six years later, in 1503, the new Spanish governor of Hispaniola, Nicolás de Ovando, visited Xaraguá ostensibly to visit Anacaona. Behechio had died since the last Spanish visit and appears to have been succeeded by his royal sister. According to Taíno custom, Anacaona had arranged for his most beautiful wife, Guanahattabenecheuá, to be buried alive with him. Ovando tricked the assembled Taíno chiefs and burned them alive. Due to her royal status, Anacaona was given the honor of being hanged, thus bringing to an end the Taíno kingdom of Xaraguá.

See also: Behechio (Taíno chief); Caonabo (Taíno chief); Columbus, Christopher; Duhos; Taíno (Arawak)

References

Las Casas, B. 1992. *A Short Account of the Destruction of the Indies.* London: Penguin Books; Sauer, C. O. 1969. *The Early Spanish Main.* Berkeley, CA: University of California Press; Wilson, S. M. 1990. *Hispaniola: Caribbean Chiefdoms in the Age of Columbus.* Tuscaloosa, AL: University of Alabama Press.

Anegada (BVI)

Anegada is a flat limestone atoll in the northeast of the British Virgin Islands. It has an area of 39 sq km, has a resident population of less than 200, and is the most remote island in this group. Recent archaeological reconnaissance discovered two prehistoric Amerindian sites, a series of conch-shell platforms, and a variety of resources that may have attracted the interest of Amerindians.

Previous archaeological investigations of Anegada in 1937 and 1974 had been brief, and focused mainly on large heaps of discarded conch shells, one of which yielded a radiocarbon date of ca. A.D. 1250. Anegada would have been attractive during pre-Columbian times as it has freshwater wells, salt ponds, and abundant marine resources. Unlike most other Caribbean islands, Anegada's coastal strip revealed no evidence of prehistoric occupation, though this may be due to natural events such as storm action.

Two sites were discovered: Anegada I is a dark-earth midden with shell and bone, and late Ceramic Age pottery; Anegada II is also a dark-earth midden that produced only a few pottery fragments and a manatee bone. More impressive were three large rectangular platforms some 50-cm-high made of discarded Queen Conch (*Strombus gigas*) shells; though their purpose is currently unknown. Anegada appears to have been visited only sporadically in pre-Columbian times.

See also: St. John (USVI); Tortola (BVI)

References

Davis, D., and K. Oldfield. 2003. Archaeological Reconnaissance of Anegada, British Virgin Islands. *Journal of Caribbean Archaeology* 4: 1–11; Gross, J. M. 1975. The Archaeology of Anegada Island. *Journal of the Virgin Islands Archaeological Society* 2: 12–16.

Anguilla

Anguilla is the most northerly of the Leeward Islands and is only 56 sq km in area. A low-lying coral island, it takes its name from its eel-like shape ("anguilla" being Spanish for eel). The majority of the 11,000 population is of African descent.

Anguilla's archaeological past is little investigated by comparison with other islands, although some forty-two sites are known. The earliest evidence for prehistoric

occupation dates to around 1500 B.C., during the Archaic Period, and is by definition preceramic. This initial settlement probably took the form of temporary hunter-gatherer camps housing small bands who gathered mollusks and various plant foods. They typically made tools from the shellfish they collected as well as from locally available stone.

The pottery-making Saladoid peoples arrived between A.D. 300 and A.D. 600, and built several substantial villages at Rendezvous Bay and Sandy Ground. At the turn of the first millennium a new wave of Amerindians arrived from the Greater Antilles, bringing with them a more sophisticated shamanic religion and political organization. Between about A.D. 900 and A.D. 1200, Anguilla's occupation by these probably Taíno peoples reached its greatest density. There were some 14 villages at this time with a total population of perhaps 2,000 people. Fish bones indicate they were harvesting both inshore and deep-sea species, and ceramic griddles suggest they were making cassava bread.

Archaeological sites have also yielded evidence of spiritual beliefs, such as the three-pointer stones known as *zemís,* and fragments of tubes that may have been part of hallucinogenic snuffing paraphernalia. Especially significant in this respect is Fountain Cavern, which contains petroglyphs and an unusual stalagmite statue with a sculpted head overlooking a pool of fresh water. Some archaeologists have interpreted this figure to be Yúcahu, the supreme Taíno deity, the invisible lord of fertility whose name meant "spirit of cassava." Currently, this important site is being developed into Anguilla's first national park, which will also house a museum. Anguilla's indigenous inhabitants disappeared during the 1600s, decimated by European disease and probably also the effects of slave raiding.

Although some believe that Christopher Columbus discovered Anguilla in 1493, others claim that the island first appears in European history in 1564, when it was mentioned by the French. Whichever is true, the island seems to have been ignored for the best part of a century until settled by the British in 1650. During its early colonial history, not only the French but also the Caribs attempted unsuccessfully to invade the island. Anguilla stayed British during the tumultuous eighteenth and nineteenth centuries and in 1980 became a British dependent territory. Today, the island's Carnival is held at the beginning of August, and features Calypso competitions and the crowning of a Carnival Queen.

See also: Caribs; Carnival (Trinidad); Cassava (manioc); Saladoid; Zemís
References
Brenda, C., and P. Colville. 1997. *Anguilla: Tranquil Isle of the Caribbean.* London: Macmillan; Crock, J. G., J. B. Peterson, and N. Douglas. 1994. Preceramic Anguilla: A View from Whitehead's Bluff Site. *Proceedings of the Fifteenth Congress of the International Association for Caribbean Archaeology.* San Juan, Puerto Rico: Centro de Estudios Avanzados de Puerto Rico y el Caribe; Douglas, N. 1990. The Fountain: An Amerindian Ceremonial Cavern on Anguilla, Its Petroglyphs and Other Finds, Related to Surface Archaeology of Anguilla's Major Beach Sites. *Proceedings of the Eleventh Congress of the International Association for Caribbean Archaeology,* pp. 141–152; Douglas, N. 1991. Recent Amerindian Finds on Anguilla. *Proceedings of the Thirteenth International Congress for Caribbean Archaeology, Held at Willemstadt, Curaçao, on July 24–29, 1989,* pp. 576–588. Willemstadt: Curaçao; Petersen, J. B., and D. R. Watters. 1991. Amerindian Ceramic Remains from Fountain Cavern, Anguilla, West Indies. *Annals of the Carnegie Museum* 60: 321–357.

Anse Des Pères (site, St. Martin)

Anse des Pères is a Late Cedrosan Saladoid site located 30 meters inland from the bay of the same name on St. Martin. It is dated to between A.D. 750 and A.D. 950.

The site appears to have been a single-occupation small village site, with pottery similar to that found at contemporary Leeward Islands sites of Golden Rock and Indian Creek. Pottery finds included a large number of almost complete vessels with typical white-on-red (W-O-R) and polychrome painting, and incised designs, including zone-incised cross-hatching (zic) ware. Cassava griddle fragments were also found.

Everyday objects included stone axes and pestles made of chert and volcanic rock, and tools made of flint and quartz, the former imported from Antigua. Shellfish such as West Indian Top Shell (*Cittarium pica*) and Queen Conch (*Strombus gigas*) featured in everyday life, both as food and for making jewelry and functional items such as scrapers. Shell beads, pendants, and square or rectangular plaques were made as well as mother-of-pearl disks.

See also: Golden Rock (site, St. Eustatius); Indian Creek (site, Antigua); Saladoid; Zic pottery
References
Hofman, C. L., and M.L.P. Hoogland (eds.). 1999. *Archaeological Investigations on St. Martin (Lesser Antilles),* pp. 63–125. Archaeological Studies Leiden University 4. Leiden.

Antigua

Antigua is the largest of the Leeward Islands with an area of 174 sq km. Low-lying and composed of volcanic rock and coral, Antigua has a population of around 64,000, the majority of whom are of African descent.

Antigua's archaeological past is far better known than that of many other islands. It appears to have been first occupied during the Archaic Period (5000 B.C. to 2000 B.C.), when groups of hunter-gatherers were attracted by the island's unusual geology that included outcrops of chert ideal for making stone tools. This, combined with Antigua's abundant marine resources, probably accounts for the fact that the island has the largest number of Archaic Period sites in the Caribbean, many of which occur on Crabb's peninsula on the northeast part of the island.

One of the best known of these early sites is Jolly Beach, which, from the quantity of Casimiroid-style stone tools discovered, was probably a workshop area. Other early sites have revealed layers of mollusk shells, reflecting the type of lifestyle practiced by the first Antiguans. In the southeast corner of the island is another well-known site called Indian Creek that belongs to the later Saladoid Period (A.D. 1 to A.D. 600). Characteristic white-on-red (W-O-R) and zone-incised cross-hatching (zic) pottery has been found, as have incense burners, cassava baking ceramic griddles, and three-pointer *zemís*. The site seems to be a central plaza surrounded by middens. In 1998, what may prove to be the largest Saladoid settlement on Antigua was discovered at the site of Royall's.

Following the demise of the Saladoid tradition came the appearance of the locally named Mill Reef culture (A.D. 600 to A.D. 900) belonging to the Troumassoid Period, which in turn was succeeded by the local Mamora Bay culture that lasted from A.D. 900 to A.D. 1100. The change from Saladoid to post-Saladoid peoples is reflected in the move from inland to coastal settlements, away from agriculture and toward fishing.

Christopher Columbus arrived in 1493 during his second voyage of exploration and appears to have seen no indigenous inhabitants. He reportedly named the island after the church of Santa Maria de la Antigua in Seville. A lack of fresh water together with Carib attacks discouraged Spanish and French colonization until 1632, when the English successfully settled there.

An important part of Antigua's colonial heritage from this time is Betty's Hope Estate, which has attracted the attention of historical archaeologists. The estate was founded during the mid-seventeenth century, initially to grow tobacco, though it soon became a sugar plantation under the ownership of Sir Christopher Codrington. At this time also, African slaves were imported to work the cane fields. Those parts of the plantation that have been investigated include the original sugar mill (1674), the postemancipation pay office (1834), and the twentieth-century overseer's house. It is thought that there may be as many as three cemeteries associated with the site. Betty's Hope illustrates the archaeology of the early colonial period, highlighting the beginnings of African-Caribbean culture, and also shows how such sites developed during the later nineteenth and twentieth centuries.

View over English Harbour and Nelson's Dockyard from Shirley Heights (Courtesy Nicholas J. Saunders)

Antigua's importance to Britain, however, was naval and strategic as well as economic. Historical archaeologists and naval historians have investigated this aspect of the island's eighteenth- and nineteenth-century heritage, which is concentrated at what is today called Nelson's Dockyard at English Harbour. The young Nelson was stationed here between 1784 and 1787, along with Prince William Henry, the Duke of Clarence, who later became King William IV. Today, the whole area is a national park, with a museum and art center. Overlooking English Harbour is Shirley Heights, where exists the remains of the British Navy's ammunition magazines and a small museum with audiovisual displays about the island's history. Antigua remained under British control until, together with the small island of Barbuda, it became fully independent in November 1981.

Antigua's capital is St. John's, and during the island's Carnival (end of July to beginning of August), its streets fill up with people dancing accompanied by steel and brass bands. The capital also has an interesting Anglican cathedral, and a thriving museum and archives in the former courthouse that displays artifacts from the prehistoric and colonial periods of Antigua's past.

See also: Archaic Period; Betty's Hope (site, Antigua); Casimiroid; Indian Creek (site, Antigua); Jolly Beach (site, Antigua); Nelson's Dockyard (Antigua); Saladoid; Slavery; Sugar; White-on-Red Pottery (W-O-R); Zemís; Zic Pottery

References

B. Carstensen, 1993. *Betty's Hope: An Antiguan Sugar Plantation.* St. John's, Antigua: Betty's Hope Trust; D. Davis, 2000. *Jolly Beach and the Preceramic Occupation of Antigua, West Indies.* Yale

University Publications in Anthropology 84. New Haven, CT: Yale University Press; B. Dyde, 1993. *Antigua and Barbuda: The Heart of the Caribbean.* London: Macmillan Caribbean; M. Etherington, and V. Richards. 2003. *The Antigua and Barbuda Companion.* Northampton, MA: Interlink Publishing Group; D. B. Gaspar, 1985. *Bondsmen and Rebels: A Study of Master-Slave Relations in Antigua.* Baltimore: Johns Hopkins University Press; D. B. Gaspar, 1988. Slavery, Amelioration, and Sunday Markets in Antigua, 1823–1831. *Slavery & Abolition* 9, pp. 1–28; D. V. Nicholson, 1983. *English Harbour, Antigua: An Historical and Archaeological Sketch.* St. John's, Antigua: Antigua Archaeological and Historical Society; D. V. Nicholson, 1983. *The Story of the Arawaks in Antigua and Barbuda.* St. John's, Antigua: Antigua Archaeological Society & Linden Press; D. V. Nicholson, 1994. *Heritage Landmarks, Antigua and Barbuda.* St. John's, Antigua: Museum of Antigua and Barbuda; I. B. Rouse, and B. F. Morse. 1999. *Excavations at the Indian Creek Site, Antigua, West Indies.* New Haven, CT: Yale University Publications in Anthropology, No. 82.

Arauquinoid (pottery)

Arauquinoid pottery was a prehistoric ceramic style that, together with pottery of the Guayabitoid series, originated from the Barrancoid cultures in northeastern South America, the Orinoco Valley, and Trinidad. Arauquinoid ceramics replaced those of the preceding Barrancoid tradition around A.D. 500. Some archaeologists believe Arauquinoid developed out of the Barrancoid while others remain to be convinced. What is more certain is that the use by Arauquinoid potters of incised and punctated geometric motifs, and of freshwater sponge spicules in the distinctive *cauixí* temper, locate these ceramics firmly within a broader pan-Amazonian pottery-making tradition known as the Incised and Punctate Horizon.

Arauquinoid ceramics belonged to a people who had made a significant advance in subsistence by mastering the domestication and preparation of maize, carbonized fragments of which are commonly found in early sites belonging to this culture. The abundant remains of ceramic griddles at these sites, normally recognized as diagnostic evidence of manioc cultivation, would now seem to indicate the preparation of maize cakes as well. The earliest Arauquinoid culture, known as Corozal, seems to have developed in the middle Orinoco Valley and appears to be transitional between the earlier Saladoid-Barrancoid complex and a more fully developed Arauquinoid tradition. Typical Arauquinoid features include finely incised designs sometimes filled in with red paint, and simple human-like faces on the body of the pottery vessel.

Between the sixth and seventh centuries A.D., Arauquinoid populations of the middle Orinoco increased, possibly as a consequence of maize cultivation, and expanded into the Guianas and Trinidad. The pure Arauquinoid culture known as the Macapaima Complex is called Bontour on Trinidad, and Guayabita on the eastern coast of Venezuela. Macapaima pottery is even less decorated than earlier Arauquinoid ceramics, though the distinctive cauixí temper persists in some items, such as the ceramic griddles presumably exchanged by Trinidad's Bontour people with Amerindians inhabiting southwest Tobago. There also seems to have been extensive trading in Arauquinoid times between Trinidad and the middle Orinoco; roller stamps used for decorating the body and ceramic whistles known as ocarinas appear to have made their way from the mainland to Trinidad, and shell-tempered Bontour pottery appears in the Lower Orinoco.

See also: Guayabitoid (pottery); Trinidad and Tobago

References

Boomert, A. 1985. The Guayabitoid and Mayoid Series: Amerindian Culture History in Trinidad during Late Prehistoric and Protohistoric Times. *Proceedings of the Tenth International Congress for the Study of the Pre-Columbian Cultures of the Lesser Antilles, Martinique 1983,* pp. 93–148; Boomert, A. 2003. Agricultural Societies in the Continental Caribbean. In J. Sued-Badillo (ed.), *General History of the Caribbean: Vol. 1, Autochthonous Societies,* pp. 165–167, 175–180. Paris: UNESCO; Roosevelt, A. C. 1980. *Parmana: Prehistoric Maize and Manioc Subsistence along the Amazon and Orinoco,* p. 188. London: Academic Press.

Archaic Period

Although the first evidence of human presence in various parts of Mesoamerica and South America ranges between 20,000 and 8,000 years ago, it seems that the Island Caribbean was not populated until somewhere between 5000 B.C. and 4000 B.C. Archaeological sites from this time are often assigned either to the so-called Lithic Age (4000 B.C. to 2000 B.C.) or the Archaic Age (2000 B.C. to ca. 500 B.C.). However, as the distinction between the two is dependent on the appearance in the Archaic of grinding stones and shell artifacts, and as both are, most importantly, preceramic, they are sometimes lumped together. This practice will be followed here where most hunter-gatherer preceramic cultures will be regarded as belonging to the Archaic Period, a time that ends with the appearance of the first pottery-making Saladoid peoples in the first few centuries B.C. Some archaeologists divide the Archaic into two series of peoples and cultures, the Casimiroid and Ortoiroid, though others reject this division.

The earliest Archaic Period sites discovered so far are those of Banwari Trace and St. John Oropuche in Trinidad, dated to around 5500 B.C. Both belong to the Ortoiroid series that takes its name from the site of Ortoire, also on Trinidad. It is possible that at this time Trinidad was still connected to the South American mainland and so was not strictly speaking an island, though this hardly diminished its role in the early populating of the Island Caribbean.

Ortoiroid material culture, found in sites that are usually shell middens, includes bone spearpoints, rough stone tools for chopping and grinding, hammerstones, and manos and metates. The Ortoroid way of life was evidently based on hunting, gathering, and fishing, with a focus on the exploitation of shellfish. At Banwari Trace, the remains of freshwater mollusks, pig, and monkey were discovered. Some of these sites appear short-lived and are typically situated near mangrove swamps and beaches; sometimes human burials are found within them. Two other Ortoroid sites belonging to the local Boutbois culture have been discovered in Martinique. On the offshore islands of Venezuela, early evidence of Archaic Period human occupation has been discovered on Cubagua, where at the sites of Cubagua and nearby Manicuare, flaked-stone tools and shell tools indicate a basic maritime economy. Somewhat later, around 1500 B.C., are the early Bonairean sites of Lagun and Gotomeer.

Only slightly younger than the Ortoiroid sites of Trinidad are others dating from 4000 B.C. to 3500 B.C. on Cuba to the north in the Greater Antilles. Here, early sites such as the Levisa rockshelter date to at least 3300 B.C. and have yielded flaked-stone tools, animal bones, and shells. The Cuban site of Seboruco has yielded dates of between ca. 4000 B.C. and 1000 B.C., although one investigator believes it may date as far back as 6000 B.C. Other Cuban sites, such as Funche Cave, Painted Cave, and Hoyo del Muerto, have dates around 2000 B.C. or younger. Also dating to around 2000 B.C., and not dissimilar to Seboruco, are Archaic sites discovered on Hispaniola (modern Haiti and the Dominican Republic), such as Barrera-Mordán/Casimira, Pedernales, and Couri.

Often located near mangrove swamps, these sites were occupied by hunter-gatherer groups, while others of similar appearance have yielded large stone blades—the so-called stemmed points—that may have been used to hunt now-extinct large mammals. On nearby Puerto Rico, Archaic Period sites have been discovered at Caño Hondo and Cerillo, among others, and at Angostura and Maruca, human burials have been found.

Although disputed by some (see following), the Casimiroid subdivision of the Archaic Period is thought to include the inhabitants of Cuba and Hispaniola (modern Haiti and the Dominican Republic) between 4000 B.C. and 400 B.C. The Casimiroid itself has been further divided into three subseries, the Casimiran, the Courian, and the Redondan—all based on specific assemblages of material culture from individual type-sites. The Casimiran people may have originally come either from Central America or South America. At the type-site of Casimira in southwestern Dominican Republic, stone tools have been found dating to between 2610 B.C. and 2165 B.C., and in neighboring Haiti, to around 3620 B.C.

People of the later Courian subseries left remains at the type-site of Couri on Haiti and at El Porvenir in the Dominican Republic dating to between 2630 B.C. and A.D. 240. Their more elaborate stone tools may indicate a wider range of prey, and sophisticated items such as stone beads and shell jewelry suggest a more developed social and ritual life. The cultural remains of the subsequent Redondan subseries on Cuba, from sites such as Cayo Redondo, span the period 2050 B.C. to A.D. 1300, and include shell middens as well as painted cave sites. On Antigua in the northeastern Lesser Antilles, at least twenty-four sites are known that seem to be related to the Casimiroid tradition. One of these sites, Jolly Beach (ca. 1800 B.C.), seems to have been a workshop area where stone flakes were struck from the abundant pebbles, though manos, metates, and simple beads have also been discovered.

On nearby St. Martin, the site of Norman Estate is assigned to the Archaic Period, yielding flint flakes, river pebbles, and shell artifacts made from Queen Conch (*Strombus gigas*). It has been dated to between ca. 2350 B.C. and 1800 B.C. Similar dates have been given to the earliest evidence for human occupation on St. Kitts, dating to around 2150 B.C. and evidently focused on an economy dominated by the collection of shellfish. On St. Thomas (U.S. Virgin Islands), the Archaic Period site of Krum Bay has been dated from ca. 880 B.C. to 225 B.C. and has given its name to the local culture of that time. Krum Bay culture settlements were located near the sea and appear only to have been open-air sites.

They consist of shell middens, within which have been found basic stone tools, celts, and pendants made either from stone, bone, or shell.

The identification of the Casimiroid as a distinctive cultural tradition highlights several critical issues with the archaeology of Archaic Period sites in the Island Caribbean. These issues concern archaeological theory and methodology. The central issue is how to interpret the complex nature of these early archaeological sites. For example, it may ultimately be the case that a particular site assigned to a specific Archaic (i.e., preceramic) culture on the basis of its stone tools is in fact simply a specific "activity location" of a later, perhaps ceramic culture. Sites without pottery are by definition aceramic, but not necessarily preceramic. For example, the site of Bois Neuf in Haiti possesses stone tools that considered alone suggest a preceramic (Archaic) culture, but the presence of pottery in more recent levels reveals a Taíno date of ca. A.D. 1490. Some sites, especially those located near good stone resources, may be multiperiod, but if no pottery is found they may be designated as purely Archaic and the range of stone tools present may be used to construct a single (and nonexistent) cultural entity, thereby distorting interpretation of this and other sites.

A similar interpretive problem still surrounds the identification of the first preceramic human inhabitants of Cuba. These people were given the name Ciboney and have been defined by their simple technology and cave-dwelling habits; they are assumed to be the ancestors of the Guanahatabey people who lived nearby at the time of the European arrival. Apart from confusion about the actual name Ciboney, archaeologists disagree on interpretation of the patchy and possibly propagandistic historical record and the archaeological evidence. The crucial question is whether or not the Guanahatebays can be considered a relic of the Archaic Period surrounded by more sophisticated pottery-using Taíno peoples, or are a creation of the current inability to understand the incomplete historical and archaeological evidence.

Problems surrounding the investigation, interpretation, and naming of the Island Caribbean's various first human settlers will continue. What is certain, however, is that in most but not all parts of the region, pottery-using Saladoid peoples arrived from South America between around 500 B.C. and 200 B.C. They ushered in a new age of cultural development that increasingly isolated and marginalized any surviving remnants of Archaic Period societies.

See also: Antigua; Banwari Trace (site, Trinidad); Casimiroid; Cuba; Guadeloupe; Guanahatabey; Jolly Beach (site, Antigua); Krum Bay (site, St. Thomas); Margarita Island (Venezuela); Norman Estate (site, St. Martin); Ortoiroid; St. Kitts and Nevis; St. Thomas (USVI); Trinidad and Tobago

References
Allaire, L., and M. Mattioni. 1983. Boutbois et le Goudinot: Deux gisements acéramiques de la Martinique. *Proceedings of the Ninth International Congress for the Study of Pre-Columbian Cultures of the Lesser Antilles, Dominican Republic, August 2–8, 1981,* pp. 27–38; Boomert, A. 2000. *Trinidad, Tobago and the Lower Orinoco Interaction Sphere,* pp. 55–69. Alkmaar, the Netherlands: Cairi Publications; Cruxent, J. M., and I. Rouse. 1969. Early Man in the West Indies. *Scientific American* 221 (5): 42–52; Davis, D. 2000. Jolly Beach and the Preceramic Occupation of Antigua, West Indies. *Yale University Publications in Anthropology* 84. New Haven, CT: Yale

University Press; Guarch, J. M. 2003. The First Caribbean People: Part 1, The Palaeoindians in Cuba and the Circum-Caribbean. In J. Sued-Badillo (ed.), *General History of the Caribbean: Vol. 1, Autochthonous Societies,* pp. 93–118. Paris: UNESCO; Harris, P.O.B. 1973. Preliminary Report on Banwari Trace, A Preceramic Site in Trinidad. *Proceedings of the Fourth International Congress for the Study of Pre-Columbian Cultures of the Lesser Antilles, St. Lucia 1971,* pp. 115–125; Kozlowski, J. K. 1974. *Preceramic Cultures in the Caribbean.* Zeszyty Naukowe, Uniwerstytet Jagielloński, 386, Prace Archeologiczne, Zezyt 20. Krakow; Lundberg, E. R. 1989. *Preceramic Procurement Patterns at Krum Bay, Virgin Islands.* Ph.D. dissertation, University of Illinois, Urbana; Pantel, G. A. 1988. *Precolumbian Flaked Stone Assemblages in the West Indies.* Ph.D. dissertation, University of Tennessee, Knoxville; Pantel, G. A. 2003. The First Caribbean People: Part 2, The Archaics. In J. Sued-Badillo (ed.), *General History of the Caribbean: Vol. 1, Autochthonous Societies,* pp. 118–133. Paris: UNESCO; Rouse, I. 1992. *The Tainos: Rise and Decline of the People Who Greeted Columbus,* pp. 62–67. New Haven, CT: Yale University Press.

Areíto

Areíto is the Taíno word that refers to their ceremonies and dances. In early encounters, the Spanish were welcomed and entertained by the Taíno, who arranged areítos in their honor as a type of elite hospitality. In 1496, when Christopher Columbus's brother Bartolomé visited the Taíno kingdom of Xaraguá in Hispaniola, he was welcomed by Behechio, his sister Anacaona, and an assembly of Taíno nobility who were singing and dancing to music produced by drums and rattles. One Spanish account records that thirty of Behechio's wives appeared completely naked except for a small cotton skirt called a *nagua*. In festive mood, the women sang and danced and carried palm tree branches in their hands.

Areítos usually took place in the plaza or cleared area fronting the chief's house and temple. These areas are also called dance grounds, or dance courts for the Classic Taínos, where they form a bounded area lined with earthen embankments and/or standing stones sometimes decorated with images of *zemís*. This suggests that areítos were also associated in some way with ancestor worship. One account of an areíto tells how men and women purified themselves by vomiting before entering the council house, whereupon they sang the praises of the chief ancestors and asked for the favors of the *zemís*. All levels of society were integrated by the ceremonies and dances of the areítos. They were undoubtedly an important part of Taíno social, political, and ceremonial life, though some of their more subtle meanings are now lost.

See also: Anacaona (Taíno queen); Ball-Game; Behechio (Taíno chief); Cohoba; Zemís

References

Arévalo, M. G., and L. A. Chanlatte Baik. 1976. *Las espátulas vómicas sonajeras de la cultura Taína.* Santo Domingo, the Dominican Republic: Fundación García Arevalo; Lovén, S. 1935. *Origins of the Tainan Culture, West Indies,* Göteborg, Sweden: Elanders; Rouse, I. 1992. *The Tainos: Rise and Decline of the People Who Greeted Columbus.* New Haven, CT: Yale University Press; Wilson, S. M. 1990. *Hispaniola: Caribbean Chiefdoms in the Age of Columbus.* Tuscaloosa, AL: University of Alabama Press.

Aruba

Located 25 km off the Venezuelan mainland, Aruba is 31.5 km long and 10 km wide, and has an area of 184 sq km. Its 70,000 inhabitants are a mix of the original Amerindian population, and Spanish and Dutch colonizers. As Aruba never had a plantation economy, the island is one of the few in the Caribbean without a major African presence.

Archaeological excavations have revealed some evidence of preceramic occupation. As on Bonaire and Curaçao, this early occupation was probably by seminomadic hunter-gatherers from the mainland. Influences from Venezuela probably swept over the island between 1000 B.C. and A.D. 1000, by which time peoples of the Dabajuroid ceramic tradition had arrived. It was probably these Amerindians who brought the Arawakan language to Aruba, and whose descendants were the people called Caquetio by the first European explorers.

Several important Dabajuroid settlement sites have been excavated in recent years. At the site known as Tanki Flip (A.D. 950 to A.D. 1250), investigations have found evidence of perhaps 100 inhabitants living in large oval-shaped and small structures, and surrounded by Dabajuroid pottery, hearths or kilns, stone tools, animal bones, and thousands of shell fragments. Almost 300 shell items were complete and many were made of Queen Conch (*Strombus gigas*), including two notable pieces—a frog-shaped pendant and a curved-shell mask pendant. So rich is the quantity and variety of objects made from shell that the Aruba Archaeological Museum has organized an interdisciplinary research project to investigate them across the island as well as to analyze its own collections. Human burials were also found.

Another Dabajuroid site is that of Santa Cruz, which may have had occupation dating to historic times. Posthole evidence suggests potato-shaped dwellings, some of which have human burials inside, others without. Altogether, some thirty burials have been discovered, of children as well as adults, some in upturned urns, and including a woman interred with her griddle—evidence of manioc consumption. A historic-period burial of an Amerindian woman revealed she had been interred with 2,500 black and white glass beads—evidence of the value of these early exchanges between Europeans and the island's local inhabitants.

Europeans first saw Aruba, along with Bonaire and Curaçao, when the Spaniard Alonso de Ojeda and the Italian Amerigo Vespucci arrived in 1499. On observing the Aruba Amerindians living in houses built on piles over the sea, Vespucci named the mainland Venezuela (little Venice). The Spanish maintained a small presence on Aruba between 1527 and 1636, when the Dutch arrived and took possession of the island. In 1678, the Peace of Nijmegan formally recognized Dutch sovereignty of Aruba, Bonaire, and Curaçao. Aruba's Amerindian peoples seem not to have been exterminated but rather absorbed into the general European population. Between the sixteenth and eighteenth centuries, they supervised European livestock such as cattle, sheep, and horses, and were generally left alone, though they appear to have maintained their own cultural contacts with mainland Amerindians. At this time they inhabited the north of the island where, it is said, the last indigenous-speaking individuals were interred in burial urns in 1800.

The British occupied Aruba several times during the early nineteenth century, and in 1954, Aruba and its two companion islands was granted domestic autonomy. In 1986, Aruba withdrew from the Netherlands Antilles, and is now an autonomous member of the Kingdom of the Netherlands.

Due to Aruba's geography and history, and the focus of Caribbean historical archaeologists on plantation sites, to date little historical archaeology has been carried out on the island. The only significant work has been investigations of the remains of the short-lived gold-working activities between 1824 and 1915. There is an archaeological museum in the capital of Oranjestadt. Culturally, while Dutch is the official language, the everyday local dialect is Papiamento—a mix of Portuguese, Dutch, Spanish, and English with African and Indian influences. The main festival is Carnival, which takes place during the two weeks that precede Lent.

See also: Bonaire; Curaçao; Dabajuroid; Pearls (gems); Tanki Flip (site, Aruba)

References

Boerstra, E.H.J. 1976. Burying the Dead in Pre-Columbian Aruba. *Proceedings of the Sixth International Congress for the Study of Pre-Columbian Cultures of the Lesser Antilles, Point-à-Pitre, Guadeloupe, July 1975,* pp. 125–133; Haviser, J. B. 2001. Historical Archaeology in the Netherlands Antilles and Aruba. In P. Farnsworth (ed.), *Island Lives: Historical Archaeologies of the Caribbean,* pp. 60–81. Tuscaloosa: The University of Alabama Press; Josselin de Jong, J.P.B. 1918. The Praecolumbian and Early Postcolumbian Aboriginal Population of Aruba, Curaçao, and Bonaire. *Internationales Archiv für Ethnographie* 24 (3): 51–114; Stienstra, P. 1988. The Economic History of Gold Mining on Aruba, Netherlands West Indies, 1824–1920. In L. J. van der Steen (ed.), *Studies in Honour of Dr. Pieter Wagenaar Hummelinck,* pp. 227–254. Utrecht, the Netherlands: Koninklijke van de Gaarde; Tacoma, J. 1991. Precolumbian Human Skeletal Remains from Curacao, Aruba, and Bonaire. *Proceedings of the Thirteenth International Congress for Caribbean Archaeology, Curacao 1989,* pp. 802–812; van Heekeren, H. R. 1963. Prehistorical Research on the Islands of Curaçao, Aruba, and Bonaire in 1960. *Nieuwe West-Indische Gids* 43: 1–25; Versteeg, A. H. 1993. Settlement Patterns within the Dabajuroid Santa Cruz Site (Aruba). *Proceedings of the Fifteenth Congress of the International Association for Caribbean Archaeology,* pp. 1–6; Versteeg, A., and S. Rostain (eds.). 1997. The Archaeology of Aruba: The Tanki Flip Site. *Publications of the Archaeological Museum of Aruba* No. 8. Aruba/Amsterdam; Versteeg, A., and A. C. Ruiz. 1995. Reconstructing Brasilwood Island: The Archaeology and Landscape of Indian Aruba. *Publications of the Archaeology Museum of Aruba* No. 6. Oranjestadt, Aruba.

Atajadizo

The Atajadizo culture was the first example of the Chican Ostionoid (Taíno) subseries in eastern Hispaniola (modern-day Dominican Republic). Named after the archaeological site where it was discovered, it developed out of the previous local Punta style around A.D. 800.

Made by the so-called Anadel people, Atajadizo pottery represents a style that favored bowls with constricted mouths, rims, and handles decorated with modeled or appliqué human and animal head lugs, and feet attached to the base of the vessel. Curving incised designs and dots, sometimes alternating with rectilinear incisions, were used as decoration both on the inside and outside of the vessel. These designs recall those of the contemporary Meillac pottery used farther west. Archaeologists call the Atajadizo style "modeled-incised," thereby differentiating it from the Punta and Meillac styles, though whether it originated with the Barrancoid or Cedrosan Saladoid is still unclear. Somewhat later, around 950, the Atajadizo people developed a further variation of their Chican Ostionoid pottery with less surface polishing and more intricate incised designs. This is called the Guayabal style after the archaeological site where it was discovered.

Some investigators regard the Atajadizo as an intermediate stage of cultural development, during which time there was a growing population and a consequent intensification of agriculture, as suggested by the increased frequency of ceramic cassava griddles. What is certain is that at this time there is a great variety of local social and cultural developments in the Greater Antilles, and a proliferation of local pottery styles.

See also: Barrancoid; Hispaniola; Meillacan; Ostionoid; Taíno (Chican Ostionoid)

References
Calderon, F. L. 1976. Preliminary Report on the Indian Cemetery "El Atajadizo," Dominican Republic. *Proceedings of the Sixth International Congress for the Study of Pre-Columbian Cultures of the Lesser Antilles, Point-à-Pitre, Guadeloupe, July 1975,* pp. 295–303; Keegan, W. F. 1992. *The People Who Discovered Columbus: The Prehistory of the Bahamas,* pp. 17–18. Gainesville, FL: University Press of Florida; Rouse, I. 1992. *The Tainos: Rise and Decline of the People Who Greeted Columbus,* pp. 110–111, 115. New Haven, CT: Yale University Press; Veloz Maggiolo, M., E. Ortega, M. Sanoja, and I. Vargas. 1976. Preliminary Report on Archaeological Investigations at El Atajadizo, Dominican Republic. *Proceedings of the Sixth International Congress for the Study of Pre-Columbian Cultures of the Lesser Antilles, Point-à-Pitre, Guadeloupe, July 1975,* pp. 283–294; Veloz Maggiolo, M., I. Vargas, M. Sanoja, and F. Luna Calderón. 1976. *Arqueología de Yuma (Dominican Republic),* pp. 28–72. Santo Domingo, Dominican Republic: Taller.

B

Balboa, Vasco Núñez de

Vasco Núñez de Balboa (ca. 1475–1519) was a Spanish explorer famous for being the first European to see the Pacific Ocean. He was also responsible for making contact with Amerindians along the Caribbean coast of Panama and adjacent Colombia, observing their customs and habits including their goldworking traditions.

While his early life is somewhat shadowy, by 1500 Balboa was in the West Indies, having joined an expedition led by Juan de la Cosa and Rodrigo Bastidada to the Tierra Firme (Panama and Colombia) of the southwestern Caribbean, around the Gulf of Urabá. After this he lived for a while at the Spanish settlement of Salvatierra de la Sabana in southwestern Hispaniola.

In 1510, Balboa returned to the Gulf of Urabá, reportedly as a stowaway, with Martín Fernández de Enciso's expedition to relieve the settlement of Saint Sebastián. This town had been abandoned by the conquistador Alonso de Ojeda and left in the charge of Francisco Pizarro, the future conqueror of the Inca empire. Surrounded by hostile Amerindians, the situation at Saint Sebastián was untenable. Balboa advised that the Spanish move instead to the western side of the Gulf of Urabá near the Amerindian village of Darién. Here, he noted, the indigenous population inhabitants were more friendly and did not use poisoned arrows. Balboa was thus responsible for the founding of Santa María la Antigua del Darién, one of the most successful Spanish settlements on the Caribbean coast of Tierra Firme.

Balboa was duly made a justice of the new settlement and ultimately tried and sentenced to death the conquistador Diego de Nicuesa, who was deemed to have exceeded his authority by claiming control over Darién. Balboa then outmaneuvered Enciso, who returned to Hispaniola leaving Balboa in command of the town. Learning from his own and others' experiences on Hispaniola, Balboa did not upset the local political arrangements of native chiefs (caciques), nor did he extort tribute or divide up the local population as virtual slave labor. Instead he cleverly inserted himself into the native system, becoming a type of supreme white chief, protecting the Amerindians from abuse by the Spanish. This attitude brought peace to the region and offerings of Amerindian gold, food, and voluntary labor to Darién. As a result, the new Spanish settlement flourished.

Like many conquistadors, Balboa was motivated by gold. He soon became convinced that there was a local source somewhere to the west of the town. In 1511, he organized an expedition along the Caribbean shores of the province of Careta north of Darién, where he befriended an Amerindian chief and was given golden artifacts. The Caretans guided him north to the great chief Comogre, whose territory stretched from the central area of the Isthmus of Panama eastward to the Caribbean coast. Comogre entertained his guests in lavish style in a great hall from whose rafters hung the desiccated cadavers of his ancestors wearing golden face masks. Balboa received golden jewelry and sealed an alliance with Comogre, who told him of a great sea to the west.

In 1512, Balboa mounted an expedition south in search of a great chief called Dabeiba, whose land was reportedly rich in gold. He didn't find the chief or his lands and returned to Darién, from where he wrote to the king of Spain of his explorations and discoveries and of his plans to mount a new expedition to the west. The king's reaction was to send a relief expedition under Pedro de Ávila, who was charged with investigating Balboa's recent activities and to start proceedings against him for his treatment of Enciso.

Balboa's second expedition westward sighted the Pacific Ocean on 27 September 1513. He famously walked through the surf and claimed the giant sea for Spain. He then visited Amerindian villages along the western part of Panama, finding golden artifacts and learning of rich pearl fisheries maintained by the native inhabitants, but could not locate a source for the gold. Frustration turned to anger and he began terrorizing the local people, holding chiefs for ransom and committing all types of cruelties.

In June 1514, de Ávila arrived in Darién and immediately began raiding and antagonizing the Amerindians so painstakingly pacified by Balboa. As the natives resisted and disease spread, the state of Darién worsened. Balboa unceasingly complained to the king about de Ávila's activities but judiciously kept clear of Darién. De Ávila, however, had him arrested, tried for treason, and executed. In many ways, Balboa can be considered as the man who transcended the Caribbean—opening new vistas for exploration and expanding European knowledge concerning the size of the world and the disposition of land and sea.

See also: Cuna

References

Anderson, C.L.G. 1971. *Life and Letters of Vasco Nuñez de Balboa, Including the Conquest and Settlement of Darien and Panama*. Westport, CT: Greenwood Press; Romoli, K. 1953. *Balboa of Darien: Discoverer of the Pacific*. New York: Doubleday; Sauer, C. O. 1969. *The Early Spanish Main*. Berkeley, CA: University of California Press.

Ball-Game

At the time of Columbus's arrival in the Caribbean, the Taínos played a rubber ball-game known as *batey* in custom-made rectangular ballcourts. Apart from recreation, these ball-games almost certainly possessed political and cosmological dimensions, as did similar games played throughout Mesoamerica and parts of northern South America. The Spanish witnessed the Taíno ball-game firsthand, commenting on its popularity and the remarkable elasticity of the solid rubber ball. They observed that wagers were often laid on the outcome, with the chiefs (caciques) offering prizes of food for winners of important intervillage contests.

Spanish accounts tell how the game was played by two teams, each of which numbered between ten and thirty players. The objective was to keep the ball in motion and move it into the opposing team's end of the court. This had to be achieved without using either hands or feet. As in Mesoamerica, ball-game players wore special equipment for protection and perhaps also to more accurately deflect the ball by using the shoulder or hip. The so-called stone collars and elbow stones may have been based on wooden prototypes and were possibly worn as belts, with more elaborate examples serving a ceremonial function. Fragments of these items have been found associated with ballcourts at many different sites. Each team took turns in serving the ball, watched by spectators either seated on the earthen embankments that flanked the court, or, if they were high-ranking individuals, seated on their ceremonial stools or *duhos*. Both women and men played batey, though not against each other.

In pre-Taíno times, during the Saladoid and Ostionoid Periods, archaeology indicates the ball-game had been played in a variety of simpler types of courts that were often little more than open spaces, as at Maisabel in Puerto Rico. Despite their normally rectangular shape, it is sometimes difficult to differentiate between plazas that were ballcourts and those that may have been used as dance courts or for ceremonial or religious purposes. Whether rectangular, square, oval, or circular, all such plazas could be multipurpose.

By Classic Taíno times, there appear to have been two main types of ballcourts—those within a village that were used by the local inhabitants, and others in the countryside, possibly used for contests between teams representing different villages. In Puerto Rico, the countryside location of the most sophisticated ballcourts has been explained by their being situated on the territorial boundaries of different chiefdoms—an interpretation that would support a political role for at least some of the contests.

Archaeologists have identified early examples of ballcourts in Puerto Rico at the sites of Bronce and Tibes. These were lined with slabs of stone set upright or laid flat and were associated with human burials—a practice abandoned in later times when separate cemeteries came into being. From south-central Puerto Rico, the practice of building ballcourts appears to have spread eastward to St. Croix in the Virgin Islands and westward to Hispaniola (the Dominican Republic and Haiti) and thence to eastern Cuba. At the Salt River site on St. Croix, there is the easternmost example of a Classic Taíno ballcourt. It is a single, stone-lined clearing in the middle of a village area, with several of its slabs decorated with crude petroglyphs. Fragments of stone belts have been found at the site and an adjacent cemetery suggests a religious and ritual dimension for the court, perhaps associated with ancestor worship.

Moving west through the Dominican Republic, ballcourts become less numerous but larger in size. The biggest is a circular structure at the site of Corrales de los Indios that may have been the major village of the Taíno chief Caonabo. Farther west, in Haiti and eastern Cuba, ballcourts tend to be of simpler construction, flanked only by earthen embankments. North of Haiti, on Middle Caicos Island, several possible dance or ballcourts have been found lined with rocks rather than slabs. One appears to be associated with a chief's house and it has been suggested that some of the stones were astronomically aligned. This site is thought to be a Classic Taíno outpost.

To date, the most elaborate grouping of plazas or courts has been found at Caguana (or Capá) in the mountainous country of central Puerto Rico. The site spans the Ostionan and Chican Periods and has been heavily reconstructed. While Caguana boasts a number of courts, most have an uncertain function, and only one has been identified as a ballcourt due to its rectangular shape. Lined with undecorated stones on each of its four sides, it lies adjacent to a larger square plaza referred to as a dance court, and is surrounded by a number of variously shaped plazas. Caguana may have been the seat of the powerful chief Guarionex.

Until recently, it was believed the Taíno ball-game had been introduced from Mesoamerica, where the game was played in large sophisticated ballcourts and was accompanied by human sacrifices. The Classic Maya especially considered the ballgame to have important symbolic and mythological significance. Today, archaeologists consider it equally likely that the Caribbean ball-game was a parallel development from similar types of activities in village plazas throughout the tropical rainforest areas of the circum-Caribbean mainland.

See also: Atajadizo; Caguana/Capá (site, Puerto Rico); Caonabo (Taíno chief); Duhos; Guacanagarí (Taíno chief); Maisabel (site, Puerto Rico); Ostionoid; Saladoid; Salt River (site, St. Croix); St. Croix (USVI)

References
Alegría, R. E. 1983. Ball Courts and Ceremonial Plazas in the West Indies. *Yale University Publications in Anthropology* No. 79. New Haven, CT; Eckholm, G. 1961. Puerto Rican Stone Collars as Ballgame Belts. In S. K. Lothrop (ed.), *Essays in Pre-Columbian Art and Archaeology,* pp. 356–371. Cambridge, MA: Harvard University Press; Faber Morse, B. 1990. The Pre-Columbian Ball and Dance Court at Salt River, St. Croix. *FOLK: Journal of the Danish Ethnographical Society* 32: 45–60; Lovén, S. 1935. *Origins of the Tainan Culture, West Indies,* pp. 86–99, Göteborg, Sweden: Elanders; Scarborough, V. L., and D. R. Wilcox (eds.). 1991. *The Mesoamerican Ballgame.* Tucson, AZ: The University of Arizona Press; Stern, T. 1949. The Rubber-Ball Games of the Americas. *Monographs of the American Ethnological Society* No. 17, New York.

Banwari Trace (site, Trinidad)

Banwari Trace is located on the edge of the Oropuche Lagoon in southern Trinidad. In 1969, archaeological excavations revealed a mix of marine and terrestrial fauna ranging from freshwater mollusks to the remains of pig, deer, alligator, and howler monkey. The changing variety and frequency of shells is regarded as an indicator of changing environmental conditions leading to adaptive changes in subsistence strategies by the inhabitants. Stone tools, such as blades, scrapers, and projectile points, together with a fragment of a serpentine bowl, appeared to be made variously from local as well as mainland South American materials. Human remains were found scattered across the surface of the site, and in 1978 a complete human skeleton was removed. Most significant, the oldest levels of the site were radiocarbon dated to about 5000 B.C., which makes it the oldest Archaic Period site—and thus the earliest evidence for human occupation—in the Island Caribbean. The artifacts have been assigned by archaeologists to the Ortoiroid culture.

See also: Ortoiroid; Trinidad and Tobago

References

Boomert, A. 2000. *Trinidad, Tobago, and the Lower Orinoco Interaction Sphere*, pp. 55–69. Alkmaar, the Netherlands: Cairi Publications; Harris, P.O.B. 1971. *Banwari Trace: Preliminary Report on a Preceramic Site in Trinidad, West Indies*. Pointe-a-Pierre: Trinidad and Tobago Historical Society (South Section); Harris, P.O.B. 1973. Preliminary Report on Banwari Trace: A Preceramic Site in Trinidad. *Proceedings of the Fourth International Congress for the Study of Pre-Columbian Cultures of the Lesser Antilles, St. Lucia 1971*, pp. 115–125; Veloz Maggiolo, M. 1971–1972. Localizan enterramiento Meso-Indio en Trinidad. *Revista Dominicana de Arqueólogia e Antropólogia* 2/3: 300–302.

Barbados

Barbados is 34 km long by 22.5 km wide, and is the easternmost of all the Caribbean Islands. It has a population of over 260,000, most of whom are of African descent, with some mixed-race people.

Barbados was first settled by the village-living and pottery-making peoples of the later (Barrancoid influenced) Saladoid tradition, who journeyed there by canoe from South America, perhaps via Trinidad. The early colonizers cleared the land for horticulture probably between A.D. 350 and A.D. 650, an activity that may have upset the delicate balance of the island's ecosystem. After 650, a series of locally inspired pottery styles developed out of the earlier Saladoid tradition and lasted until around 1100. The umbrella term for these local styles, on Barbados and throughout the Island Caribbean, is the Troumassoid. The final era of prehistoric occupation on Barbados is called the Suazoid, which came to an end either just before or soon after Europeans arrived in the region during the late fifteenth century.

One of Barbados's most important archaeological sites is Chancery Lane, which appears to have been occupied for over 1,000 years by a succession of Amerindian peoples. Typical Saladoid pottery-like ceramic cassava griddles have been found, as has evidence of later Troumassoid and Suazoid presence. Another multiperiod site is Heywoods, which also has Saladoid remains but is dominated by finds from later periods, including the remains of an unusual Troumassoid Period round house fringed by coral fragments. Of a similar late date are the sites of Silver Sands and Hillcrest, all of which are dated to around A.D. 1000.

It is unclear who was the first European to see Barbados or when this might have happened. Probably the earliest reference to the island is the Spanish mention of the Isla de los Barbudos in 1518. Barbados's name is commonly ascribed to Portuguese navigators who named the island after the bearded fig trees that they saw. Early landings make no mention of Amerindians and it seems likely that by this time, if not earlier, the last Suazoid inhabitants had left the island.

In 1627, the English successfully colonized the island and within a few decades there were about 40,000 Europeans living there. Most were small-scale farmers, who left after the establishment of larger-scale sugar plantations during the 1650s. At this time, some of the poorer colonizers lost their livelihood, were pushed onto less desirable land, and became economically marginalized as the still-existing group known as the Poor Whites. The location of Barbados outside the main arc of Caribbean islands meant that it avoided the colonial period conflicts between the French and British.

Today, Barbados's African-Caribbean peoples refer to themselves as Bajans, and popular culture is a mix of African and Caribbean traditions. While most people belong to the Anglican Church, the services are musically vibrant occasions with handclapping gospel hymns that recall African rhythms rather than European Christian singing. In 1957, Pastor Granville Williams returned to Barbados from Trinidad and founded the Spiritual Baptist Church that teaches the pan-African idea of the Black Divinity. Mysticism is at the heart of this movement and the followers wear white robes and colored sashes with cloth tied around their heads—hence their popular name as Tie-Heads. This faith is an indigenous Barbadian development that is a true fusion of Christian and African elements.

During services, bells are sounded, a conch shell is blown, and there is much foot-stomping and handclapping. Their worship involves the whole body, which they move by bowing and spinning in front of the altar. A distinctive feature is the practice of so-called Mourning Ground rituals—purification prayers and meditations undertaken by those baptized in the faith—that take place in an especially sacred part of the church known as the Mourning Ground. There are currently two specially built Spiritual Baptist churches—the Zion Apostolic Temple at Richmond Gap and the Jerusalem Apostolic Cathedral at Ealing Grove.

Today, the largest festival on the island is called Cropover and derives from slavery days on the sugar plantations. It begins with the blessing of the last sugar canes to be harvested. Parades and calypso competitions take place prior to Kadooment Day on the first Monday in August. Commemorating the arrival of the first white settlers is the Holetown Festival held in February, and leading up to Independence Day on 30 November is the National Independence Festival of Creative Arts.

Bridgetown, the capital, has a statue of Lord Nelson, a Parliament building dating to 1872, St. Michael's cathedral dating to 1789, and an early-nineteenth-century synagogue on the site of an earlier version built by Jews who left Brazil in the seventeenth century. Bridgetown also has the so-called Garrison Area, a grouping of nineteenth-century military structures that includes a group of thirty cannon, and the Barbados Museum, which exhibits items of natural history and colonial period heritage. Beyond the capital are vestiges of the island's colonial history such as Morgan Lewis Mill, Gun Hill, and Farley Hill House. Harrison's Cave has a small exhibition of Amerindian objects.

> **See also:** Chancery Lane (site, Barbados); Dogs; Heywoods (site, Barbados); Hillcrest (site, Barbados); Historical Archaeology; Newton Plantation (Barbados); Orisha/Shango (Trinidad); Saladoid; Silver Sands (site, Barbados); Slavery; Suazey/Suazoid; Sugar; Troumassoid

References

Beckles, H. M. 1990. *A History of Barbados: From Amerindian Settlement to Nation State.* Cambridge: Cambridge University Press; Boomert, A. 1987. Notes on Barbados Prehistory. *Journal Barbados Museum Historical Society* 38 (1): 8–43; Bullen, R. P., and A. K. Bullen. 1968. Barbados Archaeology 1966. *Proceedings of the Second International Congress for the Study of Pre-Columbian Cultures of the Lesser Antilles, Barbados,* pp. 134–144. Barbados; Corruccini, R. S., J. S. Handler, R. J. Mutaw, and F. W. Lange. 1982. Osteology of a Slave Burial Population from Barbados, West Indies. *American Journal of Physical Anthropology* 59: 443–459; Drewett, P. L. 1991. *Prehistoric Barbados.* London: Institute of Archaeology and Archetype Publications; Guglin, T. 1974. *The Spiritual Baptist Church of Barbados: A Description of an Afro-Christian Religion.* Unpublished manuscript. University of the West Indies, Cave Hill, Barbados; Handler, J. S. 1997. An African-Type Healer/Diviner and His Grave Goods: A Burial from a Plantation Slave Cemetery in Barbados. *International Journal of Historical Archaeology* 1 (2): 91–130; Handler, J. S., and F. W. Lange. 1978. *Plantation Slavery in Barbados: An Archaeological and Historical Investigation.* Cambridge, MA: Harvard University Press; Hughes, G. 1750. *The Natural History of Barbados in Ten Books.* London: privately published; Inniss, L. 1985. *Vestiges of an African Past in Barbadian Culture.* Unpublished manuscript. University of the West Indies, Cave Hill, Barbados; Kremser, M., 2001. African-Derived Religions in Barbados. In S. D. Glazier (ed.), *Encyclopedia of African and African-American Religions,* pp. 41–43. New York: Routledge; Sloane, H. 1707. *A Voyage to the Islands Madera, Barbados, Nieves, S. Christophes, and Jamaica with the Natural History of the Herbs and Trees, Four-Footed Beasts, Fishes, Birds, Insects, Reptiles, etc. of the Last of Those Islands.* London: privately published.

Barrancoid

The Barrancoid peoples take their name from the sites of Los Barrancos and Barrancas on the banks of the lower Orinoco River in Venezuela. Barrancoid culture seems to have developed between 1500 B.C. and 1000 B.C., possibly out of the local Ronquinan Saladoid tradition. Its peoples moved northward to the mouth of the Orinoco river delta, perhaps displacing or bypassing other Saladoid groups as they went. They brought settled village life, cassava (manioc) cultivation, and elaborate pottery to the Archaic Period peoples of the central coast of Venezuela.

By around A.D. 500, they appear to have traveled by canoe across the Columbus Channel to Trinidad, where Barrancoid pottery appears associated with Saladoid ceramics at the sites of Palo Seco and Erin on the south coast of the island. From Trinidad, Barrancoid peoples made their way northward to Tobago, arriving in the Lesser Antilles just after A.D. 350. Between this time and A.D. 500, Barrancoid influence in the area was at its height but faded soon after. Barrancoid influence is apparent in the pottery of the Virgin Islands and at the site of Sorcé on the island of Vieques, Puerto Rico.

In many ways, Barrancoid ceramics are an elaboration on previous Cedrosan Saladoid styles. Some archaeologists regard it simply as a baroque phase of the Saladoid. Typically, Barrancoid pottery is made with quartz sand or grit temper. Its main shapes are bowls, jars, bottles, and cone-shaped incense burners perhaps used for the ritual taking of hallucinogens. Distinctive decoration includes elaborate incision and modeling, simple line and/or spiral decoration, and anthropomorphic and zoomorphic hands, feet, and faces. Often, such intricately modeled and incised features are in the form of *adornos*—the decorative lugs and handles of ceramics. Sometimes individual animals can be identified and monkeys, caiman, king vultures, and macaws have all been recognized in Barrancoid ceramic imagery.

The mechanisms by which Barrancoid influences appear on, or associated with, Saladoid pottery, remain poorly understood and the relationship between the two styles is problematic. A common expression is to describe ceramics of this period as Saladoid with Barrancoid influences. Nevertheless, the discovery of Barrancoid pottery in Cedrosan Saladoid sites in Trinidad and Tobago, and of typically Saladoid zic (zone-incised cross-hatching) pottery in Lower Orinoco locations suggests trade as an important mechanism. Barrancoid peoples appear to have been masters of long-distance trade, especially by canoe. Sites such as Sorcé on Vieques (offshore Puerto Rico) and others in Montserrat and Tobago have been referred to by archaeologists as Saladoid/Barrancoid ports of trade.

See also: Cedros (site, Trinidad); Montserrat; Palo Seco (site, Trinidad); Saladoid; Trinidad and Tobago; Zic Pottery

References

Allaire, L. 1999. Archaeology of the Caribbean Region. In F. Salomon, and S. B. Schwartz (eds.). *The Cambridge History of the Native Peoples of the Americas: Vol. III, South America Part 1,* pp. 702–706, 719, Cambridge: Cambridge University Press; Boomert, A. 2000. *Trinidad, Tobago, and the Lower Orinoco Interaction Sphere,* pp. 118–125, 202–216. Alkmaar, the Netherlands; Rouse, I. 1992. *The Tainos: Rise and Decline of the People Who Greeted Columbus,* New Haven, CT: Yale University Press.

Behechio (Taíno chief)

Behechio Anacaochoa was the principal chief (cacique) of the province of Xaraguá in southwestern Hispaniola at the time of Columbus's arrival in 1493. Like other Taíno lords, he had many titles, one of which, Tareigua Hobin, meant "prince resplendent as copper." His sister, Anacaona, was married to Caonabo, the chief of the neighboring province of Maguana. Today there is no archaeological evidence for Behechio's village, which probably lies beneath Haiti's capital city of Port-au-Prince.

In January 1497, Christopher Columbus's brother, Bartolomé, arrived in Xaraguá with his men. They were welcomed by Behechio who arranged for songs and dances (*areítos*) in Bartolomé's honor, feted him with palms and branches, and feasted him on fish from the rivers and the sea. Knowing of the Spaniards' actions elsewhere, Behechio was probably hoping to appease the powerful strangers. The Spaniards were housed in twos and threes in different houses within the village, with Bartolomé staying in the great house of Behechio where the festivities were held. From later accounts it is known that this house could hold upward of eighty people.

Bartolomé informed the Taíno chief that Christopher Columbus expected him to offer tribute as a token of subservience to the Spanish Crown. Behechio protested that as he knew gold was the only tribute acceptable to the Spanish he could not comply, as his kingdom was poor in gold. Bartolomé replied that he would accept food—especially cassava—as well as cotton in lieu of gold and the two finally agreed. In this way, Behechio gained a reprieve for his people from the fate of other Taíno on the island.

Several months later, on hearing from Behechio that the tribute was ready, Bartolomé returned to Xaraguá. He was again received with great hospitality by Behechio, his sister Anacaona, and thirty-two lesser chiefs, and was supplied with cotton, fish, cassava, and root crops. Such was the quantity of gifts that Bartolomé arranged for a caravel to sail around the island and anchor offshore. When they heard this, Behechio and Anacaona accompanied the Spanish to the coast, stopping for the night in one of Anacaona's houses where the Spaniards saw cotton goods, *duhos,* and artful wooden sculptures—some of which Bartolomé received as gifts. The next day, Behechio and Anacaona were invited onboard the Spanish ship and were duly impressed by its size and maneuverability and especially by the firing of its lombard guns.

Six years later, in 1503, when the Spanish Governor of Hispaniola Nicolás de Ovando visited Xaraguá, Behechio had died and apparently been succeeded by his royal sister. Anacaona and many of the lesser chiefs were tricked and then murdered and the village devastated.

See also: Anacaona (Taíno queen); Areíto; Caonabo (Taíno chief); Columbus, Christopher; Gold; Guacanagarí (Taíno chief); Guarionex (Taíno chief); Taíno (Arawak)

References
Las Casas, B. 1992. *A Short Account of the Destruction of the Indies.* London: Penguin Books;
Sauer, C. O. 1969. *The Early Spanish Main.* Berkeley, CA: University of California Press;
Wilson, S. M. 1990. *Hispaniola: Caribbean Chiefdoms in the Age of Columbus.* Tuscaloosa, AL: University of Alabama Press;

Betty's Hope (site, Antigua)

Although the first crops grown by the British on Antigua were tobacco, indigo, and ginger, by 1674 sugar had become king. The dominance of sugar accelerated from 1684, when Sir Christopher Codrington arrived on the island bringing with him ideas and technology for large-scale cultivation. By the 1750s, Antigua had over 150 sugar mills, among which was Codrington's original estate called Betty's Hope, after his daughter.

Located in the limestone center of Antigua, the original plantation had been founded in the early 1650s by Antigua's governor Christopher Keynell, but after his death was sold by his widow to Codrington in 1674. So successful was Codrington at transforming the plantation into a profitable business that other Antiguan plantation owners soon abandoned other crops and focused on sugar. In many ways, Betty's Hope was like any other large sugar plantation; a small number of European overseers supervised a large number of Africans (first as slaves, then as free laborers) in an enterprise that was both industrial and agricultural. The workers at Betty's Hope developed great skill as boilers, distillers, and craftsmen that gave the estate a superior reputation.

Historic windmills of Betty's Hope sugar plantation on the island of Antigua (Reinhard Eisele / Corbis)

In 1990, Betty's Hope Trust was formed, with the aim of restoring the plantation as an open-air museum and interpretation center. Today, there is a visitor center/museum located in an old cotton house storeroom, and of the two surviving sugar-cane windmills, one has been completely restored with cane-crushing machinery in working order and new sails attached. As part of the ongoing research and restoration program, the plantation has been surveyed and photographed by historical archaeologists, the vegetation cleared, surface collections made, and test pits dug. So far, the original 1674 sugar mill, the postemancipation pay office, and the overseer's house have been investigated. It is thought that there may be as many as three cemeteries associated with the site. Future projects include restoring the underground catchment area (cisterns) where the cane juice collected after crushing, and investigating the Great House and slave village.

Betty's Hope illustrates the archaeology of the early colonial period, highlighting the beginnings of African-Caribbean culture, and also shows how such sites developed during the later nineteenth and twentieth centuries. More than just a historical plantation, Betty's Hope represents a focus for Antiguan history, and through its development as an open-air museum, it has become an important tourist attraction. In some ways, Betty's Hope remains as important a part of the wider Antiguan economy today as it was before, though now for tourism rather than sugar.

See also: Antigua; Galways Plantation; Historical Archaeology; Slavery; Sugar

References

Carstensen, B. 1993. *Betty's Hope: An Antiguan Sugar Plantation*. St. John's, Antigua: Betty's Hope Trust; Dyde, B. 1993. *Antigua and Barbuda: The Heart of the Caribbean*. London: Macmillan Caribbean; Gaspar, D. B. 1985. *Bondsmen and Rebels: A Study of Master-Slave Relations in Antigua*. Baltimore: Johns Hopkins University Press; Goodwin, C. M. 1994. Betty's Hope Windmill: An Unexpected Problem. *Historical Archaeology* 28 (1): 99–110; Murphy, R. 1989. Betty's Hope Old North Mill Excavated. *Antigua Historical and Archaeological Society Newsletter* 27 (1): 5; Murphy, R. 1993. The Importance of Betty's Hope in a Caribbean Historical Perspective. *Antigua Historical and Archaeological Society Newsletter* 42: 5; Nicholson, D. V. 1994. *Heritage Landmarks: Antigua and Barbuda*. St. John's, Antigua: Museum of Antigua and Barbuda.

Birds

The trees and skies of the Caribbean vibrate with the dazzle and calls of a seemingly endless variety of birds. Located on migration routes between North and South America, some Caribbean islands have endemic species such as Grenada's yellow-billed parrot, while others, like Trinidad, have over 400 species of primarily South American birds. Like all Amerindian peoples, those inhabiting the Island Caribbean saw birds as spirit beings, the natural avatars of shamans, able to break the bonds of earth and fly up to the spirit realm. Shimmering plumage, flapping wings, and echoing calls have an ineffable quality, and it is no surprise that avian symbolism figures prominently in pottery and jewelry from Saladoid times to the Taíno Period.

The association of birds with shamans and hallucinogenic trance is illustrated by a seventeenth-century legend concerning the Chaima people who lived around the margins of Trinidad's Pitch Lake. The Chaima believed they had offended spirits of the dead by unwittingly hunting their souls, which had transformed into hummingbirds. As a punishment, their village sank into the earth and Pitch Lake appeared. Hummingbirds drink the nectar of the tobacco plant, and shamans can transform into them in order to obtain tobacco for their curing séances. Such ideas are well documented for the Venezuelan Warao who regularly visited Trinidad, and who believed that tobacco shamanism was invented in the House of Tobacco Smoke, created out of nothingness by the Creator Bird of Dawn. Farther north, in the Greater Antilles, a Taíno myth tells how women were created when *inriri* birds (woodpeckers) were tied to sexless bodies and, thinking they were attached to tree trunks, pecked a hole where a woman's sexual parts are found.

The natural beauty of bird plumage usually outweighed their value as food. In the richly elaborate headdresses and costumes of Amerindians, the symbolism of color, shininess, and texture added to the value of feathers, and so birds were hunted with arrows designed to stun rather than damage the bird.

Archaeologically, sophisticated avian imagery first appears on carved-stone pendants of the Saladoid people from Puerto Rico, Grenada, and Trinidad. Identified by the distinctive beak as probably the South American king vulture, the bird grasps a turtle or human head in its claws. Many bird images previously identified as parrots or condors may in fact be the king vulture. In the Windward Islands also, some stone axes have a distinctive profile that may be the juxtaposed heads of the king vulture. It is thought possible that these objects were used not as axes but rather as platforms for snuffing hallucinogenic powder. Such associations are explicit in Taíno carved-wood *zemí* bird figures, where the body has a circular platform attached from which the hallucinogenic *cohoba* powder was snuffed by shamans through tubes.

Bird imagery, in pottery decoration (*adornos*), whistles and flutes, headdresses and regalia, as well as mythology, was an integral part of indigenous Caribbean culture. When Africans arrived they too used avian symbolism to express their identity and beliefs. African-derived ideas informed metalworking, as in the power of blacksmiths conceptualized as the anvil bird whose ominous call sounds like clashing metal. Today, the Caribbean's rich birdlife attracts many visitors and adds to the region's thriving ecotourism industry.

See also: Shamanism; Taíno (Arawak); Tobacco; Trinidad and Tobago; Warao; Zemís
References
Arrom, J. J., and M. García-Arévalo. 1988. El murciélago y la lechuza en la cultura Taína. *Serie Monográfica* 24. Santo Domingo, Dominican Republic: Fundación García Arévalo; Benson, E. P. 1997. *Birds and Beasts of Ancient Latin America,* pp. 68–92. Gainesville, FL: University Press of Florida; Bond, J. 1971. *Birds of the West Indies.* Boston: Houghton Mifflin; Boomert, A. 2001. Raptorial Birds as Icons of Shamanism in the Prehistoric Caribbean and Amazonia. In W. H. Metz, B. L. van Beek, and H. Steegstra (eds.). *Patina: Essays Presented to Jay Jordan Butler on the Occasion of his 80th birthday,* pp. 99–123. Groningen, the Netherlands: Groningen State University; Ffrench, R. 1992. *A Guide to the Birds of Trinidad and Tobago.* London: Christopher Helm; Reina, R. E., and K. M. Kensinger (eds.). 1991. *The Gift of Birds: Featherwork of Native South American Peoples.* Philadelphia: University Museum of Archaeology and Anthropology, University of Pennsylvania; Wilbert, J. 1985. The House of the Swallow-Tailed Kite: Warao Myth and the Art of Thinking in Images. In G. Urton (ed.), *Animal Myths and Metaphors in South America,* pp. 145–182. Salt Lake City, UT: University of Utah Press.

Black Legend

The Black Legend was the name given to the European views about the cruel and intolerant behavior of the Spanish in the Americas, and especially the Caribbean. Although such attitudes existed long before the twentieth century, the term seems to have been first publicized by the Spanish writer Julián Juderías y Loyot in his book of the same name published in 1914.

The origins of the attitudes represented by the Black Legend are commonly believed to have originated in the work of Bartolomé de Las Casas, who charged the Spanish conquistadors with decimating the native peoples of the Caribbean, most notably in his widely read and translated *Brevíssima relación de la destruición de las Indias* (*A Short Account of the Destruction of the Indies*), published in 1552. Theodore de Bry's graphic depictions of murder, rape, and savagery, which illustrated his editions of Las Casas's work, fixed indelible images of the horror of Spanish treatment of the Amerindians in the European mind. While Las Casas's book was published in the sixteenth century when Spain was a major power, within 100 years the country's imperial position was declining—censorship followed, and the *Brevíssima relación* was banned. There is little doubt that Spain's adversaries in those empire-building times, particularly England and Holland, seized on this evidence as propaganda against the Spanish.

The twentieth-century development of the Black Legend was tied both to the disappearance of the Spanish empire and political developments within Spain itself. Right-wing tendencies, especially during the period of General Franco, attacked the liberalism that had allowed Las Casas to make his criticisms and what followed was a period of historical revisionism that denied these accusations. More recently, Las Casas's work has been reviewed in a more positive light and it has been realized that much of the information used to substantiate the legend came from pro-Spanish writers such as the eyewitness Oviedo. Today, most scholars agree that the Black Legend was based mainly on fact and began with the activities of Christopher Columbus himself. When Columbus arrived in Hispaniola in 1492 there were perhaps 3 to 4 million Taíno inhabitants, but by 1516 the number had declined to maybe only 12,000. Disease was a major killer, but cruelty and abuse played a major part and established the characteristic Spanish treatment of Amerindians henceforth.

See also: Disease; Las Casas, Bartolomé de; Oviedo y Valdés, Gonzalo Fernández de
References

Chaunu, P. 1964. La Légende Noire Antihispanique. *Revue de Psychologie des Peuples,* pp. 188–223; Conley, T. 1992. De Bry's Las Casas. In R. Jara and N. Spadaccini (eds.). *Amerindian Images and the Legacy of Columbus,* pp. 103–131. Minneapolis: University of Minnesota Press; Gibson, C. (ed.). 1971. *The Black Legend: Anti-Spanish Attitudes in the Old World and the New.* New York: Random House; Keen, B. 1992. Black Legend. In S. A. Bedini (ed.), *The Christopher Columbus Encyclopedia,* pp. 69–71. London: Macmillan; Sánchez, J. P. 1989. The Spanish Black Legend: Origins of Anti-Hispanic Stereotypes. *Encounters, A Quincentennial Review* (Winter): 16–22.

Bonaire

The first Bonaireans arrived from the neighboring island of Curaçao sometime around 1500 B.C. They were seminomadic hunter-gatherers of the Archaic Period and left their traces at the oldest known Bonairean site of Lagun. By 2,000 years ago, they had become well-adapted to the island's environment, with changes in their ways of life reflected in developments in the types of tools they used, which have been found at such sites as Lac Bay and Gotomeer.

At this time, the adjacent mainland of Venezuela was being invaded by more advanced peoples, who made polychrome pottery, practiced horticulture, especially cassava (manioc) cultivation, and lived in permanent villages. Originating from the area of the middle Orinoco, and speaking a form of the Caquetio language, they colonized Bonaire over the next 300 years, adapting to its island conditions and assimilating its earlier inhabitants. By A.D. 470, prehistoric Bonairean sites such as Wanapa, Amboina, and Fontein shared what archaeologists call the Ocumaroid ceramic tradition.

By 800 A.D., a new wave of people had established themselves on the Venezuelan coast and soon became a major influence on Bonairean culture. Perhaps 1,000 people lived on the island at this time, disposing of their dead in inhumation or urn burials along with grave goods within the village boundary. Between 1000 and 1400, the island was dominated by the peoples of the Dabajuroid ceramic tradition, who have left a rich archaeological record including crude pottery figurines, jars, thick cassava griddles, and pottery disks probably used as spindle whorls for making cotton. The presence of manos and metates used in preparing maize suggests a mixed diet supplemented by fish, shellfish, and crabs. Large pottery urn vessels have been interpreted as evidence for the consumption of an intoxicating drink made from the fermented maguey plant. Shell ornaments depicting frogs, birds, and small spotted felines together with polished basalt celts suggest a sophisticated ceremonial and spiritual life. It is thought that the island's rock paintings were also part of Bonairean religious life, marking sacred places in the landscape.

One artifact that spans both the Archaic and Ceramic Periods of Bonairean prehistory is the tool used to process the *cocuy* plant. This plant provided food and yielded a valuable fiber used for making rope, nets, and hammocks.

During the fifteenth and sixteenth centuries, Europeans arrived, bringing disease and slave raiding to Bonaire—activities that subsequently produced a mixed-blood Amerindian/European or mestizo population, and, a century later, mixed Amerindian/African peoples known as *zambos*. During this time, the Dutch first conquered and then colonized Bonaire, destroying the Amerindian villages of Fontein and Rincon. An indigenous presence nevertheless continued into the eighteenth century, with Amerindians raiding European livestock and establishing mestizo communities at Antriol and Nord Saliña. By the early twentieth century, there were probably no pure-blooded Amerindian peoples left, though today there remains a strong, if romanticized, notion of Amerindian identity on the island.

See also: Archaic Period; Curaçao; Dabajuroid

References
Haviser, J. B. 1990. Perforated Prehistoric Ornaments of Curaçao and Bonaire, Netherlands Antilles. *Journal of the Society of Bead Research,* Vol. 2; Haviser, J. B. 1991. *The First Bonaireans.* Willemstad: Archaeological-Anthropological Institute of the Netherlands Antilles. Curaçao; Haviser, J. B. 1995. Toward Romanticized Amerindian Identities among Caribbean Peoples: A Case Study from Bonaire, Netherlands Antilles. In N. L. Whitehead (ed.), *Wolves from the Sea,* pp. 157–170. Leiden, the Netherlands: KITLV Press; Josselin de Jong, J.P.B. 1918. The Praecolumbian and Early Postcolumbian Aboriginal Population of Aruba, Curaçao, and Bonaire. *Internationales Archiv für Ethnographie* 24 (3): 51–114; Josselin de Jong, J.P.B. 1920. The Praecolumbian and Early Postcolumbian Aboriginal Population of Aruba, Curaçao, and Bonaire. *Internationales Archiv für Ethnographie* 25: 1–26; Tacoma, J. 1991. Precolumbian Human Skeletal Remains from Curacao, Aruba, and Bonaire. *Proceedings of 13th International Congress for Caribbean Archaeology, Curacao 1989,* pp. 802–812; van Heekeren, H. R. 1963. Prehistorical Research on the Islands of Curaçao, Aruba, and Bonaire in 1960. *Nieuwe West-Indische Gids* 43: 1–25.

Breton, Father Raymond

The Dominican Father Raymond Guillaume Breton (1609–1679) sailed in May 1635 to be part of the mission on the French Caribbean island of Guadeloupe. He stayed nineteen years, during which time he made important studies of the language of the Carib inhabitants and became known as the Apostle to the Caribs.

Breton collected valuable ethnographic information on the life and beliefs of the Caribs of Dominica, though his main claim to fame is a two-part dictionary of the Carib language. This work contains such words as *petun* (tobacco), *mapoya* (evil spirits), *boïyako* (witch doctor), *lambies* (sea-shells), and *ouicou*, a drink made of cassava and water. Breton's dictionary may in fact have been a joint effort by the French missionaries assembled on the island rather than an individual work, at least as it appeared in its original form in 1647. Two versions of a later work that incorporated the original material are thought to have been produced by Breton alone and today are located in the Bibliothèque National in Paris and the archives of the Propaganda Fide in Rome.

More recent linguistic work, notably by anthropologist Douglas Taylor, suggests that Breton misunderstood much of what he saw and heard. Breton believed that Carib men and women spoke different tongues, the former a Cariban language, the latter an Arawakan one. In reality, it seems, the mother tongue of both sexes was Arawakan. However, when the seafaring men gathered together in the men's house they spoke a "men-only" language that mixed their native Arawakan tongue with words borrowed from their South American trading partners—a difference of gender and status rather than of pure linguistics.

See also: Caribs; Dominica; Languages

References
Breton, P. R. 1665. *Dictionnaire caraïbe-françois.* Auxerre, France; Hulme, P. and N. L. Whitehead (eds.). 1992. *Wild Majesty: Encounters with Caribs from Columbus to the Present Day,* pp. 107–116. Oxford: Oxford University Press; Petitjean Roget, J. 1963. The Caribs as Seen through the Dictionary of Reverend Father Breton. *Proceedings of the First International Congress for the Study of Pre-Columbian Cultures of the Lesser Antilles,* pp. 43–68; Taylor, D. 1954. Diachronic Note on the Carib Contribution to Island Carib. *International Journal of American Linguistics* 20: 28–33; Taylor, D. 1977. *Languages of the West Indies.* Baltimore: Johns Hopkins University Press.

C

Cacao

Cacao *(Theobroma cacao),* the principal constituent of chocolate, was a widely traded commodity in pre-Columbian times, especially among Mesoamerican civilizations. In Central America, it was grown in native plantations from the southeastern Mayan area to the Pacific coast of Guatemala and down to Costa Rica. Although it seems not to have been native to the Island Caribbean, it was present on the Caribbean coast of Nicaragua and a wild variety may have grown in northern South America before the European conquest.

In Mesoamerica, cacao was highly esteemed. Mixed with water, chili, and other flavorings, it was consumed as a high-status beverage. It was especially favored by the Maya, many of whose beautiful polychrome ceramic vases bear glyphic texts identifying them as cacao drinking vessels. Cacao pods are depicted on pottery from the sites of Copán in Honduras and Lubantuun in Belize, a part of the Mayan world that must have produced much cacao. So important was cacao in the social, economic, and religious lives of the Maya, that it had its own god. Ek Chuah, the deity of merchants, was also the patron of cacao. Those who owned cacao plantations honored him annually in a ceremony designed to ensure the continued fertility of the cacao trees. This ceremony saw the sacrifice of a dog with cacao-colored spots, offerings of feathers and iguanas to images of the gods, and gifts of long pods of cacao beans given to participating officials. During later Post-Classic Mayan times, cacao was an important item transported in seagoing canoes along the Caribbean coast of the Mayan world.

Cacao seeds extracted from the pod also served as currency in Central America from pre-Columbian times to the twentieth century. Among the Aztec, for whom there is detailed information, one obsidian blade cost 5 cacao beans, a turkey 100 beans, and a necklace of fine jade beads in the order of 60,000 beans.

If cacao's cultural significance in the Island Caribbean had been marginal during pre-Columbian times, its role was transformed after European arrival. Introduced usually by the Spanish, cacao became the basis of many plantations whose architectural and landscape remains now form part of the Caribbean's historical archaeological record.

This is especially true in Trinidad, where the period 1870 to 1920 was regarded as the most recent of several golden ages of cacao production. In 1920, there were some

Drying cacao beans on the Lopinot Estate, Trinidad (Courtesy Nicholas J. Saunders)

200,252 acres of the island under cacao cultivation with some 62 million pounds of cacao exported that year. Today, the remains of former cacao plantations can be seen in many parts of Trinidad, as can the so-called Cocoa Panyols—mixed-blood descendants of Amerindian/African/Spanish workers who came from Venezuela during the nineteenth century to work the cacao plantations.

> *See also:* Cocoa Panyols; Historical Archaeology; Maya; Trinidad and Tobago
> **References**
> Coe, S. D., and M. D. Coe. 1996. *The True History of Chocolate.* London: Thames and Hudson; Moodie-Kublalsingh, S. 1994. *The Cocoa Panyols of Trinidad: An Oral Record.* London: British Academic Press; Sauer, C. O. 1950. Cultivated Plants of South and Central America. In J. H. Steward (ed.), *Handbook of South American Indians* 6: 538–540. Smithsonian Institution, Bureau of American Ethnology Bulletin 143. Washington, DC: U.S. Government Printing Office; Shephard, C. Y. 1932. *The Cacao Industry of Trinidad.* Port of Spain, Trinidad;

Caguana/Capá (site, Puerto Rico)

The Taíno site of Caguana, also known as Capá, lies in the mountain country of central Puerto Rico, and is dated to between A.D. 1000 and A.D. 1450, with its peak occurring in the last 150 years of that period. Set near the Tanamá River in a limestone landscape whose many caves and rock shelters may have had spiritual and mythological significance for the Taíno, Caguana is the most elaborate grouping of plazas and ballcourts known in the Caribbean. Archaeologically, it spans the Ostionan and Chican Periods, and today has been heavily reconstructed and designated the Caguana Indian Ceremonial Park. Caguana appears to have been a ceremonial center, with little evidence of habitation other than perhaps some chiefs' houses and temple remains. The site seems to have been surrounded by a countryside dotted with single farm-like structures and thus gives the impression of being the political center of a dispersed population, perhaps even of a network of related chiefdoms. In keeping with this interpretation, Caguana is dominated by specialized architecture in the form of plazas and courts where ceremonial dances, processions, and the ball-game took place.

The central Plaza A is lined on its western side with stone slabs that are decorated with petroglyph images from Taíno mythology. The iconographic study of these images by José R. Oliver suggests that the central figure is a Taíno chief (cacique) flanked by a pair of anthropomorphic beings interpreted as ancestors on his right, with a pair of low-ranking descendants to his left. These in turn are flanked by bird-shaped creatures carved in profile. The central chiefly figure wears what appears to be a gold (guanín) pectoral as a mark of social status, typical of the elite items commented upon by the early European explorers. Given the important role of powerful spirit-laden images known as zemís in Taíno religion, it could be that these intriguing petroglyphs functioned as zemís in their own right, perhaps articulating Taíno visions of the cosmos.

Although Caguana is thought by some archaeologists to have been the seat of the powerful Taíno chief Guarionex, others disagree,

One of the elaborate series of ceremonial courts at Caguana, central Puerto Rico (Courtesy Nicholas J. Saunders)

citing other equally important chiefs of the region. It seems likely that as the Spanish appear not to have known about the site, it was abandoned before they arrived in 1508.

See also: Ball-Game; Puerto Rico; Taíno (Arawak); Zemís

References

Alegría, R. E. 1983. Ball Courts and Ceremonial Plazas in the West Indies. *Yale University Publications in Anthropology* No. 79. New Haven, CT; Lovén, S. 1935. *Origins of the Tainan Culture, West Indies,* pp. 86–99, Göteborg, Sweden: Elanders; Mason, J. A. 1941. A Large Archaeological Site at Capá, Utuado, with Notes on Other Puerto Rican Sites Visited in 1914–1915. *Scientific Survey of Puerto Rico and the Virgin Islands,* Vol. 18 (2). New York: New York Academy of Sciences; Oliver, J. R. 1998. *El Centro ceremonial de Caguana, Puerto Rico. Simbolismo iconográfico, cosmovisión y el poderió caciquil taíno de Borinquén.* British Archaeological Reports International Series 727. Oxford: Archaeopress; Oliver, J. R. 2000. Gold Symbolism among Caribbean Chiefdoms: Of Feathers, *Çibas,* and *Guanín* Power among Taíno Elites. In Colin McEwan (ed.), *Pre-Columbian Gold: Technology, Style, and Iconography,* pp. 205–206. London: British Museum Press; Oliver, J. R. 2002. *The Proto-Taíno Monumental Cemís of Caguana: A Political-Religious "Manifesto."* Unpublished manuscript.

Caimito, El

El Caimito culture was a pottery-making society in eastern Hispaniola (modern day Dominican Republic) between ca. 300 B.C. and A.D. 120.

Poorly understood, previous explanations of its origins invoked trans-Caribbean voyages from Colombia, though today these are no longer taken seriously. Recent investigations suggest that El Caimito in Hispaniola and Hacienda Grande in Puerto Rico were contemporaries. It may be that Hacienda Grande people influenced the El Caimito style via trade as the ceramic traits of the former appear, albeit in cruder form, in the latter's pottery. El Caimito ceramics are unimaginative and crudely made, with decoration limited to basic modeling and incisions.

Apart from pottery, El Caimito material culture includes stone, bone, and shell items that are similar to objects made by the earlier Courian Casimiroid people of Hispaniola (in present day Haiti). Flint blades and stone axes are typical, but significantly, cassava griddles are missing, suggesting that at least this form of agriculture was not practiced. Settlement sites are small and similar to those of the El Porvenir culture—a contemporary society of the Courian Casimiroids—in the adjacent part of Hispaniola that is now the Dominican Republic. Some archaeologists believe that El Caimito culture was a creative synthesis of El Porvenir and Hacienda Grande traditions.

See also: Casimiroid; Hacienda Grande

References

Rouse, I. 1992. *The Tainos: Rise and Decline of the People Who Greeted Columbus,* pp. 90–92, 110–111. New Haven, CT: Yale University Press; Veloz Maggiolo, M., M. E. Ortega, and P. P. Peña. 1974. *El Caimito: Un antiguo complejo ceramista de las Antillas Mayores.* Museo del Hombre Dominicano, Serie Monográfica 30. Santo Domingo, the Dominican Republic: Ediciones Fundación García Arévalo.

Caonabo (Taíno chief)

Caonabo, whose name meant "he who is like gold" or "King of the Golden House," was one of the principal Taíno chiefs (caciques) of Hispaniola at the time of Columbus's arrival in 1493. He ruled over the area known as Maguana in the southwest of the island. Today, Caonabo's village has been identified with the archaeological site of Corrales de los Indios—a great circular enclosure south of the Cordillera Central. Caonabo's wife by royal marriage was Anacaona, the sister of another great chief, Behechio, whose kingdom of Xaraguá was adjacent to that of her husband.

In 1494, Caonabo had been blamed by Guacanagarí for burning the Spanish settlement of La Navidad and killing its inhabitants and thus Columbus regarded him as a dangerous enemy. He is reported to have been a relatively old man, though knowledgeable and possessed of a keen wit. Stories of his capture by the Spanish vary—some saying Columbus caught Caonabo himself, others that the honor went to Alonso de Hojeda. According to the latter version, Hojeda arrived at Caonabo's village and invited the chief to ride a horse. Hojeda knew that the Taíno admired European metals that they called *turey* (i.e., *guanín*), regarding it as a precious and sacred material that they believed came from the sky. With Caonabo mounted on a horse, Hojeda invited him to test the supernatural power of European *turey* by trying on a pair of brightly polished manacles. Caonabo agreed, whereupon the manacles were clasped shut and the chief captured. Columbus decided to send Caonabo back to Spain but the chief appears to have died en route of unknown causes.

> **See also:** Anacaona (Taíno queen); Behechio (Taíno chief); Columbus, Christopher; Gold; Guacanagarí (Taíno chief); Guarionex (Taíno chief); Taíno (Arawak)
>
> **References**
> Las Casas, B. 1992. *A Short Account of the Destruction of the Indies.* London: Penguin Books;
> Sauer, C. O. 1969. *The Early Spanish Main.* Berkeley, CA: University of California Press;
> Wilson, S. M. 1990. *Hispaniola: Caribbean Chiefdoms in the Age of Columbus.* Tuscaloosa, AL: University of Alabama Press;

Carib Territory/Waitukubuli Karifuna Community (Dominica)

In 1902, the British administrator Henry Hesketh Bell recommended to the British government the creation of a Carib territory on the east coast of Dominica. The territory is some 8.8 sq km in area, and today is inhabited by approximately 3,400 people who live mainly in three communities: Salybia, Bataka, and Sinecou. Close to Sinecou is the L'escalier Tete Chien or "Snake's Staircase," a geological dike that resembles a huge serpent emerging from the sea to climb onto the island. The French term *tete chien* is the local Dominican name for boa constrictor due to its dog-like head. It features in Carib mythology and folklore, and one local saying has it that when there are no Caribs left on the island the great serpent will return to the sea.

Bell had clearly formulated his ideas about the Dominican Caribs before arriving on the island in 1899. He had decided that the original inhabitants should be guaranteed

permanent title to an officially recognized area on the island they once occupied in its entirety. To this end he visited the remote and wild east coast communities where, since the eighteenth century, Carib peoples had gathered in part to escape the depredations of Europeans. The result of this visit, informed by his avocational interest in anthropology, was a letter written on 26 July 1902 to Joseph Chamberlain, the secretary of state for Britain's colonies. It outlined the main features of Carib life and history, Bell's own suggestions for setting up a reserve, and importantly included a professionally surveyed plan by A. P. Skeat of the proposed area. He recommended also that the Carib chief be awarded a small stipend.

In less than a year, on 4 July 1903, Bell announced that the Carib Reserve was officially established.

Despite this unique development, conditions on the island for the Caribs remained poor. In 1930, the fatal shooting by two police officers of two Caribs accused of smuggling in Salybia led to civil unrest known as the Carib War. In a clear case of overreaction by the British, marines and extra police officers were drafted into Dominica and the warship HMS *Delhi* sailed from Trinidad and fired flares and starshells to intimidate the Caribs. Chief Jolly John gave himself up in Roseau, Dominica's capital, and was arrested. Together with five other Caribs, he was charged with wounding police officers and taking goods, though the case against all of the accused collapsed in court the following year.

Despite this legal victory, the unpopular British administrator of Dominica refused to reinstate Jolly John as chief, holding him responsible for the two deaths. There followed an official investigation into the conditions of the Carib Reserve on Dominica and into the incident. The final report recommended that the Carib Reserve be maintained but that Jolly John not be reinstated, that a new chief be elected by the Caribs, and that he should work with a government-appointed officer whose duty it would be to look after them. In fact, the post of chief was suspended in 1931 and only reactivated in 1952 when a Carib council was established deciding that a new Carib chief be appointed every five years. In addition, the Carib Territory has a parliamentary representative who sits in the House of Assembly in Roseau and is also elected every five years. It was only in 1970 that the first road was cut through the territory, with telephone and electricity following a decade later.

The most important anthropological investigations carried out in the Carib Territory were those of Douglas Taylor. A linguist by training, Taylor spent many years living and working in Dominica and documenting the island's Carib language, culture, and folklore. It was Taylor who observed the traditional Carib philosophy of life and death, shamanism, curing, the making of canoes, trading, hunting, fishing, basketmaking, agriculture, house-building, cooking, and astronomy. Perhaps most important were his critical insights into the nature of the Carib language, notably that Carib men and women spoke different languages. Men appear to have possessed a "men-only" language, used when they gathered together in the "men's house." This seems to have been a mix of their own Arawakan tongue spiced with Cariban words borrowed from their South American Carib trading partners. Carib women, who did not share this special type of language, spoke only in the traditional Arawakan tongue.

In 1994, Jacob Frederick, a local artist and keeper of traditional Carib knowledge, had the idea of building and sailing a large seagoing canoe along the islands south to South America. He wanted to test the seaworthiness of Carib canoes, engender pride and confidence among Dominica's Carib people, make contact with other indigenous peoples, and perhaps bring back crafts and knowledge that Dominica's Caribs had lost during the intervening centuries.

By 1997, the traditional dugout canoe was ready to sail. It was called the *Gli Gli*—the Carib name for a small hawk and an indigenous symbol of bravery. It had been built under the supervision of the Dominican Carib master canoe builder Etien Charles from a tree felled in the island's rainforest. At 35 feet long (compared to the 80-foot-long canoes of earlier times), it was the largest canoe built in living memory, and it took forty people two days to drag it to Salybia. It was here that the traditional methods of canoe construction played their part, with the stretching of the interior section by using heated rocks and water, and the building up of the sides with wooden planks. Fitted with sails, seats, rudder, and oars, it was launched in November 1996 after having been anointed with coconut water and gommier smoke. The journey took in such islands as St. Vincent, Grenada, and Trinidad and went on to make emotional reunions with indigenous peoples of the mainland.

Today, there is an increasing sense of identity and self-worth among the Dominican Caribs, boosted in part by tourism (particularly ecotourism) and the income generated by the commercial manufacture of traditional Carib arts and crafts, from paintings to intricate basketware. The Waitukubuli Karifuna Development Committee (the name means

"Dominican Caribs" in the Carib language) is the focus for this cultural revival and has built several traditional buildings in Salybia as well as the new church of St. Marie of the Caribs decorated with murals portraying Carib history, including the arrival of Christopher Columbus. Inside the church, the altar is a traditional Carib canoe. More recently, the Kalinago Center has been established in the island's capital of Roseau.

Since 1976, there have been ideas and rejuvenated plans for a Carib cultural village to be built on four acres of land in the center of the Carib territory. These plans included provision for handicraft workshops, a canoe-building shed, a cassava-making hut, and a restaurant serving local food. The idea is to provide a focus for tourism and to offer a coherent and managed environment for the maintenance and appreciation of Carib culture in the modern world. In March 2002, the completed Carib Model Village at Salybia played host to the Condor and Eagle Indigenous Action Summit, which was attended by representatives of some 41 million indigenous American peoples. Among other issues discussed was the creation of an environment for cooperative and tourist-based partnerships between the participants and Dominica's Caribs, characterized by peaceful coexistence and sustainable development.

See also: Breton, Father Raymond; Caribs; Cassava (manioc); Columbus, Christopher; Dominica; Garifuna (Black Caribs); Jolly John; Kalinago/Kalina; Santa Rosa Carib Community (Arima, Trinidad)

References
Birge, W. G. 1900. *In Old Rousseau, Reminiscences of Life as I Found it in the Island of Dominica and among the Carib Indians.* New York: Isaac H. Blanchard; Boucher, P. B. 1992. *Cannibal Encounters: Europeans and Island Caribs 1492–1763.* Baltimore: Johns Hopkins Press; Breton, P. R. 1665. *Dictionnaire caraïbe-françois.* Auxerre, France; Fermor, P. L. 1950. *The Traveller's Tree: A Journey through the Caribbean Islands,* pp. 98–130. London: John Murray; Honychurch, L. 1975. *The Dominica Story: A History of the Island.* London: Macmillan; Honychurch, L. 1997. Crossroads in the Caribbean: A Site of Encounter and Exchange on Dominica. *World Archaeology* 28 (3): 291–304; Hulme, P. 2000. *Remnants of Conquest: The Island Caribs and Their Visitors, 1877–1998.* Oxford: Oxford University Press; Hulme, P., and N. L. Whitehead. 1992. *Wild Majesty: Encounters with Caribs from Columbus to the Present Day,* pp. 231–353. Oxford: Clarendon Press; A. Layng, 1983. *The Carib Reserve: Identity and Security in the West Indies.* Washington, D.C.: Rowman and Littlefield; Layng, A. 1985. The Caribs of Dominica. *Ethnic Groups* 6 (2–3): 209–221; Petitjean Roget, J. 1963. The Caribs as Seen through the Dictionary of Reverend Father Breton. *Proceedings of the First International Congress for the Study of Pre-Columbian Cultures of the Lesser Antilles,* pp. 43–68; Rouse, I. B. 1948. The Carib. In J. H. Steward (ed.), *Handbook of South American Indians 4,* pp. 547–566. Washington, D.C.: Smithsonian Institution; Taylor, D. 1938. The Caribs of Dominica. *Bureau of American Ethnology Bulletin* 119, Anthropological Papers No. 3. Washington, DC.

Caribs

The Caribs appear to have been late arrivals in the Caribbean, sailing large seagoing canoes from South America perhaps around A.D. 1400 and colonizing the Lesser Antilles, especially the Windward Islands of Dominica, Martinique, St. Vincent, and Guadeloupe. Although the Caribs have been little investigated by archaeologists, most experts agree that their material culture, economy, and spiritual beliefs are most closely associated with peoples of the Guianas in northern South America. It seems most likely that the Caribs of the eastern Caribbean were indeed recent arrivals from the South American mainland—a view supported also by their continuing close trade relationships with this area. The name "Carib" is itself a corruption of the Taíno words *cariba* and *caniba,* which they applied to the fierce and dangerous people of the Lesser Antilles who, they told the Spanish, raided them for their marriageable women.

The language spoken in the Lesser Antilles by the Island Caribs (or Kalinago) seems to have belonged to the same Arawakan linguistic family as did the Taíno language. Somewhat confusingly, this bears no relationship to the Cariban linguistic family spoken by South American Caribs (or Karinya). To further complicate matters, the seafaring Island Carib men appear to have possessed a "men-only" language used when they gathered together in the men's house; this appears to have been a mix of their own Arawakan tongue spiced with Cariban words borrowed from their South American Carib trading partners—in other words, a difference of gender and status rather than of pure linguistics.

Economic and Artistic Life

Carib culture was mainly based on agriculture. Although it was similar to the Taíno in this respect, there were also important differences, not least in the less intensive nature of their use of the land. A particularly notable difference was the Carib production of manioc beer, which was neither made nor consumed by the Taíno. Both bitter and sweet manioc were grown and used to make cassava bread that was baked on griddles; together, the bread, beer, and stews known as pepper pot combined as a gastronomic focal point for intervillage gatherings. Other plant foods included sweet potatoes, yams, beans and peppers, and these were supplemented with bananas, papayas, and pineapple. Tobacco was rolled into cigars and smoked, and there is some evidence that these may have served as a type of currency. While tobacco was chewed, there is no evidence it was made into powdered snuff.

Fishing was clearly important to such an island economy and the Carib employed a variety of strategies, including nets, bows and arrows, hook and line, harpoons, and beating a poisonous wood on the water that stupefied the fish. Among other maritime resources exploited were crabs, shellfish, sea turtles, and manatees, though there is some suggestion that these last two animals could be subject to taboos. Eels it seems were avidly avoided. On land, Caribs hunted lizards and the agouti (*Dasyprocta aguti*), which had been introduced from South America and which may have substituted for the hutia (*Isolobodon portoricensis*), which was not present in the Lesser Antilles. Birds were hunted probably more for their plumage than as food, and were stunned with cotton-tipped arrows or poisonous smoke.

Carib arts and crafts were more simple than those of the Taíno. They used red-and-black painted calabash containers and also made a basic type of undecorated pottery associated with the Cayo style known from the historical period on St. Vincent and that possessed similarities with ceramics from the Guianas. The excavation of a Cayo site on St. Vincent yielded part of a ceramic pot inlaid with European glass beads, indicating that this was a historic-period Carib deposit. Basketry was also a feature of domestic life and has continued to the present day. Cotton weaving was practiced mainly to make hammocks and bracelets that were sometimes elaborated by adding polished stone beads, coral, and shell.

Carved-wood stools and a variety of well-made dugout canoes were made; the latter had their sides built up with planks sewn together with twine fibers and calked with bitumen. Some were large enough to carry fifty people. Carib men were evidently great seagoing traders and apart from interisland voyages they journeyed great distances to South America, where they obtained at least some of their items of gold (*guanín*) jewelry. Their most prized possession was the *caracoli,* a crescent-shaped gold object that varied in size and could be worn as bodily adornment in the ear or nose or, for the larger examples, as pendants. During the sixteenth century the Carib obtained and used European metal goods such as iron griddles, axes, and knives. Known for their warlike behavior, the Caribs made highly decorated wooden war clubs, blowguns, and longbows whose arrows were tipped with stingray spines and sometimes dipped in poison.

Although they didn't make or worship *zemí* figures like the Taíno, the Carib nevertheless appear to have worn small figurines of stone or wood around their necks to protect against evil spirits, and also to decorate their seagoing canoes (pirogues). Zoomorphic and geometric designs decorated war clubs and gourds. One of the best-known features of Island Carib art is the body of rock art, or petroglyphs that are found engraved onto cliffs and large boulders in many of the Lesser Antilles. On St. Vincent, these images, which may well belong to several periods of the island's prehistory, are small scale but spectacular. The most accessible are those at Layou north of the capital, Kingstown, and at Yambou east of the town. At Yambou there are several locations, one of which is especially interesting as it has been Christianized by a wayside calvary. In Caura Valley high in the mountains of the Northern Range on Trinidad is the famous Carib Stone, which may have been carved by the Caribs and which depicts a series of stylized anthropomorphic figures.

Society, Culture, and Politics

Carib society was less sophisticated than that of the Taíno, and was characterized by egalitarian social organization. It seems that Carib men called themselves Kalinago and women Kalipuna. Although there were no chiefs, a local headman appears to have been the main authority in Carib villages. Wider political authority encompassing several islands did sometimes occur when a war leader organized raids on Puerto Rico and especially the coastal areas of South America. The temporary authority wielded by these individuals may have been misconstrued by Europeans, who seem often to have regarded them as major chiefs based on their prior experience of the Taíno.

Carib villages tended to be built on the windward side of an island so as not to be vulnerable to surprise attacks. A nearby stream was preferred and settlements were generally small, consisting of an oval-shaped men's house (*carbet*), smaller dwellings for women, and areas for storage. The political center of Island Carib villages was the communal meeting place of the men's house. Although future archaeological investigation may change existing views, there currently appears to be little evidence that Carib villages had either central plazas, ballcourts, or temples.

Religion and Mythology

Carib religion, like that of the Taíno, was based on the shamanic traditions of South America. In this magical worldview, plants, animals, and landscapes were infused with spirituality associated both with ancestors and the immanent powers of nature. There were strong ties to mythology and these were acted out in rituals and ceremonies that bound the social and supernatural realms. Carib shamans (*boyes*) were the society's healers and the arbiters of this world. They controlled the forces of life and death through a typically Amerindian philosophy based on analogical symbolic reasoning. This indigenous view of life saw philosophical connections between objects, people, natural phenomena, and social events in a holistic way—tied together by invisible strands of power and bloodlines of kinship.

Carib religion was less developed than that of their Taíno neighbors to the north. They had few recognizable gods and lacked the distinctively Taíno worship of *zemí* images. Malign spirit-beings known as *mabouya* seem to have been associated with disease, hurricanes, earthquakes, and eclipses. They were invisible but betrayed their presence by an evil smell. Shamans possessed a *mabouya* as a personal spirit and cajoled them and constrained their power by making offerings of cigar smoke and food. During nocturnal séances, shamans sought to manipulate the *mabouya* in order to cure illness within their own group, send illness to others, divine the future, or influence the outcome of warfare. Sometimes *mabouya* were believed to reside in the bones of ancestors and so shamans wrapped them in cotton and kept them in their houses.

Good spirits among the Carib were called *akamboue*. They were invisible by day but transformed into bats at night. It was believed that each Carib had one of these as their own personal guardian spirit, known as an *ichieri,* whose duty it was to convey the soul of its owner to heaven upon death. As with all shamanistic beliefs, however, good and evil spirits are relative beings—sending and curing illness illustrates how what is evil for one group is beneficial to another. The Carib philosophy of life and death is reflected in their treatment of the dead, whom they apparently feared, never speaking their names again. Once satisfied that the deceased had not been killed by sorcery, they washed and painted the body and placed it in an open pit in the carbet, which was left open for ten days. Sometimes the bodies were burned, along with their belongings, and on some occasions the ashes were mixed into a drink and consumed in an act of ritual cannibalism.

Island Carib mythology is poorly documented compared to that of the Taíno, which itself is not especially rich. The French missionaries who collected ethnographic information during the seventeenth century have left only a sketchy outline. As with all Amerindian mythology, the Caribs regarded the earth as the anthropomorphized Mother who provided the ingredients of life. The Carib world itself was brought into being when a man known as Louquo descended from heaven bringing knowledge of manioc (cassava) agriculture and the plant itself, and proceeded to make the earth and the fish from pieces of baked cassava bread.

Astronomy seems to have figured prominently in Carib mythology. Many celestial bodies were personified as anthropomorphic beings such as the male Sun, the female Moon (*houiou*), and the stars. Carib astronomy is little known but what details survive illustrate its typically Amerindian nature. The star known as Achinoin was associated with rain and lightning, another called Couroumon created the tides and waves, and a third known as Savacou was a transformed bird who controlled thunder. Other phenomena like eclipses, comets, and rainbows all figured in Carib mythological thought. Despite these clear cultural differences, the Carib did share with the Taíno a view of a spiritually animated universe in which all things possessed sacred and secular importance that was acknowledged in rituals designed to make sense of physical and spiritual life.

Cannibalism

One of the most dramatic and endlessly misrepresented aspects of Carib culture is the issue of cannibalism. During Christopher Columbus's first voyage in 1492, he heard stories from the Taíno of islands rich in gold to the east (i.e., the Lesser Antilles) but inhabited by fierce warriors who not only raided the Taíno for women but who also consumed human flesh. In one sense, the accusations of cannibalism and militarism drew the Spanish closer to the Taíno and made the Caribs the perfect scapegoat for Spanish conquest and subjects for enslavement.

It is still a matter of debate whether or not the Caribs of the Lesser Antilles did actually raid the Taínos of Hispaniola during pre-Columbian times, though it is thought probable that they did attack Taíno villages in Puerto Rico. Most experts agree that whatever the truth about these wife-gathering raids, the Carib peoples maintained a stronger and much closer association with mainland South America. Nevertheless, after the Spanish arrival and settlement of Puerto Rico, it is well documented that Caribs did make raids and appear to have used the nearby island of St. Croix as a base. Whatever the pre-Spanish situation between the Taíno and Carib, the former clearly understood how to acquire a powerful new ally against the traditional foe.

The early Taíno accusations of Carib cannibalism stuck and became a defining feature in the imaginations and literary traditions of Europe of the savage behavior of indigenous peoples in the Caribbean (and the Americas more generally). So entrenched did this become that the terms "cannibal" and "cannibalism," themselves derived from the name "Carib," displaced the previous Greek term "anthropophagy" to describe eating human flesh. It was not until Columbus's second voyage in 1493 that the Spanish saw a Carib island firsthand. They went ashore on Guadeloupe and observed several human bones in Carib dwellings (though no Caribs) and assumed these to be the remains of a cannibal feast.

There is little doubt that the Spanish exaggerated ideas of Caribs engaging in orgiastic feasts of human flesh in order to justify their own slave raiding activities and colonizing ambitions. The simplistic idea of "peaceful Taínos (Arawaks) and warlike Caribs" had always been a useful fiction, and the Spanish soon began labeling any Amerindian who resisted attack or enslavement a Carib. It is certain, however, that the Spanish also misunderstood what they did observe firsthand. The evidence from Guadeloupe and elsewhere suggests the Island Caribs practiced ritual cannibalism like their South American cousins.

Throughout lowland Amazonia, Amerindian societies displayed a variety of attitudes toward warfare and the proper treatment of the dead. It was often the case that warriors ritually consumed a piece of the enemy's flesh to acquire his strength and aggressiveness. This was not a unique case, but rather part of their worldview, where essence and spirit could be transferred from one type of life to another. This way of thinking saw Amazonian warriors eating part of the flesh of the jaguar in order to absorb its hunting prowess. In a similar vein was the eating or drinking of the powdered bones of a dead relative as a mark of respect and to keep the essence of the deceased loved one literally and figuratively within the bodies of their family. The Europeans encountered such behavior across South America and either willfully or accidentally labeled it as evidence of savage pagan practices. Shorn of their ideological and philosophical subtleties, similar activities by Island Caribs recently arrived in the Lesser Antilles from South America could easily lead to accusations of wild cannibalistic feasts.

The Caribs in History

It was not until the seventeenth century and the activities of French missionaries in Dominica, Guadeloupe, and Martinique that Europeans came into prolonged and regular contact with Caribs and aspects of their society and culture began to be recorded. As the Carib scholar Louis Allaire has observed, "Carib society as we know it today is in many respects a seventeenth century creation. What changes occurred in Carib society during the momentous sixteenth century during which the Spanish, French, English and Dutch explored and colonised the Caribbean is unknown. However, it can be suggested that their indigenous ways of life must have been affected to some degree by almost a century of albeit sporadic and distant relationships with Europeans."

Arguably the single most influential figure in documenting Carib culture was the Dominican Father Raymond Guillaume Breton (1609–1679), who lived in the region for nineteen years. Known as the Apostle to the Caribs, Breton collected much ethnographic information on Carib culture but is famous today mainly for his dictionary of the Carib language. This work contains such words as *petun* (tobacco), *lambies* (sea-shells), and *ouicou,* the typically Carib beer made of manioc and water.

Knowledge of the Island Caribs is clearly entangled with European propaganda, misunderstandings, and comparatively little archaeological research and is complicated by the late arrival of the Caribs in the region. This picture becomes more even complex when other evidence is introduced. The idea that Carib culture was influenced by Taínos fleeing their Greater Antillean homelands to escape the Spanish is currently unproven. More confusing is the situation on Trinidad, Tobago, and Grenada, which appear to have received a very late influx of Cariban-speaking Caribs from the South American mainland and who maintained a separate ethnic identity from the Island Caribs.

Carib history during the era of European colonialism took many twists and turns. Perhaps the most surprising development was that of the Black Caribs, or Garifuna, of St. Vincent. The island had been home to the Island Caribs at the time of the European arrival and it was here that during the 1980s the Cayo style of ceramics was identified and attributed to the Carib population. The Caribs of St. Vincent welcomed escaped African slaves who eventually became assimilated into their society, adopting their language and way of life. The offspring of mixed race unions produced the so-called Black Caribs, differentiated from the original Yellow Carib inhabitants. In 1763, the British occupied St. Vincent and the Caribs fought a guerrilla war that lasted until 1796. A year later, 4,000 were rounded up and deported to the island of Roatán off the coast of Honduras in Central America.

Soon after their arrival, the Garifuna moved to the mainland and began settling along the Caribbean coastline. As they moved they encountered other free black peoples who had come originally from the French islands of Haiti and Guadeloupe and who appear to have adopted Garifuna cultural traditions, especially in religion, music, and dance. Today, the Garifuna, as well as their culture, have been described as truly hybrid. Starting with some 2,000 people in 1797 there are now some 200,000 Garifuna living in communities in Central America and the United States. Many Garifuna settled in the Stann Creek area of Belize (formerly British Honduras) around 1800 and the site has recently been renamed Dangriga—its original Garifuna name. Today, on the remote northeast coast of St. Vincent itself are the two poor Black Carib villages of Sandy Bay and Owia.

On Dominica, Carib history has been particularly eventful during the twentieth century. In 1902, the British administrator Hesketh Bell recommended the creation of a Carib territory on the east coast centered on the settlement of Salybia. In 1930, the fatal shooting of two Caribs by police officers led to civil unrest known as the Carib War, during which the chief, Jolly John, was arrested. A Carib Council was established in 1952 and arrangements made for a new Carib chief to be appointed every five years. Today, there is a reawakening of Dominican Caribs' sense of identity, boosted in part by tourism and the commercial manufacture of Carib basketware. The Waitukubuli Karifuna Development Committee (the name means "Dominican Caribs" in the Carib language) is the focus for this cultural revival and has built several traditional buildings in Salybia as well as the new church of St. Marie of the Caribs, decorated with murals portraying Carib history and with a traditional canoe as its altar.

The most recent example of the resurgence of interest in their indigenous past by Caribbean peoples has taken place on Trinidad. The island's unique mix of African and Asian peoples, and underlay of Spanish, French, and English influences, has nevertheless led to stirrings of an Amerindian consciousness. Little known outside the island, the Santa Rosa Carib Community of the town of Arima is made up of the descendants of Kalipuna Amerindians from St. Vincent, Trinidad's own Mission Amerindians, Venezuelans of mixed Amerindian-Spanish blood, and African slaves. In recent years they have taken inspiration from the Roman Catholic festival of Santa Rosa, whose statue is kept in the local church, itself built on land once occupied by an Amerindian village.

Today, their attempts to reclaim their Amerindian identity focus on the community center in Arima, where they make cassava bread by traditional methods first brought to Trinidad 2,000 years before by the Saladoid peoples. They weave cassava squeezers, build *ajoupa* houses with local materials gathered from the forest, and collect the folklore names and knowledge of Trinidad's trees, flowers, and medicinal plants. While some of these skills have been passed down by elders, such as the figurehead Carib Queen, others have been transmitted by visiting indigenous groups from Guyana. There is little direct continuity between Trinidad's indigenous past and the Santa Rosa Caribs at Arima; yet, however mixed their ancestry, Amerindian blood flows through the veins of many of the town's inhabitants.

Throughout the Caribbean, the scattered groups of indigenous peoples have forged links with their more numerous and influential cousins in Guyana, Venezuela, and Belize. Calling themselves the Caribbean Organization of Indigenous Peoples, they seek recognition as the original inhabitants of the Caribbean, to gain formal title to land, and to reclaim, at least symbolically, the sacred landscapes of their ancestors.

See also: Breton, Father Raymond; Carib Territory / Waitukubuli Karifuna Community (Dominica); Cassava (manioc); Columbus, Christopher; Dominica; Garifuna (Black Caribs); Guadeloupe; Jolly John; Kalinago / Kalina; Martinique; Pepper Pot; Santa Rosa Carib Community (Arima, Trinidad); Shamanism; St. Vincent and the Grenadines; Suazey / Suazoid; Tobacco; Trinidad and Tobago; Troumassoid

References

Allaire, L. 1977. *Later Prehistory in Martinique and the Island Caribs: Problems in Ethnic Identification.* Ph.D. dissertation, Yale University; Allaire, L. 1980. On the Historicity of Carib Migrations in the Lesser Antilles. *American Antiquity* 45: 238–245; Allaire, L. 1997a. The Lesser Antilles before Columbus. In S. M. Wilson (ed.), *The Indigenous People of the Caribbean,* pp. 20–28. Gainesville, FL: University Press of Florida; Allaire, L. 1997b. The Caribs of the Lesser Antilles. In S. M. Wilson (ed.), *The Indigenous People of the Caribbean,* pp. 177–185. Gainesville. FL: University Press of Florida; Boomert, A. 1982. The Rock Drawings of Caurita. *Naturalist Magazine* 4 (6): 38–44: Woodbrook, Trinidad; Boomert, A. 1986. The Cayo Complex of St. Vincent: Ethnohistorical and Archaeological Aspects of the Island-Carib Problem. *Antropológica* 66: 3–68; Boomert, A. 1995. Island Carib Archaeology. In N. L. Whitehead (ed.), *Wolves from the Sea: Readings in the Anthropology of the Native Caribbean,* pp. 23–36. Leiden, the Netherlands: KITLV Press; Boucher, P. B. 1992. *Cannibal Encounters: Europeans and Island Caribs 1492–1763.* Baltimore: Johns Hopkins Press; Breton, P. R. 1665. *Dictionnaire caraïbe-françois.* Auxerre, France; Davis, D. D., and R. C. Goodwin. 1990. Island Carib Origins: Evidence and Nonevidence. *American Antiquity* 54: 37–48; N. L. González, 1988. *Sojourners of the Caribbean: Ethnogenesis and Ethnohistory of the Garifuna.* Urbana, IL: University of Illinois Press; Hulme, P. 2000. *Remnants of Conquest: The Island Caribs and Their Visitors, 1877–1998.* Oxford: Oxford University Press; Hulme, P., and N. L. Whitehead. 1992. *Wild Majesty: Encounters with Caribs from Columbus to the Present Day.* Oxford: Clarendon Press; Layng, A. 1983. *The Carib Reserve: Identity and Security in the West Indies.* Washington, D.C.: Rowman and Littlefield; Layng, A. 1985. The Caribs of Dominica. *Ethnic Groups* 6 (2–3): 209–221; Myers, R. 1984. Island Carib Cannibalism. *Nieuwe West-Indische Gids* 58: 147–184; Petitjean Roget, J. 1963. The Caribs as Seen through the Dictionary of Reverend Father Breton. *Proceedings of the First International Congress for the Study of Pre-Columbian Cultures of the Lesser Antilles,* pp. 43–68; Rouse, I. B. 1948.

The Carib. In J. H. Steward (ed.), *Handbook of South American Indians 4*, pp. 547–566. Washington D.C.: Smithsonian Institution; Taylor, D. M. 1951. *The Black Caribs of British Honduras.* New York: Viking Fund Publications in Anthropology No. 17; Verin, P. M. 1968. Carib Culture in Colonial Times. *Proceedings of the Second International Congress for the Study of Pre-Columbian Cultures of the Lesser Antilles, St. Ann's Garrison, Barbados*, pp. 115–120; Whitehead, N. L. 1984. Carib Cannibalism: The Historical Evidence. *Journal Societe des Americanistes* Vol. 70, pp. 69–87; Whitehead, N. L. 1988. *Lords of the Tiger Spirit: A History of the Caribs in Colonial Venezuela and Guyana 1498–1820.* Dordrecht, the Netherlands: Foris Publications.

Carnival (Trinidad)

The origins of Carnival can be traced back to the arrival of French immigrant planters in the Caribbean, particularly in Trinidad during the 1780s. Originally it seems that Carnival was the preserve of the resident Spanish and French aristocracy—a polite mix of balls, dressing up in masks and costumes, and visiting house to house. At this time, Trinidad's remaining Amerindians pointedly ignored the event, and African slaves were prohibited from taking part.

After the abolition of slavery in 1834, however, Carnival in Trinidad quickly transformed into street festivities celebrated by the free African-Caribbean population. For most of the rest of the nineteenth century, Carnival developed a characteristic satirical flavor that saw the British colonial rulers mocked for their appearance and behavior. One example was the carnivalesque figure of Dame Lorraine, who poked fun at the eccentricities of the white plantocracy.

The British elite, for their part, complained of the degenerate behavior, wild abandon, and socially undermining and immoral effects of the event. After violent disturbances during the 1870s and especially the so-called Canboulay Riot of 1881, the chief of police Captain Baker imposed restrictions; Carnival was reduced from three days to two, drumming was outlawed, and the *canboulay* (see following) procession of stick-fighting bands of men, which opened the festivities and had its roots in slavery, was banned. The change in Carnival to today's more respectable celebrations probably had less to do with colonial restrictions than the idea of a more peaceful type of competition between participating groups that became a feature of the festivities in the last decade of the nineteenth century. Competition now pervades all aspects of modern Carnival—from singers to musicians, dancers, and costume-makers.

Today's Carnival in Trinidad (also known as Mas', short for "masquerade") has a well-established structure. The first signs of the events to come are a series of fetes that serve as a long, drawn-out warming-up period. Fetes can be impromptu parties in private houses, or larger public events such as the ones held annually in the Oval—the main cricket ground in Port of Spain. At some of these pre-Carnival fetes, what are known as Old Mas' bands dressed in rudimentary costumes may compete with each other. It is, however, during *J'Ouvert* (see following) that these bands come into their own and take to the streets. On the Sunday night of Carnival week—set annually for the week of Ash Wednesday—a series of events that has seen competitions between kings and queens of the different Mas' bands and also between steel bands culminates with the event called *Dimanche Gras*. Here, the King and Queen of Carnival are chosen as is the Calypso Monarch. After these events have ended, many people go on to a fete and stay until daybreak.

In the spirit of the festivities, Carnival itself officially begins as Dimanche Gras ends. At 2:00 A.M. on Monday, J'Ouvert (adapted from *jour ouvert,* French for "daybreak") is a boisterous predawn procession that sees bands and their followers pouring into the streets from all the different fetes and making their way into the center of Port of Spain. J'Ouvert seems to be the real soul of Carnival for many Trinidadians, and lasts well into the morning. The origins of J'Ouvert can be traced back to the nineteenth-century Canboulay—itself a reenactment of previous slave processions that saw the plantation workers called out to deal with fires resulting from the burning of the sugar cane in the fields before harvesting. Its name is a corruption of the French *cannes brulées* (burning canes). The rest of Carnival Monday is considered a warmup for the following celebrations, with many of the masquerade bands not surprisingly under strength and costumes incomplete.

The next day, Carnival Tuesday, is the big event that sees the Mas' bands parading from one competition site to another in Port of Spain throughout daylight hours. The main judging place for the bands is the grandstand at the Queen's Park Savannah in the center of town, whose stage can support even the several thousand performers of the largest bands. It is here that the judges name the Band of the Year and the audience acclaims a People's Choice at the end of the day. Although Carnival officially ends at midnight, in recent years festivities have continued into the Lent period with shows of the various Carnival champions in concert and Last Lap fetes in various parts of town.

Carnival is a mosaic of cultural influences filtered through Trinidad's multicultural past and multiethnic present. This is particularly evident in the dancing and music that is a focus of the celebrations. Trinidadian Carnival dancing has its own distinctive moves: its more energetic form referred to as "jumping up," and a more sedate shuffling movement used during the long road marches called "chipping." Equally distinctive is "wining," which involves an energetic and suggestive swiveling of the hips.

A central feature of Carnival is the tents. Already in evidence by the 1840s, tents were originally backyard structures of bamboo and thatch—smoke-filled, candlelit, and ruled by a king and queen. Nowadays, calypso tents start early in the New Year and are usually located in local meeting halls. It is here that small groups of singers and dancers congregate to practice and they often feature a well-known singer such as Lord Kitchener, Sparrow, and David Rudder. The year's new songs are perfected and range from biting satire to rhythmic dance music. Jokes and witty commentary by a resident master of ceremonies weave together the different musical styles. A series of judges tour the tents and select twenty-four star singers to perform in San Fernando, Trinidad's second town, in a semifinal from which seven are chosen to compete for the title of Calypso Monarch. In addition, the most-played calypso song during Carnival is chosen as that year's Road March and the artist becomes the Road March King.

The so-called Mas' Camps are the bases for the Mas' bands—the main components of Carnival. Each band/camp can have as many as 4,000 members and is organized by one of

Trinidad's most accomplished creative organizers such as Peter Minshall and Wayne Berkeley. Every year each camp adopts a theme, from nature, history, culture, or folklore, that is reflected in its costumes—the most elaborate of which are worn by its king and queen. Those who take part in Carnival by joining a masquerade band are referred to as "playing Mas.'"

There are two aspects of Trinidad Carnival that today are inseparable from the event itself—steel-band music (also known as pan) and Calypso singing. Coming from a background of traditional African drumming, pan originated in the poorer parts of Port of Spain during the 1930s—partly as a long-delayed response to the outlawing of Carnival drumming in the previous century. Although percussion had been available through the beating of bamboo and miscellaneous metal objects, an increasingly sophisticated use of shaped and cut metal containers came to dominate many bands. In 1945, the first steel bands made their appearance, using the cut-down ends of oil drums, and playing ever more sophisticated tunes. In the early days, the new music was not readily accepted. Belonging to a band was akin to being a gang member and violence between bands was common. Today, steel bands have broadened their appeal, band members now include women and middle-class Trinidadians, and the distinctive sound has an international following.

Steel band orchestras have a variety of different pans that are cleverly tuned by raising areas of the drum's surface in accord with its musical notes. In the months leading up to Carnival, the orchestras practice in panyards throughout the island, perfecting their arrangements of tunes for that year. The focus of Carnival for steel-pan orchestras is the Panorama competition that begins with about seventy orchestras and is whittled down to finalists who compete in Port of Spain before enthusiastic audiences. The key to winning is a special ten-minute arrangement whose performance combines individual skills and tight collective playing.

Calypso has far more ancient roots with origins in songs that praised and satirized native rulers in West Africa and that were kept alive by the slaves who came to Trinidad. As Carnival developed during the nineteenth century, Calypso became a way of making scandalous public comment on the island's white British colonial society. In the first two decades of the twentieth century it continued to evolve—its French patois dropped in favor of English—and it became both respectable and commercialized, though never lost its satirical bite. Calypso singers adopted memorable stage names, such as Attila the Hun, Terror, Panther, and Executor, often prefixed by Lord or Mighty. Arguably the greatest exponent of Calypso has been the Mighty Sparrow, whose singing dominated the genre from the 1950s to the 1980s, though the evergreen Lord Kitchener is probably as famous and even older. More recently, Shadow, Calypso Rose, Chalkdust, Tambu, and David Rudder have risen to prominence. All Calypsonians are quick, stylish, and extroverted, blending new and old musical styles but retaining the heart of clever and witty social comment in a changing world.

See also: Individual islands; Trinidad and Tobago

References

Anthony, M. 1989. *Parade of the Carnivals in Trinidad 1839–1989*. Port of Spain, Trinidad: Circle Press; Butcher, J. 1989. Peter Minshall: Trinidad Carnival and the Carnivalesque.

International Review of African American Art 8 (3): 39–48; Cowley, J. 1996. *Carnival, Canboulay, and Calypso: Traditions in the Making.* Cambridge: Cambridge University Press; Eastman, R., and M. Warner-Lewis. 2000. Forms of African Spirituality in Trinidad and Tobago. In J. K. Olopuna (ed.), *African Spirituality,* pp. 403–415; Hill, D. R. 1993. *Calypso Calaloo: Early Carnival Music in Trinidad.* Gainesville, FL: University Press of Florida; Lewis, S. (ed.). 1989. Contemporary Art of Trinidad and Tobago. *International Review of African American Art* 8: 8–64; Mason, P. 1998. *Bacchanal!: The Carnival Culture of Trinidad.* Philadelphia: Temple University Press; Nunley, J. W. 1988. Masquerade Mix-Up in Trinidad Carnival: Live Once, Die Forever. In J. W. Nunley and J. Bettleheim (eds.). *Caribbean Festival Arts: Each and Every Bit of Difference,* pp. 85–116. Seattle: University of Washington Press; Nurse, K. 1999. Globalization and Trinidad Carnival: Diaspora, Hybridity, and Identity in Global Culture. *Cultural Studies* 13: 661–690; Regis, L. 1999. *The Political Calypso: True Opposition in Trinidad and Tobago 1962–1987.* Gainesville, FL: University Press of Florida; Riggio, M. C. 1998. Resistance and Identity: Carnival in Trinidad and Tobago *TDR* 42 (3): 7–23; Stuempfle, S. 1995. *The Steel-Band Movement: The Forging of a National Art in Trinidad and Tobago.* Philadelphia: University of Pennsylvania Press.

Casimiroid

The Casimiroid peoples lived between 4000 B.C. and 400 B.C. on the two largest islands of the Greater Antilles, Cuba and Hispaniola (modern day Haiti and the Dominican Republic). Casimiroid culture is usually divided into three subseries: the Casimiran, the Courian, and the Redondan.

The Casimiran subseries is found on both islands during the Lithic Period. These people may have originally come either from Central America or South America. At the archaeological type-site of Casimira and also that of Barrera-Mordán in southwestern Hispaniola (Dominican Republic) were found the remains of workshops where stone tools had been made. These sites are dated to between 2610 B.C. and 2165 B.C. The Vignier III site in adjacent Haiti, which has yielded stone tools and shells, has been dated to ca. 3620 B.C. Excavations at several rock shelters in central Cuba revealed not only the typical stone tools but also evidence of everyday life such as animal bones and seashells. One of these sites, the Levisa rockshelter, is dated to ca. 4190 B.C. Recent investigations suggest that all Casimiran peoples shared the same way of making their flaked-stone tools with variations being due to different available raw materials and local style of working.

The people of the Courian subseries followed those of the Casimiran on Hispaniola. Two local cultures, the Couri in Haiti and the El Porvenir in the Dominican Republic have been dated to between 2630 B.C. and A.D. 240. Possibly living in small bands, the Couri people may have moved seasonally between the coast and inland, taking advantage of the resources of both. They appear to have made more elaborate stone tools than their Casimiran predecessors, with larger, more sophisticated blades being used as spear-points to hunt sloths and manatees. The Couri also made conical pestles and mortars to prepare food and a variety of possible ritual implements such as stone balls, disks, and dagger-like objects, as well as elaborate stone beads and shell jewelry.

The Redondan subseries in Cuba currently has two local cultures—Guayabo Blanco and Cayo Redondo—dated to between 2050 B.C. and A.D. 1300. The distinctive feature of these two cultures is the presence of triangular shell gouges, a tradition that may have originated in Florida. The Redondan people have left shell midden sites on Cuba's coast, but they also lived in caves whose walls they painted and in whose floors they buried their dead. Flaked-stone tools continued to be made though less well than those of the Courian peoples. Perhaps significantly, Redondan ground-stone tools became most sophisticated in eastern Cuba, a short sea passage away from Courian culture in Hispaniola.

See also: Archaic Period; Cuba

References
Cruxent, J. M., and I. Rouse, 1969. Early Man in the West Indies. *Scientific American* 221 (5): 42–52; Kozlowski, J. K. 1974. *Preceramic Cultures in the Caribbean.* Zeszyty Naukowe, Uniwerstytet Jagielloński, 386, Prace Archeologiczne, Zezyt 20. Krakow; Pantel, G. A. 1988. *Precolumbian Flaked Stone Assemblages in the West Indies.* Ph.D. dissertation, University of Tennessee, Knoxville; Rouse, I. 1992. *The Tainos: Rise and Decline of the People Who Greeted Columbus,* pp. 62–67. New Haven, CT: Yale University Press; Rouse, I., L. Allaire, and A. Boomert, 1985. Eastern Venezuela, the Guianas, and the West Indies. Unpublished manuscript (C. Meighan, comp.). *Chronologies in South American Archaeology.* New Haven, CT: Yale University, Department of Anthropology.

Cassava (manioc)

Cassava, or manioc (*Manihot esculenta*), is also widely known as yuca throughout Central and South America. It was, and remains, one of the most important food plants for indigenous tropical forest peoples. Although there are a number of different varieties of manioc, all are perennial shrubs with starchy roots, and all belong to the same species. Within this variety, there are two main types—sweet and bitter—a distinction based on the latter's high concentration of toxic hydrocyanic (prussic) acid.

Sweet manioc has the wider distribution, and is easily converted into food by being baked or boiled. Bitter manioc, however, is poisonous, and requires expert knowledge of complex processing techniques in order to render it safe for eating. Despite this, bitter manioc is often preferred as a food by Amerindian peoples due to its higher starch content and suitability for making flour, bread, and various beverages.

The earliest evidence for cassava consumption is about 2000 B.C. in the Orinoco basin of Venezuela. Unfortunately, as manioc is not propagated through seeds, direct traces of the plant are difficult to identify archaeologically. There are indirect traces, however, in the durable equipment used to process and cook the plant, such as small, chipped stones used to grate the manioc, and ceramic griddles used to bake cassava bread.

Cassava is traditionally grown in fields known as *conucos* or *chagras.* These have been cleared from the forest by the slash-and-burn technique, where trees are felled with axes, and the area then burned to provide an ash-enriched soil for the growing not only of manioc, but chilis, bananas, maize, and pineapples. Soil is heaped together to conserve moisture, then several manioc cuttings planted in each mound. This simple but effective tech-

nique allows each conuco to support two or three successive plant-
ings over some four years.

In the Island Caribbean, on Hispaniola (modern day Haiti and the
Dominican Republic), the sixteenth-century Spanish chronicler

Women peeling manioc
root in Bequia, St.
Vincent and the
Grenadines (Dean
Conger / Corbis)

Cassava (manioc)   57

Oviedo recorded that the Taíno planted their cassava at the start of the lunar month so that the crop grew with the phases of the moon. The Taíno also encouraged growth by placing or burying *zemí* figures of stone or wood in the cassava garden to supernaturally protect the crop and ensure its potency. Today, in lowland Amazonia, manioc gardens are associated with fertility and sexuality, as places where menstruating women take refuge, unmarried couples have sex, and babies are born. The process of planting hard manioc cuttings in soft, yielding soil is itself seen as full of sexual imagery.

Although cassava can be harvested after eight months, its starch-rich tubers can be left in the ground for up to two years without spoiling. In South America today, and possibly in the prehistoric Caribbean, manioc is usually harvested by women, with some 45 kg of tubers sufficient to feed a family of five for a week. While men are hunting or fishing, women clean and peel the tubers, then grate them against rough stones, or with a special grater made from wood studded with chips of flint or quartz. It can take four women seven hours to grate 54 kg of cassava.

The grated cassava, now a wet pulp, is placed in a basket sieve and pounded until the toxic prussic acid leaches out into a pot beneath the sieve. An alternative way of removing bitter manioc's toxic liquid is squeezing. Various methods can be used but the most widespread utilizes a tubular basket of plaited palm leaves, vine, or reed stems, and called variously the *tipiti, matapi,* or Carib Snake—some of which can be 3 meters in length. Manioc pulp is first pushed inside, the upper part of the tipiti is then hung from a roof beam, and the lower part has a large pole threaded through it upon which women and children sit, thereby stretching the tipiti and squeezing the prussic acid out into a pot.

Whichever method is used, the resulting liquid's starch—known as tapioca—settles at the bottom of the pot and is used to make bread and beverages. The still poisonous juice can be boiled with chilis to form the sauce known as *cassarip,* the base of the stew known as pepper pot. Manioc juice is also used as a fish poison and for ridding dogs of fleas. In the Island Caribbean during the sixteenth century, it was reported that indigenous peoples committed suicide by drinking the raw juice to escape maltreatment by the Spanish.

When squeezing has finished, manioc pulp is sieved, dried, and pounded for several days, each activity further aiding the detoxification process. The final product is then made into two types of flour—fine-sieved if it is to be baked into bread on a griddle, and coarser if it is to be toasted as farinha. Various types of beer, or *chicha,* and nonalcoholic drinks are made from cassava and often drunk in large quantities during feasts that may last several days.

The varied processes and techniques used to grow cassava and transform it into food and drink find a symbolic dimension in which acts of cassava processing are used metaphorically to describe the world of myth and acts of social reproduction. Current Amazonian societies, such as the Barasana, enshrine cassava imagery in their mythology. For the Barasana, Romi Kumu was the "Woman Shaman" who fashioned the world, and who dropped her ceramic cassava griddle to make the earth. Another important figure is Manioc-Stick Anaconda, who burned himself to death in an act that paved the way for the annual burning of Barasana manioc gardens.

Baking cassava bread on a griddle (Courtesy Nicholas J. Saunders)

This rich body of mythic associations among modern indigenous peoples probably was mirrored in the Caribbean during pre-Columbian times. Here too, the female cycle and human reproduction were associated with the planting of cassava, and Yúcahu, the supreme Taíno deity, was the invisible lord of fertility whose name meant "spirit of cassava."

See also: Maize; Pepper Pot; Saladoid; Santa Rosa Carib Community (Arima, Trinidad); Taíno (Arawak); Zemís

References

Carneiro, R. L. 1983. The Cultivation of Manioc among the Kuikuru of the Upper Xingú. In R. B. Hames and W. T. Vickers (eds.). *Adaptive Responses of Native Amazonians*, pp. 65–111. London: Academic Press; Hugh-Jones, C. 1988. *From the Milk River: Spatial and Temporal Processes in Northwest Amazonia*, pp. 174–192. Cambridge: Cambridge University Press; Mowat, L. 1989. *Cassava and Chicha: Bread and Beer of the Amazonian Indians.* Princes Risborough, UK: Shire Publications; Rivière, P. 1987. Of Women, Men and Manioc. *Etnologista Studier* 38: 178–201; Roosevelt, A. C. 1980. *Parmana: Prehistoric Maize and Manioc Subsistence along the Amazon and Orinoco.* London: Academic Press.

Cayman Islands

The Cayman Islands, made up of Grand Cayman, Cayman Brac, and Little Cayman, are a British Crown colony. Grand Cayman is 35 km long, 6.4 km wide, and has an area of 197 sq km. Cayman Brac is 9 km long and .6 km wide, and Little Cayman is 6 km long and .6 km wide. The total population of around 30,000 is of mixed African and European origin.

Christopher Columbus was the first European to see the Cayman Islands in 1503, at which time he called them Las Tortugas after the many turtles he observed. By 1523 they had been rechristened Lagartos—the Spanish for alligators or large lizards, and they then became the Caymanas, after the Carib word for crocodiles. European explorers soon hunted the local turtles to extinction as an easy source of food on their Caribbean voyages.

Archaeological survey and excavations suggest that while the Cayman Islands were likely known and visited by Amerindians during prehistory, there were either no sizeable settlements, or if there were, the evidence has either disappeared or not yet been located. Nevertheless, while there would appear to be no pre-Columbian archaeology on the Caymans, the islands are rich in their historical archaeological heritage, particularly in underwater sites.

Many ships met their end on the reefs that circle each of the three Cayman Islands. For this reason, the maritime geography of the islands is primarily responsible not only for the 325 shipwrecks in and around the islands, but also for the distinctive nature of Cayman history, language, and folklore. During the 1700s, when the islands were a dependency of Jamaica, the mix of piracy and salvage that became known locally as "wrecking" came to dominate Cayman culture. The reefs, wrecked ships, castaways, and salvaged artifacts that featured in everday Cayman life manifested themselves in local styles of clothing, house-building, and boat-building traditions, such as the so-called catboat used to catch turtles. These varied aspects of Cayman life are documented today in the National Museum on Grand Cayman.

It is shipwrecks, however, that have dominated Cayman life and continue to do so through underwater archaeology and heritage management. One of the most important shipwreck sites is that thought to belong the *Santiago,* a ship carrying a wealth of goods plundered from the Aztecs by Hernán Cortés between 1519 and 1521. When it was discovered in 1970 in shallow water off a hotel beach in Grand Cayman, silver bars, jewelry, and Aztec gold figurines came to light. A key to identifying the wreckage was a signet ring belonging to Rodrigo de León, captain of the *Santiago* when it disappeared in 1522. A more recent maritime loss was that known as the Wreck of the Ten Sail—a fleet of ten ships that sank in 1794 and were investigated in the 1980s and 1990s. In 1994, Queen Elizabeth II unveiled a commemorative monument overlooking the reefs where the ships were lost, known henceforth as Queen's View.

See also: Ten Sail, Wreck of the; Tortola (BVI); Underwater Archaeology

References
Biondi, J., and B. Bell, 2002. *Insight Pocket Guide Cayman Islands.* Singapore: Insight Guides; Brunt, M. A., and J. E. Davies (eds.). 1994. *The Cayman Islands: Natural History and Biogeography.* Dordrecht, the Netherlands: Kluwer; Considine, J. L., and J. L. Winberry, 1978. The Green Sea Turtle of the Cayman Islands. *Oceanus* 21 (3): 50–55; Doran, E. B. 1953. *A Physical and Cultural Geography of the Cayman Islands.* PhD. dissertation, University of California, Berkeley; Drewett, P., S. J. Scudder, and I. R. Quitmyer. 2000. Unoccupied Islands? The Cayman Islands. In P. Drewett (ed.), *Prehistoric Settlements in the Caribbean: Fieldwork in Barbados, Tortola, and the Cayman Islands,* pp. 5–16. London: Archetype Publications; Ebanks, S. O. 1983. *Cayman*

Emerges: A Human History of Long-Ago Cayman. Georgetown, Grand Cayman: Northwester Company; Leshikar, M. E. 1993. *The 1794 "Wreck of the Ten Sail," Cayman Islands, British West Indies: A Historical Study and Archaeological Survey.* PhD dissertation, Texas A&M University. Ann Arbor, MI: University Microfilms; Leshikar, M. E. 1997. Underwater Cultural Resource Management: A New Concept in the Cayman Islands. *Underwater Archaeology,* pp. 33–37; Smith, R. C. 1985. The Caymanian Catboat: A West Indian Maritime Legacy. *World Archaeology* 16 (3): 329–336; Smith, R. C. 2000. *The Maritime Heritage of the Cayman Islands.* Gainesville, FL: University Press of Florida; Stokes, A. V., and W. F. Keegan, 1996. A Reconnaissance for Prehistoric Archaeological Sites on Grand Cayman. *Caribbean Journal of Science* 32 (4): 425–430.

Cayo (pottery)

Despite many European reports about encounters with Caribs, it has proven difficult to identify archaeologically these newcomers to the eastern Caribbean. The invisibility of any distinctively Island Carib material culture lasted until the 1980s. In 1986, the Dutch archaeologist Arie Boomert reassessed pottery found on St. Vincent during the early 1970s, identifying what he called the Cayo style and attributing it to the Island Caribs. Confirmation of his work seemed to come in the 1990s when Cayo ceramics were discovered alongside European materials such as pieces of sixteenth- and seventeenth-century Spanish olive jars. Particularly notable was the discovery of a fragment of Carib pottery decorated with European glass beads—an item that encapsulates the attraction for Caribbean Amerindians of European shiny objects.

Cayo ceramics appear associated with those belonging to the Koriabo complex of coastal Guiana both in their shapes and decoration, such as the incision of thin lines, grooved motifs, modeled face designs, and appliqué fillets. While most of these ceramics were tempered with local volcanic sand, the distinctive use of tree-bark ash temper (known as *caraipé*)—a typically South American mainland practice, often used in Koriabo pottery and unknown in the Lesser Antilles—suggested direct sea contacts between the two areas. All together, this evidence provides archaeological support for the ethnohistorical evidence given to French missionaries by the Island Caribs concerning their own mythical (and actual) origins in South America, and their movement into the Lesser Antilles in the centuries immediately preceding European arrival. Although no Cayo site has been investigated in depth, Cayo pottery has been found in all the islands from Tobago in the south to Dominica in the north.

It seems clear that Boomert's original insights were correct, and that Cayo ceramics originated in South America and came to the Windward Islands of the Lesser Antilles perhaps as early as A.D. 1250, where they continued to be made, albeit with some changes, during the early historical period of European exploration and colonization.

See also: Aesthetic of Brilliance; Caribs; St. Vincent and the Grenadines

References
Allaire, L. 1994. Historic Carib Site Discovered! *St. Vincent Archaeological Project Newsletter.* Winnipeg: University of Manitoba; Boomert, A. 1986. The Cayo Complex of St. Vincent: Ethnohistorical and Archaeological Aspects of the Island-Carib Problem. *Antropológica* 67:

33–54; Boomert, A. 1995. Island Carib Archaeology. In N. L. Whitehead (ed.), *Wolves from the Sea: Readings in the Anthropology of the Native Caribbean*, pp. 23–35. Leiden, the Netherlands

Cedros (site, Trinidad)

Cedros is one of the most important archaeological sites in the Caribbean. It is a partly destroyed shell midden located on the southwest tip of Trinidad within sight of mainland Venezuela. It was excavated by John Bullbrook and Irving Rouse in 1946. They discovered conch, clam, and oyster shells together with painted pottery (mainly bowls and jars), ceramic griddles, and anthropomorphic and zoomorphic *adornos*. There were two corrected radiocarbon dates yielding 190 B.C. and A.D. 100.

Rouse made it the type-site for his Cedros subseries of the Saladoid ceramic series, that is, the first pottery tradition in Trinidad that he considered originated with the Ronquinan Saladoid peoples who lived along the Orinoco River from 2000 B.C. to 550 B.C. before spreading north. Its wider significance lies in the fact that it represents the introduction of a settled, horticultural, village-based life not only to Trinidad but the whole Island Caribbean. White-on-red (W-O-R) and zic (zone-incised cross-hatching) pottery found at Cedros has become known as Cedrosan Saladoid, and is a useful diagnostic marker for ceramic-period archaeology in many parts of the Caribbean.

See also: Ronquinan; Saladoid; Trinidad and Tobago; White-on-Red Pottery (W-O-R); Zic Pottery

References

Boomert, A. 2000. *Trinidad, Tobago and the Lower Orinoco Interaction Sphere*, pp. 131–145. Alkmaar, the Netherlands; Olsen, F. 1974. *On the Trail of the Arawaks*, pp. 234–256, 365–373. Norman, OK: University of Oklahoma Press; Rouse, I. B. 1947. Prehistory of Trinidad in Relation to Adjacent Areas. *MAN* (o.s.) 47 (103): 93–98; Rouse, I. B. 1953. Appendix B: Indian Sites in Trinidad. In: J. A. Bullbrook, *On the Excavation of a Shell Mound at Palo Seco, Trinidad, B.W.I.*, pp. 96–97, 102–105, 109–110. New Haven, CT: Yale University Publications in Anthropology 50.

Chancery Lane (site, Barbados)

Chancery Lane is a multicomponent site on the south coast of Barbados that was probably inhabited for the whole of Barbados prehistory. Excavated at various times since the 1930s, the site's millennium-long occupation is probably the result of its favorable location. At the time of occupation, the site was a sandrock bench overlooking a sea inlet. With time, advancing sand dunes and storm damage appear to have covered the site and cut off the inlet, leaving a salt marsh, part of which survives today. It may have been these events that led to the site's abandonment.

The site has yielded several human burials and various areas of rubbish middens. The burials, mostly of adults, are usually found in natural hollows in the sandrock base. The presence of post-holes may suggest a dwelling, and excavations have also yielded evidence of food preparation, including fish and shellfish remains and cassava baking in the typical ceramic griddles.

Most of Chancery Lane's pottery seems to belong to the Saladoid/Barrancoid Period and style. Typically Saladoid zic (zone-incised cross-hatching) ware is present, as is possibly also white-on-red (W-O-R), and a later style known as Caliviny Polychrome. A pottery shard that shows incisions of a turtle-shell pattern may once have been part of a larger effigy vessel. Cassava griddles have been found, as have remains of so-called incense burners. There is also evidence of later Troumassoid and final Suazoid occupation. As is to be expected at such a site, there are rich remains of seashells, particularly of Queen Conch (*Strombus gigas*), from which axes/adzes, scrapers, and punches as well as several beads were made.

See also: Barbados; Saladoid; White-on-Red Pottery (W-O-R); Zic Pottery
References
Boomert, A. 1987. Notes on Barbados Prehistory. *Journal Barbados Museum Historical Society* 38 (1): 8–43; Bullen, R. P., and A. J. Bullen, 1968. Barbados Archaeology 1966. *Proceedings of the Second International Congress for the Study of Pre-Columbian Cultures of the Lesser Antilles,* pp. 134–144; Drewett, P. L. 1987. Archaeological Survey of Barbados. *Journal of the Barbados Museum* 38: 44–80; Drewett, P. L. 1991. *Prehistoric Barbados,* London: Institute of Archaeology and Archetype Publications; Taylor, R. V. 1986. Archaeological Events in Barbados. *Journal Barbados Historical Society* 37 (4): 337–342.

Chichén Itzá Cenote (site, Mexico)

Beneath Mexico's waterless Yucatán Peninsula is an extensive series of collapsed limestone caves and tunnels that extend out beneath the Caribbean seabed. In many of these underground locations the Maya deposited human sacrifices, pottery, and the remains of animals. Such caverns are known in the Yucatán as cenotes, a term that is a Spanish corruption of the Mayan word *ts'onot,* meaning a natural well.

The large cenote at the Mayan city of Chichén Itzá seems to have had a mainly religious purpose. The site's name means "at the mouth of the well of the Itzá (people)." Here, human sacrifices and items of gold and jade were cast into the well from a platform located on one of its sides. Although this practice appears to have ended around the thirteenth century, it may be that more mundane offerings are still made to this day by local farmers praying for rain.

The well at Chichén Itzá, and the sacrifices that took place there, were first described by the Spanish priest Diego de Landa around 1566 when he described Mayan offerings to the rain god Chac. Many attempts to retrieve these items have been made. The first real success was by Edward Herbert Thompson who became U.S. consul in the Yucatán and bought the ancient site in 1894. He spent years dredging the well and recovering large quantities of archaeological materials that were donated to Harvard University's Peabody Museum and the Field Museum of Natural History in Chicago—some of which later ended up back in Mexico. Although amateur divers subsequently tried to explore the cenote, the lack of visibility in its dark waters hampered their efforts. However, from 1960 to 1961, the Mexican archaeologist Román Piña Chan, together with the Mexican Explorers and Divers Club (CEDAM), spent four months bringing hundreds of artifacts to the surface. Damage to fragile artifacts led to the project's cancellation by the Mexican authorities.

The most scientifically valuable and professional investigation was carried out from 1967 to 1968 by CEDAM, in association with Mexico's National Institute of Anthropology and History (INAH). This project saw the well's water level lowered and the part of the site exposed being investigated by traditional archaeological techniques. For the rest of the site that was still underwater, the water was treated in order to clean it and improve visibility, and then explored by scuba divers.

The layer of silt and mud at the bottom of the well created an anaerobic environment that preserved such fragile objects as wooden artifacts, rubber, textiles, basketry, and even balls of the ritually important copal incense. Items retrieved during the various excavations include parts of three broken atlatls, or spearthrowers, several wooden manikin scepters with faces decorated in gold and mosaic, cotton and vegetable textile fragments, and wooden figurines covered with a skin of rubber and painted blue. Textile and basketry preservation allowed identification of many of the techniques used by the Maya, including coiling, plaiting, tapestry, and twill. Golden items were more often in fact *tumbaga*—a pre-Columbian alloy of gold and copper—though thousands of pure copper bells were also recovered. Other objects included pottery, obsidian, bone, and shell, as well as pectorals and thousands of beads fashioned from the green jade so prized by the Maya.

The wealth of materials recovered from Chichén Itzá's great cenote have permitted archaeologists to suggest two distinct phases for the Mayan use of the well. The first period relates to militaristic influence from central Mexican Toltec peoples between 750 and 1150, and the second, which appears to be more like Post-Classic Mayan culture encountered later by the Spanish, dates to between 1250 and 1450. Although many of these objects remain unstudied, it is thought that most were cast into the cenote as sacrificial offerings to gods, spirits, and ancestors as part of a cult that centered on water and fertility rites.

See also: Maya; Underwater Archaeology

References

Coggins, C. C. 2001. A Soft Economy: Perishable Artifacts Offered to the Well of Sacrifice, Chichén Itzá. In B. A. Purdey (ed.), *Enduring Records: The Environmental and Cultural Heritage of Wetlands,* pp. 83–91. Oxford: Oxbow; Coggins, C. C., and O. C. Shane III (eds.). 1984. *Cenote of Sacrifice, Maya Treasures from the Sacred Well at Chichén Itzá.* Austin, TX: University of Texas Press; Lothrop, S. K. 1952. Metals from the Cenote of Sacrifice, Chichén Itzá, Yucatán. *Memoirs of the Peabody Museum, Harvard University* X (1). Cambridge, MA; Piña Chán, R. 1968. Exploración del Cenote Sagrado de Chichén Itzá: 1967–68. *Boletín del Instituto Nacional de Antropología e Historia* 32: 1–3; Proskouriakoff, T. 1974. Jades from the Cenote of Sacrifice, Chichén Itzá, Yucatán. *Memoirs of the Peabody Museum, Harvard University* X:2. Cambridge, MA; Tozzer, A. M. 1957. Chichén Itzá and Its Cenote of Sacrifice. *Memoirs of the Peabody Museum, Harvard University* 11–12. Cambridge, MA; Vesilind, P. J. 2003. Watery Graves of the Maya. *National Geographic* 204 (4) (October); 82–102; Willard, T. A. 1926. *The City of the Sacred Well.* New York: The Century Co.

Clifton Plantation

Clifton Plantation on the Bahamas is known particularly well for the period of its ownership by William Wylly between 1815 and 1821. Wylly was attorney general of the Bahamas during this time, and while never in favor of the abolition of slavery, he was a controversial figure and a Methodist who believed in reforming the conditions of all slaves. This liberal attitude brought him into conflict with the Bahamian House of Assembly and in 1821 he moved to St. Vincent.

Clifton Plantation had about forty-four slaves during Wylly's tenure, about ten of whom were African-born, the rest second-generation creoles. Historical archaeological investigations at Clifton have identified seven slave cabins and a slave kitchen, which included typical artifacts such as ceramics, metal, glass, tobacco pipes, and the remains of fish and shellfish.

By comparing the pottery of the slave quarters with that found in the planter's house and other plantations, it appears that the slaves made their own choices as to the type and decoration of their ceramics. Although there is no evidence of African traditions as such, the slaves clearly favored colors and designs of English pottery that coincidentally accorded with those of their traditional African material culture. This accords well with Wylly's attitudes toward his slaves, whom he encouraged not only to earn cash wages and participate in the wider economy but also possibly to retain elements of their African aesthetic and religious traditions.

See also: Drax Hall (site, Jamaica); Galways Plantation; Historical Archaeology; Newton Plantation (Barbados); Slavery; Sugar

References

Wilkie, L. A. 2001a. Communicative Bridges Linking Actors through Time: Archaeology and the Construction of Emancipatory Narratives at a Bahamian Plantation. *Journal of Social Archaeology* 1 (2): 225–243; Wilkie, L. A. 2001b. Evidence of African Continuities in the Material Culture of Clifton Plantation, Bahamas. In J. Haviser (ed.), *African Sites Archaeology in the Caribbean,* pp. 264–276. Princeton, NJ: Markus Wiener; Wilkie, L. A., and P. Farnsworth. 1997. Daily Life on a Loyalist Plantation: Results of the 1996 Excavations at Clifton Plantation. *Journal of the Bahamas Historical Society* 19: 2–18.

Cocoa Panyols

During the nineteenth century and up to 1920, Venezuelan peasants and agricultural laborers journeyed to Trinidad to find work on the cocoa (cacao) plantations. They gravitated to and mixed with the resident and mainly rural descendants of Spanish peasants to form a uniquely Trinidadian community. During the twentieth century they became known as the Cocoa Panyols, deriving their name from a local corruption of *español.*

Panyols of Venezuelan and Trinidadian origin shared a mixed racial origin, with Amerindian, Spanish, and African ancestors. They took great pride in their language, customs, music, and agricultural prowess, forming a tight-knit community in Trinidad's multiracial society. It was probably their intimate knowledge of the land and its flora and fauna that, together with their indigenous origins, made the Panyols such sensitive and accomplished cocoa growers. As such, they were of crucial importance to the Trinidadian cocoa industry.

The Cocoa Panyols lived between four worlds: Amerindian, Spanish, African, and the British who controlled Trinidad at the time. Mainly uneducated, the Panyols lived and worked in the rural areas of cocoa plantations, especially in the valleys and foothills of Trinidad's Northern Range. Here, in isolated settlements, they maintained their language, customs, and religion, and found work as independent cocoa planters or hired hands. The Caura Valley was recognized as the quintessential Panyol area in British Trinidad until the 1940s, when the colonial government moved the inhabitants en masse in order to build a dam. Many made their way to the adjacent Arouca Valley and established themselves at the site of the old Lopinot cocoa estate. Although this move dislocated Panyol society, in fact their self-sufficient way of life had been in decline since 1921.

Today, while Panyol culture and their Spanish language have largely disappeared, some customs have survived by filtering into general Trinidadian folklore. Most notable are the Spanish songs and music known as parang—a modern Trinidadian rendering of the Spanish word *parranda* (to make merry). Parang music is played, appropriately, on European stringed instruments like the *cuatro,* mandolin, and violin, and is accompanied by percussion instruments such as the Amerindian maracas. In modern Trinidad, parang is more popular than in the past and is a common feature of Christmas festivities, where it is enjoyed by all Trinidadians.

See also: Cacao; Santa Rosa Carib Community (Arima, Trinidad); Trinidad and Tobago
References
Chauharjasingh, A. S. 1982. *Lopinot in History,* Port of Spain, Trinidad: Columbus Publishers; Moodie-Kublalsingh, S. 1994. *The Cocoa Panyols of Trinidad,* London: British Academic Press.

Cohoba

In 1495, during his second voyage of discovery, Christopher Columbus observed a native religious ritual on the island of Hispaniola (modern Haiti and the Dominican Republic). He saw the local Taíno using a double-branched cane to snuff powder from an elaborately carved circular table attached to the head of a *zemí* figure. Known as *cohoba,* this hallucinogenic powder intoxicated those who inhaled it.

By snuffing cohoba, Taíno chiefs (caciques) and shamans (*bohitu*) communed with the spirit world, especially ancestor spirits resident within trees and wooden zemí figures. The ensuing visions were often part of curing sessions in which the illness-inducing spirits were interrogated and a cure suggested. Chiefs would often take cohoba while sitting on a wooden *duho* stool, itself made from a powerful spirit-wood and covered with intricate patterns of circles and spirals. These sacred designs may have been inspired by hallucinogenic imagery experienced during cohoba intoxication. Throughout Mesoamerica and South America, shamans and rulers sat on such seats of power, sometimes carved in the shape of an animal, which were believed to connect the sitter with the spirit realm.

Cohoba evidently played an important role in Taíno ritual life and associated mythology. In one creation myth, four brothers escaped from Yaya, the supreme spirit, by escaping to their grandfather's house. When one asked for some cassava the grandfather became enraged and spat on the boy's back. The spittle transformed into cohoba, allowing the Taíno to contact the grandfathers (i.e., ancestors) through ritual. The symbolic relationship between cohoba, tobacco, and food (especially cassava), is embodied in a myth that identifies *guanguayo* as the shaman's tobacco spittle that, when mixed with cohoba, has a purifying and hallucinogenic effect on the taker. Guanguayo may also be identified as the mucous that streams from the shaman's nose after he has ingested cohoba and that in South America is identified symbolically with semen.

For many years, it was believed that cohoba was a powdered form of the strong variety of tobacco known as *Nicotiana rustica*. It is now recognized that it was made from the pulverized seeds of *Anadenanthera peregrina,* a mimosa-like tree that is related to *A. colubrina,* the source of the sacred *huilca* snuff used in South America.

> **See also:** Cassava (manioc); Columbus, Christopher; Duhos; Shamanism; Tobacco; Trees, Spiritual Importance of; Zemís
>
> **References**
> Columbus, C. 1969. *The Four Voyages,* Harmondsworth, UK: Penguin Books; Saunders, N. J., and D. Gray, 1996. Zemís, Trees, and Symbolic Landscapes: Three Taíno carvings from Jamaica. *Antiquity* 70 (270): 801–812; Stevens-Arroyo, A. M. 1988. *Cave of the Jaqua: The Mythological World of the Tainos.* Albuquerque, NM: University of New Mexico Press; Veloz Maggiolo, M. 1971. El rito de la cohoba entre los aborigenes antillanos. *Revista dominicana de arqueología y antropología* 29 (1–2): 201–216; Wilbert, J. 1987. *Tobacco and Shamanism in South America,* New Haven, CT: Yale University Press;

Columbus, Christopher

The Life, 1451–1506

Christopher Columbus was born Cristoforo Columbo in Genoa, Italy, sometime between 25 August and 31 October 1451, probably in the building next to the city's Olivella gate where his father Dominico was warden. Both his father and his mother, Susanna Fontanarossa, were associated with the weaving industry. He had two younger brothers, Bartolomé and Diego, both of whom would be lifelong supporters and closely associated with his ventures in the Americas. Apart from a basic education and literacy in Latin, the young Columbus was well drilled in the technical and mathematical aspects of the import-export business by his father, who had diversified into the wine trade. He appears to have been mainly self-taught in those aspects of astronomy, geography, and geometry that would be needed for the navigational skills that became such an essential part of his life. These skills were doubtless honed from the age of thirteen or fourteen, when he probably started participating in maritime trading voyages.

Given Genoa's status as a center of maritime trade it is not surprising that Columbus joined his father's thriving textile and wine trade in 1470 and journeyed throughout the

Mediterranean. In 1472 he was in Tunisia and a year later in the Genoese trading center on the Greek island of Chios. By 1476 he had moved to Lisbon and begun working for Genoese companies that sent him on voyages north to Iceland and Britain and south to the Gulf of Guinea. In August of that year he was involved in a naval battle between a Genoese convoy and a French fleet—the disastrous consequences of which apparently saw Columbus's ship sunk and the young man having to swim 11 or 12 km to the Portuguese shore.

It was probably during these formative years that Columbus first heard stories speculating what might lie on the other side of the Atlantic. The more rumors he heard and the more experienced in navigation he became, the more he considered the trading prospects of opening up a westerly route to the spice-rich Orient across the Atlantic rather than around the southern tip of Africa. It was during this period that he probably learned of the existence of the counterclockwise winds and currents off Africa that would carry a vessel westward.

Working for the influential Genoese Centurione family, Columbus was able to make a good marriage to Felipa Perestrello y Moniz. Tragedy followed the birth of their son, Diego, as Felipa died soon after. Realizing that he needed royal patronage to make his dreams of discovery a reality, Columbus first approached King João II of Portugal sometime around 1484 but was rejected on the advice of the king's panel of experts, who considered his navigational calculations inaccurate. Nothing daunted, Columbus turned his attentions to petitioning the newly joined kingdoms of Aragon and Castile and their monarchs Ferdinand and Isabella. In 1488 he had his second son, Fernando, by Beatriz Enríquez de Arana, though he never married her.

Cultivating two noblemen, the Count of Medinaceli and the Duke of Medina Sidonia, Columbus managed to obtain an audience with Queen Isabella in early 1486. Columbus used his powers of persuasion to good effect and added that he would use the gold he would discover during his voyage to liberate Jerusalem from the Muslims. For several years the two monarchs supported him financially while his ideas were examined by a special commission. At the end, however, the Spanish examiners were no more impressed by Columbus's calculations than the Portuguese had been and they voted to reject his proposal. Further possibilities appeared in quick succession with Portugal for a second time, then France and England, but nothing came of them.

Columbus's luck was about to change, however. As 1491 ended, he had a second chance to argue his case at court. Although the proposal was officially rejected a second time, this decision was almost immediately reversed and he was given permission to put together an expedition. This change of fortune may have been due in part to behind-the-scenes maneuverings by two of his supporters—Luis de Santángel and Francesco Pinelli—and their persuading Ferdinand that such an expedition could be financed cheaply at little risk and had great economic potential. The motive was purely financial on all sides. It was probably also affected by the feeling of confidence that followed the surrender of Granada, the last Moorish kingdom in Spain, in January 1492. The triumph of the Christian *reconquista* of the Iberian peninsula ended centuries of Islamic presence and was a turning point in European history. The military energy and religious fervor of those engaged in this campaign would soon need a new outlet, and for better or worse, the Americas provided such an opportunity.

Whatever the cause of his unexpected success, Columbus pressed his case and in the so-called *Santa Fe Capitulations* of 17 April 1492 he received the following main guarantees: his title was to be Admiral of the Ocean Sea (as the Atlantic was then known) and he would be allowed to pass on these rights and prerogatives to his heirs in perpetuity; he would be viceroy and governor-general of all the lands he discovered; he could expect 10 percent of all the wealth he discovered; and he had the choice as to whether to pay one-eighth of the expenses involved in sending a ship to the New World in return for the same percentage of any profit. While all of these rights and privileges were dependent on his expedition being successful, they were nonetheless astonishing and it may well be that the Spanish monarchs later regretted such largesse. Columbus was also furnished with royal letters of introduction to the rulers he expected to meet, such as the Great Khan of China and, most importantly, two caravels from the port of Palos near Seville. In making the arrangements for the voyage, Columbus's key partner was Martín Alonso Pinzón, a member of the Pinzón shipping family in Palos with whom he had a difficult but respectful relationship.

Columbus's four voyages to the Americas are described separately in the following sections. It was in November 1504, after having spent twelve years engaged in these momentous expeditions interspersed with periods back in Spain awaiting renewed royal support, that he returned to Spain for the last time. His greatest champion in his own mind had always been Queen Isabella, who died some two weeks after his return. Columbus found himself bereft of royal support, and his health, which had deteriorated seriously in the Caribbean, began to worsen. Over the next few months he became increasingly bitter about the injustices (as he saw them) of his situation. He felt that the terms of the *Capitulations* had not been honored, specifically that he had been cheated of the 10 percent of the wealth of the lands he had discovered. He was particularly worried about the crown honoring his son's inheritance privileges. An audience with Ferdinand went badly, his health worsened even more, and within weeks of an interview with Isabella's successors to the Castilian throne—Juana and Felipe—Columbus died on the night of 20 May 1506.

Throughout his life, Columbus retained his affection for his native city of Genoa. In several letters he refers to a bequest to the city's San Giorgio Bank of 10 percent of his wealth to care for the city's poor. Yet he had always been a difficult man, usually trusting only his family, always an outsider, and never becoming a Castilian citizen. Many were jealous and he seemed to make enemies easily. Like many who achieve greatness, his strengths were also his weaknesses.

For a man who traveled the world so extensively during life, his journeys did not end with death. He was first buried at Valladolid, then transferred in 1509 to Cuevas near Seville, and then again in 1541 across the Atlantic to Santo Domingo on Hispaniola, where his remains were placed by the altar in the cathedral alongside his brother, Bartolomé, and his son Diego. In 1759 they were transferred to Cuba and in 1898 back across the ocean to the cathedral in Seville. There is a contrary view, however, that a coffin inscribed with Columbus's name discovered in Santo Domingo during the nineteenth century contains the admiral's remains.

The First Voyage (3 August 1492–15 March 1493)

On 3 August 1492, Columbus set sail from Palos with three ships—the *Santa Maria,* the *Niña,* and the *Pinta.* On board were some ninety men, most of whom were experienced seamen. Their number also included a Jew who spoke Chaldean and Arabic as well as Hebrew—a talent that would facilitate translations with the Oriental peoples whom Columbus expected to meet. Ferdinand and Isabella also sent two representatives to look after their interests. The little fleet arrived first at the Canary Islands, where, after repairs to the *Pinta*'s rudder, it finally set sail for the Americas on 6 September. Although by the standards of the time this was a voyage into the unknown, Columbus's ships took advantage of the northeast trade winds that blew from Africa westward.

Christopher Columbus receives ritual gifts from the cacique Guacanagarí on Hispaniola. Engraving by Theodore de Bry (1528–1598). (Stapleton Collection / Corbis)

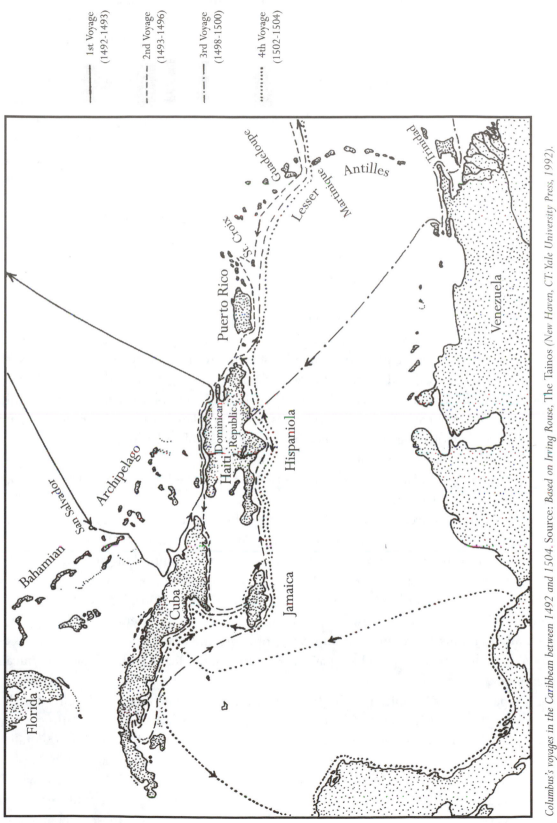

1st Voyage
(1492–1493)

2nd Voyage
(1493–1496)

3rd Voyage
(1498–1500)

4th Voyage
(1502–1504)

Florida

Bahamian

San Salvador

Archipelago

Cuba

Jamaica

Haiti

Dominican
Republic

Hispaniola

Puerto Rico

St. Croix

Guadeloupe

Martinique

Lesser

Antilles

Trinidad

Venezuela

Columbus's voyages in the Caribbean between 1492 and 1504. Source: Based on Irving Rouse, The Tainos (New Haven, CT: Yale University Press, 1992).

The crews of the three ships were anxious during the voyage and Columbus and Martín Pinzón readily interpreted the sighting of birds, clouds, and whales as indicators that they were nearing landfall. But by early October, with no land in sight, the crews were more restless than ever and it seems as if some were ready to mutiny. On 11 October flotsam was observed in the sea and hopes began to rise. Columbus himself saw a light in the distance the same night and urged his men to keep a lookout, adding a personal gift of a silk doublet to the royal reward of 10,000 *maravedís* to the first person to see land.

At 2:00 A.M. on Friday, 12 October, Rodrigo de Triana, who was high in the rigging of the *Pinta,* sighted land and claimed the reward—though Columbus himself took the money on the basis of his prior if ambiguous sighting. For the last 500 years, historians and archaeologists have argued about the true location of the island that was Columbus's landfall. Its native name was Guanahaní, and Columbus renamed it San Salvador. It was then known as Watlings Island until it reverted back to San Salvador in the twentieth century. In recent years, it has been suggested that the first European landfall was in fact on Grand Turk in the Turks and Caicos Islands.

Columbus went ashore and took possession of the island for the king and queen of Spain. He established an enduring tradition of exchange with the native peoples by giving them glass beads. He also noted that they were of a timid nature and would be easy to enslave and convert to Christianity. While he seized seven Amerindians to take back to Spain, he paradoxically also treated others well, providing them with food and gifts. Throughout these first contacts Columbus was keen to learn of the sources for the gold ornaments that the natives wore in their noses. His journal makes many references to gold and, as many scholars have noted, this established a template for the European interactions with the indigenous peoples of all the Americas.

After leaving San Salvador, the fleet cruised through the Bahamas, and learned from the natives of an island called Cipangu that was rich in gold and spices and inhabited by great merchants. Searching for this island, Columbus reached Cuba on 28 October and believed that he had reached Cathay (China). He was so convinced of this that he sent an expedition into the interior armed with letters from the Spanish king and queen in the hope of contacting the Great Khan. As these exploratory trips continued without any real sign of success, Columbus's crew became disenchanted. On 20 November Martín Pinzón separated himself with the *Pinta* from the rest of the fleet. By 5 December, Columbus and his remaining two ships were offshore the island known to the natives as Bohío, which he rechristened La Española (Hispaniola; modern Haiti and the Dominican Republic).

Hispaniola was inhabited by the Taíno (Arawak), whom he initially identified as the people of the Great Khan. On Christmas Day 1492, as the two ships were sailing along Hispaniola's north coast, the *Santa Maria* ran aground. With the help of the local Taíno chief, Guacanagarí, the Spanish salvaged everything of value from the stranded flagship and brought it ashore. The Taíno entertained the Spanish at a feast during which Columbus exchanged a pair of gloves and a shirt for gold jewelry and a gold-encrusted mask. As the two sides were unable to speak each other's language, these exchanges al-

Celebrating "Discovery Day" with a reenactment of Columbus's landing in southern Trinidad (Courtesy Nicholas J. Saunders)

most certainly were misunderstood. It was Guacanagarí who first told Columbus of the gold-rich land known as Cibao in the center of the island.

This news, together with the fact that Columbus's remaining ships could not transport everyone back to Spain, led to the establishment of La Navidad—the first European settlement in the New World. Columbus's idea was that during his absence these men would locate and collect gold, ready for his return. La Navidad was built from the salvaged remains of the *Santa Maria* and thirty-eight volunteers were left behind when Columbus sailed for Spain in the *Niña* on 16 January 1493, after having been rejoined by Pinzón in the *Pinta*.

The two ships sailed north to pick up the westerly winds, became separated during a storm, and sighted the Portuguese islands of the Azores on 15 February. Driven by another storm, Columbus finally landed in Portugal on 4 March, where he had an audience with the Portuguese King João before leaving for Spain and arriving back in Palos on 15 March, some seven and a half months after leaving. After having navigated a different route, the *Pinta* arrived within a few hours of Columbus. Pinzón died within a few days of his arrival, leaving no record of what he must have seen while separated from Columbus. On 20 April, Columbus reported to the Spanish king and queen, who were holding court in Barcelona. At the peak of his career, Columbus was granted a coat of arms and confirmed in the various privileges promised to him at the outset.

The Second Voyage (25 September 1493–11 June 1496)

Within a month of his royal reception in Barcelona, Columbus had received a commission to undertake a second voyage. Unlike the first, this was to include colonization as well as exploration. While Columbus clearly had in mind the exploitation of gold, the royal permission and instructions emphasized the good treatment that should be accorded to the local Amerindians and their conversion to Christianity. Columbus's own sons, Diego and Fernando, meanwhile had joined the Spanish court as royal pages.

On 25 September 1493, Columbus set sail from Cádiz with 17 ships and 1,200 men, including 20 cavalrymen plus their horses, 5 religious advisers—2 priests and 3 lay brothers—and his youngest brother, Diego. This second expedition included two people who were to write significant historical accounts of future events—Dr. Chanca, his personal physician, who recorded the establishment of the new settlement of La Isabela, and Father Ramón Pané, a Heironymite priest whose responsibilities included documenting the language, customs, and beliefs of the local Taíno.

The Canaries were once again visited en route and a quick transit of the Atlantic brought the fleet to the island of Dominica on 3 November. Sailing north from here, Columbus discovered several islands of the Lesser Antilles on his way to Hispaniola. On one island, named Guadeloupe, the Spanish observed human bones in a recently vacated Carib village that they interpreted as evidence of the cannibalistic feasts described to Columbus by the Taíno during the first voyage. On arrival in Hispaniola, Columbus found La Navidad in ruins and his men dead. Guacanagarí prevaricated, accusing other more powerful Taíno chiefs, notably Caonabo, of having attacked and killed the Europeans. Perhaps through a combination of such plausible deniability and the Spanish need of a powerful Taíno ally, Guacanagarí's excuses were accepted, and he came back into favor. La Navidad, however, was not rebuilt, and a new settlement known as La Isabela was founded in January 1494.

Accompanied by Guacanagarí, Columbus led a joint Spanish/Taíno expedition into Hispaniola's mountainous heart on 12 March in search of the golden riches of Cibao, to punish Caonabo, and to establish the fort of Santo Tomás. After this adventure, Columbus left Diego in charge and set off on 24 April to explore the southern coastline of Cuba, returning at the end of September. Arriving back at La Isabela, Columbus found his brother Bartolomé had arrived from Spain with three ships and he quickly appointed him *adelantado* (governor). This act led to accusations of nepotism and the taking of Bartolomé's ships by some of the discontented colonizers, who then sailed back to Spain and set about spreading rumors of Columbus's high-handed behavior.

There was trouble also between the Spanish and the local Taíno on Hispaniola. Columbus mounted a year-long expedition into the center of the island that treated the Amerindians with savage brutality but appeared to have the desired effect—bringing peace to Hispaniola. During this incursion, the Taíno chief Guarionex played a central role in dealing with the Spanish, famously offering to feed them in lieu of paying tribute by gold mining—a practice he told Columbus his people knew nothing of. Columbus declined the offer and built the fort of Concepción de la Vega on a hill strategically overlooking Guarionex's village, which was where he also temporarily settled Ramón Pané.

Back in Spain, Ferdinand and Isabella had appointed a judicial inquiry to investigate the stories of Columbus's mismanagement on Hispaniola. When the investigator, Juan Aguado, arrived in the Caribbean and treated Columbus in a humiliating fashion, the latter returned to Spain in March 1496 to defend himself personally. Once there, he adopted the appearance of a penitent, dressing in a priest's robe and carrying chains wherever he went. He was to spend two years in Spain constantly writing letters and reports in attempts to convince the king and queen to allow him to undertake a third voyage.

During his elder brother's absence, Bartolomé put down a revolt of Taíno chiefs and threw Guarionex in jail, though he quickly released him as a calming influence on the local Amerindian population. Abuses of Guarionex's family by a faction of the Spanish colonizers led by Francisco Roldán led to the Taíno chief taking refuge with Mayobanex, chief of the Macorix people. Both men were subsequently captured by Bartolomé Columbus. In January of 1497, Bartolomé also visited Behechio Anacaochoa, principal chief of the Taíno of Xaraguá in southwestern Hispaniola. Although the Spanish were welcomed and feasted by the Taíno, Bartolomé's demands for tribute in gold were said to be impossible to satisfy, and food and cotton were offered instead—an arrangement accepted by Bartolomé. Several months later Bartolomé returned to Xaraguá to collect the tribute and it was at this time that Behechio and his royal sister, Anacaona, gave gifts to the Spanish of cotton goods, ceremonial carved-wood stools (*duhos*), and artful wooden sculptures.

By early 1498 Christopher Columbus was back in favor in Spain. He received royal affirmation of his title of viceroy and governor of the Indies and permission for another expedition. It also seems likely that this new voyage was designed in part to confirm the existence and location of a large continent rumored to exist opposite southern Africa and south of the Caribbean—South America.

The Third Voyage (30 May 1498–September/October 1500)

Columbus's six ships sailed out of the Guadalquivir River in May 1498. After calling at Madeira and the Canary Islands, the fleet divided into two, with three ships going to Hispaniola and the other three under Columbus's command sailing farther south to the Cape Verde Islands and then turning west across the Atlantic. After being becalmed in the infamous windless region known as the doldrums, Columbus's ships finally sighted land on 31 July. The three mountain peaks that announced landfall signaled the discovery of the most southerly Caribbean island of Trinidad.

The small fleet sailed along the island's southern shore, meeting Trinidad's Amerindian peoples when they landed to take onboard fresh water. They continued westward, finally entering the Gulf of Paria through the so-called Serpent's Mouth between Trinidad and the mainland, and finally set foot on the South American continent on 4 August. On 15 August off the island of Margarita, Columbus decided to sail north across uncharted Caribbean waters and head for Hispaniola. Before he left, it seems that he had recognized that while Trinidad was an island, his other landfall had been the much rumored landmass of South America. This was due partly to the quantity of fresh water emerging from the mouth of the Orinoco River.

On 31 August, the fleet arrived in Santo Domingo on Hispaniola's southern coast, which had been founded in his absence (though on his orders) by Bartolomé when La Isabela was finally abandoned. The situation between the Spanish on Hispaniola had deteriorated during Columbus's absence and Francisco Roldán now had the upper hand—partly due to his view that there should be no restrictions either on goldmining activities or the use of Amerindians as forced labor. Roldán was left in virtual control of the southern part of the island, though small bands of rebels held out in other areas. Hispaniola's internal strife accelerated when Alonso de Hojeda arrived in September 1499 and joined the anti-Columbus rebels. Columbus appealed to the Spanish monarchs for help but the result of their sending Francisco de Bobadilla was that the three Columbus brothers refused to accept his authority, were quickly arrested, and were sent back to Spain in chains, arriving in October 1500.

Columbus took advantage of his situation, walking the streets of Cádiz and Seville in the chains that he refused to have removed and that he hoped would gain his sovereigns' sympathy. Ferdinand and Isabella seemed to fall for the ruse, granted him an audience, and promised to restore his rights and privileges. During the following months he studied the Bible and rejuvenated his old idea of restoring Muslim-occupied Jerusalem to Christendom. His musings on these issues were gathered together in his *Book of Prophecies*. Perhaps spurred on—and certainly aggrieved—by the appointment of Don Nicolás de Ovando as governor-general of Hispaniola, Columbus renewed his petitions at the Royal Court to be allowed a fourth expedition. His efforts bore fruit on 14 March 1502.

The Fourth Voyage (3 April 1502–7 November 1504)

Christopher Columbus's fourth and final voyage—comprised of four ships—began on 3 April 1502. Instructed to continue his exploration of the mainland he had previously discovered, he took with him his son Fernando and his brother Bartolomé. It is clear, however, that he still clung to the belief that he could discover a sea route to the East Indies. The fleet arrived in Martinique on 15 June after a rapid ocean crossing of just twenty-one days.

Disobeying specific instructions not to call at Hispaniola, Columbus arrived offshore Santo Domingo on 29 June but was denied permission to dock by Governor Ovando. Warning the authorities that a hurricane was approaching, Columbus found shelter down the coast, but Ovando ignored the threat and allowed a large fleet to sail for Spain. Nineteen ships and 500 men were lost, including Columbus's earlier nemesis, Francisco de Bobadilla. From Hispaniola, Columbus sailed past Cuba and arrived off Cape Honduras on 30 July. The Amerindian peoples of this region seemed far more advanced than those of the Caribbean islands and the Spanish observed that they had metalworking technology. Columbus had touched the boundaries of the great Mesoamerican civilizations but that momentous discovery eluded him. He turned east instead of west and thereby left greater fortune, if not greater fame, to Hernán Cortés seventeen years later.

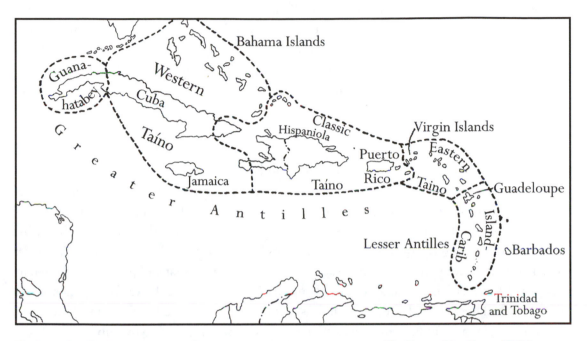

The Amerindian Caribbean at the time of Columbus. Source: *Based on Irving Rouse,* The Tainos *(New Haven, CT: Yale University Press, 1992).*

Columbus's voyaging took him along the Caribbean coast of present day Honduras and Costa Rica. By 6 October he had reached the area of the Guaymi Amerindians at Chiriqui in Panama. Encouraged by his own wishful thinking, Columbus believed he had reached the East Indies and was following the coast of the Malay Peninsula. Buffeted by contrary winds and slowed by countercurrents, the fleet spent Christmas 1502 in the vicinity of today's Panama Canal. At the beginning of 1503 he anchored at the mouth of the Belén River near Veragua and discovered gold during an inland exploration in the area. Plans to build a town to exploit this discovery had to be abandoned when relations with the Guaymi deteriorated and several Spaniards were killed. A failure to careen his ships meant that they were now taking on water to a dangerous degree and Columbus decided to cut his losses and return to Hispaniola.

Bad weather and navigational mistakes took the ships off course to Cuba, from where they were then blown away from Hispaniola toward Jamaica. The now hardly seaworthy ships were beached at what is now St. Ann's Bay on Jamaica's north coast near a Taíno village. Columbus and his 115 men were now stranded, though two canoes of Europeans and local Amerindians under the command of Columbus's supporter Diego Méndez managed to journey to Hispaniola and raise the alarm. Back in Jamaica, the Taíno were bringing less and less food and the situation was deteriorating. Columbus gambled on an event that spoke volumes concerning the different worldviews and knowledge of Europeans and Caribbean Amerindians. Using almanac information, he predicted a lunar eclipse on 29 February 1504 that astonished the Taíno and food supplies were restored. It was more than a year after they had been stranded that Columbus and his men were finally rescued in June 1504. After a brief layover in Hispaniola he sailed for Spain, arriving on 7 November.

See also: Black Legend; Caribs; Cuba; Dominica; Dominican Republic; Gold; Guacanagarí (Taíno chief); Guadeloupe; Haiti; La Isabela (site, Dominican Republic); La Navidad/En Bas Saline (site, Haiti); New Seville (site, Jamaica); Pané, Father Ramón; Taíno (Arawak); Trinidad and Tobago; Turks and Caicos

References
Bourne, E. G. 1906. Columbus, Ramón Pané, and the Beginnings of American Anthropology. *Proceedings of the Antiquarian Society* 17, pp. 310–348; Columbus, C. 1969. *The four voyages of Christopher Columbus.* Harmondsworth, UK: Penguin; Columbus, C. 1988. *Select Documents Illustrating the Four Voyages of Columbus.* (Trans. C. Jane). New York: Dover; Cundall, F. 1894. The Story of the Life of Columbus and the Discovery of Jamaica. *Journal of the Institute of Jamaica* 2: 1–79; Deagan, K. A. 1987. Columbus's Lost Colony. *National Geographic* 172 (5): 672–675; Deagan, K. A., and J. M. Cruxent. 2002. *Columbus's Outpost among the Taínos: Spain and America at La Isabela, 1493–1498.* New Haven, CT: Yale University Press; Dor-Ner, Z. 1991. *Columbus and the Age of Discovery.* London: HarperCollins; Dunn, O., and J. E. Kelley (eds.). 1989. *The Diario of Christopher Columbus's First Voyage to America, Abstracted by Fray Bartolomé de Las Casas.* Norman, OK: University of Oklahoma Press; Fernández-Armesto, F. 1991. *Columbus.* Oxford: Oxford University Press; Floyd, T. 1973. *The Columbus Dynasty in the Caribbean, 1492–1526.* Albuquerque, NM: University of New Mexico Press; Fuson, R. E. 1987. *The Log of Christopher Columbus.* Camden, NJ: International Marine Publishing; Gerbi, A. 1985. *Nature in the New World: From Christopher Columbus to Gonzalo Fernandez de Oviedo.* (Trans. J. Moyle). Pittsburgh: University of Pittsburgh Press; Keith, D. H., T. L. Carrell, and D. C.

Lacey. 1990. The Search for Columbus's Caravel *Gallega* and the Site of Santa María Belén. *Journal of Field Archaeology* 17: 123–140; S. A. Morrison, 1942. *Admiral of the Ocean Sea: A Life of Christopher Columbus.* Boston: Little, Brown; Morrison, S. E. 1940. The Route of Columbus along the North Coast of Haiti and the Site of La Navidad. *Transactions of the American Philosophical Society* 31 (4): 239–285; Nader, H. 1992a. Christopher Columbus: Columbus in Spain. In S. A. Bedini (ed.). *The Christopher Columbus Encyclopedia* Vol. 1, pp. 187–198. New York: Simon and Schuster; Nader, H. 1992b. Christopher Columbus: The Final Years, Illness, and Death. In S. A. Bedini (ed.). *The Christopher Columbus Encyclopedia* Vol. 1, pp. 198–204. New York: Simon and Schuster; Phillips, W. D., and C. R. Phillips, 1992. *The Worlds of Christopher Columbus.* Cambridge: Cambridge University Press; Sale, K. 1992. *The Conquest of Paradise.* London: Papermac/Macmillan; Stannard, D. E. 1992. *American Holocaust: Columbus and the Conquest of the New World.* Oxford: Oxford University Press; Taviani, P. E. 1985. *Christopher Columbus: The Grand Design.* London: Orbis.

Conch

Prehistoric inhabitants of the Island Caribbean exploited the vast resources of marine shellfish both as food and as raw material for making a wide variety of artifacts, from simple scrapers and needles to musical instruments. This is evident from huge heaps of shells known as middens found throughout the region from the earliest times. The shell midden at Erin in Trinidad alone is estimated to have over 100 million shells.

The largest and single most important gastropod was the Queen Conch (*Strombus gigas*), though the smaller West Indian Crown Conch (*Melongena melongena*) was also culturally significant. Queen Conch prefers relatively shallow water and a sandy sea-floor, in contrast to West Indian Crown Conch, which prefers mud flats and mangrove swamps. The Lucayan Amerindians of the Bahamas were renowned for their diving abilities to retrieve Queen Conch, so much so that they were later forced by the Spanish to become pearl divers.

Throughout the Caribbean region, Queen Conch was exploited as a nutritious food, and for the production of tools, figurines, decorative inlay, and jewelry. Sometimes the economic dependence on the species was overwhelming, as in Saladoid times in Puerto Rico, and post-Saladoid Barbados. Perhaps emerging from its value as a plentiful food source, the ritual importance of Queen Conch might be seen as inspiring the shape of the small three-pointed stone *zemís*. Perhaps also, this religious significance was reinforced by its shell being burned as part of the production of the ritually important hallucinogenic *cohoba* snuff. Conch-shell trumpets are known from Taíno sites, and historical sources mention them being played in Taíno musical celebrations known as *areítos*.

As the largest example of its type, Queen Conch may have been associated with the fertility of the sea. This role may have been enhanced by the occasional discovery of a pearl inside, as such objects were themselves highly regarded as symbols of life and regeneration.

See also: Cohoba; Pearls (gems); Saladoid; Zemís

References
Antczak, M. and A. Antczak. 1987. Algunas consideraciones sobre la identificación del material arqueológico de concha: El caso del *Strombus gigas* en el Archipélago de Los Roques, Venezuela.

Boletín Asociación Venezolana de Arqueología 4: 28–37; Carstarphen, D. 2000. *The Conch Book.* Miami, FL: Pen and Ink Press; Dacal Moure, R. 1978. *Artefactos de Concha en las Communidades Aborigenes Cubanas.* Havana: Universidad de la Habana; Hesse, R. C., and K. Orr Hesse, 1977. The Conch Industry in the Turks and Caicos Islands. *Underwater Naturalist* 10: 4–9; Morris, P. A. 1973. *A Field Guide to Shells of the Atlantic and Gulf Coasts and the West Indies.* Boston: Houghton Mifflin; Sutty, L. A. 1978. A Study of Shells and Shelled Objects from Six Precolumbian Sites in the Grenadines of St. Vincent and Grenada. *Proceedings of the Seventh International Congress for the Study of Pre-Columbian Cultures of the Lesser Antilles,* pp. 195–210. Centre de recherches caraïbes, Université de Montréal, Montréal.

Coralie (site, Turks and Caicos)

The Coralie site is located on the northwest part of Grand Turk Island in the Turks and Caicos. It is important because it has yielded archaeological evidence concerning a period of Caribbean prehistory about which little is known.

The site was discovered in 1992, and it was soon realized that it dated to the earliest period of occupation by pottery-making peoples in the Bahamas. Radiocarbon dates ranging between A.D. 705 and A.D. 1170 confirmed this, proving that Coralie's inhabitants were the ancestors of the later Taínos. Excavations revealed pottery that belonged to the Ostionan Ostionoid style, and that seems to have been imported from the Greater Antilles to the south rather than made at the site itself. Two types of pottery were found, the better-made fineware, and the less sophisticated coarseware. Fragments from boat-shaped bowls were found, as were zoomorphic ceramic pieces (a turtle head and a flipper) that appeared originally to have come from a turtle effigy bowl. The presence of ceramic cassava griddles indicated that cassava bread was baked and consumed at the site. Overall, it appeared that pottery had been in short supply and consequently had been overused and had become fragile.

An analysis of faunal remains showed that Coralie's inhabitants had consumed large quantities of green turtle, iguana, snakes, and birds, as well as Queen Conch. Unusually, these Amerindians also seem to have hunted large fish, including shark, barracuda, groupers, and snappers. Excavation also identified the location of large house posts of a dwelling that was probably abandoned and simply rotted away. There was also evidence for rebuilding perhaps necessitated by the burning of old insect-infested dwellings and maybe also in response to a rise in sea level that occurred in 700.

See also: Ostionoid; Turks and Caicos

References

Keegan, W. H. 1997. *Bahamian Archaeology: Life in the Bahamas and Turks and Caicos Before Columbus.* Gainesville, FL: University Press of Florida.

Cozumel

Cozumel is a coral island situated 16 km off the northeastern coast of Mexico's Yucatán peninsula. During Classic Mayan times (A.D. 250 to A.D. 800), it was unimportant, but with the advent of the Post-Classic Period (1300 to 1519) it became a strategic and influential trading and pilgrimage center.

Cozumel's rise to power was the result of a shift during Post-Classic times away from land trade and toward canoe-based sea commerce. This was a consequence of the rise to power of the merchant seamen of the Putun Maya. Cozumel became the major port-of-trade in a coastal trading system that included Tulum, Tancah, and the Isla de Mujeres, and which connected the Yucatán with Honduras, Nicaragua, and Panama. Important Cozumel families may have exercised political influence in the great mainland city of Mayapan and further west in the region of Campeche and Tabasco.

For many years, archaeologists regarded Cozumel as a cultural backwater in the Mayan world. More recently, the island's role in the Putun Maya trading sphere has been recognized. In their large seagoing canoes, the Putun transported cotton, honey, cacao beans, and salt, as well as objects of obsidian, jade, and the ritual items of jaguar skins and quetzal feathers. Contact with the mainland, especially Mayapan, is also well attested in the Puuc style of pottery and the ceramic figurine incense burners so important in Ix Chel's rituals.

The Putun may have blended the spiritual, the commercial, and the defensive in the series of small coastal shrines that may also have served as watchtowers. Many major settlements are inland, dominated by structures—houses, temples, and shrines—built with stone foundations, mud walls, stone benches and altars, and topped with thatched roofs. One of the most recognizable structures found by archaeologists is the apiary, which yielded large amounts of honey and wax, for both local consumption and trade.

It was the Spanish priest Fray Diego de Landa who first commented that the Maya regarded Cozumel as a center of pilgrimage akin to the Christian Jerusalem and Rome. As with Tulum, and the northeastern part of Yucatán more generally, there were strong cosmological and mythical associations between the east, the Caribbean sea, and the worship of the Lady of the Rainbow—the moon goddess Ix Chel, supernatural wife of the god Itzamná. Cozumel was the main center for Ix Chel's worship, and devotions and offerings were made especially at the site of San Gervasio. Although associated with medicine, and regarded as patron deity of traders and pilgrims, Ix Chel was most closely identified with fertility and especially with women who wished to become pregnant or were about to give birth. The Ahkin (Priest of the Sun), would hide behind giant ceramic images of the goddess and served as an oracle, answering the questions put to the deity by the female pilgrims.

Sailing from Cuba in 1518, the Spaniard Juan de Grijalva made his first Mexican landfall at Cozumel—at the sight of which the local Maya fled. A year later, the future conqueror of Mexico, Hernán Cortés, repeated the act and spent several days destroying temples and shrines, and casting down their idols. Such acts, together with the Spaniards' subsequent dismantling of buildings for raw materials with which to build their towns, led to the wholesale destruction of the pre-Columbian Mayan architecture of Cozumel. As with so many abandoned Mayan sites, it was John Lloyd Stephens and Frederick Catherwood who, in 1843, rediscovered the Mayan ruins of Cozumel, reporting small shrines near the town of San Miguel. Between 1916 and 1922, the first extensive archaeological survey investigated the island's ruins, and in the early 1970s a second survey of Mayan settlement patterns was carried out by a team from Harvard and the University of Arizona.

See also: Cacao; Maya; Tancah (site, Mexico); Tulum (site, Mexico)
References
Fernandez, M. A. 1945. Exploraciones arqueologicas en la Isla Cozumel, Quintana Roo. *Annals of the Institution of Anthropology and History* 1: 107–120; Freidel, D. A., and J. A. Sabloff, 1984. *Cozumel: Late Maya Settlement Patterns,* Orlando, FL: Academic Press; Sabloff, J. A. 1977. Old Myths, New Myths: The Role of Sea Traders in the Development of Ancient Maya Civilization. In E. P. Benson (ed.), *The Sea in the Pre-Columbian World,* pp. 67–88. Washington, DC: Dumbarton Oaks; Sabloff, J. A., and W. L. Rathje (eds.). 1975. A Study of Changing Pre-Columbian Commercial Systems: The 1972–1973 Seasons at Cozumel, Mexico. *Monograph 3 of the Peabody Museum of Archaeology and Ethnology.* Cambridge, MA.

Creole / Creolization

Since the arrival of Christopher Columbus in 1492, the Caribbean has been regarded as a mixing pot of cultures, ethnicities, religions, and languages. Amerindians, Europeans, Africans, and others from India, China, and the Middle East have all contributed to Caribbean societies, though the African element is the most visible.

The hybrid cultures, languages, and traditions that have evolved over 500 years are often called Creole. Creolization, the process of mixing to create something new, usually refers to the formation of a new language as a result of two linguistic traditions coming into contact. Different definitions exist even here, however. Some specialists believe that a creole language develops out of a local pidgin (defined as a short-lived makeshift jargon to facilitate initial exchanges between groups); others consider pidgins and creoles as entirely different and unrelated, and a true creole language created by the children of first- or second-generation parents.

Creole cultures developed in different ways on different islands, depending on which was the dominant European culture, the density of African slaves, and the particular historical trajectory of each island. For example, English colonies were much slower to develop creole societies than the Spanish or French due to English colonists initially keeping to themselves and not interbreeding or adapting their material culture and traditions with African elements. The term *criolla* is sometimes used simply as the Spanish equivalent of English "creole." More accurately and widely, it is used to identify a specific type of creole society in which Spanish influence is dominant and is specifically applied to those born in the Caribbean of European parents.

The term "creole" has also been applied more widely to music, cuisine, and architecture, where, variously, indigenous Amerindian influences (for example in musical instruments and available plant foods) have joined with European and African traditions to create distinctive musical forms (such as rumba, salsa, and calypso), food dishes, and architectural styles.

See also: Languages; Music

Crocodile

In the Caribbean region, the American crocodile (*Crocodylus acutus*) is found in southern Florida, the Antilles, Central America, Colombia, and Venezuela. In the Island Caribbean, only Cuba has its own species, the Cuban crocodile (*Crocodylus rhombifer*). Both species can reach over 5 meters in length and are as dangerous to humans today as they undoubtedly were in the past.

These powerful saurians are notoriously difficult to kill—a fact that, together with their fearsome appearance and ability to live on land and in water, must have made a deep impression on native Amerindian peoples. Crocodilian imagery appears sometimes on Saladoid ceramics, and a special religious reverence for these animals is indicated for the natives of Panama, among whom the most common anthropozoomorphic goldwork figurines display crocodilian features. Equally significant, among the Maya of Yucatán, the crocodile or caiman was a much venerated deity and identified with the creator god Itzamna. During Colonial times, the Yucatec Mayan god Itzam Cab Ain was identified as the "great earth caiman" associated with the flood.

While early European explorers commented on their great numbers, especially on the Caribbean coasts of the Central and South American mainland, there was evidently confusion as to whether or not they were (or were related to) iguanas or snakes. During his first voyage, Christopher Columbus reported crocodiles as serpents, capturing one on Small Island in the Bahamas. Until the recent discovery in a Bahamian archaeological site of a crocodile leg bone, it was believed that these animals were not present in the area at this time. One of the earliest reports comes from an acquaintance of Oviedo, a Dr. Codro who journeyed to the Indies and made a study of the region's great lizards, i.e., crocodiles and caimans. At Darién, on the Caribbean coast of Colombia, Martín Fernández de Enciso wrote from personal experience in his 1519 *Suma de Geographía* of lizards as big as bullocks with dorsal scales so tough that ten lances bounced off them.

In 1503, while returning to Hispaniola on his fourth voyage (1502 to 1504), Christopher Columbus discovered several small islands that he christened the Islas Tortugas (the Turtle Islands), so completely were they covered with these creatures. By 1523, however, they appeared on a map as Lagartos (lizards/crocodiles) and by 1530 their name had changed again to Caymanas (caiman) after the Amerindian word for crocodiles. Although it was the edible turtles that attracted European seafarers to the Cayman Islands, in 1586 Sir Francis Drake had cause to taste crocodile and pronounced it edible. Interestingly, the first edition of Peter Martyr's *De Orbe Novo* contained a map of Mexico's Yucatán peninsula on which there was but one place name—a Caribbean coastal location marked as Bahía de Lagartos (Bay of Lizards/Crocodiles).

Although the various species of crocodiles in the Caribbean region have been much reduced, today they still survive on the larger islands and along the coastal margins of the mainland. They continue to pose a threat to humans. In 1990, somewhat ironically, a man was killed in Panama by a crocodile when he jumped into a river chasing a wounded iguana. In Jamaica, folk tales tell of a character called Brer Alligator in the same manner as the more famous Brer Rabbit.

> *See also:* Columbus, Christopher; Martyr, Peter; Maya; Turtles
> *References*
> Guggisberg, C.A.W. 1972. *Crocodiles.* Newton Abbot, UK: David and Charles.

Cuba

Cuba is the largest Caribbean island, 1,250 km long by 191 km at its widest point, and it lies only 145 km south of Florida on the U.S. mainland. The population is about 11 million, some two-thirds being the descendants of Spanish settlers and the balance black and mulatto. Today there are no Amerindian inhabitants on the island.

Cuba was first settled in prehistoric times by Casimiroid peoples between 4000 B.C. and 400 B.C. The Casimiran subseries (which developed into the early Ciboney culture) is found on the island during the Lithic Period, its peoples coming possibly from Central or South America. Sites of this period tend to be workshops where stone tools were manufactured and usually date to around 2000 B.C., though one of the earliest, the Levisa rockshelter, dates to ca. 4190 B.C. The excavation of these sites typically reveals stone tools, animal bones, and seashells. Some archaeologists believe that this simple level of society persisted in western Cuba until European contact, living in caves, gaining a living from fishing, and never inventing pottery. They are commonly called the Guanahatabey culture.

The subsequent Redondan subseries (also known as the later Ciboney) is divided into two local cultures—Guayabo Blanco and Cayo Redondo—with dates ranging from 2050 B.C. to A.D. 1300. The distinctive feature of these two cultures is the presence of triangular shell gouges. The Redondan people left shell midden sites on Cuba's coast, but they also lived in caves whose walls they painted and in whose floors they buried their dead. Interestingly, the ground-stone tools they made are the most sophisticated in eastern Cuba, a short sea passage away from Courian culture in Hispaniola (modern Haiti and the Dominican Republic). Pottery and agriculture appeared around A.D. 800 and may have been a Ciboney creation, though it could have been introduced into Cuba from outside. The local Bani culture is the name given to the Cuban variation of the Meillacan people who appear to have moved here from Hispaniola around this time.

The Taíno people seem to have entered Cuba around the third century A.D. and developed a successful agricultural village life up until the arrival of Europeans, by which time they numbered somewhere between 100,000 and 150,000. Eastern Cuba has the greatest number of sites, including the ceremonial center at Laguna de Limones and the petroglyph cave site of La Patana. It is the area of the Maniabón Hills in the eastern province of Holguín, however, that has the greatest single density of Taíno occupation, such as La Campana, El Mango, and the rich burial ground at Chorro de Maíta. In 1994, Canada's Royal Ontario Museum began excavations at the waterlogged Taíno site of Los Buchillones, from which extraordinarily well-preserved wooden artifacts have been recovered.

First visited by Europeans during Christopher Columbus's first voyage of discovery on 27 October 1492, it was conquered in 1511 by the Spanish conquistador Diego de Velázquez in a particularly vicious and bloody campaign. During the subjugation of the island, the chronicler Bartolomé de Las Casas, acting a chaplain, was tricked by his superiors into placating the Amerindians, whereupon they were captured, tortured, and killed. In 1518, the Spaniard Juan de Grijalva sailed from Cuba to make his first Mexican landfall at Cozumel, and soon afterward the conquistador Hernán Cortés left the island to conquer Mexico. In 1526, the first African slaves were brought to Cuba, though their use on sugar plantations did not occur until the 1590s. Soon afterward, tobacco became an important industry and in 1717 its cultivation and sale was established as a Spanish monopoly.

During the nineteenth century, several slave rebellions and civil uprisings occurred and were crushed. In 1898, U.S. forces occupied the island after their victory over the Spanish fleet at Santiago de Cuba in the Spanish-American War. Cuba's first president, Tomás Estrada Palma, took over the government in 1902 under the patronage of the United States, which reserved the right to intervene in Cuban affairs until 1934.

Today, Cuban culture is an effervescent mix of African and Hispanic influences particularly in its music and folk religions. Musically, the combination of African percussive rhythms and Spanish guitar has created such vibrant styles as rumba, *trova, son,* and *danzón*—the last two being the inspiration for the internationally better-known salsa and cha-cha, respectively. In religion, Roman Catholicism is the major faith with some 40 percent nominally Catholic. In fact, the mestizo nature of Cuban society blends African and Catholic elements in Santería. This folk religion brings together Catholic saints and the animistic beliefs of the African Yoruba culture that sees the natural world as infused with spiritual energies.

Due to its recent history as a communist state, Cuba has been denied the vast amounts of tourist money that has so transformed other Caribbean islands. One fortunate result is that many fine examples of early Spanish colonial architecture have escaped development. In Havana, Cuba's capital, splendid colonial buildings survive in the old city that is now designated a UNESCO World Heritage Site. In the Plaza de Armas, located in the heart of the old city, is the National Museum of Natural History of Cuba. Outside Havana, Santa Clara in the island's center was the site of the last battle of Fidel Castro's Cuban revolution, and Trinidad on the south coast preserves much Spanish colonial architecture. At the eastern end of Cuba is Santiago de Cuba, whose Colonial Museum is the island's oldest, being founded by Cortés in 1516. Cuba's national hero, José Martí, is buried nearby in the Santa Efigenia cemetery. Between 16 and 19 April, this town plays host to one of the island's most colorful annual events—the Festival de Caribe—during which the streets come alive with African music and dancing.

See also: Casimiroid; Columbus, Christopher; Cozumel; Guanahatabey; Las Casas, Bartolomé de; Los Buchillones (site, Cuba); Meillacan; Santería

References
Bergad, L. W., F. García Iglesias, and M. Carman Barcia. 1995. *The Cuban Slave Market 1790–1880*. Cambridge: Cambridge University Press; Dacal Moure, R., and M. Rivero de la

Calle. 1996. *Art and Archaeology of Pre-Columbian Cuba.* Pittsburgh: University of Pittsburgh Press; Davis, D. D. 1995. Revolutionary Archaeology in Cuba. *Journal of Archaeological Method and Theory* 3 (3): 159–188; Dominguez, L. 1978. *Arqueología colonial Cubana: dos estudios.* Havana: Editorial de Ciencias Sociales; Graham, E., D. M. Pendergast, J. Calvera, and J. Jardines. 2000. Excavations at Los Buchillones, Cuba. *Antiquity* pp. 263–264; Guarch, J. M. 1978. *El Taíno de Cuba: Ensayo de reconstrucción etno-histórica.* Academia de Ciencias de Cuba, Instituto de Ciencias Sociales, Havana; Hagedorn, K. J. 2001. *Divine Utterances: The Performance of Afro-Cuban Santeria.* Washington, DC: Smithsonian Institution Press; Luis, W. 2000. *Culture and Customs of Cuba.* Westport, CT: Greenwood Publishing Group; Mason, M. A. 2002. *Living Santeria: Rituals and Experiences in an Afro-Cuban Religion.* Washington, DC: Smithsonian Institution Press; Osgood, C. 1942. The Ciboney Culture of Cayo Redondo, Cuba. *Yale University Publications in Anthropology* 25. New Haven, CT: Yale University Press; Rouse, I. B. 1942. Archaeology of the Maniabón Hills, Cuba. *Yale University Publications in Anthropology* No. 26. New Haven, CT: Yale University Press; von Humboldt, A. 2001. *The Island of Cuba.* Princeton, NJ: Markus Wiener.

Cuna

The Cuna live today mainly on the San Blas Islands off Panama's Caribbean coast. At the time of European arrival they and the Cueva lived on the adjacent mainland of Panama. In 1513, the Spanish conquistador Vasco Núñez de Balboa explored the area from his base at Darién and was entertained lavishly by the Amerindian chief (cacique) Comogre, who also gave the Spaniards gold and slaves. The relationship between the Cuna and Cueva remains unclear with some scholars believing the former to be the descendants of the latter while others consider the Cuna to have moved into the Cueva homeland after the latter had been decimated by disease and Spanish depredations. In any event, it seems as if the name Cuna first appeared during the seventeenth century.

Early European reports mentioned the Cuna's light, smooth skin, chestnut hair, and sparkling eyes. From the beginning, Europeans noticed the pacific nature of the Cuna, a philosophy that abhorred violence except in self-defense, and a belief in one god. In the face of ravages by Spanish conquistadors and European adventurers, the early Cuna are said to have refused to fight and simply turned their back on their farms and land and retreated into the jungles and mountains.

In the mid-nineteenth century, the Cuna divided into two groups. The mainland Cuna now live on the western Pacific shores of Panama and around the Gulf of Uraba, and the Atrato River valley in Colombia. The island Cuna inhabit around sixty of the several hundred San Blas islands offshore of Panama's Caribbean coast. Both groups share the same language and dress, yet while the mainland Cuna have remained isolated, their island cousins have been drawn inexorably closer to the modern world through trade and tourism. Today there are about 40,000 Cuna, who refer to themselves as Tule, or the "Sons of God."

The digging of the Panama Canal, which began in 1904, brought social and political unrest to the Cuna as outsiders began infiltrating their territory. A Tule republic was declared in 1919, combining both mainland and island communities. A declaration of inde-

pendence was followed by the killing of Panamanian police on Tigre Island. In 1925 a peace treaty was signed by Panamanian officials and Cuna leaders aboard the USS *Cleveland* and since that time the Panamanian government has kept a low profile. Tension between the two still exists though the Cuna are now permitted to police themselves. The Cuna flag is a circle representing a Cuna woman's gold nose-ring superimposed on a swastika—an ancient Cuna motif.

Traditional Cuna culture has survived to a considerable degree, unlike that of most indigenous peoples of the Caribbean region. Today, as in the past, the Cuna represent themselves through the making and wearing of their traditional dress. It is the women who, being highly regarded in Cuna society, have served as the guardians of culture, philosophy, and values. A woman's blouse, onto which is sewn a brightly colored decorative appliqué design called a *mola,* is the most important emblem of the female role, along with the typical gold nose-ring. While the mola has been affected by changing twentieth-century fashions and now also appears on menswear, it retains its place as a source of Cuna identity and independence.

Early observations of Cuna dress are scarce, though one report mentions their "curiously embroidered" cotton skirts. The first detailed description and illustration of the mola was written by Lady Richmond Brown, who visited the San Blas Islands in 1922, though the earliest known mola dates only to 1909. Mola designs appear not to have originated in the complex designs of body painting and tattoo noted by the earliest explorers, of which the thin black line down the middle of the women's noses is the most visible sign.

The voyage of Lionell Wafer to the Cuna region was recorded in his *A New Voyage and Description of the Isthmus of America.* Written in 1681, though not published until 1933, it provides rich insight into Cuna ideas of color and design that are so much part of the mola tradition. Wafer describes their love of bright colors, the designs of birds, animals, and humans, and the use of natural pigments, such as black from the *Genipa americana* and red from the *Pterocarpus draco,* or dragon's-blood tree, used in traditional tattooing. He also describes the knee-length skirts worn by Cuna women and notes in detail the growing, spinning, and dyeing of cotton.

Like all indigenous circum-Caribbean peoples except the Maya, the Cuna lived originally in an oral tradition. After European contact they seem to have developed an unusual type of picture-writing, at first using balsa-wood boards and then paper. Once the secretive and deeply metaphorical language had been deciphered, these were realized to be often complete songs or myths. Their translation revealed a wealth of information about how the Cuna saw themselves and their mythical origins, including a creator deity called Olocupinele, a sacred mountain of creation called Takarkuna, and a great culture hero named Ibeorgun. It was the latter who bestowed the gift of speech on the Cuna, taught them picture-writing, and showed them how to carve wooden staffs and figurines (*nuchus*) used by shamans in curing ceremonies.

The religious and spiritual dimensions of Cuna society reveal a typically Amerindian worldview where the power of shamans (*neles*), their songs and chants, brings order and meaning to life. Neles are able to magically talk with ancestor spirits, can converse with animals, and have the power to avert natural disasters such as earthquakes and hurricanes. Cuna ceremonial chanters called *kantules* sing in a secret code almost impossible for an outsider to comprehend. The few words that are understood reveal an ancient world where a mirror's image, the heat of the sun, or an echo are all manifestations of animating spirit force known as *purba.* All living things—whether plant, animal, or human—partake of purba and are thus joined together in a spiritual continuum. Such animistic ideas typically embrace cultural activities and natural phenomena. A tree whose leaves are attacked by a parasite is left marked with beautiful designs and anyone who rubs the liquid from these leaves into their eyes is able to make beautiful molas.

Traditional Cuna social life centers around nightly meetings called *congressos.* Here, the villagers congregate in a large hut to discuss politics and the day's events, and to air their grievances. Kantules may also recite stories from Cuna myth and history. The chiefs recline in their hammocks, smoke tobacco, and preside over events. Congressos are a favorite scene for the mola-makers.

Women are cherished in Cuna society. While they carry culture through their molas, they also deal with business and trading activities and guard the proceeds as shown by the wearing of a money-box key around the neck. Marriage is almost exclusively within the Cuna community and while women are expected to marry young, it is they who choose a husband. In many ways, Cuna attitudes toward women are linked to their spiritual philosophy and are summed up in the creation myth known as *Mu-Dup*—which sees the Earth Mother giving birth to all life as an expression of love.

See also: Balboa, Vasco Núñez de; Shamanism; Tobacco
References
Herrera Porras, T. 1978. *Cuna Cosmology.* (Trans. Anita McAndrews). Washington, DC: Three
Continents Press; Nordenskiöld, E. 1925. A Historical and Ethnological Survey of the Cuna
Indians. *Comparative Ethnological Studies* 10, Göteborg Museum, Göteborg, Sweden;
Nordenskiöld, E. 1929. The Relationship Between Art, Religion, and Magic Among the Cuna
and Choco Indians. *Journal de la Société des Américanistes* 21: 141–158; Puls, H. 1999. *Textiles of
the Kuna Indians.* Princes Risborough, UK: Shire; Stout, D. B. 1948. The Cuna. In J. H.
Steward (ed.), *Handbook of South American Indians* 4: 257–269. Washington, DC: Smithsonian
Institution; Wassén, S. H. 1938. Original Documents from the Cuna Indians of San Blas,
Panama. *Etnologiska Studier* 6: 1–178; Wafer, L. 1933. *A New Voyage and Description of the Isthmus
of America.* London: The Hakluyt Society.

Curaçao

Curaçao is the largest of the five islands of the Netherlands Antilles. Lying offshore of
Venezuela's coast, it is 65 km long, 11 km wide, with an area of 448 sq km, and has a cosmopolitan population of about 170,000.

Archaeological investigations have included an island-wide survey in 1982 that documented both pre-Columbian and historic-period sites. There are at least ninety-seven
prehistoric Amerindian sites on Curaçao, about one-third belonging to the Archaic Period
(2540 B.C. to 1840 B.C.), and half belonging to the ceramic period that spanned the years
from A.D. 450 to the arrival of Europeans. About 10 percent of sites have petroglyphs.

During the Archaic Period there appears to have been one major permanent site, sixteen semipermanent sites, and ten other sites where resources were extracted or worked.
At this time, Curaçao was lightly populated with hunter-gatherer groups mainly exploiting turtle and crabs for food and limestone and shale for tools. The following ceramic period was associated by the technology and decoration of pottery with the Dabajuroid culture of the Venezuelan mainland. Dabajuroid culture originated around Lake Maracaibo in
western Venezuela, and spread to the offshore islands that included Bonaire and Curaçao
as well as Aruba before A.D. 1000. At this time, there were more specialized strategies for
acquiring food, especially the Queen Conch (*Strombus gigas*), and tools were now being
made from chert and basalt. There are seven permanent settlement sites and up to forty-
two extraction sites known for this period.

Europeans stepped ashore on Curaçao, along with Bonaire and Aruba, when the
Spaniard Alonso de Ojeda and the Italian Amerigo Vespucci arrived in 1499. The Spanish
kept a small colony there between about 1520 and 1634; the Spanish site of Gaito has
yielded a radiocarbon date of 1610. In 1634, the Dutch arrived and took control. The
French briefly held the island in 1713, and the English between 1801 and 1803, and again
between 1807 and 1816. Curaçao became a trading hub for the region and so commerce
rather than plantations was the driving force in the economy. Nevertheless, the Dutch
slave trade saw large numbers of Africans pass through. Slave revolts occurred in 1750 and
1795, and eventual emancipation in 1863, after which Chinese, Lebanese, and others arrived, giving Curaçao its current multiethnic population.

Archaeologists have investigated a range of sites, including the protohistoric Spanish-Amerindian site of San Hironimo, a seventeenth-century Protestant cemetery beneath a synagogue in Willemstadt, a contemporary slave camp at Zuurzak, and an African settlement in the Kenepa area whose dwellings have been compared to traditional West African houses. Modern Afro-Curaçaon ideas of ethnic identity and continuity with their slave forebears have also recently been investigated by archaeologists. They studied the continuing tradition of building what has been called the single greatest icon of African cultural heritage on the island—the traditional thatch *kunuku* houses.

Of more recent times, investigations have been made at a nineteenth-century Dutch fort, several contemporary optical telegraph sites, twentieth-century salt warehouses, and a World War II observation post. Underwater archaeology has also received attention with the 1986 discovery and investigation of the British ship *Mediator,* which sank in 1884 at the entrance to Willemstadt harbor, and is the focus of a public education program on Curaçao's maritime heritage.

See also: Aruba; Bonaire; Dabajuroid; Historical Archaeology; Los Roques Islands (Venezuela); Margarita Island (Venezuela); Underwater Archaeology

References

Allen, R. M. 1991. The Folk Material Culture Related to Food Quest and Food Production in Curaçao Culture. *Proceedings of the Thirteenth International Congress for Caribbean Archaeology,* pp. 462–476; Boldero, E. 2003. *"Skin Deep": How and to What Extent Has the Physical Decay of Curaçao's Monuments Had an Impact in Its Society?* Unpublished BSc dissertation, University College London; Curaçao Tourist Board, 2001. *Curaçao: The Official Island Guide.* Willemstadt: Curaçao Tourist Board; Fonk, H. 1999. *Curaçao: Architectural Style.* Willemstadt: Curaçao Style Foundation; Haviser, J. B. 1987. Amerindian Cultural Geography on Curaçao. *Natuurwetenschappelijke Studiekring voor Suriname en de Nederlandse Antillen* No. 120. Amsterdam; Haviser, J. B., and N. Simmons-Brito. 1995. Excavations at the Zuurzak Site: A Possible 17th-Century Dutch Slave Camp on Curaçao, Netherlands Antilles. *Proceedings of the Fifteenth International Congress for Caribbean Archaeology,* pp. 71–82; Josselin de Jong, J.P.B. 1918. The Praecolumbian and Early Postcolumbian Aboriginal Population of Aruba, Curaçao, and Bonaire. *Internationales Archiv für Ethnographie* 24 (3): 51–114; van Heekeren, H. R. 1963. Prehistorical Research on the Islands of Curaçao, Aruba, and Bonaire in 1960. *Nieuwe West-Indische Gids* 43: 1–25.

D

Dabajuroid

The Dabajuroid cultural tradition was a long-lived phenomenon that originated around Lake Maracaibo in western Venezuela. It is thought that Dabajuroid peoples may share a common ancestry with the Saladoid peoples, perhaps in the area of the Upper Orinoco. The Dabajuroid tradition began with the local Rancho Peludo ceramic style around 1800 B.C. At this time, coarsely made pottery was decorated with appliqué fillets and fabric and mat impressions, though modeled human heads are also known.

There is little evidence for social complexity among the different local variations of Dabajuroid culture, which seem to have been simple village-based farming communities. Early sites have revealed thick ceramic cassava griddles indicative of bitter manioc cultivation. As time went on, Dabajuroid cultures increasingly adopted maize, as shown by the corn-grinding manos and metates that have been recovered from later sites. Some investigators see the Dabajuroid peoples as introducing maize agriculture to this whole region.

The series of local Dabajuroid cultures have been clustered together and called the Macro-Dabajuroid group. During this period there was an increase in overall population, one consequence of which was an expansion into the small offshore islands of Curaçao, Bonaire, and Aruba, with some influence extending perhaps as far as Barbados and the Lesser Antilles. The wider expansion of the Macro-Dabajuroid peoples seem associated also with the spread of Arawakan languages into the Island Caribbean.

Coastal and island variants of the Dabajuroid peoples dominated Bonaire between A.D. 1000 and A.D. 1400, making crude pottery figurines, large ceramic urns, polished basalt celts, and shell ornaments depicting frogs and birds. The presence of ceramic griddles and manos and metates suggests a mixed economy of cassava and maize supplemented by fish, mollusks and crabs.

See also: Aruba; Bonaire; Curaçao; Los Roques Islands (Venezuela); Maize
References
Allaire, L. 1999. Archaeology of the Caribbean Region. In F. Salomon and S. B. Schwartz (eds.). *The Cambridge History of the Native Peoples of the Americas: Vol. III, South America Part 1,* pp. 702, 715–716, Cambridge: Cambridge University Press; Bruhns, K. O. 1994. *Ancient South America,* pp. 152–153. Cambridge: Cambridge University Press; Haviser, J. B. 1991. *The First Bonaireans.* Archaeological-Anthropological Institute of the Netherlands Antilles. Willemstad:

Curaçao; Oliver, J. R. 1989. *The Archaeological, Linguistic and Ethnological Evidence for the Expansion of Arawakan into Northwestern Venezuela and Northeastern Colombia.* Ann Arbor, MI: University Microfilms; Oliver, J. R. 1997. Dabajuroid Archaeology, Settlements, and House Structures: An Overview from Mainland Western Venezuela. In A. H. Versteeg and S. Rostain (eds.). *The Archaeology of Aruba: The Tanki Flip Site,* pp. 363–429. Publications of the Archaeological Museum of Aruba 8.

Darién (Panama)

The region of Darién, a narrow part of the Isthmus of Panama, with both a Caribbean and a Pacific coast, played an unexpected and momentous role in the history of European colonization of the Americas and beyond. In 1510, Vasco Núñez de Balboa arrived in the Gulf of Urabá on the Caribbean coast of present day Colombia. He advised the Spanish Crown that the early settlement of Saint Sebastián was untenable due to hostile natives, and that a new town should be built among friendlier Amerindians on the western shore of the Gulf. Soon afterward, the Spanish founded Santa María la Antigua del Darién, one of their most successful settlements on the Caribbean coast of Tierra Firme.

Balboa did not offend the local Amerindians, but cleverly positioned himself in native society, becoming a type of supreme white chief, protecting them from Spanish abuse. This behavior brought peace to the region and offerings of Amerindian gold, food, and labor. Consequently, Darién flourished, and Balboa used it as a base from which to explore the region searching for gold—the town had become part of the search for fabulous riches later conceived as El Dorado. On his first expedition, Balboa befriended local Amerindian chiefs and received gold jewelry in return, and during his second, the Pacific Ocean was sighted on 27 September 1513. He promptly claimed it for Spain. During his absence from Darién, however, Balboa's rival, Pedro de Ávila, took control, subsequently capturing Balboa and having him tried and executed for treason.

It was at Darién that Gonzalo Fernández de Oviedo y Valdés (1478–1557) had his introduction to the Americas. Oviedo was a Spanish official who lived most of his life in the Caribbean and is one of the most important chroniclers of the region's geography and native peoples. He first journeyed to the Indies in 1514, where he became the official inspector of gold smelting at Darién. A man of his times, Oviedo supervised the looting of two Amerindian tombs in the area in search of gold. The Spanish settlement of Darién attracted many different types of people during these early years, such as the lawyer Martín Fernández de Enciso, who wrote from personal experience in his 1519 *Suma de Geographía* of lizards as big as bullocks with dorsal scales so tough that ten lances bounced off them.

In 1681, the English journalist Lionel Wafer arrived in the area and was kept as a guest there by local Amerindians. His experiences were published in his *A New Voyage and Description of the Isthmus of America,* providing rich insight into Cuna religious beliefs, clothing, tattooing, and social life. Throughout the 1680s, buccaneers made their way to the South Seas overland from the Caribbean through the Darién region. It was due to this strategic location that the area attracted the attention of Scottish settlers.

In July 1698, five ships left Scotland and arrived offshore in Caledonia Bay in November, inspired by William Patterson's belief that a Scottish settlement in the area could hold the key to trade between the Atlantic and Pacific oceans—a less fanciful idea in the days before the Panama Canal than it might seem today. Unaccustomed to the harsh physical conditions; afflicted by malaria, dysentery, and yellow fever; and plagued by lack of supplies, the colony and the planned town of New Edinburgh quickly ran into trouble. In addition to these problems, perhaps the main reason for the colony's collapse was the Scottish failure to realize how vital this region was for the transhipment of Spain's wealth from Pacific South America to the Atlantic Caribbean, and thence to Spain. The Spanish could never tolerate foreign interference in such a valuable location. In the background, the international political intrigues of the time between the English, Dutch, and, unusually, the Spanish meant that the English wished to avoid antagonizing the Spanish and so their navy did not support the Scottish settlers.

In 2003, archaeologists from Bristol University in the United Kingdom returned to the area to locate and excavate the site. They discovered the remains of Fort St. Andrews, the sunken wreck of a ship in the nearby harbor, and a number of coins and tools, together with a hearth and a pocket sundial. The evidence of musket and cannon balls inside the fort suggests far bloodier encounters between the settlers and the Spanish than the ambiguous historical records suggest. These discoveries highlight the potential of historical archaeology to throw new light on the past.

In all, the Scottish venture in Darién cost some 2,000 lives and around £200,000 of investors' money. The denouement was even more momentous, as Scotland was virtually bankrupted when the colony failed. In return for England paying off the huge debt, Scotland agreed to the 1707 Act of Union between the two countries. A small, short-lived settlement on the rainforest shores of Panama's Caribbean coast had changed the course of British and perhaps European history.

See also: Balboa, Vasco Núñez de; Cuna; El Dorado; Oviedo y Valdés, Gonzalo Fernández de
References
Horton, M. 1979. *A preliminary report of the archaeological project of Operation Drake;* Prebble, J. 2002. *The Darien Disaster.* London: Pimlico; Romoli, K. 1953. *Balboa of Darien: Discoverer of the Pacific.* New York; Sauer, C. O. 1969. *The Early Spanish Main.* Berkeley, CA: University of California Press; Wafer, L. 1933. *A New Voyage and Description of the Isthmus of America.* London: The Hakluyt Society.

Disease

Disease was the secret killer of Amerindian peoples throughout the Americas after 1492. The Caribbean was at the forefront of this confrontation between Europeans, who had gained considerable immunity over previous centuries, and the indigenous population, who, after thousands of years of geographical, cultural, and microbial isolation, had no such protection.

When Christopher Columbus arrived in the New World, he observed what he described as a healthy and vital people who seemed to suffer none of the epidemics that had so ravaged Europe in medieval times. This was true but also misleading. While the Caribbean Taíno and Carib peoples did not suffer from European diseases, they and their mainland cousins suffered considerably from their own afflictions. Modern archaeological research, aided by paleopathology, has shown that the study of Amerindian teeth and bones can reveal the presence of a range of indigenous diseases long before Europeans arrived.

In the Caribbean, and especially in Mexico and Peru, its seems as if death rates had markedly increased in the centuries immediately preceding 1492. This may well have been due to the incremental effects of an increasingly sedentary agricultural way of life that gathered ever larger densities of people together in villages and cities, rendering them more susceptible to infectious diseases. The evidence of human remains is supported by selective but graphic images in pre-Columbian art that depict a variety of indigenous afflictions from cleft palate to skin diseases. It seems as if prehistoric Amerindians suffered from pneumonia, tuberculosis, arthritis, dysentery, and various nutritional diseases, as well as parasites such as tapeworm and hookworm. Mental problems, real or imagined, were also present as shown by the number of skulls that had undergone surgery. This took the form of trepanning—the removal of sections of skull bone that subsequently healed and regrew—though many of these were probably the result of wounds sustained in battle.

A great debate has raged for many years concerning the sexually transmitted disease syphilis. Although it now appears as if this was a purely American disease brought back to Europe, the picture remains unclear as other diseases leave similar markings on human bones.

Apart from the range of indigenous American afflications, it is true that Amerindian peoples had never been exposed, or built any resistance to, the variety of killer diseases that had recently swept through Europe. These often originated in the Mediterranean, a densely populated sinkhole of Old World diseases brought by contact and trade with Asia and Africa. Initially, these had decimated European populations until, over time, they developed immunity.

Probably the greatest killer of Amerindians was smallpox, which ravaged the Americas repeatedly from around 1520. To this can be added measles, typhoid, cholera, bubonic plague, yellow fever, and malaria, among others. Sometimes diseases spread in advance of Europeans, as most famously with the death of the Incan emperor Huayna Capac in 1527, some five years before the Spanish arrived in Peru. A timetable for the first outbreaks of the major diseases includes: smallpox, 1520 to 1524; typhoid, 1528; measles, 1531 to 1533; influenza, 1559; cholera, 1832 to 1834; and malaria, 1830 to 1833. Such was the destruction of native American peoples that it was only around 1900, 400 years after Columbus, that indigenous population numbers began slowly to recover. There is no doubt that combined with maltreatment, slavery, and harsh tribute, disease wiped out the majority of Amerindian populations in the Caribbean within a short time. When Christopher Columbus came to Hispaniola in 1492 there were perhaps 3 to 4 million Taíno, but by 1516 this had declined to maybe only 12,000.

See also: Columbus, Christopher

References

Cook, N. D. 1993. Disease and Depopulation of Hispaniola, 1492–1518. *Colonial Latin American Review* 2: 213–245; Cook, N. D. 1998. *Born to Die: Disease and New World Conquest, 1492–1650.* Cambridge: Cambridge University Press; Cook, N. D., and W. G. Lovell (eds.). 2001. *"Secret Judgements of God": Old World Disease in Colonial Spanish America.* Norman, OK: University of Oklahoma Press; Crosby, A. W. Jr. 1973. *The Columbian Exchange: Biological and Cultural Consequences of 1492.* Westport, CT: Greenwood Press; Denevan, W. (ed.). 1976. *The Native Population of the Americas in 1492.* Madison, WI: University of Wisconsin Press; Guerra, F. 1985. La epidemia americana de influenza en 1493. *Revista de Indias* 45: 325–347; Lovell, W. G. 1992. "Heavy Shadows and Black Night": Disease and Depopulation in Colonial Spanish America. In K. W. Butzer (ed.), *The Americas Before and After 1492: Current Geographical Research. Annals of the American Association of Geographers* 82 (3): 426–443; Newman, M. T. 1976. Aboriginal New World Epidemiology and Medical Care, and the Impact of Old World Disease Imports. *American Journal of Physical Anthropology* 45: 667–672; Verano, J. W., and D. H. Ubelaker, 1991. Health and Disease in the Pre-Columbian World. In H. J. Viola and C. Margolis (eds.). *Seeds of Change: A Quincentennial Commemoration,* pp. 209–223. Washington, DC: Smithsonian Institution Press.

Dogs

Dogs (*Canis familiaris*) first appeared in the Caribbean with the arrival of the Saladoid peoples and their village- and horticulture-based society during the fifth century B.C. Dog faces are one of the typical images of Saladoid *adornos,* and they also appear as large, hollow ceramic effigy vessels.

According to Christopher Columbus, these Amerindian dogs were small and without a bark, and reportedly howled or whined—their Taíno masters called them *aon.* Europeans noted (in hindsight, with irony and hypocrisy) that Caribbean Amerindians used their dogs for hunting and lavished affection on them but would also eat them. In fact, these apparently inoffensive hounds became extinct before their Amerindian masters when the Spanish ate vast numbers to stave off hunger during the 1494 famine.

It is thought there may have been two types of dog present in the Caribbean at the time of European contact. Apart from the aon, there was possibly another that was buried alongside humans and whose canine teeth were perforated for stringing in necklaces. This possible second variety was larger and not eaten, and may have been used for hunting the large rodent known as the hutia (*Isolobodon portoricensis*). Today, these Amerindian dogs may have genetic descendants in the mixed breed known as *satos*. The remains of dogs have been found in human burials in Puerto Rico, at the Hacienda Grande site, and at the offshore site of Sorcé on Vieques Island, where no less than twenty were discovered—some with their legs tied together. To date, the most famous artistic representation of a dog from a funerary context is a hollow effigy vessel from Puerto Rico.

The physical remains of other dogs have been found archaeologically on the island of Middle Caicos in the Bahamas, and also at the later Suazoid site of Silver Sands in Barbados.

The symbolic and spiritual role of dogs among prehistoric Caribbean societies has been interpreted as a mythic substitution for larger, fiercer animals that dominated the religious beliefs of lowland Amazonian societies from South America—themselves the ancestors of the Saladoid peoples. In these mainland cultures, the jaguar (*Panthera onca*) was the most powerful symbolic animal, associated with shamans, sorcery, and the spirits of fertility and death. As the jaguar does not exist in the Island Caribbean, it is thought that the nearest fang-bearing animal, the dog, took its place in spiritual beliefs, perhaps also as a symbol of manly status and hunting prestige. This plausible explanation is complicated by the fact that in South America several types of dogs also existed, one of which was used in hunting prey animals as well as the jaguar, and the best and most ferocious of which would be metaphorically compared to the jaguar itself.

Another type of dog also played an important and cruelly tragic role in the early years of European contact and conquest. These were the huge European mastiffs taken by the conquistadors to the New World and used to terrorize and hunt down the local Amerindian peoples. Bartolomé de Las Casas records in his *Short Account of the Destruction of the Indies* how, in the Caribbean islands and on the mainland, these dogs were encouraged to develop a taste for native flesh, whereupon they were let loose on the Amerindians and tore them to pieces. More recently, up until the 1930s, Warao Amerindians from Venezuela traveled by canoe to the southernmost Caribbean island of Trinidad in order to trade hunting dogs for the island's tobacco and other goods—a practice that probably extended back to early contact and maybe prehistoric times.

See also: Hacienda Grande; Las Casas, Bartolomé de; Saladoid; Silver Sands (site, Barbados); Warao

References

de Las Casas, B. 1992. *A Short Account of the Destruction of the Indies.* London: Penguin; Mattioni, M., and R. P. Bullen, 1974. Precolumbian Dogs in the Lesser and Greater Antilles. *Proceedings of the Fifth International Congress for Caribbean Archaeology, Antigua 1973,* pp. 162–165; Roe, P. G. n.d. *The Domesticated Jaguar: The Symbolism of South Amerindian Dogs from a Lowland Perspective.* Unpublished manuscript; Roe, P. G. 1995. Eternal Companions: Amerindian Dogs from Tierra Firma to the Antilles. *Proceedings of the Fifteenth International Congress for Caribbean Archaeology, San Juan, Puerto Rico 1993,* pp. 155–172; Schwartz, M. 1997. *A History of Dogs in the Early Americas.* New Haven, CT: Yale University Press; Varner, J. G., and J. J. Varner, 1983. *Dogs of the Conquest.* Norman, OK: University of Oklahoma Press.

Dominica

Dominica is 47 km long by 26 km wide, with an area of 751 sq km. Its population of some 72,000 is mainly of African descent with the important exception of some 2,000 descendants of the original Carib inhabitants. Dominica is a mountainous island of volcanic origin.

(opposite) Traditional method of making a Carib seagoing canoe, Carib Territory, Dominica (Courtesy Nicholas J. Saunders)

Dominica's cultural importance is largely due to its colonial period history as home to the Caribs who called the island Waitukubuli. Very little is known of its pre-Carib archaeology. It seems there is evidence for ca. 3000 B.C. Archaic Period hunter-gatherers who left their chipped- and ground-stone tools and conch-shell gouges at

coastal and riverine locations. Saladoid settlers arrived sometime in the century before Christ, bringing with them a sophisticated agricultural village life, which included their well-made pottery with its decorative zoomorphic *adornos* featuring images of parrots, turtles, and frogs. Around A.D. 1000, a new wave of South American peoples, the Caribs, arrived, dominating the island perhaps by warfare or more subtle means such as intermarriage.

Christopher Columbus was the first European to see Dominica on 3 November 1493, but the Spanish failed to exploit this and instead Dominica was fought over for centuries by the Caribs, French, and British despite several times being declared a neutral zone by the two imperial powers. The Treaty of Paris finally ceded the island to Britain in 1763. Despite several short-lived French occupations, and problems with the island's Maroons, Britain kept control until 3 November 1978, when Dominica became a fully independent member of the British Commonwealth.

Dominica's identification with the Carib peoples has been a dominant factor in its late prehistoric and colonial history, though today the descendants are of mixed blood. In 1635, the Dominican Father Raymond Guillaume Breton arrived in the Caribbean and spent nineteen years studying Dominica's Carib people, compiling a unique two-part dictionary of their language. In 1902, the British administrator Hesketh Bell recommended the creation of a Carib territory on the east coast, centered on the settlement of Salybia.

In 1930, the fatal shooting of two Caribs by police officers led to civil unrest known as the Carib War, during which the chief Jolly John was arrested. Partly as a long-delayed consequence of these events, a Carib Council was established in 1952, and arrangements made for a new Carib chief to be appointed every five years as well as a separate parliamentary representative to be elected, also for five years. In Dominica today, as throughout the Caribbean, there is a reawakening of indigenous peoples' sense of identity, boosted in part by tourism and the commercial manufacture of Carib basketware, alongside the making of canoes by traditional Carib methods.

While English is the official language, many Dominicans also speak creole French, a historical legacy that has become part of their culture and that, through the publication of a dictionary in 1991, has led to its increasing appearance in print. French influence is also present in religion, as over 70 percent of Dominicans belong to the Catholic faith. Dominica's annual carnival takes place on the Monday and Tuesday before Ash Wednesday, with its focus in the island's capital at Roseau. It is currently more French-style masquerade than the increasingly popular pan-Caribbean, Trinidad-style Carnival that is developing elsewhere. Folk dances and music feature especially on Independence Day festivities between 3 and 4 November, and women's colorful national dress—*la wobe douillete*—appears on Creole Day on the last Friday in October.

See also: Breton, Father Raymond; Caribs; Carnival (Trinidad); Jolly John

References

Allaire, L. 2003. Agricultural Societies in the Caribbean: The Lesser Antilles. In J. Sued-Badillo (ed.), *General History of the Caribbean: Vol. 1, Autochthonous Societies,* pp. 195–227. Paris: UNESCO; Birge, W. G. 1900. *In Old Rousseau, Reminiscences of Life as I Found It in the Island of*

Dominica and among the Carib Indians. New York: Isaac H. Blanchard; Fermor, P. L. 1950. *The Traveller's Tree: A Journey through the Caribbean Islands.* London: John Murray; Honychurch, L. 1995. *The Dominica Story: A History of the Island.* London: Macmillan; Honychurch, L. 1992. *Dominica: Isle of Adventure.* London: Macmillian; Honychurch, L. 1997. Crossroads in the Caribbean: A Site of Encounter and Exchange on Dominica. *World Archaeology* 28 (3): 291–304; Petitjean Roget, H. 1978. Reconnaissance archéologique à l'île de la Dominique. *Proceedings of the Seventh International Congress for the Study of Pre-Columbian Cultures of the Lesser Antilles,* pp. 81–97. Montreal: Centre de Recherches Caraïbes, Université de Montréal.

Dominican Republic

The Dominican Republic comprises the eastern two-thirds of the island of Hispaniola (the western remainder is Haiti), and has an area of 48,443 sq km. Its population of 8 million is a mix of white, African, and mestizo. Hispaniola's Taíno name, Quisqueya, is still used today in the Dominican Republic.

Archaeologically, the Dominican Republic's heritage extends from around 4000 B.C. to the present day, and is a rich mix of the prehistoric, colonial, and historically recent. Sites dating to the Casimiroid people have been found at the type-site of Casimira and Barrera-Mordán in the southwest, where stone-tool workshops have been dated to between 2610 B.C. and 2165 B.C. The arrival of the Saladoid peoples is marked by the Hacienda Grande culture, whose type-site on the island's north coast is dated to between ca. 400 B.C. and A.D. 500. Pottery is typically Cedrosan Saladoid, featuring white-on-red (W-O-R) and zic (zone-incised cross-hatching) ware, as well as three-pointers, jewelry, and modeled anthropomorphic and zoomorphic images. Around 400, Hacienda Grande culture evolved, first into the Cuevas culture and then the Ostiones culture.

Taking its name from this culture/site, the Ostionoid cultural tradition appeared around 500 and went through several cultural variations. The entire Ostionoid tradition is dated to the period 500 to 1500, the final variation being known as Chican Ostionoid, the name given to archaeological remains of the Taíno peoples encountered by Columbus in 1492. During Taíno times, Hispaniola seems to have been divided into chiefdoms (*cacicazgos*), those in the eastern part being identified with the chiefs Mayobanex, Guarionex, and Higuanamá (Higüeyo). Recent investigations at the underwater site of Mantanial de la Aleta have revealed basketry, gourds, pottery, and an extraordinary range of carved-wood artifacts. This site dates to between A.D. 1035 and A.D. 1420, and seems to have been only, or mainly, a ritual and ceremonial location.

Hispaniola was first encountered by Christopher Columbus on Christmas Day 1492 when the *Santa Maria* ran aground. The local Taíno chief Guacanagarí helped the Spanish retrieve their valuables and exchanged gold jewelry and a gold-encrusted mask for a pair of gloves and a shirt from Columbus. Columbus's men built La Navidad—a small stockaded settlement—in what today is inside the border of Haiti but found it destroyed and its men killed when Columbus returned the following year. As a consequence, in 1494, Columbus built La Isabela farther east (in modern Dominican Republic) as the first permanent European settlement in the Americas. This site, a location of historically important interactions between Europeans and the indigenous Taíno, was occupied for five years and has recently been intensively excavated by the archaeologists K. A. Deagan and J. M. Cruxent.

Investigations yielded the material culture of everyday life such as coins, merchant's weights, majolica ceramics, fragments of Spanish armor, and items of jewelry from glass bracelets to finger rings. Although La Isabela was abandoned in 1497 when the new city of Santo Domingo was founded, archaeological work has identified continuing habitation by pirates, smugglers, and later fishermen, and today the site is a national park. The recent discovery of pictographs at Jose Maria Cave in the East National Park has been interpreted as representing Taíno tribute of food to the Spanish around 1500. The nation's archaeological heritage also includes many underwater wrecks, such as that of the *Monte Cristi,* an English-built merchantman whose cargo containing glass beads suggests trade with Amerindian peoples.

Today, museums, community heritage centers, and art and craftwork movements are starting to reclaim and revitalize aspects of Taíno culture and history. Traditional Taíno cassava-making techniques survive, as do many place names, animal names, and those of plants—the Dominican stew known as *salcocho* probably descends from Amerindian pepper pot. Natural medicines survive in rural areas though they are threatened by modern pharmaceuticals, and rural housing incorporates Taíno names and forms. The Dominican Taíno are extinct as a society, but elements of their culture survive, as does their genetic heritage.

Nevertheless, the country's society is a rich blend of European and African traces as well. The creole nature of society is reflected in the nation's music, particularly the merengue—a symbol of Dominican culture. A feature of African inheritance is *gaga,* an African-derived spirituality popular among Haitian immigrant workers. Similar to Vodoun, it incorporates shamanic elements suggestive of Amerindian influence, and has an annual ceremony similar to the cropover celebrations on Barbados.

See also: Caimito, El; Guacanagarí (Taíno chief); Hacienda Grande; Haiti; La Aleta (site, Dominican Republic); La Isabela (site, Dominican Republic); Music; Ostionoid; Taíno (Arawak)

References
Alegría-Pons, J. F. 1993. *Gaga y Vudu en la Republica Dominicana.* San Juan, PR: Editiorial Chango-Prieto; Andrade, M. J. 1930. Folk-Lore from the Dominican Republic. *Memoirs of the American Folklore Society* 23. New York: American Folklore Society; Austerlitz, P. 1977. *Merengue: Dominican Music and Dominican Identity.* Philadelphia: Temple University Press; Brown, I. Z. 1999. *Culture and Customs of the Dominican Republic.* Westport, CT: Greenwood Publishing Group; Deagan, K. A., and J. M. Cruxent, 2002. *Columbus's Outpost among the Taínos: Spain and America at La Isabela, 1493–1498.* New Haven, CT: Yale University Press; Ferbel, P. J. 2002. Not Everyone Who Speaks Spanish is from Spain: Taíno Survival in the 21st Century Dominican Republic. KACIKE: The Journal of Caribbean Amerindian History and Anthropology. *http://www.kacike.org/FerbelEnglish.html;* Guitar, L. 1998. *Cultural Genesis: Relationships among Indians, Africans, and Spaniards in Rural Hispaniola, First Half of the Sixteenth Century.* Ann Arbor, MI: University Microfilms; Guitar, L. 2002. Documenting the Myth of Taíno Extinction. KACIKE: The Journal of Caribbean Amerindian History and Anthropology. *http://www.kacike.org/GuitarEnglish.html;* Moya Pons, F. 1995. *The Dominican Republic: A National History.* New Rochelle, NY: Hispaniola Books; Rosenburg, J. C. 1979. *El Gaga—*

religion y sociedad de un culto de Santo Domingo. Santo Domingo, the Dominican Republic: Universidad Autonoma de Santo Domingo; Scott, J. F. 1985. *The Art of the Taino from the Dominican Republic.* Gainesville, FL: University of Florida; Vega, B. 1980. *Los cacicazgos de La Hispaniola.* Santo Domingo, the Dominican Republic: Museo del Hombre Dominicano; Wilson, S. M. 1990. *Hispaniola: Caribbean Chiefdoms in the Age of Columbus.* Tuscaloosa, AL: University of Alabama Press.

Drake Manuscript

The Drake Manuscript, more accurately the French work entitled *Histoire Naturelle des Indes,* appears to have been part of a personal record of Sir Francis Drake's privateering exploits in the Caribbean. Essentially this was raiding Spanish treasure galleons and ports such as Santo Domingo on Hispaniola in 1586, during which he even took the church bells of the city. One page of the manuscript shows a sketch-map of the Spanish port of Nombre de Dios in Panama—used for the transshipment of gold from Peru in South America.

According to the Spaniards Nuño da Silva and Francisco de Zarate, whom he captured, Drake kept painters on board his ship whose duty it was to illustrate the wildlife and native inhabitants of the West Indies. There are over 200 captioned illustrations in the *Histoire* in styles that suggest the work of at least two artists. Typically, some images are rendered more or less scientifically, while others are sheer fantasy, but all have been arranged according to their subject. Special attention is given to the natural history of the Caribbean, such as a painting of bananas, labeled *Plantainnes,* and also to the native practices of agriculture and hunting, such as the image of an Amerindian in Trindidad using an elaborate parrot trap. Also, undoubtedly for propaganda reasons, the *Histoire* illustrates the cruelties visited by the Spanish on the Amerindians in the forced labor of the gold mines.

References

Cummins, A. 1997. European Views of the Aboriginal Population. In S. M. Wilson (ed.), *The Indigenous People of the Caribbean,* pp. 46–55. Gainesville, FL: University Press of Florida; Drake, Sir Francis. 1963. *The World Encompassed, by Sir Francis Drake, Being His Next Voyage to That to Nombre de Dios.* London: Hakluyt Society.

Drax Hall (site, Jamaica)

The Drax Hall estate was founded in 1699 by William Drax near St. Ann's Bay on the north coast of Jamaica. In 1762 it was acquired by William Beckford, at which time some 533 acres were under sugar cultivation. The investigation of the long-abandoned and -forgotten site during the 1980s combined archaeology with historical research and provided valuable insights into the changing lives of African slaves and free laborers on a Jamaican sugar plantation.

Archaeology and history complemented each other in this investigation, with archaeology testing the validity of historical accounts, and historical information adding to the detail of slave life where artifacts were too fragile to survive in the ground. The investigation

· COMME · LES · YNDES ·

fom la Chasse au poisson

Les yndien allам au boꝛt della Mer ſoiant Le –
poisson ſe Joue deʃſus leaue promptemen
Le flechent Le faiſam mouriꝛ Car eʃtam
frappé Il ne peult plus nager ny aller
au fons deleaue

How the Indians hunt for fish, *from the Drake
Manuscript, also known as the* Histoire Naturelle
des Indes *(Natural history of the Indies) (The
Pierpont Morgan Library / Art Resource)*

located and excavated the Old Village, identified as the slave quarters, and the Great House, where the estate overseer lived. Documentary evidence revealed that there were about 300 slaves on the estate during the eighteenth and early nineteenth centuries.

Comparing the size and materials of the Great House with the Old Village revealed tremendous differences in social status. The Great House was built of cut-and-fitted limestone, had three floors with some 5,000 sq meters of floor space, and an overall area some ten times that of a slave house. Archaeological research identified that the Old Village slave dwellings had between one and three rooms, and mainly had wattle-and-daub walls and thatched roofs. There was also a marked absence of window glass compared to the Great House.

Great numbers of artifacts behind the slave houses indicated a range of activities, including a garden plot, fruit trees, and the growing of medicinal plants. Evidence of traditional West African material culture was found, such as coarse earthenware pottery (*yabbas*), which showed a continuity with traditional African pottery-making traditions. These items continued for a time in the Old Village despite the availability of cheap imports from Britain. This may have been due to the need or desire to retain traditional African methods of food preparation and consumption. An example of this was the remains of a hearth fire and tripod behind the slave house on which a large iron pot kept the evening meal of yams and akee simmering for communal consumption. By comparison, historical documents show that the Europeans living in the Great House consumed more expensive foods, such as pickled meats, rabbits, and coffee.

Despite the presence of African objects, the majority of items found at Drax Hall were European imports, suggesting a change over time from making and using African types of objects to assimilating European types as a distinctive Afro-Jamaican culture emerged, particularly in the group of items associated with kitchen activities. Another interesting discovery was the slave habit of recycling, such as recarving and reusing parts of smoking pipes, and carving delftware disks for possible use as gaming pieces. Traces of individuality also survive, as in an inscribed belt buckle.

The investigation also identified changes in the lives of ex-slaves after the abolition of slavery in 1807. Those ex-slaves who remained at the Old Village did so as rent-paying tenants, and tended to be the economically marginalized older individuals who retained their previous ways of living. The study of their food remains revealed a postemancipation increase in obtaining and consuming locally grown plants, shellfish, chickens, and goats. This was possibly one way of making up for the fresh meat and salted fish that the estate had previously supplied to its slaves and that ended with emancipation. One consequence of this was a boom in the numbers of local shopkeepers and middlemen to supply this shortfall in food—all of which now had to be bought.

See also: Betty's Hope (site, Antigua); Galways Plantation; Historical Archaeology; Jamaica; Newton Plantation (Barbados); Slavery; Sugar

References
Armstrong, D. V. 1985. An Afro-Jamaican Slave Settlement: Archaeological Investigations at Drax Hall. In T. A. Singleton (ed.), *The Archaeology of Slavery and Plantation Life,* pp. 261–287.

San Diego: Academic Press; Armstrong, D. V. 1990. *The Old Village and the Great House: An Archaeological and Historical Examination of Drax Hall Plantation, St. Ann's Bay Jamaica.* Urbana, IL: University of Illinois Press; Higman, B. W. 1988. *Jamaica Surveyed: Plantation Maps and Plans of the Eighteenth and Nineteenth Centuries,* pp. 99–102. Kingston: Institute of Jamaica.

Dudley, Sir Robert

Sir Robert Dudley, illegitimate son of the Earl of Leicester, sailed from Plymouth in December 1594 bound for the West Indies and, according to the suspicious Sir Walter Ralegh, for the coast of Guiana.

Dudley's importance to the Caribbean, like Ralegh's (whose arrival he preceded by just a few weeks), was in his contact with and observations of the indigenous inhabitants of Trinidad and the Orinoco River delta. He was the first Englishman to see and comment favorably on the good-quality tar of Pitch Lake so useful in calking boats. Some Amerindians came aboard his ships at this time, trading food and tobacco for knives, bells, and glass beads. From these he heard of a nearby mine of marcasite that, while its shininess was esteemed by the locals, was realized not to be pure gold but fool's gold (pyrites). He acquired samples nonetheless.

Dudley made valuable observations of the native metallurgical tradition associated with the manufacture of elite jewelry, particularly crescent-shaped pectorals. He noted local names for gold (*calcouri*), silver (*perota*), copper (*arrara*), bracelet (*techir*), and the valuable greenstones known as *tacorao*. He also learned of the trade in these items between Trinidad, South America, and the Island Caribbean, and of a mainland gold mine near a town called Orocoa.

Anchored off Trinidad's east coast, he organized an expedition inland in search of an Amerindian named Braio—a metalsmith of some repute whose name he had been given by several Amerindian chiefs. The expedition was unsuccessful, though it entered an empty Amerindian village at night and apparently observed metal dross left over from metalworking activities. Dudley's expedition foreshadowed the better-known explorations of Sir Walter Ralegh and are important for a number of reasons, not least the making of a short but important word list.

See also: Gold; Pitch Lake (site, Trinidad); Ralegh, Sir Walter; Trinidad and Tobago
References
Boomert, A. 1984. The Arawak Indians of Trinidad and Coastal Guiana, ca. 1500–1650. *Journal of Caribbean History,* 19 (2): 123–188; Warner, G. F. (ed.). 1969 [1899]. *The Voyage of Robert Dudley [. . .] to the West Indies, 1594–1595.* London: Hakluyt Society.

Duhos

Duhos were ceremonial seats made by the Taíno of the Greater Antilles, especially the islands of Hispaniola (modern Haiti and the Dominican Republic) and Puerto Rico, though examples have also been found in the Bahamas, Turks and Caicos, and Jamaica. As seats of power, duhos shared a common symbolism with shamans' benches and lordly thrones found throughout Mesoamerica and South America. Their distinctive shape and decoration, however, make duhos unique to the Island Caribbean. It seems likely that the greatest quantity and most elaborately decorated examples were made between A.D. 1200 and A.D. 1500 as status-related items among the emerging Taíno chiefdoms.

Duhos were usually made of wood but sometimes also in stone, especially in Puerto Rico. In Taíno belief, the natural world was animated by spirits, and both wood and stone possessed spiritual qualities before being made into duhos. Trees were especially important, functioning as a magical medium for communicating with the supernatural. Spirit trees talked to Taíno shamans (behiques) and chiefs (caciques) and were then cut down and carved into duhos and zemí images. Duhos and other objects derived part of their power from the ways in which the Taíno conceived of the world.

Duhos were carved into a variety of anthropomorphic and zoomorphic shapes, often with an animal head projection. Many have a characteristically high and sloping backrest. Wooden duhos typically display excellent craftsmanship and are often covered with intricate patterns of circles and spirals that may have originated as sacred designs inspired by hallucinogenic imagery during cohoba rituals. The most sophisticated duhos were inlaid with pieces of shell, bone, or guanín. Some duhos, especially those made from the hard guayacán (ironwood) tree, retain traces of having been highly polished, a feature that may be associated with a pan-Amerindian "aesthetic of brilliance," where shininess indicated the presence of spiritual power.

The sophistication of many duhos indicates their status as elite objects used on ceremonial occasions as a mark of respect for visiting dignitaries and a status symbol for the owner. When Christopher Columbus visited a Cuban chief he was offered a guanín-inlaid duho to sit on. Duhos embodied political power for Taíno chiefs and as such were probably regarded as personal or family property. The control of duho manufacture and distribution was a privilege of the elite. In the Taíno chiefdom of Xaraguá, in southeast Hispaniola (modern Haiti), the female chief Anacaona appears to have controlled the production of duhos on the small offshore island of Gonâve. When Bartolomé Columbus visited the area in A.D. 1496, Anacaona showed him the workshop whose prestige items may have been made by women. She presented him with objects made of black polished wood, including fourteen beautifully carved duhos.

Some duhos may have been so closely identified with their owner that on death the body of the deceased was buried sitting upright on his ceremonial seat, perhaps literally supported by the ancestor whose spirit inhabited the wood. As a mark of their social and political standing, Taíno shamans and chiefs sat on carved and polished wooden duhos to watch the ceremonial ball-game known as batey while lesser people crouched on their stone equivalents.

Given the spirituality of the Amerindian worldview, it is not surprising that duhos possessed an important religious dimension. During cohoba-snuffing rituals, shamans and chiefs sat on their sacred seats to commune with the ancestors. As with the mainland equivalent of the shaman's bench, sitting on an animal-shaped stool carved out of sacred wood was a way of connecting the sitter with spirit realm.

One unusual feature of duhos was the Taíno habit of secreting them away in inaccessible caves. It is not known whether this was part of pre-Columbian ritual behavior that saw caves as sacred and mythical places, or whether it simply served in later years to hide them from the Spanish, who regarded such objects as pagan idols. Whatever the reason, this practice preserved many duhos for later discovery. A cache of three duhos was discovered in Cartwright Cave on Long Island in the Bahamas and today over 100 examples are known.

See also: Aesthetic of Brilliance; Anacaona (Taíno queen); Ball-Game; Columbus, Christopher; Cohoba; Taíno (Arawak); Zemís

References

de Hostos, A. 1951, The "Duho" and Other Wooden Objects from the West Indies, In *Anthropological Papers: Papers Based Principally on Studies of the Prehistoric Archaeology and Ethnology of the Greater Antilles,* pp. 77–84, San Juan: Office of the Historian, Government of Puerto Rico; Helms, M. W. 1986, Art Styles and Interaction Spheres in Central America and the Caribbean: Polished Black Wood in the Greater Antilles, *Journal of Latin American Lore* 12 (1): 25–43; Lehmann, H. 1951, Un 'duho' de la civilization taíno au Musée de l'Homme, *Journal de la Société des Américanistes* 40: 153–161; Ostapkowicz, J. M. 1997. To be Seated with "Great Courtesy and Veneration": Contextual Aspects of the Taíno Duho, In Fatima Bercht, Estrellita Brodsky, John Alan Farmer, and Dicey Taylor (eds.). *Taíno: Pre-Columbian Art and Culture from the Caribbean,* pp. 56–67, New York: The Monacelli Press.

E

El Dorado

The legend of El Dorado, "the gilded man," is one of the most enduring myths of the Americas. As much European fantasy as Amerindian reality, it was fueled in part by the wealth of gold, silver, and gemstones taken by the Spanish during their conquest of the Aztec and Inca empires between 1519 and 1532. So unexpected were these vast treasures that they incited an ever greater gold-lust among the Spanish, who deluded themselves into believing that golden cities full of jewels lay just beyond every horizon.

European explorers brought to the Americas typically medieval ideas concerning the nature of gold. Not only was it the standard of wealth in Europe and the undiscovered secret of the alchemists' quest, but it was also thought to be engendered by heat. In the European imagination, the tropical parts of the Americas were bound to be rich in gold. The search for the precious metal underwrote the Spanish explorations of the Caribbean, and Columbus and his colleagues quickly noticed the small gold jewels worn by the Taíno chiefs. In fact, these were not pure gold but an alloy of gold, silver, and copper known as *guanín*.

The Island Caribbean helped stimulate the Spanish desire for gold and in 1512 an expedition left the town of Darién on Colombia's northern Caribbean coast in search of an Amerindian chief named Dabeiba who was supposed to possess great treasures of gold. While this expedition was unsuccessful, some gold was looted from ancient tombs in the region. Gold-lust reached fever pitch, however, after the conquest of the Aztecs between 1519 and 1521 in Mexico, and the Inca empire of South America in 1532. The vast wealth acquired by these conquests helped shape the idea of an even richer kingdom built of gold.

The most famous story behind the El Dorado legend originated among the Muisca people of Colombia in South America. Muisca rituals took place at Lake Guatavita, in a ceremony celebrating the appointment of a new chief. After a period of seclusion, the ruler-to-be arrived at the lake shore, where he was stripped of his clothing and his body smeared with sticky resin onto which was blown a glittering layer of gold dust. Accompanied by four lesser chiefs adorned with golden jewelry, the gilded man was paddled out into the center of the lake on a raft itself richly adorned and bearing four braziers smoking with sacred incense. Those left behind on the shore blew flutes and trumpets, and sang. On reaching the center of the lake, silence fell, and the new chief cast his gold into the lake, with his companions doing likewise. The offerings now made, they returned to the shore, where the chief was received as the new ruler.

Whatever the truth or otherwise of this story, for the Muisca, gold possessed supernatural qualities as an incorruptible metal infused with cosmological power. Mixed with copper and known as *tumbaga,* its transformation into sacred images by metalsmiths was regarded as a magical process that recombined the mystical elements of life. Yet, for most Amerindians, gold was but one shiny substance among many: pearls, shells, minerals, rainbows, and water all shared a sacredness that has been called the "aesthetic of brilliance." Such ideas were incomprehensible to Europeans, who saw preciousness only in commercial terms.

As a place, El Dorado was a legend, though as an idea it was an ever-changing symbol of unimaginable wealth. So fertile was this idea that El Dorado was located in many different places, both within and beyond the borders of European exploration. In 1595, Sir Walter Ralegh was searching for it on the other side of the continent in Guiana, while Spanish expeditions to drain Lake Guatavita continued throughout the sixteenth and seventeenth centuries, with the latest attempt abandoned only in 1914.

See also: Aesthetic of Brilliance; Amazons; Gold; Ralegh, Sir Walter

References

Bray, W. 1978. *The Gold of El Dorado.* London: Times Newspapers; Hemming, J. 1978. *The Search for El Dorado.* London: Michael Joseph; Nicholl, C. 1996. *The Creature in the Map: Sir Walter Ralegh's Quest for El Dorado.* London: Vintage; von Hagen, V. W. 1974. *The Golden Man: The Quest for El Dorado.* Farnborough, UK: Saxon House; Whitehead, N. L. 1997. *The Discoverie as Ethnological Text.* In *Sir Walter Ralegh, The Discoverie of the Large, Rich and Bewtiful Empyre of Guiana.*:60–116. (Transcribed, annotated, and introduced by N. L. Whitehead.) Manchester, UK: Manchester University Press.

Elenan

Elenan is the name given to the local variation of the Ostionoid culture that developed from the Saladoid in the Leeward Islands and Virgin Islands around A.D. 600. It developed eventually into the Eastern Taínos between 900 and 1200. In this respect, it is the equivalent of the Meillacan Ostionoid for the Western Taínos of Hispaniola.

Originally, the territory of the Elenan peoples extended from central Puerto Rico through the Leeward and Virgin Islands to Guadeloupe, being replaced by Taíno (Chican Ostionoid) in the former area and by the Island Caribs on Guadeloupe. Elenan culture created the earliest known formal dance and ballcourts at the sites of Tibes and El Bronce in central southern Puerto Rico. These two sites occupied what has been called the frontier between Elenan and Ostionan peoples. Available evidence indicates that the practice of building ballcourts spread from here east to the Virgin Islands and west to Hispaniola and eastern Cuba. These earliest courts, unlike later Taíno examples, incorporated burials.

Throughout, Elenan peoples continued to occupy the ancestral Saladoid sites of Maisabel, Hacienda Grande, and Sorcé on Puerto Rico, Salt River on St. Croix, and Indian

Creek on Antigua. Excavation of these sites indicates that an increasing population relied on intensifying their exploitation of marine resources and began deep sea fishing.

Material culture also changed. Simpler shapes in pottery were adopted along with a crude form of white-on-red (W-O-R) decoration, accompanied by the loss of zic (zone-incised cross-hatching) incision and modeled designs. Later, thick-walled bowls were made and these in turn were influenced by the emerging Taíno (Chican Ostionoid) styles coming out of Hispaniola and spreading east through Puerto Rico and across to the Leeward Islands. Other items persisted from earlier times to the Elenan Period, such as three-pointers that became increasingly decorated as time went by. At the Indian Creek site on Antigua, the central part of the site may have been used to play the ball-game.

See also: Antigua; Ball-Game; Hacienda Grande; Indian Creek (site, Antigua); Maisabel (site, Puerto Rico); Meillacan; Ostionoid; Salt River (site, St. Croix); Zemís

References

Allaire, L. 1985. The Archaeology of the Caribbean. In C. Flon (ed.), *The World Atlas of Archaeology,* pp. 370–371. Boston: Portland House; Davis, D. D., and R. C. Goodwin. 1990. Island Carib origins: Evidence and Nonevidence. *American Antiquity* 54: 37–48; Hall, C. K., and G. Hatt. 1924. Archaeology of the Virgin Islands. *Proceedings of the Twenty-First International Congress of Americanists,* Part 1, pp. 29–42. The Hague, the Netherlands; Hofman, C. L., and M.L.P. Hoogland. 1991. Ceramic Developments on Saba, N. A. (350–1450 A.D.). *Proceedings of the Fourteenth Congress of the International Association for Caribbean Archaeology.* Barbados; Robinson, L. S., E. R. Lundberg, and J. B. Walker. 1983. *Archaeological Data Recovery at El Bronce, Puerto Rico: Final Report, Phases 1 and 2.* Christiansted, St. Croix: St. Croix Archaeological Services; Wing, E. S. 1990. Animal Remains from the Hacienda Grande Site, Puerto Rico. Appendix. In I. Rouse and R. E. Alegría (eds.). Excavations at Maria de la Cruz Cave and Hacienda Grande Village Site, Loiza, Puerto Rico. *Yale University Publications in Anthropology* No. 80. New Haven, CT.

Encomienda

The *encomienda* was an institution born of the Spanish experience with native Caribbean peoples. In effect, it was a system of subjugation created by Nicolás de Ovando during his time as governor of Hispaniola between 1502 and 1509. Although loosely based on a system of land grants in Spain, as a mechanism for aiding colonization it was a New World phenomenon, developed in the Caribbean and exported across Spanish America, from Mexico to Paraguay.

The essence of the encomienda was the granting to a Spanish conquistador or colonist a number of Amerindians, sometimes entire villages, who were obligated to provide food, material goods, and their labor for no financial recompense. The *encomendero* was supposed to provide instruction in the Christian faith and guidance on becoming civilized, as well as legal and military protection. There were some benefits for the Amerindians inasmuch as they retained their language and culture, as well as—at least in theory—legal title to village territory. They also continued to be responsible to their own chief (cacique), who in turn was controlled by the encomendero. In practice, however, the encomienda was a form of virtual slavery and widely abused by the encomenderos as a way of enriching themselves. Overworked, underfed, and forced to live in unsanitary conditions, Amerindians easily fell prey to European diseases. Those who escaped were hunted down with specially trained hunting dogs and ripped apart.

The encomienda was legally constituted by a series of Spanish laws formulated between 1512 and 1514. In 1542, the New Laws were passed in response to petitions made by the Dominican Order in which they blamed the encomienda system for the maltreatment of Amerindians and the calamitous decline in the native population. While the excesses of earlier encomienda practice—such as obligatory labor and personal service to the encomendero—were outlawed, these rulings were widely flouted. Attempts to abolish the encomienda system completely, notably by Bartolomé de Las Casas, failed in practice due to the refusal of encomenderos to comply and their threats of insurrection. Nevertheless, by around 1600, the encomienda was no longer an economically significant practice although indigenous labor was widely used to establish haciendas.

See also: Agüeybana (Taíno Chief); Las Casas, Bartolomé de

References
Keith, R. G. 1971. Encomienda, Hacienda, and Corregimiento in Spanish America: A Structural Analysis. *Hispanic American Historical Review* 51: 431–446; Lockhart, J. 1969. Encomienda and Hacienda: The Evolution of the Great Estate in the Spanish Indies. *Hispanic American Historical Review* 49: 411–429; Zavala, S. 1935. *La encomienda indiana.* Madrid: Imprenta helénica.

G

Galways Plantation

Galways Plantation on the island of Montserrat lasted for 300 years as a typical, medium-sized Caribbean sugar plantation. In its very ordinariness it gives valuable insights into the life and times of its inhabitants.

Galways Plantation was established around 1660 by the Irishman David Galway. At first, it covered some 1,300 acres, with its buildings and processing plant at the base of Galways Mountain, and the cane fields higher up the slopes. This arrangement may have contributed to the estate's decline by the early eighteenth century. By 1830, the estate had changed hands, possibly as a result of

Vegetation overgrows the stone arched ruins at the Galways Plantation, Montserrat. (Kelly-Mooney Photography / Corbis)

new European investors taking advantage of the sugar boom. One consequence was modernization and relocation of the cane-processing buildings and estate house higher up the mountain. During the eighteenth century, a longer growing season, more fertile soil, and better water supplies benefited the plantation but also brought problems. Erosion caused by clearing land for cane fields and buildings caused problems with water runoff that necessitated the construction of elaborate drainage systems.

The estate's African slaves better understood and accommodated themselves to the new environment than their white owners. Despite repressive laws, they familiarized themselves with the subtleties of soil, moisture, and local vegetation, growing plants for food and raw materials that they sold to each other and the planters on Sundays. They grew Amerindian cassava on a large scale and used European materials to process it. In many inventive and resourceful ways they produced a new African-Caribbean culture, and through it expressed their resistance to the European plantocracy and their own enslavement. Today, this creative use of the land stands as the most important feature of local life for the slaves' descendants. The plantation ended, but the gardens, springs, and places of the mountain live on in local folklore, forever associated with the spirits of the "old time people."

See also: Antigua; Betty's Hope (site, Antigua); Clifton Plantation; Drax Hall (site, Jamaica); Historical Archaeology; Montserrat; Newton Plantation (Barbados); Slavery; Sugar

References
Pulsipher, L. M. 1991. Galways Plantation, Montserrat. In H. J. Viola and C. Margolis (eds.). *Seeds of Change: A Quincentennial Commemoration,* pp. 139–159. Washington, DC: Smithsonian Institution Press; Pulsipher, L. M., and C. M. Goodwin, 1982. A Sugar-Boiling House at Galways: An Irish Sugar Plantation in Montserrat, West Indies. *Post-Medieval Archaeology* 16: 21–27; Pulsipher, L. M., and C. M. Goodwin, 1999. Here Where the Old Time People Be: Reconstructing the Landscapes of Slavery and Post-Slavery Era in Montserrat, West Indies. In J. B. Haviser (ed.), *African Sites Archaeology in the Caribbean,* pp. 9–37. Princeton, NJ: Markus Wiener Publishers.

Garifuna (Black Caribs)

The origin of the present-day Garifuna people lies with the so-called Black Caribs of St. Vincent. Before 1763, St. Vincent was populated by Amerindians of Island Carib culture among whom were living some 700 French farmers and their priests. The Island Carib population, also known as Kalinago, spoke their own language—a mix of South American Carib words and Arawak vocabulary, both of which belong to the Arawakan family of languages. Today, the Garifuna—a variant spelling of Kalipuna/Karaphuna, as these people are also known—still speak a form of the original Island Carib language.

The arrival of African slaves on St. Vincent may have been due to Carib raiding on neighboring European-controlled islands that used slaves on their sugar plantations. There is also a story that around 1635, several ships were wrecked off St. Vincent and their cargo of African slaves made it to the island. Escaped slaves may also have journeyed from Barbados with favorable currents to arrive on St. Vincent.

Whatever the truth, these Africans eventually became assimilated into Carib society, adopting their language, technology, horticulture, aesthetics of personal adornment, and the practice of canoe-making. The offspring of mixed-race unions produced the so-called Black Caribs, differentiated from the original Yellow Carib inhabitants. Over time, the former possibly became more reproductively successful, and thus St. Vincent's native population would have become increasingly Africanized. In 1763, the British occupied St. Vincent and the Caribs and the French settlers combined forces in a guerrilla war that lasted until 1796, when French forces surrendered. Although the Caribs held out a little longer, eventually over 4,000 were rounded up by the British and moved offshore early in 1797 to the island of Balliceaux, where some 2,400 died, probably of typhus or yellow fever.

Typically for the time, and despite the fact that Black Caribs and Yellow Caribs were biologically and culturally indistinguishable, the British often allowed those with lighter skins to go free while imprisoning those with darker skins. Having identified—and in a sense created—the Black Caribs as the troublemakers, they deported some 2,000 of them across the Caribbean to the island of Roatán off Honduras in Central America in April 1797.

Within weeks, the Garifuna moved to the mainland and began spreading along the Caribbean coastline of Honduras and beyond, usually in small groups following a headman and living near European settlements. Initially, the Spanish employed the men as soldiers while the 806 women who had made the journey returned to their traditional practices of weaving cotton cloth and sleeping mats and growing cassava and other staple crops. As the Garifuna moved around, they encountered other free black peoples who had come originally from the French islands of Haiti and Guadeloupe and who appear to have adopted Garifuna cultural traditions, especially in religion, music, and dance.

As time passed, the military usefulness of Garifuna men was replaced by an appreciation of their hardworking nature, intelligence, and honesty, as well as their apparent immunity to many of the tropical diseases that afflicted the indigenous Amerindian population. It was men who built the houses, cleared the forest, made canoes, practiced basketry, and fished. The willingness of Garifuna men to travel widely in their work and often be away from home for considerable lengths of time meant that it fell to the women to preserve their religion—spiritual beliefs based on ancestor worship.

Today, the Garifuna themselves, as well as their culture, have been described as truly hybrid. Starting with the forced transportation of some 2,000 people in 1797, there are now some 200,000 Garifuna living in communities in Central America and the United States. Around 1800, many Garifuna had moved to the area of Stann Creek in present day Belize (formerly British Honduras). Recently, Stann Creek has been renamed Dangriga—the name given to it by its original Garifuna inhabitants. Commemorating this historic influx of Garifuna into the area has been the recognition of 19 November as Settlement Day.

See also: Caribs; Maroons; Miskito; St. Vincent and the Grenadines; Taíno (Arawak)

References

Craton, M. 1986. From Caribs to Black Caribs: The Amerindian Roots of Servile Resistance in the Caribbean. In G. Y. Okihiri (ed.), *In Resistance: Studies in African, Caribbean, and Afro-American*

History, pp. 96–116. Amherst, MA; González, N. L. 1988. *Sojourners of the Caribbean: Ethnogenesis and Ethnohistory of the Garifuna.* Urbana, IL: University of Illinois Press; González, N. L. 1997. The Garifuna of Central America. In S. M. Wilson (ed.), *The Indigenous People of the Caribbean,* pp. 197–205. Gainesville, FL: University Press of Florida; Hulme, P., and N. L. Whitehead (eds.). 1992. *Wild Majesty: Encounters with Caribs from Columbus to the Present Day,* pp. 170–179. Oxford: Oxford University Press; Taylor, D. M. 1951. The Black Caribs of British Honduras. *Viking Fund Publications in Anthropology* No. 17. New York.

Gold

Gold, pure and in alloy form, played a vital role in the Spanish conquest and colonization of the Caribbean, and in the disappearance of its indigenous peoples. It whetted the Spanish appetite for precious metals soon to be found in vast quantities in the native empires of Aztec Mexico and Incan Peru. These discoveries gave rise in the European imagination to the legend of El Dorado.

The Caribbean was not a gold-rich area. Many deposits were alluvial, found in the rivers of Hispaniola (modern Haiti and the Dominican Republic), Cuba, Puerto Rico, and along the Caribbean shores of Venezuela. Nevertheless, in the 150 years between A.D. 1500 and A.D. 1650, at least fifty tons of gold were produced in the Antilles, mainly by Taíno slave laborers working for Spanish overlords. Much of this was probably melted-down Taíno artifacts. Indigenous valuations of gold differed from those of the Europeans, and the mutual misunderstandings about this precious metal were an integral part of early Amerindian-Spanish relationships.

For the Taíno of the Greater Antilles, the importance of gold and its alloys is revealed by its being enshrined in creation myths and materialized in the shimmering ornaments worn as status symbols by paramount chiefs. The Taíno recognized several types of sacred metal, of which pure gold, or *caona,* was the least potent and valuable. Artifacts made from caona were simply hammered nuggets of alluvial gold. Far more sacred and spiritually charged was *guanín,* an alloy of copper, gold, and silver. Guanín represented a sophisticated knowledge of metallurgy not possessed by the Taíno, and so by definition came from elsewhere—over the horizon in South America. It was this exotic quality that contributed to the magical powers and attraction of guanín for the Taíno.

Across the Island Caribbean, and in mainland South America and Mesoamerica, metals were seen as sensorial stimulants, used for decoration, adornment, and to symbolize status and power by visually expressing elite connections to supernatural beings. The true power of metal jewelry and ornaments lay in the symbolic associations of their color, shape, and smell, and the belief that through their jingling sounds and flashing appearance they could enhance the hallucinogenic visions of shamans and chiefs. Illustrating how different were Amerindian and European ideas of gold was the special odor attributed by the Taíno to guanín, which they related to sex and fertility, the pungent-smelling tagua-tagua plant (*Passiflora foetida*), the golden-flowered and equally odiferous guanina plant (*Cassia occidentalis*), and the iridescent feathers of the Cuban *guani* hummingbird. This suggests that for the Taíno, there was a class of materials known as guanín that shared a similar smell, color, and sacredness.

When the Spanish arrived in the Caribbean, the Taíno were immediately attracted to European items made of brass, whose smell they regarded as similar that of guanín. They called it *turey*, a sacred material full of numinous power, which came from the sky, i.e., a distant cosmic domain. The Spanish were surprised that not only could they trade common brass objects for gold and pearls, but that the guanín metal the Taíno valued so highly was, for them, nothing but low-quality gold mixed with copper and some silver.

For Amerindians, the special nature of gold was related also to the pan-Amerindian "aesthetic of brilliance," where the shininess of objects and natural phenomena indicated the presence of spiritual power. Light, and the shiny objects that trapped it, possessed healing and energizing qualities that promoted fertility and symbolized high social status. In Taíno mythology, one story tells how the culture hero Guayahona received *guanines* (jewelry made of guanín) to wear around his arms and neck. This included nose rings, ear plugs, lip plugs, necklaces, and bracelets. Pure gold, caona, was used especially to decorate the mouth, ears, and eyes of the chiefly *duho* seats.

In other myths, guanín appears to have been identified with the iridescent rainbow bridge that connected the sky and the underworld—a view supported by the discovery of crescent- or rainbow-shaped guanín objects in Taíno archaeological sites. These myths may have acted as a sacred charter for the social status of chiefs who could claim their shiny metal jewels as power objects conferred on Guayahona in primordial times.

So closely entwined are indigenous concepts of power, prestige, and light throughout native America, that gods and chiefs often have epithets and names that refer to shinyness and brilliance. On Hispaniola, the Taíno chief Behechio held the title Tureywa Hobin ("Shiny as Sky-Brass" or "king as dazzling and heavenly as guanín"), while other chiefs had names such as Caonabo and Anacaona, which incorporated the word for gold, caona.

See also: Aesthetic of Brilliance; El Dorado; Guarionex (Taíno chief)

References
Oliver, J. R. 2000. Gold Symbolism among Caribbean Chiefdoms: Of Feathers, Çibas, and *Guanín* Power among Taíno Elites. In C. McEwan (ed.), *Pre-Columbian Gold: Technology, Style, and Iconography*, pp. 196–219. London: British Museum Press; Saunders, N. J. 1998. Stealers of Light, Traders in Brilliance: Amerindian Metaphysics in the Mirror of Conquest. *RES: Anthropology and Aesthetics* 33: 225–252; Saunders, N. J. 2002. "Catching the Light": Technologies of Power and Enchantment in Pre-Columbian Goldworking. In J. Quilter and J. W. Hoopes (eds.). *Gold and Power: In Ancient Costa Rica, Panama, and Colombia.* Washington, DC: Dumbarton Oaks; Whitehead, N. L. 1997. *The Discoverie* as Ethnological Text. In *Sir Walter Ralegh, The Discoverie of the Large, Rich and Bewtiful Empyre of Guiana*, pp. 60–116. (Transcribed, annotated, and introduced by N. L. Whitehead.) Manchester, UK: Manchester University Press.

Golden Rock (site, St. Eustatius)

Occupied between the seventh and ninth centuries A.D., Golden Rock is the largest and most important archaeological site of the Saladoid Period on the island of St. Eustatius in the Netherlands Antilles. Situated in the middle of the island, in an area suitable for cassava cultivation, the village could have supported between 80 and 100 people. Apart from horticulture, available food resources include fish, shellfish, crabs, iguana, agouti, and birds. While these resources indicate the people of Golden Rock could have been self-sufficient, they may also have engaged in long-distance trade, as suggested by eighty-one quartz beads found in a child's grave and which did not originate on the island.

Total excavation of the Golden Rock site allowed archaeologists to identify six prehistoric houses. Three were of a size and sophistication that led to their identification as *maloccas*—the name given to large communal houses from Amazonian South America. The substantial post-holes were arranged in a circular form, though one building appears to have supported a roof in the shape of a Hawksbill turtle shell or carapace and has been called the Sea Turtle House. While several houses appear to have been destroyed by fire, the last to be built had its upright beams removed—perhaps to be reused elsewhere.

The Saladoid ceramics are of a high quality, with typical zic (zone-incised cross-hatching) pottery being found in all levels. Often highly polished, these pottery remains included zoomorphic *adornos,* decorated bowls, and handles. Intriguingly, only a small number of the village's occupants were buried within the village area. The remains of everyday life also included tools made from coral, the end-pieces or spurs of several spearthrowers, mother-of-pearl pendants, and shell plaques. Perhaps indicative of some religious belief or ritual act was the discovery of an upturned skeleton/shell of a Hawksbill sea turtle in the lowest (oldest) level of the village's occupation.

> *See also:* Saladoid; Zic pottery
> *References*
> Versteeg, A. H. 1989. The Internal Organization of a Pioneer Settlement in the Lesser Antilles. In P. E. Siegel (ed.), *Early Ceramic Population Lifeways and Adaptive Strategies in the Caribbean,* pp. 171–192. Oxford: British Archaeological Reports International Series 506; Versteeg, A. H., and K. Schinkel (eds.). 1992. *The Archaeology of St. Eustatius: The Golden Rock Site.* Amsterdam: St. Eustatius Historical Foundation.

Great Inagua Island

Great Inagua Island is the third-largest island in the Bahamas archipelago. It is mainly a low-lying, swampy environment at whose heart is Lake Windsor. Its Lucayan name was Inawa or "small eastern island." It was long thought that there was no permanent prehistoric Amerindian occupation, but archaeological survey and excavation by William Keegan between 1984 and 1993 cast doubt on this by locating at least thirteen sites, several of which appeared to indicate permanent habitation.

It appears that the earliest Amerindian occupation of the Bahamas belonged to the spread of Ostionoid peoples through the region between A.D. 600 and A.D. 1200. Archaeological survey discovered large quantities of seashells and pottery at Union Creek, some of which appeared to be imported (i.e., belonging to the Meillacan culture of Hispaniola, a local variation of the Ostionoid tradition), while others belonged to the later and indigenous Palmetto (i.e., Lucayan Taíno) style. Another site was found at Smith Sloop

Point that yielded seashells, fragments of cassava griddles, and again a mix of imported (Meillacan style) and local Palmetto ceramics. Several other sites yielding Palmetto-style pottery were discovered, though one, designated GI-11 and consisting almost totally of burned shell fragments, has been interpreted as a farmstead.

Investigations at a cave near Salt Pond Hill yielded imported Meillacan pottery, and nearby was found a mix of seashells and imported and Palmetto ceramics. Natural salt deposits may have attracted prehistoric peoples but only yielded one piece of Palmetto pottery. This scattered but important archaeological evidence, together with geographical location and the evidence of sea currents, suggests that Grand Inagua, rather than one of the Caicos Islands, may have been the first island in this area to be colonized.

See also: Coralie (site, Turks and Caicos); Lucayans; Palmetto; Taíno (Arawak); Turks and Caicos

References
Keegan, W. H. 1993. Inagua Archaeology. *Miscellaneous Project Report* 51. Gainesville: Department of Anthropology, Florida Museum of Natural History; Keegan, W. H. 1997. *The People Who Discovered Columbus.* Gainesville, FL: University Press of Florida.

Grenada

Grenada is the southernmost of the Windward Islands in the eastern Caribbean. Volcanic in origin, with a tropical wet-forest vegetation, it is 34 km long and 19 km wide. Together with its associated islands, which include Carriacou and Petit Martinique, it has an area of 344 sq km. About 80 percent of the 100,000 inhabitants of Grenada and its associated islands are of African descent.

Grenada's archaeological past is less well known than that of many other Caribbean islands, although in prehistory it was the strategic stepping-stone from Trinidad and Tobago in the south to the rest of the Island Caribbean. The archaeologist Ripley Bullen conducted the first modern professional excavations on the island, and in 1964 investigated the site of Pearls nearby the airport. For twenty-five years very little serious archaeology was conducted apart from a brief survey by the French archaeologist Henri Petitjean-Roget in the 1980s. More recently, the Pearls site has been investigated again by William Keegan.

Grenada appears to have been first settled during Saladoid times, the best-known site from this time being Pearls on the east coast, located next to the modern airport. Typical zoomorphic *adornos,* almost complete pots, and greenstone figures of frogs are typical objects that have been recovered and illustrate the nature of settlement between ca. 300 B.C. and A.D. 400. Also investigated have been sites from the Suazoid culture (A.D. 1000 to A.D. 1450), which took its name from the site of Savannah Suazey on the island. During this time, Grenada's indigenous inhabitants lived near beaches and mangrove swamps, their diet consisting mainly of mollusks, fish, and turtles. Suazoid people disappeared before Europeans arrived and were replaced by Carib peoples from mainland South America who called the island Camerhogue.

Christopher Columbus arrived in Grenada in 1498, during his third voyage to the New World. He christened the island Concepción, which soon became Mayo, and finally

Granada after the Spanish city, though the spelling subsequently changed to Grenada. From the time of European contact until the mid-seventeenth century, the island was successfully defended by the Caribs. In 1650, a French force landed, and after initially friendly contact, killed their hosts. According to popular belief, those who escaped the slaughter preferred to commit suicide rather than surrender, which they did by jumping to their deaths from the spot known as Morne des Sauteurs or Carib Leap on the north coast.

Having lost the indigenous workforce, the French imported African slaves to work the fields of sugar, tobacco, cocoa, and coffee. The island was a pawn in the imperial chess game between France and Britain, passing back and forth until finally being awarded to Britain in 1783 in the Treaty of Versailles. Not long afterward, the British introduced nutmeg that, together with cloves and mace, has thrived so much that today Grenada is known as the Spice Island. In 1795, Julian Fedon led a slave revolt, and in 1834 slavery was abolished. Granted full independence from Britain in 1974, Grenada today is a member of the British Commonwealth.

The African-Caribbean inhabitants of Grenada and Carriacou still practice their spiritual ceremonies in the form of feasts known as *saracas*—a word originating from Arabic-influenced West African terms given to various rituals associated with ancestor worship—though these appear not to include spirit possession. On Carriacou, the main feast in such events is called a Big Drum Dance where participants divide into African-derived kin groups such as Ibo and Mandingo, and celebrate their ethnic identity. More recently, Shango-derived ceremonies have become prominent in which Yoruba deities (*orishas*) are invoked in the Yoruba language. Known as "Queens," elder women of standing in the community organize the building of temporary shrines and also pilgrimages to sacred places such as lakes and rivers. Orisha deities such as Ogun, Eshu, and Oshun are worshipped, and, as elsewhere in the Caribbean, they can take possession of some of individual worshippers. This ecstatic dimension to Shango is thought to be one reason for the religion's popularity in Grenada.

While Big Drum and Shango rituals are a central feature of Grenadian spiritual life, they have also influenced local hybrid religions that draw on Christianity. Shango Baptists and Spiritual Baptists (the latter sometimes called Shouters) mix Protestantism and African spiritualities and regard both as complementary aspects of belief rather than as opposed religions.

Today, Grenada's cultural life centers on the island's capital of St. George, with its vibrant mix of eighteenth-century French houses and Georgian-style English ones. Many of the public buildings, such as the parliament, Catholic cathedral, and supreme court are nineteenth century. The National Museum exhibits African materials as well as items associated with the growing of sugar and spice. The Historical Society Museum on the island of Carriacou exhibits Amerindian objects. Grenada's Carnival takes place on the second weekend of August, during which time the island's capital of St. George comes alive with steel bands, dancing, a pageant, and a colorful parade through the town's streets. Elsewhere, August also sees the Rainbow City cultural festival that is held at Grenville on the east coast. A month or so earlier, at the end of June, is the blessing of the fishing nets and boats that is especially well seen at the small fishing port of Gouyave on the west coast and is called the Fisherman's Birthday.

See also: Caribs; Columbus, Christopher; Obeah; Orisha/Shango (Trinidad); Pearls (site, Grenada); Saladoid; Suazey/Suazoid

References

Bullen, R. P. 1964. *The Archaeology of Grenada, West Indies.* Gainesville, FL: University Press of Florida; Cheng, P. G., and G-K. Pang. 2000. *Grenada.* Tarrytown, NY: Benchmark Books; Honychurch, L. 2002. The Leap at Sauteurs: The Lost Cosmology of Indigenous Grenada. *http://www.uwichill.edu.bb/bnccde/grenada/conference;* Keegan, W. H. 1993. Archaeology at Pearls, Grenada: The 1990 Field Season. *Miscellaneous Project Report* 47. Gainesville, FL: University of Florida. Department of Anthropology, Florida Museum of Natural History; McDaniel, L. 1998. *The Big Drum Ritual of Carriacou.* Gainesville, FL: University Press of Florida; Polk, P. A. 1993. African Religion and Christianity in Grenada. *Caribbean Quarterly* 39 (3–4): 74–81; Pollak-Eltz, A. 1993. The Shango Cult and Other African Rituals in Trinidad, Grenada, and Cariiacou and their Possible Influences on the Spiritual Baptist Faith. *Caribbean Quarterly* 39 (3–4): 12–25.

Guacanagarí (Taíno chief)

Guacanagarí was the Taíno chief (cacique) of the populous Marien province in northern Hispaniola at the time of Columbus's arrival in 1492. He was the first great chief whom Columbus met, and the encounter between the two greatly influenced the course of many of the tragic events that followed. Guacanagarí's name (or title), like those of other Taíno rulers, included the prefix *gua,* which relates to the Taíno word for the sacred gold-copper-silver alloy known as *guanín.*

When Columbus's flagship, the *Santa Maria,* became grounded, Guacanagarí's people came out in canoes to help the Spanish salvage the wreck, storing the goods in two of their own buildings. The Taíno chief entertained the Spanish at a feast during which Columbus exchanged a pair of gloves and a shirt for gold jewelry and a gold-encrusted mask. In the meetings between Columbus and Guacanagarí that followed, the Taíno chief gave his guest a golden crown, and Columbus reciprocated by giving a necklace of colored glass beads, a woolen cape, and a silver ring. With the two sides unable to speak each other's language, these exchanges almost certainly were misunderstood, though Guacanagarí's status among his own people and neighboring tribes was probably enhanced by his alliance with such powerful strangers. It was from Guacanagarí that Columbus first heard of Cibao, a land rich in gold in the heart of Hispaniola.

Guacanagarí's hospitality led Columbus to establish La Navidad—the first European settlement in the New World—near the chief's village, the latter of which has now been identified as the archaeological site En Bas Saline. Columbus left thirty-eight men behind when he returned to Spain in January 1493. On his return the following year, he found La Navidad in ruins and his men dead. Guacanagarí prevaricated, blaming other more powerful Taíno chiefs, notably Caonabo, accusing them of having attacked and killed the Europeans. Whatever the truth, Guacanagarí accompanied Columbus's expedition into the island's interior in search of the golden riches of Cibao and to punish Caonabo. Born a chief, Guacanagarí died destitute, abandoned by his European allies when his usefulness was exhausted.

> *See also:* Caonabo (Taíno chief); Columbus, Christopher; Gold; Guarionex (Taíno chief); Taíno (Arawak)
>
> **References**
> Las Casas, B. 1992. *A Short Account of the Destruction of the Indies.* London: Penguin Books; Sauer, C. O. 1969. *The Early Spanish Main.* Berkeley, CA: University of California Press; Wilson, S. M. 1990. *Hispaniola: Caribbean Chiefdoms in the Age of Columbus.* Tuscaloosa, AL: University of Alabama Press;

Guadeloupe

The island of Guadeloupe in the eastern Caribbean has an area of 1,510 sq km and is in fact two islands—Basse-Terre and Grand-Terre—separated by the narrow strait of the Salée River. The population is around 200,000 and the island is the second most important of the French Antilles after Martinique.

Although one of the archaeologically least known of the major Caribbean islands, there is evidence that early Saladoid peoples arrived during the period 100 B.C. to A.D. 100. Perhaps dating from this time are the striking petroglyphs from the Pérou River, first mentioned by the French missionary Father Raymond Breton in 1647 and rediscovered in 1990. Guadeloupe's prehistoric inhabitants seem to have produced large quantities of well-made carved items, particularly as shell ornaments, during the period of Barrancoid influence between A.D. 350 and A.D. 650. At this time also, many of three-pointed *zemí* figures were made. There is substantial archaeological evidence for the succeeding Troumassoid Period between 650 and 1200, when pottery styles became somewhat less complex, and parallel white lines painted onto a red background made their appearance as pottery decoration.

Also at this time, as elsewhere in the Lesser Antilles, was the appearance of clay spindle whorls, and the distinctive footed griddle whose three substantial supporting legs replaced the earlier legless variety. Perhaps significantly, this had disappeared by the time the historic Carib peoples arrived from South America around 1450. Equally intriguing is the evidence from the site of Morel that indicates that while Guadeloupe's inhabitants continued making their three-pointed zemís at this time, they adopted the unusual practice of deliberately breaking them, perhaps for ritual reasons.

With the passing of the Troumassoid Period and arrival of the Suazey Period (ca. 1200 to 1450), Guadeloupe is well known by evidence from the late period occupation at Morel, whose plain conical pottery seems to some archaeologists to have little connection with Suazoid ceramics and perhaps to be oriented more toward developments in the Leeward Islands. An important multiperiod site that appears to span a millennia of cultural developments, from the earliest Saladoid to what is known as the Suazan Troumassoid (i.e., 450 to 1400), is that of Anse à la Gourde. Here, at levels dated to ca. A.D. 1000, has been excavated a settlement, surrounded by a horseshoe-shaped midden, whose house remains contained some sixty human burials interred with quantities of high-quality shell work and pottery. After 1450, and the arrival of the Caribs from South America, archaeological evidence for this sophisticated type of material culture disappears.

Christopher Columbus was the first European to see Guadeloupe during his second voyage in 1493. He named Sainte-Marie of Guadeloupe after the Virgin of Guadeloupe in Extremadura in Spain, the patron saint of sailors; its original Carib name seems to have been Turuqueira or Caroucaera. It was on Guadeloupe that Europeans had their first contact with Carib peoples. Already informed during his earlier encounters with the Taíno (Arawak) that these islands were home to man-eating Caribs, Columbus's landing party went ashore with many preconceptions. In a week-long stay, they encountered no Caribs, but did find quickly abandoned homes and fields as well as excellent-quality woven cloth. They also saw human bones hanging in several Carib houses, which they interpreted as the remains of a cannibal feast. So far, no archaeological evidence of Carib occupation has been discovered.

As with Martinique, the Spanish never settled on Guadeloupe and it was left to the French to colonize it in 1635. At first, the 350 French settlers were welcomed by their Carib hosts. The Europeans were ill prepared for the conditions they experienced, however, and soon began to run out of food. They took to raiding Carib gardens and stealing food, thereby initiating a long and bitter struggle that ended with the migration of many Caribs in the early 1640s. In 1660, the French governor moved the remaining Carib families to land northeast of Grande-Terre at first considered infertile but subsequently incorporated into expanding sugar-cane plantations. By 1882, a group of fifteen Caribs survived in northern Grande-Terre, and these were soon absorbed into the general population.

Never as prosperous as Martinique, Guadeloupe saw its first African slaves around 1650. By 1761, the British had captured the island as a bargaining chip that was then returned to France in exchange for French Canada in 1763. Recently, archaeological excavations have begun to investigate this tumultuous history, especially seventeenth-, eighteenth-, and nineteenth-century plantations associated with the growing of sugar, coffee, and indigo. These investigations have an added significance on Guadeloupe, as they can add crucial insights into an unusual sequence of events that saw slavery abolished as early as 1794, only to be bloodily re-established by Napoleon in 1802, and then finally abolished again in 1848. To date, some thirty African slave-village sites have been identified.

Archaeological investigations at the sugar plantation site Habitation Murat have uncovered buildings and machinery associated with the site, and excavations of the indigo works at La Gouffre have documented coral and limestone tanks used in the indigo-making process. New sites were revealed after the devastating hurricanes of 1995, some of which were colonial-period cemeteries. At the site of Anse de la Petite Chapelle, human remains have been found in an early-seventeenth-century chapel, with an associated cemetery perhaps still in use at the time of the World War I (1914 to 1918). Similar cemetery sites have been found at Anse du Vieux-Fort and Morne Dauphine, while at Anse Sainte-Marguerite over seventy burials were discovered, mostly in coffins. Local tradition has it that this was a slave cemetery, but no unequivocal scientific evidence is yet available to verify this.

Today Guadeloupe, like Martinique, has a distinctive cultural mix of French and African cultures. Creole is widely spoken, using French words but an African grammar, and music blends European and African instruments and forms. Some aspects of folk culture recall earlier times and attitudes, such as a national costume that, for women, incorporates a skirt hitched up to reveal a cotton petticoat. During the eighteenth and nineteenth centuries, only white women could wear silk petticoats and "petticoat inspectors" stood at church doors to check colored women as they entered.

See also: Breton, Father Raymond; Caribs; Dominica; Historical Archaeology; Hueca, La (Puerto Rico); Martinique; Slavery; Suazey/Suazoid; Sugar; Troumassoid

References
Annezer, J. C., D. Bégot, and J. Manlius, 1980. L'univers magico-religieux: l'example de la Guadeloupe. In J-C Bonniol (ed.), *L'histoire antillais,* pp. 459–478. Fort-de-France, Martinique: Dajani; Breton, Father R. 1978 [1647]. *Relations de l'île de la Guadeloupe.* Bibliothèque d'histoire antillaise 3. Basse-Terre: Société d'histoire de la Guadeloupe; Clerc, E. 1968. Sites Précolombiens de la côte Nord-Est Grande Terra de la Guadeloupe. *Proceedings of the Second International Congress for the Study of Pre-Columbian Cultures of the Lesser Antilles,* Barbados, pp. 47–60. Barbados; Clerc, E. 1973. Les trois-pointes des sites précolombiens de la côtes nord-est de la grande terre de la Guadeloupe. *Proceedings of the Fourth International Congress for the Study of the Pre-Columbian Cultures of the Lesser Antilles,* St. Lucia 1971, pp. 199–214; Courtaud, P., A. Delpuech, and T. Romon, 1999. Archaeological Investigations at Colonial Cemeteries on Guadeloupe: African Slave Burial Sites or Not? In J. B. Haviser (ed.), *African Sites Archaeology in the Caribbean,* pp. 277–290. Princeton, NJ: Markus Wiener Publishers; Delpuech, A. 2001. Historical Archaeology in the French West Indies: Recent Research in Guadeloupe. In P. Farnsworth (ed.), *Island Lives: Historical Archaeologies of the Caribbean,* pp. 21–59. Tuscaloosa, AL, and London: The University of Alabama Press; Hofman, C. L., A. Delpuech, and M.L.P. Hoogland, 1999. Excavations at the Site of Anse a la Gourde, Guadeloupe: Stratigraphy, Ceramic Chronology, and Structures. *Proceedings of the Eighteenth International Congress for Caribbean Archaeology,* pp. 162–172; Kelly, K. G. 2002. African Disapora Archaeology in Guadeloupe, French West Indies. *Antiquity* 76 (292): 333–334; Mason, K.O.T. 1885. *The Guesde Collection of Antiquities in Pointe-à-Pître, Guadeloupe, West Indies, from the Smithsonian Report for 1884,* pp. 731–837. Washington, DC: Government Printing Office; Michelin, 2001. *Michelin Green Sightseeing Guide to Guadeloupe and Martinique.* French and European Publishing.

Guanahatabey

The Guanahatabeys of western Cuba were first mentioned in a letter sent by the Spanish conquistador Diego Velázquez de Cuellar to the Spanish king in April 1514. Velázquez, and later Bartolomé de Las Casas, both scathingly referred to savages who lived in caves rather than houses, who had no agriculture, and who ate mainly fish. Yet, as neither of these two Spaniards visited western Cuba, their information must have been secondhand, perhaps coming from the more sophisticated Taíno (Arawak) people they encountered on the island. Such stories may also have been influenced by Taíno ideas and mythology, or perhaps by the Spaniards misunderstanding what they were told. The issue of who the Guanahatabeys were has become enveloped in confusion and supposition, and has had serious implications for the culture history of the Island Caribbean well beyond the shores of Cuba.

The historical reports of the contact-period Guanahatabeys soon became entangled with archaeology, as early-twentieth-century excavations in western Cuba discovered sites without pottery (i.e., aceramic). It was an easy step to suggest that such sites belonged to the primitive Guanahatabeys, who in turn probably represented vestiges of the earliest human occupation of the Caribbean, predating the pottery-using, village-dwelling, and agriculturalist Taíno, whom the Spanish encountered in the eastern part of Cuba and the Greater Antilles. The name "Ciboney" was given to the culture that produced these archaeological remains, and the link with the Guanahatabeys was forged.

However, the apparent equivalence between the Ciboney and Guanahatabey was itself a result of confusion in reading the historical records. In his 1516 petitioning of the Spanish Crown for the missionization of Cuban Amerindians, Las Casas clearly differentiated between the Guanahatabeys and Ciboneys (as well as others) on ethnic and geographical grounds. The Guanahatabeys were Amerindians living on the Cape of Cuba, whereas the Ciboney were reported as being slaves to the powerful Taíno chiefs of that island. Despite the absence of any known connection between these two groups, their names had now become interchangeable, with Guanahatabey referring to the contact-period Amerindians, and Ciboney their archaeological ancestors.

Once this dubious connection had been made, the Ciboney/Guanahatabey had a straightforward cultural identity that could be exported—applied to any Caribbean archaeological site that lacked pottery. As long as the evidence was aceramic, it was clearly Ciboney. Apart from this unproven assumption, there was also the error in assuming that sites that lacked pottery (aceramic by definition) were the same as those that were preceramic, and therefore had to belong to the Archaic Period of which the Ciboney were the exemplar. This was, and in part remains, a seriously flawed circular argument that impedes rather than advances archaeological knowledge.

Furthermore, such primitive people had survived not only until European contact in Cuba but also in other isolated locations such as southwestern Haiti, though this assumption, like others, appears to have been due at least in part to more confusion in the historical record. It was further argued that these primitive peoples had been pushed into remote and marginal locations by the expansion of the more sophisticated and powerful pottery-using Saladoid peoples and subsequently by their descendants the Taíno (Arawak).

What had begun as a misnaming of one hardly-known Amerindian Cuban society—the Guanahatabey—had become an error-ridden archaeological dogma for interpreting critical events during 7,000 years of Caribbean prehistory, from the Archaic Period to the arrival of the Europeans. The crucial questions remain unanswered: Who were the Guanahatabey? Who were the people, erroneously called Ciboney? Who produced Cuba's aceramic sites (and how many of these are preceramic)? Did any non-pottery-using Amerindian groups survive until European contact? And what, if any, provable and meaningful connections exist between all or any of these groups?

See also: Archaic Period; Cuba
References
Keegan, W. F. 1989. Creating the Guanahatabey (Ciboney): The Modern Genesis of an Extinct Culture. *Antiquity* 63 (239): 373–379; Osgood, C. 1942. The Ciboney Culture of Cayo Redondo, Cuba. *Yale University Publications in Anthropology* 25. New Haven, CT: Yale University Press; Rouse, I. B. 1948. The Ciboney. In J. H. Steward (ed.), *Handbook of South American Indians 4,* pp. 497–503. Washington, DC: Smithsonian Institution; Rouse, I. 1992. *The Tainos: Rise and Decline of the People Who Greeted Columbus,* pp. 20–21. New Haven, CT: Yale University Press; Sauer, C. O. 1969. *The Early Spanish Main,* pp. 184–185. Berkeley, CA: University of California Press; Valdés, P. G. 1948. The Ethnology of the Ciboney. In J. H. Steward (ed.), *Handbook of South American Indians 4,* pp. 503–505. Washington, DC: Smithsonian Institution.

Guarionex (Taíno chief)

Guarionex was a Taíno chief (cacique) on Hispaniola at the time of the island's exploration and conquest by Christopher Columbus. The name may well have been a title rather than a personal name. What is certain is that Guarionex was the preeminent leader of the Magua chiefdom in north-central Hispaniola, the seat of the populous province of Cayabo, the third of five native provinces of the island.

Through persuasion, personality, and kinship ties, Guarionex commanded a number of lesser chiefs within Cayabo, and could call on their labor and manpower in times of need. One of his subchiefs is reported to have offered him 16,000 armed men with which to fight the Spanish. The Spanish, however, misunderstood the nature of Taíno leadership, and often referred erroneously to Guarionex and the great chiefs of the other four provinces as kings.

Guarionex played a central role in dealing with the Spanish, preferring diplomacy and accommodation to confrontation. When Christopher Columbus moved into Guarionex's domain in late A.D. 1495, the chief and his subordinates offered almost no resistance. Having gained control of the Magua district, Columbus renamed it the Vega Real, and commanded the local chiefs to arrange for every person of fourteen years and older to render tribute in gold or cotton. It was Guarionex who explained to Columbus that the effects of European disease, a food shortage, and the fact that the Taínos knew nothing about gold mining meant that this was impossible. He famously offered to plant cassava along the length of his kingdom to feed the Spanish in lieu of gold payments, but Columbus declined.

The Spanish built the fort of Concepción de la Vega on a hill strategically located to overlook Guarionex's settlement by the banks of the Río Verde. It was Guarionex's village that Christopher Columbus chose to be the temporary home of the friar Ramón Pané so that he could learn about Taíno religion. His report is the only eyewitness source for such matters. For two years Pané attempted to convert Guarionex to Christianity but without success. After he departed, the Christian shrine and images that he had left behind were destroyed.

In 1497, Guarionex was still struggling to meet Spanish demands for tribute, but appeared to be unable to restrain his subordinate chiefs from raising a rebellion. Bartolomé

Columbus put down the uprising, captured Guarionex, and put him in jail, though he soon released him as a calming influence on the local population. After further maltreatment by the Spanish, who had now divided into two rival factions, and after his wife had been raped by Francisco Roldán, Guarionex gave up his power and fled north, seeking refuge with Mayobanex, chief of the Macorix people. Failing to appreciate, or perhaps unwilling to believe, that Guarionex no longer had authority, Bartolomé Columbus ravaged the mountainous home of Mayobanex and captured both chiefs. Mayobanex died in captivity while Guarionex was kept prisoner until 1502, when the decision was made to send him back to Spain in chains.

In an ironic twist of fate, Guarionex was put aboard a ship of the Spanish fleet that also carried a wealth of golden treasure extorted from the Taíno on Hispaniola. This included the so-called Great Nugget, reportedly as big as a loaf of bread. Ignoring the onset of the hurricane season, the fleet set sail and promptly sank off the southeast coast of the island with great loss of life, including Guarionex. For the great Taíno chief, it may have seemed that Guabancex, the Taíno "Lady of the Hurricane Winds" had reclaimed both his spirit and his gold.

See also: Cassava (manioc); Columbus, Christopher; Gold; Guacanagarí (Taíno chief); Pané, Father Ramón; Taíno (Arawak)

References

Las Casas, B. 1992. *A Short Account of the Destruction of the Indies.* London: Penguin Books; Sauer, C. O. 1969. *The Early Spanish Main.* Berkeley, CA: University of California Press; Wilson, S. M. 1990. *Hispaniola: Caribbean Chiefdoms in the Age of Columbus.* Tuscaloosa, AL: University of Alabama Press;

Guayabitoid (pottery)

Guayabitoid pottery was a prehistoric pottery style that, together with the Arauquinoid ceramic tradition, followed the Barrancoid cultures of northeastern South America sometime around A.D. 500. It is particularly well known from Trinidad around 1200, as at the site of Icacos in the southwest of the island and at a time when the Venezuelan coastal region was occupied by peoples belonging to the Macro-Dabajuroid cultural complex. There appears to be no Guayabitoid presence farther north in the Lesser Antilles.

See also: Arauquinoid (pottery); Dabajuroid; Mayoid (pottery); Trinidad and Tobago

References

Boomert, A. 1985. The Guayabitoid and Mayoid Series: Amerindian Culture History in Trinidad during Late Prehistoric and Protohistoric Times. *Proceedings of the Tenth International Congress for the Study of the Pre-Columbian Cultures of the Lesser Antilles, Martinique 1983*, pp. 93–148.

H

Hacienda Grande

Hacienda Grande culture is an early local form of the Saladoid tradition. It is called after the archaeological site of the same name located on the north coast of Puerto Rico. Hacienda Grande culture flourished between ca. 400 B.C. and A.D. 500.

Hacienda Grande pottery is typically Cedrosan Saladoid, featuring white-on-red (W-O-R) painted ceramics and zic (zone-incised cross-hatching) ware, as well as modeled anthropomorphic and zoomorphic images in the form of *adornos*. These two characteristic types of pottery continued to be made until around A.D. 400, when in quick succession they disappeared as the Cedrosan Saladoid came to an end. The material culture of the Hacienda Grande people includes ceramic cassava griddles, stone adzes, three-pointer *zemís*, hallucinogen-snuffing vessels, beads and pendants made from various minerals, bone, and shell, and wooden items inlaid with mother-of-pearl. As at Maisabel, Hacienda Grande appears not to have had a formal ballcourt.

The relationships between the Hacienda Grande and the roughly contemporary La Hueca cultures of Puerto Rico remain poorly understood, though there are general similarities between the pottery-making traditions and economic lives of both. While the dates from early Hacienda Grande are earlier than the La Hueca site of Punta Candelero, there is a Hacienda Grande occupation overlying the La Hueca layers at the site of Sorcé on the island of Vieques. At the same time as this occurred, around A.D. 240, there are signs that Hacienda Grande people had spread to southeastern Hispaniola (modern Dominican Republic) at the site of La Caleta, where they seem to have displaced the local El Caimito people, whose pottery makers may have copied the more sophisticated ceramics of the newcomers.

Around 400, Hacienda Grande culture evolved into a final Saladoid variation (or subseries) known as Cuevas, and then into the Ostiones culture. At Hacienda Grande itself, as at Maisabel and Sorcé, these developments appear not to have interrupted the occupation of the settlement. Interestingly, while there is no evidence for Spanish conquest-period presence at Hacienda Grande, the site was occupied by some of the first African slaves in the Americas.

See also: Hueca, La (Puerto Rico); Maisabel (site, Puerto Rico); Ostionoid; Puerto Rico; Saladoid; White-on-Red pottery (W-O-R); Zemís; Zic Pottery

References

Chanlatte Baik, L. A. 1995. Presencia Huecoide en Hacienda Grande, Loiza, Puerto Rico. *Proceedings of the Fifteenth International Congress of Caribbean Archaeology, Puerto Rico, 1993,* pp. 501; Roe, P. G. 1985. A Preliminary Report on the 1980 and 1982 Field Seasons at Hacienda Grande (12PSj7–5): Overview of Site History, Mapping, and Excavations. *Proceedings of the Tenth International Congress for the Study of the Pre-Columbian Cultures of the Lesser Antilles,* pp. 151–180. Montréal; Rouse, I., and R. E. Alegría. 1990. Excavations at Maria de la Cruz Cave and Hacienda Grande Village site, Loiza, Puerto Rico. *Yale University Publications in Anthropology,* No. 80. New Haven, CT; Wing, E. S. 1990. Appendix: Animal Remains from the Hacienda Grande Site, Puerto Rico. In I. Rouse and R. E. Alegría (eds.). *Excavations at Maria de la Cruz Cave and Hacienda Grande Village site, Loiza, Puerto Rico.* New Haven, CT: Yale University Publications in Anthropology, No. 80.

Haiti

Haiti comprises the western one-third of the island of Hispaniola (the eastern remainder is the Dominican Republic), and has an area of 27,700 sq km. Unlike the mixed population of the Dominican Republic, 95 percent of Haiti's 7 million people are of pure African descent. The majority of these speak a creole language that developed out of French.

The earliest evidence for human presence in Haiti is Archaic Period Casimiroid sites such as Vignier III, whose stone tools and shells have been dated to 3620 B.C. Subsequently, the Courian culture (the equivalent of the Dominican El Provenir culture) is dated to between 2630 B.C. and A.D. 240. The Courians made elaborate stone tools whose large blades were used as spear-points to hunt sloth and manatees. They also made pestles and mortars, stone beads, and shell jewelry. During the later Taíno (Chican Ostionoid) Period, the local culture on Haiti is represented by the Carrier style of pottery.

Hispaniola was first encountered by Christopher Columbus on Christmas Day 1492 when the *Santa Maria* ran aground. The local Taíno chief Guacanagarí appeared friendly and helped the Spanish retrieve their valuables. One consequence was that Columbus built a small stockaded settlement known as La Navidad nearby. When he returned to Spain in early 1493 he left thirty-nine men there. On his return, the settlement had been destroyed and the men killed. Recent archaeological excavations have identified the site of En Bas Saline as Guacanagarí's village, but no definite location for La Navidad has yet been found.

In the southwest Taíno chiefdom of Xaraguá, the principal chief was Behechio Anacaochoa, whose sister, Anacaona, was married to Caonabo the chief of the neighboring province of Maguana. There is no archaeological evidence today for Behechio's village, which may lie beneath Haiti's capital city of Port-au-Prince. It was the Columbus family's dealings with Behechio and Anacaona and the visits they made to Xaraguá that provided much information on the Hispaniolan Taíno, from the ceremonial dances (*areítos*) with which they were entertained, to the black polished-wood *duhos* made by women on the small offshore island of Gonâve that they received as gifts. Subsequent cruelty and torture of the Taínos by Nicolás de Ovando led to the disappearance of indigenous Amerindian life.

The formative exchanges between the Taínos and the Spanish have left distinctive archaeological traces. The town of Puerto Real was one such melting pot—a true colonizing settlement. It was built in 1503 over an aboriginal shell midden with Taíno pottery, and was typical of Spanish efforts to make self-sufficient use of local resources and Amerindian labor. It's inhabitants raised cattle and mined gold but also engaged in slave raiding against the Lucayans of the Bahamas. Recent excavations have yielded locally-made pottery that supports the historical records of Spanish men taking Taíno women as wives or concubines. By 1576, Amerindian peoples had largely disappeared through disease and maltreatment, and over 30,000 African slaves had been brought to Hispaniola. At Puerto Real, Taíno pottery disappears and is replaced by typically African-style ceramics.

The investigations by historical archaeologists have thrown much light on early encounters between Europeans and Taínos. It was the Africans, however, who shaped the postcontact realities of Haitian life, particularly during the period that saw Haiti become the largest producer of sugar in the Caribbean and that characterized French control between 1697 and 1804, when this part of Hispaniola was known as Saint Domingue.

Tensions between the French plantocracy and their African slaves were exacerbated in the wake of the French Revolution of 1789, and in 1791 thousands of Europeans were slaughtered when slaves rebelled. From the ensuing chaos (accelerated by appalling French torture of their slaves), the ex-slave Francois-Dominique Toussaint (more commonly Toussaint L'Ouverture) emerged as a charismatic leader and brilliant strategist. He joined the Spanish against the French, then the French against the English who had invaded in 1794. By 1801, he was militarily and politically supreme, created a new constitution and declared himself governor general for life. In 1802 he was defeated and captured by Napoleonic forces and died in prison in France a year later. In 1804, Toussaint's lieutenant, Jean-Jacques Dessalines—also an ex-slave—declared himself emperor and renamed Saint Domingue as Haiti, though he was assassinated two years later.

One feature of this difficult history was the role of traditional African spiritualities, mixed with Catholicism and sometimes also with remnant Taíno beliefs. Most famous of these syncretistic African-Caribbean religions is Haitian Vodoun (more widely known as voodoo). Vodoun beliefs see the natural world as animated by powerful multidimensional gods and spirits with whom humans converse through prayers, offerings, music, and dance. The colonial French rulers regarded Vodoun as a threat, giving strength and unity to plantation slaves and undermining the sugar-based economy.

Today, apart from religion, the vibrancy of African-Haitian culture manifests itself in arts and crafts, such as wood carvings, leatherwork, papier maché, and folk paintings of Vodoun scenes. Celebrations such as Mardi Gras (Carnival), Rara, and Day of the Dead, bind Haitian society with masked dancing and African-inspired music, though Jamaican reggae, Cuban *son,* and *zouk* from Martinique are more modern influences. Most recently traditional drumming and electronic instruments have given birth to the so-called voodoo beat.

See also: Casimiroid; Columbus, Christopher; Dominican Republic; Guacanagarí (Taíno chief); La Navidad/En Bas Saline (site, Haiti); Music; Puerto Real (site, Haiti); Slavery; Sugar; Taíno (Arawak); Toussaint L'Ouverture; Vodoun

References

Alexis, S. 1949. *Black Liberator: The Life of Toussaint Louverture.* London: Ernest Benn; Arthur, C. 2002. *Haiti in Focus: A Guide to the People, Politics, and Culture.* Northampton, MA: Interlink Publishing Group; Cosentino, D. (ed.). 1995. *Sacred Arts of Haitian Vodun.* Los Angeles: UCLA Fowler Museum of Cultural History; Deagan, K. A. 1989. The Search for La Navidad, Columbus's 1492 Settlement. In J. T. Milanich and S. Millbrath (eds.). *First Encounters.* Gainesville, FL: University Press of Florida; Deagan, K. A. 1995. *Puerto Real: The Archaeology of a Sixteenth-Century Spanish Town in Hispaniola.* Gainesville, FL: University of Florida Press; Desmangles, L. G. 1992. *The Faces of the Gods: Vodou and Roman Catholicism in Haiti.* Chapel Hill: University of North Carolina Press; Ewen, C. R. 1991. *From Spaniard to Creole: The Archaeology of Cultural Formation at Puerto Real, Haiti.* Tuscaloosa, AL, and London: The University of Alabama Press; Laguerre, M. S. 1989. *Voodoo and Politics in Haiti.* New York: St. Martin's Press; McAlister, E. A. 2002. *Rara: Vodou, Power, and Performance in Haiti and Its Diaspora.* Berkeley, CA: University of California Press; Morrison, S. E. 1940. The Route of Columbus along the North Coast of Haiti and the Site of La Navidad. *Transactions of the American Philosophical Society* 31 (4): 239–285; Nicholls, D. 1985. *Haiti in Caribbean Context: Ethnicity, Economy, and Revolt.* London: MacMillan; Rouse, I. B. 1939. Prehistory in Haiti: A Study in Method. *Yale University Publications in Anthropology* No. 21. New Haven, CT; Wilson, S. M. 1990. *Hispaniola: Caribbean Chiefdoms in the Age of Columbus.* Tuscaloosa, AL: University of Alabama Press.

Heywoods (site, Barbados)

Heywoods is a late prehistoric, Troumassoid/Suazoid site on the northwest coast of Barbados radiocarbon dated to between A.D. 830 and A.D. 1040. The site was heavily disturbed by sugar-cane agriculture in historic times and the construction of the coastal road.

The ceramic remains are poorly preserved, though red-painted shards were found. Also discovered were the remains of large cauldron-like vessels, cassava-baking griddles with foot supports, and anthropomorphic and zoomorphic decorative lugs. Finger-marking seems to have been the only decorative technique used, though several fragments may have had the white-on-red paint remains of the style known as Caliviny Polychrome. There are a handful of shards that may be, or be related to, the Saladoid style, though this may indicate a local development of the Troumassoid/Suazoid style on Barbados. The shellwork at Heywoods is primarily Queen Conch (*Strombus gigas*), and usually takes the form of adzes and small tools.

See also: Barbados; Suazey/Suazoid; Troumassoid

References

Boomert, A. 1987. Notes on Barbados Prehistory. *Journal Barbados Museum Historical Society* 38 (1): 8–43; Bullen, R. P., and A. J. Bullen, 1968. Barbados Archaeology 1966. *Proceedings of the Second International Congress for the Study of Pre-Columbian Cultures of the Lesser Antilles,* pp. 134–144; Drewett, P. L. 1991. *Prehistoric Barbados.* London: Institute of Archaeology and Archetype Publications.

Hillcrest (site, Barbados)

Hillcrest is a multiperiod but mainly late prehistoric Troumassoid/Suazoid site on the Atlantic facing the east coast of Barbados. It is situated on a promontory some 30 to 35 meters above sea level.

Excavations revealed the remains of a small round house fringed by circle of coral fragments and midden refuse and dated to ca. A.D. 870. The site had a long prehistoric occupancy beginning with Saladoid peoples and ending in Suazoid times. Most pottery appears to be bowls, though there are some large cauldron-like vessels and cassava-baking footed griddles. Decoration includes finger-marking, incision, and punctation. There are some red-slipped and zic (zone-incised cross-hatching) style Saladoid/Barrancoid pottery remains, though most ceramics belong to the later Troumassoid Period. Shellwork is rare and mainly conch though probably ornamental items appear to have been highly polished. Intruding into the prehistoric levels are historic period materials, mainly nineteenth- and twentieth-century clay pipes, glass, and metalwork.

See also: Barbados; Saladoid; Suazey/Suazoid; Troumassoid

References

Boomert, A. 1987. Notes on Barbados Prehistory. *Journal Barbados Museum Historical Society* 38 (1): 8–43; Bullen, R. P., and A. J. Bullen, 1968. Barbados Archaeology 1966. *Proceedings of the Second International Congress for the Study of Pre-Columbian Cultures of the Lesser Antilles,* pp. 134–144; Drewett, P. L. 1991. *Prehistoric Barbados.* London: Institute of Archaeology and Archetype Publications.

Historical Archaeology

Historical archaeology is a multidisciplinary endeavor that combines archaeological techniques, historical methods, and textual evidence. Its main focus is the period that begins with European colonial expansion during the early fifteenth century, and thus it is global in extent. For this reason, it has been referred to as the archaeology of colonialism. As historical archaeology can, by definition, investigate any site after this time, from an English cotton mill in Yorkshire to an abandoned whaling station in the South Atlantic, it is perhaps more usefully regarded as the archaeology of the capitalist transformation of the world. This broad definition clearly includes aspects of what is also known as industrial archaeology and underwater archaeology.

The Caribbean was a prime area for such economic and social transformation in its plantations; the mass enslavement and transportation of Africans; and the arrival of many different peoples, cultures, and religions from around the world, including Hindus and Sikhs from India, Muslims from the Middle East, and Chinese as well as Protestant and Catholic Christians from Britain, Holland, Spain, and France. All of these have left distinctive archaeological signatures on the cultural landscape, sometimes suggestively mixed with the remains of the region's indigenous Taíno or Carib inhabitants. For this reason, historical archaeology in the Caribbean can be concerned equally with investigating the remains of early Spanish settlements on Hispaniola (modern Haiti and the Dominican

Republic); British and French plantation houses and associated remains on Tobago and Guadeloupe, respectively; colonial Dutch architecture on Curaçao; or African slave villages and their burials on Barbados.

A brief overview of historical archaeology in the Caribbean reveals the extraordinary richness of this new type of investigation as well as the patchy way in which it is developing on different islands. For example, on the Dutch side of the island of Sint Maarten/St. Martin, various surveys have been carried out, including one of the underwater shipwreck site of the *Proselyte*. Few detailed excavations have been attempted, a notable exception being work at the site of Fort Amsterdam in 1987. Similarly, on Saba investigation has been limited, though survey and mapping has been carried out and revealed many previously unknown rural villages of the last 200 years. On Curaçao, the Spanish-Amerindian site of San Hironimo has been excavated, and investigations into postemancipation slave houses in the Kenepa area have been compared to traditional West African forms. Also on Curaçao, World War II structures and a seventeenth-century Protestant cemetery beneath a synagogue in Willemstadt have been studied and underwater surveys conducted on the shipwrecks of the eighteenth-century *Alphen* and the nineteenth-century *Mediator*.

Elsewhere, surveys have documented historical monuments, such as the remains of 111 standing sugar-cane mills on Antigua; maps and plans of plantations on Jamaica; and similar structures on Barbuda, Anguilla, and the Bahamas. Although archaeological excavations of military sites (mainly forts) are rare, historical research into their plans and buildings is less so, and valuable research has been carried out at Shirley Heights on Antigua and Cabrits on Dominica. The archaeology of the Maroons is a topic that spans the material remains of indigenous Amerindians, escaped African slaves, and Europeans in a typically Caribbean way. Detailed excavations have been carried out at the Jamaican Maroon site of Nanny Town, and other sites exist on Antigua, Hispaniola, Dominica, and Cuba.

On Jamaica, at the site of New Seville, investigations have explored an area that was originally a Taíno village, then the Spanish town of Sevilla la Nueva founded on the orders of Diego Columbus in 1509, then a transshipment port for African slaves, and, from 1655, a British sugar plantation. At Puerto Real on Hispaniola, established in 1503, long-term excavations have focused on the town's nature as a colonial rather than simply exploitative settlement. Investigations have surveyed the site and located high- and low-status buildings through the presence of European glass and Spanish majolica pottery (in the former) and locally made pottery (in the latter). This archaeological finding supports historical documents that report Spanish men taking Taíno women as wives or concubines, and who used (perhaps made) local pottery for domestic purposes. This indigenous ceramic style was replaced by typical African-style pottery when African slaves began to replace the disappearing Taíno.

Investigations have also taken place in the area of La Navidad on northern coast of Hispaniola. This was the first European settlement in the Americas built on Christopher Columbus's orders near to the village of the Taíno chief Guacanagarí. The archaeological

site of En Bas Saline is thought to be the Amerindian village, and while La Navidad has not yet been identified, some scholars believe it might be nearby at Caille Brûlee.

One of the Caribbean's best-known historical archaeological investigations has been at Port Royal in Jamaica. Situated on the island's south coast, much of Port Royal fell into the sea during the 1692 earthquake. Investigations have combined the study of historical documents such as wills and probate inventories with underwater excavation techniques to study styles of building, identify the makers and owners of individual items from silver cutlery to pewter plates, and even retrieve the remains of children caught up in the disaster.

Despite the extraordinary breadth and scope of historical archaeology, to date most investigations of this type have focused on investigating plantations (plantation archaeology). Within this, they have emphasized the study of the material remains of African slavery. One key aim of plantation archaeology to date has been to throw light on the everyday lives and beliefs of those who were almost exclusively disenfranchised, unable to record their own lives in their own words, yet on whose exploitation a global economy, and arguably the modern world, was built.

Plantation economies transformed the physical and cultural landscapes of the Island Caribbean in many ways. Plantation archaeology seeks to document and interpret this variety in order to understand the everyday lives of slave communities and their interactions with the European plantocracy. Archaeological investigations at the eighteenth-century estate at Drax Hall, Jamaica, have illuminated the changing lives of African slaves and free laborers on this Jamaican sugar plantation. Comparing the remains of the slave quarters and the overseer's Great House, marked differences in status between the former's wattle-and-daub architecture and the latter's cut-and-fitted limestone buildings were documented. The plantation's slaves initially made typically West African earthenware pottery (yabbas), but over time they incorporated European items, thus creating a distinctive Afro-Jamaican type of material culture. Especially interesting was the slave habit of recycling, whether recarving and reusing parts of smoking pipes, or carving delftware disks for possible use as gaming pieces.

The rich body of information on everyday life from Drax Hall is supplemented by evidence of the changing practices in slave burials from Newton Plantation on Barbados. Here, it was found that earlier burials were oriented toward the east and later ones toward the west. This suggests the earlier ones were of African-born individuals or first-generation creoles facing toward their homeland, whereas the later west-facing burials belonged to individuals whose burial practices had been influenced in some way by Christian European practices and beliefs. The fact that west-facing burials were positively correlated with the presence of coffins (a European influence) perhaps reinforces this view. One unusual burial has been interpreted as that of an African-born witch doctor or Obeahman, due to his elaborate African-style necklace of cowrie shells, drilled dog teeth, glass beads, and drilled fish vertebrae.

Across the Caribbean, many slave cemeteries have been located, although only a small proportion has been excavated. Each in its own way preserves a unique record of the life and death of slave communities on islands as varied in their economies and geographies as in their dominant British, French, Spanish, or Dutch cultures.

Caribbean plantations were of many different types, ranging from coffee and cacao (cocoa), to sugar and tobacco. The diversity in the physical remains of such varied undertakings offers historical archaeologists the opportunity to investigate a wide range of research topics. Coffee works and water mills have been studied at Balenbouche Estate on St. Lucia, sugar plantations investigated on Montserrat, Jamaica, Cuba, and Antigua (to mention just a few)—some of which began as tobacco plantations—and on Guadeloupe the intricate mechanics of producing indigo have been documented.

It is the remains of sugar plantations, however, that have attracted most attention from historical archaeologists, not only because of their number but also because of the irony (and guilt) of enslaving untold numbers of Africans to produce a luxury sweetener for the European palate. The remains of sugar plantations are uniform and easily identified. On Nevis, at the Coconut Walk Estate, historical documentation has been supplemented by archaeological identification of an early animal-powered mill for pressing cane juice, a later windmill, a boiling house, and a small stone-and-mortar lime kiln. Similar remains have been found at many sugar plantation sites across the Caribbean, such as Habitation Murat on Guadeloupe, Betty's Hope on Antigua, and Whim Estate on St. Croix.

Apart from documenting an ever-increasing number of plantation sites and their remains, historical archaeologists have in recent years become adept at recognizing a variety of more subtle aspects of slave life revealed in material culture. The presence of an Obeahman in Newton Plantation on Barbados has been mentioned, but of wider significance is the recognition of traditional African technologies in pottery making, metalworking, and the transformation of European materials into African forms that mark the beginnings of uniquely African-Caribbean culture.

On St. Croix, archaeologists have identified a distinctive type of pottery, called Afro-Cruzan ware, which, by virtue of being hand-molded and made mainly into bowls and olla shapes, stands in contrast to the European glazed and wheel-turned tradition. On Puerto Rico, similarly, characteristically non-European-style ceramics were made by slaves and their free descendants and are known as criollo ceramics. Typically Caribbean, is the fact that these types of pottery appear to have been associated with cooking and eating specific types of foods by most of Puerto Rico's peoples, not just those of African descent.

Such African-Caribbean earthenware pottery has been found on a number of islands, such as Antigua, Barbuda, St. Martin, and St. Thomas, much of which is regarded as a creolized style, a mixing of African and European traditions, and perhaps just occasionally with indigenous Amerindian influence as well. On St. Eustatius, in 1983, 1,300 shards of African-Caribbean pottery were found in the ruins of an eighteenth-century synagogue that had evidently been subsequently used as a rubbish dump. These undecorated ceramics, generically called coarseware, were apparently used in the cooking of pepper pot stew, itself an Amerindian dish, and also for storage. Other uses include percussion instruments for dances, and as magical items in Obeah. What is clear, is that for African-Caribbean peoples, traditional non-European ceramics could often possess a variety of uses that might not be apparent from their appearance. In other words, plain and superficially uninteresting pottery was a way for African slaves and their descendants to negotiate and express their identity and resistance to the white-dominated society who claimed to own them.

The reuse of traditional technology to reinforce spiritual beliefs, to cut across religions such as Vodoun and Shango, to mobilize African origins in a white world and yet to appear mundane, can also be seen in metal objects. Historical archaeologists have shown how African metalworking techniques made their way from Africa to the Caribbean, and were manifested in beliefs concerning the supernatural power of blacksmiths conceptualized as the Anvil bird, whose ominous call sounds like clashing metal. Skilled African-Caribbean smelters, casters, and blacksmiths may have produced what Europeans regarded as functional items—from wrought-iron gates to fences—but archaeological evidence suggests that foundries sometimes served also as sites for traditional African religious activities. In Orisha ceremonies today, the deity Ogun is still associated with iron and war.

Historical archaeology in the Caribbean is a recent development compared with prehistoric archaeology. There are many areas and topics still to receive attention; these include the study of sometimes impressive World War II installations, nineteenth- and twentieth-century estate houses in rural Trinidad, the remains of the Garifuna (Black Carib) sites on St. Vincent, the development of dock facilities, the interrelationships between different types of sites on islands that changed hands (mainly between the British and French) during the colonial period, and the effects of tourism on issues of heritage and reconstruction—to mention just a few.

Despite still being in its infancy, historical archaeology in the Caribbean has demonstrated a remarkable sophistication in revealing the diversity of ways in which African peoples came to terms with their enslavement and subsequent emancipation, among themselves and in their relations with others. The merging of archaeology and history is proving a powerful way of investigating aspects of the Caribbean's colonial and more recent past that was once thought to be not only worthless but also beyond recovery.

See also: Antigua; Betty's Hope (site, Antigua); Drax Hall (site, Jamaica); Galways Plantation; Guadeloupe; Jamaica; La Isabela (site, Dominican Republic); La Navidad/En Bas Saline (site, Haiti); Maroons; Newton Plantation (Barbados); Obeah; Pepper Pot; Port Royal (Jamaica); Puerto Real (site, Haiti); Slavery; St. Croix (USVI); St. Lucia; Sugar; Trinidad and Tobago

References

Deagan, K. 1987. *Artifacts of the Spanish Colonies of Florida and the Caribbean, 1500–1800: Vol. 1, Ceramics, Glassware, and Beads.* Washington, DC: Smithsonian Institution Press; Deagan, K. 1988. The Archaeology of the Spanish Contact Period in the Caribbean. *Journal of World Prehistory* 2 (2): 187–225; Deagan, K. 1995. *Puerto Real: The Archaeology of a Sixteenth-Century Spanish Town in Hispaniola.* Gainesville, FL: University of Florida Press; Deagan, K., and J. M. Cruxent. 2002. *Archaeology at La Isabela: America's First European Town.* New Haven, CT: Yale University Press; Farnsworth, P. 1996. The Influence of Trade on Bahamian Slave Culture. *Historical Archaeology* 30 (4): 1–23; Farnsworth, P. (ed.). 2001. *Island Lives: Historical Archaeologies of the Caribbean.* Tuscaloosa, AL, and London: The University of Alabama Press; Goodwin, C. M. 1982. Archaeology on the Galways Plantation. *Florida Anthropologist* 35 (4): 251–258; Handler, J. S. 1972. An Archaeological Investigation of the Domestic life of Plantation Slaves in Barbados. *Journal of the Barbados Museum and Historical Society* 34: 64–72; Handler, J. S. 1997. An African-Type Healer/Diviner and his Grave Goods: A Burial from a Plantation Slave Cemetery in Barbados. *International Journal of Historical Archaeology* 1 (2): 91–130; Handler, J. S., and F. W. Lange. 1978. *Plantation Slavery in Barbados: An Archaeological and Historical Investigation.* Cambridge, MA: Harvard University Press; Haviser, J. B. (ed.). 1999. *African Sites Archaeology in the Caribbean.* Princeton, NJ: Markus Wiener; Haviser, J. B. 2001. Historical Archaeology in the Netherlands Antilles and Aruba. In P. Farnsworth (ed.), *Island Lives: Historical Archaeologies of the Caribbean,* pp. 60–81. Tuscaloosa, AL, and London: The University of Alabama Press; Haviser, J. B., and N. Simmons-Brito. 1995. Excavations at the Zuurzak Site: A Possible 17th-Century Dutch Slave Camp on Curaçao, Netherlands Antilles. *Proceedings of the Fifteenth International Congress for Caribbean Archaeology,* pp. 71–82; Higman, B. W. 1974. A Report on Excavations of Montpelier and Roehampton. *Jamaica Journal* 8 (2–3): 40–45; Higman, B. W. 1988. *Jamaica Surveyed.* Kingston: Institute of Jamaica; Honychurch, L. 1983. *The Cabrits and Prince Rupert's Bay.* Roseau, Dominica: Dominica Institute; Hume, N. I. 1968. A Collection of Glass from Port Royal, Jamaica, with Some Observations on the Site, Its History, and Archaeology. *Historical Archaeology* 2: 5–34; Mathewson, R. D. 1972. Jamaican Ceramics: An Introduction to 18th-Century Folk Pottery in West African Tradition. *Jamaica Journal* 6: 54–56; Ohm, C. C. 1995. *Landscapes and Plantations on Tobago: A Regional Perspective.* Unpublished Ph.D. dissertation. Department of Anthropology, University of Florida, Gainesville, FL; Watters, D. R. 1980. Observations on the Historic Sites and Archaeology of Barbuda. *Archaeology and Anthropology* 3 (2): 125–154; Watters, D. R. 1994. Mortuary Patterns at the Harney Site Slave Cemetery, Montserrat in Caribbean Perspective. *Historical Archaeology* 28 (3): 56–73; Watters, D. R. 1997. Historical Documentation and Archaeological Investigation of Codrington Castle, Barbuda.

Annals of the Carnegie Museum 66 (3): 229–288; Weik, T. 1997. The Archaeology of Maroon Societies in the Americas: Resistance, Cultural Continuity, and Transformation in the African Disapora. *Historical Archaeology* 31 (2): 81–92; Wilkie, L. A. 1997. Secret and Sacred: Contextualizing the Artifacts of African-American Magic and Religion. *Historical Archaeology* 31 (4): 81–106; Yentsch, A. E., and M. C. Beaudry. 1992. *The Art and Mystery of Historical Archaeology: Essays in Honor of James Deetz.* Boca Raton, FL: CRC Press.

Hope Estate (site, St. Martin)

Hope Estate in northeastern St. Martin is one of the most important archaeological sites in the Lesser Antilles. It belongs to the Saladoid Period and has been dated to between ca. 400 B.C. and A.D. 650.

Investigations indicate several distinct and separate occupation phases, one belongs to the La Hueca Saladoid culture (or subseries) and is called Hope Estate 1. Its pottery typically has thin walls, appears as goblets, dishes, and jars with curving incised designs and lacks sophisticated painted decoration, although white paint is used to fill in the incisions and some vessels have a red slip. Both animal and human shapes decorate the pottery in the form of *adornos.* Ceramic cassava griddles are also present.

The second phase of occupation is known as Hope Estate 2 and belongs to the Cedrosan Saladoid culture (or subseries). This pottery is more robust than the La Hueca style, and has white-on-red (W-O-R) and polychrome painted decoration in typical Cedrosan Saladoid style. There are a variety of forms, including bowls of different shapes, so-called hallucinogen-snuffing vessels and ceramic cassava griddles. Both styles share the distinctive zoned-incised cross-hatched decorative technique known as zic ware.

Stone tools, such as axes and adzes, appear to have been made from local raw materials, notably tephrite, although chert was imported from elsewhere. Also imported were the typically favored exotic minerals of jadeite, amethyst, carnelian, and serpentine, which were used for manufacturing ceremonial items such as beads and amulets. These items arrived at the site already made, and probably were obtained through trade, exchange, or direct exploitation of sources, some of which may be on other Caribbean islands. For some minerals, long-distance trade with South America is a possibility. In both cases, extended canoe voyages would have been required.

Everyday life seems to have centered around the gathering of local shallow-water shellfish, especially West Indian Top Shell (*Cittarium pica*), which was cooked and eaten in a soup. The shell remains of various species were used to make scrapers and axes and also two unusual cups. Shell jewelry also was made, including beads and pendants and mother-of-pearl disks produced from the inner layers of oysters. More generally, the presence of the hardwood known as *Guaiacum officinale* suggests the possibility that the resin from this tree was employed in curing sexual diseases, as such a use is documented from early Spanish times. Five adult burials of the Cedrosan Saladoid culture were discovered, only one of which yielded any mortuary gifts. Dating to the period after A.D. 600, they came from a now partly destroyed cemetery and appear similar to those found at the Golden Rock site on St. Eustatius.

References
Haviser, J. B. 1991. Preliminary Results of Test Excavations at the Hope Estate Site (SM-026), St. Martin. *Proceedings of the International Congress for Caribbean Archaeology* 13: 647–666; Hofman, C. L., and M.L.P. Hoogland. (eds.). 1999. *Archaeological Investigations on St. Martin (Lesser Antilles)*, pp. 129–250. Archaeological Studies Leiden University 4. Leiden, the Netherlands; Wing, E. S. 1995. Rice Rats and Saladoid People as Seen at Hope Estate. *Proceedings of the Fifteenth International Congress for the Study of Pre-Columbian Cultures of the Lesser Antilles*, pp. 219–232.

Hueca, La (Puerto Rico)

La Hueca culture has been identified from the archaeological remains of two sites in Puerto Rico—Sorcé on the southern side of Vieques Island and Punta Candelero (possibly founded by the former) on the mainland opposite. It appears to have been a local variation (also called subseries) of the Saladoid tradition. La Hueca culture flourished between around 160 B.C. and A.D. 500.

The material culture of Sorcé and Punta Candelero appears sufficiently different from that of the similarly Saladoid and generally contemporary Hacienda Grande people to warrant a distinct identity (i.e., La Hueca). At both sites were found typically Saladoid three-pointer *zemís*, stone pendants, small ornaments and jewelry of shell, mother-of-pearl and greenstone. La Hueca pottery includes so-called hallucinogen-snuffing vessels and zic (zone-incised cross-hatching) ware. La Hueca artisans did not paint their ceramics but instead rubbed white or red paint onto the zic designs, which they extended to cover areas usually painted in Saladoid pottery.

Another distinctive feature of La Hueca material culture is the distinctive carved-stone bird-head pendants that were apparently made at Punta Candelero and that appear similar to avian imagery on Barrancoid pottery. The Orinoco source of Barrancoid pottery suggests long-distance island-hopping canoe travel, and it is thought that Sorcé may have been a port of trade, strategically located at the entrance to the Greater Antilles. The relationships between the La Hueca and Hacienda Grande cultures are problematical, however; while dates from Punta Candelero are later than early Hacienda Grande dates, at Sorcé the La Hueca people seem to have been followed by a period of Hacienda Grande occupation.

References
Chanlatte Baik, L. A. 1981. *La Hueca y Sorcé (Vieques, Puerto Rico): Primeras migraciones agroalfereras Antillanas—Nuevo esquema para los procesos culturales de la arqueología Antillana.* Santo Domingo, the Dominican Republic; Chanlatte Baik, L. A. 1983. *Catálogo arqueología de Vieques: Exposición del 13 del Marzo al 22 de Abril de 1983.* Río Pedras: Museo de Antropología, Historia y Arte, Universidad de Puerto Rico; Narganes Storde, Y. M. 1991. Secuencia cronológica de dos sitios arqueólogicos de Puerto Rico (Sorcé, Vieques y Tecla, Guayanilla). *Proceedings of the*

Thirteenth International Congress for Caribbean Archaeology Held at Willemstadt, Curaçao, on July 24–29, 1989, pp. 628–646. Willemstadt; Oliver, J. 1999. The "La Hueca Problem" in Puerto Rico and the Caribbean: Old Problems, New Perspectives, Possible Solutions. In C. L. Hofman and M.L.P. Hoogland (eds.). 1999. *Archaeological Investigations on St. Martin (Lesser Antilles),* pp. 253–297. Archaeological Studies Leiden University 4. Leiden, the Netherlands; Rodríguez, M. 1991. Arqueología de Punta Candelero, Puerto Rico. *Proceedings of the Thirteenth International Congress for Caribbean Archaeology Held at Willemstadt, Curaçao, on July 24–29, 1989,* pp. 605–627. Willemstadt.

I

Igneri

Igneri is a name sometimes applied to the Saladoid peoples. Whereas Saladoid is now an accepted term among archaeologists to describe the first pottery-using horticulturalists to enter the Island Caribbean, the name Igneri comes from the ethnography of the Lesser Antilles.

Caribs from mainland South America entered the Lesser Antilles in the years immediately preceding European arrival. Calling themselves Kalina, scholars now refer to them as Island Caribs to avoid confusion with those who live on the mainland. The Island Caribs settled in Guadeloupe and Martinique and told Europeans that when they arrived they had conquered an ethnic group called the Igneri whose name they adopted. The newcomers were essentially group of marauding warriors who killed or expelled the Igneri men from their homelands and took their women as wives. They were able to impose some aspects of their culture on the Igneri such as the practice of the men living together in a men's house. While the men engaged in long-distance canoe trade, the women practiced the traditional Igneri form of agriculture and worshipped household *zemís*. Today, many linguists refer to the Island Carib language as Igneri.

See also: Caribs; Guadeloupe; Martinique; Saladoid
References
Rouse, I. 1992. *The Tainos: Rise and Decline of the People Who Greeted Columbus,* pp. 21–25. New Haven, CT: Yale University Press.

Indian Creek (site, Antigua)

Indian Creek is an archaeological site located in the southeastern corner of Antigua, along a small stream and some 800 meters from the sea. First discovered in 1956, it is made up of a ring of middens with a small central plaza that may have been a dance- or ballcourt.

The earliest evidence for prehistoric settlement belongs to the late Saladoid age known locally as the Indian Creek Period (A.D. 1 to A.D. 600). During this time, both white-on-red (W-O-R) and zic (zone-incised cross-hatching) pottery is present, with white geometric and spiral designs painted on a dark red background. Some cylindrical vessels may have been incense burners, while others are the remains of cassava-baking griddles. Many tools are made from seashells, especially Queen Conch (*Strombus gigas*), as are three-pointer *zemí* pieces, while cowrie shells have been made into decorative beads.

The next phase of Indian Creek's occupation was the Mill Reef Period (600 to 900), named after the local site of that name and which belongs to the early Troumassoid age. Zic pottery disappears and only W-O-R remains, though it is thicker and much coarser than before. Barrancoid influence from South America may account for new rectilinear incised designs. From these occupation levels have come a carved manatee bone and frog carved from conch shell.

Indian Creek's last inhabitants flourished between 900 and 1100 in the Mamora Bay Period. By this time, the quality of the site's pottery had declined even further, with bowls and jars being thick and poorly fired. Scratching and scoring are the main decorative techniques. Conch shell continues to be the preferred material for making tools, although a beautiful mask/face was also made from this material. Several three-pointers were found from this period as well as olive shell ornaments. Antigua appears to have been abandoned some time after 1100 and had no indigenous population at the time of the European arrival in 1492.

> *See also:* Antigua; Troumassoid; White-on-Red (W-O-R) Pottery; Zemís; Zic Pottery
> **References**
> Jones, A. R. 1985. Dietary Change and Human Population at Indian Creek, Antigua. *American Antiquity* 50 (3): 518–536; Rouse, I. 1974. The Indian Creek Excavations. *Proceedings of the Fifth International Congress for the Study of Pre-Columbian Cultures of the Lesser Antilles, Antigua, July 22–28, 1973,* pp. 166–176; Rouse, I., and B. Faber Morse. 1999. Excavations at the Indian Creek Site, Antigua, West Indies. *Yale University Publications in Anthropology* No. 82. New Haven, CT.

Indian Warner

Thomas "Indian" Warner (1657–1676) was, according to some accounts, the son of Sir Thomas Warner, governor of St. Kitts, and a Carib woman. The uncertainty and scandal that surrounded his life and death places him in the position of many unacknowledged individuals who lived between two worlds in the early days of contact and colonization in the Americas. Such people have been seen variously as traitors, intermediaries, and intercultural agents, their often ambiguous attitudes toward Europeans inevitably attracting exaggerations and legends in accounts of their extraordinary lives.

Despised by his contemporaries because of his mixed parentage, Indian Warner apparently went to live with the Caribs of Dominica. With his brown skin and black hair, he was accepted and rose to a position of some influence. Lord Willoughby, governor of Dominica, considered Warner useful in bringing the island's Caribs over to the British side in the conflicts with France. In 1668 he gave Warner a commission and Warner seems to have had some success, as the commission was renewed after Willoughby's death. However, suspicions were gathering. Warner is reported to have been ambiguous in his attitudes toward Carib raids on English Antigua, and perhaps to be growing too close to the French.

Philip Warner, Indian Warner's legitimate white half-brother, commanded a party of English soldiers that was sent to Dominica in response to the attack on Antigua. Philip feigned affection for his brother but, after getting him and his Carib companions drunk, ordered his soldiers to kill them all. Philip Warner was sent to England and imprisoned in the Tower of London but was subsequently shipped to Barbados and acquitted.

See also: Caribs

References

Hulme, P., and N. L. Whitehead. 1992. *Wild Majesty: Encounters with Caribs from Columbus to the Present Day,* pp. 89–106. Oxford: Clarendon Press.

J

Jamaica

Jamaica is 235 km long and 82 km at its widest point, with an area of 10,992 sq km. The majority of the 2.5 million inhabitants are of West African descent, with the balance being of Chinese, East Indian, and British origin.

Jamaica was first settled in prehistoric times by Ostionoid peoples who, as part of their colonization of the Greater Antilles, introduced pottery sometime around A.D. 500. This was the foundation from which emerged the subsequent Meillacan culture, known in its local variations from Hispaniola and Cuba as well as Jamaica. The Jamaican variant, called White Marl, appears to have colonized the whole island and lasted into historic times, forming the base of the Taíno culture that watched Christopher Columbus land for the first time in 1494.

Spanish occupation began in 1509 at the site Sevilla la Nueva (New Seville) by St. Ann's Bay on Jamaica's north coast at the spot where Columbus had been stranded for a year during his fourth voyage in June 1503. This site was adjacent to a large Taíno village. During Spanish rule, Jamaica was always an economic backwater, and, having no gold, was used as a point of transshipment in the slave trade. As the Amerindian labor force declined through mistreatment and disease, it was replaced with imported African slaves. In 1655, an English force arrived and effectively took over the island, the Spanish finally leaving altogether a few years later. During this time the African slaves and their descendants joined the remnants of the Taíno in the mountains where, becoming known as Maroons, they established the villages of Accompong in the west and Nanny Town in the east, from where they fought the English until 1795.

During the early years of English rule, Jamaica's great sugar plantations were established and the island also became a refuge for pirates. Port Royal on the south coast was the lair of the buccaneer Henry Morgan until it was destroyed by an earthquake in 1692. The disaster killed around 5,000 people. The site was then rebuilt to serve as a base for the Royal Navy, and today remains of that time still survive. The Port Royal site also houses Jamaica's Archaeological Museum in which are kept many of the objects retrieved by underwater archaeologists from the now-sunken early port.

The remains of the great sugar estates form an important part of Jamaica's historical and archaeological heritage. Jamaica had probably the highest percentage of slaves working in large plantations in the Americas. It is thus easy to understand how, during the eighteenth and nineteenth centuries, the plantation was a dominant institution in Jamaican society. One of the best known estates archaeologically is Drax Hall founded in 1699 by William Drax near St. Ann's Bay. Its excavation during the 1980s provided detailed insights into the lives of the slaves who lived, worked, and died there, and also revealed the changes that took place after the abolition of slavery in 1807 (enacted in 1838). The Drax Hall story was repeated across Jamaica in varying degrees.

Jamaica gained its independence from Britain in 1962 and became a member of the British Commonwealth. Today, Jamaica's prehistoric archaeological and colonial period heritage is administered by the Jamaica National Heritage Trust based in Kingston. The Trust looks after the old Great Houses of the previous plantation owners, and the remains at Port Royal and St. Ann's Bay. The mid-eighteenth-century Gordon House in Kingston is now the Jamaican legislature, and Jamaica House is the official residence of the prime minister. Not far from Kingston is Spanish Town, the island's first capital founded in 1534. The town is in part a time capsule of eighteenth-century English architecture, with a Georgian main square, the House of Assembly, and the 1714 Cathedral Church of St. James, the oldest in the English-speaking Caribbean. Jamaican colonial history is represented in the museum at Spanish Town and its prehistoric heritage at the White Marl Arawak Museum just outside town.

In popular imagination, Jamaican culture is dominated by reggae, a musical style made famous internationally by Jamaica's first superstar, Bob Marley. Blending African rhythms and electronic music with lyrics of social comment, reggae is strongly associated with Rastafarianism—the Jamaican religion that regards the late emperor of Ethiopia, Haile Selassie or Ras Tafari, as divine. Rastafarians wear their hair in long dreadlocks, often smoke cannabis (ganja), avoid pork, and believe that God (Jah) will lead black people to the promised land of Zion. While Carnival is a recent introduction to Jamaica, there is an annual reggae festival called Sun Splash.

Despite the high profile of Rastafarianism, today most Jamaicans are Protestants of the Anglican, Baptist, and Methodist varieties, to mention just a few. Roman Catholics, Muslims, Jews, and Hindus all practice their faiths in the modern Jamaica. In the countryside especially, there is also an underlying folk belief in Obeah, the Jamaican variant of Haitian Voudon. Mixing African, Christian, and possibly also Taíno influences, Obeah beliefs see the world as animated by spiritual forces. During the nineteenth century, the descendants of African slaves believed that ceiba (or silk-cotton) trees gathered together after sunset; even today the ceiba is commonly called the God Tree and is associated with *duppies,* or ghosts.

See also: Drax Hall (site, Jamaica); Maroons; New Seville (site, Jamaica); Obeah; Paradise Park (site, Jamaica); Port Royal (Jamaica); Rastafarianism; Slavery; Sugar; Taíno (Arawak); Trees, Spiritual Importance of

References

Alleyne, M. C. 1988. *Roots of Jamaican Culture.* London: Pluto Press; D. V. Armstrong, 1990. *The Old Village and the Great House: An Archaeological and Historical Examination of Drax Hall*

Plantation, St. Ann's Bay Jamaica. Urbana, IL: University of Illinois Press; Barrett, L. 1977. *The Rastafarians: The Dreadlocks of Jamaica*. Boston: Beacon Press; Beckwith, M. W. 1929. *Black Roadways: A Study of Jamaican Folk Life*. Chapel Hill, NC: University of North Carolina Press; Campbell, M. C. 1990. *The Maroons of Jamaica 1655–1796*. Trenton, NJ: Africa World Press Inc.; Dance, D. C. 1985. *Folklore from Contemporary Jamaicans*. Knoxville, TN: University of Tennessee Press; Davis, S., and P. Simon. 1977. *Reggae Bloodlines: In Search of the Music and Culture of Jamaica*. London: Heineman Educational; Jahn, B., and T. Weber. 1998. *Reggae sland: Jamaican Music in the Digital Age*. New York: Da Capo Press; Marx, R. F. 1973. *Port Royal Rediscovered*. New York: Doubleday; Mordecai, M., and P. Mordecai. 2000. *Culture and Customs of Jamaica*. Greenwood Publishing Group; Zahedieh, N. 1986. Trade, Plunder, and Economic Development in Early English Jamaica, 1655–1689. *Economic History Review* 4 (2): 205–222;

Jolly Beach (site, Antigua)

Jolly Beach is the site of a flint workshop on a small island off the northern coast of Antigua. It belongs to the Archaic Period (5000 B.C. to 2000 B.C.), and its tools are identified as similar to those of the Casimiroid tradition (4000 B.C. to 400 B.C.). By definition, Jolly Beach is preceramic and is one of perhaps forty similarly Archaic Period sites on the island.

The stone artifacts are mainly flakes struck from pebbles and blades made from prepared flint cores. Some ground-stone artifacts were also found, alongside manos and metates, net sinkers, a conical pestle, and simple beads and pendants. Other typical tools are celts made from conch shell. The other Antiguan sites of this period are unlike Jolly beach inasmuch as they are shell middens, reflecting the suitability of this part of the island for fishing and collecting shellfish.

See also: Archaic Period; Casimiroid

References
Davis, D. 1982. Archaic Settlement and Resource Exploitation in the Lesser Antilles: Preliminary Information from Antigua. *Caribbean Journal of Science* 17: 107–122; Davis, D. 1993. Archaic Blade Production on Antigua, West Indies. *American Antiquity* 58: 37–48; Davis, D. 2000. Jolly Beach and the Preceramic Occupation of Antigua, West Indies. *Yale University Publications in Anthropology* 84. New Haven, CT: Yale University Press; Rouse, I. 1992. *The Tainos: Rise and Decline of the People Who Greeted Columbus,* p 65. New Haven, CT: Yale University Press.

Jolly John

Thomas Jolly John was the chief of the Dominican Caribs during the so-called Carib War of 1930. After unrest at the Carib settlement of Salybia during which police officers shot and fatally wounded two Caribs, Jolly John was arrested in the island's capital of Roseau and later charged with wounding police officers and retrieving smuggled goods from them. The trial took place in 1931; however, the prosecution case collapsed and all Caribs concerned were acquitted.

Despite this legal victory, E. C. Eliot, the British administrator of Dominica, refused to reinstate Jolly John as chief, holding him responsible for the two deaths. There followed an official investigation into the conditions of the Carib Reserve on Dominica and the incident. This was published in 1932 and recommended that the reserve be maintained but that Jolly John was wholly unfit to be chief, as he had no influence over the Carib people. The report nevertheless advised that Jolly John should be replaced by a chief elected by the Caribs and that he should work with a government-appointed officer whose duty it would be to look after the Carib people. In fact, the post of chief was suspended in 1931 and only reactivated in 1952.

See also: Caribs; Dominica

References

Hulme, P., and N. L. Whitehead (eds.). 1992. *Wild Majesty: Encounters with Caribs from Columbus to the Present Day,* pp. 283–285, 291–293. Oxford: Oxford University Press.

K

Kalinago / Kalina

Kalinago is the name often given to the Caribs inhabiting the Windward Islands when Europeans arrived in order to differentiate them from the mainland Caribs of South America, the Kalina or Kariña. The Kalinago regarded themselves as Caribs; hence the similarity of names. Originally, they had lived in the coastal area of the Guianas and in eastern coastal Venezuela, and it is from one, or perhaps both, of these areas that some Kalina traveled north to become the Kalinago.

The Kalinago language seems to have belonged to the same Arawakan linguistic family as did the Taíno language. Somewhat confusingly, this bears no relationship to the Cariban linguistic family spoken by South American Caribs (Kalina). The seafaring Kalinago Carib men had a "men-only" language used when they gathered together in the men's house. This seems to have been a mix of their own Arawakan tongue spiced with Cariban words borrowed from their South American Kalina trading partners—in other words, a difference of gender and status rather than of pure linguistics.

See also: Caribs; Igneri; Languages

Key Marco (site, Florida, USA)

Key Marco is one of the Americas' most important archaeological sites. Situated in southwest Florida, it was discovered by Frank Hamilton Cushing in 1895. The waterlogged nature of the site preserved some of the most astonishing wooden artifacts ever discovered in the Americas.

Cushing's expedition to the low-lying coastal mangrove region of Marco Island excavated the area misleadingly called the Court of the Pile Dwellers. Shell middens dominate the area, but the court appears to have been artificially made and associated with a canal. When the site was drained, the mud had preserved many exquisite wood items, as well as innumerable artifacts of shell, stone, and bone. Particularly notable wooden objects included eight complete anthropomorphic masks to which Cushing gave such memorable names as Pelican Man and Hawksbill Turtle Man; zoomorphic figureheads of a pelican, turtle, deer, and wolf; and a beautiful kneeling anthropomorphic feline—

Cushing's Panther Man (shaman?). Birds, snakes, spearthrowers (atlatls), and wooden stools were also recovered.

The presence of many ceremonial items suggests this was a ceremonial site rather than a political center. No stratigraphy and incomplete excavation makes it impossible to date the beginnings of the site, though the absence of European artifacts indicates a late-fifteenth-century date for its unexplained abandonment and suggests it was built by the Calusa people who occupied the area when Europeans arrived. The wetland nature of Key Marco on Florida's Caribbean coast makes it a valuable comparison for the Taíno sites of Los Buchillones (Cuba) and La Aleta (Dominican Republic).

See also: La Aleta (site, Dominican Republic); Los Buchillones (site, Cuba); Underwater Archaeology

References

Cushing, F. H. 1897. Exploration of Ancient Key Dwellers' Remains on the Gulf Coast of Florida. *Proceedings of the American Philosophical Society* 25 (153): 329–448; Gilliland, M. 1989a. *Key Marco's Buried Treasure: Archaeology and Adventure in the Nineteenth Century.* Gainesville, FL: University Press of Florida; Gilliland, M. 1989b. *The Material Culture of Key Marco, Florida.* Gainesville, FL: University Press of Florida; Milanich, J. T. 1994. *Archaeology of Precolumbian Florida.* Gainesville, FL: University Press of Florida; Purdy, B. A. 1996. *Indian Art of Ancient Florida.* Gainesville, FL: University Press of Florida.

Krum Bay (site, St. Thomas)

The Archaic Period site of Krum Bay on the island of St. Thomas (USVI) is one the most unusual and best-documented archaeological sites of this early stage of human occupation in the Island Caribbean.

The site has been dated to between ca. 880 B.C. and 225 B.C., and has given its name to the local culture of that time. Krum Bay culture settlements are located near either the sea or mangrove swamps, and so far appear only to have been open-air sites. They are small shell middens, within which are found basic stone tools and chipped-stone celts (axes), as well as roughly fashioned jewelry in the form of pendants made either from stone, bone, or shell. A typical stone tool is the edge-grinder, with its distinctive facets along the edges rather than over the surface. Sometimes the Krum Bay people buried their dead within these middens, though whether this was for practical or spiritual reasons (or both) is not known. Krum Bay inhabitants relied on the sea for their food and raw materials, and their occupation seems to have been short-lived and intermittent.

The Krum Bay culture is one of two that belong to the so-called Ortoiroid tradition, the other being the Coroso culture of Puerto Rico. The main difference between these two contemporary groups is that for reasons as yet unexplained, the Coroso people inhabited caves as well as open-air sites.

See also: Archaic Period; Ortoiroid; St. Thomas (USVI)

References

Bullen, R. P. 1973. Krum Bay, a Preceramic Workshop on St Thomas. *Proceedings of the Fourth International Congress for the Study of Pre-Columbian Cultures of the Lesser Antilles, St. Lucia 1971,* pp.

10–114; Lundberg, E. R. 1985. Interpreting the Cultural Associations of Aceramic Deposits in the Virgin Islands. *Journal of Field Archaeology* 12: 201–212; Lundberg, E. R. 1989. *Preceramic Procurement Patterns at Krum Bay, Virgin Islands.* Ph.D. dissertation, University of Illinois, Urbana; Rouse, I. 1992, *The Tainos: Rise and Decline of the People Who Greeted Columbus,* pp. 62–68. New Haven, CT: Yale University Press.

L

La Aleta (site, Dominican Republic)

La Aleta is a Taíno site in the southeastern Dominican Republic (the eastern half of Hispaniola), within which a flooded cavern is known as the Mantanial de la Aleta (Spring of the Fin). The site dates to between A.D. 1035 and A.D. 1420. The watery conditions and anoxic environment of the cavern have preserved such normally fragile items as basketry, gourds, and carved-wood artifacts. Perhaps due to the presence of the cavern, La Aleta appears to have been a ritual and ceremonial center rather than a heavily populated town, an impression reinforced by the presence of four ceremonial plazas.

La Aleta is located in an area of limestone (karst) geology in the territory of the conquest-period Taíno chiefdom of Higüey. It is one of many cave sites in this part of the island, and only one of a handful that have been investigated. Most such sites are dry caves used by the Taíno to bury their dead, decorate the walls with paintings and carvings (petroglyphs), and perhaps contact ancestral spirits. As with other Amerindian peoples, the Taíno considered caves as entrances to the watery underworld, which for them was known as *coaybay,* the "house of the dead." Caves featured prominently in Taíno cosmogonic myths as places of emergence and as the homes of the spirits of the dead—the *opía*—who transformed into bats and flew out of their cave-roosts at night to feed on guava fruit. It is thought that La Aleta's cavern may have been visited by the Spanish chronicler Bartolomé de Las Casas during his participation in the conquest of the region in 1503 and mentioned in his early writings.

The cavern features an underwater hill at a depth of about 35 meters, upon which are scattered well-preserved stone tools, pottery, wooden items, and baskets. Archaeologists believe that these cultural materials were deliberately and carefully placed here as offerings to gods and ancestral spirits. The wooden items include a small *duho,* decorated bowls, several hafts for holding axe-heads, a *macana* (war club), and fragments of a canoe paddle and crocodile figurine. One small bowl has been interpreted as being associated with the *cohoba* ritual where participants snuffed hallucinogenic powder to enter a trance and contact the spirits. An integral part of Taíno cohoba ceremonies was ritual vomiting, perhaps as an act of purifying the body for its possession by spirits. As an aid to this act of ritual cleansing, the Taíno made so-called vomiting spatulas from shell, bone, and wood—

an example of the latter also being found at La Aleta. Gourd vessels are some of the most frequently found items in La Aleta's watery cavern and so far are unique; one example is decorated with Taíno designs typical of their Chican Ostionoid pottery. Also unique are the fragments of Taíno basketry that have been retrieved.

Pottery finds include elaborate adorno imagery of a turtle possibly associated with Taíno mythology, and another whose handles take the form of bats. It seems likely that some of these ceramics came from beyond La Aleta itself, suggesting that the cavern's religious importance may also have had a wider political dimension. Also found were the seeds of the guácima tree (*Guazuma ulmifolia*) that is a source of food and medicine. The Mantanial de la Aleta may well have had more than local significance and be intricately embedded as a sacred place in Taíno mythology and political ideology. Unlike many other similar but smaller caves, such as the Cueva de Chico, La Aleta was clearly much more than a source of the cool, sweet water that so impressed Las Casas.

See also: Dominican Republic; Duhos; Los Buchillones (site, Cuba); Taíno (Arawak); Trees, Spiritual Importance of:; Underwater Archaeology; Zemís

References

Arévalo, M. G., and L. A. Chanlatte Baik. 1976. *Las espátulas vómicas sonajeras de la cultura Taína.* Santo Domingo, the Dominican Republic: Fundación García Aravalo; Beeker, C. D., G. W. Conrad, and J. W. Foster. 2002. Taíno Use of Flooded Caverns in the East National Park Region, Dominican Republic. *Journal of Caribbean Archaeology* 3: 1–26; Conrad, G. W., J. W. Foster, and C. D. Beeker. 2001. Organic Artifacts from the Manantial de la Aleta, Dominican Republic: Preliminary Observations and Interpretations. *Journal of Caribbean Archaeology* 2: 1–20; Conrad, G. W., J. Foster, C. Beeker, L. Uhls, M. Brauner, M. Veloz Maggiolo, and E. Ortega. 1997. Images of Conquest. *Archaeology* July/August: 60–61; Foster, J. W., and C. D. Beeker. 1997. The Conquest of a Sinkhole: Initial Archaeological Investigations at El Manantial de la Aleta, East National Park, Dominican Republic. *Underwater Archaeology* pp. 27–32.

La Isabela (site, Dominican Republic)

La Isabela was the first permanent European settlement in the Americas. It was founded on 6 January 1494 during Christopher Columbus's second voyage to the Americas (1493 to 1496) after he discovered that the small wooden fort of La Navidad he had left behind during his first voyage earlier that year had been destroyed and its garrison killed. Named for the queen of Spain, La Isabela was built on that part of the northern coast of Hispaniola that is today the Dominican Republic. It was the site of historically important interactions between Europeans and the indigenous Taíno peoples for five years before it was abandoned.

Recently, ten years of scientific research led by the archaeologists K. A. Deagan and J. M. Cruxent have revealed a wealth of information about La Isabela. Excavations have brought to light the material culture of everyday life such as coins, merchants' weights, colorful majolica ceramics, fragments of Spanish armor, and items of jewelry from glass bracelets to finger rings. More substantial remains included a metalworking furnace, and a pottery kiln displaying Spanish-Moorish influence. The town's stone-built buildings, the

Excavation of La
Isabela, founded by
Columbus on
Hispaniola in 1493
(Jim Sugar / Corbis)

only surviving remnants of fifteenth-century architecture in the Americas, were also investigated. Christopher Columbus's fortified house and associated watchtower were explored, as was the church and its adjacent cemetery. The latter revealed a mix of European bodies simply buried in a shroud together with the remains of local Taíno Amerindians. What was important about these investigations was that apart from bringing to light evidence from the historical site itself, new light was cast on the nature of early European colonialism in the process of formation.

The location was a rocky promontory, chosen for its proximity to the local Bahabon-ico River, cultivable land, abundance of fish, and strategic position on Amerindian routes to the supposedly gold-rich interior of the island. In 1987, a similar fifteenth-century site was located nearby that is known as Las Coles. This may be the site referred to by the contemporary chronicler Dr. Chanca as Cuidad Marta, and suggests that the Spanish settlement known as La Isabela was in reality at least two separate locations, separated by a limestone quarry useful as a source of building materials. The passengers of the seventeen ships of the second voyage populated the town with builders, craftsmen, farmers, and priests, as well as soldiers and sailors. To impress civil order on the settlement a town council (*cabildo*) was also established. The layout of the town reflected Spanish urban traditions, with a central plaza, a stone-built church, a barracks, a house for Columbus himself, a storehouse, and some 200 thatch-roofed houses for the inhabitants.

Despite the best intentions and efforts of the Spanish, La Isabela seemed doomed almost from the beginning. This was because it was based mainly on the idea of a Spanish settlement transplanted across the Atlantic rather than a rethinking of ideas based on different environmental conditions (notably hurricanes), the availability (or not) of local resources, and a (then) numerous indigenous Taíno population increasingly antagonized by the depredations of the settlers. The townspeople soon began to fall prey to disease, probably including dysentery, influenza, and perhaps syphilis, as well as exhaustion and food shortages. The Taíno, bullied and forced into working for the Spanish, began to rebel and soon many Spanish colonizers began to mutiny. When Columbus returned to the town at the end of March 1494, after an expedition into the interior, he found more settlers had died from illness and two-thirds of the buildings had been destroyed by fire. The efforts required to start rebuilding did nothing to improve the temper of the remaining colonists.

Columbus then left on another expedition, this time to explore Cuba and Jamaica, during which time his brother Bartolomé arrived with much-needed food for the town. His ships, however, were commandeered by many disgruntled colonists, including the influential Pedro de Margarite, who sailed to Spain and started spreading rumors about Columbus's mismanagement and high-handed behavior. The remaining settlers were further angered when Columbus, who was ill on his return and remained so for several months, appointed his brother *adelantado* (governor)—accusing him of nepotism.

In the winter of 1494, a relief fleet arrived under Antonio de Torres, and La Isabela's inhabitants enjoyed the fruits of new supplies of food, wine, medicine, and clothing. Another military expedition against the increasingly hostile Taíno saw Columbus bring some 1,600 Amerindians back to La Isabela as slaves, from where over 500 were taken back to Spain on the returning relief fleet, accompanied by yet more dissatisfied colonists. In June of the following year, La Isabela suffered a hurricane that sank four ships moored at anchor, and the town saw the construction of the first European ship built in the Americas from the salvaged remains of the wrecks. Nevertheless, by 1595, just over a year after its foundation, the original population of around 1,700 men (a figure that included ships' crews, some of whom had already departed by February 1494) had fallen to some 630. A year later it was 300 people.

During October 1495, Juan de Aguado arrived from Spain with royal orders to investigate the way Christopher Columbus was running the island. He interviewed those inhabitants of La Isabela who were not healthy enough to be out fighting the Taíno or searching for gold and found them not surprisingly highly critical of the admiral. Columbus decided yet again to return to Spain and defend himself but another hurricane kept both him and Aguado trapped in La Isabela while new ships were built. The fleet finally left in March 1496, leaving the island under the governorship of Bartolomé Columbus, and La Isabela under the control of Francisco de Roldán as chief magistrate. It appears that even before he departed, Christopher Columbus had given much thought to moving the town.

In July 1496, another fleet arrived at La Isabela with news that sounded the death knell of the town. Apart from much-needed supplies, Peralonso Niño, the fleet's commander, brought royally approved letters from Columbus giving Bartolomé permission to found a new settlement near the gold mines at Santo Domingo on the south coast and to abandon La Isabela. This took place throughout the remainder of the year, though by 1497 there was still a reduced population at La Isabela. These unfortunate inhabitants continued to suffer from illness and food shortages that together killed perhaps some 300 individuals by the time Bartolomé returned from the south in early 1497. In May of that year, Roldán led an uprising against the Columbus brothers, seizing supplies, killing Spanish livestock, and forcing Diego Columbus, who had been left in charge, to take refuge in his elder brother's fortified stone-built house. Roldán and perhaps seventy supporters then roamed the countryside of Hispaniola attracting more disillusioned settlers to his side by promises of women, food, and gold instead of the hardships they had experienced under Columbus.

By the end of 1497, these events and the progress made in building Santo Domingo combined to see the final abandonment of La Isabela. From 1498 onward, ships from Spain bypassed the town and headed straight for Santo Domingo. Although left in ruins, La Isabela's buildings were not forgotten. In fact, such was the miserable folk memory of the site that the belief grew up that it was haunted by the ghosts of all those who had suffered and died during its brief life. Some thirty years after it had been abandoned, the chronicler and theologian Bartolomé de Las Casas reused some of the building stone to construct the Franciscan *convento* at nearby Puerto Plata, initiating a practice that continued into the nineteenth century. Throughout this period, La Isabela's location and ruined buildings nevertheless proved attractive to both smugglers and fishermen. Famous English sea rovers such as John Hawkins and Sir Richard Grenville engaged in illicit activities there during the sixteenth century. In the early part of the twentieth century the small fishing village of El Castillo was established at the site. Today, the old sea-facing plaza area has been designated a national park.

See also: Columbus, Christopher; Dominican Republic; Guacanagarí (Taíno chief); Guarionex (Taíno chief); La Navidad/En Bas Saline (site, Haiti); Puerto Real (site, Haiti); Taíno (Arawak)

References
Chiarelli, B. 1987. La Isabela. (Special issue). *International Journal of Anthropology* 2 (3):195–253; Deagan, K. A. 1992. La Isabela, Foothold in the New World. *National Geographic* 181 (1): 40–53; Deagan, K. A. 1995. *Puerto Real: The Archaeology of a Sixteenth-Century Spanish Town in Hispaniola,* Gainesville, FL: University Press of Florida; Deagan, K. A., and J. M. Cruxent. 2002a. *Archaeology at La Isabela: America's First European Town.* New Haven, CT: Yale University Press; Deagan, K. A., and J. M. Cruxent. 2002b. *Columbus's Outpost among the Taínos: Spain and America at La Isabela, 1493–1498.* New Haven, CT: Yale University Press; Ortega, E., and J. Guerrero. 1988. *La Isabela y la arqueología en la ruta de Colón.* San Pedro de Macorís, Dominican Republic: Universidad Central de Este.

La Navidad/En Bas Saline (site, Haiti)

La Navidad, located on the north coast of Hispaniola near Cap Haïtien (in present day Haiti), was the first European settlement in the Americas. It was here on Christmas Eve 1492 that Christopher Columbus's flagship the *Santa Maria* grounded on a coral reef. On Christmas Day, the Spanish salvaged the cargo with the help of a Taíno chief named Guacanagarí and his people, whose village was less than 2 km away. The rescued supplies were stored in two buildings that the chief made available to the Spanish.

While enjoying Guacanagarí's hospitality for several weeks, Columbus exchanged gifts with the Taíno chief, though it is doubtful that either party realized the significance of this for the other. Notably, Columbus gave Guacanagarí a necklace of glass beads and a woolen cape in exchange for a golden crown. It was during several such meetings that Columbus heard of Cibao, a land rich in gold in the center of the island.

Probably unable to fit all his men onto the two remaining ships, the *Niña* and *Pinta,* and doubtless wishing to discover the source of Guacanagarí's gold, Columbus left thirty-nine men behind when he sailed for Spain in early 1493. The *Santa Maria* was stripped of much its timber planking, and this was used to build a small fortress near, or perhaps adjacent, to the Taíno village. These first settlers were given food, a boat, and orders to search for gold.

When Columbus returned on his second voyage in November of the same year, the fort had been burned, his men killed, and their supplies scattered among the local inhabitants in the surrounding area. Various stories circulated: that the Spanish had argued among themselves, that they had died of disease, and that their behavior toward the Taíno—lusting after their women and gold artifacts—had led to their killing. Columbus interrogated Guacanagarí, who at first prevaricated and then blamed other, more powerful Taíno chiefs, notably Caonabo, accusing them of having attacked and killed the Spanish. Columbus appears to have believed Guacanagarí's story.

Today, some scholars believe that the large archaeological site of En Bas Saline is the location of Guacanagarí's village. Certainly, excavations have revealed Chican Ostionoid (Taíno) artifacts and burials dated to the last period of aboriginal occupation. The presence of Spanish trade goods reinforces the identification. However, there has been no definitive identification of the site of La Navidad itself though Caille Brûlee, on the shore near Cap Haïtien, has been recently suggested.

See also: Columbus, Christopher; Guacanagarí (Taíno chief); La Isabela (site, Dominican Republic); Taíno (Arawak)

References
Deagan, K. A. 1987. Columbus's Lost Colony. *National Geographic* 172 (5): 672–675; Deagan, K. A. 1988. The Archaeology of the Spanish Contact Period in the Caribbean. *Journal of World Prehistory* 2 (2): 187–225; Deagan, K. A. 1989. The Search for La Navidad, Columbus's 1492 Settlement. In J. T. Milanich and S. Millbrath (eds.). *First Encounters.* Gainesville, FL: University Press of Florida; Deagan, K. A., and J. M. Cruxent. 2002. *Columbus's Outpost among the Taínos: Spain and America at La Isabela, 1493–1498.* New Haven, CT: Yale University Press; Fuson, R. E. 1987. *The Log of Christopher Columbus.* Camden, London: International Marine Publishing; Hodges, W. H. 1983. *The Search for La Navidad: Further Inquiry.* Unpublished manuscript. Musée de Guahabá, Limbé; Morrison, S. E. 1940. The Route of Columbus along the North Coast of Haiti and the Site of La Navidad. *Transactions of the American Philosophical Society* 31 (4): 239–385.

La Sorcé (site, Vieques, Puerto Rico)

La Sorcé is a Saladoid site on the offshore island of Vieques, Puerto Rico. Together with the mainland Puerto Rican site of Punta Candelero, La Sorcé has been regarded as representing a subseries of the Saladoid, known as Huecan Saladoid (160 B.C. to A.D. 500), though some archaeologists regard them as having arrived before the Saladoids and directly from the eastern Andes in South America.

The ceramics from this site lack the white-on-red (W-O-R) painted pottery so typical of the Saladoid, but does have the other main component, zic (zone-incised cross-hatching) ware. On Vieques, potters rubbed white or red paint into the typical zic incisions. Pottery at La Sorcé also displays influence of the later Barrancoid peoples (around A.D. 500), and the site itself is regarded by some as port-of-trade during Saladoid/Barrancoid times.

Typical artifacts found at La Sorcé include three-pointer *zemís,* stone pendants, small ornaments, and jewelry of shell, mother-of-pearl, and greenstone, as well as so-called incense burners and hallucinogen-snuffing vessels. Many of these items possess sophisticated zoomorphic imagery. No less than twenty dog burials have been found at the site, some of which had their legs tied together presumably as part of ritual activity. There was a long and complex period of prehistoric occupation at La Sorcé, whose final dates are around 1540.

See also: Barrancoid; Elenan; Hueca, La (Puerto Rico); Saladoid; White-on-Red Pottery (W-O-R); Zic Pottery

References

Chanlatte Baik, L. A. 1976. *La hueca y sorcé (Vieques, Puerto Rico): Nuevo esquema para los procesos culturales de la arqueología antillana.* Santo Domingo, the Dominican Republic: Fundación García Arévalo; Chanlatte Baik, L. A. 1981. *La Hueca y Sorcé (Vieques, Puerto Rico): Primeras migraciones agroalfereras Antillanas—Nuevo esquema para los procesos culturales de la arqueología Antillana.* Santo Domingo, the Dominican Republic; Narganes Storde, Y. M. 1991. Secuencia cronológica de dos sitios arqueólogicos de Puerto Rico (Sorcé, Vieques y Tecla, Guayanilla). *Proceedings of the Thirteenth International Congress for Caribbean Archaeology Held at Willemstadt, Curaçao, on July 24–29, 1989,* pp. 628–646. Willemstadt.

Landfall, Columbus's First

Controversy has long surrounded the identification of Christopher Columbus's first landfall in the Americas. Much of the effort spent on this issue is disproportionate to its significance. While it is important to pinpoint the landing spot so as to identify Columbus's route and his unique descriptions of the Lucayan inhabitants, this does not affect the momentous consequences of Columbus's arrival for the Americas' indigenous peoples or the rest of the world.

Land was spotted at 2:00 A.M. on Friday, 12 October 1492. It seems that the native name of the island was Guanahaní and Columbus quickly renamed it San Salvador. It then became known as Watlings Island until it reverted back to San Salvador in the twentieth century. At least ten islands have been identified as Guanahaní, most famously Samana Cay, Egg Island, and Grand Turk. Most identifications have been ingenious, employing evidence ranging from ocean currents, mistakes in historical sources, and computer-generated models. The key problem for all theories is the lack of Columbus's original logbook;

only abstracts and copies have survived. Today, archaeological evidence of Spanish artifacts in a Lucayan site on San Salvador, while hardly conclusive, probably favors that location over the alternatives.

Whatever the truth, Columbus went ashore and took possession of the island for the king and queen of Spain, and established an enduring tradition of exchange with the native peoples by giving them glass beads and quizzing them over the source of their gold ornaments.

See also: Bahamas; Columbus, Christopher; Lucayans

References

Hoffman, C. A. Jr. 1987. Archaeological Investigations at the Long Bay Site, San Salvador, Bahamas. In D. T. Grace (ed.), *Proceedings of the First San Salvador Conference, Columbus and His World,* pp. 237–245. Fort Lauderdale, FL: CCFL Bahamian Field Station; Keegan, W. H. 1992. *The People Who Discovered Columbus: The Prehistory of the Bahamas,* pp. 183–205. Gainesville, FL: University Press of Florida; Molander, A. 1983. A New Approach to the Columbus Landfall. *Terrae Incognitae* 15: 113–149.

Languages

The Caribbean is a mosaic of islands and cultures. Its unique geography and dramatic prehistoric and recent European- and African-influenced history has left an indelible mark on the people and their languages. Today, even more than in prehistory, many different tongues can be heard throughout the region.

At the time of the European arrival, there were two main languages: those spoken by the Taíno (Arawak) in the Greater Antilles, and the Carib of the Lesser Antilles. Although different from each other, they both belong to the same Arawakan linguistic family that probably first entered the region with the Dabajuroid peoples.

Different forms or dialects of the Taíno language were spoken in the Bahamas, Jamaica, Puerto Rico, eastern Cuba, and Hispaniola (modern Haiti and the Dominican Republic). In some places, remnants of non-Taíno peoples still spoke their own language, about which almost nothing is known. Knowledge of the Taíno language has come through the Spanish who transcribed what they heard phonetically into European script. These words reflected the nature of their military, economic, and geographical interactions with the Taíno, such as *macaná* (to kill), *serra* (to exchange), *cayos* (islands), *caona* (gold), and many important trees such as the jagua (genip tree) and the ceiba. Some Taíno words have passed through Spanish into common English usage, such as *tabac* (tobacco), *maíz* (maize), *huracán* (hurricane), *hamaca* (hammock), and *savana* (savannah).

The Taíno language flourished in the Island Caribbean for perhaps 2,000 years, but within 50 years of Columbus's arrival in 1492 it had been destroyed, along with the culture that spoke it. Although pure-blooded Taínos disappeared soon after the European arrival, their mixed-blood descendants still live in Puerto Rico, Cuba, and the Dominican Republic. In rural areas many Taíno words survived, while in recent years the revival of cultural and ethnic awareness has seen a resurgence of their use.

In Puerto Rico (native Borinquén), one such group calls itself the Jatibonicu Taino Tribal Nation of Boriken and actively promotes its own heritage, language, and arts and crafts. Today, the word *bohío,* originally a Taíno rectangular house, is now commonly applied to small rural houses.

The language of the Island Caribs (Kalinago) belonged to the same Arawakan linguistic family as that spoken by the Taíno to the north, and Arawaks from mainland South America. Island Carib language (somewhat confusingly) bore no relationship to the Cariban linguistic family spoken by South American Caribs (Karinya). To complicate matters further, while Island Carib women spoke this language of Arawakan affiliation, their seafaring men seem to have also had a "men-only" language used when they gathered together in the men's house. This appears to have been a pidgin language (see following), a mix of their own native Arawakan tongue and Cariban words borrowed from their South American Carib trading partners—in other words, a difference of gender and status rather than of pure linguistics. This pidgin may have developed on the South American mainland as a way for Arawakan-speaking and Cariban-speaking tribes to communicate and engage in trade.

Many of the Island Carib words that have been passed down were gathered by the French Dominican Father Raymond Breton (1609–1679), who lived among the Caribs for nineteen years. In his famous dictionary, *La Dictionnaire Caraïbe-François,* published in 1665, he recorded such important terms as *eyeri* (man), *bwayé* (shaman), *petun* (tobacco), *lambies* (sea-shells), *mwiná* (house), and *ouicou,* the typically Carib beer made of manioc and water. It was Breton who first noticed that Carib men and women often spoke what seemed to be two different languages. It was only the later painstaking work of anthropologist Douglas Taylor that proved that Breton had misunderstood the situation and that all Island Caribs spoke an Arawakan language but the men also had an extra "men-only" tongue. Today, the Garifuna, descendants of the Black Caribs of St. Vincent who live on the Caribbean coasts of Belize and Honduras, still speak a form of the original Island Carib language.

With the arrival of the Spanish, French, British, and Dutch, Amerindians needed a way of communicating during these momentous encounters. Early hybrid languages, known as pidgins, evolved, and these are regarded as a type of temporary make-do jargon that helped initial exchanges between these radically different peoples. Later, with the arrival of Africans, a whole new set of languages was added to the mix and again, initial and makeshift pidgins were used. With the children of first- or second-generation parents, however, a new and more sophisticated creole language evolved, heavily influenced by the dominant European language spoken on a particular island. Some specialists believe that a fully fledged creole language develops out of a local pidgin, whereas others consider pidgins and creoles as entirely different and unrelated. Whatever the truth, the colonial history of the Caribbean has given rise to French creole, English creole, and Spanish *criolla* languages. These hybrid tongues do not stand alone—they are an integral part of their respective creole cultures that embrace music, religion, and cuisine as well as language.

The twentieth century saw the emergence of a new way of speaking associated with Rastafarianism on Jamaica. Although it is English and thus not a new language, it uses words from the Bible to express new concepts: "Babylon" refers to the period of slavery between the sixteenth and nineteenth centuries, and "Zion" is the African homeland. New idiomatic expressions were also invented, such as "Irie" (refers to happiness) and "I and I" used instead of "we" or "you and I," representing the concept of the oneness of two people. "Rasta talk" is the latest linguistic creation of the Caribbean's dramatic history.

See also: Breton, Father Raymond; Caribs; Creole/Creolization; Dominica; Garifuna (Black Caribs); Rastafarianism; Taíno (Arawak)

References
Aikhenvald, A. Y. 1999. The Arawak Language Family. In R.M.W. Dixon and A. Y. Aikhenvald (eds.). *The Amazonian Languages,* pp. 64–106. Cambridge: Cambridge University Press; Baluntansky, K., and M.-A. Sourieau. 1998. *Caribbean Creolization: Reflections on the Cultural Dynamics of Language, Literature, and Identity.* Gainesville, FL: University Press of Florida; Breton, P. R. 1665. *Dictionnaire caraïbe-françois.* Auxerre, France; Rat, J. N. 1897. The Carib Language, as Now Spoken in Dominica, West Indies. *Journal of the Anthropological Institute* 27: 293–315; Taylor, D. M. 1977. *Languages of the West Indies.* Baltimore: Johns Hopkins University Press; Taylor, D., and I. Rouse. 1955. Linguistic and Archaeological Time Depth in the West Indies. *International Journal of American Linguistics* 21 (2): 105–115; Todd, L. 1990. *Pidgins and Creoles.* London: Routledge.

Las Casas, Bartolomé de

Bartolomé de Las Casas (1484–1566) was born in Seville, and became famous as a historian and theologian, but mainly as the defender of the Indians and arguably a founding figure in anthropology. His firsthand experience of the atrocities of early-sixteenth-century Spanish colonialism in the Caribbean and his advocacy of Amerindian rights based on eyewitness observations of indigenous life make Las Casas a peerless figure in the history of the Caribbean and Latin America.

As an eight-year-old boy, Las Casas watched as Columbus paraded his Caribbean Amerindians along the streets of Seville on returning from his momentous first voyage to the New World in 1493. Later that year, Las Casas's father and several uncles accompanied Columbus on his second voyage and five years later the eighteen-year-old Bartolomé journeyed to Hispaniola (modern Haiti and the Dominican republic) to manage his father's estate. Although clearly troubled by what he saw of the Spanish treatment of the Taínos, he nevertheless took part in the expedition of the conquistador Juan de Esquivel to subjugate the Taíno of eastern Hispaniola's Higüey province.

In 1506, Las Casas returned to Spain where he was ordained a priest and subsequently journeyed back to Hispaniola in the company of Christopher Columbus's son Diego. He was granted land, Indians, and mining rights along with a duty to convert the Taíno allotted to him as his *encomienda*—a system that required Amerindians to render food, goods, and labor to the Spanish. Unlike many Spanish colonizers, Las Casas treated his Amerindians well but remained concerned primarily with the economic profitability of his estate.

In 1511, the conquistador Diego de Velázquez conquered Cuba in a cruel and bloody campaign. Las Casas, acting as a chaplain, subsequently joined the Spanish forces of Pánfilo de Narváez, who had been invited by Velázquez to join the expedition. Las Casas was used by the conquistadors to placate the Amerindian's fears and gather them together

Bartolomé de Las Casas, a sixteenth-century Spanish historian, was the earliest crusader for human rights in the New World. (Bettmann/Corbis)

163

whereupon they were captured. While in Cuba, he was an eyewitness to the many atrocities committed against the native population, an experience that changed his mind about Spanish activities in the Caribbean. He gave up his own encomienda and, in 1515, accompanied the Dominican Antonio Montesino back to Spain to petition the Spanish King Ferdinand to abolish the encomienda system responsible for so much cruelty and destruction.

Ferdinand died in 1516 and was succeeded by Cardinal Francisco Jimenez de Cisneros acting as regent. Las Casas proposed, and Cisneros accepted, that that the encomienda system be replaced by settling the Amerindians in self-supporting villages overseen by the Spanish with each village rendering labor for the gold mines and the *encomenderos* receiving financial compensation. Cisneros appointed Las Casas "Protector of the Indians," but the plan failed miserably and Las Casas returned again to Spain.

In 1517, Cisneros died and the new king, Carlos I, came to the throne. He supported Las Casas's ideas but a new project that combined colonization of Venezuela with converting the Amerindians and exploiting the resources of gold and pearls also failed. Las Casas became deeply disillusioned and retreated from the world into the Dominican convent in Santo Domingo on Hispaniola.

In 1531, after ten years of seclusion, he reemerged, advocating a revolutionary new approach to the Indian problem. He now argued for Amerindian self-determination and their inalienable rights to their own land. All Spanish activity in these areas since 1492 he deemed to have been illegal, and the only responsibility of the Spanish was to convert the indigenous peoples to Christianity. His basic ideas of abolishing encomiendas and denying Spanish colonists' control over Amerindians' lives was accepted by King Carlos as it coincided with his efforts to curb the growing power and autonomy of the colonists.

The disaster of the Caribbean experience, which saw the indigenous population virtually exterminated by maltreatment, slavery, overwork, and disease, influenced Spanish royal ideas about the treatment of native peoples more widely, particularly in Mexico and Peru. While there were powerful supporters of a new way of dealing with Amerindians, it was Las Casas's firsthand experience of events in the Caribbean and deep knowledge of Catholic theology that made him such an effective propagandist for Amerindian rights. He argued eloquently for the unity of humankind and the equality of all races.

His beliefs and ideas were articulated powerfully in several important works. His *Brevíssima relación de la destruición de las Indias* (A Short Account of the Destruction of the Indies), published in 1552, related the horrors he had witnessed during the Spanish conquest of Cuba and similar events in Central and South America. On a grander scale, the *Apologética historia sumaria* laid out his ideas in an erudite and comparative fashion, though it was not published until 1909. Especially valuable was his *History of the Indies,* written between 1527 and 1562 but not published until 1875, which included an abstract of the lost original manuscript of Christopher Columbus's diary account of his epic 1492 voyage. An admirer of Columbus, Las Casas nevertheless regarded the admiral's fall from grace and subsequent imprisonment as divine punishment for his abuses against the Caribbean Taíno and Carib.

See also: Columbus, Christopher; Cuba; Encomienda; Martyr, Peter; Pané, Father Ramón; Puerto Real (site, Haiti)

References

Conley, T. 1992. De Bry's Las Casas. In R. Jara and N. Spadaccini (eds.). *Amerindian Images and the Legacy of Columbus,* pp. 103–131. Minneapolis: University of Minnesota Press; Friede, J., and B. Keen (eds.). 1971. *Bartolomé de Las Casas in History: Toward an Understanding of the Man and His Work.* DeKalb: Northern Illinois University Press; Hanke, L. 1952. *Bartolomé de Las Casas, Historian: An Essay in Spanish Historiography.* Gainesville, FL: University of Florida Press; Henige, D. 1992. To Read is to Misread, To Write is to Miswrite: Las Casas as Transcriber. In R. Jara and N. Spadaccini (eds.). *Amerindian Images and the Legacy of Columbus,* pp. 198–229. Minneapolis: University of Minnesota Press; Las Casas, B. 1971. *Bartolomé de Las Casas: History of the Indies.* Ed. and trans. A. M. Collard. New York: Harper and Row; B. de Las Casas, 1992. *A Short Account of the Destruction of the Indies.* Harmondsworth, UK: Penguin.

Los Buchillones (site, Cuba)

Los Buchillones is a Taíno site on the north coast of Cuba. Its existence was suspected after local inhabitants began finding well-preserved wooden artifacts in a lagoon in the 1980s. In 1997, excavations began and immediately found a wealth of wooden items, including eyed-needles, dishes with elaborate handles, several wooden handles with stone axe blades still hafted, miniature *duhos,* and fragments of *zemís.* This unique find of wooden items doubled the total already known for the whole of the Antilles.

The radiocarbon dating of the considerable wood remains of Los Buchillones has revealed occupation ranging between A.D. 1200 and A.D. 1620—a cultural life for the site of at least 400 years. With a length of 1.5 km from east to west, and possibly 100 meters north to south, the site is currently the largest known from prehistoric Cuba.

Although it was originally thought that the underwater finds represented ritual deposits by the Taíno, the discovery of domestic stone tools and pottery along with the remains of beams and rafters of a circular building indicated that this was a submerged village site. Preservation was so good that even sections of the original palm-thatch roofing of the building were recovered. The minimal disturbance of the structural elements of the building displayed the original layout, and suggested a nonviolent end to the site as well as the almost immediate creation of a stable anoxic environment.

Further excavations in 1999 encountered the remains of another well-preserved structure, smaller than the first and rectangular in shape. Once again large amounts of roof thatch had been preserved alongside food remains, pottery, and stone tools. It seems likely that although no historical records have yet been discovered to indicate such a practice in this region, some of the buildings may have been built on piles over water. An important lesson for investigating such waterlogged sites was thus learned inasmuch as the depositional history of the site—the ways in which its buildings collapsed and were so well preserved—resulted from a complex series of events and was not a straightforward case of the sea covering and eroding cultural remains. This is in part due to the constant changes in local environment involving erosion, deposition, and the movement of water—processes that were presumably active at the time of occupation as well as since.

It also highlights how different the environment of Los Buchillones is today from what it was in Taíno times.

Perhaps the most surprising aspect of the excavations at Los Buchillones, apart from the preservation, are the implications of the radiocarbon dates that indicate Taíno occupation may have lasted until the seventeenth century. This evidence was supplemented by the discovery of European majolica pottery, one piece of which had been shaped into a triangular object—perhaps an example of the well-known practice of Amerindians acquiring shiny European objects as ritual items akin to their own shell, bone, and gold (*guanín*) jewelry.

Accepted wisdom regards the indigenous Amerindians of Cuba as having disappeared through conquest, disease, maltreatment, and absorption into Spanish society within a few decades of Spanish arrival at the end of the fifteenth century. Evidence from Los Buchillones suggests that a culturally intact village community still existed and was still building traditional houses well over 100 years after Spanish occupation. Although there are currently no specific historical documents to aid interpretation, the presence of high-status carved-wood items at the site suggests the possibility that the site was abandoned quickly, perhaps through the forced exodus of the inhabitants due to Spanish discovery of the village. It may be that its location had concealed the village from the Spanish for many years and that Los Buchillones was the longest-surviving Taíno community on Cuba, and in the Caribbean.

See also: Cuba; Duhos; La Aleta (site, Dominican Republic); Taíno (Arawak); Trees, Spiritual Importance of; Underwater Archaeology; Zemís

References
Dacal Moure, R., and M. Rivero de la Calle. 1996. *Art and Archaeology of Pre-Columbian Cuba.* Pittsburgh: University of Pittsburgh Press; Graham, E., D. M. Pendergast, J. Calvera, and J. Jardines. 2000. Excavations at Los Buchillones, Cuba. *Antiquity* 74, pp. 263–264; Guarch, J. M. 1978. *El Taíno de Cuba: Ensayo de reconstrucción etno-histórica.* Academia de Ciencias de Cuba, Instituto de Ciencias Sociales, Havana; Pendergast, D. M., E. Graham, J. A. Calvera, and M. J. Jardines. 2001. Houses in the Sea: Excavation and Preservation at Los Buchillones, Cuba. In B. A. Purdy (ed.), *Enduring Records: The Environmental and Cultural Heritage of Wetlands,* pp. 71–82. Oxford: Oxbow Books.

Los Roques Islands (Venezuela)

The Los Roques archipelago lies 135 km off the Caribbean coast of Venezuela. The forty-five islands of the group are small and arid with no indigenous animals. They appear to have been regularly visited during prehistoric times by the Valencia people of the mainland, who belonged to the Arauquinoid cultural tradition (ca. A.D. 900 to A.D. 1500). Twenty-seven archaeological sites have been discovered on eighteen of the islands, and these belong to Amerindians who occupied the islands on a seasonal basis, exploiting the maritime resources. In particular they dived for Queen Conch (*Strombus gigas*) and West Indian Top Shell (*Cittarium pica*), and also hunted turtles.

Investigations on the small coral island of Dos Mosquises in the western part of the archipelago yielded the remains of 303 ceramic figurines. Some appeared as pregnant women, others as mothers with babies, masked individuals, deformed people, while some are shown standing and others seated. The archaeological site appeared to be a temporary campsite, a base from which hunting and fishing was carried out and which also yielded remains of meals of turtle and fish. Dating to between 1300 and 1500, the ceramic remains all belonged to the Valencia culture and so had been brought to the island from the mainland.

See also: Arauquinoid (pottery); Conch
References
Antczak, A. 1999. *Late Prehistoric Economy and Society of the Islands Off the Coast of Venezuela: A Contextual Interpretation of the Non-Ceramic Evidence.* PhD dissertation, Institute of Archaeology, University College London; Antczak, M. 2000. *"Idols" in Exile: Making Sense of Prehistoric Human Pottery Figurines from Dos Mosquises Island, Los Roques Archipelago, Venezuela.* PhD dissertation, Institute of Archaeology, University College London.

Lovers' Retreat (site, Tobago)

Lovers' Retreat is one of Tobago's most important and well-documented prehistoric archaeological sites. Its favorable location on a rocky headland on the island's leeward coast may be partly responsible for its long period of occupation—a millennium at least.

Lovers' Retreat was discovered in 1943 by the archaeologist Thomas Cambridge, and has been heavily investigated (and damaged) since that time by a succession of archaeologists, collectors, and developers who have removed vast quantities of pottery, human remains (burials), and midden material. The midden site, which is totally of the ceramic period, is regarded as having three sections, each of which belongs to a separate stage of Tobago's prehistoric cultural development. The first, Section A, which has human burials, belongs to the early Saladoid-era Friendship Complex (A.D. 250 to A.D. 750), a period in which the inhabitants hunted armadillos, peccaries, turtle, and shark, and whose pottery featured red-and-black painted bowls and incised anthropomorphic and zoomorphic decoration.

Section B of the midden belongs to Tobago's subsequent Golden Grove Complex, whose pottery is distinguished by being of two types: finely made and highly polished red-brown items assumed to be of a ceremonial nature, and rougher, yellow-gray domestic ware. Some items may be trade pieces from Trinidad, especially those in typically Arauquinoid style, but more obvious are increasingly close associations with the Suazoid series from the Windward Islands that, together with radiocarbon evidence, suggests a date of ca. A.D. 1200.

Section C belongs to the Plymouth Complex (A.D. 1150 to A.D. 1400), whose pottery developed out of the Golden Grove–style and retained the clear distinction between well-made ceremonial and coarser domestic ceramics. Unsurprisingly, the material culture of this period also shows close affinities with that of the Windward Islands Suazoid style.

See also: Saladoid; Suazey/Suazoid; Trinidad and Tobago
References
Boomert, A. 1996. *The Prehistoric Sites of Tobago: A Catalogue and Evaluation,* pp. 68–77. Alkmaar, the Netherlands; Harris, P.O.B. 1980. Excavation Report: Lovers Retreat Period IV, Tobago.

Proceedings of the Eighth International Congress for the Study of the Pre-Columbian Cultures of the Lesser Antilles, St Kitts 1979, pp. 524–552.

Lucayans

The indigenous inhabitants of the Bahamas (including Turks and Caicos) are known today as the Lucayans, whose name derives from their own term for "island men." The Lucayans shared a common ancestry with the Taínos of the Greater Antilles through the Ostionoid peoples who originally settled the islands between ca. A.D. 600 and A.D. 1200 in their canoes—the impressive size of which was commented upon by Columbus.

The exact point of departure for this colonization is disputed between Cuba, Hispaniola (modern Haiti and the Dominican Republic), and Inagua, the southernmost island of the Bahamas archipelago. The Cuban case is supported by the presence of Meillacan influences in the locally made Bahamian Palmetto–style pottery on Long Island. The case for Hispaniola lies partly in that it is geographically much closer than Cuba, especially to the Turks and Caicos islands. The presence of apparently imported (and thus pre-Palmetto) pottery, and the fact that most Caicos sites are adjacent to salt pans—salt being a major trade item—reinforced this explanation. Another significant factor was the presence of one site that, by its size and organization, suggested (earlier) Classic Taíno rather than (later) local Lucayan origins.

The Cuban and Hispaniolan hypotheses nevertheless have problems raised by recent archaeological research. These have led to a third theory, a variation of the second, that the initial colonization took place from northern Hispaniola via the island of Great Inagua during the Ostionoid Period. The proximity of Great Inagua to Hispaniola, together with favorable winds and currents, make it a prime location for early occupation. This is reinforced by archaeology, which has shown that Inaguan sites contain an abundance of imported ceramics.

While the exact origins of the Lucayans is still debated, evidence suggests that once established, they became expert horticulturalists, cultivating perhaps fifty different types of plant foods. Sweet and bitter cassava, corn, sweet potatoes, chili peppers, and tobacco were paramount, and these were supplemented by hunting and fishing—with parrotfish, turtles, and shellfish being varied by occasional land mammals such as the large rodent known as the hutia (*Isolobodon portoricensis*). The large, thick-walled Palmetto ceramics would have been ideal for making the stew known as pepper pot.

Current evidence indicates that many Lucayan villages were located between the sea and a swampy area, probably to take advantage of different prey species and the availability of fresh water. As with their Taíno cousins, Lucayan villages were often composed of houses arranged in a circle around a central plaza in which dances and public events took place. On Grand Turk, the Lucayans made shell disk beads and wove them into belts that may have served as a symbolic record of political relationships between different groups. Lucayan lifeways were successful and it is estimated that when Europeans first arrived, the indigenous population numbered somewhere between 40,000 and 80,000.

The identity and date of the first European to encounter the Lucayans is still disputed and is tied to an ongoing debate concerning the identification of the site where Christopher Columbus first set foot on the Americas in October 1492. There appears a strong case for Columbus having first landed on Grand Turk rather than San Salvador in the Bahamas, though it is possible that the first European to see the islands was Juan Ponce de León. Archaeological evidence of European objects, such as Spanish earthenware pottery, found in Lucayan sites on San Salvador, Long Island, Samana Cay, and elsewhere, appears to support the case for early Spanish-Lucayan contact. Such items, however, could have been traded between different Lucayan groups or introduced later, and so the picture is still unclear.

Another explanation is tied to the fate of the Lucayans in that within twenty years of the Spanish arrival in the Caribbean, the Lucayan people had disappeared from history. As the Bahamas lay astride the route back to Europe, many Lucayans were kidnapped on an ad hoc basis, such as those taken by Amerigo Vespucci. However, the real disaster came on 3 May 1509 with a decree by the Spanish Crown that legitimated slave raiding—one consequence of which was that the Lucayan islands were systematically depopulated to provide manpower for gold-mining enterprises on nearby Puerto Rico and Hispaniola, and pearl diving at the island of Cubagua off Venezuela's Caribbean coast. These slaving expeditions among Lucayan villages may have been responsible for the Spanish objects found there today.

Within a generation, the first of the Americas' inhabitants encountered by Europeans had disappeared and when two further Spanish slaving raids swept through the islands in 1520 they failed to see even a single Lucayan.

See also: Duhos; Great Inagua Island; Hispaniola; Meillacan; Ostionoid; Palmetto; Pearls (gems); Pepper Pot; Puerto Real (site, Haiti); Taíno (Arawak); Turks and Caicos

References

Aarons, G. A. 1989. The Lucayan Duhos: 1828–1988. *Journal of the Bahamas Historical Society* 11: 3–11; Berman, M. J., and D. M. Pearsall. 2000. Plants, People, and Culture in the Prehistoric Central Bahamas: A View from the Three Dog Site, An Early Lucayan Settlement on San Salvador Island, Bahamas. *Latin American Antiquity* 11: 219–239; de Booy, T. 1912a. Lucayan Artifacts from the Bahamas. *American Anthropologist* 15: 1–7; de Booy, T. 1912b. Lucayan Remains on the Caicos Islands. *American Anthropologist* 14 (1): 81–105; Granberry, J. 1979–1981. Spanish Slave Trade in the Bahamas, 1509–1530: An Aspect of the Caribbean Pearl Industry. 3 parts. *Journal of the Bahamas Historical Society* 1, 2, and 3; Granberry, J. 1980. A Brief History of Bahamian Archaeology. *Florida Anthropologist* 33: 83–93; Granberry, J. 1991. Lucayan Toponyms. *Journal of the Bahamas Historical Society* 13 (1): 3–12; Keegan, W. F. 1985. *Dynamic Horticulturalists: Population Expansion in the Prehistoric Bahamas.* PhD. dissertation. Ann Arbor, MI: University Microfilms; Keegan, W. F. 1986. The Ecology of Lucayan Fishing Practices. *American Antiquity* 51 (4): 816–825; Keegan, W. F. 1992. *The People Who Discovered Columbus: The Prehistory of the Bahamas.* Gainesville, FL: University Press of Florida; Keegan, W. F. 1997. *Bahamian Archaeology: Life in the Bahamas and Turks and Caicos Before Columbus.* Nassau: Media Publishing; Winter, J., and D. M. Pearsall. 1991. A Wooden Mortar of the Lucayans. *Proceedings of the Fourteenth International Congress for Caribbean Archaeology, Barbados,* pp. 586–590.

M

Maisabel (site, Puerto Rico)

Maisabel is a large, early Cedrosan Saladoid site on the north coast of Puerto Rico. It has been the subject of multidisciplinary archaeological investigations that indicate it may represent the beginnings of a social and political complexity that led to the emergence of Ostionoid culture and that culminated in the appearance of powerful Taíno chiefdoms from ca. A.D. 1200 onward.

Some 20 ha in size, Maisabel is composed of a series of middens arranged like a horseshoe around a central plaza, some part of which may have served as an area for communal dances or the ball-game—though there is no evidence for a formal ball-court. Also in the center of the site is a cemetery that, although mainly Saladoid, includes some later Ostionoid burials. The general lack of grave goods in the twenty-three burials excavated suggests that if differences in social status existed, it was not considered important to show them after death. This lack of differentiation may indicate a communal nature for Maisabel society. The central location of the cemetery, surrounded by mounds, may indicate a ceremonial nature for the site, perhaps related to ancestor worship. A large Ostionoid Period house was found in between the two largest middens and seems to belong to the eighth century A.D. Twelve burials were found and excavated from beneath this structure.

Analysis of the remains of everyday life at Maisabel shows that the inhabitants were adept at exploiting a range of economic and food resources, from horticulture (notably cassava) to hunting and fishing. No less than 155 animal species are present in the archaeological remains, including, notably, the large rodent known as the hutia (*Isolobodon portoricensis*), doves, parrot-fishes, grouper, limpets, and conch. The most important food, however, seems to have been the blue land crabs (*Cardisoma guanhumi*) that were easily obtainable from the nearby mangrove swamps. It seems that at Maisabel, as at other contemporary Saladoid sites, the land crab population was increasingly overhunted. This led to a decline in numbers found archaeologically that may itself represent a population collapse of the crab population. Whatever the cause, Maisabel's inhabitants switched their attention increasingly to the range of other available maritime resources.

See also: Hacienda Grande; Ostionoid; Puerto Rico; Saladoid

References
Budinoff, L. 1991. An Osteological Analysis of Human Burials Recovered from Maisabel, an Early Ceramic Site Located on the North Coast of Puerto Rico. *Proceedings of the Twelfth International Congress of Caribbean Archaeology, Cayenne, French Guiana, 1987,* pp. 45–51; de France, S. D. 1990. Zooarchaeological Investigations of an Early Ceramic Age Frontier Community in the Caribbean: The Maisabel Site, Puerto Rico. *Antropológica* 73–74: 3–180; Roe, P. G. 1991. The Petroglyphs of Maisabel: A Study in Methodology. *Comptes Rendus des Communications du Douzième Congrès International d'Archeologie de la Caraïbe, Cayenne, Guyane Française,* pp. 317–370. Martinique: Association Internationale d'Archeologie de la Caraïbe; Siegel, P. E. 1989. Site Structure, Demography, and Social Complexity in the Early Ceramic Age of the Caribbean. In P. E. Siegel (ed.). *Early Ceramic Population Lifeways and Adaptive Strategies in the Caribbean,* pp. 193–245. Oxford: British Archaeological Reports International Series 506; Siegel, P. E., and P. G. Roe. 1991. Maisabel Archaeological Project: A Long-Term Multidisciplinary Investigation. *Proceedings of the Twelfth International Congress of Caribbean Archaeology, Cayenne, French Guiana, 1987,* pp. 109–115.

Maize

Maize (*Zea mays*) takes its name from the Taíno word *ma-hiz,* and quickly became known to Europeans as Indian corn. It appears to have been first domesticated in Mesoamerica before 3500 B.C. and spread eventually to South America, though some scholars maintain an older variety was domesticated separately in the Greater Antilles at an unknown date.

Christopher Columbus was the first European to observe maize being cultivated by the Lucayans in the Bahamas. Samples taken back to Spain were initially grown as curiosities, but by the sixteenth century it had been introduced into Africa and soon spread around the world.

Maize is a cost-efficient, high-protein cultigen, and it is thought that its domestication during the third millennium in the Orinoco basin led to a population explosion that rippled out first to the Guianas and then through Trinidad north to the Island Caribbean around A.D. 500. The first maize cultivators in South America are known archaeologically as the Osoid peoples, who subsequently influenced the Corozal culture—the earliest group associated with the making of Arauquinoid pottery. By about 1000, maize cultivation was increasingly part of the Dabajuroid culture that flourished on the Venezuelan offshore island of Curaçao and at the site of Tanki Flip on Aruba. Around the same time (ca. 1200), maize also appeared in the Bahamas to the north.

Unlike Amerindians of mainland Mesoamerica and South America, the Taíno appear to not have brewed beer from their maize nor to have made bread (tortillas) from corn flour. They preferred to grow it in forest clearings and to eat the individual kernels. Unlike the dominant cassava, maize seems to have played no role in their religion. Nevertheless, it may be that the Taíno used it as feed for their domesticated animals, pounding it in wooden mortars rather than the otherwise diagnostic stone mano and metate. Whatever the truth, maize kernels have been found at the site of the Taíno village at En Bas Saline on Haiti's north coast—where Columbus built his ill-fated first settlement of La Navidad.

See also: Arauquinoid (pottery); Cassava (manioc); Tanki Flip (site, Aruba)

References

Bush, M. B., D. R. Piperno, and P. A. Colinvaux. 1989. A 6,000-Year History of Amazonian Maize Cultivation. *Nature* 340: 303–305; Keegan, W. F. 1987. Diffusion of Maize from South America: The Antillean Connection. In W. F. Keegan (ed.). *Emergent Horticultural Economies of the Eastern Woodlands,* pp. 329–344. Carbondale, IL: Southern Illinois University; Newsom, L. A. 1994. Zea Mays in the West Indies: The Archaeological and Early Historic Record. In S. Johannesen and C. A. Hastorf (eds.). *Corn and Culture in the Prehistoric New World,* pp. 203–217. Boulder, CO: Westview Press; Roosevelt, A. C. 1980. *Parmana: Prehistoric Maize and Manioc Subsistence Along the Amazon and Orinoco.* London: Academic Press;

Margarita Island (Venezuela)

Margarita Island, belonging to Venezuela, is made up of one island in two parts that are joined by an 18-km-long sandspit, and two smaller offshore islands of Cubagua and Coche.

Archaeological excavations on Margarita have not yet revealed any great depth of occupation. As on other small islands of the area, the main feature is shell middens indicative of temporary camps like that of Gire-Gire that perhaps were used in the exploitation of the once-rich pearl beds. Most of the pottery is plain with no decoration, and the rare painted item is probably tradeware brought in from elsewhere. There are also some ceramics that have modeled *adornos* and small modeled heads on D-shaped handles, and fragments of griddles suggest that manioc was prepared and eaten on the island. Apart from pottery, some petaloid celts (stone axe heads) have been found, along with hammerstones and mortars. Worked shell is rare, though crude conch-shell ornaments have been discovered. By around A.D. 1000, Amerindians of the Dabajuroid culture from Lake Maracaibo had arrived on the island.

Margarita was first seen by Europeans, and subsequently named by Christopher Columbus, in August 1498 during his third voyage. It was Alonso de Hojeda, however, who was the first Spaniard to step ashore on the island in the following year. In early accounts of sailors in this area it was reported that sea monsters known as tritons could be seen cavorting in the waves.

It is the small offshore island of Cubagua that is better known to history, as it was the center first of an Amerindian, then Spanish pearl-diving industry. The island also has a currently well-documented early prehistoric, Archaic Period occupation. At the archaeological sites of Cubagua and Manicuare there is evidence suggesting Amerindian occupation by around 2225 B.C. These people appear to have been clearly adapted to a maritime way of life that included fishing and collecting shellfish. They made flaked-stone tools, though most of their spearpoints, axes, beads, and pendants were fashioned from shells. As on Margarita, by A.D. 1000 people belonging to the Dabajuroid culture were living on the island.

Cubagua was initially known to the Spanish as Pearl Island, and here they engaged in trade with local Amerindians who exchanged large quantities of pearls for shiny European objects like glass beads, mirrors, and items made of brass, copper, and iron. So important were these exchanges for the Spanish that in 1508, with a dwindling number of local native divers available, large numbers of Lucayan Amerindians were taken from the Bahamas and forced to dive for pearls off Cubagua. Their working conditions were harsh and by 1518 the Bahamas had been totally depopulated and African slave divers had begun to be imported.

The huts of the early Spanish settlers were replaced by the building of Nueva Cadiz, which flourished along with the burgeoning trade in pearls. In 1529, for example, 345 kg of pearls came from the pearl beds of nearby Coche Island in just one month. By 1531 there were 1,000 people living in Nueva Cadiz but within a few years there were signs of serious depletion of the pearl beds and the Spanish began moving to nearby Margarita. The town's problems were exacerbated by pirate attacks and in 1541, after what has variously been seen either as a hurricane or an earthquake and tidal wave, the town was abandoned. The ancient pearl wealth of Margarita and Cubagua has echoes in folklore and religion today. In the church of the Virgen del Valle on Margarita, the figure of the Madonna has two dresses, one adorned with diamonds, the other with pearls.

See also: Columbus, Christopher; Dabajuroid; Lucayans; Pearls (gems)

References
de Booy, T. 1915–1916. Notes on the Archaeology of Margarita Island, Venezuela. In *Contributions to the Museum of the American Indian, Heye Foundation,* Vol. 2, No. 5. New York; Donkin, R. A. 1998. *Beyond Price, Pearls and Pearl-Fishing to the Age of Discoveries.* Philadelphia: Transactions of the American Philosophical Society; Osgood, C., and G. D. Howard. 1943. An Archaeological Survey of Venezuela. *Yale University Publications in Anthropology* No. 27, pp. 1–153; Romero, A., S. Chilbert, and M. G. Eisenhart. 1999. Cubagua's Pearl-Oyster Beds: The First Depletion of a Natural Resource Caused by Europeans in the American Continent. *Journal of Political Ecology* 6: 57–77; Rouse, I., and J. M. Cruxent. 1963. *Venezuelan Archaeology,* New Haven, CT: Yale University Press; Sauer, C. O. 1969. *The Early Spanish Main.* Berkeley, CA: University of California Press.

Maroons

"Maroon" is the name applied to escaped slaves in the wider Caribbean region, and *marronage* the term given to the practice of running away from plantations. Maroon is an anglicized form of the Spanish term *cimarrón,* which was itself based on a Taíno (Arawak) word. Originally, cimarrón was the name given to cattle that had turned feral and escaped to the hill country of Hispaniola (modern Haiti and the Dominican Republic). It was soon applied also to the Taíno Amerindians who had similarly fled the depredations of their new Spanish masters. It quickly took on the meanings of "fierce" and "wild," and by the 1540s was mainly being applied to African-Caribbean slaves who had run away from their owners. Slaves escaped their bondage also in mainland South America (from the Guianas to Brazil, Colombia, and Peru) as well as in Mexico and parts of the United States. In these countries, Maroons were variously known as *palenques, mocambos,* or *ladeiras.* Today, the descendants of the first Maroons still live in Jamaica, Suriname, French Guiana, and Belize.

Maroons settled in their own communities either on the fringes of the plantations from which they had escaped or in isolated areas that protected them from raids. These communities forged their own cultural traditions in opposition to the European society that had enslaved them. In some places, such as Haiti, marronage was responsible for preserving enclaves of African religious beliefs such as Vodoun, as well as facilitating the mixing of new hybrid spiritualities where individuals belonging to different African tribes came together.

The first Jamaican Maroons may well have been the surviving remnants of the island's Taíno population escaping from Spanish servitude. Nevertheless, marronage in Jamaica is most commonly associated with some 1,500 slaves of African descent who took the opportunity of freedom offered by their former Spanish masters when the British took the island in 1655. As the Spanish departed for Cuba, the newly freed slaves took to the hills and soon began engaging in guerrilla attacks on the British.

Organizing themselves into small bands, the Maroons began raiding the plantations of their former masters, stealing and killing cattle, carrying off slaves, and sowing fear and resentment among the white settlers. In 1690 in the area of Clarendon, one such group belonging to the African Coromantee tribe fled their plantation and joined their comrades in the isolated heart of Jamaica. Further localized slave uprisings occurred in 1694 and 1702, and after a crackdown by the planters and militia, more slaves escaped to swell the numbers of the Maroons.

Jamaican planters increasingly resented the fact that Maroon communities remained unpunished and acted as a magnet and refuge for runaway slaves. When the British authorities responded to the threat, the small groups of Maroons operating in the western-central part of Jamaica came together and appointed an overall chief called Cudjoe (also spelled Kojo) to lead them, along with his brothers Accompong and Johnny. Cudjoe was a brave and resourceful warrior of whom it was said that he never lost a battle against the British. His success and fame soon attracted other scattered groups of Maroons—many with their own languages and ethnic traditions. These events led to the so-called First Maroon War that lasted from 1720 until 1739. The British suffered militarily against the cleverly camouflaged Maroon fighters and their guerrilla tactics and could never achieve a decisive victory.

After Cudjoe's ambush and massacre of British soldiers at Peace Cave in 1738, the British signed a peace treaty ending hostilities and granting these western or Leeward Maroons their freedom, 15 ha of land, and limited self-governance. Cudjoe was appointed chief commander of Trelawney Town. In return, the Maroons had to agree to help defend Jamaica against foreign invasion and return any future runaway slaves to their owners. In 1739, a similar treaty was signed with Chief Quao of the eastern or Windward Maroons and with this the First Maroon War came to an end. Today in Jamaica, the two main Maroon communities of the Leewards and Windwards still survive and flourish. The Windward Maroons occupy the villages of Moore Town and Charles Town in the Blue Mountains of eastern Jamaica. Moore Town is said to have been founded by the renowned female Maroon warrior, Nanny, who is now a Jamaican national hero. Granny Nanny, as she was known, was a skilled and cunning guerrilla fighter whose exploits and character have been embroidered over the centuries to such an extent that history and legend are hopelessly intertwined.

Nanny is said to have practiced obeah witchcraft and to have had such supernatural power that she could spirit away slaves from plantations. She is also alleged to have caught the white man's bullets in midflight and returned them at speed to their owners. Nanny played an important role during the First Maroon War and is believed to have opposed the peace treaty signed by Cudjoe. She was finally killed in 1734 when the British Captain Stoddart, accompanied by Amerindians brought from Central America's Mosquito Coast and tracker dogs, attacked and destroyed the village of Nanny Town. Archaeological investigations at the site have revealed not only Maroon objects but items belonging to Taíno Amerindians as well, thus raising new questions about the relations between the two groups. Nowadays, every October, celebrations take place in Moore Town that honor the redoubtable Granny Nanny.

In the western part of the island, the Leeward Maroons live in and around the settlement of Accompong in the remote area known as the Cockpit Country. Accompong New Town today is relatively new, having been moved from the ancestral location of Cudjoe's time that is now sacred ground. Every January, celebrations in honor of Cudjoe are held in Accompong and the festivities attract thousands of visitors to watch the singing of the so-called Treaty Songs, the dancing of ancestral Maroon War dances, and the telling of folk tales.

Daily life in Jamaican Maroon communities was simple and hard but free. People lived in small houses with thatched roofs and earth floors. Maroons practiced a basic form of agriculture with the women cultivating such staples as maize and yams. These foods were supplemented by the men, who concentrated on hunting wild boar and, in the early days, anything they could plunder from the white man's plantations. They also bred cattle and raised pigs and chickens. After the peace treaty of 1739, Maroons would also ransom escaped slaves they had captured. As Maroon communities were often made up of different African societies, their languages also varied. European accounts of everyday Maroon life noted the mix of African languages together with the use of broken Spanish and English. The Maroons appear to have devised a unique way of communicating that did not depend on dialect or language. This was the cow's horn, or *abeng,* with which each Maroon could be summoned by his own individual call. It is said that in the Cockpit Country the blast of the abeng could be heard up to 15 km away and it is still used in festivals and funerals.

Aside from Jamaica, Hispaniola, and elsewhere in the Island Caribbean, Maroon communities also existed in mainland areas of North and particularly South America. One of the most unusual of these groups is the so-called Seminole Maroons. This group originated with slaves who escaped their masters in South Carolina and Georgia and made their way to Spanish Florida during the eighteenth century. Here, they associated themselves with the local Seminole Amerindians but kept their own distinctive cultural traditions. In 1842, after the Seminole War, they were forcibly removed, along with their Amerindian allies, to Oklahoma and subsequently many ended up in Mexico, Texas, and the Bahamas.

In those parts of South America that fringe the Caribbean, Maroon societies also survive today. In Suriname and French Guiana, six communities have a combined population of around 60,000. Apart from being politically distinct, these groups also differ in their basic ways of life, such as language, dress, marriage customs, and diet. These differences are most marked between the groups of Saramaka, Matawi, and Kwinti who live in central Suriname and those of the Ndyuka, Aluku, and Paramaka who occupy an area that spans eastern Suriname and western French Guiana. The Saramaka's ancestors began escaping from Dutch plantations in Suriname during the seventeenth century, fought their previous owners for almost 100 years, then signed a peace treaty in 1762. The Aluku crossed from Suriname to French Guiana between 1776 and 1777 and eventually signed a treaty jointly with the French and Dutch in 1860. As with other Caribbean Maroons, their society is strongly matrilineal. Religious practices vary, and can focus on spirit possession, the interpretation of visionary dreams, and consulting objects known as oracle bundles.

The religious life of these Maroon communities is full of elaborate participatory ritual, and includes special languages such as Púmbu and Papá, drumming rhythms, and invocations to ancestors. Snake gods (*vodu*) and warrior gods (*komanti*) are often at the heart of religious beliefs and prayers. Misfortune, childbirth, and illness are all considered the consequences of antisocial behavior that can be alleviated by talking to spirits. The most elaborate ritual expressions focus on funeral ceremonies that can last for several months and involve hundreds of people. Dancing, singing, and the carrying of the coffin as part of divinatory rites are all practiced during such events. Although some inroads have been made by Christianity among the Maroons of Suriname, in general the ever-changing nature of their religious and ritual life makes their beliefs the most rooted of all in their African origins.

The artistic and material life of mainland South American Maroons—especially those in Suriname—is particularly rich and creative, especially in relation to rituals associated with birth, reaching adulthood, and death. As anthropologists Richard and Sally Price have observed, Maroon art is not a static leftover from seventeenth-century Africa but a creative and innovative adaptation and development of an African heritage to the new social and environmental conditions of the Americas.

For example, where the first Maroons possessed basic clothing and rustic wood carvings, the twentieth century saw an explosion of stunning and seemingly African wooden sculptures, multicolored textiles, and calabashes elaborately carved inside and out by men and women with newly created tools. Stringed musical instruments made from wood and stingray tails, elaborately carved-wood attaché cases, and artfully designed and decorated folding stools are all new forms ingeniously made and for sale to tourists and museums. Throughout the twentieth century, it is African ideas about aesthetics, color, and the place of art in everyday life that has survived and not a simple fossilized adherence to African objects and forms.

While many consider contemporary Maroon societies and their material culture to be totally African and displaced to the Americas as a consequence of slavery, the situation is more complex. Maroon people themselves, their beliefs, practices, values, and the cultural world of objects they make, undoubtedly originate in the varied tribes of Africa. Yet, as with African-Caribbean peoples more generally, they are remarkably open and inventive and elements of their religious beliefs and material culture are dynamic, creating new hybrid forms that are neither purely African nor American but truly African-American. Some Maroons, like the Aluku of French Guiana, have funerary customs influenced by the local Amerindians, and, more widely, the creole languages they speak are a mix of primarily European words with African and Amerindian additions.

The place of the Maroons in the contemporary cultural and political life of the Caribbean and adjacent areas of South America is ambiguous. The colonial realities that created marronage are long gone and the once isolated Maroon communities are increasingly accessible. The attitude of modern postcolonial governments (for whom eighteenth- and nineteenth-century peace treaties are an embarrassing and anachronistic legacy of colonial rule), and the pressures of tourism and the global economy are all impinging on Maroon culture and identity, whether in Jamaica or Suriname. The younger generation, as the carriers of Maroon culture into the future, is increasingly attracted to the westernized towns and cities of their own countries and beyond, and consequently their connections to their ancestral homelands and traditions are weakened. In response, groups of Maroon elders and representatives are actively promoting links to pan-Amerindian networks of indigenous peoples, documenting their own cultural patrimony, and promoting educational programs in efforts to secure the survival of their remarkable heritage.

See also: Jamaica; Nanny Town (site, Jamaica); Obeah; Shamanism; Slavery; Sugar; Vodoun

References
Agorsah, E. K. 1992. Archaeology and the Maroon Heritage in Jamaica. *Jamaica Journal* 24 (2): 2–9; Agorsah, E. K. 1993. Archaeology and Resistance History in the Caribbean. *The African Archaeology Review* 11: 175–196; Agorsah, E. K. (ed.). 1994. *Maroon Heritage: Archaeological, Ethnographic and Historical Perspectives.* Kingston: Canoe Press; Barker, D., and S. Balfour. 1988. Afro-Caribbean Agriculture: A Jamaican Maroon Community in Transition. *The Geographical Journal* 154 (2): 98–208; Besson, J. 1995. The Creolization of African-American Slave Kinship in Jamaican Free Village and Maroon Communities. In S. Palmie (ed.). *Slave Cultures and the Cultures of Slavery,* pp. 195–202. Knoxville, TN: The University of Tennessee Press; Bilby, K. 1980. Jamaica's Maroons at the Crossroads: Losing Touch with Tradition. *Caribbean Review* 9 (4): 18–21, 49; Campbell, M. C. 1990. *The Maroons of Jamaica 1655–1796.* Trenton, NJ: Africa World Press Inc; Dunham, K. 1946. *Journey to Accompong.* New York: Henry Holt & Co.; Gottlieb, K. L. 2000. *The Mother of Us All: A History of Queen Nanny, Leader of the Windward Jamaica Maroons.* Trenton, NJ: Africa World Press; de Groot, S. W. 1985. A Comparison between the History of Maroon Communities in Surinam and Jamaica. *Slavery and Abolition* 6 (3): 173–184; Heuman, G. (ed.). 1982. *Out of the House of Bondage: Runaways, Resistance, and Maroonage in Africa and the New World.* London: Frank Cass; Kopytoff, B. K. 1976. The Development of Jamaican Maroon Ethnicity. *Caribbean Quarterly* 22 (2–3): 33–50; McFarlane, M. 1977. *Cudjoe the Maroon.* London: Allison and Busby; Picart, L. 1995. The Trelawny Maroons and Sir John Wentworth: The Struggle to Maintain their Culture 1796–1800. *Collections of the Royal Nova Scotia Historical Society* Vol. 44, pp. 165–187; Price, R. 1996. *Maroon*

Societies: Rebel Slave Communities in the Americas. Baltimore and London: The John Hopkins University Press; Price, R., and S. Price. 1990. *Maroon Arts.* Boston: Beacon Press; Weik, T. 1997. The Archaeology of Maroon Societies in the Americas: Resistance, Cultural Continuity, and Transformation in the African Disapora. *Historical Archaeology* 31 (2): 81–92;

Martinique

The island of Martinique in the eastern Caribbean is 65 km long and 31 km wide, and is dominated geographically by the active volcano Mount Pelée. With a population of around 400,000, it is the most important island of the French Antilles that include Guadeloupe, Saint-Martin, and Saint Barthélémy.

The island appears to have first been occupied during the preceramic Ortoiroid Period (ca. 2000 B.C. to 400 B.C.). Two sites in the central part of the island belonging to the local Boutbois culture have yielded crudely made stone flakes and edge-grinding tools. The arrival and settlement of Saladoid peoples with their agricultural village life seems to have been constantly disrupted by the volcanic activity of Mount Pelée. At the Saladoid site of Vivé, a layer of ash has preserved a living floor that shows the arrangement of house posts, pottery, grinding stones, and ceramic griddles indicating the cultivation and processing of manioc. There is no evidence for the consumption of maize.

Vivé pottery is typically Saladoid, though arguably somewhat more geometrical in decoration than elsewhere. At this time, sites were located on the northeast coast in an area of poor fishing and hunting resources, and this is reflected in the archaeological remains. The site of Vivé also preserved the transition between the Saladoid and subsequent Barrancoid Period (A.D. 350 to A.D. 650) in two layers separated by volcanic ash. New Barrancoid influences in pottery are evident at the site of Diamant, and in general the period sees an increase in the number of sites across the island. From around 650 to 1200, the local L'Espérance pottery style appears with simplified shapes and decoration, representing a local manifestation of the Troumassoid style. At this time also, the appearance of shell middens indicates changing subsistence patterns and a focus away from the land and toward the sea. The last phase of Troumassoid came with the locally called Paquemar pottery style, which sees thick-walled ceramics with burnished surfaces and decorated with scrolls and triangles.

Around 1000 to 1200, Troumassoid culture on Martinique is replaced by evidence of the Suazey tradition that lasted until ca. 1450. This period saw the introduction of new types of pottery with finger indentations, a renewed appearance of *adornos,* and clay disks decorated with human faces. There were, however, continuities with the preceding Troumassoid peoples as shown by the material culture at the site of Anse Trabaud on the south coast. After 1450, Martinique seems to have been populated by Carib peoples, though archaeological evidence is scant so far. Martinique seems to have featured in the mythology of the Taíno peoples of the Greater Antilles. According to one legend, the Taíno culture hero Guayahona took all the women from Hispaniola to live in the island of Matinino (Martinique) where they lived without men, and in one variation were turned into frogs. In this way, Matinino/Martinique inadvertently figured in the European expectation of finding Amazons in the Caribbean.

Columbus arrived either in 1493 or 1502 (the date is disputed) and promptly named the island Martinica, supplanting the similar-sounding Carib name Madinina. The presence of the Carib population, however, prevented Spanish colonization. It was only in 1635 that the island was permanently settled by French colonizers from St. Christopher, and the Caribs were soon pushed into the eastern part of the island. Despite various crises in their relations with the Caribs, it was not until 1658 that the French finally decided to extinguish all trace of Carib presence and massacred men, women, and children. Most survivors left for Dominica and St. Vincent, though a few took refuge in the mountains.

With the Caribs removed, sugar-cane cultivation based on slave labor imported from Africa became the economic mainstay. The wealth produced by sugar plantations led to heightened rivalry between the French and English, the latter occupying the island several times during the eighteenth century. In 1848, when slavery was abolished, migrant workers from India came to Martinique to replace the freed plantation slaves. Immediately after the World War II, the island first became a French department and in 1974 a region. It is now officially part of France.

Today, Martinique society is a distinctive mix of French and African cultures. Creole is widely spoken, using French words but an African grammar, and music blends European and African instruments and forms. A recent modern variation called *zouk* has become internationally famous. The main cultural event is carnival, known as Mardi Gras, which takes place in February. Other spectacular hybrid events include a procession of black and white "devils" on Ash Wednesday, kite-fights at Easter, and Toussaint in November, when candlelight processions make their way to local cemeteries. In the capital of Fort-de-France, there is an archaeological museum, and at St. Pierre a modern village and museum have been built on the remains of the original capital of the island that was destroyed when Mount Pelée exploded in May 1902. At Les Trois-Ilets in the south of the island, is the sugar-cane museum illustrating this important part of Martinique's colonial history.

See also: Caribs; Dominica; Guadeloupe; Saladoid; Suazey; Troumassoid
References
Allaire, L. 1977. *Later Prehistory in Martinique and the Island Caribs: Problems in Ethnic Identification.* Ph.D. dissertation, Yale University; Allaire, L. 2003. Agricultural Societies in the Caribbean: The Lesser Antilles. In J. Sued-Badillo (ed.). *General History of the Caribbean: Vol. 1, Autochthonous Societies,* pp. 195–227. Paris: UNESCO; Delawarde, J-P. 1983. *La sorcellerie à la Martinique et dans les voisines: ses positions et ses réactions dans ses rapports avec le culte chrétien ambiant.* Paris; Dessalles, P., E. Forster, and R. Forster (eds.). 1996. *Sugar and Slavery, Family and Race: The Letters and Diary of Pierre Dessalles, Planter in Martinique, 1808–1856.* Baltimore: Johns Hopkins University Press; Mattioni, M. 1982. *Salvage Excavations at the Fond-Brulé Site, Martinique, Final Report.* University of Manitoba Anthropology Papers 27. Winnipeg: University of Manitoba; Michelin, 2001. *Michelin Green Sightseeing Guide to Guadeloupe and Martinique.* French and European Publishing; Petitjean Roget, H. 1978. Note sur un vase Arawak trouvé à la Martinique. *Proceedings of the Seventh International Congress for the Study of Pre-Columbian*

Cultures of the Lesser Antilles, pp. 99–115. Montreal: Centre de Recherches Caraïbes, Université de Montréal; Petitjean Roget, J. 1970. Archaeology in Martinique. *Parallèles* 36–37: 48–67; Rosemain, J. n.d. *La musique dans la société antillaise: 1635–1902, Martinique, Guadeloupe.* Paris: L'Hamattan; Tomich, D. W. 1990. *Slavery in the Circuit of Sugar: Martinique and the World Economy, 1830–1848.* Baltimore: Johns Hopkins University Press.

Martyr, Peter

Peter Martyr, more accurately Pietro Martire D'Anghiera (ca. 1457–1526), was an Italian humanist and native of Milan whose importance to the Caribbean lay in the fact that he published the first account of the New World of the Americas.

In 1488, D'Anghiera moved from Italy to Spain, where he became a chaplain at the royal court. Appointed to the Council of the Indies in 1518, he listened to the eyewitness accounts of the New World given by Christopher Columbus and various conquistadors and explorers, and read the many official reports and documents concerning these momentous events. He saw Amerindians brought back to Spain, tasted new spices, held golden nuggets and heavy pearls in his hands, and pored over new maps. He even had one Amerindian dress up in various costumes and perform his war dances. D'Anghiera's most famous work is the *De rebus oceanis et Orbe Novo decades,* a series of letters and pamphlets written to colleagues and friends, including his powerful patron Cardinal Ascanio Sforza, between 1493 and 1525.

These accounts spread the news of the discoveries in the New World throughout Europe. They were full of unique insights, facts, and fantasies that tell of the commercial anxieties and intellectual ferment caused by these events. He reports on the gold, silver, geography, animals, and other "marvellous things" found in the Caribbean and beyond, and presents his idea of the Americas as a golden world whose noble savages lived a peaceful existence. These views proved influential in shaping European ideas about, and activities in, the New World, contrasting the rational European man with either the natural innocence or cannibalistic savagery of Amerindians.

The fame of *De Orbe Novo* led in 1524 to his being put in charge of the abbey of Sevilla la Nueva (New Seville) on the north coast of Jamaica—a town built in 1509 on the site where Christopher Columbus had been shipwrecked during his fourth voyage. Although he never left Europe, the income from this abbacy allowed D'Anghiera to pay for the building of a stone church for Sevilla la Nueva, whose remains have since been investigated by archaeologists.

See also: Columbus, Christopher; Jamaica; Las Casas, Bartolomé de; Pané, Father Ramón

References
d'Anghiera, P. M. 1912. *De Orbe Novo: The Eight Decades of Peter Martyr D'Anghiera.* New York: Burt Franklin; Gerbi, A. 1986. *Nature in the New World: From Christopher Columbus to Gonzalo Fernández de Oviedo,* pp. 50–75. Pittsburgh: University of Pittsburgh Press; Pagden, A. 1982. *The Fall of Natural Man: The American Indian and the Origins of Comparative Ethnology.* Cambridge: Cambridge University Press.

Maya

The Mayan civilization of Mesoamerica was in part a Caribbean phenomenon. Divided into the Preclassic (2000 B.C. to A.D. 250), Classic (A.D. 200 to A.D. 850), and Post-Classic Periods (A.D. 750 to A.D. 1521), it featured hydraulic agriculture, cities and ceremonial centers, a complex dual-calendar system, sophisticated hieroglyphic writing, and an elaborate and religiously inspired art style.

Although most of Mayan civilization was an internal Mesoamerican development, the proximity of the Caribbean exercised considerable influence. This was especially true during the Post-Classic Period and the events surrounding the European conquest and early colonization of the Yucatán peninsula. It is these Caribbean-related aspects of Mayan culture that will be the focus here.

The Late Post-Classic Period of Mayan civilization before the Spanish arrival was in many ways a pale shadow of the glories of the Classic era whose great cities of Tikal, Palenque, and Copán flourished in the tropical rainforest of the Mayan lowlands. During the Late Post-Classic, Mayan society saw a move away from land-based trade in favor of seaborne trading. Extensive trade-networks were interlaced around the Yucatán coast, north to eastern Mexico, and south to Honduras, Nicaragua, Costa Rica, and Panama. The greatest mainland coastal settlement at this time was Tulum on the eastern coast of Yucatán, which flourished as a trading port and religious-cult center between A.D. 1200 and A.D. 1519. Although its architecture—such as the Temple of the Diving God—is shoddy by comparison with other sites, the temple and town were strategically located for maritime trade and the pilgrimage cult of the Mayan moon goddess Ix Chel.

Nearby was another important Mayan maritime trading settlement known as Tancah. Its surviving architecture spans some 600 years, beginning around A.D. 1000 and ending sometime in early colonial times. It is mainly famous today for its fourteenth-century murals that depict scenes of maritime conflict. It may be that around this time that region came under the control of the sea-trading Mayan group known as the Putun. Together with Tulum, Tancah appears to have been at the heart of a pilgrimage area, perhaps associated with the religious and astronomical beliefs concerning the planet Venus, whose glyph has been found carved on the wall of the site's cenote (underground well).

Another place that played an important role in late Mayan history and the early years of European exploration was the island of Cozumel, some 16 km off Yucatán's northeastern coast. It too was an important trading and ritual center, perhaps the pivotal location and major port-of-trade in a commercial network that included Tulum, Tancah, and the Isla de Mujeres. It was on Cozumel that the Putun blended the spiritual, commercial, and defensive aspects of their culture in the series of small coastal shrines that may also have served as watchtowers. It was the Spanish priest Fray Diego de Landa who first commented that the Maya regarded Cozumel as a center of pilgrimage akin to the Christian Jerusalem and Rome, and the focus of the worship of Ix Chel at such sites as San Gervasio.

The trading Maya of Mesoamerica's Caribbean coast entered European history during Christopher Columbus's fourth voyage (April 1502 to November 1504), when he reached the island of Guanaja off Cape Honduras. Offshore of Honduras, near the Bay Islands, Columbus's expedition encountered a large seagoing Mayan trading canoe. From its size, and some thirty passengers, as well as its cargo of cacao, copper bells, axes, metalworking equipment, and clothing, it was obvious that the people of this region were far more advanced than those of the Caribbean islands. Despite hearing stories of sophisticated peoples who traded in great markets and wore large quantities of jewelry, Columbus did not take advantage of his luck and so missed the opportunity of the very wealth that he had spent so long searching for.

During the following years, a handful of other Spaniards arrived on the Caribbean coast of Mayan Yucatán. In 1511, a shipwrecked crew were cast ashore in eastern Yucatán and only two Spaniards survived the ensuing capture by Mayan lords. Gerónimo de Aguilar ended up serving a local Mayan ruler, and Gonzalo de Guerrero moved south to Chetumal, where he married a local ruler's daughter.

In 1517, a new Spanish expedition led by Francisco Hernández de Córdoba landed at several locations, including Isla de Mujeres and Champoton. The Maya at the latter place fought so ferociously that despite superior weaponry the Spanish retreated to Cuba, where Córdoba died of his wounds. The next year, Juan de Grijalva's expedition landed on the island of Cozumel and then, farther south, saw the imposing coastal town of Tulum. He then retraced his steps and sailed around the Yucatán peninsula and up the eastern coast of Mexico, where he was the first European to hear of the great Aztec civilization. In the

Chichen Itza, the "El Castillo" pyramid (Courtesy Nicholas J. Saunders)

wake of the stories told by Grijalva back in Cuba, Hernán Cortés was put in charge of a further expedition in 1519.

Cortés's first port-of-call was Cozumel where he spent several days destroying many of the Mayan idols of Ix Chel and erecting Christian crosses. Hearing of "bearded men" on the adjacent mainland, he went to investigate and discovered Aguilar, whom he rescued and employed as an interpreter. Moving north then southwest around Yucatán, Cortés arrived at Tabasco, where he was given a local girl named Marina who was fluent in both the Mayan and Aztec languages. Both Aguilar and Marina were to play decisive roles in Cortés's subsequent conquest of Aztec Mexico between 1519 and 1521.

In the years following the Spanish conquest, the Yucatán Maya were subdued by Francisco de Montejo, who had been a member both of the Grijalva and Cortés expeditions. In 1526, Montejo received permission from the Spanish Crown to conquer and colonize the Yucatán, a process that began the following year but was not completed until 1546. The invasion made good progress, encountering little resistance until 1528 at Chauaca. Here the local Maya fought tenaciously but were defeated. The decisive battle, however, took place at Ake near the modern town of Tizimin where traditional Mayan weapons and tactics again were no match for the Spanish. Over 1,000 Mayan warriors were killed and the psychological effect was so traumatic that all Mayan resistance in the area collapsed. Further engagements followed, including an episode where Montejo's emissaries failed to persuade the long-abandoned Aguilar to leave his Mayan family and rejoin the Spanish.

Montejo's second phase of conquest lasted from 1531 until 1535, during which time he based himself at Champoton. In 1531, the Mayan ruler Ah Canul surrendered and Montejo sent his son to the old Mayan city of Chichén Itzá in the area controlled by the Cupules. It was here that Montejo the younger established a royal city but was forced to abandon it when the Cupules rose against him. Father and son were reunited at Dzibikal but soon afterward news arrived of Francisco Pizarro's conquest of the fabulously wealthy Incan empire in Peru. Yucatán had yielded little gold in seven years of fighting and many soldiers left for South America. With his army depleted, Montejo abandoned the conquest.

In 1541, Montejo the elder formally handed over the conquest to his son, who promptly established his base of operations at Campeche. The powerful Xiu Maya submitted to the Spanish but those of Ah Canul refused. In a campaign against them, Montejo's cousin established the city of Mérida in central northern Yucatán where he received Tutul Xiu, the ruler of Mani, the most powerful independent Mayan kingdom. The conversion of Tutul Xiu to Christianity led to further submissions in western Yucatán but in the east, Mayan towns either held out or submitted and then rebelled. The largest of these rebellions occurred in 1546 and involved an alliance of many different Mayan groups. This was provoked in large part by the behavior of local Spanish soldiers such as Alonso Pacheco, who enslaved, tortured, and murdered the local Maya as well as stealing their crops. In revenge, the Maya killed Spaniards residing in the area and were only defeated by an expedition led by Montejo himself.

Chichén Itzá, the Observatory and the "El Castillo" pyramid in the background (Courtesy Nicholas J. Saunders)

After twenty years, the Spanish had finally ended over two millennia of Mayan civilization in the Yucatán and ushered in a new colonial era for the Mayan lands of the Caribbean. Yet, over the following centuries, Mayan slaves escaped their masters and took refuge in the forests. Uprisings were inspired by those who received divine prophecies from the gods and who subsequently wrote them down, most famously in *The Books of Chilam Balam*. Throughout the colonial period, the Yucatán Maya found ways of resisting their Spanish overlords, making idols of their gods to be distributed throughout the peninsula, maintaining underground religious movements, talking of prophecies of the end of Spanish rule, and sometimes killing Spaniards and their supporters. Even as late as 1848, the so-called Maya Caste War saw thousands of Mayas and whites die in fighting provoked mainly by agrarian reform. Ironically, the Maya of Caribbean Mexico proved far more difficult to subdue than the warrior Aztecs of central Mexico, who had been defeated almost 500 years before.

See also: Cacao; Chichén Itzá Cenote (site, Mexico); Columbus, Christopher; Cozumel; Tancah (site, Mexico); Tulum (site, Mexico); Underwater Archaeology

References
Chamberlain, R. S. 1948. *The Conquest and Colonization of Yucatan, 1517–1550.* Washington, DC: Carnegie Institution of Washington Publication 582; Clendinnen, I. 1978. *Ambivalent Conquests: Maya and Spaniards in Yucatan, 1517–1570.* Cambridge: Cambridge University Press; Craine, E. R., and R. C. Reindorp (trans. and eds.). 1979. *The Codex Pérez and the Book of Chilam Balam of Maní.* Norman, OK: University of Oklahoma Press; Freidel, D. A., and J. A. Sabloff. 1984. *Cozumel: Late Maya Settlement Patterns.* Orlando, FL: Academic Press; Lothrop,

S. K. 1924. *Tulum: An Archaeological Study of the East Coast of Yucatan*. Washington, DC: Carnegie Institution of Washington Publication 335; Miller, A. G. 1977. The Maya and the Sea: Trade and Cult at Tancah and Tulum. In E. P. Benson (ed.). *The Sea in the Pre-Columbian World*, 97–138. Washington, DC: Dumbarton Oaks; Miller, A. G. 1982. *On the Edge of the Sea: Mural Painting at Tancah-Tulum, Quintana Roo, Mexico*. Washington, DC: Dumbarton Oaks; Sabloff, J. A. 1977. Old Myths, New Myths: The Role of Sea Traders in the Development of Ancient Maya Civilization. In E. P. Benson (ed.). *The Sea in the Pre-Columbian World*, pp. 67–88. Washington, DC: Dumbarton Oaks; Sharer, R. J. 1994. Epilogue: The Spanish Conquest, *The Ancient Maya*, pp. 731–754. Stanford, CA: Stanford University Press.

Mayoid (pottery)

Mayoid pottery, possibly related to the Koriabo ceramic complex of coastal Guiana, was a late development, arriving in Trinidad in the years immediately preceding European arrival, almost certainly brought by Amerindians from the mainland. Mayoid pottery appears to have been used alongside the earlier Arauquinoid ceramic style in some Trinidadian sites, possibly as trade items. It has been found at the coastal site of Guayaguare in southeastern Trinidad.

It seems to have been made well into the historic period, appearing in the Amerindian mission villages established in Trinidad by Capuchin monks from 1687. These missions are known to have been populated with Nepoio Amerindians, a group that also occupied the lower reaches of the Orinoco River, further indicating a mainland origin for this pottery style. A distinctive feature of Mayoid ceramics is that their fabric always includes a temper called *caraipé*, made from the ash of burned bark of the small tree *Licania apetala*. The most common Mayoid pottery shape is a simple necked jar whose only decoration is a nicked rim, which is occasionally painted black. Its shape recalls the so-called buck pot, also from mainland northeastern South America, that was used to cook the Amerindian stew known as pepper pot.

> **See also:** Arauquinoid (pottery); Cayo (pottery); Pepper Pot; Trinidad and Tobago
> **References**
> Allaire, L. 2003. Agricultural Societies in the Caribbean: The Lesser Antilles. In J. Sued-Badillo (ed.). *General History of the Caribbean: Vol. 1, Autochthonous Societies*, p 186. Paris: UNESCO; Boomert, A. 1985. The Guayabitoid and Mayoid Series: Amerindian Culture History in Trinidad during Late Prehistoric and Protohistoric Times. *Proceedings of the Tenth International Congress for the Study of the Pre-Columbian Cultures of the Lesser Antilles, Martinique 1983*, pp. 93–148; Boomert, A. 1995. Island Carib Archaeology. In N. L. Whitehead (ed.). *Wolves from the Sea: Readings in the Anthropology of the Native Caribbean*, pp. 23–35. Leiden:

Meillacan

Meillacan culture, a local variation or subseries of the Ostionoid tradition, succeeded that of the earlier Ostiones people in the Cibao valley of northern Hispaniola. Here they innovated ridged-field agriculture and then, starting sometime before A.D. 800, moved into Jamaica and Cuba in the footsteps of their Ostiones forebears.

Unlike the Saladoid and Ostiones cultures, the Meillacan peoples made unpainted pottery, though it was distinctive due to its textured surfaces, decorated with rectilinear incisions, cross-hatched designs, punctations, appliqué clay ridges, and small geometric and zoomorphic lugs. This unique ceramic style has inspired speculation as to a non-Caribbean source for the tradition, with Guyana and the Orinoco River having been suggested, though an evolution from local preceramic peoples of the Courian Casimiroid tradition is also a possibility. In material culture, Meillacans continued to use ceramic griddles for baking cassava bread, and to make objects of stone, bone, and shell, some as *zemí* figures for religious worship.

In Jamaica, Meillacan peoples spread out from the earlier Ostiones foothold (the locally known Little River culture) in the south to colonize the whole island. It seems as if this local Meillacan White Marl culture persisted until historic times on Jamaica. In Cuba, the local Meillacan Bani culture seems to have represented the introduction and spread of a pottery-making agricultural society that replaced or assimilated the earlier Archaic Period society of the Redondan Casimiroid peoples, sometimes also referred to as Ciboney. On Hispaniola, where the original Meillacan culture had evolved from the earlier Ostiones culture, further changes saw the emergence of the Chican Ostionoid peoples (i.e., the Taíno) around A.D. 1200.

See also: Casimiroid; Cuba; Jamaica; Ostionoid; Taíno (Arawak)

References

Allaire, L. 1999. Archaeology of the Caribbean Region. In F. Salomon and S. B. Schwartz (eds.). *The Cambridge History of the Native Peoples of the Americas: Vol. III, South America Part 1,* pp. 717–725, Cambridge: Cambridge University Press; Rouse, I. 1992. *The Tainos: Rise and Decline of the People Who Greeted Columbus,* pp. 96–99, New Haven, CT: Yale University Press; Veloz Maggiolo, M., E. Ortega, and A. Caba Fuentes. 1981. *Los modos de vida Meillacoides y sus posibles orígenes: Un estudio interpretativo.* Santo Domingo, the Dominican Republic: Museo del Hombre Dominicano.

Miskito

The Miskito people of the Caribbean coasts of Honduras and Nicaragua are of mixed Amerindian, African, and European ancestry. In 1797, the British brought around 2,000 Garifuna (Black Caribs) from St. Vincent, leaving them on the island of Roatán off Honduras. They soon moved to the mainland where they encountered many free blacks, slaves who had previously escaped from Haiti and Guadeloupe, as well as local Amerindian peoples, the Sumo and Paya. These different peoples were all influenced by each other and, variously, by Spanish and English settlers. The African element was dominant, however, and the result was a mixed-heritage group that became known as Miskito.

The Miskito forged strong cultural links with the English and with buccaneers, raiding other tribes and Spanish towns in order to take prisoners for the slave trade and being paid in guns, ammunition, and tools. Although the English never had total or direct control over them, the Miskito admired and adopted aspects of English culture, including language and dress. So close was this relationship that Miskito sometimes journeyed to

Jamaica with their hunting dogs onboard English ships to help track down escaped slaves (Maroons).

Even Miskito political structure reflected aspects of the English system, as they had offices that included a king, governor, and admiral. In 1687, the British in Jamaica recognized the king of Mosquitia as an ally against the Spanish. The Miskito kings lived in that part of coastal Nicaragua known as Bluefields after 1687, and have regarded themselves as a British protectorate since 1740, refusing to recognize the Nicaraguan government. In 1894, part of the Miskito coast was annexed by Nicaragua, and Britain ceded any rights in the area to Nicaragua as well.

In July 2002, the Council of Elders in Bilwi announced the creation of an independent nation, the Communitarian Nation of Moskitia, that incorporates 280 communities and 7 ethnic groups—mestizos, Miskitos, Sumos, Ramas, Afro-Nicaraguans, Garifuna, and Creoles.

> *See also:* Garifuna (Black Caribs); Maroons
> **References**
> Conzemius, E. 1932. Ethnographic Survey of the Miskito and Sumu Indians of Honduras and Nicaragua. *Bureau of American Ethnology Bulletin* 106. Washington, DC: Smithsonian Institution; Helms, M. W. 1971. *Asang: Adaptations to Culture Contact in a Miskito Community:* Gainesville, FL: University of Florida Press; Nietschmann, B. 1973. *Between Land and Water: The Subsistence Ecology of the Miskito Indians, Eastern Nicaragua.* New York: Seminar Press.

Molasses Reef Wreck

The earliest European shipwreck found to date, and once erroneously announced to the world's press as Columbus's caravel the *Pinta,* is named after the Molasses Reef in the Turks and Caicos Islands on which it ran aground sometime in the early sixteenth century.

The site was discovered in 1976 in a remote area, but in water only 6 meters deep, by treasure hunters who removed several artifacts. After many illegal activities, the Turks and Caicos government requested the help of the Institute of Nautical Archaeology at Texas A&M University. Excavations began in 1982 over an area of some 6,000 sq meters, but not before treasure seekers had further damaged the site with explosives. Despite these depredations, the Molasses Reef wreck is unusual inasmuch as it is the earliest that has so far been exhaustively and scientifically excavated.

The early date of the wreck was indicated by several discoveries. Late-fifteenth- and early-sixteenth-century objects, including Spanish pottery, and wrought-iron, breech-loading cannon (*bombardetas*) were found, and the style of hull architecture was also typical of that time. In addition, swivel guns (*versos*) were found alongside crossbows and swords. In all, some 10 tons of artifacts were recovered, scientifically studied, and conserved. Insights gained include the fact that some of the ship's stone ballast had probably been loaded in Lisbon and added to other ballast stones of black limestone from Bristol in England. An unusual feature was the relative lack of personal possessions, a paucity of ceramics, an absence of coins, and armaments that appear to have been stowed rather than ready for use.

Although heavily damaged, it was possible to suggest that the ship had at least three masts, was about 19 meters long, and probably sank somewhere between 1510 and 1530. The presence of glass beads suggests the ship may have been trading with local Amerindians, and/or perhaps also engaged in the trade in native Lucayans who lived on the Turks and Caicos and who were in demand as slave labor in Hispaniola (modern Haiti and the Dominican Republic). If this was the case, it may explain why there are no archival records of its voyage, and thus so far no clue as to its identity. All recovered objects were returned in 1990 to the National Museum in the Turks and Caicos.

See also: Nuestra Señora de Atocha, Wreck of; *Nuestra Señora de la Concepción,* Wreck of; *Nuestra Señora de las Maravillas,* Wreck of; Underwater Archaeology

References

Keith, D. H. 1987. *The Molasses Reef Wreck.* PhD dissertation, Texas A&M University. Ann Arbor, MI: University Microfilms; Keith, D. H. 1997. Molasses Reef Wreck. In J. P. Delgado (ed.). *Encyclopedia of Underwater and Maritime Archaeology,* pp. 279–281. London: British Museum Press; Keith, D. H., J. A. Duff, S. R. James, T. J. Oertling, and J. J. Simmons. 1984. The Molasses Reef Wreck, Turks and Caicos Islands, B.W.I.: A Preliminary Report. *International Journal of Nautical Archaeology and Underwater Exploration* 13: 45–63.

Montserrat

Montserrat is 18 km long by 11 km wide, with an area of 101 sq km, and has a population of some 11,000, mainly of African descent. It is of volcanic origin, and still active.

Montserrat's earliest prehistoric artifacts date to around 250 B.C. and belong to the period of Saladoid expansion through the area, as illustrated by the finding of characteristic white-on-red (W-O-R) ceramics. The first major occupation appears at the site of Trants and dates to around A.D. 200. Trant's occupants appear to have been the Saladoid predecessors of the later Taíno. Together with the islands of Vieques, St. Croix, and Grenada, Montserrat may have functioned as a port-of-trade, serving the maritime trade in stone beads and zoomorphic pendants. Of the twenty-nine varieties of mineral identified—including carnelian, quartz, amethyst, and turquoise—not one occurred on the island. The inhabitants of Montserrat were importing stone jewelry made from exotic minerals, though may also have been involved in making some items as well.

Christopher Columbus first sighted Montserrat on 11 November 1493, naming it Santa Maria de Montserrate after the Spanish monastery where Ignacio de Loyola experienced his vision to found the Jesuits. At this time, the island appears to have had no or few indigenous inhabitants, though its name is reported as being Alliouagana, a Carib name for "place of the prickly bush."

It was Thomas Warner from Britain who first settled the island colony with Irish Catholics, whereupon it became a place of refuge for all of that faith. In the mid-seventeenth century, African slaves were imported and Montserrat became a plantation economy based on sugar. Despite periodic Carib raids on the island during the seventeenth century, several French invasions in the eighteenth century, and a slave uprising in 1786, the island retained its stability, remaining British throughout. Today, Montserrat is a British dependent territory.

Due to its unusual history, Irish influence is apparent in food, dance, and music, mixing with the otherwise dominant African elements. Calypso, steel bands, and costumed masquerades are a feature of Montserrat popular culture, especially during the Christmas season. Dancing and healing are combined in the activities of the *jumbie* dancers, and African and imported musical instruments blend together in the island's musical repertoire. While St. Patrick's Day is celebrated on 17 March across the island, Montserrat's favorite festivities occur at Christmas, from 12 December to New Year's Day.

The island's capital of Plymouth has a museum built within the restored remains of a sugar mill tower, and which contains paintings by local artists and a variety of pre-Columbian artifacts recovered during archaeological excavations on the island. Historical archaeology is also a feature of Montserrat's heritage, with investigations of the eighteenth-century Galway sugar plantation having identified the Great House and boiling house, among other buildings.

See also: Caribs; Columbus, Christopher; Galways Plantation; Saladoid; Slavery; Sugar
References
Akenson, D. H. 1997. *If the Irish Ran the World: Montserrat, 1630–1730.* Montreal, Quebec: McGill-Queens University Press; Dobbin, J. D. 1986. *The Jombee Dance of Montserrat: A Study of Trance Ritual in the West Indies.* Columbus: Ohio State University Press; Fergus, H. A. 1994. *Montserrat, A History of a Caribbean Colony.* London: MacMillan; Pulsipher, L. M., and C. M. Goodwin. 1982. *Galways Plantation, Montserrat West Indies, 1981 Field Report.* Knoxville, TN: University of Tennessee, Department of Geography; Watters, D. 1994. Archaeology of Trants, Montserrat. *Annals of Carnegie Museum* 63 (3): 215–237.

Music

Caribbean music, like music anywhere in the world, is more than entertainment. It embodies ideas of ethnic and political identity, self-image, and the struggle against adversity. It represents ways of dealing with life through satire, irony, and sheer physical enjoyment, and in many instances also is intimately associated with folklore beliefs and spiritual activities. During the pre-Columbian period, music was an integral part of indigenous Amerindian life, and in the last 500 years, the music of the Caribbean has reflected, and continues to reflect, the melting pot of peoples, cultures, and religions that the region became after Columbus's 1492 arrival.

Pre-Columbian Music

Before Europeans arrived, the indigenous Taíno and Carib peoples used music to express and reinforce their spiritual view of the world and of their place within it. Their music was an integral part of their philosophy of life, as it was in their original homeland of South America. They used singing and chanting to maintain ideas of community, praising ancestors and the spirits of the forest. The shape of musical instruments and the sounds they made often replicated different types of birds, the ultimate spirit familiar that represented the soul of the shaman as he journeyed up into the supernatural realm. Drums could summon ancestors, and when combined with fasting, induced ritual trance in shamans and audience alike.

Amerindian singing, chanting, whistling, percussion, and dancing connected social life to the spiritual breath that permeated the universe. Human breath had magical power to summon spirits, and shamans blew protective and purifying spells over people and food alike. Typical of Amerindian music and its close associations with shamanism and spirituality is the case of the Warao of the Orinoco river delta opposite Trinidad. For the Warao, songs and chants have a numinous quality that can protect the singer from malign spirits. Warao shamans use several types of rattles, deer-bone flutes, cane flutes, conch trumpets, as well as more recent introductions such as violins and small guitars called *cuatros.*

The most important Warao rattle is the *hebu mataro* or calabash rattle, some 70 cm long with a wooden handle, slits, and decorated with red and yellow feathers of the cotora parrot. Inside the rattle are several small quartz fragments that glow when the rattle is shaken at night. Shamans use the hebu mataro to cure illness, the glowing light of the quartz helping to convince the patient of the shamans' powers. Curing songs accompany these performances, while other shamanic songs provide help in childbirth, canoe paddling, and traveling on foot through the jungle. Warao society illustrates how embedded music is in their rituals, practices, and mythology. This distinctively Amerindian attitude to music was in all probability broadly similar during pre-Columbian times throughout the Caribbean region and beyond.

The integrated nature of music, religious life, and worldview for pre-Columbian peoples is seen most clearly for the Island Caribbean in the Taíno *areíto*—a social and political ceremonial event that featured singing, music, dancing, and feasting. Like all Amerindians, the Taíno had no stringed instruments, playing rattles, rasps, drums, whistles, and flutes instead. In early encounters, the Spanish were welcomed and entertained by the Taíno who arranged areítos in their honor as a type of elite hospitality. Areítos usually took place in the plaza or cleared area fronting the chief's house, temple, and *zemí* images, suggesting perhaps that areítos were associated in some way with ancestor worship.

While only the remains of bone or ceramic flutes and conch-shell trumpets are found archaeologically, rare drawings made by European explorers and chroniclers provide an insight into a musical world that has largely disappeared. Perhaps the most famous scene is that included in the written works of Gonzalo Fernández de Oviedo y Valdés, which shows a Taíno H-drum, so-called because of the distinctive cuts made into the surface of a hollowed-out log. Similarly shaped drums are known from Mexico and Costa Rica. The Carib of the Lesser Antilles had many of the same type of instruments, including calabash rattles, flutes made from bamboo and from bone, panpipes, conch-shell trumpets, and snail-shell rattles tied to arms and legs.

The Caribbean Maya of the Yucatán also played flutes, rattles, and drums, and these are known archaeologically and from early Spanish accounts that describe their use in religious ceremonies. Most information on pre-Columbian music, however, comes from central and western Mexico and the great culture area of Peru that lay beyond the Caribbean basin. Nevertheless, the shared nature of Amerindian worldview and musical practices can be assumed, as depicted in the colorful murals of the Classic Mayan city of Bonampak that depict Mayan men dressed in animal costumes and playing a variety of musical instruments.

Historical and Modern Music

The arrival first of Europeans, and then Africans, transformed the musical world of the Caribbean. The introduction of stringed instruments, and then African percussion and chanting, combined to produce a dazzling variety of local musical styles—an inventiveness that continues today in Jamaican reggae, French Caribbean *zouk,* Trinidadian steel-drum orchestras, Cuban rumba, and merengue from the Dominican Republic, to mention just a few.

Much African-Caribbean music takes the form of telling folk tales through song and dance, accompanied by an array of percussion instruments. There is also Christian influence and perhaps some traces from the original Amerindians, some of whom came into contact with African slaves who escaped their servitude and took refuge in mountains and forests throughout the Caribbean area.

Today, in mainland South America, the descendants of these Maroon communities still make stringed musical instruments from wood and stingray tails to sell as tourist souvenirs. Ritual songs, known as *juka* in Suriname and *jawbone* in Jamaica, are still sung and reflect their multiethnic African ancestry. The Garifuna—descendants of the so-called Black Carib peoples of St. Vincent who were forcibly relocated by the British to Central America in the late 1700s—also have their own distinctive musical traditions. A typical Garifuna group from the Caribbean coast of Guatemala has several skin-headed drums made from a tree trunk, gourd rattles, and sometimes a conch-shell trumpet. These instruments accompany a singer and chorus in several different styles such as *chumba* and *yankunú.* Other groups use electric instruments to play more modern Caribbean music. The Garifuna use their different songs to accompany religious services, funerals, and to celebrate the sacred ancestor cult of Chugu and Dugu.

African-Caribbean music is often intimately associated with the great syncretic religious movements such as Santería, Vodoun, and Orisha/Shango. Before emancipation, slaves often used mundane items such as ceramic pots, sticks, and iron hoes as impromptu musical instruments that also had a role in Obeah witchcraft unsuspected by the European slave owners.

Music in the Dominican Republic is described as creole and has moved away from earlier Spanish influences to incorporate African forms. At Saints' festivals the *Salve* is a sung rosary and is mainly performed by women, although different versions have evolved in different parts of the island. The merengue is a symbol of the creole nature of Dominican society and culture. This typical dance music is played on an accordion, tambora, and marimba, and blends European, African, and possibly Taíno influences.

Today, Cuba is a center for distinctive African-American music in its effervescent mix of African and Hispanic influences. The combination of African percussive rhythms and Spanish guitar has created such vibrant styles as rumba, *trova, son,* and *danzón*—the last two being the inspiration for the internationally better known salsa and cha-cha, respectively. African influence predominates in the music of Santería, with two-headed drums (*batás*), gourds covered with bead nets (*shekere*), and steel hoe blades (*hierro*) being the main instruments. With the emergence of Cuban nationality between 1790 and 1868, various musical styles influenced from Europe and Africa took on a distinctively Cuban nature. In western Cuba this took the form known as *punta campesino* and in eastern Cuba a mixture of strings and percussion became known as *son.* Elsewhere, the urban music known as rumba developed in the suburbs of Havana and included its own distinctive percussion instruments known as congas.

In Puerto Rico, the sung rosary (*rosario cantato*) is an important local musical tradition. There are various types, some sung within a church and others outside, though mostly they are all accompanied by the cuatro. An African form is known as the *bomba,* and originated among slaves and ex-slaves at birthdays, weddings, and the end of the harvest. Typical of the Puerto Rican creole tradition is the *décima,* a combination of poetry and music, though the largest quantity of music belongs to the genre known as *seis.* Perhaps beginning as early as the mid-sixteenth century, seis incorporates African influences in its rhythms, and is played by several cuatro players and a singer of décimas. A final form is the *plena,* which developed as dance music around 1900, with guitar, concertina, and tambourine, with singing added after a few years.

Until the recent resurgence of interest in Cuban music, Jamaican reggae and its predecessor, ska, had dominated the international music scene in terms of Caribbean music since the late 1960s. Reggae was made famous internationally by Jamaica's first superstar, Bob Marley and his group, the Wailers. Blending African rhythms and electronic music with lyrics of social comment, reggae is strongly associated with Rastafarianism—the Jamaican religion that regards the late emperor of Ethiopia, Haile Selassie (or Ras Tafari), as divine.

In the French Antilles, notably Martinique and Guadeloupe, and those islands that had at one time belonged to France, much French influence remains in local musical traditions. Today, Martinique society is a distinctive mix of French and African cultures. Creole is widely spoken, and local music blends European and African instruments and forms. A recent modern variation called zouk has become internationally famous. In St. Lucia, French patois known as *Kwéyòl* is still widely spoken, although English is the official language, and zouk is a favorite. In Trinidad, which had seen Spanish, then French, and finally English influence, varied European musical forms have blended with African, Amerindian, and Indian styles to produce probably the most varied musical landscape in the Island Caribbean.

Trinidad's multicultural society has created many different types of music. Calypso has ancient roots with origins in songs that praised and satirized native rulers in West Africa and that were kept alive by the slaves who came to Trinidad. Calypso developed throughout the nineteenth and twentieth centuries, and singers adopted memorable stage names, such as Atilla the Hun, Terror, and Panther, usually prefixing these with Lord or Mighty, such as the world famous Lord Kitchener and Mighty Sparrow, whose singing dominated the genre from the 1950s to the 1980s. More recently, Shadow, Calypso Rose, and Chalkdust have risen to prominence. All Calypsonians are quick, stylish, and extroverted, blending new and old musical styles but retaining the heart of clever and witty social comment in a changing world.

Equally inventive is Trinidadian steel-band music (also known as *pan*). Originating against a background of traditional African drumming, pan began in the poorer parts of Port of Spain during the 1930s—partly as a long-delayed response to the outlawing of Carnival drumming in the previous century. In 1945, the first steel bands appeared, using the cut-down ends of oil drums and playing ever more sophisticated tunes. Despite an early reputation for violence, steel bands today have broadened their appeal to include women and middle-class Trinidadians. These and other Trinidadian musical forms appear during Carnival where competitions choose the best talents for a year.

Less well-known internationally, but equally important for Trinidad's multicultural society and traditions, is the music of the Cocoa Panyols—a community whose ancestry is a mix of Venezuelan peasant farmers, the descendants of Trinidad's Spanish peasantry, Africans, and Amerindians. The name derives from a Trinidadian corruption of the term *español*. While much of Cocoa Panyol culture has disappeared, their distinctive music known as Parang has survived. Parang music is played on European stringed instruments like the cuatro, mandolin, and violin, and accompanied by percussion instruments, such as the Amerindian maracas. Parang is more popular today than in the past, and is a common feature of Christmas festivities where it is enjoyed by all Trinidadians.

See also: Areíto; Carnival (Trinidad); Cocoa Panyols; Cuba; Dominican Republic; Garifuna (Black Caribs); Jamaica; Maroons; Obeah; Puerto Rico; Rastafarianism; Santería; Shamanism; Trinidad and Tobago; Vodoun; Warao

References
Arrivillaga Cortés, A. 1990. La música tradicional Garífuna en Guatemala. *Latin American Music Review* 11 (2): 251–280; Austerlitz, P. 1977. *Merengue: Dominican Music and Dominican Identity.* Philadelphia: Temple University Press; Basso, E. 1985. *A Musical View of the Universe.* Philadelphia: University of Pennsylvania Press; Behague, G. H. (ed.). 1994. *Music and Black Ethnicity: The Caribbean and South America.* Miami: University of Miami, North-South Center; Berrian, B. F. 2000. *Awakening Spaces: French Caribbean Popular Song, Music, and Culture.* Chicago: University of Chicago Press; Bilby, K. 1988. The Caribbean as a Musical Area. In S. Mintz and R. Price (eds.). *Caribbean Contours,* pp. 181–218. Baltimore: The Johns Hopkins University Press; Boggs, V. W. (ed.). 1992. *Salsiology.* New York: Excelsior Music Publishing Company; Cornelius, S., and J. Amira., 1992. *The Music of Santería: Traditional Rhythms of the Batá Drums.* Crown Point, ID: White Cliffs Media; de Boyrie Moya, E. 1971. Tres flautas-ocarinas de manufactura alfarea de los indígenas de la isla de Santo Domingo. *Revista dominicana de arqueología y antropología* 1 (1): 13–17; Guibault, J. 1993. *Musical Traditions of St. Lucia, West Indies: Dances and Songs from a Caribbean Island.* Smithsonian/Folkways Recordings SF 40416. Washington, DC; Hammond, N. 1972. Classic Maya Music. Part 2: Rattles, Shakers, Raspers, Wind, and String Instruments. *Archaeology* 25 (3): 222–228; Hill, D. R. 1993. *Calypso Calaloo:*

Early Carnival Music in Trinidad. Gainesville, FL: University Press of Florida; Manuel, P. 1990. *Essays on Cuban Music: Cuban and North American Perspectives.* Lanham, MD: University Press of America; Manuel, P., K. Bilby, and R. Largey. 1995. *Caribbean Currents: Caribbean Music from Rumba to Reggae.* Philadelphia: Temple University Press; O'Brien-Rothe, L. 1976. Music in a Maya Cosmos. *The World of Music* 18 (3): 35–42; Olsen, D. A. 2002. *Music of El Dorado: The Ethnomusicology of Ancient South American Cultures.* Gainesville, FL: University Press of Florida; Olsen, D. A., and D. E. Sheehy (eds.). 2000. *The Garland Handbook of Latin American Music.* New York: Garland Publishing; Pacini Hernández, D. 1995. *Bachata: A Social History of a Dominican Popular Music.* Philadelphia: Temple University Press; Potash, C. (ed.). 1997. *Reggae, Rasta, Revolution: Jamaican Music from Ska to Dub.* New York: Schirmer Books/Prentice Hall; Robertson, C. (ed.). 1992. *Musical Repercussions of 1492: Exploration, Encounter, and Identities.* Washington, DC: Smithsonian Institution Press; Whylie, M., and M. Warner-Lewis. 1994. Characteristics of Maroon Music from Jamaica and Suriname. In E. K. Agorsah (ed.). *Maroon Heritage: Archaeological, Ethnographic, and Historical Perspectives,* pp. 139–148. Kingston: Canoe Press.

N

Nanny Town (site, Jamaica)

Nanny Town in the Blue Mountains of northeast Jamaica is named after the redoubtable Maroon leader Granny Nanny, who carried on a skilled guerrilla war with the British until she was killed in 1734 and the settlement destroyed.

The lost site of Nanny Town was relocated in 1967 in a loop of the Stony River deep in the Blue Mountains. Preliminary excavations were made in 1973, but it wasn't until the 1990s that extensive excavations took place, discovering the remains of five rectangular stone buildings covered with tropical vegetation, some species of which are still used for their medicinal properties. Surprisingly, the earliest levels yielded Amerindian ceramic artifacts, the second phase (1655 to 1734) is associated with Maroon occupation, with earthenware pottery, pipe bowls, musket balls, and glass, and the third phase after 1734 is represented by short-lived British fortifications, with European ceramics, medicine bottles, and possibly a flag pole posthole.

Preliminary interpretations suggest the Nanny Town site was occupied by the Jamaican Taíno, possibly before European contact, but certainly afterward when they escaped their enslavement by the Spanish and took refuge there. They were then joined and subsequently absorbed by escaped African slaves. In this scenario, the first Jamaican Maroons were the Taíno, and only later a hybrid of (mainly) African and Taíno. This view accords well with the history of the preceding Spanish control of Jamaica, which records that Spanish troops entered the region to recapture escaped Taíno slaves.

See also: Historical Archaeology; Jamaica; Maroons

References
Agorsah, E. K. 1992. Archaeology and the Maroon Heritage in Jamaica. *Jamaica Journal* 24 (2): 2–9; Agorsah, E. K. 1993a. Archaeology and Resistance History in the Caribbean. *The African Archaeology Review* 11: 175–196; Agorsah, E. K. 1993b. Nanny Town Excavations: Rewriting Jamaica's History. *Jamaican Geographer (Newsletter of the Jamaican Geographical Society)* 8 (1): 6–8; Agorsah, E. K. 1994. Archaeology of Maroon Settlements in Jamaica. In K. Agorsah (ed.). *Maroon Heritage: Archaeological, Ethnographic, and Historical Perspectives,* pp. 163–187. Kingston: Canoe Press; Bonner, T. 1974. The Blue Mountain Expedition. *Jamaica Journal* 8 (2–3): 46–50.

Nelson's Dockyard (Antigua)

Nelson's Dockyard at English Harbour on Antigua is one of the most famous of the Caribbean's historical sites. Its location attracted the native population long before Europeans arrived as Archaic Period and later Taíno remains have been found at the site. First mention of the site was in 1671 when an English naval ship took shelter there from a hurricane. Its safety as a port and strategic value were quickly realized and it was soon being used by ships in need of refitting. In 1725, work began on the buildings of the dockyard and they continued to be used by the Royal Navy until 1889.

During the eighteenth and early nineteenth centuries, English Harbour was an important naval base in the rivalries between Great Britain and France, and the various episodes of the Napoleonic Wars. At this time many famous English admirals visited Antigua, including Rodney, Cochrane, Hood, and Nelson, who had first docked in English Harbour in 1784 as captain of *HMS Boreas*. During these years, there were some 5 officers and 327 men at the base, most of the latter being African slaves who had specialized as shipwrights and sailmakers.

Many of the buildings are excellent examples of Georgian architecture, investigated and restored by historical archaeologists and enthusiasts beginning in 1931 and continuing to the present. The dockyard includes a boat- and mastyard, a slipway, and even some of the original columns. There is a lumber and copper store (1789), a pitch and tar store (1788), a pay office (1805), and a small museum displaying artifacts retrieved from the site. Many of the restored buildings now house tourist facilities.

Various relics from English Harbour's historic past have been reused at the site, including unusable cannon upturned as bollards, sailor's graffiti dating to the 1740s, and cauldrons originally used for boiling pitch to calk (i.e., make watertight) the wooden hulls of sailing ships. Nearby is Fort Berkeley, which protected the entrance to the harbor, and Clarence House, where King William IV lived in the 1780s while he was a midshipman. Overlooking the harbor, Shirley Heights is a group of ruined eighteenth-century fortifications including the officers' quarters and nearby ammunition magazines. English Harbour benefited from the founding of the Friends of English Harbour Society in 1951, and has been a national park since 1985.

See also: Historical Archaeology

References
Jane, C.W.E. 1982. *Shirley Heights: The Story of the Redcoats in Antigua*. English Harbour, Antigua: Nelson's Dockyard National Park Foundation; Nicholson, D. V. 1983. *English Harbour, Antigua: A Historical and Archaeological Sketch*. St. John's, Antigua: Antigua Archaeological and Historical Society; Nicholson, D. V. 1995. Mud and Blood: Artifacts from Dredging and the Naval Hospital, English Harbour, Antigua. *Proceedings of the Fifteenth Congress of the International Association for Caribbean Archaeology 1993*, p 45. San Juan, Puerto Rico: Centro de Estudios Avanzados de Puerto Rico y el Caribe.

New Seville (site, Jamaica)

New Seville (Sevilla la Nueva) in Jamaica was founded by the Spanish conquistador Juan de Esquivel in 1509 on the orders of Diego Columbus, the son and heir of Christopher Columbus. In establishing New Seville, Diego was carrying out his father's wishes to claim the island through colonization at a time when the Spanish crown was disputing its original agreement with the Columbus family.

Located on the island's north coast, at the harbor called Santa Gloria in what is today St. Ann's Bay, the town took root at the site where Christopher Columbus and his other son, Ferdinand, had been stranded for a year from June 1503 during his fourth voyage. In recent years underwater archaeologists have searched for the remains of Columbus's wrecked caravels. Despite press reports to the contrary, and the finding of small but more recent boats offshore, these have not been located. This site itself was near a Taíno village called Maima whose food resources of fish, turtles, and cassava had fed Columbus during his enforced stay. Archaeological investigations have found Taíno pottery in the area and there are reports of a carved-wood *zemí* figure having been discovered, though this is now lost.

Esquivel began building the settlement and constructing a Franciscan monastery for the converting of local Taíno to Christianity. Like many conquistadors, however, he abused his position and used the Amerindians for his own purposes. Las Casas was especially critical, blaming Esquivel for not tending to the spiritual well-being of the Taíno and working them mercilessly to produce maize, cotton, and cassava for sale to Cuba and the mainland.

When Esquivel died in 1512, he was succeeded by Francisco de Garay, whose governorship lasted until 1523. Under Garay, estates were established in the region to grow food that could be exchanged with Spanish settlers on the mainland for slaves. During Spanish rule, Jamaica was always an economic backwater, and, having no gold, was used to provision the more prosperous areas of Spain's Caribbean empire. The slaves were transported across the Caribbean to New Seville, which thus served as the point of transshipment for human cargoes en route to Santo Domingo in Hispaniola. During his tenure, Garay also built a grand governor's mansion in Renaissance style and several sugar mills. These mills were a sign of Jamaica's future. As the Amerindian labor force declined through maltreatment and disease, they were replaced with imported African slaves.

Garay resigned the governorship of Jamaica in 1523 and sailed to Mexico in an unsuccessful attempt to make his fortune. He was replaced by Pedro de Mazuelo. In 1524, Peter Martyr was awarded the abbacy at New Seville and used this income to begin building a stone church. This was never completed, however, probably because Mazuelo, like so many others, diverted labor resources to his own ends. The death knell of New Seville was sounded in 1533 when Mazuelo received royal permission to move the capital from Jamaica's north coast to the southern part of the island near to his new sugar mill. Originally called Seville, it later became Santiago de la Vega. After the English capture of Jamaica in 1655, the site and its locale became a sugar plantation worked by imported

African slaves. Today, New Seville belongs to the Jamaican people and is administered by the Jamaican National Heritage Trust.

See also: Columbus, Christopher; Jamaica; Martyr, Peter

References

Aarons, G. A. 1983 and 1984. Sevilla la Nueva: Microcosm of Spain in Jamaica. (Parts 1 and 2). *Jamaica Journal* 16 (4) and 17 (7); Chaunu, H., and P. Chaunu. 1955–1959. *Seville et l'Atlantique 1504–1650.* Eight vols. Paris: P. A. Colin.

Newton Plantation (Barbados)

Newton Plantation lies in the parish of Christ Church in southern Barbados. It is one of the best historically documented of all Barbadian plantation sites, with evidence covering the period 1683 to 1922, though especially detailed between 1794 and 1823.

As with many plantation sites, the documentation of Newton refers mainly to the plantocracy, and relatively little is known of the life and times of the slaves upon which it depended. It is this gap in knowledge that plantation archaeology (as a particular type of historical archaeology) in general seeks to fill. Despite many structural similarities, plantations varied across the Caribbean as did the experience of their slaves. One consequence of this variation is that different plantation sites offer different opportunities for archaeological research. Between 1972 and 1973, excavations at Newton focused on the slave cemetery, investigating the material ways in which African slaves came to terms with death in a foreign land, surrounded by European culture, and the influence of Christian beliefs and mortuary rituals.

The proximity of the cemetery to the slave village, and the fact that the burials were within the plantation and not in the Anglican churchyard or the Protestant mission, were an early indication that this was a slave cemetery and probably of preemancipation date. Altogether, some ninety-two burials were found, several of which had their incisor teeth filed, strongly suggesting that these individuals had been born in Africa rather than Barbados. Particularly unusual was Burial 72, which had an elaborate African-style necklace composed of cowrie shells, drilled dog teeth, glass beads, and drilled fish vertebrae, as well as a distinctive clay pipe. This type of material culture suggests a person of special social status, and, as he was old, he may have been a highly regarded elder or a practitioner of folk medicine. Given the prevalent belief in Caribbean slave communities of malevolent and benevolent spirits and sorcery, this individual may have been an Obeahman (or witch doctor). The east-facing orientation of the body toward Africa indicates burial during the early years of slavery on Barbados, and perhaps suggests that this was an African-born individual.

Small quantities of locally made earthenware pottery were associated with the burials. The production of this type of ceramic began about 1650, and it is known that male slaves were involved. Unlike elsewhere in the Caribbean, the technology used on Barbados was almost completely European, i.e., wheel-thrown and fired in a kiln. Nevertheless, the discovery of three shards indicated the presence of more traditional African techniques that did not employ these methods. A variety of clay pipes and fragments were also found, the most common being those made from white clay. Historical documents reveal that tobacco smoking was a special treat for slaves, and that tobacco and perhaps the pipes were sometimes used to exchange for food. Glass beads were also discovered and seem to have been used by the slaves to make bracelets, necklaces, and anklets, and to have been widely available throughout the island.

At least twenty-nine of the excavated burials included the remains of coffins, and possibly another twenty-three were similarly interred. These were identified by the presence of metal handles and nails in the burials, and sometimes also by metal flakes resting on the chest. In general, archaeological stratigraphy indicates that the earlier burials were oriented toward the east and later ones toward the west. This may be evidence that the earlier ones were of African-born individuals or first-generation creoles facing toward their homeland, whereas the later west-facing burials belonged to individuals whose burial practices had been influenced in some way by Christian European practices and beliefs. This possibility is reinforced by the fact that west-oriented burials were positively correlated with the presence of coffins—again a European influence.

An important conclusion of the Newton excavations, supported by similar investigations elsewhere in the Island Caribbean, is that slave status cannot be confirmed by archaeological evidence alone. It is dependant on location, historical records, and educated conjecture. Material culture, left unaided, is not sufficiently diagnostic—a fact that argues strongly for the interdisciplinary approach of historical archaeology.

See also: Barbados; Drax Hall (site, Jamaica); Historical Archaeology; Jamaica; Obeah; Slavery; Sugar

References

Handler, J. S. 1972. An Archaeological Investigation of the Domestic Life of Plantation Slaves in Barbados. *Journal of the Barbados Museum and Historical Society* 34: 64–72; Handler, J. S. 1997. An African-Type Healer/Diviner and His Grave Goods: A Burial from a Plantation Slave Cemetery in Barbados. *International Journal of Historical Archaeology* 1 (2): 91–130; Handler, J. S., and R. Corrucini. 1983. Plantation Slave Life in Barbados: A Physical Anthropological Analysis. *Journal of Interdisciplinary History* 14: 65–90; Handler, J., and F. W. Lange. 1978. *Plantation Slavery in Barbados: An Archaeological and Historical Investigation.* Cambridge, MA: Harvard University Press.

Norman Estate (site, St. Martin)

Norman Estate is a preceramic Archaic Period site on the north side of St. Martin. The shell midden has no pottery and has yielded flint flakes, river pebbles, and shell artifacts. It has been dated to between ca. 2350 B.C. and 1800 B.C.

Severely damaged due to road construction, the site appears to be a 20-cm-thick deposit of shells, stone artifacts, and faunal remains. The stone tools include hammerstones, rubbing stones, flints, and flint cores from which individual flint tools would have been struck. Shellfish remains were plentiful and included mainly the species known locally as Turkey Wing (*Arca zebra*) and Tiger Lucina (*Codakia orbicularis*). While these represented species that were eaten, shell artifacts were made only from Queen Conch (*Strombus gigas*), and include part of a shell axe and a shell gouge. It appears as if these early peoples fished with traps set near shallow coral reefs and specialized in catching parrotfish.

See also: Archaic Period; Jolly Beach (site, Antigua)
References
Hofman, C. L., and M.L.P. Hoogland. (eds.). 1999. *Archaeological Investigations on St. Martin (Lesser Antilles)*, pp. 25–60. Archaeological Studies Leiden University 4. Leiden.

Nuestra Señora de Atocha, *Wreck of*

The *Nuestra Señora de Atocha* is one of many Spanish galleons whose wrecks have been commercially exploited—primarily by treasure hunters—rather than investigated by archaeologists. Despite this, the many dazzling objects that have been recovered provide valuable insights into seventeenth-century life and provide archaeologists with at least the opportunity to study them before they are sold. The *Atocha* was a 500-ton Spanish vice-flagship that was sunk by a hurricane in the Florida Keys on 4 September 1622. In fact, a long line of debris on the seabed indicated it had been struck by two separate storms that dispersed wreckage over a large area. The *Atocha* was part of the annual fleet from the Caribbean to Spain, and had been custom built in Havana, Cuba, in 1620 to serve as an official treasure galleon. Archival research in Spain has recently located the shipwright's original contract.

When the fleet left Havana, it was carrying thousands of passengers as well as a large quantity of private and royal treasure from Spain's American colonies. The *Atocha* itself was carrying some 550 people, of which only 5 survived. While some ships of the fleet, such as the *Margarita,* were salvaged by the Spanish at the time, no trace of the *Atocha* was found.

The modern search for the *Atocha* was the obsession of Mel Fisher, an experienced scuba diver and treasure hunter. In 1966 he began surveying 192,000 km of the seabed and in 1971, as a portent of things to come, the initial identification of one of the ship's iron anchors was accompanied by the discovery of a 2.5-m-long gold chain. The subsequent recovery of gold coins, all dating to before 1622, indicated that this was the wreck of one of the 1622 treasure galleons. Confirmation that this was the *Nuestra Señora de Atocha* came when the markings on recently recovered silver bars tallied with those on the ship's manifest. Several bronze cannon were later discovered, but it was only in 1985, after fifteen years of searching, that Fisher's divers located the main part of the wreck. It was not long before extraordinary finds were made, including raw emeralds, silver ingots, boxes of coins, and objects of silver and gold, such as elaborate drinking cups or ewers. Perhaps more valuable historically was the recovery of what is thought to be the pilot's chest, which contained not only coins, but also three rare bronze astrolabes—a device used mainly for timetelling and surveying. One unusual find was seeds of the *Bidens alba* plant that subsequently flowered and is thought to have been used as animal fodder.

By the end of 1986, the wreck of the *Nuestra Señora de Atocha* was revealed as one of the richest treasure wrecks ever discovered: 130,000 silver coins, 956 silver ingots, 15 gold chains, 115 gold bars, and 315 emeralds were just some of the precious items recovered and that had an estimated total value at that time of some $25 million.

See also: *Nuestra Señora de la Concepción,* Wreck of; *Nuestra Señora de las Maravillas,* Wreck of; Underwater Archaeology

References

Kane, R. E., R. C. Kammerling, R. Moldes, J. I. Koivula, S. F. McClure, and C. P. Smith. 1989. Emerald and Gold Treasures of the Spanish Galleon *Nuestra Señora Atocha*. *Gems and Gemology* 25(4): 196–206.; Mathewson, R. D. III. 1986. *Treasure of the Atocha*. New York; Moore, D. 1997. *Nuestra Señora de Atocha*. In J. P. Delgado (ed.). *Encyclopedia of Underwater and Maritime Archaeology,* pp. 298–299. London: British Museum Press.

Nuestra Señora de la Concepción, *Wreck of*

The *Nuestra Señora de la Concepción* (also known as the *Almiranta*) was a 600-ton Spanish vice-flagship that sank in 1641, foundering on the Silver Shoal reefs off the north coast of Hispaniola. She was on a journey from Havana, Cuba, to Spain, when a storm damaged her masts and steering and she drifted out of control. Regaining steerage, Admiral Villavivencio advised against the course taken by his pilots but to no avail. The result was that the *Concepción* ran onto reefs, and only 194 of the original 532 people aboard survived. In the weeks that followed, Villavivencio failed in his attempts to salvage the cargo.

At least four more unsuccessful attempts were made to locate the *Concepción* and its treasure during the seventeenth century. It was not until 1687 that the English captain William Phips relocated the wreck that was now covered in coral and managed to retrieve one-quarter of a million pounds (possibly $50 million at today's value), for which he received a knighthood from the king and the governorship of the then-British colony of Massachusetts. Some twenty expeditions in the twentieth century, including one by the famous scuba explorer Jacques Cousteau, failed to find the wreck again. It was only when the historian Peter Earle found the logbook of Phip's ship and published it that the treasure hunter Burt Webber was able to relocate the wreck once more.

Digging down through the remains of Phip's rum bottles and tools as well as coral growths—many of which had silver coins embedded in them—Webber located the *Concepción's* cargo holds. Apart from the gold and silver coins, chains, and tableware that he sought, equally valuable historically were finds of glass beads, wooden cups, pottery, and a marble statue and astrolabe—a device used mainly for timetelling and surveying. Perhaps the most startling discovery was of a sealed wooden chest that contained rare Ming Dynasty Chinese porcelain and silver tableware, and, in a secret compartment, some 1,440 congealed silver coins. Altogether, the quantity and diversity of artifacts recovered represented a major collection of utmost historical and archaeological significance as well as of commercial value—some $10 million. Today, part of the *Concepción's* treasure is housed in the Museo de las Casas Reales in Santo Domingo, Dominican Republic.

See also: Molasses Reef Wreck; *Nuestra Señora de Atocha,* Wreck of; *Nuestra Señora de las Maravillas,* Wreck of; Underwater Archaeology

References

Borrell, C. P. 1983. *Historia y rescate del galeon Nuestra Señora de la Concepción.* Santo Domingo, the Dominican Republic; Earle, P. 1980. *The Treasure of the Concepción: The Wreck of the Almiranta.* New York: Viking Press; Grissim, J. 1980. *The Lost Treasure of the Concepción.* New York; Smith, R. C. 1997. *Nuestra Señora de la Concepción.* In J. P. Delgado (ed.). *Encyclopedia of Underwater and Maritime Archaeology,* pp. 299–300. London: British Museum Press; Peterson, M. 1980. *The Treasure of the Concepción.* Chicago: John G. Shedd Aquarium.

Nuestra Señora de las Maravillas, *Wreck of*

The *Nuestra Señora de las Maravillas* (also known as the *Maravilla*) was a seventeenth-century Spanish treasure galleon that sank in January 1656. Having run into shallow waters, she then collided with another ship in her convoy, and foundered on nearby reefs. She broke into two sections during the night, and in the morning, only 56 survivors of the original 700 passengers and crew were found alive. Over the next three years, the Spanish managed to salvage about one-quarter of her precious cargo. The *Maravilla* had been loaded with gold and silver treasure from Spain's wealthy colonies in Mexico and South America—perhaps five times that on board the *Nuestra Señora de Atocha.*

In 1960, the treasure hunter Robert Marx conducted archival research into the *Maravilla* in Seville, Spain, and located a copy of her manifest. In 1972, Marx formed the company Seafinders with the oceanographer Willard Bascom, and began searching the Little Bahama Bank. On one dive, Marx found a single gold coin dated to 1655 and this convinced him he had found the long-sought-after wreck. The expedition soon found four of the *Maravillas*'s iron anchors, two bronze cannon bearing the coat of arms of King Philip IV of Spain, and silver bars, silver plates, and hundreds of coins often congealed into solid lumps of silver. In the days that followed the initial discovery some 5 tons of silver bars and 50,000 silver coins were retrieved, together with golden disks, gold jewelry, and hundreds of raw emeralds. The commercial imperative of these activities, and the extraordinary richness of the site, is underlined by Marx's comment that he didn't consider it a good day unless at least $250,000 worth of treasure was discovered.

Typical of the aftermath of such discoveries, fantastic rumors and the jealousies of other treasure hunters soon put legal blocks on further salvage work by Marx's company. Since 1986, other treasure-seeking companies have investigated the site, and in 1988 a spectacular 100-carat emerald was found and valued at $1 million. Thousands more silver coins, gold chains, lockets, and rings have been retrieved, along with gold bars and ingots, and, more unusually, a complete elephant tusk.

The *Maravilla* is an example of the discovery of a historically important wreck, and the removal of its extraordinary cargo by a succession of professional treasure hunters rather than underwater archaeologists. While great wealth and astonishing artifacts have been recovered, the political intrigues and maneuverings between profit-motivated companies have replaced careful scientific investigation.

See also: Molasses Reef Wreck; *Nuestra Señora de Atocha,* Wreck of; *Nuestra Señora de la Concepción,* Wreck of; Underwater Archaeology

References

Marx, R., and J. Marx. 1993. *The Search for Sunken Treasure: Exploring the World's Great Shipwrecks,* pp. 81–85. Toronto: Key Porter Books.

O

Obeah

Like other African-Caribbean spiritual practices, such as Santería, Vodoun, and Shango, Obeah is an animistic religion that sees the natural world as alive with spirits of ancestors and supernatural forces. In this worldview, as late as the nineteenth century in Jamaica, descendants of African slaves believed that silk-cotton trees gathered together after sunset, and even today that tree is commonly called the God Tree, associated with *duppies,* or ghosts. Sometimes referred to as Afro-Caribbean shamanism, Obeah is far less well known and researched than its more high-profile relatives. Obeah is shrouded in secrecy, and even the meaning of its name is unclear; some consider that it originated from *Obeye*—the name given to a supernatural force that resides in African sorcerers—while others see the West African Akan word *Obayifo* (witch) as the likely source. Those who practice it are known as Obeahmen, and can be considered a mix of shaman, sorcerer, and Vodoun witch doctor. Obeah is often divided into two types known as "science" and "bush magic"; adherents of the former use commercial charms and conjuring books while the latter prefer the more traditional talismans of dog teeth, bones, feathers, and minerals.

Today, Obeah is increasingly a catch-all term for many different types of spiritual activity, often appearing to blend with other African-Caribbean religions and influenced also by other faiths such as Islam, Hinduism, and Christianity. In Trinidad and Tobago, for example, Obeah is mixed with Orisha in several different forms. Originally, Obeah was practiced solely by enslaved West Africans brought to the Caribbean to work on plantations. Its origins can be traced particularly to the peoples of Dahomey and the Ashanti, arriving in the Caribbean during the seventeenth century. The colonial British rulers of the time used the term Obeah indiscriminately to describe any type of magical or mystical activities by African slaves. Such was the reputation of Obeahmen for evildoing that they were often blamed for misfortune, unrest, and disaster on plantations by the European planters and African slaves alike.

Although usually credited with malign influence, in fact the Obeahmen who arrived on the first slave ships had the same supernatural qualities possessed by indigenous Amerindian shamans. They were ritual specialists who guarded their society's spiritual and ethical traditions; they were supernatural warriors who could kill at a distance, steal souls, raise the dead, and cure and send illness. While Taíno and Carib shamans were also accomplished herbalists, the African Obeahmen seem to have specialized in using plants to conduct apparently miraculous cures and to send magical death through poisoning.

Apart from their role as living links between the traditions of Africa and the new African-Caribbean society that was coming into being, Obeahmen also played an important political role during the slavery period. Their ostensibly religious meetings could be used to disguise opportunities for planning insurrection. Obeahamen were often believed to be at the heart of slave rebellions and of less violent forms of resistance. Often charismatic individuals, Obeahmen were believed to be able to protect their followers from the white man's weapons by rubbing special powders or substances on their body. In one case, recorded by Edward Long in his 1774 *History of Jamaica,* one Obeahman was believed to be able to catch the white man's bullets in his hand and hurl them back at those who had fired them. Whatever the credibility of such stories, they served to embolden the slaves and make the plantation owners anxious.

Obeahmen made their followers swear bloody oaths of secrecy on pain of death to carry out any instructions that they might be given. These rites of obedience and the other rituals associated with Obeah involved a host of objects and materials deemed to be powerful weapons in the right hands. Plant poisons, powdered glass, gun powder, bird beaks, and animal teeth were all considered ingredients in Obeah sorcery. Eventually, rigorous searches of slave quarters every two weeks were carried out by the white planters, and in Jamaica increasingly harsh penalties were imposed for their possession. The link between Obeah witchcraft and slave unrest was finally recognized in 1816 when a law was enacted that sentenced the guilty to deportation. If anyone died through being poisoned, the occupant of the house where Obeah poisons were found was judged to have committed murder and could be hanged or burned. Obeahmen also sold their services, sometimes being commissioned to poison one person on behalf of another. More often, perhaps, they were employed for more mundane purposes—to cure illness, divine the future, or unmask an adulterer or thief. They were paid in food or money but might also might defer payment by requesting a future favor. An astute Obeahman could build up a network of people who owed such favors and so achieve great personal power and influence. The ability of Obeahmen to be in one place while someone died in another location was presented as a sign of his ability to kill at a distance, whereas in fact he had simply called in a favor owed to him by someone else.

Obeahmen flourished in the harsh and often cruel conditions of slavery in the Caribbean. The injustices that white plantation owners and overseers visited on the slaves were such that acts of rebellion, large and small, were also desperate forms of resistance against oppression. In the hothouse conditions of plantation life, where slaves outnumbered their white owners, it is not surprising that Obeahmen were feared equally by their African-Caribbean compatriots and European masters. These situations magnified and emphasized the malign aspects of Obeah sorcerers at the expense of their equally important role as healers, ritual experts, and keepers of cultural traditions.

See also: Historical Archaeology; Newton Plantation (Barbados); Orisha/Shango (Trinidad); Santería; Shamanism; Slavery; Sugar; Vodoun

References
Bell, H. H. 1970 [1889]. *Obeah, Witchcraft, and the West Indies.* Westport, CT: Negro Universities Press; Hedrick, B. C., and J. E. Stephens. 1977. It's a Natural Fact: Obeah in the Bahamas. *Museum of Anthropology Miscellaneous Series* No. 39. Greeley, CO: University of Northern Colorado Museum of Anthropology; Kalafou, A. n.d. *Obeah: Afro-Caribbean Shamanism;* Long, E. 1774. *History of Jamaica.* London: T. Londwes.; Morrish, I. 1982. *Obeah, Christ, and Rastaman: Jamaica and its Religions.* Cambridge, MA: James Clarke Press; Schuler, M. 1979. Myalism and the African Religious Tradition in Jamaica. In M. E. Graham and F. W. Knight (eds.). *Africa and the Caribbean: The Legacies of a Link.* Baltimore: Johns Hopkins University Press; Sereno, R. 1948. Obeah: Magic and Social Structure in the Lesser Antilles. *Psychiatry* 11 (1): 15–31; Williams, J. J. 1932. *Voodoos and Obeahs: Phases of West India Witchcraft.* New York: Dial Press.

Orisha / Shango (Trinidad)

In Trinidad, the descendants of West African Yoruba peoples who came to the island both as freemen and slaves during the nineteenth century have preserved a rich tapestry of spiritual beliefs. Originally called Shango, this African-derived religious movement is now more commonly known as Orisha. Like Vodoun and Santería, Orisha is a hybrid religion—a vibrant mix of African spiritualities and Roman Catholicism.

Orisha's early development in Trinidad is seen in two ways: first, the Christian element was possibly adopted to help disguise the outlawed African beliefs. A second and increasingly popular explanation is that African and Catholic elements evolved together and gradually merged to create the new hybrid religion. As with other places in the Americas, notably Mexico and Peru, indigenous spirits and deities were identified with those Catholic saints most closely identified with them. In Trinidad, however, these deities—the *orisha*—were not Amerindian but African, and specifically Yoruba. Since the 1950s, several elements of Hinduism have been incorporated into Orisha rituals, a fact indicative of the faith's open and tolerant nature in Trinidad's multiethnic society. Today, Orisha has become a vehicle for establishing and celebrating African identity in Trinidad and to this extent the Catholic dimension is sometimes elided.

The mixing of different types of African religious beliefs with Orisha is well illustrated by the case of Trinidad's Rada people who came originally from Dahomey in the mid-nineteenth century. Gathering around the Dahomean diviner and herbalist known as Papa Nanee, they held their religious rituals in his residential compound, which included a house of the gods, or *vodunkwe*. Nanee and his followers were typically accused of practicing Obeah by Trinidad's British colonial rulers—the term being a catch-all accusation of witchcraft and sorcery for anyone involved in African spiritual activities. Although Rada shares a common African heritage and several deities with the Orisha movement, it is a distinct faith, with such deities as Dada Segbo (the creator), Dangbwe (serpent), and Sakpata (the earth god). Ritual celebrations are called sacrifices as many types of small animals are sacrificed to the deities in order to ask for blessings for children, ward off illness, and honor the ancestors. Papa Nanee died in 1899, and today Rada is a much-reduced faith and overshadowed by the burgeoning interest in Orisha.

Originating in the polytheistic Yoruba religious beliefs and rituals of West Africa, Orisha focuses on spirit possession, ancestor worship, divination, and herbalism. The main deity (orisha) is Obatala, who is flanked by the powerful Ogun, god of iron and war; Shango is a weather god associated with storms; Oya is similarly identified with weather in the form of wind; and the female Oshun is mistress of the waters. Spirit possession, as with Amerindian shamanism, is a key feature of Orisha as the deities take over their devotees. Induced by flickering candlelight and rhythmic drumming, possession is controlled by the leader of an Orisha shrine whose responsibility it is to identify the spirit being invoked. The faith is learned from an early age with infants and young children being brought to the shrine.

Orisha ceremonies are called feasts (*ebo* in Yoruba) and take place in the shrine-leader's yard and house. This ceremonial space has several components—the *palais* where music and dancing occur, and the *chapelle* that contains an altar adorned with flags, pictures of saints, and ritual objects of the Orisha deities that include so-called shango-stones (also called thunderstones), and stools dedicated to the gods. The main event is an annual feast that lasts between two and four days, during which spiritual ties between the deities and the followers are rejuvenated through the offerings of food and sacrificial animals. A ceremony begins with Christian prayers and sometimes hymns. As the prayers end, the drumming begins, and worshippers gather in a circle and start to sing to the deity called Eshu. This is followed by songs sung to Ogun, who finally signals his arrival by possessing the head of a worshipper. Subsequently, other devotees are also possessed by different gods. While many people may be possessed at the same time, on some occasions it is possible that no orishas will appear. Those who are possessed are called the "horses" or "mounts" of the gods who possess them.

The worship of ancestors, distant and recent, is the central feature of Orisha. Ancestors are prayed to and worshipped in a context of respect for age and experience, where living elders, or "old heads," have a special place in society. This feature of the religion is part of the wider nonhierarchical nature of the faith. Highly individualistic, Orisha has no books, and works only on the basis of the oral tradition where chants, songs, and prayers are learned by rote. Consequently, a large degree of independence is exercised by shrine leaders, who determine which deities will be worshipped during a given feast. Leaders serve as spiritual guides for shrine members who may belong to the local community or perhaps who live in larger towns elsewhere but who recognize the shrine as a spiritual home. Each feast is attended by a small coterie of active participants and a larger group of onlookers.

Today in Trinidad, Orisha is becoming increasingly Africanized as younger, more politically active devotees seek to stress their African roots. There are nevertheless two distinct trends: one championed by those who wish to purify and emphasize the African content of Orisha, and a second whose supporters stress the innovative and inclusive nature of Trinidadian Orisha over its purely African content.

Previously regarded with suspicion, the religion is now opening up to the public, and attracting members of the island's artistic community. The government has recognized it as a legitimate religion and partly as a consequence it has attracted an ever-increasing number of followers. Orisha priests can now conduct legal marriage services and the annual events of Orisha Family Day and the Oshun Festival have heightened its public profile. There are perhaps 150 Orisha shrines spread throughout the country and somewhere between 10,000 and 20,000 worshippers.

See also: Obeah; Santería; Trinidad and Tobago; Vodoun
References
Carr, A. T. 1989. *A Rada Community in Trinidad.* Trinidad and Tobago: Paria Publishing; Henry, F. 1957. African Powers in Trinidad: The Shango Cult. *Anthropological Quarterly* 30 (2): 45–59; Houk, J. T. 1995. *Spirits, Blood, and Drums: The Orisha Religion of Trinidad.* Philadelphia: Temple University Press; Laird, N. 1992. Shango Worship in Trinidad. In G. Besson and B. Brereton (eds.). *The Book of Trinidad,* pp. 368–374. Port of Spain, Trinidad: Paria Publishing; Lum, K. A. 1999. *Praising His Name in the Dance: Spirit-Possession in the Spiritual Baptist Faith and Orisha Work in Trinidad, West Indies.* Amsterdam: Harwood; Simpson, G. E. 1965. *The Shango Cult in Trinidad.* San Juan: University of Puerto Rico; Warner-Lewis, M. 1991. *Guinea's Other Sons: The African Dynamic in Trinidad Culture.* Dover, MA: The Majority Press.

Ortoiroid

People of the Ortoiroid culture arrived in the northern Island Caribbean from South America by around 2000 B.C. and had disappeared by ca. 400 B.C. Taking the name from the shell midden site of Ortoire in southeast Trinidad, Ortoiroid artifacts are found in sites along the banks of the Orinoco River in South America north to Puerto Rico.

The earliest evidence for Ortoiroid culture dates to ca. 5000 B.C. at Banwari Trace in Trinidad. Other sites are located mainly along the island's south and southeast coast, though one has been identified at Milford on nearby Tobago. Such sites typically are dominated by shell middens composed of fresh- and seawater species used mainly for food. Ortoiroid artifacts are simply made with few defining features. They include bone spearpoints and barbs and also perforated animal teeth for stringing as jewelry. Roughly made stone tools include manos, metates, and pestles for preparing vegetables, and simple stone choppers, hammerstones, and coarsely chipped stone. Farther north, in Martinique, two Ortoiroid sites belonging to the local Boutbois people are known and are dominated by edge-grinding pebbles. In Antigua, some twenty-four Ortoiroid shell-midden sites have been found, mainly in areas suitable for fishing and shellfish gathering, and which typically have roughly made metates, manos, and net sinkers.

At the northern end of its distribution, Ortoiroid objects are common and well known enough to permit the identification of two separate cultures—called Coroso in Puerto Rico and Krum Bay in the Virgin Islands. While the Coroso people inhabited caves as well as open spaces, the Krum Bay people lived only in open areas. All sites were small shell-middens in which the dead were sometimes buried and which were located near mangrove swamps and beaches. In both areas, edge-grinders are typical and occasionally simple stone, bone, and shell jewelry is found.

Ortoiroid peoples relied on the sea for their food and raw materials, and their occupation seems to have been short-lived and intermittent. Their material culture included bone as well as stone tools, but they seem to have left little evidence of artistic activities apart from occasional roughly made jewelry items.

See also: Antigua; Archaic Period; Banwari Trace (site, Trinidad); Jolly Beach (site, Antigua); Krum Bay (site, St. Thomas); Martinique; Trinidad and Tobago

References
Allaire, L., and M. Mattioni. 1983. Boutbois et le Goudinot: Deux gisements acéramiques de la Martinique. *Proceedings of the Ninth International Congress for the Study of Pre-Columbian Cultures of the Lesser Antilles, Dominican Republic, August 2–8, 1981,* pp. 27–38; Boomert, A. 2000. *Trinidad, Tobago, and the Lower Orinoco Interaction Sphere,* pp. 54–87. Alkmaar, the Netherlands; Davis, D. D. 1982. Archaic Settlement and Resource Exploitation in the Lesser Antilles: Preliminary Information from Antigua. *Caribbean Journal of Science* 17: 107–122; Lundberg, E. R. 1989. *Preceramic Procurement Patterns at Krum Bay, Virgin Islands.* Ph.D. dissertation, University of Illinois, Urbana; Lundberg, E. R. 1991. Interrelationships among Preceramic Complexes of Puerto Rico and the Virgin Islands. *Proceedings of the Thirteenth International Congress for Caribbean Archaeology, Willemstadt, Curaçao, July 24–29, 1989,* pp. 73–85; Rouse, I. 1992. *The Tainos: Rise and Decline of the People Who Greeted Columbus,* pp. 62–67. New Haven, CT: Yale University Press.

Osoid

The Osoid ceramic series appeared around 1000 B.C. on the boundary between the eastern foothills of the Andes and the seasonally flooded western llanos. It is noteworthy because it is regarded as the first polychrome-painted ceramic style in the Americas. It was from the Osoid peoples that the color-painting of pottery diffused to the Barquisimeto region, home to the Tocuyanoid ceramic tradition of western Venezuela. From here it spread to the central Venezuelan coast and to the Middle Orinoco valley. The Osoid people also grew maize, which was taken up by the Corozal culture, the oldest group associated with the Caribbean Arauquinoid pottery tradition. By the sixth and seventh centuries A.D., Arauquinoid peoples had moved into the Guianas and Trinidad. The Osoid people thus represent one of the many South American roots of Caribbean culture.

See also: Arauquinoid (pottery)

References
Boomert, A. 2003. Agricultural Societies in the Continental Caribbean. In J. Sued-Badillo (ed.). *General History of the Caribbean: Vol. 1, Autochthonous Societies,* pp. 150–151, 169–172. Paris: UNESCO; Zucchi, A. 1972. New Data on the Antiquity of Polychrome Painting from Venezuela. *American Antiquity* 37: 439–446.

Ostionoid

The Ostionoid cultural tradition (or series) is named after the Ostiones culture that developed out of the Saladoid Period Cuevas culture in eastern Hispaniola (modern Dominican Republic) around A.D. 500. The Ostiones culture is recognized as one of several variations or subseries of the more inclusive Ostionoid tradition—these include the Ostionan Ostionoid itself, the Elenan Ostionoid, and the Chican Ostionoid (or Classic Taíno). The Ostionoid tradition itself was a uniquely Island Caribbean phenomenon, with none of the South American mainland characteristics of its Saladoid predecessors. The Ostiones peoples, and the later local subseries that developed from them, date the whole Ostionoid tradition to the period ca. A.D. 500 to A.D. 1500.

Ostiones pottery was less varied and sophisticated than that of the Saladoid Period. Zic (zone-incised cross-hatching) and white-on-red (W-O-R) decoration disappeared, as did the intricate modeling of anthropozoomorphic imagery. It was replaced by simple black smudging, very basic modeling, and an orange-red slip applied to the whole of the typically thin and hard ceramic vessel. It is widely referred to as redware.

The appearance of Ostiones pottery and its varied local types represented a true movement of peoples. Ostiones people appear to have been the first human settlers to colonize Jamaica ca. A.D. 500. They introduced pottery making and agriculture westward to Cuba and then east to Puerto Rico and beyond, though the nature of their interaction with the preexisting Archaic Period people of these islands is not well known. What is more certain is that Ostiones peoples were the first to systematically colonize the forested highland interiors of the Greater Antilles.

The Ostiones culture of Hispaniola was the precursor of cultural diversification in the Greater Antilles and adjacent areas. It laid the foundations for the emergence of locally variable Ostionoid traditions or subseries, such as the Meillacan culture in Hispaniola, Cuba, and Jamaica, the Elenan culture in the Leeward and Virgin Islands, and the Palmetto culture in the Bahamas. On Hispaniola, the local Ostiones culture that had developed into the Meillacan culture lasted only until ca. 1200 when it was succeeded by the Chican Ostionoid, the name given to archaeological remains of the classic Taíno peoples encountered by Columbus in 1492.

See also: Columbus, Christopher; Cuba; Elenan; Jamaica; Meillacan; Palmetto; Taíno (Arawak); White-on-Red Pottery (W-O-R); Zic Pottery

References
Allaire, L. 1999. Archaeology of the Caribbean Region. In F. Salomon and S. B. Schwartz (eds.). *The Cambridge History of the Native Peoples of the Americas: Vol. III, South America Part 1*, pp. 717–720, Cambridge: Cambridge University Press; Rouse, I. 1992. *The Tainos: Rise and Decline of the People Who Greeted Columbus*, pp. 72–73, 92–96, New Haven, CT: Yale University Press.

Oviedo y Valdés, Gonzalo Fernández de

Gonzalo Fernández de Oviedo y Valdés (1478–1557), usually known simply as Oviedo, was a Spanish official who lived most of his life in the Caribbean and is one of the most important chroniclers of the region's geography and native peoples.

Oviedo first journeyed to the Indies in 1514, where he became the official inspector of gold smelting at Darién on Colombia's northern Caribbean coast. In 1532 he became the official chronicler of the Indies and a year later he was also appointed governor of the fortress of Santo Domingo on Hispaniola.

Oviedo's main interest seems to have been natural history, and he described and made drawings of the astonishing wealth of new plants, animals, and fish of the New World. In 1526, he published the first of two important books, *De la natural historia de las Indias* (*Natural History of the Indies*), in which he dealt with the fauna and flora of Hispaniola, and coastal Colombia and Panama (known then as Tierra Firme). He comments on the therapeutic qualities of trees and fruits, describes the exuberance of the tropical rainforest in equally florid terms, and is fascinated by a fight between flying fish, seagulls, and dorados. He seems perplexed by native American tigers (i.e., jaguars), which do not seem as fleet of foot as their Asian cousins, and by American lions (i.e., pumas), which are not as fierce as African ones.

Between 1535 and 1557, he published a second, more substantial work, the *Historia general y natural de las Indias, islas y Tierra Firme del mar Océano* (*The General and Natural History of the Indies, Islands and Tierra Firme of the Ocean Sea*). Here he supplemented descriptions of natural history already made with now famous drawings—such as an Amerindian hammock and a canoe—with accounts of Spanish activities in the Americas. While a patriotic Spaniard and royal servant, Oviedo spared no one. He describes the squabbles between the Spaniards of Galicia and Castille, and the Basques and Catalans, and detailed the difficulties and cruelties of the conquistadors. Typically, he related the bloody use of hunting dogs by the Spanish to run down escaped Amerindians, and how they had acquired a taste for the natives and ripped them to pieces. Yet, taken together, these two publications contain a wealth of information, including the first scientific descriptions of rubber trees, the tobacco plant, cinnamon, and the narcotic coca leaf.

Oviedo's views of the Americas' native peoples have often been misunderstood. While he exhibited real humanity toward the Amerindians, and blamed the Spanish for not converting them, he also saw them as savage, lazy, bestial, and given to idolatry. Yet even here he spoke with authority, having studied in depth their religion, language, and marriage rites, and admired their costumes and dances. For Oviedo, it often seems as if there was little to choose between the savagery of the natives and the cruelties and vanities of the Spanish.

See also: Columbus, Christopher; Las Casas, Bartolomé de; Vespucci, Amerigo

References

Gerbi, A. 1986. *Nature in the New World: From Christopher Columbus to Gonzalo Fernández de Oviedo,* pp. 129–406. Pittsburgh: University of Pittsburgh Press; Fernández de Oviedo, G. 1959. *The Natural History of the West Indies.* Chapel Hill, NC: University of North Carolina Press; Fernández de Oviedo, G. 1979. *Sumario de la natural historia de las Indias.* México: Fondo De Cultura Economica.

P

Palmetto

Palmetto is the name given to the archaeological remains of the Amerindian people who inhabited the Bahamas and Turks and Caicos islands at the time of Columbus's arrival in 1492, and who are known ethnohistorically as the Lucayan Taínos.

There are several theories concerning the origins of the people and their material culture. One view is that around A.D. 800, Meillacan Amerindians from northeastern Hispaniola began journeying to the Turks and Caicos to exploit local resources of salt and fish. They settled there over the next 100 years, developing the Palmetto style of ceramics that they then carried to the Bahamas. An alternative view is that Meillacans from northwestern Hispaniola moved into the southern Bahamas due to overpopulation at home and from there settled the rest of the Bahamas and the Turks and Caicos islands. Recent evidence from the island of San Salvador suggests a more complex origin, where the pottery of the Ostionan people evolved into Palmetto in the southern Bahamas and into Meillacan in northwestern Hispaniola. Whatever their origin, by the twelfth century A.D. these prehistoric peoples had evolved into the Lucayan Taínos and were the first Amerindians to encounter Europeans.

Due to the poor quality of clay available in this area, Palmetto pottery is inferior to that elsewhere in the Caribbean. It is thick, fragile, and mostly made with crushed shell as a temper. The remains are mainly bowls and decoration is rare, though the impressions of matting often occur. The remains of griddles indicate cassava growing and baking. Stone, bone, and shell artifacts are similar to those of the Ostionan and Meillacan cultures, though the ceramics are quite different.

See also: Meillacan; Ostionoid; Taínos (Arawak); Turks and Caicos

References

Hoffman, C. A. Jr. 1970. The Palmetto Grove Site on San Salvador, Bahamas. *Contributions to the Florida State Museum, Social Sciences* 16, pp. 1–26. Gainesville, FL; Keegan, W. F. 1985. Dynamic Horticulturalists: Population Expansion in the Prehistoric Bahamas, pp. 297–299. PhD. dissertation. Ann Arbor, MI: University Microfilms; Rouse, I. 1992. *The Tainos: Rise and Decline of the People Who Greeted Columbus,* pp. 99–104. New Haven, CT: Yale University Press; Sears, W. H., and S. D. Sullivan. 1978. Bahamas Prehistory. *American Antiquity* 43 (1): 3–25; S. D. Sullivan, 1981. *Prehistoric Patterns of Exploitation and Colonization in the Turks and Caicos Islands.* PhD. dissertation, University of Illinois, Urbana.

Palo Seco (site, Trinidad)

Palo Seco is an important archaeological site on the southern coast of Trinidad. Its significance is twofold. It is currently the only major prehistoric Trinidadian site to be extensively excavated and published, and it was chosen as the type-site of one of two periods of Saladoid ceramic development on Trinidad. In other words, the prehistoric people of Palo Seco were among the first Trinidadians to practice agriculture, live in villages, and make sophisticated pottery. Ceramics of the Palo Seco complex are found throughout Trinidad.

The archaeological site of Palo Seco is composed of at least two middens overlooking the Columbus Channel, which separates Trinidad from Venezuela. A layer of charcoal in the earliest level suggests that the first inhabitants may have burned the forest undergrowth in order to settle there. What remains today are at least two oval middens, which have Cedros-style pottery overlain by slightly later Palo Seco–style ceramics that show evidence of Barrancoid influence and that date to around 50 B.C.

This later Palo Seco pottery is fairly thick, coarse and soft, and usually in the form of bowls with flaring rims. Both zic (zone-incised cross-hatching) and white-on-red (W-O-R) ceramics are present, with red, white, and black paint applied before firing. The most famous examples of Palo Seco–style pottery are the modeled "water bottle" from a human burial at the nearby site of Erin and the unique effigy cassava beer bottle found underwater off the island of Gaspar Grande, northwest Trinidad. More generally, the modeled geometric and anthropozoomorphic *adornos* show increasing Barrancoid influence in the monkeys, birds, felines, and possibly turtles and frogs that they depict.

Palo Seco's middens are densely packed with shells of various types and interspersed with layers of earth and cultural matter. Altogether, some twenty-six species of shells are represented, though their frequencies change over time. Eleven human burials have been discovered.

> *See also:* Barrancoid; Cedros (site, Trinidad); Saladoid; Trinidad and Tobago; White-on-Red (W-O-R) Pottery; Zic Pottery
>
> **References**
> Boomert, A. 2000. *Trinidad, Tobago, and the Lower Orinoco Interaction Sphere,* pp. 145–169. Alkmaar, the Netherlands; Bullbrook, J. A. 1953. On the Excavation of a Shell Mound at Palo Seco, Trinidad, B.W.I. *Yale University Publications in Anthropology* No. 50. New Haven, CT; Rouse, I. 1947. Prehistory of Trinidad in Relation to Adjacent Areas. *MAN* (o.s.) 47 (103): 93–98.

Pané, Father Ramón

Father Ramón Pané was a Spanish Catholic priest from Catalonia who described himself as "a poor friar of the Order of Saint Jerome." He journeyed with Christopher Columbus on his second voyage to the Americas in 1494. His assignment was to live among the indigenous Taíno of Hispaniola (modern Haiti and the Dominican Republic), learn their language, and study their customs and beliefs. Although Pané was not an anthropologist, his written record, *An Account of the Antiquities of the Indians,* is a uniquely informative eyewitness account and has earned its author the title of "the first ethnographer of the Americas."

Soon after his arrival, Pané went to live in the village of the Taíno chief Mayobanex in northern Hispaniola, where he began learning the indigenous language. A year later, in the spring of 1495, he moved to the village of another chief, Guarionex, where he stayed for several years and during which time he wrote his account. Seeing that Guarionex was not likely to convert, Pané left and went to another chief called Mabiatué, who had expressed an interest in becoming Christian.

Pané's work is remarkable for its insight, detail, and sensitivity. Although as a priest he was bound to try to convert the Taíno, he respected them as human beings and was the first to expose the abuses that they suffered at the hands of the Spanish colonizers. The main part of his work deals with Taíno religious beliefs and moral philosophy, and illustrates a sophisticated understanding and discernment of complex issues. He noted, for example, how the spirit of a living person is the anthropomorphic *goeíza* while that of a deceased individual is the *opía*. He recorded an insightful story of a spiritually animated tree that calls out for a shaman who, after conducting certain rituals, interrogates the tree, then cuts it down in order to make a sacred carved-wood *zemí*.

In other parts of his report, Pané described long and symbolically complex creation myths and charts the role of culture heroes like Guayahona. He described the activities of shamans, their snuffing of the hallucinogenic *cohoba* powder, and their medicinal knowledge. Importantly, he named and described such major deities as Guabancex, the "Lady of the Hurricane Winds"; Baibrama, the deity identified with the cultivation and consumption of cassava; and Yúcahu, the supreme Taíno deity whose name (somewhat confusingly) means "spirit of cassava."

After its completion in 1498, Pané gave his report to Columbus and promptly disappeared from history. His account was summarized by the Italian humanist Peter Martyr and the Spanish chronicler and priest Bartolomé de Las Casas, and was included in full by Christopher Columbus's son Fernando in his biography of his father. Fernando Columbus died in 1539 without publishing his work, which was then taken to Venice and hastily and incompletely translated into Italian by Alfonso de Ulloa and published posthumously. Today, both Pané's and Fernando Columbus's original manuscripts are lost, leaving only the two summaries and the error-ridden Italian translation. In 1999, however, the Pané scholar José Juan Arrom published the definitive critical translation in English—*An Account of the Antiquities of the Indians*—which has ensured Pané's place in the forefront of American anthropology.

See also: Cassava (manioc); Cohoba; Guarionex (Taíno chief); Shamanism; Taíno (Arawak); Zemís

References

Arrom, J. J. 1992. Fray Ramón Pané, Discoverer of the Taíno People. In R. Jara and N. Spadaccini (eds.). *Amerindian Images and the Legacy of Columbus,* pp. 266–290. Minneapolis: University of Minnesota Press; Bourne, E. G. 1906. Columbus, Ramón Pané and the Beginnings of American Anthropology. *Proceedings of the Antiquarian Society* 17: 310–348; Pané,

Fray Ramón. 1999. *An Account of the Antiquities of the Indians.* (J. J. Arrom, ed.). Durham, NC, and London: Duke University Press.

Paradise Park (site, Jamaica)

Paradise Park is an important and recently investigated Taíno site in the county of Westmoreland, southwest Jamaica. Located in coastal dunes, it is in fact two sites—Paradise dated to ca. A.D. 850 (Ostionan Period), and Sweetwater, dated to ca. A.D. 1450 (Meillacan Period). Between 1998 and 2002, it was excavated by archaeologists from the Jamaica National Heritage Trust (JNHT), the Florida Museum of Natural History, and the University of the West Indies.

These two sites are important because they have yielded evidence of different lifeways for early and late Taíno peoples against a background of comparatively little archaeological research and knowledge about prehistoric Jamaica. The evidence of stone tools, faunal remains, and pottery from the two sites highlights the differences between the two cultures that occupied them. The Paradise site yielded substantial remains of marine species (turtles, fish bones, and Queen Conch shells), a large number of flaked stone tools, and typical redware pottery. The Sweetwater site, in contrast, yielded a clean plaza area, Meillacan-Period pottery of the Jamaican Montego Bay style (only known previously from the north coast), a greenstone axe, stone tools made from different chert sources, fewer Queen Conch (*Strombus gigas*) shells, and the remains of crocodiles, birds, and the hutia (*Isolobodon portoricensis*). These investigations are adding much-needed detail to the sequence and development of prehistoric Jamaican culture.

> *See also:* Jamaica; Ostionoid; Taíno (Arawak)
> *References*
> Howard, R. R. 1965. New Perspectives on Jamaican Archaeology. *American Antiquity* 31 (2): 250–255; Keegan, W. H. 2002. Earthwatch Paradise Park, 2002. *http://flmnh.ufl.edu/anthro/caribarch/paradiseParkEW2002.htm.*

Pearls (gems)

According to the Roman naturalist Pliny, pearls form when dew falls into oysters. In the Americas, where dew and oysters were abundant, European explorers expected to find vast quantities of the gems. Among pre-Columbian peoples, the translucent qualities of pearls were held in high esteem. They were associated with water, fertility, and the ritual and economic importance attached to the shells that yielded them: Atlantic pearl oyster (*Pinctada*), Atlantic wing oyster (*Pteria*), and sometimes Queen Conch (*Strombus gigas*).

For some Amerindian societies, pearls were regarded as miniature symbols of the sea as the "mother of fertility," to whom they were given as votive offerings. For others, pearls held the human soul and were buried in vast quantities with the dead. Together with other brilliant materials like gold, jade, and iridescent bird feathers, pearls shared a ritual importance that saw sacredness and power manifested as glittering objects—the pan-Amerindian "aesthetic of brilliance."

Pearls were the focus of early exchanges between Europeans and native Caribbean peoples, playing an important role in the encounter between the Old and New Worlds. They were traded for shiny European objects like glass beads, mirrors, and items made of brass, copper, and iron. During Columbus's third voyage in 1498, on the "Pearl Island" of Cubagua, a sailor smashed a glazed ceramic dish, exchanging its shiny fragments for a string of pearls. The first financially profitable voyage to the Americas was that of Pedro Alonso Niño in 1499, who traded tin, copper bells, and glass beads for ninety-six pounds of Venezuelan pearls.

The European passion for American pearls had far-reaching consequences. In 1508, large numbers of Lucayan Amerindians were taken from the Bahamas and forced to dive for pearls off Cubagua, due to their expertise in diving 30 meters or more for conch. The value of a Lucayan slave diver reached 150 gold ducats but within 10 years the Bahamas had been completely depopulated and the Lucayans were extinct. For Lucayan pearl divers life was hard; they dived from sunrise to sunset, were weighed down with heavy stones, given little respite between dives, and suffered from pressure-induced hemorrhages and shark attacks. Equally tragic, the origins of European slave trading along Africa's Guinea coast was partly driven by the demand for African pearl divers to replace the decimated Amerindian population. Ironically, pearls taken by the Spanish from their slave divers were in turn acquired by English corsairs who raided Spanish treasure fleets on the high seas.

Despite these setbacks and the cruelty toward the slave divers, the rewards for the Spanish were enormous. In one month alone in 1529, 345 kg of pearls came from the island of Coche nearby Margarita and Cubagua. In 1543, the fleet of Martín Alonso Pinzón took 9,000 ducats worth of pearls back to the Spanish Crown.

Europeans soon called the Americas the "Land of Pearls." The gems quickly became a fashion accessory for European royalty and nobility, worn by the Hapsburgs, Medicis, Stuarts, and Tudors. The famous pear-shaped Huerfana pearl weighed 31 carats, and passed from Panama's Amerindians in 1515 to a succession of Spanish noblewomen until acquired by Isabella, wife of the emperor Charles V (1500–1558). When England's Queen Elizabeth I died, her body was draped with pearl necklaces, earrings, and pendants. So profitable did the gems become that higher-valued Persian pearls were taken to the Americas, sold to affluent Hispano-Americans, and the profits used to purchase cheaper American pearls that had a ready market in Europe among people of more modest means. By the early 1530s, overexploitation of the pearl beds of Cubagua had led a serious decline in production and, by 1541, after several natural disasters, the Spanish left Cubagua for Margarita.

In the opalescent luster of pearls, Amerindians and Europeans each saw symbols of beauty, wealth, and power. Yet, where Amerindians saw pearls as embodiments of bright and sacred cosmic energy, Europeans saw commercial value indicated by flawlessness, size, and color. The European lust for Caribbean pearls epitomized both the entrepreneurial spirit and the unparalleled greed of the Age of Discoveries.

See also: Aesthetic of Brilliance; Margarita Island; Gold; Slavery

References

Donkin, R. A. 1998. *Beyond Price, Pearls and Pearl-Fishing to the Age of Discoveries*. Philadelphia: Transactions of the American Philosophical Society; Kunz, G. F., and C. H. Stevenson. [1908] 1993. *The Book of the Pearl*. New York: Dover; Mester, A. M. 1990. *The Pearl Divers of Los Frailes: Archaeological and Ethnohistorical Explorations of Sumptuary Good Trade and Cosmology in the North and Central Andes*. Ph.D. Dissertation, University of Illinois at Urbana-Champaign. Ann Arbor, MI: University Microfilms; Morris, P. A. 1973. *A Field Guide to Shells of the Atlantic and Gulf Coasts and the West Indies*. Boston: Houghton Mifflin; Romero, A., S. Chilbert, and M. G. Eisenhart. 1999. Cubagua's Pearl-Oyster Beds: The First Depletion of a Natural Resource Caused by Europeans in the American Continent. *Journal of Political Ecology* 6: 57–77; Sauer, C. O. 1969. *The Early Spanish Main*. Berkeley, CA: University of California Press; Saunders, N. J. 1999. Biographies of Brilliance: Pearls, Transformations of Matter and Being, ca. A.D. 1492. *World Archaeology* 32 (2): 243–257.

Pearls (site, Grenada)

The archaeological site of Pearls is located on the windward eastern coast of Grenada on rich agricultural land near the mouth of the Simon River. The archaeologist Ripley Bullen investigated the area in 1964 and made a collection currently in the Florida Museum of Natural History. In August 1988 and January 1989, the Foundation for Field Research sponsored further work at the site. This consisted of surface surveys and test excavations that were followed in August 1989 by investigations led by William Keegan to ascertain the layout of the site and the impact of new airport construction.

It appears that the site had been heavily looted for many years. Many complete Saladoid pots and zoomorphic adorno handles were acquired and subsequently sold to tourists at the airport. The ceramics included bowls, bottles, and incense burners. In 1987, a greenstone pendant was discovered and soon other similar items of a frog-like shape were dug up. The combined results of the scientific investigations and looted objects indicated that the site was an ideal location to investigate cultural developments during Saladoid/Huecoid times (ca. 300 B.C. to A.D. 400). Pearls's importance lay in the fact that its artifacts showed stylistic similarities with objects from other islands in the Lesser Antilles, South America, and Puerto Rico—the latter's small offshore island of Vieques possessing the type-site of La Hueca, which gave its name to the Huecoid style.

The recent excavations have highlighted shortcomings in Ripley Bullen's original work and have also shown that the site itself had a complex layout. Multidisciplinary investigations revealed details of the site's surface and subsurface structure by using geophysical methods, aerial photography, and the specialized analysis of human bones and plant remains, thereby placing the rich pottery and greenstone finds in a broader cultural context. After years of neglect, the Pearls site was beginning to be investigated in a scientific way to identify the prehistoric or modern nature of soil formations, to establish a stratigraphy, and to reveal that the depth and richness of middens cannot be established solely from surface appearance.

See also: Grenada; Saladoid; Suazey/Suazoid

References
Bullen, R. P. 1964. *The Archaeology of Grenada, West Indies.* Gainesville, FL: University Press of Florida; Bullen, R. P. 1968. Some Arawak Ceramic Variations between Grenada, Barbados, St. Lucia, and Eastern Trinidad. *Proceedings of the Second International Congress for the Study of Pre-Columbian Cultures in the Lesser Antilles, Barbados,* pp. 81–86. Barbados; Bullen, R. P. 1970. The Archaeology of Grenada, West Indies, and the Spread of Ceramic People in the Antilles. *Proceedings of the Third International Congress for the Study of Pre-Columbian Cultures of the Lesser Antilles, Grenada,* pp. 147–152. Grenada; Keegan, W. F. 1991. Archaeology at Pearls, Grenada: The 1990 Field Season. *Miscellaneous Project Report* No. 47, Florida Museum of Natural History, Gainesville, FL; Keegan, W. F., and A. Cody. 1989. Progress Report on the Archaeological Excavation at the Site of Pearls, Grenada, August 1989. *Miscellaneous Project Report* No. 44, Florida Museum of Natural History, Gainesville, FL.

Pepper Pot

Pepper pot stew was a staple meal of indigenous Caribbean peoples when Christopher Columbus arrived, and is still widespread among South American tropical rainforest societies. The basic ingredient is *cassarip,* a savory sauce made from the initially poisonous juice left over from cassava squeezing. This juice is mixed with chili peppers and then boiled for several hours. Squash, beans, peanuts, meat, fish, and water are then added, cooked, and kept simmering over a fire in a large ceramic bowl. In South America today, and possibly among indigenous peoples of the Island Caribbean in the past, there is a rich symbolism associated with the preparation and consumption of pepper pot. Embodying ideas of sexuality, gender roles, and transformation, pepper pot is made by women and offered to visitors as a traditional gesture of hospitality. Among some tribes it is also a symbolic invitation for visiting men to associate with nubile women.

See also: Cassava (manioc)

References
Hugh-Jones, C. 1988. *From the Milk River: Spatial and Temporal Processes in Northwest Amazonia,* pp. 224–226. Cambridge: Cambridge University Press; Mowat, L. 1989. *Cassava and Chicha: Bread and Beer of the Amazonian Indians.* Princes Risborough, UK: Shire Publications.

Pitch Lake (site, Trinidad)

Pitch Lake, also known as La Brea, is a unique natural phenomenon—a lake of bubbling and hardened asphalt in south-central Trinidad. Long known to Trinidad's Amerindian inhabitants, it was first noticed by Europeans when the Spanish settled the island in 1592. The first English report was by Robert Dudley early in 1595, and then, more famously, by Sir Walter Ralegh a few months later. Europeans regarded it as natural curiosity but remarked on the usefulness of its pitch to calk their boats.

Around the lake's raised margins, extensive archaeological remains have been found. An early indicator of human presence is a wide scatter of flint and chert together with stone tools that appear to date to between 5000 B.C. and 500 B.C. Another site was probably a village belonging to the Saladoid peoples and dated to between ca. A.D. 300 and A.D.

650. It yielded various mollusk remains, a fragment of a cassava griddle, and pieces of elaborate pottery including zoomorphic ceramic
images (*adornos*) of birds, frogs, and bats.

During the seventeenth century, Amerindian tradition tells how
the local Chaima people offended spirits of the dead by hunting
their souls, which had transformed into hummingbirds. As a punishment their village sank into the earth and Pitch Lake appeared.
There may be a symbolic connection between hummingbirds and
tobacco shamanism enshrined in this myth, as hummingbirds suck
the nectar of the tobacco plant, and shamans were believed to transform into hummingbirds in order to obtain tobacco for curing and trance. Variations on this myth were once
common, and some identified the lake as a portal to the spirit world. There appears to
have been a large population of Amerindian descent living around Pitch Lake until the
nineteenth century.

From the 1930s until the early 1970s, various wooden artifacts have been recovered, well preserved, from the asphalt at Pitch Lake. There are some ten objects in all,
including a bowl, mortar, oval seat, wooden paddles, so-called weaving sticks, and a
zoomorphic four-legged wooden stool in the shape of a feline, perhaps a jaguar or
ocelot. The stool is similar to shamans' benches well known from South America. These
remarkable finds may either have been lost or deliberately thrown into the lake as ritual offerings where they remained until the churning action of the liquid pitch eventually disgorged them.

See also: Shamanism; Tobacco; Trinidad and Tobago

References

Anderson, A. 1979. An Account of the Bituminous Lake or Plain in the Island of Trinidad. *Philosophical Transactions of the Royal Society* 79, pp. 65–70; Assee, S. 1972. When the Pitch Lake Swallowed Up the Chaimas. *Trinidad Guardian,* July 31. Port of Spain, Trinidad; Boomert, A. 1984. Aspects of Pitch Lake; The Pitch Lake in History; The Pitch Lake in Amerindian Mythology; The Pitch Lake in Archaeology. *The Naturalist Magazine* 5 (11): 11–47 (Trinidad); Boomert, A. 2000. *Trinidad, Tobago, and the Lower Orinoco Interaction Sphere,* pp. 297–300, 454–457. Alkmaar, the Netherlands.

Port Royal (Jamaica)

Port Royal began life as Fort Cromwell in 1655, located on a spit of land jutting out into Kingston harbor on Jamaica's south coast. This strategic position controlled access to the harbor and soon attracted a population of sailors, merchants, and craftsmen. Named Port Royal in 1660 after Charles II became king of England, the original building was appropriately renamed Fort Charles. These developments spurred the growth of the town until by the late seventeenth century it had become the largest and most important English port in the New World.

As Port Royal grew, so did its relationship with privateers and buccaneers, and this lasted into the eighteenth century. After 1670, the port became the center for the Caribbean trade in slaves and sugar as well as the proceeds of high-seas piracy. Attracting ever greater wealth, Port Royal became known as "the wickedest city in the world," with a population estimated at about 8,000. In a good year, several hundred ships would make this port of call. At this time, Port Royal was a cosmopolitan mix of peoples and faiths, with Anglicans, Jews, and Roman Catholics rubbing shoulders with each other and the rougher members of society.

During the eighteenth century there were the beginnings of a shift in Jamaica's economy toward the great plantations and much of this was funded with the wealth funneled through Port Royal. At 11:43 A.M. on 7 June 1692, disaster struck when an earthquake hit the area and over half of Port Royal fell into the sea. Altogether, some 5,000 people died during and after the event that, while tragic, also created one of the world's most important underwater archaeological sites. Although the town made a dramatic recovery, a fire and subsequent hurricanes and earthquakes led to its final disappearance in 1722.

Today, much of Port Royal lies almost intact beneath the waters offshore Kingston. Ever since the disastrous earthquake, divers have retrieved objects from the submerged streets and houses. In recent years, however, the technology and increasing sophistication of underwater archaeology have allowed ever-more detailed information to be gathered and analyzed. In 1981, the Jamaica National Heritage Trust (JNHT) joined forces with Texas A&M University and the Institute of Nautical Archaeology to investigate the underwater portions of the old port. For ten years, investigators explored the seventeenth-century remains clustered around the commercial heart of the port along Lime Street. One major finding was the ad hoc nature of the settlement, with well-built brick buildings alongside timber-framed structures clearly not designed to last.

French expedition exploring Port Royal, Jamaica, showing habitat, wildlife, and Indian encampment. Engraving by Theodore de Bry (1528–1598).

The preservation of these buildings is informative of how they developed as Port Royal became more important. One building had three rooms, several of which have been tentatively identified as a tavern and a cobbler's shop. Details such as the herringbone style of brickwork, wooden door sills, hearths, and ovens have all been investigated. Many artifacts have also been recovered, such as silver cutlery, Chinese porcelain, and pewter plates and drinking vessels. More poignantly, the remains of several children have been found in the ruins, illustrating the terrible speed of the disaster that overtook the port.

Adding valuable insights to the understanding of Port Royal's rich archaeological record has been historical research into the port's seventeenth-century documentary records. Wills, probate inventories, and miscellaneous documents have helped identify the possible makers and owners of objects retrieved from the site. One example is Simon Benning, identified as a maker of pewter ware. Benning came from Tottenham in Middlesex, England, where he spent seven years learning his trade before traveling to Barabados, where he lived for six or seven years before moving on to Jamaica. He appears in the 1680 census of Port Royal and his will, written on 8 March 1683, names his wife, Susanna, and three children and identifies properties he owned in Port Royal. During the underwater excavations, over fifty pewter plates and dishes were found with Simon Benning's touchmark—a pineapple flanked by "S" and "B" and all surrounded by a rope border.

The story of Port Royal and its inhabitants illustrates how, by cooperation between historians, archaeologists, and a range of specialists, a living picture of a place can be painstakingly reconstructed.

See also: Historical Archaeology; Jamaica; Underwater Archaeology

References

Buisseret, D. J. 1966. Port Royal 1655–1725. *The Jamaican Historical Review* 6: 21–28; Fox, G. L. 1999. The Kaolin Clay Tobacco Pipe Collection from Port Royal, Jamaica. In P. Davey (ed.). *The Archaeology of the Clay Tobacco Pipe.* Oxford, British Archaeological Reports International Series 809; Gotelipe-Miller, S. 1990. *Pewter and Pewterers from Port Royal, Jamaica: Flatware before 1692.* Unpublished Master's thesis. Department of Anthropology, Texas A&M University, College Station, TX; Hamilton, D. L. 1986. Port Royal Revisited. *Underwater Archaeology Proceedings from the Society for Historical Archaeology Conference 1986,* pp. 73–81; Hamilton, D. L. 1991. A Decade of Excavations at Port Royal, Jamaica. *Underwater Archaeology Proceedings from the Society for Historical Archaeology Conference, Richmond, Virginia, 1991,* pp. 90–94; Link, M. C. 1960. Exploring the Drowned City of Port Royal. *National Geographic Magazine* 117 (1): 151–183; Pawson, M., and D. J. Buisseret. 1975. *Port Royal Jamaica.* Oxford: Clarendon Press; Priddy, A. 1975. The 17th- and 18th-Century Settlement Pattern of Port Royal. *Jamaica Journal* 9 (2–3): 8–10; Zahedieh, N. 1986. Trade, Plunder, and Economic Development in Early English Jamaica, 1655–1689. *Economic History Review* 4 (2): 205–222.

Puerto Real (site, Haiti)

The town of Puerto Real was established on the north coast of Hispaniola (in modern day Haiti) in 1503 by the Spanish governor Nicolás de Ovando as part of his attempts to pacify the local Taíno inhabitants of the region. It lasted for some eighty years.

Puerto Real was one of thirteen settlements founded by the Spanish during their colonization of Hispaniola. Never large, and often economically marginal, the town was typical of Spanish efforts to make use of local resources and indigenous people in order to be self-sufficient. The total population of the town, including its subject local Taíno inhabitants, may have been in the region of 500 to 600 people, though only a fraction of these would have been full-fledged citizens according to Spanish law. The town was governed by the local *cabildo,* and the whole region was initially under the control of the chief magistrate Lucas Vásquez de Ayllón, appointed by Ovando in 1506. By 1511, Puerto Real was part of the diocese of Concepción de la Vega, whose parish curate was appointed by the archbishop at Santo Domingo on Hispaniola's south coast.

Puerto Real's inhabitants engaged in gold mining and cattle raising. Soon after founding the town, the Spanish discovered and began working a famous copper mine at Morne Rouge whose deposits contained a good portion of gold. To help work this mine, the Spanish King Ferdinand sent one of the first shipments of African slaves to the Americas in 1505. The mine never lived up to expectations, however, and by 1530 it was all but exhausted. Apart from copper, Puerto Real's inhabitants dealt in cattle hides that were more valuable than the meat at the time, and were destined for Europe and other colonies.

For the first decades of its life, Puerto Real was also the starting point for slave raids to the Bahamas in search of labor to replace the Taíno depleted by maltreatment and disease.

In April 1532, Puerto Real was involved in one of the early slave uprisings when a local chief (cacique) and his supporters killed a Spanish family and their Indian retainers. By 1576, Amerindian peoples had largely disappeared and there were already over 30,000 Africans on Hispaniola—a situation that led to racial mixing whose offspring were called mulatos. Disease, the decline in local and Spanish population, and the town's isolation led to its final abandonment around 1578. In a final irony, much of Puerto Real's rock and brick was scavenged from the town during the sixteenth century and used to build a sugar plantation by the French who had gained control of this part of Hispaniola.

Abandoned, despoiled, and forgotten, the ruins of Puerto Real were lost for 400 years until 1978 when they were rediscovered by Dr. William Hodges and investigated archaeologically. Puerto Real's significance was that it was one of the first European towns in the Americas whose purpose was to colonize rather than simply exploit the New World. As such, it represented an opportunity for historical archaeologists to understand colonialism and the rise of Hispanic-American culture.

Multidisciplinary investigations included historical research, a geographical and ecological assessment of the region, a survey of the town's layout and boundaries, and the location of the town plaza and church. There was also excavation of houses of high and low economic status indicated by the contrasting presence of European glass and Spanish majolica pottery in the former, and a paucity of European materials and the presence of indigenous pottery in the latter. The presence of locally produced kitchenware pottery (almost 50 percent of the total recovered) represents a significant adaptation to local conditions and supports the historical records of Spanish men taking Taíno women as wives or concubines.

Archaeological investigations confirmed Puerto Real had been built with strong linear features and building orientations indicating it followed the rectangular grid plan characteristic of Spanish settlements in the New World. This layout appears to have been present even in 1503 when the first palisade structure was built and that was clearly influenced by local Taíno architectural traditions. Underlying the first levels of European activity was evidence of an aboriginal shell midden with Meillacan-Ostionoid pottery. Somewhat later, there is evidence for a cemetery where indigenous peoples were buried, often in shallow graves. A masonry-built church decorated with gargoyles represented the high point in the life of Puerto Real. As the indigenous peoples disappeared they were replaced by African slaves and this is probably reflected in the change from Taíno pottery types to a new variation known as Christophe Plain and that appears to have been a typically African style. Puerto Real's eventual demise is marked by destruction of the church (including the churchdoor padlock in the locked position) and evidence for squatter settlement within its ruins.

See also: Jamaica; La Isabela (site, Dominican Republic); La Navidad/En Bas Saline (site, Haiti); Meillacan

References

Cook, N. D. 1993. Disease and Depopulation of Hispaniola, 1492–1518. *Colonial Latin American Review* 2: 213–245; Deagan, K. 1995. *Puerto Real: The Archaeology of a Sixteenth-Century Spanish Town in Hispaniola,* Gainesville, FL: University Press of Florida; Deagan, K., and J. M.

Cruxent. 2002. *Columbus's Outpost among the Taínos: Spain and America at La Isabela, 1493–1498.* New Haven, CT: Yale University Press; Ewen, C. R. 1991. *From Spaniard to Creole: The Archaeology of Cultural Formation at Puerto Real, Haiti.* Tuscaloosa, AL: The University of Alabama Press; McEwan, B. G. 1986. Domestic Adaptation at Puerto Real, Haiti. *Historical Archaeology* 20 (1): 44–49; Reitz, E. J. 1990. Early Spanish Subsistence at Puerto Real, Hispaniola. *Proceedings of the Eleventh Congress of the International Association for Caribbean Archaeology,* pp. 442–447. San Juan, Puerto Rico: Fundación de Arqueología e História de Puerto Rico; Williams, M. W. 1986. Subsurface Patterning at Sixteenth-Century Spanish Puerto Real, Haiti. *Journal of Field Archaeology* 13 (3): 283–296.

Puerto Rico

Puerto Rico is the smallest of the Greater Antilles, and has an area of 8,768 sq miles. Volcanic mountains and tropical rainforests dominate the heart of the island, although its northern part is limestone karst. After the Spanish-American War of 1898, Spain ceded the island to the United States and today it is a U.S. overseas commonwealth territory, with a population of some 3.7 million.

Archaeologically, Puerto Rico has a rich and impressive pre-Columbian past. The earliest human occupation dates to around 1000 B.C. and belongs to the so-called Coroso culture of the Ortoroid Period. At this time, the hunting and gathering inhabitants lived both in caves and in open areas. Sites are typically small shell middens, with rather basic stone tools and sometimes simple bone and shell jewelry. It was the Coroso people who must have confronted the first Saladoid pottery-making peoples when they arrived somewhere around 430 B.C. At this time, the earliest local form of Saladoid culture is known as Hacienda Grande—named after the type-site on the island's north coast where it flourished between ca. 400 B.C. and A.D. 500.

Hacienda Grande pottery, with its white-on-red (W-O-R) and zic (zone-incised cross-hatching) styles, also has anthropomorphic and zoomorphic decorative *adornos*. Zemís, cassava griddles, and jewelry made from various minerals were all characteristic features at this time. Overlapping with Hacienda Grande is the La Hueca culture known from the sites of Sorcé and Punta Candelero, and dating to between 160 B.C. and A.D. 500. While also belonging to the Saladoid tradition on Puerto Rico, and sharing, for example, the practice of interring dogs with human burials, the La Hueca people were distinctive in their making of bird-head pendants of carved stone. Somewhere around A.D. 400, Hacienda Grande society evolved into the culture known as Cuevas, and then again into the succeeding Elenan culture of the Ostionoid tradition—whose later forms included the fully fledged Taíno culture. The mainly Saladoid site of Maisabel seems to represent an increase in social and political complexity in prehistoric Puerto Rico, and experienced cultural evolution as indicated by the presence of Ostionoid Period burials and buildings. The Elenan culture that replaced the Saladoid in Puerto Rico saw the development of formal dance and ballcourts at the sites of Tibes and El Bronce.

During Classic Taíno (Chican Ostionoid) times, the size, distribution, and sophistication of village sites and associated ballcourts increased in line with developments in social

Massive ramparts flank the heavily fortified gateway to Old San Juan town, Puerto Rico (Courtesy Nicholas J. Saunders)

and political organization. It may be that some of the largest ball-courts were located on the territorial boundaries between two chiefdoms and therefore had a political role. The most elaborate group of plazas or courts known to date is at Caguana (or Capá) in the center of the island.

Puerto Rico was first seen by Europeans when Christopher Columbus and Juan Ponce de León landed on the island on 19 November 1493 during the second voyage, though the inhabitants, fearing they were raiding Caribs, retreated into the hinterland. At the time, the island, called Borinquén by its Taíno inhabitants, seems to have been the frontier between the Taíno to the west and the Caribs to the east. In 1508, Ponce de León founded the first European settlement there nearby the present site of San Juan, to where it was moved two years later. A paramount chief during this period was Agüeybana and at first both he and the other inhabitants acquiesced to Spanish demands that they work for them in encomiendas, and especially in searching the rivers for gold. Several years of maltreatment by the Spanish provoked a short-lived rebellion in 1511 organized by Agüeybana who was quickly caught and executed. In the years that followed, Old World diseases and continued abuse by the Spanish led to the virtual disappearance of the Taíno peoples as identifiable communities. By the end of the nineteenth century, just a small population survived in the western part of the island.

Today, there are significant remains of Puerto Rico's pre-Columbian past across the island. In the center is the Caguana Indian Ceremonial Park with its ballcourts and dance plazas set in a distinctive limestone scenery that probably had spiritual significance for the Taíno inhabitants. Another center of archaeological interest is the museum at Ponce on the south coast, and the nearby Tibes Indian Ceremonial Center that incorporates Elenan Period (i.e., pre-Taíno) ballcourts and plazas in which some 200 human burials (including those of children) have been found. There is also a replica Taíno village at the site.

Puerto Rico's rich archaeological and historical past includes much that is post-Taíno. The sixteenth-century demise of these native inhabitants led to labor shortages that saw African slaves imported to work sugar plantations and the vast cattle ranches that had become an important feature of the island's economy. The characteristically non-European–style pottery made by these slaves and their freed descendants is referred to as *criollo* ceramics. They have been found in house and fortress remains in San Juan, and date to the 100 years between the late eighteenth and late nineteenth centuries. As these ceramics were found alongside glazed European pottery, it seems likely that their typical vessels—ollas and *cazuelas*—were used to prepare meals enjoyed not just by the African-descended peoples but by most of the island's population regardless of wealth or social position. In this instance, historical archaeology has illuminated the very beginnings of the distinctive Spanish-American culture and tastes of Puerto Rican society.

Puerto Rico's strategic location made it a point of military defense for the Spanish against the competing imperial powers of France and England. It was an important stopover for the annual fleet that sailed between Spain and her American colonies. Between 1533 and 1540, the Governor's Palace at San Juan was built to protect not just against European attackers but raiding Caribs as well. In 1591, the great fortress of San Felipe del Morro was built at the entrance to San Juan's harbor, and in 1772 the landward side of the city was similarly protected by the construction of the vast Fort San Cristóbal. Despite this, an English seaborne force under the Earl of Cumberland took the fort and the town in 1598 but were forced to retire when struck with fever.

Today, the El Morro fort and its surrounding neighborhood of Old San Juan preserves much colorful colonial Spanish architecture. One of these buildings, the sixteenth-century Dominican convent, now houses the Institute of Culture, and another, the Casa Blanca, built in 1523, was the family house of the Ponce de León family for 250 years and is now a historical museum. The museum that is part of the University of Puerto Rico holds displays of the island's archaeological and historical heritage.

The Spanish soul of the island is particularly evident in the local folklore musical traditions of the island's interior—mountain music preserved and sung by the rural peasants known as *jíbaros*. In the countryside also, elements of mixed Amerindian-African culture survive in folklore beliefs concerning landscape and plants. Where, during Taíno times, the silk-cotton tree (*Ceiba pentandra*) was a principal "spirit tree" from which carved-wood *zemí* figures were made, today it is still revered as a spirit tree. In recent years, like many other Caribbean islands, Puerto Rico has seen the resurgence of indigenous Amerindian identity—a development greatly aided by the Internet. The Jatibonicu Taino Tribal Nation of Boriken call themselves the "Great People of the Sacred High Waters" and occupy several villages in Puerto Rico's mountainous heartland. They promote their own heritage, arts and crafts, and indigenous language, and maintain close relationships with other Taíno and non-Taíno indigenous groups in the Caribbean and beyond.

See also: Agüeybana (Taíno chief); Ball-Game; Hacienda Grande; Hueca, La (Puerto Rico); Maisabel (site, Puerto Rico); Meillacan; Ortoiroid; Taíno (Arawak); Trees, Spiritual Importance of; White-on-Red Pottery (W-O-R); Zic Pottery

References

Alegría, R. E. 1974. *Discovery, Conquest, and Colonization of Puerto Rico 1493–1599.* San Juan, Puerto Rico: Colección de Estudios Puertorriqueños; Anderson-Córdova, K. 1990. *Hispaniola and Puerto Rico: Indian Acculturation and Heterogeneity, 1492–1550.* Ph.D. dissertation, Yale University. Ann Arbor, MI: University Microfilms; Chanlatte Baik, L. A. 1976. *La hueca y sorcé (Vieques, Puerto Rico): Nuevo esquema para los procesos culturales de la arqueología antillana.* Santo Domingo, the Dominican Republic: Fundación García Arévalo; Curet, A. L. 1992. House Structure and Cultural Change in the Caribbean: Three Case Studies from Puerto Rico. *Latin American Antiquity* 3: 160–174; Curet, A. L., and J. R. Oliver. 1998. Mortuary Practices, Social Development, and Ideology in Precolumbian Puerto Rico. *Latin American Antiquity* 9 (3): 217–239; deFrance, S. D. 1989. Saladoid and Ostionoid Subsistence Adaptations: Zooarchaeological Data from a Coastal Occupation on Puerto Rico. In P. E. Siegel (ed.). *Early Ceramic Population Lifeways and Adaptive Strategies in the Caribbean,* pp. 57–77. Oxford: British Archaeological Reports International Series 506; deFrance, S. L. 1990. Zooarchaeological Investigations of an Early Ceramic Age Frontier Community in the Caribbean: The Maisabel Site, Puerto Rico. *Antropológica* 73–74: 3–180; Fernandez, R., S. Mendez Mendez, and G. Cueto. 1998. *Puerto Rico Past and Present.* Greenwood Publishing Group; Goodwin, R. 1975. *Villa Taina de Boqueron: Excavation and Analysis of an Early Taino Site in Puerto Rico.* San Juan, Puerto Rico: Interamerican University Press; Magaña, C. S. 1999. Crillo Pottery from San Juan de Puerto Rico. In J. B. Haviser (ed.). *African Sites Archaeology in the Caribbean,* pp. 131–143. Princeton, NJ: Markus Wiener Publishers; Oliver, J. R. 1998. *El Centro ceremonial de Caguana, Puerto Rico. Simbolismo iconográfico, cosmovisión y el poderió caciquil taíno de Borinquén.* Oxford: British Archaeological Reports International Series 727, Archaeopress; Rodríguez, M. 1989. The Zoned Incised Crosshatch (Zic) Ware of Early Precolumbian Ceramic Age Sites in Puerto Rico and Vieques Island. In P. E. Siegel (ed.). *Early Ceramic Population Lifeways and Adaptive Strategies in the Caribbean,* pp. 249–266. Oxford: British Archaeological Reports International Series 506; Roe, P. G. 1991. The Best Enemy is a Killed, Drilled, and Decorative Enemy: Human Corporeal Art (Frontal Bone Pectorals, Belt Ornaments, Carved Humeri, and Pierced Teeth) in Pre-Columbian Puerto Rico. *Proceedings of the Thirteenth International Congress for Caribbean Archaeology, Willemstadt, Curaçao,* pp. 854–873. Curaçao: Archaeological-Anthropological Institute of the Netherlands Antilles; Rouse, I. B., and R. E. Alegría. 1990. *Excavations at Maria de la Cruz Cave and Hacienda Grande Village Site, Loiza, Puerto Rico.* New Haven, CT: Yale University Publications in Anthropology, No. 80; Siegel, P. E. 1999. Contested Places and Places of Contest: The Evolution of Social Power and Ceremonial Space in Prehistoric Puerto Rico. *Latin American Antiquity* 10 (3): 209–238.

R

Ralegh, Sir Walter

The Elizabethan explorer Sir Walter Ralegh (1552–1618) journeyed to the Caribbean in 1595, spending time on Trinidad before making his way up the Orinoco River in search of the golden land of El Dorado. The events of this expedition are recorded in Ralegh's fascinating but problematical book, *The Discoveries of the Large, Rich and Bewtiful Empyre of Guiana*, which was first published in 1596.

Ralegh's importance for the Caribbean lies in his ethnographic observations of the island of Trinidad and the adjacent mainland region of the Orinoco delta, as well as in his contribution to the El Dorado legend. Arriving off southwest Trinidad on 22 March 1595, Ralegh stepped ashore on an island already claimed, if only sparsely settled, by the Spanish. He made his way up the island's west coast where he was impressed by Pitch Lake, regarding it as a natural curiosity and remarking on the usefulness of its pitch for calking his ships. He conversed with the indigenous inhabitants, noting such names as the Carinepagotos, Nepoios, and Yao, among others.

One of his informants, a local chief called Cantyman, supplied details on the Spanish dispositions at their main town of San José de Oruña, which Ralegh quickly attacked and overcame, razing the buildings and freeing local chiefs imprisoned by the Spanish. Ralegh also captured the governor, Antonio de Berrio, an ageing conquistador who had made many expeditions in search of El Dorado. Ralegh appears to have gotten on well with many of the island's native peoples, addressing them in a speech during which he displayed a portrait of his queen, who became in their tongue Ezrebeta Cassipuna Aquerewana or "Elizabeth the Great Princess."

Ralegh retraced his steps to the southwest tip of Trinidad where, according to Spanish records, he built a small fort with the help of local Amerindians at or near a native village called Curiapan. Recent archaeological investigations have searched for the site of this fort but so far without success. At Curiapan, Ralegh prepared for his Orinoco expedition and interrogated Berrio, from whom he undoubtedly received valuable information concerning the geography and native peoples of that region—long familiar to the Spanish. Today, there is still debate over to what extent Ralegh's book simply synthesizes in English knowledge already well known to the Spanish and to what extent it reflects his own discoveries and insights.

Ralegh finally set out for the Orinoco in five boats, rowing up the river where he encountered the Tivitivas, the modern Warao. Meetings with different Amerindian groups followed, as did the acquisition of some golden artifacts as well as the realization that much gold was alluvial in nature. Yet the location of the golden city of Manoa, founded by the mythical Inca-related Epuremi tribe on the shores of a great inland lake, eluded him. Ironically, he noted the existence of what he called marcasite (fool's gold) and shiny quartz stones valued by the native inhabitants. Although Ralegh never found his El Dorado, gold was discovered in the nearby highland area during the nineteenth century, embedded in veins of this same white quartz.

See also: Aesthetic of Brilliance; Amazons; Dudley, Sir Robert; El Dorado; Gold; Trinidad and Tobago; Warao

References

Ralegh, Sir Walter. 1997. *The Discoverie of the Large, Rich and Bewtiful Empyre of Guiana* (Transcribed, annotated, and introduced by N. L. Whitehead). Manchester: Manchester University Press; N. J. Saunders, and A. Chauharjasingh. n.d. *Inventory of Archaeological Sites in Trinidad and Tobago. Report 4, Counties of Victoria and St. Patrick.* University of the West Indies, St. Augustine, Trinidad.

Rastafarianism

Rastafarianism in popular imagination is associated with Jamaica, reggae music, dreadlocks, and the smoking of ganja (marijuana). These internationally recognized features, however, are only the most publicized and sometimes misunderstood and misrepresented aspects of a set of deeply held spiritual beliefs and attitudes.

Rastafarianism is a religion that emerged in Jamaica during the 1930s and that took its inspiration from the Old Testament of the Bible. It was the black nationalist teachings of the Jamaican-born Marcus Garvey (1887–1940) that gave biblical prophecies a powerful and emotive appeal. Garvey's pan-Africanist message galvanized the social and political aspirations of the impoverished working-class African peoples of the island during the 1920s and 1930s through his Universal Negro Improvement Association (UNIA). Garvey believed that integrating black people into white society was useless, and that instead they should focus on restoring their dignity by abandoning the white man's world and returning to Africa. "If Europe is for Europeans, then Africa is for the black people of the world," Garvey said. Today, there are over one million Rastafarians worldwide, mainly still of Afro-Caribbean descent.

There are several important features and tenets of Rastafarianism, and like all aspects of the religion, language and biblical references play a key role. First is the belief that King Haile Selassie of Ethiopia (1892–1975)—known as "Ras Tafari"—is a living messiah whose mission is to lead all Africans to a promised land of freedom and justice. Selassie is regarded as the ultimate manifestation of Jah (God)—one of the supreme being's four avatars, the others being Jesus Christ, Moses, and Elijah. Some Rastas consider the white man's god to be the devil. Rastas believe that all black peoples can trace their ancestry back to King David through the founding of Ethiopia during the tenth

*Rastafarian Ras Moses teaches a fellow
Rastafarian from a Bible, Barbados. (Tony
Arruza/Corbis)*

century B.C. by a son conceived by the Queen of Sheba while on a visit to King Solomon in Israel.

Rastafarianism's name refers to Ras (Prince) Tafari Makonnen, who in 1930 was crowned as Emperor Haile Selassie of Ethiopia. This event was seen as the fulfilment of a prophecy by Marcus Garvey that predicted the coronation of a black king in Africa and that itself seemed to echo a similar Biblical reference in the book of Psalms. Haile Selassie was crowned "King of Kings, Lord of Lords, and the conquering lion of the Tribe of Judah," and is regarded as being the 225th in an unbroken line of Ethiopian kings descended from King David. Further enhancing Selassie's reputation was the fact that Ethiopia was the only sub-Saharan African country to escape colonialism, and Selassie the only black leader accepted by European royalty.

The cruelty and oppression that Africans suffered at the hands of the white people during the transatlantic slavery days of the sixteenth to nineteenth centuries is referred to as "Babylon," and the African homeland they aspire to is known as "Zion," a term also used to mean heaven. Other linguistic characteristics of the faith include the expression "I and I" used instead of "we" or "you and I," which represents the concept of the oneness of two people and the presence of God and his love in everyone. The word "Irie" refers to happiness and good things, "livification" instead of dedication removes the phonetic associations with death, and "I-tal" food refers to organic or natural sustenance uncontaminated by modern chemical additives or processes. Unacceptable foods are those of modern scientific origin, those that originate in "unclean" scavenging animals such as pigs, crabs, and lobsters, and even milk, coffee, and alcohol. The completely I-tal Rasta is a vegetarian.

The reading of Old Testament stories, particularly the identification of Ethiopia as Zion, recast for a new period of black empowerment in Caribbean history, was given credibility in the minds of early Rastas by the presence of the Falashas—the Jewish community in Ethiopia. The most widespread association of Rastafarianism is with Eastern Orthodox Christianity, though the patriarchs of that faith do not recognize the Rastas. Early forms of the religion were influenced variously by African and indigenous Amerindian spiritualities, Judaism, and Hinduism—reflecting the region's multicultural mosaic of peoples and faiths. Rastafarians also revere an ancient Ethiopian holy book, the Kebra Negast, as a sacred text. They consider the standard Bible as having been tampered with to promote a white-oriented view of religion and so have adopted instead an alternative "Black Man's Bible" known as the Holy Piby.

Ganja smoking is an important part of Rastafarianism for many (though not all), and may have been influenced by the cannabis-smoking mystics of India. Rastas consider that it helps meditation and that its use is sanctioned in the Bible where they identify it with the term "herb" in Genesis 3:18: "Thou shalt eat the herb of the field"; and in Exodus 10:12: "Eat every herb of the land." While some features of Rasta belief have been accepted in Western societies as part of the faith, ganja smoking is not recognized and remains as illegal for Rastas as for everyone else.

Dreadlocks also are a feature of the faithful though not universal. Rastas find biblical support for this hairstyle in Leviticus 21:15: "They shall not make baldness upon their head, neither shall they shave off the corner of their beard. . . ." However, dreadlocks also serve to emphasize the distinctive kinky hair of Africans in contrast to the straight hair of Caucasians and so make a powerful visual statement of difference. It may also be that symbolically they associate Rastas with Jah/Haile Selassie in his role as the Lion of Judah standing against the depredations of Babylon. Rastafarianism's sacred colors are red (for the blood of martyrs), green (for Zion's abundant vegetation), and gold (for the wealth of Africa). Along with these emblematic colors, the Rasta symbol of the lion stands for the male principle, and Haile Selassie in his manifestation as Jah (the Lion of Judah).

Rastafarian religious observances are of two types: a "reasoning," or small gathering of Rastas to smoke ganja and discuss social issues or those relating to the faith, and a "binghi" or holiday, numbering several hundred and that can go on for days and includes dancing, music, feasting, and ganja smoking. Special events in the Rasta calendar include 6 January—Haile Selassie's ceremonial birthday; 21 April—the anniversary of Selassie's 1966 visit to Jamaica; 23 July—Haile Selassie's actual birthday; 17 August—Marcus Garvey's birthday; and 2 November—the coronation of Haile Selassie as emperor of Ethiopia. It is interesting that Selassie himself was never a Rasta; he subscribed to Eastern Orthodox Christianity, remained ambivalent to his apotheosis by Rastafarianism, and told Jamaica's Rasta leaders that they should not return to Ethiopia until the island's own population had been liberated.

Although the early tenets of Rastafarianism included a hatred of white people and a promised revenge against their treatment of Africans as slaves, these extreme ideas have now mostly disappeared. Acknowledging Haile Selassie as Jah (God) and seeking a symbolic return to Africa remain, but today most Rastas no longer believe in black supremacy. The Bible is regarded as teaching tolerance and liberation to all people.

In its recent, post-1960s history, Rastafarianism was boosted not only by Haile Selassie's visit to Jamaica, but also by its association with reggae music, and especially the superstar status of Bob Marley and the Wailers, who spread both around the world. Music and faith became intertwined. Today, Rastafarianism is not a highly organized religion, though most belong to the so-called House of Dreads (Nyabinghi) and are divided into two main groups—the Bobos and the Twelve Tribes of Israel. Increasingly, Rastafarianism is moving away from its original form and becoming secularized; women are playing a more vocal role and arguing against the faith's original male-dominated ethos. Rasta colors are now a fashion statement rather than a symbolic code of belief, and dreadlocks similarly no longer identify only a true believer.

See also: Jamaica; Maroons; Obeah; Santería; Vodoun

References

Barrett, L. 1977. *The Rastafarians: The Dreadlocks of Jamaica.* Boston: Beacon Press; Barrett, L. 1988. *Rastafarians: Sounds of Cultural Dissonance.* Boston: Beacon Press; Bilby, K. 1982 Three Resistance Movements in Jamaica: The Maroons, Garveyism, and the Rastafarians. *Journal of the Afro-American Historical and Genealogical Society* 3 (1): 33–39; Campbell, H. 1985. *Rasta and Resistance: From Marcus Garvey to Walter Rodney.* London: Hansib Publishing Ltd.; Chevannes, B. 1998. *Rastafari and Other African-Caribbean Worldviews.* Piscataway NJ: Rutgers University Press; Morrish, I. 1982. *Obeah, Christ, and Rastaman: Jamaica and its Religions.* Cambridge, MA: James

Clarke Press; Clark, P. 1994. *Black Paradise: The Rastafarian Movement.* San Bernadino: Borgo Press; Hausman, G. 1997. *The Kebra Negast: The Book of Rastafarian Wisdom and Faith from Ethiopia and Jamaica.* New York: St. Martin's Press; Jahn, B., and T. Weber. 1998. *Reggae Island: Jamaican Music in the Digital Age.* New York: Da Capo Press; Landman-Bouges, J. 1977. Rastafarian Food Habits. *Cajanus* 9 (4): 228–234; Murrell, N. S., W. D. Spencer, and A. A. McFarlane (eds.). 1998. *Chanting Down Babylon: The Rastafari Reader.* Kingston: Ian Randle Ltd.; Rowe, M. 1980. The Women in Rastafari. *Carribean Quarterly* 26 (4): 13–21; Watson, S. 2002. *The Archaeology of Rastafari.* Unpublished Master's thesis. School of Archaeological Studies, University of Leicester; van De Berg, W. R. 1998. Rastafari Perceptions of Self and Symbolism. In P. B. Clarke (ed.) *New Trends and Developments in African Religions,* pp. 159–175. Westport, CT: Greenwood Press; Waters, A. M. 1985. *Race, Class, and Political Symbols: Rastafari and Reggae in Jamaican Politics.* New Brunswick, NJ: Transaction Books; Williams, K. M. 1981. *The Rastafarians.* London: Ward, Lock Educational.

Ronquinan

The Ronquinan culture, a variation (or subseries) of the Saladoid tradition, occupied the middle and lower Orinoco River in present-day Venezuela. It takes its name from the archaeological site of Ronquín (ca. 1600 to 1100 BC), strategically located at a point where a seasonal stream enters the Orinoco River and that is consequently rich in marine resources. From the abundant pottery shards that litter the site, it has been calculated that the Ronquín Period here had a population of around 128 individuals and lasted for around 500 years. Overall, the wider phenomenon of Ronquinan culture has been dated to between ca. 2000 B.C. and 550 B.C.

Ronquinan peoples lived mainly in villages located atop the natural forested levees of the Orinoco River banks. They cleared these areas for slash-and-burn agriculture that included the growing of cassava as indicated by the presence of ceramic cassava griddles. They must also have been masters of environmental diversity, however, taking advantage of the region's annual flooding in horticulture, hunting, fishing, and opportunistic foraging.

Ronquinan material culture is dominated by their pottery, which arguably created the Saladoid tradition. These include animal effigy bowls, large necked-jars, and thick cassava griddles that were supported over the fire by baked clay cylinders called *topia*. Decoration included variations of white-on-red (W-O-R) painting, linear and curving incised designs, simple cross-hatching, and modeled zoomorphic images as *adornos*.

Ronquinan peoples moved out from the Orinoco River delta and spread along the coasts of Guyana and Venezuela, where they developed a further variation of their culture known as the Cedrosan Saladoid subseries. It was the bearers of this cultural tradition who eventually took to seagoing canoes and colonized Trinidad and the Island Caribbean as far north as Puerto Rico, displacing the earlier Archaic Period peoples as they went.

See also: Barrancoid; Saladoid; White-on-Red Pottery (W-O-R)
References
Roosevelt, A. C. 1980. *Parmana: Prehistoric Maize and Manioc Subsistence Along the Amazon and Orinoco,* pp. 195, 222–249. New York: Academic Press; Rouse, I. 1978. The La Gruta

Sequence and Its Implications. In E. Wagner and A. Zucchi (eds.). *Unidad y Variedad: Ensayos anthrópologicos en homenaje a José M. Cruxent,* pp. 203–229. Caracas: Ediciones CEA-IVIC; Rouse, I. 1992. *The Tainos: Rise and Decline of the People Who Greeted Columbus,* pp. 75–77, New Haven, CT: Yale University Press; Rouse, I., J. Cruxent, and A. C. Roosevelt. 1976. Ronquin Revisited. *Proceedings of the Sixth International Congress for the Study of Pre-Columbian Cultures of the Lesser Antilles, Point-à-Pitre, Guadeloupe, July 1975,* pp. 117–122.

S

Saladoid

Saladoid is one of most important terms in Caribbean archaeology. It refers, variously, to a type of pottery, or ceramic assemblage (whose local variations are called subseries), and to the people who made it. It also serves also as a chronological marker for cultural development. It was the Saladoid people who introduced pottery making to the Island Caribbean, lived a settled life in the region's first villages, and brought agriculture, the worship of sacred *zemí* figures (probably as part of an ancestor cult), and possibly also the earliest version of the ball-game.

Saladoid takes its name from the archaeological type-site of Saladero in the Orinoco river valley of Venzeuela. At some time just before 2000 B.C., Saladoid-style pottery first appeared along the lower and middle Orinoco river valley. Archaeologists have called this the Ronquinan Saladoid subseries. This style later spread to the coastal parts of Guiana and eastern Venezuela, where it developed into another subseries called the Cedrosan Saladoid after the type-site of Cedros in Trinidad. It was this variation of Saladoid pottery which, around 500 B.C., its makers carried with them as they journeyed by canoe to Trinidad. From here, they island-hopped northward, reaching Puerto Rico somewhere around 430 B.C., according to the earliest evidence from the site of Hacienda Grande.

Cedrosan Saladoid pottery is of two distinct types: white-on-red (W-O-R) and zic (zone-incised cross-hatching). W-O-R is defined by white paint applied to red, especially on bell-shaped bowls that have flanged rims and D-shaped strap handles. Zic pottery is characterized by cross-hatch decoration and is found on similar bowl-shaped vessels with D-shaped handles. Both types share common materials, shapes, and designs. Saladoid pottery is considered some of the most sophisticated ceramics produced in this area of the Americas.

Typical of Cedrosan Saladoid pottery are the decorative *adornos*—three-dimensional images of fantastical anthropomorphic and zoomorphic creatures. Natural animals also appear, such as monkeys, bats, turtles, and dogs, though these probably possessed supernatural dimensions as well. The shapes and designs of Saladoid pottery, particularly elaborate incense burners and effigy vessels, indicate not only the technical skills of master potters, but also suggest a rich tradition of religious and mythological beliefs—part of a typical shamanic worldview, where people, animals, and supernatural creatures blended into each other.

The spread of Cedrosan Saladoid peoples across the Caribbean had a major impact on the region's geographical and cultural landscapes. Previous Archaic Period hunters and gatherers disappeared, either killed, assimilated, or pushed beyond the advancing Saladoid frontier. The shape of the land also changed, as Saladoid settlers made more varied and efficient stone tools, felled larger trees, and cleared more extensive areas for their villages and fields. They grew cassava (manioc), sweet potato, cotton, and tobacco. Settled village life was characterized by a rich variety of material culture, from stone axes and grinding stones (manos and metates), to ceramic cassava griddles, drills, and a variety of artistic endeavors, such as carved and decorated human arm bones and skulls. Jewelry was also popular, made from perforated human and animal teeth, mother-of-pearl, and trade beads of amethyst, quartz, and turquoise.

The sea continued to play an important role in the everyday and religious lives of Saladoid peoples. Not only did canoe travel link the islands with each other, but also with the mainland of South America, particularly the area around the mouth of the Orinoco River. The Caribbean islands and the adjacent South American mainland seem to have formed an interaction sphere of diverse but connected peoples, languages, and landscapes.

It was the maritime aspect of Saladoid societies that had an enduring effect on their cultural development. During the period A.D. 350 to A.D. 500, Cedrosan Saladoid pottery became increasingly elaborate and sculptural. It appears to have been influenced by ceramic styles made by the Barrancoid peoples of the Lower Orinoco in Venezuela, and which were disseminated by maritime trade, perhaps focusing on specialized villages acting as ports of trade, as have been found on the islands of Tobago and Montserrat. The description "Saladoid with Barrancoid influences" is commonly used for this type of pottery. Saladoid-Barrancoid pottery declined from around A.D. 600, and was replaced by peoples and pottery known as Ostionoid.

See also: Ball-Game; Barrancoid; Cassava (manioc); Ostionoid; Shamanism; White-on-Red Pottery (W-O-R); Zemís; Zic Pottery

References
Allaire, L. 2003. Agricultural Societies in the Caribbean: The Lesser Antilles. In J. Sued-Badillo (ed.). *General History of the Caribbean: Vol. 1, Autochthonous Societies,* pp. 195–227. Paris: UNESCO; Rodríguez, M. 1997. Religious Beliefs of the Saladoid People. In S. M. Wilson (ed.). *The Indigenous People of the Caribbean,* pp. 80–87. Gainesville, FL: University Press of Florida; Roe, P. G. 1989. A Grammatical Analysis of Cedrosan Saladoid Vessel Form Categories and Surface Decoration: Aesthetic and Technological Styles in Early Antillean Ceramics. In P. E. Siegel (ed.). *Early Ceramic Population Lifeways and Adaptive Strategies in the Caribbean,* pp. 267–382. Oxford: British Archaeological Reports International Series 506; Rouse I. 1992. *The Tainos: Rise and Decline of the People Who Greeted Columbus,* pp. 82–89. New Haven, CT: Yale University Press.

Salt River (site, St. Croix)

Located on a small peninsula near a sheltered harbor, the Salt River site on the island of St. Croix was the largest coastal site on the island at the time of the European arrival. It was occupied continuously for some 1,500 years. In 1587, the Englishman John White observed local inhabitants, but soon afterward the indigenous people had disappeared, probably due to Spanish raids. In 1923, archaeological investigations by Gudmund Hatt uncovered the island's only known dance- or ballcourt, measuring some 30 meters by 25 meters. Excavations revealed an 8-meter-long row of gray sandstone slabs, several of which were engraved with crude petroglyphs—one of which depicted what has been interpreted as "the mother of the sky god," while another had a carving of a frog with a human face.

Simple anthropomorphically carved stones were located on the northwest side of the court. A startling find was of a 42-cm-long column shaped from local coral and thought to be the base for a triangular head, also of coral, found nearby—the two portions perhaps forming a *zemí* cult image. Other artifacts included smaller coral heads, shell-disk jewelry, fragments of stone ball-game regalia, and two types of three-pointer figures—several made from conch shells, and two from stone decorated with anthropomorphic faces. The artifacts seemed to fit with site's pottery, which was dated between ca. A.D. 1200 and A.D. 1500.

Human remains were also discovered. Apart from numerous disarticulated bones, there were four deliberately buried skeletons, two of which were found mixed with seashells and fish and manatee bones in a midden. A fifth skeleton, belonging to an infant, was found inside a decorated ceramic bowl along with pieces of shell. These ambiguous remains have been seen variously as evidence for and against cannibalism. Most recently, they have been interpreted as an indication of the zemí cult that centered on ancestor worship associated with bones of the dead.

See also: Ball-Game; Conch; St. Croix (USVI); Zemís

References
Faber Morse, B. 1989. Saladoid Remains and Adaptive Strategies in St. Croix, Virgin Islands. In P. E. Siegel (ed.). *Early Ceramic Population Lifeways and Adaptive Strategies in the Caribbean,* pp. 29–42. Oxford: British Archaeological Reports International Series 506; Faber Morse, B. 1990. The Pre-Columbian Ball and Dance Court at Salt River, St. Croix. *FOLK: Journal of the Danish Ethnographical Society* 32: 45–60; Faber Morse, B. 1997. The Salt River Site, St. Croix, at the Time of the Encounter. In S. M. Wilson (ed.). *The Indigenous People of the Caribbean,* pp. 36–45. Gainesville, FL: University Press of Florida; Hatt, G. 1924. Archaeology of the Virgin Islands. *Proceedings of the Twenty-First International Congress of Americanists.* Part 1, pp. 29–42. The Hague, the Netherlands.

Santa Rosa Carib Community (Arima, Trinidad)

In Trinidad, with its unique mix of African and Asian peoples, and underlay of Spanish, French, and English influences, there have been stirrings of Amerindian consciousness since the 1970s. Little known outside the island, the so-called Caribs of Arima are a mixed-blood community made up of the descendants of Kalipuna Amerindians from St. Vincent, Trinidad's own Mission Amerindians, Venezuelans of mixed Amerindian-Spanish blood, and African slaves.

In 1974 they reconstituted themselves as the Santa Rosa Carib Community, taking part of their inspiration from the annual Roman Catholic festival of Santa Rosa de Lima, whose statue is kept in the local church, itself built on land once occupied by an Amerindian village. During the annual festival, the statue of Santa Rosa is garlanded with white, pink, and red flowers and paraded around the town before being taken back into the church. The Santa Rosa festival began during the early nineteenth century when the old, indigenous beliefs—though weak—were stronger than today. In part, this hybrid or syncretic Trinidadian development reflects wider changes in Central and South America, where many indigenous peoples assimilated their ancient beliefs to Christianity and the new political and economic order that it represented.

Santa Rosa is the patron saint of Arima. The association began in 1759 when the Capuchin Mission there was dedicated to her. Although Santa Rosa lived her whole life in Lima, Peru, where she dedicated herself to looking after the poor (Amerindians and slaves), Trinidadian tradition tells how she appeared to three Carib hunters in the Arena forest near to Arima and in the vicinity of a former mission site where a number of priests had been massacred in 1669. This apparition led to the conversion to Christianity of an entire Amerindian tribe and helped strengthen the bond between the church and the native peoples.

Originally there seems to have been a ceremonial figurehead of a Carib King but this has disappeared and been replaced by a Carib Queen. From one perspective, this can be seen as an echo of pre-Columbian tradition of the elite status of women known from the fifteenth-century case of Anacaona among the Taíno of Hispaniola.

Today, the Arima Carib Community's attempts to reclaim its Amerindian identity focus on the community's center in Arima, where the people make cassava bread by traditional methods first brought to Trinidad 2,000 years before by the Saladoid peoples. The importance of traditional food production and consumption in establishing indigenous identity cannot be overstated, as cassava (*Manihot esculenta*) is the quintessential Amerindian food. The community acquires its starch-rich cassava tubers from several sources, usually older Trinidadians who have maintained cassava gardens and traditional horticultural knowledge—even of the difficult and dangerous techniques of preparing the more nutritious and longer-lasting but potentially lethal variety of bitter cassava.

Cassava production also requires traditional arts and crafts skills be mastered. The single most important and visually striking feature of this is the squeezing of the grated wet cassava pulp in a tubular basket of plaited palm leaves known variously in Trinidad as the Carib Snake, *coulève, sebucan,* or *tipiti.* The pulp is pushed inside, the upper part of the tipiti is hung from a roof beam, and the lower part has a large pole threaded through it upon which women and children sit, thereby stretching the tipiti and squeezing out the juice into a pot. The method for making these objects has been relearned at Arima, where small and large varieties are made for sale by the community as is the baked cassava bread. Once again, this practice associates the Carib community at Arima with age-old Caribbean beliefs about cassava, of which the most famous is Yúcahu, the supreme Taíno deity, the invisible lord of fertility whose name meant "spirit of cassava."

Statue of Santa Rosa being carried through the streets of Arima during her annual festival (Courtesy Nicholas J. Saunders)

Another conscious act of reclaiming their heritage is the restarting of the Smoke Ceremony, knowledge of which was retained by the elders of the community, some of whom were centenarians. Originally an Amerindian prayer preserved as the "Prayer of the Indian" in Spanish, today it is an offering to the Great Spirit, asking for fertility and blessings. Resin is collected from the forest, dried and mixed with tobacco and then burned on a fire surrounded by four men, one for each of the directions of the earth. As the Indian Prayer is recited to the accompaniment of percussive music, a bird feather is cast on the flames. In recent years the ceremony was performed at the unveiling of the statue to the Amerindian Chief Hyarima.

While the evidence for Hyarima in Trinidad history is slight, his role as a symbol of emerging Amerindian consciousness is more significant. He seems to have been a chief of the local Nepoyo tribe who lived at Arima and who fought with the Dutch against the Spanish in 1637. He took part in the last battle between Europeans and the local Amerindians on the outskirts of Arima, an event known as the Arena Massacre. In 1931, F. E. M. Hosein, the mayor of Arima, enshrined history and imagination in his miracle play entitled *Hyarima and the Saints*.

Sir Ralph Woodford, the British governor of Trinidad from 1813, was particularly interested in the Amerindians of Arima, as was a successor, Lord Harris, from 1846 to 1854. It was Harris who gave a cannon to the local community; it was originally placed on Calvary Hill and is said to have been fired instead of the traditional blowing of the conch shell in order to summon the inhabitants for the annual celebrations and on the actual day of the Santa Rosa festival.

The Arima Caribs are concerned to foster all aspects of Trinidad's Amerindian past. A few kilometers west of Arima—along what was originally an Amerindian trail—the forestry department has built the Cleaver Woods National Park, which features an Amerindian *ajoupa,* or typical long-house of the island's Mission Indians. Built in the traditional fashion from palm leaves, bamboo, and wattle-and-daub, this building provides a unique insight into the skills of the indigenous peoples. Members of the Carib community weave intricate palm-leaf fans and baskets, and make other handicrafts and structures from the local straw called *tirite.* They also collect the folklore names and knowledge of Trinidad's trees, flowers, and medicinal plants, such as *moriche,* a hammock made from palm; *cocorite,* an edible palm; *timite,* a palm used for thatching; and *balbac,* a wild apple whose branches exude a sap that stuns fish and was used in aboriginal times.

While some of the community's skills have been passed down by elders, such as the Carib Queen, others have been transmitted by visiting indigenous groups from mainland South America, notably Guyana. In 1992 there was a large international gathering of the region's indigenous peoples at Arima as part of the Carifesta celebrations. In recent times, the Carib community has made attempts to gain title to a piece of land in the ancestral Calvary Hill district of Arima, with the intention of building a traditional Carib village.

It is important to state that there is little direct continuity between Trinidad's indigenous past and the Santa Rosa Caribs at Arima. The community and their president, Ricardo Bharath, are fully aware of its mixed-blood ancestry. The name "Carib" has been adopted not to identify specifically with Caribs but rather as a sign that they are proud of their Amerindian heritage in general. Since the early 1990s, another member of the community, Cristo Adonis, has taken on the mantle of an Amerindian shaman, drawing on popular modern notions of shamanism as well as knowledge of Arima's own aboriginal traditions.

In recent years the Santa Rosa Carib Community has forged ever-closer links with other indigenous peoples across the Caribbean and South America—notably Dominica, St. Vincent, Guyana, and Venezuela. They are now part of a pan-Amerindian movement of indigenous ethnic minorities who are trying to establish a place in the modern world. After hundreds of years during which the remnants of Trinidad's indigenous peoples were marginalized and silent, they have begun to find a voice.

See also: Anacaona (Taíno queen); Caribs; Cassava (manioc); Cocoa Panyols; Dominica; Shamanism; St. Vincent and the Grenadines; Trinidad and Tobago

References
Ahee, C. B. 1992. *The Carib Community of Arima, Five Hundred Years after Columbus.* Unpublished Caribbean Studies dissertation. University of the West Indies, St. Augustine, Trinidad; Almarales, B. 1994. *The Santa Rosa Carib Community from 1974–1993.* Unpublished Caribbean Studies dissertation. University of the West Indies, St. Augustine, Trinidad; Boomert, A. 1982. Our Amerindian Heritage. *Naturalist Magazine* 4 (4): 26–61: Woodbrook, Trinidad; Brereton, B. 1996. *An Introduction to the History of Trinidad and Tobago.* Oxford: Heinemann; Chauharjasingh, A. S. n.d. *A Dictionary of Trinidad and Tobago Folklore.* Unpublished manuscript; de Verteuil, A. 1999. Spirit of the Americas. *Caribbean Beat (BWIA International Airways Magazine)* (40) (November/December): 40–47; de Verteuil, A., and N. J. Saunders. 1998. *The First*

Trinidadians. Television documentary. Port of Spain, Trinidad: Pearl and Dean (Caribbean) Ltd.; Forte, M. C. 1999. From Smoke Ceremonies to Cyberspace, Globalized Indigeneity, Multisited Research, and the Internet. *Paper Presented at the 25th Annual Meeting of the Canadian Anthropology Society.* Université Laval, Québec; Forte, M. C. 2001a. "Our Amerindian Ancestors": The State, the Nation, and the Revaluing of Indigeneity in Trinidad and Tobago. *Paper Presented at the Fourth Biennial Conference of the Australian Association for Caribbean Studies.* Australian National University, Canberra, 8–10 February; Forte, M. C. 2001b. *Re-Engineering Indigeneity: Cultural Brokerage, the Political Economy of Tradition and the Santa Rosa Carib Community of Arima, Trinidad, and Tobago.* Unpublished PhD dissertation, University of Adelaide; Forte, M. C. 2001c. The Relationship of the Caribs of Arima with the Caribs of Dominica, 1992–1997. *http://www.centrelink.org/fntt/Dominica.html;* Forte, M. C. 2001d. The Relationship of the Caribs of Arima with the Tainos of Puerto Rico and the USA. *http://www.centrelink.org/fntt/History.html;* Hosein, F.E.M. 1976. *Hyarima and the Saints: A Miracle Play and Pageant of Santa Rosa.* Marabella, Trinidad; Mowlah-Baksh, J. S., and E. Reyes, (ed.). 1978. *The Carib Community.* Arima: Santa Rosa Carib Community; Santa Rosa Carib Community. 1998. We, the Carib Community of Trinidad and Tobago. *http://www.members. tripod.com/~SRCC1CaribCommunity/weone.htm.*

Santería

Santería is one of several syncretistic African-Caribbean religions, the other main ones being Vodoun (voodoo) and Obeah. Santería, which means "the Way of the Saints," is just one of the popular names given to this religion, others being Lukumi, Candomble Jege-Nago, and the pejorative term "macumba." The full and proper name is Regla de Ocha, which means "the Rule of the Orisha"—*orisha* being the African term for deities and guardian beings. Santería has developed as a mixed religion, drawing on the rituals, beliefs, and imagery of African spiritualities and Roman Catholicism. In the Caribbean today, Santería is mainly concentrated in Cuba.

The origins of Santería began during the sixteenth century, when Europeans brought vast numbers of West African peoples to the Caribbean to work as slaves, mainly on their sugar plantations. Many of these slaves belonged to the Yoruba peoples of modern Nigeria and they brought with them elements of their indigenous African spiritual beliefs. These beliefs were part of a philosophy of life that saw the natural world as animated by powerful gods and spirits with whom humans had to converse through ritual prayers, offerings, music, and dancing. Consequently, the orishas are seen as multidimensional spirit beings, intimately concerned with the earthly life of humans. At this fundamental level, African beliefs shared much with the shamanistic ideas of indigenous Amerindian peoples. In its early years of development, Santería, along with other mixed-origin religions of the Caribbean, Mesoamerica, and South America, was influenced to an unknown degree by contacts between escaped African slaves and the remnants of indigenous Amerinidan societies with whom they initially took refuge.

When Africans first arrived in the Caribbean they were usually baptized into the Christian faith as Roman Catholics. One way of retaining their spiritual beliefs, ethnic identity, and dignity, was to realign their religious ideas with those of their new masters.

A man prays before a large homemade Santería altar in Baracoa, Cuba. (Robert van der Hilst/Corbis)

In this way, traditional African orishas became identified with Christian saints. This allowed African religion to survive, but also created something new by establishing equivalencies between two quite separate religions.

Santería is a syncretic set of beliefs and rituals that has developed over hundreds of years. Not everyone can join the faith and many of the important and spiritually deeper beliefs are not discussed with the uninitiated. Unlike Christianity or Islam, there is no book of rules for Santería, whose beliefs and rituals are passed down the generations through the oral tradition and thus are flexible, and creatively interpreted by different groups. These differences are clearly seen in the variations and emphases of followers in the Caribbean who stress their African origins, and those of Mexico, where the Roman Catholic roots are more visible. Despite the secrecy surrounding Santería, it is possible to provide an outline of the religion's philosophy and rituals.

Although it is the orishas who occupy the central focus of Santería, they themselves are under the control and protection of the supreme creator known as Olorun or Olodumare, whose name means "owner of heaven." In Santería, heaven is regarded as the invisible half of creation, and acts as a template for the other, visible half, which is the world of the living. Orishas are seen as physical manifestations of those aspects of the mysterious

Olorun that are knowable by human beings. Each orisha is associated with a Christian saint and each has a special number, colors, favorite herbs, item of food, dance move, and sign that represents its particular cosmic nature. While there are many orishas and their saintly equivalents, seven have become especially popular, and hence most powerful in Santería's pantheon.

The most powerful orisha is Obatala, whose saintly equivalent is Our Lady of Mercy, whose feast day is 24 September. His favored color is white and he is the deity of peace, purity, and intellectual endeavor. Ogun's equivalent is St. Peter, whose feast day is 29 June and whose colors are green and black. He symbolizes violence, energy, and war, works with iron, and protects against accidents (which he also can cause). Chango became identified with St. Barbara, whose feast day is 4 December, and whose colors are red and white. He is master of thunder, lightning, and fire, and, because he represents passion and virility, is the most popular orisha. Eleggua's Christian counterpart is St. Anthony, whose feast day is 13 June, and whose colors are red and black. He is the supreme sorcerer who casts unbreakable spells and divines the future without the aid of implements. Orunla is identified with St. Francis of Assisi, has his feast day on 14 October, and regards green and yellow as his colors. He personifies wisdom, only admits men to his mysteries, and is the owner of the most powerful divinatory tool, known as the "Table of Ifa." Yemaya, whose Catholic saint is Our Lady of Regla, has her feast day on 7 September and regards blue and white as her colors. She is regarded as the great mother, the giver of all life. Oshun's saintly counterpart is Our Lady of La Caridad del Cobre, with a feast day on 8 September and three favored colors—coral, aquamarine, and yellow. She controls love, sexuality, and all human pleasures, and has dominion over marriage.

In order to recharge their supernatural energy and remain active, orishas require that humans supply them with sustenance—symbolically in the form of prayer and music and physically (and symbolically) in the form of animal sacrifices, usually the blood of sacrificed chickens. In return, orishas bestow magical power, or *ashe,* on priests that enables them to accomplish their goals. Humans are as essential to the orishas as the orishas are to humans, but it is the orishas who made people, and it was the animating breath of Olorun that gave them life.

The ritual arena in which a particular orisha is worshipped and invoked includes not only animal sacrifice but also rhythmic music, dancing, and singing. These activities are aimed at pleasing the orisha and persuading it to dispense good luck and forgiveness of the sins of its followers. As the ritual reaches its height, some individuals become possessed by the orisha, who then speaks and acts as an earthly embodiment of the deity. An integral part of an orisha ceremony is the veneration of ancestors, who, named as Ara Orun or Egun, dwell in heaven, under the protection of Olorun. Ancestors live an exemplary life and are petitioned for advice concerning the moral behavior of the living. When the living die, their souls may become an ancestor, and join the invisible realm of the orishas and Olorun.

Orisha ceremonies are conducted by priests known as *santeros* or *babalochas* (if they are male), and *santeras* or *Iyalochas* (if female). As with Amerindian shamans, these ritual specialists undergo many years apprenticeship during which they learn the songs, dances, prayers, and healing methods passed down through the oral tradition. All are acknowledged herbalists, as it is plants that are the common ingredients in their ceremonial activities, particularly the casting of magical spells. There are three levels of initiation that prospective followers and those who would be priests must undergo. The first is called *Elekes,* and centers on the bestowal of necklaces on an initiate. The necklace embodies the essential qualities of an orisha, is ritually blessed and purified for seven days then presented to the initiate who is dressed all in white.

The second level is called *Eleggua and the Warriors,* during which the initiate has a priestly consultation in which all aspects of his or her life are mapped out and who then receives an image of the orisha Eleggua and an iron cauldron of the orisha Ogun in which have been placed symbolic miniature implements of his responsibilities—a knife, machete, anvil, pick, spade, hammer, and rake. Ochosi is represented by a miniature bow and arrow and Osun by a small silver cup with bells and the image of a rooster. The third and final level for those who aspire not just to be a member of the faith but a priest, is the *asiento* or "making of the saint," whose ceremonial name is *Kariocha.* This takes seven days to complete, and is followed by a period of apprenticeship that lasts an additional one year and seven days.

When the initiate becomes a fully fledged priest, he or she is expected to undertake four types of divination as part of their ritual responsibilities. These are *obi* (coconut shells), *diloggun* (cowrie shells), *okuele* (a chain of coconut-shell medallions), and the "Table of Ifa"—the latter being the most powerful oracle in the faith. Each has its own rituals and aims, and each is practiced by a priest who has mastered the appropriate level of knowledge and whose experience allows accurate interpretation of the divine replies he receives.

See also: Cuba; Obeah; Orisha/Shango (Trinidad); Shamanism; Vodoun

References
Brandon, G. 1993. *Santeria from Africa to the New World: The Dead Sell Memories.* Bloomington, IN: Indiana University Press; Cornelius, S., and J. Amira. 1992. *The Music of Santería: Traditional Rhythms of the Batá Drums.* Crown Point, ID: White Cliffs Media; Flores-Peña, Y., and R. J. Evanchuk. 1994. *Santeria Garments and Altars: Speaking Without a Voice.* Jackson, MS: University Press of Mississippi; Hagedorn, K. J. 2001. *Divine Utterances: The Performance of Afro-Cuban Santeria.* Washington, DC: Smithsonian Institution Press; Mason, M. A. 2002. *Living Santeria: Rituals and Experiences in an Afro-Cuban Religion.* Washington, DC: Smithsonian Institution Press; Vega, M. M. 2000. *The Altar of My Soul: The Living Traditions of Santeria.* New York: Ballantine Books.

Shamanism

The indigenous inhabitants of the Caribbean Islands and the adjacent mainland, like all Amerindian peoples, conceived of their world as animated by spiritual forces and articulated by myth. Ancestor spirits and the immanent forces of nature resided in every feature and phenomenon of their natural and social worlds. The reverence, respect, propitiation, and manipulation of these all-powerful, omnipresent, and dangerously ambivalent spirit beings through ritual is a distinctive feature of the spiritual beliefs known generally as shamanism. The shamanistic worldview—a natural and moral philosophy—sees spirituality residing in cultural artifacts as well as natural entities, from rivers, rocks, and mountains to animals, birds, trees, plants, ceramic figurines, and carved wood sculptures.

The arbiters of this magical world were the shamans, and their control over the forces of life and death was based on a philosophy founded on analogical symbolic reasoning. This non-Western view of the world saw connections between objects, people, natural phenomena, and social events in a holistic way—tied together by invisible strands of power. In such a spiritually charged universe, all things possessed sacred and secular importance and these were acknowledged in rituals and ceremonies designed to make sense of physical and spiritual life.

Caribbean shamans, like their North American, Mesoamerican, and South American neighbors, gained access to the spirit world through altered states of consciousness brought on variously by abstinence, chanting, music, and the taking of powerful mind-altering narcotics. Tobacco smoking was a widespread technique used to enter trance, allowing shamans to bridge the divide between the physical and spiritual worlds. Under tobacco's influence, the earth was linked to the sky, and the living communed with the ancestors. Tobacco made the shaman light and conveyed him along a celestial path of smoke to the upper realm where he conversed with spirits in order to cure or send illness and divine the future—in other words, to arbitrate between humans and supernaturals. A typical magico-religious use of tobacco in lowland South America is to blow tobacco smoke over food or wounds, thereby purifying it and warding off malign illness-causing spirits.

Tobacco shamanism is especially well documented among the Warao who inhabit the area of the mouth of the Orinoco River opposite Trinidad. Research into their use of and beliefs concerning tobacco has provided valuable insights into the possible use of tobacco among the inhabitants of the Island Caribbean. For the Warao, tobacco shamanism was invented in the House of Tobacco Smoke created out of nothingness by the Creator Bird of Dawn—an association between birds, tobacco, and shamans repeated many times in spiritual beliefs and art across South America and the Caribbean. Bird imagery in wooden sculptures and ceramic decoration is particularly evident in prehistoric Caribbean material culture. One of the most important aspects of shamanism is the ability of the shaman to use tobacco to fly up into the celestial realm. Some shamans are believed to become hummingbirds in order to suck the nectar of the tobacco plant.

Similar ideas, held in common across the Americas, also saw the ritual use of far stronger hallucinogenic substances, from mushrooms to cacti, snuff made from powdered seeds, and beverages prepared from powerful jungle vines, such as the *ayahuasca* beverage. All produce vivid colorful visions, a sense of macroscopia, microscopia, and heightened sensory awareness interpreted as supernatural presence.

While it is probable that this type of worldview was a feature of the earliest hunting and gathering peoples who occupied the Island Caribbean, it was not until around 500

B.C. and the arrival of the Saladoid peoples from South America that artifacts suggestive of shamanism became common. Images of birds, ceramics that may have been used for tobacco or hallucinogen use, and the widespread zoomorphic animal faces (*adornos*) used to decorate pottery can be interpreted as evidence of a sophisticated shamanistic religion. Saladoid-period dog burials may also indicate shamanistic beliefs, as in South America these animals are associated with the shaman and linked also to the powerful jaguar (*Panthera onca*)—the alter ego of especially powerful and dangerous shamans.

Later peoples, notably the Taíno (Arawak) and Carib inherited this view of an animistic universe, and both had shamans to intercede on their behalf with spirit forces. For the Taíno of the Greater Antilles, shamans were called *behiques,* though the chiefs, known as caciques, also possessed shamanistic powers. As a mark of their social and political status, shamans and chiefs sat on carved and polished wooden stools (*duhos*) to commune with ancestors. Duhos were sometimes decorated with circles and spirals that may have originated as designs inspired by hallucinogenic imagery during rituals that involved snuffing the powerful narcotic *cohoba* powder. The drug-induced visions were part of curing sessions in which the illness-inducing spirits were interrogated and a cure suggested.

The wood itself was regarded as sacred, coming from trees regarded as the transformed essence of ancestors. These trees were believed to communicate with shamans, talking to them especially at night, relaying messages from the other world. Sometimes these same trees were cut down and carved into duhos and *zemís*—wooden sculptures representing powerful spirits and deities. The many different types of zemí image were an important aspect of Taíno shamanism as they embodied the supernatural essence of spirits and nature. As ritual specialists, shamans could manipulate them for different purposes, petitioning them for successful harvests, hunting expeditions, warfare, curing activities, and probably also for political advantage.

The Caribs of the Lesser Antilles had shamans called *boyes.* As with the Taíno, these individuals were society's healers, diviners, and guardians of worldview. They were knowledgeable concerning illness, weather, astronomy, different types of human souls, and the supernatural forces that controlled life and death. Carib shamans possessed a *mabouya* (a malign spirit-being) as a personal spirit whose potential for causing evil was constrained through offerings of cigar smoke and food. During typically nocturnal séances, shamans sought to manipulate the mabouya to cure or send illness, foretell the future, and guarantee success in war. As these spirits sometimes inhabited the bones of ancestors, shamans wrapped these remains in cotton and kept them in their houses. It was one of many ironic coincidences of Caribbean history that the great number of enslaved African peoples transported across the Atlantic to work on Caribbean plantations possessed animistic religions similar to those of the Taíno and Carib. When African slaves escaped to the mountains or otherwise came into contact with remaining Amerindians, their worldview was probably a point of spiritual connection, despite different languages, cultures, appearances, and traditions. Where Africans had priests and witch doctors, Amerindians had shamans—and both shared a common conceptual view of the world. It is no surprise that those African-inspired Caribbean religions that still flourish today have many shamanistic features.

Santería, for example, with its spiritually animated worldview dominated by the multidimensional spirit beings called orishas, has clear shamanistic qualities. Music, dancing, and ritual petitions to the spirit world are all features shared in common with shamanism as known among indigenous Amerindian peoples. Vodoun, Obeah, and Shango similarly all possess fundamentally shamanic elements that would have been more akin to Taíno or Carib beliefs than the Protestant or Catholic Christianity of Europeans. Nevertheless, Amerindian shamanism is an inclusive and malleable type of religion that can incorporate foreign elements and redefine itself accordingly. In this sense also, Vodoun and Santería especially have been heavily influenced by Roman Catholicism. Today, the revival of interest in the Amerindian heritage and identity of the Caribbean's mixed-blood descendants of the Taíno and Carib has included a modern appreciation of shamanism where the figure of the shaman is an often colorful and media-friendly focal point for representing the community to the wider world.

See also: Aesthetic of Brilliance; Caribs; Cuna; Dogs; Gold; Obeah; Orisha/Shango (Trinidad); Pitch Lake (site, Trindidad); Saladoid; Santa Rosa Carib Community (Arima, Trinidad); Santería; Taíno (Arawak); Tobacco; Trees, Spiritual Importance of; Vodoun; Warao; Zemís

References

Boomert, A. 2001. Raptorial Birds as Icons of Shamanism in the Prehistoric Caribbean and Amazonia. In W. H. Metz, B. L. van Beek, and H. Steegstra (eds.). *Patina: Essays Presented to Jay Jordan Butler on the Occasion of His 80th Birthday.* Groningen and Amsterdam: Metz/Van Beek/Steegstra; Crocker, J. C. 1985. *Vital Souls: Bororo Cosmology, Natural Symbolism, and Shamanism.* Tucson, AZ: University of Arizona Press; Eliade, M. 1974. *Shamanism: Archaic Techniques of Ecstasy.* Princeton, NJ: Princeton University Press; Glazier, S. D. 1980. A Note on Shamanism in the Lesser Antilles. *Proceedings of the Eighth International Congress for the Study of the Pre-Columbian Cultures of the Lesser Antilles, St Kitts 1979*, pp. 447–455; Naxon, R. M. 1993. *The Nature of Shamanism: Substance and Function of a Religious Metaphor.* Albany, NY: State University of New York Press; Reichel-Dolmatoff, G. 1971. *Amazonian Cosmos.* Chicago: Chicago University Press; Reichel-Dolmatoff, G. 1975. *The Shaman and the Jaguar.* Philadelphia: Temple University Press; Reichel-Dolmatoff, G. 1979. Desana Shamans' Rock Crystals and the Hexagonal Universe. *Journal of Latin American Lore* 5 (1): 117–128; Roe, P. G. 1997. Just Wasting Away: Taíno Shamanism and Concepts of Fertility. In F. Bercht, E. Brodsky, J. A. Farmer, and D. Taylor (eds.). *Taíno: Pre-Columbian Art and Culture from the Caribbean,* pp. 124–157. New York: The Monacelli Press; Schultes, R. E., and A. Hofmann. 1980. *Plants of the Gods: Origins of Hallucinogenic Use.* London: Hutchinson; Vega, B. 1987. *Santos, shamanes y zemíes.* Santo Domingo, the Dominican Republic: Fundación Cultural Dominicana; Wilbert, J. 1987. *Tobacco and Shamanism in South America.* New Haven, CT: Yale University Press.

Silver Sands (site, Barbados)

Silver Sands is a late prehistoric Suazoid site on the south coast of Barbados. At the time of occupation it was located near a sea inlet with a salt marsh inland. Both have now been filled in by advancing sand dunes.

Excavations reveal a rich cultural debris of ceramics, shell artifacts, and food remains probably deposited as refuse middens and which have been radiocarbon dated to around

A.D. 960. Ten human interments were found in a small burial ground, including a child's skull and a body set around with coral blocks with a conch shell disk at the right shoulder. Elsewhere, more recent burials were discovered, dating to ca. 1300, which included also the remains of seven dismembered dogs.

The pottery from Silver Sands appears to belong to the latest Suazoid Period of Barbados prehistory with many examples of rough, thick pottery with fingermarks as decoration. Such was the quantity of ceramic shards that it was possible to interpret the development of pottery at the site, such as the change over time from fingertip to fingernail decoration. Cassava baking griddles with supporting feet were discovered, as were zoomorphic lugs and *adornos,* the latter including bats, and lizard and turtle heads. A beautiful anthropomorphic head or mask was found next to a human skeleton in one of the burials. Incense burners were uncovered as were spindle whorls indicating cotton clothing.

Queen Conch (*Strombus gigas*) was widely used, probably for food as well as the manufacture of shell tools such as axes and adzes. A finely made anthropomorphic figurine was found, as were shell beads and a shell pendant. Such ornaments were also made in stone as revealed by the finding of stone beads, a stone body stamp for applying paint to the body, and a polished stone pendant. Much of the site of Silver Sands had been disturbed during historic times and excavations uncovered seventeenth- to eighteenth-century European pottery and clay pipes, suggesting the presence of a now-disappeared colonial-period house.

See also: Barbados; Dogs; Suazey/Suazoid

References

Boomert, A. 1987. Notes on Barbados Prehistory. *Journal Barbados Museum Historical Society* 38 (1): 8–43; Bullen, R. P., and A. J. Bullen. 1968. Barbados Archaeology 1966. *Proceedings of the Second International Congress for the Study of Pre-Columbian Cultures of the Lesser Antilles,* pp. 134–144; Drewett, P. L. 1991. *Prehistoric Barbados,* London: Institute of Archaeology and Archetype Publications.

Sint Maarten / Saint-Martin

Sint Maarten/Saint-Martin is shared by the Dutch and French respectively. The group of islands that make up this dual national entity have a total area of 89 sq km. The total combined population is around 62,000, with about 33,500 living on Sint Maarten and 28,500 on Saint-Martin.

Archaeologically, the island has a long prehistory of occupation over 4,000 years from the Archaic Period to the time of European arrival. The Archaic occupation consists of typically preceramic shell middens with stone and shell tools and which date to around 2000 B.C., such as the site of Norman Estate on the north side of the island. Better known is the succeeding Saladoid Period with sites such as Hope Estate, dating to between 400 B.C. and A.D. 650, and bearing the characteristic traits of sophisticated white-on-red (W-O-R) pottery, zic (zone-incised cross-hatching) ware, ceramic cassava griddles, hallucinogen snuffing vessels, and zoomorphic *adornos.* Hope Estate has revealed both earlier La Hueca and later Cedrosan variants of Saladoid occupation. The inhabitants imported exotic minerals such as amethyst and carnelian already shaped for ceremonial use as beads and amulets. Somewhat later, between A.D. 750 and A.D. 950, is the Late Cedrosan Saladoid site of Anse des Pères, a small village similar to Golden Rock on St. Eustatius and whose inhabitants made shell and mother-of-pearl jewelry. In the years before European arrival, Carib peoples moved into the island and by the late fifteenth century its Carib name was reported as Sualouiga or "land of salt."

Which European was the first to see St. Martin and when is still a matter of dispute, though many believe it was Christopher Columbus during his second voyage in 1493. It was, however, the French who first settled the island in 1629, soon followed by Dutch colonists in 1631. Between 1633 and 1648, the Spanish occupied the island, driving out the French and Dutch who returned when the Spanish left. The Treaty of Mount Concordia, signed on 23 March 1648, officially divided the island between the two European nations. During the colonial period, sugar plantations were an economic mainstay, although supplemented by the extraction of salt and its sale to the United States.

In recent years, the island's wealth has been generated by tourism, particularly a thriving cruise ship industry at Sint Maarten at Philipsburg. The town has a museum that displays pre-Columbian and colonial period artifacts and nearby is the 1793 house that today is the court house and post office. The French side of the island, with its capital at Marigot, has also not escaped the influences of modern tourism. Marigot also has a historical and archaeological museum, covering the island's prehistoric and colonial periods.

Today, the island's popular culture in its Dutch variation can be seen in the huge Carnival that is held annually during the last two weeks of April. On the French side, the pre-Lent celebrations are less grand, but have a grand parade and calypso contests. More festivities take place on Bastille Day, 14 July.

See also: Anse Des Pères (site, St. Martin); Archaic Period; Golden Rock (site, St. Eustatius); Hope Estate (site, St. Martin); Norman Estate (site, St. Martin); Saladoid; White-on-Red Pottery (W-O-R); Zic Pottery

References
Barka, N. F. 1993. Archaeological Survey of Sites and Buildings, St. Maarten, Netherlands Antilles, 1. *St. Maarten Archaeological Research Series* No. 3. Williamsburg, VA: College of William and Mary, Department of Anthropology; Couture, P. 1997. *Saint Martin, Saint Barts.* Globe Pequot Press; Haviser, J. B. 1988. *An Archaeological Survey of St. Martin / St. Maarten.* Reports of the Archaeological-Anthropological Institute of the Netherlands Antilles 7. Willemstad: Curaçao; Haviser, J. B. 1995. *In Search of St. Martin's Ancient Peoples: Prehistoric Archaeology.* Philipsburg, St. Martin: July Tree Books; Hofman, C. L., and M.L.P. Hoogland (eds.). 1999. *Archaeological Investigations on St. Martin (Lesser Antilles).* Archaeological Studies Leiden University 4. Leiden, the Netherlands.

Slavery

Slave Trade

The fully developed slave trade of popular understanding did not occur immediately. In 1496, Christopher Columbus brought back some thirty Amerindians to Spain in the hope of using the Americas as a source of slaves for Europe. Queen Isabella, however, banned this treatment of her new subjects, except for those called "cannibals"—a label applied by Columbus and others to any troublesome Amerindians.

The indigenous Taíno (Arawak) were the first slaves of the Europeans in the Americas, though were not officially referred to as such. Instead, they became victims of the infamous *encomienda* system, whereby a number of Amerindians (sometimes whole villages) were given to a Spaniard and obliged to provide food, labor, and goods for free. Overworked, underfed, and prey to European diseases, Amerindians in the encomienda system were virtual slaves and their numbers quickly declined.

In 1505 black slaves were taken to Hispaniola (modern Haiti and Dominican Republic) for the first time. By 1509, Caribbean Amerindians were dying in such numbers that African slaves began to be imported specifically to replace them. According to one report, one African's work was equivalent to that of four Amerindians. In 1510, the Spanish King Ferdinand gave permission for fifty black slaves to be taken to Hispaniola to work the gold mines, and so the slave trade slowly began.

Initially, the number of African slaves was small and Spanish slave-raiding of Caribbean Amerindians continued. But, as the indigenous population collapsed, large-scale importation of African slaves began. Between 1550 and 1575, Spain's American colonies took in about 25,000 African slaves, mainly for the burgeoning sugar-cane industry. Ideally, it was thought, it took 150 slaves to maintain 100 acres of sugar cane. In 1562, the adventurer John Hawkins initiated the English slave trade by opportunistic smuggling of contraband slaves, and in 1621 the Dutch joined in.

From the 1640s, when sugar took over from tobacco, slavery increased dramatically. In 1645, Barbados had 6,000 slaves, but by 1667 there were 80,000 slaves on the island. In the last quarter of the seventeenth century, some 175,000 African slaves were brought to the British Caribbean alone, and during the eighteenth century, numbers increased again. Between 1721 and 1730, the French brought 85,000 slaves to the Caribbean and the British 100,000 between 1728 and 1732. It was calculated that the French colony of Saint-Domingue during the 1760s needed an annual influx of 15,000 slaves to maintain a viable workforce.

By the end of the eighteenth century, about 80,000 slaves a year were being transported to the Americas, most being baptized before leaving Africa, and branded on their legs or wearing bronze collars. This same century saw 11 million gallons of rum being used to pay for slaves. At the height of the slave trade during the 1780s, some 3 million slaves in the Americas, mainly on sugar-cane plantations. The relationship between slaves and profit was clear: Jamaica had 300,000 slaves in 1797 and produced 100,000 tons of sugar in 1805 and 22 million tons of coffee the year before.

Times and attitudes were changing, however. The French writer Voltaire attacked slavery throughout the mid-eighteenth century, and in 1787 a committee was set up in London to abolish the trade. In 1799, the last public sale of a black slave in England took place in Liverpool. Around this time also, William Wilberforce and Prime Minister William Pitt began championing the abolitionist cause. In 1807, a bill favoring abolition was passed and signed in the United States by President Jefferson, and a similar bill received the royal assent in Britain. Interestingly, at this time, there were still more slaves in Africa than the Americas. Illegal shipping of slaves across the Atlantic continued for many years until it was ended by the combined efforts of the British, French, Spanish, and United States navies.

The history of slavery, its social and economic dimensions and implications for the Caribbean as a whole, and for individual islands, is a vast topic that cannot be explored here. The archaeological and, more broadly, anthropological issues can, however, be outlined.

Slavery united the remnants of the indigenous Taíno peoples of the Greater Antilles with the influx of Africans. Both groups sought to escape their enslavement and it was inevitable that sometimes, as at Nanny Town in Jamaica, they would join forces. It was equally inevitable that the greater number of Africans would soon absorb the depleted Amerindian survivors. These escaped slaves became known as Maroons. Throughout the Caribbean region, Maroon communities sprang up and developed their own culture and traditions, heavily African in character, but also distinctively Caribbean. Maroon societies formed the most obvious and strident type of resistance to slavery.

Another significant result of the slave trade was the rise of hybrid religious traditions in many islands. Heavily influenced by animistic African religions but with a Caribbean slant, such movements as Vodoun (voodoo), Santería, and Obeah flourished, especially in Haiti, Cuba, and Jamaica. Obeahmen (sorcerers) were powerful individuals in the harsh conditions of slavery, feared by both their African-Caribbean compatriots and European masters. The cruelties of slave life magnified and emphasized the malign aspects of Obeah sorcerers at the expense of their equally important role as healers, ritual experts, and keepers of cultural traditions.

Today, Vodoun and Santería are important features of the cultural life of Haiti and Cuba especially, and have produced unique types of rituals, music, and dance, as well as costumes and paraphernalia—the material culture legacy of their African and Amerindian heritage and of their days of slavery.

Slavery and its aftermath have left innumerable archaeological traces as well as a rich mosaic of hybrid traditional cultures. The reorganization of native island landscapes, the introduction of new plants and animals, and the buildings and equipment associated with plantation economies—from slave villages and African-Caribbean pottery to overseer's houses and abandoned windmills—all are the legacy of slavery. Caribbean archaeology is now firmly divided into two types: the scattered and fragile remains of the pre-Columbian period, and the often highly visible and more durable remnants of the colonial period, mainly associated with slavery.

Consequences of Slavery

Slavery has been an integral part of the history of the Caribbean since Europeans arrived in 1492. Together with the plantation economies based mainly on sugar—to which it was inextricably linked—slavery changed the face of the region and left an indelible mark on the archaeological record and on traditional folk culture. Today, the Caribbean is populated mainly by the descendants of Africans who were forcibly brought across the Atlantic, mainly between the seventeenth and nineteenth centuries.

Slavery has many different types. It is certain that during pre-Columbian times, slaves in one sense or another existed in the Americas. The Aztecs had slaves who were bought and sold at a special slave market at Azcapotzalco. Some were criminals and others sold themselves into slavery for limited periods. Aztec slave numbers were small, however, perhaps 2 percent, and they never played an important economic role. No slavery existed in the pre-Columbian Caribbean before Europeans arrived.

See also: Accompong; Creole/Creolization; Drax Hall (site, Jamaica); Encomienda; Galways Plantation; Historical Archaeology; Hope Estate (site, St. Martin); Maroons; Nanny Town (site, Jamaica); Newton Plantation (Barbados); Obeah; Santería; Sugar; Tobacco; Vodoun

References
Beckles, H. M., and V. Shepherd (eds.). 2002. *Caribbean Slavery in the Atlantic World.* Princeton, NJ: Markus Wiener; Bergad, L. W., F. García Iglesias, and M. Carman Barcia. 1995. *The Cuban Slave Market 1790–1880.* Cambridge: Cambridge University Press; Bush, B. 1990. *Slave Women in Caribbean Society.* Bloomington, IN: Indiana University Press; Craton, M. 1982. *Testing the Chains: Resistance to Slavery in the British West Indies.* Ithaca, NY: Cornell University Press; Dessalles, P., E. Forster, and R. Forster (eds.). 1996. *Sugar and Slavery, Family, and Race: The Letters and Diary of Pierre Dessalles, Planter in Martinique, 1808–1856.* Baltimore: Johns Hopkins University Press; Dunn, R. S. 1972. *Sugar and Slaves: The Rise of the Planter Class in the English West Indies 1624–1713.* Chapel Hill, NC: University of North Carolina Press; Eubanks, T. H. 1992. *Sugar, Slavery, and Emancipation: The Industrial Archaeology of the West Indian Island of Tobago.* Unpublished Ph.D. dissertation. University of Florida, Gainesville, FL; Gaspar, D. B. 1985. *Bondmen and Rebels: A Study of Master-Slave Relations in Antigua.* Baltimore: Johns Hopkins University Press; Goveia, E. V. 1965. *Slave Society in the British Leeward Islands at the End of the Eighteenth Century.* New Haven, CT: Yale University Press; Hall, N. A. T. 1992. *Slave Society in the Danish West Indies: St. Thomas, St. John, and St. Croix.* Kingston: Canoe Press; Handler, J., and F. W. Lange. 1978. *Plantation Slavery in Barbados: An Archaeological and Historical Investigation.* Cambridge, MA: Harvard University Press; Higman, B. W. 1976. *Slave Population and Economy in Jamaica, 1807–1834.* Cambridge: Cambridge University Press; Knight, F. W. (ed.). 1997. *General History of the Caribbean: Vol. III, Slave Societies of the Caribbean.* London: UNESCO and Macmillan; Palmie, S. (ed.). 1995. *Slave Cultures and the Cultures of Slavery.* Knoxville, TN: The University of Tennessee Press; Rivera-Pagán, L. N. 2003. Freedom and Servitude: Indigenous Slavery and the Spanish Conquest of the Caribbean. In J. Sued-Badillo (ed.). *General History of the Caribbean: Vol. 1, Autochthonous Societies,* pp. 316–362. Paris: UNESCO; Singleton, T. A. 1985. *The Archaeology of Slavery and Plantation Life.* New York: Academic Press; Thomas, H. 1997. *The Slave Trade: The History of the Atlantic Slave Trade 1440–1870.* London: Picador.

St. Croix (USVI)

St. Croix has an area of 217.5 sq km, a population of some 55,000, and is the largest of the 68 islands that make up the U.S. Virgin Islands (USVI).

Archaeologically, the island appears to have no Archaic Period occupation and was first colonized by the village-dwelling and pottery-making horticulturalists of the Saladoid tradition in the early centuries B.C. The Saladoid is divided into local periods on St. Croix, the earlier Prosperity phase (c. 200 B.C. to A.D. 400), and the subsequent Coral Bay-Longford phase (A.D. 400 to A.D. 600). Altogether there are ten known archaeological sites from this era, including Richmond, Aklis, Prosperity, and Salt River. Typical Saladoid features include white-on-red (W-O-R) pottery, incised decoration, zoomorphic and anthropomorphic *adornos,* and cassava griddles. Frog figurines and unfinished beads in greenstone, amethyst, and carnelian suggest that St. Croix participated in an inter-island trade of these semiprecious stones.

The best-known site is that of Salt River, which has preserved the easternmost example of a Classic Taíno ballcourt in what was a large coastal site when Europeans arrived. Some of the stone slabs are decorated with crude petroglyphs. Human burials and shell-disk jewelry have also been found. The site seems to have been occupied for about 1,500 years. St. Croix and the other Virgin Islands were first seen by Europeans during Columbus's second voyage in 1493. Columbus seems to have named them Las Once Mil Virgenes after the legend of St. Ursula and her 11,000 martyred virgins. It wasn't until the seventeenth century that they were settled, with St. Croix being occupied by the English and Dutch in 1625. The island changed hands several times but remained predominantly French until between 1695 and 1696 when the colony moved to St. Domingue. During the latter half of the seventeenth century, African slaves had been imported to work the newly established sugar plantations. These flourished again after 1733, when the French sold St. Croix to the Dutch. In 1917, St. Croix, along with St. Thomas and St. John, was sold to the United States, becoming the USVI.

Today there are many remains of the colonial period of interest to historical archaeologists—especially the windmills and Great Houses once associated with the plantations. One such is the Whim Estate, which has been restored to its seventeenth-century Dutch state and houses buildings and machinery associated with sugar production as well as a museum. Historical archaeologists have also identified a distinctive type of pottery, called Afro-Cruzan ware, which, by virtue of being hand-molded and made mainly into bowls and olla shapes, stands in contrast to the European glazed and wheel-turned tradition.

The main cultural festivities take place between Christmas to the first week of January, and a colorful parade is held on the nearest Saturday to St. Patrick's Day in March. Christiansted, the island's capital, retains much of its colorful architecture and Danish charm, and in the nearby Fort Christiansvaern is the local museum.

See also: Ball-Game; Saladoid; Salt River (site, St. Croix)

References

Gartley, R. T. 1979. Afro-Cruzan Pottery: A New Style of Colonial Earthenware from St. Croix. *Journal of the Virgin Islands Archaeological Society* 8: 47–61; Highfield, A. R. 1995. *St. Croix 1493: An Encounter of Two Worlds.* St. Thomas: Virgin Islands Humanities Council; Jones, D. J., and C. L. Johnson. 1951. *Report on Historic Sites of St. Croix, Virgin Islands of the United States. Part 2, Salt River Bay Area.* San Juan, Puerto Rico: San Juan National Historic Site; Lawaetz, E. J. 1991. *St. Croix: 500 Years Pre-Columbus to 1990.* Herning, Denmark: Pout Kristensen; Morse, B. F. 1990. The Pre-Columbian Ball and Dance Court at Salt River, St. Croix. *FOLK: Journal of the Danish Ethnographical Society* 32: 45–60; Morse, B. F. 1997. The Salt River Site, St. Croix, at the Time of the Encounter. In S. M. Wilson (ed.). *The Indigenous People of the Caribbean*, pp. 36–45. Gainesville, FL: University Press of Florida.

St. Eustatius

St. Eustatius is a small island of only 21 sq km located between St. Kitts and Saba in the Leeward Islands group. Politically, it is part of the Netherlands Antilles and has a population of mixed origin that numbers about 1,800. Columbus called it Statia after St. Anastasia, but it was renamed later by the Dutch.

Despite its small size, St. Eustatius has yielded important archaeological information. The site of Golden Rock, which flourished between the seventh and ninth centuries A.D., was a Saladoid village that appears to have been economically self-sufficient and possibly also to have engaged in long-distance trade if the presence of exotic quartz beads are any indication. Archaeologists have excavated the site's prehistoric houses, one of which has been called the Sea Turtle House because it appears to have had a roof in the shape of a Hawksbill sea turtle shell or carapace—a possibly symbolic association reinforced by the discovery elsewhere on the site of an upturned skeleton and shell of the same animal.

Christopher Columbus first sighted St. Eustatius during his second voyage, but it was the Dutch who first colonized it in 1636, establishing themselves at Fort Oranje, around which the present capital of Oranjestad developed. As with other islands, St. Eustatius changed hands many times during the tumultuous seventeenth and eighteenth centuries, finally becoming Dutch for the last time in 1816. The eighteenth century was the island's golden age with a rich trade in sugar, tobacco, cotton, and slaves passing through on several thousand ships a year. So much wealth was concentrated in this small island that it was known for a time as the Golden Rock. The end began in 1781 when the British Admiral Rodney captured the island together with 150 ships and £5 million of booty, and many of the island's Jewish and Christian inhabitants fled.

Oranjestad today preserves an interesting historical legacy. In the town center is the eighteenth-century merchant's house that became Rodney's home and has been restored by the local historical foundation to serve as a museum. Archaeological artifacts from the pre-Columbian and colonial periods are displayed here. Above the town are the ruins of Fort Oranje, which include some of its original cannon. Despite its small size, St. Eustatius has attracted the attention of many archaeologists interested in both the prehistoric and colonial periods and the island has played a significant role in Caribbean archaeology.

See also: Golden Rock (site, St. Eustatius); Saladoid; Turtles

References
Attema, Y. 1976. *St. Eustatius: A Short History of the Island and its Monuments*. De Walburg Pers Zutphen. The Netherlands; Barka, N. F. 1988. Archaeology of the Jewish Synagogue Honen Dalim, St. Eustatius, Netherlands Antilles. *St. Eustatius Archaeological Research Series* No. 4. Williamsburg, VA: College of William and Mary, Department of Anthropology; Barka, N. F. 1996a. Archaeology of the Dutch Elite: The Country Estate of Johannes de Graff at Concordia, St. Eustatius, Netherlands Antilles. *St. Eustatius Archaeological Research Series* No. 9. Williamsburg, VA: College of William and Mary, Department of Anthropology; Barka, N. F.

1996b. Citizens of St. Eustatius 1781: A Historical and Archaeological Study. In R. Paquette and S. Engerman (eds.). *The Lesser Antilles in the Age of European Expansion,* pp. 223–238. Gainesville, FL: University of Florida Press; Dethlefson, E. 1982. The Historic Archaeology of St. Eustatius. *Journal of New World Archaeology* 5 (2): 73–86; Heath, B. J. 1988. *Afro-Caribbean Ware: A Study of Ethnicity on St. Eustatius.* Unpublished Ph.D. dissertation. Department of American Civilization, University of Pennsylvania, Philadelphia; van der Bor, W. 1981. *Island Adrift: The Social Organization of a Small Caribbean Community: The Case of St. Eustatius.* The Hague, the Netherlands: Smits Drukkers; Versteeg, A., and K. Schinkel (eds.). 1992. *The Archaeology of St. Eustatius: The Golden Rock Site.* Amsterdam: St. Eustatius Historical Foundation.

St. John (USVI)

St. John has an area of 41.5 sq km, has a population of some 4,000, and is the smallest of the three largest islands of the U.S. Virgin Islands (USVI). Two-thirds of the island has been designated the Virgin Islands National Park.

Archaeologically, the island appears to have no Archaic Period occupation and was first colonized by the village-dwelling and pottery-making horticulturalists of the Saladoid tradition in the early centuries B.C. Saladoid culture developed from around A.D. 600 into local variations of the succeeding Ostionoid tradition, which around 1000 became the Classic Taínos. In recent years, Taíno archaeology has developed considerably at the beach site of Cinnamon Bay, dated to between 1020 and 1490. Evidently a village site, its most remarkable feature seems to be an intact floor plan and associated remains of a *caney* or Taíno temple of the type commented on by the early sixteenth-century Spanish chroniclers. In a neat arrangement of layers that indicated hundreds of years of occupation, archaeologists discovered post-holes, bones, beads, a gold disk, and carved teeth. Ceramic adorno figures originally attached to pottery were also found, whose *zemí*-like appearance resembled similar images carved as petroglyphs elsewhere on the island. The excavations have involved local schools and businesses and bronze and silver replicas of Taíno artifacts have been made for sale.

St. John, like the other Virgin Islands, was first seen by Europeans during Christopher Columbus's second voyage in 1493. Columbus seems to have named them Las Once Mil Virgenes after the legend of St. Ursula and her 11,000 martyred virgins. It wasn't until the seventeenth century, however, that they were settled, by which time earlier Spanish slaving raids had probably depopulated them. In 1917, St. John, along with St. Thomas and St. Croix, was sold by the Danish government to the United States, becoming the USVI.

The archaeology of colonialism is also developing on St. John, as at the recently discovered eighteenth-century Danish slave house and associated cemetery at Cinnamon Bay. As on other Virgin Islands, historical archaeologists have identified the distinctive pottery made by people of African descent at various places on the island. Known as Afro-Cruzan pottery, this is low-fired earthenware, hand-molded and unglazed, and therefore in contrast with the glazed and wheel-turned European ceramics. Afro-Cruzan pottery has been found in the cooking areas of house remains in the isolated area of St. John known as the East End. Here, during the slavery period, the local economy was geared to the provisioning of plantations located in the more agriculturally rich areas of St. John. Later, this trade and exchange system was extended to other Caribbean islands, as imported pottery appears alongside the locally made Afro-Cruzan ceramics.

See also: Ostionoid; Slavery; Taíno (Arawak)

References

Acheson, P. 1999. *The Best of St. Thomas and St. John, U.S. Virgin Islands.* Two Thousand Three Associates; Armstrong, D. V. 2001. A Venue for Autonomy: Archaeology of a Changing Cultural Landscape, the East Community, St. John, Virgin Islands. In P. Farnsworth (ed.). *Island Lives: Historical Archaeologies of the Caribbean,* pp. 142–164. Tuscaloosa, AL, and London: The University of Alabama Press; Brewer, D. M., and S. Hammersten. 1988. *Archaeological Overview and Assessment, Virgin Islands National Park, St. John, U.S. Virgin Islands.* Tallahassee, FL: Southeast Archaeological Center, National Park Service; Bullen, R. P. 1962. *Ceramic Periods of St. Thomas and St. Johns Islands, Virgin Islands.* American Studies 4. Orlando, FL: William L. Bryant Foundation; Caesar, M., and P. Lundberg. 1991. The Calabash Boom Site, St. John, USVI: Preliminary Report. *Proceedings of the Twelfth International Congress for Caribbean Archaeology, French Guyana, 1987,* pp. 203–215; Hauser, M., and D. V. Armstrong. 1999. Embedded Identities: Piecing Together Relationships through Compositional Analysis of Low-Fired Earthenwares. In J. B. Haviser (ed.). *African Sites Archaeology in the Caribbean,* pp. 65–93. Princeton, NJ: Markus Wiener; Stoutamire, F. 1974. *Report of the Cinnamon Bay Site, St. John's, US Virgin Islands.* Tallahassee, FL: Southeast Archaeological Center.

St. Kitts and Nevis

St. Kitts (formerly St. Christopher) and Nevis are two small islands in the northern part of the Leeward Islands. In 1983 they became a federated single nation. St. Kitts has an area of 176 sq km, whereas Nevis has a 93-sq-km area. The combined population of both islands is around 45,000, of which some 97 percent are of African descent, with some 75 percent living on St. Kitts and 25 percent on Nevis.

Archaeologically, St. Kitts seems to have been first colonized during the Archaic Period by hunter-gatherers belonging to the Ortoiroid peoples (2000 B.C. to 400 B.C.). Sometimes called the Ciboney, these early settlers relied mainly on collecting shellfish and have been dated to around 2150 B.C. The succeeding Saladoid Period is better known, with characteristic agricultural villages being established on inland river terraces. It is thought possible that the over-exploitation of land crabs by Saladoid peoples was associated with the shift from land-based to marine food sources and a possible doubling of the population. Sometime after A.D. 1000, Carib peoples arrived and still occupied the island at the time of the European arrival. In the Carib language, St. Kitts was called Liamuiga, or "fertile land," and Nevis, Oualie. The petroglyphs found here could belong either to Carib or pre-Carib Saladoid peoples.

Both islands were first seen by Europeans during Christopher Columbus's second voyage of 1493, though St. Kitts became the first British settlement in the Caribbean in 1623, at which time there were still local Carib inhabitants. Columbus apparently named the islands San Jorges (St. Kitts), which later became San Cristobal, and San Martin (Nevis), which became Santa Maria de las Nieves—both names subsequently being anglicized and shortened to their current versions.

Around 1626 to 1628, the English governor, together with a contingent of Frenchmen, joined forces to clear St. Kitts of the increasingly troublesome Caribs. The latter's Chief Tegramond was killed and the survivors fled to other islands. At this time, tobacco was the dominant crop planted by the English, but soon large numbers of African slaves were imported to work the sugar plantations—the average annual yield for the years 1766 to 1770 being almost 11,000 tons. The island was shared by France and Britain until the Peace of Utrecht in 1713, and became a British colony in 1783.

This period of St. Kitts and Nevis colonial history has left plantation remains that are being investigated by historical archaeologists. One example is the research carried on at Coconut Walk Estate in southeast Nevis—a plantation whose historical documents refer to one owner, Edward Huggins, as a notorious abuser of his slaves. Archaeological excavations have so far concentrated on a well-preserved windmill, an earlier animal-powered mill for pressing cane juice, a boiling house, and a small stone-and-mortar lime kiln. During the late nineteenth and twentieth centuries, and after many discussions and political maneuverings, St. Kitts and Nevis became independent as a unified nation in September 1983.

Some aspects of African folk beliefs have survived on these two islands. Freely mixed with Christianity, African-Caribbean spirituality is mostly identified with Obeah, whose practitioners (Obeahmen and Obeahwomen) use typical charms of old nails, feathers, and pieces of glass to engage the spirits. Obeah spells are often aimed at securing success in life or in bestowing the ability for one person to control another—such as potions added to meals that make a man desire the woman who has spiked his food. Creatures for folk belief include *jumbies* (spirits of the dead disguised as the living), *soucouyan* (an evil person who transforms into animals), and the brilliant ball of light known as Jack o'Lantern.

Today, popular culture in St. Kitts is seen to best advantage during Carnival, held annually over Christmas and New Year, and includes calypso competitions, parades, dancing, and music in the streets, especially in the capital of Basseterre. The festival of Culturama, held between the end of July and beginning of August, is the equivalent festival on Nevis. Old African rhythms can be heard in the music of the Masquerade big drum bands and throughout the many parades of the twin-islands' festival calendar. In Charlestown, capital of Nevis, the Museum of Nevis History houses artifacts from the island's pre-Columbian and colonial periods. In recent years, archaeological investigations into the Sephardic Jewish presence on the island have begun.

See also: Caribs; Columbus, Christopher; Historical Archaeology; Obeah; Saladoid; Slavery; Sugar

References
Branch, C. W. 1907. Aboriginal Antiquities in Saint Kitts and Nevis. *American Anthropologist* 9 (2): 315–333; Dyde, B. 2002. *St Kitts: Cradle of the Caribbean.* London: Macmillan; Goodwin, R. 1979. *The Prehistoric Cultural Ecology of St. Kitts, West Indies: A Case Study in Island Archaeology.*

Ph.D. dissertation, Arizona State University, Tempe; Hamilton, C. A. 1985. *Some Belief Systems and Practices in St. Kitts.* Cave Hill: University of the West Indies; Lellouch, D. 2000. *Nevis: Queen of the Caribbean.* Charlestown, Nevis: Hummingbird Productions; Matheson, L. 1985. *The Folklore of St. Christopher's Island.* Bassterre: Creole Graphics; Merrill, G. C. 1958. *The Historical Geography of St. Kitts and Nevis, The West Indies.* Mexico City: Instituto Panamericano de Geografia e Historia; Morris, E. L. 2000. A Caribbean Feasibility—the Nevis Heritage Project. *Antiquity* 74: 267–268; Olwig, K. F. 1993. *Global Culture, Island Identity: Continuity and Change in the Afro-Caribbean Community of Nevis.* Chur, Switzerland: Harwood Academic Publishers; Richardson, B. 1983. *Caribbean Migrants: Environment and Survival on St. Kitts and Nevis.* Knoxville, TN: University of Tennessee Press; Wilson, S. M. 1989. The Prehistoric Settlement Pattern of Nevis, West Indies. *Journal of Field Archaeology* 16: 427–450; Wilson, S. M. 1999. *The Prehistory of Nevis.* Gainesville, FL: University Press of Florida.

St. Lucia

St. Lucia lies between St. Vincent and Martinique in the eastern Caribbean's Windward Islands. It has an area of some 616 sq km, and a population of around 150,000. It is considered one of the most mountainous and beautiful islands in the Caribbean. Some 90 percent of its population are of African descent.

St. Lucia's archaeological past is bound up with that of other Windward Islands, though it is one of the least investigated. As with St. Vincent and Grenada, the Carib peoples encountered by Europeans were probably latecomers and excavations have revealed an earlier, so-called Arawak occupation.

Unusually, no one knows who discovered St. Lucia or when. Popular sentiment on the island believes it was Christopher Columbus on 13 December (St. Lucy's Day) 1502, but this has been disproved by historians who have shown that the admiral never set foot on the island. Despite this, St. Lucians annually celebrate at this time, though they have changed the name from Discovery Day to National Day. An early European map shows the island marked as Santa Lucía, lending support to the idea that it was discovered, certainly claimed, but never settled by the Spanish.

What does seem beyond dispute is that the first attempt at settlement was made by the English in 1605. After spending some time among the local Caribs, observing their customs and being shown how to make cassava bread, relations broke down. The Caribs attacked the European settlement and the survivors had to flee. In 1638 another English attempt was made but after two years the Caribs attacked the settlement and hundreds were killed, the European survivors fleeing the island. A series of French intrigues followed but the Caribs continued their resistance and several French governors were killed. For over 150 years, St. Lucia was alternately French or English (though mainly French), during which time African slaves were imported to man the plantation economy that the Europeans developed. Today, this aspect of the colonial legacy is being investigated by historical archaeologists from Bristol University in Britain, with attention focusing on the eighteenth-century sugar plantation of Balenbouche Estate, where water mills, a coffee works, and slave accommodation areas have been identified.

Military actions between the two imperial powers, Carib unrest, proclamations, and various international treaties all combined to make St. Lucia's early colonial history a merry-go-round of changing fortunes. The island finally became British in 1814 by the terms of the Treaty of Paris. St. Lucia finally received its independence from Britain in 1979 and is now a full member of the British Commonwealth.

Today, much French influence remains in St. Lucian society. A French patois known as *Kwéyòl* is widely spoken although English is the official language, *zouk* music from Martinique is a favorite, and most place-names are French. There are reportedly a few Black Caribs left in some areas. Until recently, there were several African-derived creole cultural events on St. Lucia: the Flower Societies, and celebrations based on A-Bwè, Koutoumba, and Kélé—of which the latter was perhaps the most important. During the festivities of the Flower Societies, people are divided into Roses and Marguerites and hold parades, dances, and feasting, all of which are centered around the courtly figures of kings and queens. Originating in the villages south of La Sorcière Mountain, the Christmas-time singing competition of A-Bwè appears to be fading and may soon join Koutoumba—a funeral-song dance with strong African overtones that ceased in 1986 when the last drummer who could play the rhythms died. A similar fate overtook Kélé—whose rituals honored ancestral African figures and powers. It was held among families who called themselves Djiné (i.e., those born in Africa) in the island's Babonneau district but ended in 1993 with the death of the last high priest.

What made Kélé significant in African-Caribbean religions was that it showed no Christian influence but rather was a mix of traditional African spiritualities such as Shango and Ogun. It seems to have begun when Nigerian Yoruba families arrived in St. Lucia during the mid-nineteenth century. Held at New year, Easter, and at the anniversary of the recent death of an ancestor, the purpose of Kélé is to ask for good luck, protection, and good health. Interestingly, supernatural powers are believed to reside in the so-called shango-stones that are said to have come from Africa yet look like typical Amerindian axes; they possess powerful curing properties. These magical objects link people with God and were kept in homes where they formed part of the background to prayers addressed to the Yoruban god Olgun.

Carnival on St. Lucia is, like everywhere else, the high point of popular cultural life. It takes place in the days before Shrove Tuesday and Ash Wednesday at which time music, colorful costumes, and processions fill the streets. The Fisherman's Feast festivities take place on 29 June (St. Peter's Day), during which time the fishing boats are decorated. More recent has been the international success of the St. Lucia Jazz Festival that takes place in May.

St. Lucia's capital is Castries, and it contains some impressive colonial period fortifications, notably the huge fortress known as Morne Fortune, composed of Fort Charlotte and Derrière Fort. Although the town has been badly damaged by fires in its history, nineteenth- and early twentieth-century French-style houses have survived in several places. In the north of the island lies Fort Rodney, which contains a museum, and in the south the coastal town of Soufrière, which began life in 1713 when Louis XIV of France granted lands to the Devaux family, who built an estate on tobacco, coffee, and cocoa. Nearby is a luxury resort known as Jalousie Plantation, which illustrates some of the problems of archaeology in the Caribbean. Despite local protests, the resort was built on what appears to be a large Amerindian village, the tennis courts being laid over the pre-Columbian burial ground. Farther south still is Caraibe Point, where the island's last Black Caribs live.

See also: Caribs; Orisha/Shango (Trinidad); Slavery; Sugar

References

Anthony, P.A.B. 1986. The Encounter between Christianity and Culture: The Case of the "Kele" Ceremony in St. Lucia. In M. Kremser and K. R. Wernhart (eds.). *Research in Ethnography and Ethnohistory of St. Lucia,* pp. 103–120. Vienna: Ferdinand Berger and Söhne; Bullen, A. 1970. Case Study of An Amerindian Burial with Grave Goods from Grande Anse, St Lucia. *Proceedings of the Third International Congress for the Study of Pre-Columbian Cultures of the Lesser Antilles, Grenada 1969,* pp. 45–60. Grenada; Bullen, R. P., and A. K. Bullen. 1970. The Lavoutte Site, St Lucia: A Carib Ceremonial Center. *Proceedings of the Third International Congress for the Study of Pre-Columbian Cultures of the Lesser Antilles, Grenada 1969,* pp. 61–86. Grenada; Bullen, R. P., and A. K. Bullen. 1973. The Giraudy Site, Beane Field, St Lucia. *Proceedings of the Fourth International Congress for the Study of the Pre-Columbian Cultures of the Lesser Antilles, St Lucia 1971,* pp. 199–214; Devaux, R. 1976. Petroglyphs Recently Discovered at Stonefield, St Lucia. *Proceedings of the Sixth International Congress for the Study of the Pre-Columbian Cultures of the Lesser Antilles, Guadeloupe, 1975;* Jesse, C. 1966. St. Lucia: The Romance of its Place Names. *St. Lucia Miscellany,* Vol. 1. Castries, St. Lucia: St. Lucia Archaeological and Historical Society; Jesse, C. 1973a. The Caribs in St Lucia after A.D. 1605. *Proceedings of the Fourth International Congress for the Study of the Pre-Columbian Cultures of the Lesser Antilles, St Lucia 1971,* pp. 90–93; Jesse, C. 1973b. Petroglyph and Rock-Cut Basins at Dauphin, St Lucia. *Proceedings of the Fourth International Congress for the Study of the Pre-Columbian Cultures of the Lesser Antilles, St Lucia 1971,* pp. 33–34; Kremser, M., and K. R. Wernhart (eds.). 1986. *Research in Ethnography and Ethnohistory of St. Lucia: A Preliminary Report.* Vienna: F. Berger and Shone; Simpson, G. E. 1973. The Kele (Chango) Cult in St. Lucia: Research Commentaries 3. *Caribbean Studies* 13 (3): 110–116.

St. Thomas (USVI)

St. Thomas is 21 km long and less than 5 km wide, with an area of 83 sq km. It has a population of some 52,000, and is the second largest of the islands that make up the U.S. Virgin Islands (USVI).

Archaeologically, the island has an early, Archaic Period occupation, a local variation of the Ortoiroid peoples who settled the Caribbean between 2000 B.C. and 400 B.C. St. Thomas has one of these local variations named after its site of Krum Bay, the other being the Coroso culture of Puerto Rico. The earliest dates for the Krum Bay culture range between 880 B.C. and 225 B.C. Settlements were located near to the sea and appear only to have been open-air sites. They consist of shell middens, within which have been found basic stone tools and celts, and pendants made either from stone, bone, or shell.

St. Thomas, like the other Virgin Islands, was subsequently colonized by the village-dwelling, pottery-making horticulturalists of the Saladoid tradition in the early centuries B.C. From these beginnings, around A.D. 600, developed the Ostionoid series of cultures that in the Virgin Islands are known as the Elenan Ostionoid peoples. These developed eventually into the Eastern Taínos between 900 and 1200. Investigations at the Tutu site have yielded forty-two human burials, of which, so far, eight have been dated to the Saladoid Period and eleven have been assigned to the succeeding Elenan Ostionoid occupation.

St. Thomas and the other Virgin Islands were first seen by Europeans during Christopher Columbus's second voyage in 1493. Columbus seems to have named them Las Once Mil Virgenes after the legend of St. Ursula and her 11,000 martyred virgins. It wasn't until the seventeenth century, however, that they were settled, by which time earlier Spanish slaving raids had probably depopulated them. In 1665, an early Danish settlement collapsed but from 1754, when the Danish West Indies became a royal colony, St. Thomas prospered as a center of the maritime trade in African slaves. In 1917, St. Thomas, along with St. Croix and St. John, was sold to the United States, becoming the USVI.

Today, St. Thomas's carnival takes place annually between 21 and 26 April, and comprises an area mix of African ritual dancing and more Christian-influenced parades. Charlotte Amalie is the capital both of St. Thomas and the whole USVI, and has preserved many brightly colored historic buildings of the Danish period. Several forts from Danish rule also survive, such as Blackbeard's Castle dating from 1679, and the former dungeon of Fort Christian, which now serves as the Virgin Islands Museum.

See also: Archaic Period; Elenan; Jolly Beach (site, Antigua); Krum Bay (site, St. Thomas); Ortoiroid; Ostionoid; Slavery

References
Acheson, P. 1999. *The Best of St. Thomas and St. John, U.S. Virgin Islands.* Two Thousand Three Associates; Bullen, R. P. 1962. Ceramic Periods of St. Thomas and St. Johns Islands, Virgin Islands. *American Studies* 4. Orlando, FL: William L. Bryant Foundation; Bullen, R. P. 1973. Krum Bay, A Preceramic Workshop on St Thomas. *Proceedings of the Fourth International Congress for the Study of Pre-Columbian Cultures of the Lesser Antilles, St. Lucia 1971,* pp. 10–114; Righter, E., and E. Lundberg. 1993. Preliminary Report on A Prehistoric Settlement at Tutu, St. Thomas, USVI. *Proceedings of the Fourteenth International Congress for Caribbean Archaeology, Barbados, 1991,* p 561.; Wing, E. S., S. deFrance, and L. Kozuch. 1995. *Faunal Remains from the Tutu Archaeological Village, St. Thomas, USVI.* Manuscript on file at the Division for Archaeology and Historic Preservation.

St. Vincent and the Grenadines

St. Vincent is 29 km long and 18 km wide, and together with its associated islands, the Grenadines, has an area of 388.5 sq km. Most of its population is of pure or mixed African descent, of which, unusually, some 2 percent are said to be part Amerindian.

St. Vincent's archaeological past is bound up with that of the whole Windward group of islands. The earliest evidence seems to date from the late Saladoid Period culture known as Troumassoid (A.D. 600 to A.D. 1000), which was in turn replaced by peoples of the Suazoid culture. Local adaptations saw these early peoples depending on horticulture, fishing, and some gathering. During the Troumassoid Period, clay spindles whorls appeared and pottery quality was high, though in the succeeding Suazoid Period (A.D. 1100 to A.D. 1450), the quality declined dramatically. Nevertheless, some higher-standard red-painted and incised ceramics continued to be made, probably for ceremonial use. Suazoid culture appears radically different from that of the Caribs who occupied the island sometime around 1450.

Despite the many European reports about encounters with Caribs, archaeologically speaking they remained invisible until the late 1980s. In 1986, the so-called Cayo style of pottery was identified and analyzed by the Dutch archaeologist Arie Boomert and attributed to the Caribs. Dramatic confirmation came during the 1990s when Cayo ceramics were found alongside European materials, notably a fragment of Carib pottery decorated with European glass beads. Called by the Caribs Hairoun, St. Vincent has many intriguing petroglyphs and rock carvings that seem to belong to various periods of its prehistoric past. The most spectacular and (relatively) accessible are those at Layou, north of Kingstown, and Yambou, east of the capital. At Yambou there are several locations, one of which is especially interesting as it has been Christianized by a wayside calvary.

Christopher Columbus arrived in 1498, during his third voyage of exploration, but, as with Grenada to the south, Carib resistance effectively curtailed any white settlement until the eighteenth century. These people, more properly known today as Kalinago, spoke a language that mixed South American Carib words with an Arawak vocabulary. They welcomed African slaves who had either escaped from nearby islands or been shipwrecked off St. Vincent's coast. These eventually became assimilated into Carib society, adopting their language and way of life. The offspring of mixed race unions produced the so-called Black Caribs, differentiated from the original Yellow Carib inhabitants. In 1763, the British occupied St. Vincent and the Caribs fought a guerrilla war that lasted until 1796. A year later, 4,000 were rounded up and deported to the island of Roatán off the coast of Honduras in Central America.

As with so many other Caribbean islands at this time, the actions of Europeans led to labor shortages that were filled by the importation of African slaves. In St. Vincent, these were joined later by Portuguese and East Indian immigrants. A natural disaster struck in 1902 when the La Soufrière volcano erupted, killing 2,000 people and ruining much of the best agricultural land. The island became fully independent of Britain in 1979 and is now a constitutional monarchy within the British Commonwealth.

The capital of St. Vincent is Kingstown, which has preserved much architecture from colonial British times. St. George's Anglican cathedral contains a memorial floor plaque to a general who died during the Carib wars. Another legacy of that period is Fort Charlotte, overlooking Kingstown and whose cannon, some still in situ, faced inland as a defense against the Black Caribs. In the Botanical Gardens is a third generation of the breadfruit first brought to the island from Tahiti by Captain Bligh on board the *Bounty* in 1793. The archaeological museum lies within the grounds and contains artifacts from the island's pre-Columbian past, including an extraordinary Saladoid Period bat effigy ceramic pot. On the eastern, windward side of the island lie the impoverished towns of Sandy Bay, Owia, and Fancy, inhabited today by the descendants of the surviving Black Caribs.

St. Vincent's Carnival is called Vincy Mas and is held between the end of June and the beginning of July. As with similar events in other islands, it involves steel bands, costumed masquerades, and calypso singing.

See also: Caribs; Garifuna (Black Caribs); Saladoid; Suazey/Suazoid; Troumassoid

References
Bobrow, J. D., J. D. Jinkins, J. Bowrow, and M. E. Atwood, 1985. *St. Vincent and the Grenadines.* New York: W. W. Norton; Boomert, A. 1986. The Cayo Complex of St. Vincent: Ethnohistorical and Archaeological Aspects of the Island-Carib Problem. *Antropológica* 66: 3–68; Gullick, C.J.M.R. 1985. *Myths of a Minority: The Changing Traditions of the Vicentian Caribs.* Assen, the Netherlands; Kirby, E. 1977. *Pre-Columbian Monuments in Stone.* 2nd ed. The St. Vincent Archaeological and Historical Society 1969. Kingstown, St. Vincent: Reliance Press Ltd.; Sutty, L. 1993. *St. Vincent and the Grenadines.* London: Macmillan.

Suazey / Suazoid

The Suazoid culture flourished in the Lesser Antilles from ca. A.D. 1000 to around A.D. 1450. Taking its name from the Savanne Suazey site on Grenada, Suazoid culture marked a reorientation of daily life as reflected in their preference for sandy beaches and mangrove swamps. Their middens show that they ate mollusks, fish, and turtles. Suazoid represents the last truly prehistoric culture of the region. As there is no evidence of it occurring beyond the Windward Islands, it is thought to have developed and been adopted only in this part of the Caribbean. It had disappeared by the time Europeans arrived in 1498, and consequently no Suazoid site has yielded any European artifacts.

Suazoid ceramics represent a general decline in technological production and artistic styles from the previous Troumassoid tradition, though continuities exist. Most pottery vessels are characteristically poorly made with thick walls, finger marks along the rims, a variety of materials used for temper, and rough surface scratching as decoration. A small quantity of higher quality red-painted and incised ceramics were made, however, presumably for ceremonial use. This style commonly had naturalistic *adornos* shaped as flat-faced heads with facial features created by punctation and appliqué. The attachment of legs to vessels and the footed cassava griddles first introduced during the Troumassoid Period continued to be made. Other items of Suazoid material culture include clay spindle whorls, figurines, stone pestles, and shell celts and gouges, as well as clay cylinders that may have been incense burners.

From around 1200 onward, there appears to be increasing influence on Suazoid peoples from the Greater Antilles in the form of Taíno artistic imagery. A Taíno outpost, dated to ca. 1300, has recently been discovered on Saba in the Leeward Islands. Most of this influence appears related to items of religious or ritual importance, such as large three-pointer *zemís,* a *duho,* a possible hallucinogen-snuffing tube, and so-called human face masks. Most appear to have been locally made clay forms imitating more sophisticated Taíno originals of carved-wood. The Suazoid examples are decorated with typical Taíno imagery including Atabey, their major deity. Some scholars believe there is also evidence of influence from coastal Venezuela, where the Macro-Dabajuroid culture was becoming established.

Because Suazoid culture was radically different from that of the slightly later Island Caribs who occupied the same islands, it must have disappeared rapidly around 1450 for reasons that are still unclear.

See also: Caribs; Cohoba; Martinique; Taíno (Arawak); Troumassoid; Zemís
References
Allaire, L. 1991. Understanding Suazey. *Proceedings of the Thirteenth International Congress for Caribbean Archaeology, Held in Willemstadt, Curaçao, on July 24–29, 1989,* pp. 715–728; Allaire, L. 1997. The Lesser Antilles before Columbus. In S. M. Wilson (ed.). *The Indigenous People of the Caribbean,* pp. 26–27. Gainesville, FL: University Press of Florida; Bullen, R. P. 1964. *The Archaeology of Grenada, West Indies.* Gainesville, FL: University Press of Florida; Hofman, C. L., and M.L.P. Hoogland. 1991. Ceramic Developments on Saba, N. A. (350–1450 AD). *Proceedings of the Fourteenth Congress of the International Association for Caribbean Archaeology.* Barbados; Rouse, I. 1992. *The Tainos: Rise and Decline of the People Who Greeted Columbus,* pp. 129–130. New Haven, CT: Yale University Press.

Sugar

Sugar cane (*Saccharum officinarum* L.) was first domesticated around 10,000 B.C. in New Guinea, from where it soon diffused to the Philippines and India. The earliest written mention of sugar seems to be in Indian Sanskrit documents dating to around 350 B.C. However, incontrovertible evidence for sugar making by boiling sugar-cane juice to make molasses then crystallizing this into solid sugar does not occur until around A.D. 500. Ambiguous evidence for sugar production occurs in Europe between 700 and 1450, by which time the Moors were growing it in Spain as far north as Valencia. During the fifteenth century, Portuguese and Spanish expansion into the Atlantic saw sugar growing in the Canaries and Madeira, from where it was taken to the Americas on Columbus's second voyage in 1493.

The first American sugar was probably grown on Hispaniola around 1514, and was soon taken to Cuba, Jamaica, and Puerto Rico. While some Taínos may have been the first sugar workers, the expansion of plantations was only possible with the arrival of African slaves. By the late seventeenth century, the taste for sugar in northern Europe was such that it accelerated a rapid increase in Caribbean sugar plantations and in slavery. Such was the profit in sugar that the French, Dutch, and Swedes joined the English and Spanish in creating ever more sugar plantations on their respective islands. The first species of sugar to be grown was called "creole" (*Saccharum barberi*) of Mediterranean origin, but toward the end of the eighteenth century this was replaced by *Saccharum officinarum* (also known as Bourbon or Otaheite cane).

Sugar cane is a uniquely labor-intensive crop. While its cultivation is an agricultural activity, its processing is an industrial endeavor. Pieces of cane are individually laid flat in shallow trenches, and, when ripe, the cane similarly has to be cut down piecemeal. Grinding has to follow almost immediately to produce cane juice from which molasses is made, which in turn is crystallized into sugar. This series of time-sensitive linked activities requires precise scheduling, a well-organized labor force, and an efficient integration be-

Sugar-cane harvest in Trinidad (Courtesy Nicholas J. Saunders)

tween field and factory. The mass cultivation and processing of sugar was thus made possible by, and was inseparable from, mass slavery.

The eighteenth century saw the highest point of sugar production and slavery in the West Indies, with the most productive islands being British Jamaica and French Saint Domingue (Haiti). Altogether, some 2.5 million African slaves had worked on Caribbean plantations by the time slavery was abolished in the nineteenth century. The colonial history and present-day demography of the Island Caribbean—and of the world economy—is inextricably entwined with the period of African slavery that itself cannot be disentangled from sugar plantations. After emancipation, labor shortage on plantations led to a further influx of people to work sugar, including those from India, China, and Java, who added further to the cultural mosaic of the Caribbean.

Today, growing and harvesting sugar remains backbreaking and poorly paid work in the region, and is often uneconomical—vulnerable to the boom-and-bust cycles that have characterized its history. In 2000, it cost $2,440 to produce a ton of sugar on St. Kitts, which sold for only $997 a ton. Dependant on a global economy controlled by multinational companies, sugar production has become internationalized. Caribbean islands, each with varying local conditions and degrees of modernization, have been affected differently. International trade agreements threaten the future of sugar growing (and thus economic stability and historical identity) on many islands.

> **See also:** Antigua; Betty's Hope (site, Antigua); Drax Hall, (site, Jamaica); Historical Archaeology; Galways Plantation; Jamaica; Newton Plantation (Barbados); Slavery; Trinidad and Tobago

References

Barnes, A. C. 1974. *The Sugar Cane*. New York: John Wiley; Carstensen, B. 1993. *Betty's Hope: An Antiguan Sugar Plantation*. St. John's (Antigua): Betty's Hope Trust; Deerr, N. 1949. *The History of Sugar*. Vol. 1. London: Chapman and Hall; Deerr, N. 1950. *The History of Sugar*. Vol. 2. London: Chapman and Hall; Dunn, R. S. 1972. *Sugar and Slaves: The Rise of the Planter Class in the English West Indies 1624–1713*. Chapel Hill, NC: University of North Carolina Press; Eubanks, T. H. 1992. *Sugar, Slavery, and Emancipation: The Industrial Archaeology of the West Indian Island of Tobago*. Unpublished Ph.D. dissertation. University of Florida, Gainesville, FL; Galloway, J. 1989. *The Sugar-Cane Industry*. Cambridge: Cambridge University Press; Mintz, S. 1986. *Sweetness and Power: The Place of Sugar in Modern History*. Harmondsworth, UK: Penguin; Mintz, S. 1991. Pleasure, Profit, and Satiation. In H. J. Viola and C. Margolis (eds.). *Seeds of Change: Five Hundred Years Since Columbus,* pp. 112–129. Washington, DC: Smithsonian Institution Press; Pulsipher, L. M., and C. M. Goodwin. 1982. A Sugar-Boiling House at Galways: An Irish Sugar Plantation in Montserrat, West Indies. *Post-Medieval Archaeology* 16: 21–27; Ratekin, M. 1954. The Early Sugar Industry in Española. *Hispanic American Historical Review* 34: 1–19; Tomich, D. W. 1990. *Slavery in the Circuit of Sugar: Martinique and the World Economy, 1830–1848*. Baltimore: Johns Hopkins University Press; Wilkinson, A. 1989. *Big Sugar*. New York: Alfred A Knopf.

T

Taíno (Arawak)

The Taíno (also commonly called Arawak), were the first Amerindians to be encountered by Christopher Columbus in the Caribbean in 1492. At that time, they occupied the Greater Antilles (Cuba, Jamaica, Hispaniola, and Puerto Rico), as one of the two main Amerindian groups—the other being the Caribs of the Lesser Antilles. Their ancestors were the Saladoid peoples who migrated from mainland South America through Trinidad up the Lesser Antilles and arriving in Hispaniola by about 250 B.C. By around A.D. 500, these early settlers had begun to develop their own cultural features in Puerto Rico and Hispaniola and by 1000 they had established themselves in Cuba, Jamaica, and the Bahamas.

The adaptation of Saladoid peoples to local island conditions gave rise to what archaeologists call the Ostionoid cultural tradition, named after the Ostiones culture on Hispaniola (modern Dominican Republic) around A.D. 500. The Ostiones culture is but one of several local variations or subseries of the Ostionoid tradition, and represents a uniquely Island Caribbean development that lasted until European arrival in 1492. Typically Ostionoid pottery is less sophisticated than previous Saladoid ceramics; its basic modeled shapes and simple orange-red appearance has led to its being widely referred to as redware. Local developments (subseries) of the Ostionoid tradition are known as Meillacan in Hispaniola, Cuba, and Jamaica; Elenan in the Leeward and Virgin Islands; and Palmetto in the Bahamas.

On Hispaniola, the local Ostiones culture was succeeded first by the Meillacan then around 1200 by the Chican Ostionoid culture—the name given to the archaeological remains of the classic Taíno peoples encountered by Columbus. The name "Taíno" was used by the people themselves to mean "good people," and is commonly used by archaeologists to differentiate the more sophisticated Amerindians of Hispaniola and Puerto Rico from those that inhabited the smaller islands and who are sometimes referred to as sub-Taíno.

Economic and Artistic Life

At the time of the European arrival, the Taíno population of Hispaniola may have been as high as 1 million people. They lived a settled village life and practiced agriculture. Their

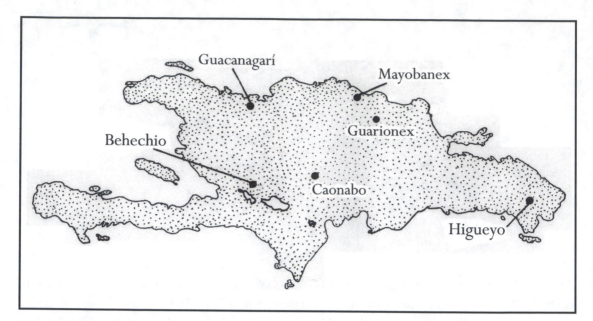

Taíno chiefs on Hispaniola at the time of Columbus. Source: *Based on Irving Rouse,* The Tainos *(New Haven, CT: Yale University Press, 1992).*

main food crops were manioc from which they made cassava bread, maize, and sweet potatoes, which they supplemented with guava, papaya, pineapple, beans, peppers, peanuts, and tobacco. Manioc and sweet potatoes were grown on heaped-up mounds of earth in fields known as *conucos.* They also grew cotton from which they manufactured items of their minimal everyday clothing and ritual paraphernalia. Domesticated plants were supplemented by hunting birds, snakes, and the large rodent known as the hutia (*Isolobodon portoricensis*). Using weirs and baskets, and fishing with nets, fish hooks, and bows and arrows, they caught a variety of marine animals such as manatees, sea turtles, clams, oysters, crabs, and different types of fish.

Taíno arts and crafts can be divided into items used for bodily adornment and those intended as either as free-standing objects or the painted and sculptural decoration of caves. Body painting was similar to that of Amerindians from South America, and consisted of designs painted in black, white, and red pigments that were prepared from plants such as annatto (*Bixa orellana*), genipap, and various minerals such as ochre. The Spanish observed that the Taíno were well-built and handsome, wore their hair long, and tattooed their faces. Body piercing was commonplace, with earrings and ear plugs, nose orna-

Taíno Amerindians on Jamaica observing the eclipse of 29 February 1504, predicted by Columbus (Courtesy Nicholas J. Saunders)

ments, and lip plugs. Feather crowns were made from multicolored bird plumage, and necklaces, amulets, bracelets, and pendants were fashioned from bone, shell, and a multitude of colorful and polished stones. Carved-stone beads and ornaments were known as *çibas* and these appear to have possessed symbolic qualities for the wearer. Gold (in fact, usually the gold-copper-silver alloy known as *guanín*) was also worn as nose-rings and was hammered into thin sheets as pendants and diadems. Jewelry made from gold was commonly referred to as *guanines*.

Woodwork was another Taíno speciality. Particularly impressive and distinctive were the *duhos*—ceremonial seats made in a distinctive curving shape with a high sloping back-rest. They were seen as connecting a person with supernatural powers and were some-times decorated with sacred swirling designs, inlaid with shell or guanín, and brightly pol-ished. Their sophistication indicates their elite status as does their use on ceremonial occasions as a mark of respect for visiting dignitaries. When Christopher Columbus vis-ited a Cuban chief he was offered a guanín-inlaid duho to sit on. Duho manufacture and distribution was a privilege of the elite. The Taíno female chief Anacaona appears to have controlled their production on the small island of Gonâve offshore of southwestern His-paniola (modern Haiti). When Bartolomé Columbus visited the area in 1496, Anacaona showed him the workshop whose prestige items may have been made by women. Duhos were not only portals to the spirit world but served also as status markers for their elite owners and sometimes were used to hold the body of a deceased cacique in the grave.

The Taínos, like any island peoples, were great navigators. They built large and so-phisticated canoes and traveled regularly between islands, maintaining a wide network of trade relationships. Through these activities they exchanged and acquired such items as polished-stone beads for bodily adornment and ritual purposes, cotton for clothing, as well as tobacco and bird feathers for their ceremonial activities. Cotton and beads were intricately worked together into composite items such as belts and figures and were commented on admiringly by the Spanish.

Most, if not all, of the sophisticated guanín goldwork items probably were obtained in down-the-line trade between islands from their original source among the great gold-working cultures of South America. Such items were regarded as elite objects, embodying mythical and supernatural power, and were the focus of ceremonial exchanges between Taíno chiefs. It is no surprise that colored stone beads, carved-wood objects, gold jewelry, and cotton items were among the valuable gifts offered to Columbus in 1492 by Guacanagarí, an important chief in northern Hispaniola. In various meetings between the two leaders, the Taíno chief gave Columbus a gold-encrusted mask and a golden crown in exchange for European colored glass beads and a woolen cape.

Society, Culture, and Politics

The political organization of the Taíno is often referred to as chiefdoms. At the top of the social hierarchy were the chiefs, or caciques, hereditary leaders who inherited their position through their mother's line. This matrilineal descent system gave great status to high-born women in Taíno society, and rules of residence and inheritance may well have been what anthropologists call avuncular (i.e., reckoned through the mother's brother). Sexual equality appears to have been well established in Taíno society, both in practice and in religious and ritual activities.

The importance of the female element is seen in the fact that major Taíno gods were both male and female and that men and women worshipped them on an equal basis. *Zemí* images also were male and female. Generally speaking, women were responsible for most horticultural work and food preparation and men for fishing and warfare. Sometimes, women like Anacaona could play a leading role in politics and dynastic affairs; the egalitarian nature of the society is revealed by the fact that women owned property in their own right.

Male caciques practiced polygamy, having perhaps as many as thirty wives. This was a consequence not just of their exalted social position, but also of necessity, inasmuch as many marriages were little more than the cementing of political alliances between different Taíno chiefdoms. It is known that in Hispaniola caciques maintained regular contact with each other, often making official visits, engaging in the exchange of prestige gifts, and forging alliances. The caciques stood out in the magnificence of their dress and jewelry, and were permitted to eat only specially prepared food. They wielded ritual as well as political power, may have been able to demand tribute in labor and goods, and lived in larger more sophisticated houses than other people.

In the Greater Antilles, the major caciques often controlled large areas within which several smaller villages were ruled by subordinate lesser chiefs. At the time of the Spanish conquest, the island of Hispaniola is thought to have been divided into five major chiefdoms or *cacicazgos*. Another principal cacique was Agüeybana in Puerto Rico (native Borinquén). He organized a rebellion against the Spanish but was caught and executed. From the class-conscious Spanish it is known that below the cacique were Taíno nobles called *nitaínos* and then manual workers known as *naborías*.

Taíno social and political organization is reflected in the sophistication of settlement size and location. Villages, called *yucayeques*, could be situated either near the coast or in inland river valleys. They ranged from small hamlets of seven or eight huts to larger villages of dozens, sometimes hundreds of communal houses known as *bohíos*, within which extended families lived. In the center of these settlements was the typically Amerindian plaza, kept level and clean for a variety of social and religious activities, such as ceremonial dances and ball-games.

According to the Spanish chronicler Bartolomé de Las Casas, Taíno houses were built of strong wood poles and fragrant-smelling straw in a bell shape. These houses were airy and spacious, and could house on average ten individuals, each one sleeping in cotton sheets suspended at either end from wooden posts—whose name *hamacas* has given us the modern word "hammock." Located prominently by the plaza, the chief's house was the largest of all. According to Peter Martyr D'Anghiera, it was decorated with multicolored branches artfully plaited together. Known as a *caney*, this structure served many purposes besides being the chief's residence. It functioned as a council house, a place to receive high-ranking visitors, and perhaps as a temple.

All levels of society were integrated by an elaborate ceremonial life that included dances, singing, and chanting, known collectively as *areítos*, and by the ball-game. When visiting other villages or welcoming the Spanish, the Taíno would stage areítos as a type of elite hospitality. These took place in the village plaza or a specially cleared area fronting the chief's house and temple. One account of an areíto tells how men and women purified themselves by vomiting before entering the council house whereupon they sang the praises of the chief's ancestors and asked for the favors of the zemís. Areítos were undoubtedly an important if not fully understood feature of Taíno social, political, and ceremonial life.

In their everyday life, the Taínos greatly enjoyed the ball-game known as *batey*, often played in custom-made rectangular ballcourts, was not only for recreation but possessed political and cosmological dimensions as well. Spanish accounts record that the game was played by two teams with a solid rubber ball and that the objective was to keep the ball in motion, and move it into the opposing team's end of the court without using either hands or feet. Each team took turns in serving the ball, watched by spectators seated either on the earthen embankments that flanked the court, or, if they were high-ranking individuals, seated on their ceremonial stools or duhos. The ball-game had everyday appeal as wagers were often laid on the outcome. One of the most famous groupings of such ballcourts is at the village and ceremonial center of Caguana in Puerto Rico, which may have been the seat of the powerful chief Guarionex.

The evidence for warfare in Taíno society is ambiguous, confused in part by the simplified propaganda view of the Spanish who called the Taíno friendly, and the Caribs warlike. While Taíno society appears not have been especially warlike, local battles undoubtedly took place between different chiefdoms to resolve disputes over territory. Nevertheless, it was the Carib peoples of the Lesser Antilles to the east who were the common enemy. Carib raiding parties attacked Taíno islands mainly, it seems, to acquire marriageable women. When the Spanish arrived, the Taíno told them this and added for good measure that the Caribs also were eaters of human flesh. In one sense, the accusations of cannibalism and militarism drew the Spanish closer to the Taíno and made the Caribs the perfect scapegoat for conquest and subjects for enslavement. Whatever the pre-Spanish situation between the Taíno and Carib, the former clearly understood how to acquire a powerful new ally against the traditional foe.

Religion and Mythology

Taíno religion was based on the shamanic tradition inherited from their Saladoid ancestors in South America. In this magical worldview, plants, animals, and landscapes were infused with spirit force derived from the immanent powers of nature and of their own ancestors. The ties to mythology were strong and were acted out in rituals and ceremonies that bound together the physical and supernatural realms of life. Taíno caciques and shamans (*behiques*) were the arbiters of this world and controlled the forces of life and death through a philosophy founded on analogical symbolic reasoning. This non-Western view of the world saw connections between objects, people, natural phenomena, and social events in a holistic way—tied together by invisible strands of power and kinship relationships. In this spiritually animated universe, all things possessed sacred and secular importance and were acknowledged in rituals designed to make sense of physical and spiritual life.

Religious beliefs focused on the veneration of gods and spirits known as zemís whose supernatural essence was embodied in sacred images—i.e., three-dimensional objects fashioned from stone, bone, wood, shell, clay, and cotton—sometimes in combination. Zemís could be male or female, could bring death and disease as well as help cure illness and help crops to grow. The images could be owned and some evidence suggests they were stolen and perhaps exchanged. For archaeologists, the most frequently encountered examples are the so-called three-pointers, objects of stone or shell that often appeared like miniature mountains in profile. Sometimes this shape was an integral part of a larger figure of a god or spirit.

The two major Taíno deities were Yúcahu, the invisible lord of fertility and spirit of cassava—their staple food. In zemí representations, Yúcahu is shown open-mouthed to eat away the soil thereby making room for the sprouting cassava tubers. His feet, likewise, are joined together to scratch away the earth. Yúcahu's female counterpart, and possibly his mother, was Atabey. As "Mother of Waters," she was associated with freshwater streams, ponds, and the rain needed to fertilize the cassava crops. She was also associated female fertility, childbirth, and the moon. These deities represent a concept of fertility that extends from the natural to social worlds, with images of both gods being invoked for successful childbirth. In a world of violently destructive weather, the Taíno also worshipped a female deity known as Guabancex, the "Lady of the Winds" and mistress of hurricanes. As with Amerindians elsewhere, the gods and spirits of the Caribbean Taíno symbolized their intimate relationship with the natural forces that shaped the world.

Religious activity found unique expression in the so-called *cohoba* ritual. Cohoba was a powerful hallucinogenic powder made from the pulverized seeds of *Anadenanthera peregrina,* which was snuffed through a double-branched cane sometimes from the flat table-like head attached to a sacred zemí figure. The intoxicating effect was believed to put those who inhaled it in touch with the spirit realm—the ensuing visions being part of curing sessions or bestowing the power of divination. Like all Taíno spiritual beliefs, there were strong ties between the cohoba ritual, gods, and mythology.

Taíno mythology, like religion, has its roots deep in South America—particularly in the tropical rainforests of the Amazon lowlands—though reflects Caribbean adaptations to local island conditions. Illustrating this shared heritage are ideas such as the view of trees as symbolic ladders that bridge the divide between heaven and earth, supplying the supernatural as well as physical materials for voyaging canoes and coffins for the dead. Caribbean islands, however, were not as rich in flora or fauna as South America. Consequently, the Taíno, like their Saladoid predecessors, adapted their mythological ideas. They replaced such powerful predators as the jaguar and harpy eagle with locally available animals in examples of so-called mythic substitution. In particular, it seems that dogs may have replaced the jaguar in many instances—partly because of the similarity between the fangs of both species, and partly also because even in Amazonia, some dogs are identified with jaguars. Other animals, which inhabited both islands and mainland, retained their mythical importance. Bats, for example, played a significant part in Amazonian myth, as did frogs—and both appear to have been important images portrayed as Taíno zemís.

An important feature of Taíno myth is the idea of metamorphosis, the ability to change outward appearance from animal to human forms or vice versa. Behavior and feelings too could alter, with mythic figures having superhuman animal strength, and animals possessing human sensibilities. Some animals could be tribal ancestors, some trees were the spirits of dead chiefs. The souls of the dead were believed to hide themselves during daylight hours, only to emerge at night to seek out and eat the guava fruit. Taíno myths, like all myths, are philosophical statements of how they regarded and made sense of their uniquely fragmented natural world, and were played out in mythic time.

Taíno creation myths are difficult to explain due to a lack of detailed prehistoric information and little postconquest comparative data. It appears that the deity known as *Yaya* is a prime mover, a distant god who personifies cosmic time, and whose four brothers are less powerful but more active supernatural beings. Itiba Cahubaba (Bloodied Aged Mother) their mother, is probably Mother Earth from whom all life emanates. When one of the brothers asks his grandfather for cassava bread, he is in fact discovering the use of fire used to bake the food. Cooking is the essence of civilized life and the Taíno used metaphor and allusion in their myth of the creation of people (see following).

According to the Taíno of Hispaniola, the creation of the universe spanned five eras. The first began when the supreme being Yaya killed his rebellious son, placing the bones in a gourd that he suspended from the rafters of his house. On examining the gourd one day, Yaya and his wife saw that the bones had transformed into fish, which they ate. In a variation of this story, the quadruplet sons of Itiba Cahubaba, who had died in childbirth, arrived in Yaya's garden. One of the brothers retrieved the gourd and they all gorged themselves on the fish it contained. Upon hearing Yaya returning they hastily replaced the gourd, but it broke, spilling water full of fish that covered the earth and became the ocean. The brothers fled to their grandfather's land but when one of them asked for some cassava bread, the old man became enraged and spat on the boy's back. This spittle transformed into the narcotic cohoba that all Taíno shamans used as a gateway to the spirit world.

The second era of Taíno cosmogony was the creation of the first people. According to one account, there were two caves in a land called Caonao on the island of Hispaniola. From one of the caves, the Taíno emerged into the world. When one man neglected his guard duties at the mouth of the cave he was turned to stone by the Sun. The others, who had gone fishing, were captured by the Sun and turned into trees. One of these, called Guayahona, washed himself and went out before sunrise. But he was caught by the Sun and changed into a bird that sings at dawn. From the second cave, came other, less numerous people of the Caribbean, those who did not share Taíno customs or identity. The second era ends with Guayahona calling to those remaining in the cave to come forth and populate the fertile islands of the Caribbean. In the third era, humans became civilized and women were created as sexual partners for men. During the fourth era, the Taíno spread over the Caribbean, perfected cassava production, lived in well-ordered villages and developed a sweet-sounding tongue. They lived this way until, in 1492, Columbus's arrival marked the end of the fourth era. The calamitous fifth era saw the disappearance of Taíno society by European maltreatment, disease, and assimilation.

Apart from creation myths, several other cosmogonic stories have survived that tell the origins of women and of tobacco. In the myth of the women made by birds, it is said that one day men went to bathe in the river and while they were washing it began to rain. The men were anxious to have women, but had searched in vain on many previous occasions. On this day, however, they looked up to see curious creatures falling from the branches of nearby trees. Lacking any sexual organs, these were neither men nor women. The men chased them, but every effort to seize them failed. Then the men called out to some men who were under the chief's orders and who were called *caracaracol* due to their rough hands that could get a grip on the slippery creatures. These men succeeded in catching the asexual creatures, whereupon the men who had requested their help conferred as to the best way to make them into women. They sought out a bird known as *inriri,* known to make holes in trees (i.e., a woodpecker). The men bound the hands and feet of the creatures, then attached the Inriri bird to them. The woodpecker believed the creatures to be trees and so began boring a hole in the place where a woman's sexual parts are found. In this way the myth relates how women were made for Taíno men.

The magical relationship between food, tobacco, and the hallucinogenic cohoba snuff is embodied in a myth that describes the encounter between two mythic beings—Deminán Caracaracol and an old man called Bayamanaco. In this myth, the substance known as *guanguayo* is identified as the shaman's spittle that is produced when he chews a wad of tobacco. The story relates how tobacco spittle was mixed with cohoba powder, which has a purifying and hallucinogenic effect on the taker. The tobacco here is the strong *Nicotiana tabacum,* whose narcotic, vision-inducing effects are released by fermentation in the mouth's saliva. The myth tells how Bayamanaco takes guanguayo from his nose and throws it onto Deminán—an act that may symbolize the mucous that streams from the shaman's nose after he has ingested cohoba and that in South America is also identified symbolically as semen. The ensuing visions are often part of shamanic curing sessions in which the illness-inducing spirits are interrogated and a cure suggested. Deminán's meeting with Bayamanaco suggests a shamanic curing aspect to the encounter. Bayamanaco is Deminán's grandfather, but may also be the supreme deity. Invoking one's grandfather may be more than a social greeting, perhaps associated ritually with divination and communion with the ancestors.

Of all Taíno mythical figures, Guayahona is one of the most important. As an archetypal culture hero, he departs from the cave of origin and journeys westward to the island of Guanín—a distinctly shamanic journey in cosmic time. In one myth, Guayahona rescues a woman named Guabonito from the bottom of the sea and she in turn cures him of sexual disease, placing him in isolation at a place called Guanara. Guabonito gives Guayahona many items of shiny jewelry such as çibas and guanines that he wears on his arms and around his neck. In this way, the copper-silver-gold alloy guanín becomes the gift of Guabonito to Guayahona and items fashioned from it serve as symbols of supernatural chiefly power.

The main themes of Taíno mythology concern the origins of the world, and the emergence of people from what appears to be a physical place, but which is actually a golden land located in mythic time. These themes link the physical and supernatural worlds, providing a mythic charter for the social order of Taíno society. Similarly, the ability to change form, or to deceive by physical appearance, is a recurring motif. Taíno myths play on the idea of metamorphosis, integrating everyday and sacred life, acknowledging the presence of death, but infusing spiritual power into the very fabric of their society.

After the arrival of Europeans, the Taíno lived in an uneasy relationship with the Spanish who initially treated them well, but subsequently with disdain and cruelty. Maltreatment, exacerbated by the ravages of disease against which they had no immunity, eventually led to Taíno uprisings that were mercilessly put down. Within a generation of European contact there were no independently viable Taíno communities left; military defeat, slavery, forced labor, disease, and intermarriage with Europeans and Africans had effectively destroyed the Caribbean's most advanced culture. Today, there is a rising tide of self awareness and pride in Taíno heritage among the mixed-race peoples of the Greater Antilles, many of whom have Amerindian blood running through their veins. In the Dominican Republic and Puerto Rico especially, museums, community heritage centers, and art and craftwork movements are slowly beginning to reclaim aspects of Taíno culture and history for a modern world. In Puerto Rico, the Jatibonicu Taino Tribal Nation of Boriken call themselves the Great People of the Sacred High Waters and actively promote their own heritage, language, and arts and crafts.

See also: Aesthetic of Brilliance; Agüeybana (Taíno chief); Anacaona (Taíno queen); Areíto; Ball-Game; Caguana/Capá (site, Puerto Rico); Caonabo (Taíno chief); Cassava (manioc); Cohoba; Duhos; Elenan; Gold; Guacanagarí (Taíno chief); Guarionex (Taíno chief); La Aleta (site, Dominican Republic); Los Buchillones (site, Cuba); Meillacan; Ostionoid; Palmetto; Puerto Rico; Saladoid; Shamanism; Tobacco; Zemís

References

Alegría, R. E. 1983. Ball Courts and Ceremonial Plazas in the West Indies. *Yale University Publications in Anthropology* No. 79. New Haven, CT; Bercht, F., E. Brodsky, J. A. Farmer, and D. Taylor (eds.). 1997. *Taíno: Pre-Columbian Art and Culture from the Caribbean.* New York: The Monacelli Press; Deagan, K. A., and J. M. Cruxent. 2002. *Columbus's Outpost Among the Taínos: Spain and America at La Isabela, 1493–1498.* New Haven, CT: Yale University Press; Ferbel, P. J. 1995. *The Politics of Taíno Indian Heritage in the Post-Quincentennial Dominican Republic: When a Canoe Means More than a Water Trough.* Unpublished Ph.D. dissertation. University of Minnesota, Minneapolis; Ferbel, P. J. 2002. Not Everyone Who Speaks Spanish is from Spain: Taíno Survival in the 21st Century Dominican Republic. KACIKE: The Journal of Caribbean Amerindian History and Anthropology. *http://www.kacike.org/FerbelEnglish.html.;* Fewkes, J. W. 1907. *The Aborigines of Port Rico and Neighboring Islands.* Washington, DC.: Bureau of American Ethnology, Smithsonian Institution; Guitar, L. 2002. Documenting the Myth of Taíno Extinction. KACIKE: The Journal of Caribbean Amerindian History and Anthropology. *http://www.kacike.org/GuitarEnglish.html;* Helms, M. W. 1986. Art Styles and Interaction Spheres in Central America and the Caribbean: Polished Black Wood in the Greater Antilles. *Journal of Latin American Lore* 12 (1): 25–43; Loven, S. 1935. *The Tainan Culture of the West Indies.* Goteborg, Sweden: Elanders; Oliver, J. R. 1997. The Taino Cosmos. In S. M. Wilson (ed.). *The Indigenous People of the Caribbean,* pp. 140–154. Gainesville, FL: University Press of Florida; Oliver, J. R. 1998. *El Centro ceremonial de Caguana, Puerto Rico. Simbolismo iconográfico, cosmovisión y el poderió caciquil taíno de Borinquén.* Oxford: British Archaeological Reports International Series 727, Archaeopress; Oliver, J. R. 2000. Gold Symbolism among Caribbean Chiefdoms: Of Feathers, *Çibas,* and *Guanín* Power among Taíno Elites. In C. McEwan (ed.). *Pre-Columbian Gold: Technology, Style, and Iconography,* pp. 196–219. London: British Museum Press; Pané, Fray R. 1999. *An Account of the Antiquities of the Indians.* Ed. José Juan Arrom. Durham, SC, and London: Duke University Press; Rouse, I. 1948. The Arawak. In J. H. Steward (ed.). *Handbook of South American Indians 4,* pp. 507–546. Washington, DC: Smithsonian Institution; Rouse, I. 1992. *The Tainos: Rise and Decline of the People Who Greeted Columbus.* New Haven, CT: Yale University Press; Wilson, S. M. 1990. *Hispaniola: Caribbean Chiefdoms in the Age of Columbus.* Tuscaloosa, AL: University of Alabama Press.

Tancah (site, Mexico)

Tancah was an important Mayan settlement on the east (Caribbean) coast of Mexico's Yucatán peninsula. Together with contemporary centers at nearby Tulum and on the island of Cozumel, Tancah flourished in the Late Post-Classic Period due to its location on a major sea trade route. Although the site was occupied in the Early Classic Period, Tancah's surviving architecture spans some 600 years, beginning ca. A.D. 1000 and ending sometime in early colonial times.

Tancah appears to have been an active port during the Late Post-Classic, with sea-going canoes bringing in food and raw materials such as obsidian. Sea resources were also important in everyday life as indicated by the presence of pottery shard net-sinkers probably used with henequen nets to catch parrot fish. The quantity of net-sinkers suggests Tancah was exporting fish to other places. Queen Conch (*Strombus gigas*) remains were also found in huge quantities and there was evidence also of sea turtle hunting.

Tancah is particularly famous today for its murals that are in the style of the Madrid Codex and that date to the fourteenth century A.D., and the carvings at the sacred Cenote Cave. It seems that from around 1400 to after the Spanish conquest, the Tancah-Tulum region was a pilgrimage area for many Mesoamerican peoples. This may well be due to the spiritual and fertility associations for the Post-Classic Maya of the east-facing Caribbean coast—east being associated with fertility and spiritual rebirth. These ideas in turn may have been associated with the predawn (heliacal) rising in the east of the planet Venus (Xuk Ek or Wasp Star), which was believed to be a dangerous supernatural influence. The entrance to Tancah's cenote (underground well) faces east and is covered with carved images including the glyph for Venus and calendrical date for the planet's heliacal rising. Even today the cave is feared by the local Maya who make offerings to pacify its spirit.

Tancah's murals show scenes interpreted as depicting episodes of military confrontation in the coastal area—perhaps pirates with central Mexican beliefs exacting food supplies from the local Tancah Maya while paying tribute to the gods. The westward shift of settlement at Tancah at this time may relate to the instability caused by such raids. Similar murals at Tulum and Chichén Itzá suggest that perhaps around 1450 the east coast came under the unified control of these sea-traders often identified as the Putun, and that the area subsequently enjoyed economic success and political stability well into the colonial period.

Despite the presence of the Spanish after 1519, there was continuity of precontact Mayan practices in the architectural techniques, pottery, and mural painting of the area. One building at Tancah is probably a Christian chapel, a Spanish building built with typically Post-Classic Mayan techniques. Beneath the stucco floor of the nave were found human burials that have been interpreted as Christian due to the absence of otherwise typically Mayan burial goods. Altogether, some twenty-three burials were excavated, filling every available space both inside and outside the chapel. The mix of culture and belief at this time is illustrated by the fact that three (European) iron nails were associated with one burial while another had a jadeite bead in its mouth in typically pre-Columbian fashion.

See also: Cozumel; Maya; Tulum (site, Mexico)

References

Lothrop, S. K. 1924. Tulum: An Archaeological Study of the East Coast of Yucatan. *Carnegie Institution Washington Publication* 335. Washington, DC; Miller, A. G. 1977. The Maya and the Sea: Trade and Cult at Tancah and Tulum. In E. P. Benson (ed.). *The Sea in the Pre-Columbian World*, 97–138. Washington, DC: Dumbarton Oaks; Miller, A. G. 1982. *On the Edge of the Sea: Mural Painting at Tancah-Tulum, Quintana Roo, Mexico.* Washington, DC: Dumbarton Oaks.

Tanki Flip (site, Aruba)

Tanki Flip is one of several archaeological sites on the island of Aruba that has undergone scientific investigation. Discovered in 1883, excavation took place in 1994 in advance of urban development. The site has been radiocarbon dated to between A.D. 950 and A.D. 1250, and it has been assigned to a series of local cultures clustered together and known as the Macro-Dabajuroid cultural group. Dabajuroid culture itself was a long-lived phenomenon that originated around Lake Maracaibo in western Venezuela and spread eventually to the offshore islands that included Bonaire and Curaçao as well as Aruba by around 1000. It was probably the Dabajuroid people who brought the Arawakan language to Aruba, and they may be the ancestors of the island's sixteenth-century Caquetio people. The Dabajuroid people may share a common ancestry with those of the Saladoid peoples in the Upper Orinoco area.

The Tanki Flip site appears to have been strategically located in relation to both water supply and good agricultural land, making the landscape around the settlement as much an artifact as the village itself. Excavations revealed a defensive palisade around the northern part of the settlement, within which there was evidence of perhaps 100 inhabitants living in large, oval-shaped structures, similar to the malocas of current-day Venezuelan Amerindians, and which could have housed extended families. Smaller circular dwellings were also found and may have been inhabited by single families. The village appears to have been laid out in a planned way.

Excavations revealed a rich variety and quantity of material culture remains, including 23,000 shell fragments (representing 35 shell species); 14,000 animals bones; 2,100 pottery fragments; 2,350 stones, of which 483 were recognized as tools; and 110 coral fragments, some of which were parts of artifacts. Shell, especially that of Queen Conch (*Strombus gigas*), was the most commonly found material, used evidently as food and raw material for tools and jewelry. Almost 300 complete shell items were recovered, including two notable pieces—a frog-shaped pendant and a curved-shell mask pendant. The maritime orientation that this focus on conch indicates is supported by the fact that almost 70 percent of animal bones retrieved were of fish, though the presence of manos and metates suggests maize cultivation as well.

Most Tanki Flip pottery was basic and utilitarian, consisting of items used for cooking and containing liquids. Some finer pieces were painted or polished, and some had stylized human or animal faces as *adornos*. Many hearths or kilns were also found, some of which may have been used in mortuary rites associated with drying the corpse—a practice commented on by the early European explorers. Adults and children burials were also found, some in urns, others beneath inverted bowls, some within a house structure, and others outside; altogether fifteen individuals were discovered though their burial treatment was diverse. Special caches of objects included complete pottery items, stone beads, and the bones of animals imported from the mainland.

See also: Aruba; Bonaire; Curaçao; Dabajuroid

References

Boerstra, E.H.J. 1985. A Limestone Human Figure from Tanki Leendert, Aruba, Netherlands Antilles. *Proceedings of the Tenth International Congress for the Study of the Pre-Columbian Cultures of* the Lesser Antilles, Martinique 1983, pp. 409–420; Josselin de Jong, J.P.B. 1918. The Praecolumbian and Early Postcolumbian Aboriginal Population of Aruba, Curaçao, and Bonaire. Internationales Archiv für Ethnographie 24 (3): 51–114; van Heekeren, H. R. 1963. Prehistorical Research on the Islands of Curaçao, Aruba, and Bonaire in 1960. Nieuwe West-Indische Gids 43: 1–25; Versteeg, A., and S. Rostain (eds.). 1997. The Archaeology of Aruba: The Tanki Flip Site. Publications of the Archaeological Museum of Aruba No. 8. Aruba/Amsterdam; Versteeg, A., and A. C. Ruiz. 1995. Reconstructing Brasilwood Island: The Archaeology and Landscape of Indian Aruba. Publications of the Archaeology Museum of Aruba No. 6. Oranjestadt, Aruba.

Ten Sail, Wreck of the

One of the eighteenth century's greatest maritime disasters took place in February 1794, when a merchant convoy of nine British ships and their Royal Navy escort HMS *Convert* foundered on the windward reefs of Grand Cayman Island. This occurred during the French Revolutionary Wars, and the *Convert* was in fact a recently captured French frigate, the *Inconstante*.

In a disastrous confusion of navigational errors, the *Convert* collided with one of the other ships and finally had to be abandoned, while others in the convoy had run into the shallows to the east of Grand Cayman. These nine ships, the *William and Elizabeth*, the *Moorhall*, the *Ludlow*, the *Britannia*, the *Richard*, the *Nancy*, the *Eagle*, the *Sally*, and the *Fortune*, were all wrecked on the reefs. The whole event became part of Cayman folklore and is remembered as the Wreck of the Ten Sail. Miscellaneous items from the wrecked ships were salvaged by the local population, most notably quantities of cloth made into fashionable clothing by the island's women.

During the 1970s, various French cannon began to appear outside of hotels and private houses on Grand Cayman. Investigation of the reef area discovered more cannon, ballast stones, English pottery, pipe stems, and miscellaneous ships' equipment. The quantity of finds increased in the wake of Hurricane Allen in 1980. Discoveries of glass and ceramics were also made on land at a location thought to have been the salvage dump organized by the *Convert*'s captain soon after the disaster.

Further investigations included a detailed survey of some thirty cannon discovered both underwater and on land, some of which were not only French but accorded well in size and inscribed date of manufacture with those that would have been carried by the *Inconstante/Convert*. Encouraged by these discoveries, in the 1990s the Cayman Islands National Museum sponsored a survey of a five-kilometer area thought to be the site of the disaster. Many new underwater sites were discovered, some of which represented previously unknown shipwrecks. Two sites in particular, known as French Cannon Site and the Probable Frigate Spillage Site, are thought to be the remains of the *Convert*, and other sites nearby may be the wreckage of the nine other ships.

Today, a combination of archival research, underwater archaeology, and surface surveys on land have mapped the event and its aftermath, and all have now become part of a cultural heritage landscape that featured in a 1994 exhibition at the Cayman Islands

National Museum. Also in that year, Queen Elizabeth II unveiled a commemorative monument overlooking the reefs from a location now known as Queen's View.

See also: Cayman Islands; Underwater Archaeology
References
Leshikar, M. E. 1993. *The 1794 "Wreck of the Ten Sail," Cayman Islands, British West Indies: A Historical Study and Archaeological Survey.* Ph.D. dissertation, Texas A&M University. Ann Arbor, MI: University Microfilms; Leshikar, M. E. 1997. Wreck of the Ten Sail. In J. P. Delgado (ed.). *Encyclopaedia of Underwater and Maritime Archaeology,* p. 416. London: British Museum Press; Smith, R. C. 2000. *The Maritime Heritage of the Cayman Islands,* pp. 152–161. Gainesville, FL: University Press of Florida.

Tobacco

A native plant of the Americas, tobacco was first domesticated around 5,000 years ago. This long association with Amerindian peoples accounts for its wide distribution and the similarity of the magical qualities that it is believed to possess. In pre-Columbian times, tobacco played an important role in religion, mythology, and shamanism among the indigenous inhabitants of the Caribbean region. Most of the information on tobacco and its uses, however, comes from the better-documented tribes of the mainland. The arrival of Christopher Columbus in the Caribbean in 1492 introduced tobacco to the world.

Tobacco was regarded as the gift of the gods among the many cultures of the Island Caribbean and the adjacent mainland of Central and South America. This was partly due to its physical effects on the human body, which were seen as proof of its divine origins and supernatural properties. In ceremonial life, tobacco was seen as bestowing knowledge and understanding on those who consumed it. For shamans, priests, and chiefs, consuming tobacco opened the door to a trance-like state, allowing them to bridge the divide between the physical and spiritual worlds. Under the influence of tobacco, the earth was linked to the sky and the living communed with the ancestors. Tobacco made the shaman light, elevating him in spiritual flight and conveying him along a celestial path of white tobacco smoke to the spirit realm. While such ideas are held in common across the Americas, individual societies had particular beliefs tailored to their own worldview. On the South American mainland, Araweté shamans become translucent after taking tobacco and thereby attract the spirits. Initiate shamans begin to glow under the influence of tobacco and their skin is said to give off shocks like those of an electric eel.

Across the Caribbean, tobacco was consumed in a variety of ways. It was smoked in pipes and as cigars, and rubbed into powder for snuffing. Tobacco juice was drunk and inserted anally through a tube as an enema. While tobacco was often taken in pure form, it could also be mixed with other plants, some of which were powerful hallucinogens in their own right. Practical medicinal values were often combined with spiritual ideas. Tobacco's fumigant properties were well known and were reinforced by indigenous beliefs in the magical powers of human breath, music, and song. Accompanied by ritual chanting, the shaman blows tobacco smoke over food or wounds, thereby purifying it and warding off illness-causing spirits. Tobacco's nicotine content can make it physically and psychologically addictive, and can cause nicotine poisoning if taken to excess. Such afflictions among tobacco-using shamans could be seen as a mark of their close relationship with supernatural powers.

During his second voyage of discovery in 1495, Christopher Columbus observed the local Taíno Amerindians engaged in a religious ritual that involved using a hollow cane to snuff powder from the table-like extension of a carved wood figure known as a *zemí*. He observed how this powder, known as *cohoba*, intoxicated those who inhaled it. It was thought for many years that cohoba was a powdered form of the strong variety of tobacco known as *Nicotiana rustica*. In fact, while the Taíno may have used their distinctive forked snuffing tubes for inhaling tobacco powder, it is now considered that cohoba is a quite different and far stronger hallucinogen.

Tobacco use and the rituals and paraphernalia associated with it probably arrived in the Island Caribbean from South America. Contact with tobacco-using peoples from coastal Mexico and lower Central America is also a possibility. In recent historical times, the Venezuelan Warao traveled by canoe to the southernmost Caribbean island of Trinidad in order to trade hunting dogs for the island's tobacco. A seventeenth-century Trinidadian legend preserves details of the association between the local Chaima tribe, tobacco shamanism, and hummingbirds, which are known to suck the nectar of the tobacco plant. For the Taíno of the northern Caribbean, there was a supernatural connection between cassava and tobacco in a myth that tells of the purifying and intoxicating effects of the shaman's spittle produced by chewing tobacco leaves and that appears to relate to the practice of using tobacco in curing sessions.

When Europeans arrived and observed Amerindians smoking they soon adopted the habit, taking tobacco back to Europe during the mid-sixteenth century, where it was initially used for medicinal purposes. As the habit took hold, demand surged, and in 1624 the first English settlers on St. Kitts began growing tobacco. Soon, tobacco plantations were established by the French and Dutch and worked by African slaves. Tobacco itself was used to pay for slaves in Africa, and in some places became an alternative currency. By the early 1600s tobacco was booming, with 50,000 lbs being imported annually into England alone, and in 1620 the Spanish Crown made tobacco a state monopoly as did the English Crown five years later. By this time also, previous habits of taking tobacco as snuff were being replaced by smoking it in clay pipes. However, overproduction and soil exhaustion led to a dramatic fall in prices by 1660, and tobacco was replaced by sugar as the main plantation crop.

Today, indigenous peoples of the circum-Caribbean mainland still use *Nicotiana rustica* for shamanic purposes. The less powerful *Nicotiana tabacum* is smoked as commercial cigarettes in the African-Caribbean religions of Vodoun in Haiti and Obeah in Jamaica. Among the Cuna of the San Blas islands of Panama, both men and women smoke tobacco in pipes, but only men smoke it in cigar form. Women will smoke to assist in childbirth and men in sessions of ritual divination. On ceremonial occasions held in a specially built house, young Cuna men blow smoke into the faces of the assembly as a purification and blessing.

See also: Cassava (manioc); Cohoba; Columbus, Christopher; Cuna; Dogs; Obeah; Shamanism; Taíno (Arawak); Trinidad and Tobago; Vodoun; Warao; Zemís
References
Butt, A. J. 1956, Ritual Blowing: Taling as a Causation and Cure of Illness among the Akawaio. *Timehri* 35: 37–52; Furst, P. T. 1976, Tobacco: Proper Food for the Gods, *Hallucinogens and Culture.* San Francisco: Chandler and Sharp Publishers.; Knapp, J. 1993. Elizabethan Tobacco. In S. Greenblatt (ed.). *New World Encounters,* pp. 272–312. Berkeley, CA: University of California Press; Robicsek, F. 1978, *The Smoking Gods: Tobacco in Maya Art, History, and Religion.* Norman, OK: University of Oklahoma Press; Wilbert, J. 1972, Tobacco and Shamanistic Ecstasy among the Warao Indians of Venezuela, In Peter T. Furst (ed.). *Flesh of the Gods: The Ritual Use of Hallucinogens,* pp. 55–83, New York: Praeger; Wilbert, J. 1987, *Tobacco and Shamanism in South America,* New Haven, CT: Yale University Press.

Tordesillas (Treaty of)

The Spanish conquest and colonization of the Caribbean, and the Spanish, French, Dutch, and English colonial rivalries that followed, were played out against the background of an astonishing agreement between Spain, Portugal, and the Papacy. In 1494, the Treaty of Tordesillas drew an imaginary line from the North to South Poles through the middle of the Atlantic Ocean, at a point 370 leagues west of the Cape Verde Islands. All lands, peoples, and resources west of this demarcation belonged to Spain, and everything to the east was to be the remit of Portugal. This symbolic and actual dividing up of the world (and the Americas especially) between two Catholic Christian powers had implications for the treatment of indigenous peoples in each of these areas.

The line itself appears to have been drawn originally by Pope Alexander VI in May 1493, bestowing rights of exploration to Spain on everything west of the Azores. When Portugal's King João II disputed this, negotiations between Portugal and Spain's Ferdinand of Aragon and Isabella of Castille led to a reformulated agreement that became the treaty and was signed on 7 June 1494. Attempts to survey and establish the meridian marking the line were soon abandoned, and replaced by an agreement that each country would inform the other of any new discoveries. Two important consequences of the treaty were that the Caribbean was indisputably in the Spanish sphere, and Brazil became Portuguese. Nevertheless, the Island Caribbean soon became a battleground for competing European mercantile powers, whether Catholic or Protestant.

See also: Columbus, Christopher
References
Davenport, F. 1917–1937. *European Treaties Bearing on the History of the United States and Its Dependencies to 1648.* 4 Vols. Vol. 1, No. 9, pp. 84–100. Washington, D.C.: C. E. Nowell, 1945. The Treaty of Tordesillas and the Diplomatic Background of American History. In *Greater America: Essays in Honor of Herbert E. Bolton.* Berkeley, CA: University of California Press.

Tortola (BVI)

Tortola is the largest of the sixty islands that make up the British Virgin Islands (BVI), a British Crown colony. It has a population of about 15,000, the majority of which is of

African descent. Tortola and the other British Virgin Islands were discovered by the Spanish in 1493 but were first settled by the Dutch before becoming British in 1666.

Archaeologically, the BVI received very little attention until investigated by Peter Drewett and his colleagues from University College London during the 1990s. A survey recorded thirty-three sites, though some had been lost to development. A handful of major sites included Brewers Bay, Cane Garden Bay, and Belmont Bay, almost all of which are on the northern side of the island. The pottery discovered is virtually all of the last period of the Ostionoid tradition, and include several *zemí* figures. Several sites, such as Cane Garden Bay, yielded possible Saladoid ceramics, and at Belmont there is some evidence of preceramic occupation. Tortola and its companion islands are located at the eastern extreme of the Taíno cultural area and appear to have served as a strategic crossroads between the Greater Antilles to the west and the Lesser Antilles to the east and south.

Excavations at Paraquita Bay, apart from recovering eighteenth- and nineteenth-century European glass, pottery, and clay pipes, and locating seventeenth- and eighteenth-century sailors' grave markers, also revealed the remains of prehistoric occupation. These included different types of marine resources such as shellfish, grouper, parrot-fish, and snapper, alongside bones of a large rodent known as the hutia (*Isolobodon portoricensis*). The pottery evidence suggests an Ostionoid date.

Excavations at the site of Belmont, originally discovered and briefly investigated by the Virgin Islands Historical Society in 1984 (during which time several zemí figures were found), discovered the remains of a small roundhouse, pottery, and shellfish, as well as a shell vomiting spatula and a shell trumpet.

Pottery evidence included zoomorphic and anthropomorphic *adornos* of the Elenan Ostionoid tradition (A.D. 900 to A.D. 1200), with perhaps some continuity of painted decoration from the preceding Saladoid style. Spindle-whorls and fragments of a cassava griddle were also found.

An alignment of stones with the setting sun on Midsummer Day, associated with nearby Belmont Hill, suggests the possibility that well-documented annual Taíno zemí-worship ceremonies may have taken place here. These ceremonies incorporated the ritual snuffing of hallucinogenic *cohoba* snuff, and may be associated with the discovery of the vomiting spatula and shell trumpet.

See also: Anegada (BVI); Cayman Islands; Cohoba; Elenan; Saladoid; Zemís
References
Drewett, L. 2000. Tortola Material Culture 1: Pottery. In P. Drewett, ed. 2000. *Prehistoric Settlements in the Caribbean: Fieldwork in Barbados, Tortola, and the Cayman Islands,* pp. 127–132. London: Archetype Publications; Drewett, P. 2000. *Prehistoric Settlements in the Caribbean: Fieldwork in Barbados, Tortola, and the Cayman Islands.* London: Archetype Publications; Drewett, P. 2002–2003. Feasting at the Ball Game: the Belmont Project, Tortola, British Virgin Islands. *Archaeology International* 6: 56–59; Drewett, P., and B. Bates. 2000. Settlement Archaeology on Tortola, British Virgin Islands. In P. Drewett, ed. 2000. *Prehistoric Settlements in the Caribbean: Fieldwork in Barbados, Tortola, and the Cayman Islands,* pp. 113–125. London: Archetype Publications; Wing, E. 2000. Economy and Subsistence 1: Animal Remains from Sites on Barbados and Tortola. In P. Drewett, ed. 2000. *Prehistoric Settlements in the Caribbean: Fieldwork*

in Barbados, Tortola, and the Cayman Islands, pp. 147–154. London: Archetype Publications; Hunt, G., and P. Drewett. 2000. Tortola Material Culture II: Stone and Shell Artifacts. In P. Drewett, ed. 2000. *Prehistoric Settlements in the Caribbean: Fieldwork in Barbados, Tortola, and the Cayman Islands,* pp. 133–139. London: Archetype Publications.

Toussaint L'Ouverture

Haiti was controlled by the French between 1697 and 1804 during which time it was the largest sugar producer in the West Indies and was known as Saint Domingue. In the wake of the French Revolution of 1789, tensions between the French plantocracy and their African slaves on the island led to the slaughter of thousands of Europeans in 1791. From the chaos that followed, several ex-slaves rose to prominence as military leaders. One was the charismatic and gifted strategist Francois-Dominique Toussaint (more commonly known as Toussaint L'Ouverture).

Already forty-five years old in 1791, Toussaint's ability as a horseman and inspirational leader saw him rise from his position as a physician to field commander. He joined the Spanish against the French, then the French against the English, who invaded Haiti in 1794 intent on reimposing slavery, which had been abolished the previous year. By 1797, Toussaint was in sole charge of military forces fighting the British, and within a year he had defeated them, forcing a retreat to Jamaica. He then turned his attention to the colored population that had sided with the planters against the freed slaves. His generals, Jean-Jacques Dessalines and Henri Christophe, defeated their forces and massacred some 10,000.

Toussaint was now the effective ruler of Saint Domingue and was recognized by France as governor-general in 1799. In 1801 he invaded and took control of Spanish Santo Domingo, created a new constitution, declared himself governor for life, and signed a trade agreement with the United States. France, however, now ruled by Napoleon, wished to reimpose slavery for economic reasons and sent an army of 23,000 troops under General Leclerc in 1803. Unable to defeat Toussaint's forces on their own soil, Leclerc used deception to persuade the leading black generals to desert their leader. When Toussaint surrendered, expecting a pardon, he was taken prisoner and sent to France, where he died in solitary confinement.

See also: Haiti; Slavery; Sugar
References
Alexis, S. 1949. *Black Liberator: The Life of Toussaint Louverture.* London: Ernest Benn; James, C.L.R. 1994. *The Black Jacobins.* London: Allison and Busby.

Trees, Spiritual Importance of

The spiritual importance of trees in the Caribbean was, and remains, an integral part of a worldview that sees landscape and flora animated by ancestral spirits and supernatural forces. Such views connected native Caribbean societies with their indigenous neighbors in Mesoamerica and South America, and, more recently, with folklore beliefs of African-Caribbean peoples.

Throughout lowland Amazonia, trees possess a rich cosmological symbolism that links mythology with cultural identity. Shamans use trees as spirit-ladders to the celestial world, and many societies believe that trees were once people in mythic time. Similar ideas existed among the Taíno of Hispaniola, where an origin myth records how men who failed to return to their caves before sunrise were turned into myrobolane trees. Gathered together in the forests of the night, the Taíno could hear the spirits talking and received messages from the ancestors.

Speaking-trees were a feature of Taíno belief, not least because their wood was the raw material from which magical *zemí* images and high-status objects were carved. The relationship between trees and material culture in Taíno worldview is illustrated by a unique Spanish account. This describes how, when moved by the wind, a tree called out to a passing Indian who then called on a shaman to conduct certain rites. The tree was then asked what the Indian should do with it. The tree responded, and the man cut it down and carved a zemí statue from it's trunk. In this account, the tree advertised its presence by being moved by the wind more than others nearby—a link perhaps between sacred trees and the spiritual force of hurricanes deified by the Taíno as Guabancex, the "Lady of the Winds."

The practical uses of trees also had their spiritual dimensions, and were linked to zemís in funerary rites. As in South America, where the Warao of coastal Venezuela regarded trees as anthropomorphic spirits and buried their dead in the canoes they had carved from living trunks, so in the Island Caribbean. For the Taíno, tree trunks themselves were recognized as zemís, and some image-zemís carved from them functioned as coffins, containing the remains of dead chiefs. As the archaeologist Peter Roe has observed, to be buried in a wooden zemí was to be symbolically interred within a hollow tree and thus to be assured of rebirth.

Different trees had their own unique physical and supernatural properties for indigenous Caribbean peoples. As the tallest tree in the forest canopy, the ceiba or silk-cotton tree (*Ceiba pentandra*) is the principal spirit tree for many Amazonian societies such as the Shipibo. The ceiba also grows in the Greater Antilles where it may well also have been the preeminent spirit tree. Certainly, ceiba wood was used to make an image of the Taíno god Baibrama found in Jamaica. The belief that the ceiba possessed emetic, diuretic, and antispasmodic properties is illustrative of the wider point that for the Taíno, African-Caribbean peoples, and some Europeans, trees had spiritual and medicinal qualities in their bark and leaves. The Spanish chronicler Oviedo reports that the Taíno considered a decoction of wood from the guayacán tree (*Guaiacum officinale*) was a much-valued cure for syphilis. This tree was also suitable for carving zemí images and high-status items such as an elaborate *duho* stool from western Hispaniola (modern Haiti).

For the Spanish also, trees were an immediate attraction. On arriving in the Caribbean, Christopher Columbus remarked admiringly on the abundance and variety of trees, regarding them as an endless supply of wood from which to make caravels and masts for his ships. Trees also played an ironic role in the Spanish conquest of the Caribbean. When Bartolomé Columbus visited the Taíno chiefdom of Xaraguá on Hispaniola, he was met by a people whose first act was to offer him branches and palms, and, subsequently, prestige gifts made from polished black wood, including fourteen beautifully carved duho stools.

In the centuries that followed European arrival, trees have retained their magical appeal in Caribbean folklore, especially for African-Caribbean peoples. A mix of African spiritual beliefs and perhaps also of remnant Taíno and Carib ideas have revitalized the spiritual importance of trees. In nineteenth-century Jamaica, the descendants of African slaves believed that ceiba trees assembled together at night, and even today it is referred to as a God Tree, associated with snakes, Obeah, and ghosts. In rural Puerto Rico, the ceiba is still revered as a spirit tree. And, for the new invaders of the Caribbean, the palm tree has become an icon of the Caribbean as a tourist destination.

See also: Duhos; Obeah; Warao; Zemís

References
Arrom, J. J. 1989. *Mitología y artes prehispanicas de las Antillas* (Rev. ed.), pp. 46, 49–51. México City: Siglo Veintiuno; Bourne, E. G. 1907. Columbus, Ramon Pané, and the Beginning of American Anthropology. *Proceedings of the American Antiquarian Society* (NS) 17: 310–348; Lehmann, H. 1951. Un 'duho' de la civilisation Taino au Musée de L'Homme. *Journal de la société des Américanistes* (NS) XL, pp. 53–161, & pls. I-III; Rashford, J. 1985. The Cotton Tree and the Spiritual Realm in Jamaica. *Jamaica Journal* 18 (1): 49–57; Saunders, N. J., and D. Gray. 1996. Zemís, Trees, and Symbolic Landscapes: Three Taíno Carvings from Jamaica. *Antiquity* 70 (270): 801–812; Stevens-Arroyo, A. M. 1988. *Cave of the Jaqua: The Mythological World of the Tainos.* Albuquerque, NM: University of New Mexico Press; Wilbert, J. 1977. Navigators of the Winter Sun. In E. P. Benson (ed.). *The Sea in the Pre-Columbian World,* pp. 16–46. Washington, DC: Dumbarton Oaks.

Trinidad and Tobago

The twin-island state of Trinidad and Tobago is the most southerly of the Island Caribbean nations. Trinidad has an area of 4,828 sq km and Tobago, 300 sq km. While Tobago's population of about 55,000 is almost exclusively of African descent, that of Trinidad is more mixed. People of African and Indian descent form some 80 percent of Trinidad's population of approximately 1,300,000, with the rest being of Chinese, Syrian, and European origin. Trinidad still retains much Spanish and French influence in its folk culture though the island itself was formally ceded to Britain in 1802 by the Treaty of Amiens. Trinidad and Tobago became an independent member of the British Commonwealth in 1962 and a republic in 1976.

Archaeologically, Trinidad and Tobago have a rich if divergent heritage that extends back to at least 5000 B.C. Trinidad occupies a unique geographical position by virtue of being the nearest Antillean island to mainland South America. In prehistory, as today, the island is at a strategic crossroads, as it was through Trinidad that the first Amerindians had to pass on their way north by seagoing canoes to Tobago, Grenada, Martinique, Puerto Rico, and beyond.

The first people to settle in Trinidad arrived some 7,000 years ago. They were hunters and gatherers who gained their living by fishing and collecting shellfish in the fertile waters

A typical Caribbean beach on Tobago beneath which lies an Amerindian village (Courtesy Nicholas J. Saunders)

of the sea and inland rivers and lagoons. Today their remains can be seen in shell middens such as the site of Cocal. The earliest evidence for human presence comes from the preceramic site of Banwari Trace that overlooks the Oropuche Lagoon in southern Trinidad. Excavations discovered stone tools of the Ortoiroid tradition dating to ca. 5000 B.C., a hunting-gathering lifestyle, and the earliest human skeleton yet found in the Caribbean. On Tobago, the earliest settlement belongs to a similarly hunter-gatherer society known from the shell midden site of Milford 1 and dated to around 2000 B.C.

It was in southern Trinidad that the first Saladoid peoples entered the Island Caribbean around 300 B.C. from the Orinoco river region in mainland South America. They brought a village life based on agriculture and a host of new skills and religious ideas, including the growing of cassava (manioc), sweet potato, and tobacco, the worship of *zemí* figures, and the growing, spinning, and weaving of cotton. They were also the first to make pottery. The most important Saladoid site on Trinidad is Cedros on the south coast, the type-site of the so-called Cedrosan Saladoid pottery discovered and named by the North American archaeologist Irving Rouse in 1946. Eventually, the Saladoid people sailed north to Tobago where they are known from the sites of Mount Irvine 2 and 4, Sandy Point, and somewhat later at Golden Grove and Lovers' Retreat—the two waves of arrivals dating to the period 100 B.C. to A.D. 250.

Around A.D. 200, a second wave of South American peoples arrived in Trinidad—those of the Barrancoid cultural tradition. They probably absorbed the earlier Saladoid people. The Barrancoid site of Palo Seco is strategically positioned to overlook the Columbus Channel between southern Trinidad and the Venezuelan coast. The extensive shell-midden has different types of pottery including a unique ceramic effigy bottle, and eleven human burials. The most famous Palo Seco–style pottery object is a unique effigy bottle found underwater off the island of Gaspar Grande in northwest Trinidad. During this post-Saladoid Period in Tobago, ceramic evidence indicates that cultural relationships with Trinidad seem to have faded and been replaced by interactions with the peoples of the Lesser Antilles, especially Grenada and St. Vincent.

By around 1000, the Barrancoid peoples had disappeared and a succession of other cultures arrived from South America. During the period 1150 to 1400, Tobago pottery of the so-called Plymouth Complex, such as that found at the site of Great Courland Bay, seems to have affinities with the Suazoid peoples of the Lesser Antilles rather than Trinidad where such ceramics do not occur. During historical times, northeastern Trinidad and the whole of Tobago came under the influence of the Carib peoples from the Windward Islands to the north, though contacts with mainland South America also continued. Historical evidence shows that the Caribs were present in Tobago between the sixteenth and eighteenth centuries but apart from occasional pottery finds that appear similar to those of the Carib Cayo pottery style from the Windward Islands, no unambiguously Carib material has yet been found.

Christopher Columbus discovered Trinidad in 1498 during his third epic voyage, at which time the island had a multiethnic Amerindian population of perhaps 50,000. Arawaks occupied the south coast, the Carib-speaking Carinepagoto lived in the north-

The "Carib Stone" petroglyph at Caurita, northern Trinidad (Courtesy Nicholas J. Saunders)

west, the Yao tribe occupied the Pitch Lake area, and in the east and southeast of the island were the Nepoyo. Tobago too had a mix of two major Amerindian groups—the Carib-speaking Kalina and later the Arawak-speaking Island Caribs (Kalinago). It was at Pitch Lake—a unique natural phenomenon of bubbling and hardened asphalt—that European adventurers like Sir Robert Dudley in 1592 and Sir Walter Ralegh in 1595 first observed and commented on the unusual natural phenomenon and used its bitumen for calking their ships.

The arrival of Europeans had a calamitous effect on these native peoples. Apart from those killed in battle, disease played a major role in depopulating the island, as did the Spanish practice from 1524 of raiding western parts of Trinidad for slaves to work in the pearl fisheries of Maragarita. In 1592, the Spanish took formal possession of Trinidad and by the beginning of the seventeenth century it seems there were only about 4,000 Amerindians left. These survivors were organized into *encomiendas* where they had to pay a tribute of food and labor to the Spanish colonists. When the encomienda system collapsed, the remaining Amerindians were gathered together by Capuchin missionaries in mission villages such as Savaneta, Savana Grande (now Prince's Town), and Arima. Still today, some Roman Catholic churches such as that at Mayo in central Trinidad are built over the remains of Amerindian villages. The legacy of Trinidad's last aboriginal peoples is to be found also in names like Indian Walk and Carib Street in San Fernando, and Mission Street in Tunapuna.

The rich and confusing history of Amerindian Trinidad was complicated further during the nineteenth century when Chaima Amerindians from Venezuela settled in western Trinidad. It was these peoples who told the legend of the village that was swallowed up by Pitch Lake when its inhabitants ignored ancient taboos on hunting hummingbirds, which were regarded as the souls of dead ancestors. From Pitch Lake also have come Amerindian wooden artifacts such as an oval seat, wooden paddles, and a zoomorphic four-legged wooden stool in the shape of an ocelot or jaguar.

Some Venezuelans who journeyed to Trinidad between the 1800s and 1930 came to work on the cocoa estates. Many of these were of mixed Spanish-Amerindian descent and they rejuvenated the Spanish language on the island. These workers, often called Cocoa Panyols, lived between four worlds—the Amerindian, the African, the Spanish, and the British who controlled Trinidad at the time. But it was surely their Amerindian blood that made them such sensitive and effective workers in the cocoa plantations—cocoa was after all an Amerindian gift to the Western world.

The Cocoa Panyols lived and worked in the rural areas of cocoa plantations, especially in the valleys and foothills of Trinidad's Northern Range. Here, in isolated settlements, they maintained their language, customs, and religion, and found work as independent cocoa planters or hired hands. Today, while Panyol culture and their Spanish language have largely disappeared, some customs have survived by filtering into Trinidadian folklore. Most notable are the Spanish songs and music known as Parang, a popular feature of Christmas festivities enjoyed by all Trinidadians.

With the demise of the Capuchin missions by 1850, many of the surviving Amerindians gathered together in Arima where they mixed with the Cocoa Panyols. In some parts of Trinidad there is almost certainly also some blood of the Venezuelan Warao Amerindians who up until 1930 would journey to Trinidad as their ancestors had done for millennia in order to trade parrots, hunting dogs, and hammocks. Trinidad's Amerindian past survives today in Arima where the Santa Rosa Carib Community has been rejuvenated over the past thirty years. The spirituality of the island's Amerindian ancestors finds expression in the annual Roman Catholic festival of Santa Rosa de Lima. The mixed-blood Caribs at Arima are in fact the varied descendants of the Mission Amerindians, Kalipuna Amerindians from St. Vincent, Africans, and the Cocoa Panyols. Nowadays, the ceremonial figurehead is the Carib Queen. One of the key elements of the Santa Rosa Carib Community's claim to Amerindian identity is their production of cassava bread with methods first brought by their Saladoid ancestors over two millennia before. Another is the use of the historical Amerindian chief Hyarima who fought with the Dutch against the Spanish in 1637 and who has become a symbol of the community's emerging Amerindian consciousness. Nearby Arima is the Cleaver Woods National Park, which includes a typical Amerindian *ajoupa* or long-house of the island's Mission Amerindians.

Apart from these links to the Amerindian past, Trinidad and Tobago today has a thriving religious tradition based on African spiritualities. The main feature of this legacy is Orisha/Shango—a religious movement originating with the West African Yoruba peoples who came to the island during the nineteenth century. Orisha/Shango is a vibrant hybrid mix of African beliefs and Roman Catholicism. Orisha focuses on spirit possession, ancestor worship, divination, and herbalism. The main deities are Obatala, Ogun, Shango, Oya, and Oshun. Orisha ceremonies are called feasts and take place in the shrine-leader's yard that is decorated with an altar, flags, and pictures of saints. Ceremonies begin with Christian prayers that give way to drumming and finally (though not always) to spirit possession of a worshipper. Ancestor worship is the central feature of Orisha, and today it is becoming increasingly Africanized as a younger generation seek to stress their African roots.

The tolerant multiethnic nature of Trinidadian society means that other African-derived religions (as well as Hinduism and Christianity) also flourish. There are Rastafarians and Spiritual Baptists and a more recent millennialist group known as the Earth People based on the teachings of Jeanette Macdonald, known as "Mother Earth." She developed the belief that male-dominated Christianity was false and that the world had instead been created by a woman whom embodied the natural world as Earth Mother. In this theology, white people and the modern technological world were the work of Earth Mother's rebellious son (i.e., the Christian God) whereas her way meant going back to nature and living a simple agricultural life. Rastafarians and Spiritual Baptists soon began to join the Earth People in their valley home on Trinidad's north coast. Although the group fragmented after Mother Earth's death in 1984, its importance seems to have been less in her visionary beliefs than the wider sense of a natural, earth-oriented, and fundamentally African way of life.

These various African-derived religious movements have developed against (and contributed to) the background of an equally rich folklore tradition in Trinidad and Tobago. Although it too is mainly of African origin, there is probably an element of Amerindian influence that is now beyond recall. The folklore of Trinidad and Tobago is full of magical beings: Papa Bois is the old man of the forest who has cloven feet, supernatural strength, and acts as guardian of nature's animals and trees against human depredations. He can appear to hunters as a deer and then unexpectedly resume his human form. La Diablesse is the devil woman who can appear either as an old hag or a beautiful young woman. She has the power to entrance men and make them lose their minds and sometimes their lives. Equally dangerous and even more hideous is Mama Dglo, the "mother of the waters," whose lower half is in the shape of an anaconda. She also protects nature against the thoughtless actions of humans. The *soucouyant* is an old woman who sheds her wrinkled skin at sunset and flies as a bright ball of flame in search of an unfortunate victim from whose body she sucks the lifeblood.

The geographical location of Tobago, between the Atlantic and the Caribbean, has led to Tobago having its own distinctive folklore stories. One example is the tale of Gang Gang Sara, the African witch of Golden Lane. Blown from Africa to Tobago by a storm, she searches for her family who had been transported as slaves and finally marries a man who she knew back in Africa. Mermaids also feature, and were believed to play in the island's coastal waters. Tobago mermaids were handsome and richly dressed males who consorted with beautiful fairymaids who lived in rivers and the caves behind waterfalls.

Trinidad and Tobago's rich multicultural array of religious, folkloric, and artistic traditions come together every year in Carnival, known locally as Mas' (short for masquerade). Having its origins with the French immigrant planters of the 1780s at which time it was a white-only festivity, it was taken over by Africans after the abolition of slavery in 1834. The British colonial elite regarded the street festivities and wild behavior with suspicion and banned drumming and the *canboulay* processions of stick-fighting men. Today's Carnival has a well-established structure followed every year and that focuses on competitions between steel bands, costumed participants, calypso singers, and the different Mas' bands, as well as vibrant and colorful street marches.

Carnival Tuesday is the big day that sees the Mas' bands parading from one competition site to another in Port of Spain and the judging of the bands at the grandstand at the Queen's Park Savannah in the center of town. Trinidad Carnival is a mosaic of cultural influences filtered through Trinidad's multicultural past and multiethnic present. This is particularly evident in the dancing and music that is the heart of the celebrations. A central feature of Carnival is that of the "tents"—groups of singers and dancers that practice together and feature a well-known singer such as Lord Kitchener or David Rudder. The so-called Mas' Camps are the bases for the Mas' bands—the main components of Carnival. Each band/camp can have as many as 4,000 members.

Trinidad's unique interactions with modernity are seen to best effect in steel-band music (also known as *pan*). This now internationally known part of Carnival in Trinidad began at the end of the World War II when local people started to use the cut-down ends of oil drums and play ever more sophisticated tunes. Although unpopular at the start, today it is an integral part of the festivities. The key to winning the annual competition is a special ten-minute arrangement whose performance combines virtuoso skills and tight group playing. Calypso singing is another feature of Carnival whose origins lay in the praise songs of West African societies. Known locally as Kaiso, Calypso singers such as the Mighty Sparrow, Chalkdust, and Shadow blend new and old forms and spice their songs with witty and satirical social comment.

See also: Banwari Trace (site, Trinidad); Barrancoid; Caribs; Carnival (Trinidad); Cassava (manioc); Cacao; Cocoa Panyols; Columbus, Christopher; Dudley, Sir Robert; Lovers' Retreat (site, Tobago); Obeah; Orisha/Shango (Trinidad); Ortoiroid; Palo Seco (site, Trinidad); Pitch Lake (site, Trinidad); Ralegh, Sir Walter; Saladoid; Santa Rosa Carib Community (Arima, Trinidad); Shamanism; Tobacco; Warao

References
Besson, G. 1989. *Folklore and Legends of Trinidad and Tobago.* Port of Spain, Trinidad and Tobago: Paria Publishing; Besson, G., and B. Brereton. 1992. *The Book of Trinidad.* Port of Spain, Trinidad and Tobago: Paria Publishing; Boomert, A. 1982. Our Amerindian Heritage. *Naturalist Magazine* 4 (4): 26–61: Woodbrook, Trinidad; Boomert, A. 1996. *The Prehistoric Sites of Tobago: A Catalogue and Evaluation.* Alkmaar, the Netherlands: privately published; Boomert, A. 2000. *Trinidad, Tobago, and the Lower Orinoco Interaction Sphere.* Alkmaar, the Netherlands: privately published; Bullbrook, J. A. 1953. On the Excavation of a Shell Mound at Palo Seco, Trinidad, B.W.I. *Yale University Publications in Anthropology* No. 50. New Haven, CT; Carr, A. T. 1989. *A Rada Community in Trinidad.* Port of Spain, Trinidad and Tobago: Paria Publishing; Chauharjasingh, A. S. 1982. *Lopinot in History,* Port of Spain, Trinidad and Tobago: Columbus

Publishers; Cowley, J. 1996. *Carnival, Canboulay, and Calypso: Traditions in the Making.* Cambridge: Cambridge University Press; de Verteuil, A. 1999. Spirit of the Americas. *Caribbean Beat (BWIA International Airways Magazine)* 40 (November/December): 40–47; de Verteuil, A. and N. J. Saunders. 1998. *The First Trinidadians.* TV documentary. Port of Spain (Trinidad): Pearl and Dean (Caribbean) Ltd.; Eubanks, T. H. 1992. *Sugar, Slavery, and Emancipation: The Industrial Archaeology of the West Indian Island of Tobago.* Unpublished Ph.D. dissertation. University of Florida, Gainesville, FL; Forte, M. C. 2001. *Re-Engineering Indigeneity: Cultural Brokerage, the Political Economy of Tradition and the Santa Rosa Carib Community of Arima, Trinidad and Tobago.* Unpublished Ph.D. dissertation, University of Adelaide, Adelaide, South Australia; Goucher, C., A. Chauharjasingh, and K. Agorsah. 1996. *Site Report on the Fort King George Blacksmith Shop.* Manuscript. Tobago Museum, Fort King George, Scarborough, Tobago; Hardy, J. D. Jr. 1983. Tobago: The Forgotten Island. *Naturalist Magazine* 4 (7): 8–50; Herskovits, M. J., and F. S. Herskovits. 1947. *Trinidad Village.* New York: Alfred A. Knopf; Houk, J. T. 1995. *Spirits, Blood, and Drums: The Orisha Religion of Trinidad.* Philadelphia: Temple University Press; Littlewood, R. 1993. Pathology and Identity: The Work of Mother Earth in Trinidad. Cambridge: Cambridge University Press; Mahabir, N. K. 1985. *The Still Cry: Personal Accounts of East Indians in Trinidad and Tobago During Indentureship, 1845–1917.* Tacarigua, Trinidad and Tobago: Calaloux Publications; Mason, P. 1998. *Bacchanal!: The Carnival Culture of Trinidad.* Philadelphia: Temple University Press; Moodie-Kublalsingh, S. 1994. *The Cocoa Panyols of Trinidad,* London: British Academic Press; Newson, L. 1976. *Aboriginal and Spanish Colonial Trinidad.* New York: Academic Press; Ohm, C. C. 1997. Settlement Patterning on the British Caribbean Island of Tobago. *Historical Archaeology* 3 (2): 93–106; Reyes, E. (ed.). 1978. *The Carib Community.* The Santa Rosa Carib Community, Arima, Trinidad and Tobago.; Rouse, I. B. 1947. Prehistory of Trinidad in Relation to Adjacent Areas. *MAN* (o.s.) 47 (103): 93–98; Taylor, J. 1991. *Trinidad and Tobago: An Introduction and Guide.* London: Macmillan; Warner-Lewis, M. 1991. *Guinea's Other Suns: The African Dynamic in Trinidad Culture.* Dover, MA: The Majority Press; Woodcock, H. I. 1971. *A History of Tobago.* London: Frank Cass.

Troumassoid

The Troumassoid was a late Saladoid Period culture that developed a distinctive identity between A.D. 500 and A.D. 600 and that lasted to ca. 1000, when it was replaced by the Suazoid culture. It appears to have developed differently in the northerly Leeward and Virgin Islands than in the more southerly Windward Islands.

In the Leewards, Troumassoid cultures develop into local Mamorean societies and in the Virgin Islands into the Magens Bay culture. The latter displays a similarity with cultural developments in Puerto Rico and elsewhere in the Greater Antilles where Ostionoid societies are beginning to appear.

In the Windward Islands, a greater variety of Troumassoid culture is apparent both in settlement patterns and material culture. At this time, there were specific adaptations by local societies to their islands that allowed them to expand territorially. This often meant that they depended more on horticulture and fishing and less on gathering. On Martinique, for example, this saw the inhabitants spread out from the northeastern part of the island to occupy the southeastern section.

Troumassoid pottery, like its Saladoid predecessors, was often painted red, black, and white in areas bounded by curving incised lines. Incision alone also was a common decorative technique. However, the Barrancoid influence of artistic modeling seems to have disappeared though other elements remained. As time went on, there was a general decline in quality of ceramics with cruder production and simplified red and black painting. Increasingly, pottery vessels, including cassava griddles, had legs attached or were provided with ring-shaped bases. The footed griddle, despite apparent advantages, seems never to have been adopted by the larger and more complex societies of the Greater Antilles.

It was during Troumassoid times that clay spindle whorls appeared that indicated an increased production of cotton cloth that itself suggests increased growing of cotton and a trade in the finished items. At this time also there was an increased production of salt in southeastern Martinique.

See also: Barrancoid; Martinique; Ostionoid; Saladoid; Suazey/Suazoid

References
Allaire, L. 1977. *Later Prehistory in Martinique and the Island Caribs: Problems in Ethnic Identification.* Ph.D. dissertation, Yale University, New Haven, CT; Allaire, L. 1997. The Lesser Antilles before Columbus, In S. M. Wilson (ed.). *The Indigenous People of the Caribbean,* pp. 25–26. Gainesville, FL: University Press of Florida; Bullen, R., A. K. Bullen, and E. Kirby. 1973. Dating the Troumassée Decorated Cylinder: A Horizon Style. *Proceedings of the Fourth International Congress for the Study of the Pre-Columbian Cultures of the Lesser Antilles, St Lucia 1971,* pp. 197–198; McKusick, M. 1960. *Distribution of Ceramic Styles in the Lesser Antilles, West Indies.* Ph.D. dissertation. Yale University, New Haven, CT; Rouse, I. 1992. *The Tainos: Rise and Decline of the People Who Greeted Columbus,* pp. 127–129. New Haven, CT: Yale University Press; Sutty, L. 1980. A Further Study of the Troumassée Cylinder and its Place in Arawak Society. *Proceedings of the Eighth International Congress for the Study of the Pre-Columbian Cultures of the Lesser Antilles, St Kitts 1979,* pp. 567–577.

Tulum (site, Mexico)

Tulum was an important Mayan city on the east (Caribbean) coast of Mexico's Yucatán peninsula. Together with contemporary Mayan centers at nearby Tancah and on the island of Cozumel, Tulum flourished as a port, trading center, and cult center during the Post-Classic Period (A.D. 1200 to A.D. 1519). Tulum was first seen by Europeans in 1518, during an expedition by the Spanish conquistador Juan de Grijalva. It was rediscovered and partially cleared in 1848 by John Lloyd Stephens and Frederick Catherwood. In the early twentieth century, the archaeologist Samuel Lothrop mapped the ancient city.

Tulum was first occupied around 1200, established probably by a group of the Putun Maya allied to the then-powerful inland Mayan city of Mayapan. It soon developed into a major maritime trading center. The city's 16 acres is enclosed by a defensive wall that has five small entrances and single-roomed watchtowers along the western wall. The eastern side, built on precipitous cliffs, faces the sea, and here a small building may have acted as a beacon, guiding canoes through a gap in the offshore barrier reef. Tulum's architecture is shoddy by comparison with Mayan structures elsewhere, though many of its white limestone buildings were originally covered with brilliantly colored frescoes.

Post-Classic Maya city of Tulum on the Yucatán's Caribbean coast (Courtesy Nicholas J. Saunders)

Situated in the eastern part of the city, adjacent to the sea, is Tulum's ceremonial center. Here lies the Temple of the Diving God, commonly identified either as the Mayan bee deity Ah Macehcabob, or Xuk Ek (the Wasp Star), a Mayan Venus god. Two plumed-serpent columns support the lintels of the doorways, and a stucco figure of the diving god lies in a niche above the doorway. Another important building is the Temple of the Frescoes, originally covered with polychrome murals depicting scenes from Mayan mythology, though executed in central Mexican Mixtec style and dated to ca. 1450. Here, the most famous image is believed to represent the Mayan Moon goddess Ix Chel, who grasps images of the rain god Chac. For the Post-Classic Maya, east was associated with fertility and spiritual rebirth, and the Tulum-Tancah-Cozumel area may well have been a sacred region and perhaps a focus of pilgrimage. Ix Chel was associated with human fertility and childbirth, and her image, the moon, rising out of the sea may have linked together ideas of sky, sea, society, and myth.

The Post-Classic Maya traveled along Central America's Caribbean coasts in seagoing canoes to Honduras, Nicaragua, and Panama. Christopher Columbus encountered one of these canoes laden with trade goods off the Bay Islands of Honduras. Tulum's strategic location also took advantage of canoe trade with inland Mayan centers reached by a network of rivers.

See also: Columbus, Christopher; Cozumel; Maya; Tancah (site, Mexico)

References
Barrera Rubio, A. 1985. "Littoral-Marine Economy at Tulum, Quintana Roo, Mexico." In A. F. Chase and P. M. Rice (eds.). *The Lowland Maya Postclassic,* pp. 50–61. Austin, TX: University of

Texas Press; Lothrop, S. K. 1924. Tulum: An Archaeological Study of the East Coast of Yucatan. *Carnegie Institution Washington Publication 335*. Washington, DC; Miller, A. G. 1977. "The Maya and the Sea: Trade and Cult at Tancah and Tulum." In E. P. Benson (ed.). *The Sea in the Pre-Columbian World*, 97–138. Washington, DC: Dumbarton Oaks; Miller, A. G. 1982. *On the Edge of the Sea: Mural Painting at Tancah-Tulum, Quintana Roo, Mexico*. Washington, DC: Dumbarton Oaks.

Turks and Caicos

The Turks and Caicos comprise a group of some forty islands and cays whose total area is 500 sq km. The combined population is about 13,000 of whom most are concentrated on the islands of Grand Turk, Salt Cay, South Caicos, Grand Caicos, and Providenciales.

The Turks and Caicos were inhabited at the time of Columbus's arrival by the Lucayans, a name deriving from the indigenous term for "island men." They shared a common heritage with the Taínos of the Greater Antilles through the latter's Ostionoid successors, from whom they probably separated around A.D. 600, though maintained trading links into historic times. While evidence suggests they cultivated perhaps fifty different types of plant foods, including sweet and bitter cassava, hunting and fishing were also important—with parrotfish and shellfish being complemented by land mammals. Many Lucayan villages were located between the sea and a swampy area, probably to take advantage of different prey and the availability of fresh water. As with their Taíno cousins, Lucayan villages were often composed of houses arranged in a circle around a central plaza in which dances and public events took place.

The site of Coralie on the northwestern part of Grand Turk is regarded by some archaeologists as an Ostionan colony and has been radiocarbon dated to between A.D. 705 and A.D. 1170. Excavation has revealed pieces of greenstone axes, conch-shell tools, and the remains of green sea turtles, iguanas, snakes, and birds. The pottery, all of which seems to have been imported from the Greater Antilles, belongs to the Ostionan Ostionoid style and includes cassava griddles and the remains of boat-shaped bowls.

On East Caicos are signs of several Lucayan villages together with caves containing petroglyphs, and on Middle Caicos the remains of a Lucayan ballcourt and village have been found by archaeologists at Armstrong Pond. At the end of the fifteenth century, perhaps as many as 80,000 Lucayans inhabited these islands.

The identity and date of the first European to see the islands is still disputed. There appears a strong case for Christopher Columbus having first landed in 1492 on Grand Turk rather than San Salvador in the Bahamas, though it is possible that the first European to see the islands was Juan Ponce de León. More important than this was that within twenty years of the Spanish arrival, the Lucayan people had disappeared from their homeland. They had fallen victim to the Spanish need of slaves to man the gold mines of Hispaniola and to dive for pearls off the island of Cubagua.

During the seventeenth century, traders from Bermuda settled on Grand Turk, Salt Cay, and South Caicos where they were later joined by British loyalists from the American Revolution. During this period, salt became a major commodity and brought great wealth to the Turks and Caicos islands until its demise in the 1960s. Today, the archaeological remains of the salt pan industry can be found nearby Cockburn Town, the only settlement of Grand Turk, which also houses the national museum with its display of the wreck of a sixteenth-century Spanish caravel and pre-Columbian artifacts. Salt Cay also preserves the ruins of the old salt industry, and on West Caicos are the remains of Yankee Town, a colonial-period center of sisal production.

During the nineteenth century, political control of the Turks and Caicos moved to the Bahamas, then Jamaica, then back to the Bahamas (albeit loosely) until in 1972 they became a British Crown colony. Today, cultural festivities center around the period after the August Emancipation Day on Providenciales with carnival processions culminating in the awarding of the title of Miss Turks and Caicos. Cactus Fest takes place on Grand Turk at the beginning of October, and Festarama is celebrated in July on North Caicos.

See also: Coralie (site, Turks and Caicos); Lucayans; Ostionoid; Taíno (Arawak)
References
Arthur, D., et al. 1996. *Our Country, The Turks and Caicos Islands.* London: Macmillan; de Booy, T. 1912. Lucayan Remains on the Caicos Islands. *American Anthropologist* 14 (1): 81–105; Hesse, R. C. and K. Orr Hesse. 1977. The Conch Industry in the Turks and Caicos Islands. *Underwater Naturalist* 10: 4–9; Keegan, W. H. 1997. *Bahamian Archaeology: Life in the Bahamas and Turks and Caicos Before Columbus.* Nassau: Media Publishing; Keith, D. H., J. A. Duff, S. R. James, T. J. Oertling, and J. J. Simmons. 1984. The Molasses Reef Wreck, Turks and Caicos Islands B.W.I.: A Preliminary Report. *International Journal of Nautical Archaeology and Underwater Exploration* 13: 45–63; Mason, O. T. 1877. Jadeite Celts from Turks and Caicos Islands, Also Two Low Wooden Stools. *American Naturalist* 11: 626; Sullivan, S. D. 1981. *Prehistoric Patterns of Exploitation and Colonization in the Turks and Caicos Islands.* Ph.D. dissertation. University of Illinois, Urbana, IL.

Turtles

Sea turtles were a common sight in the Caribbean at the time of Christopher Columbus's arrival in 1492, though overhunting since that time has severely reduced their numbers and today they are protected. There are three main varieties; Loggerhead (*Caretta caretta*), Hawksbill (*Eretmochelys imbricata*), and the Green turtle (*Chelonia mydas*).

Throughout Caribbean prehistory, turtles were a common food resource and probably symbolically important in religious belief and art. While Loggerhead turtles seem never to have been hunted either for their shells (carapaces) or flesh, both Hawksbill and Green turtles appear in archaeological middens across the region. Turtle remains have been found at the Courian Casimiroid site of El Porvenir in the Dominican Republic, dated to between 2630 B.C. and A.D. 240. Turtle imagery is a recurring decorative motif in early Caribbean pottery. Cedrosan Saladoid ceramics have *adornos* in turtle shape, and in at least one instance a beautiful turtle-shaped bowl with zic (zone-incised cross-hatching) incision was made.

The excavation of the Saladoid village at Golden Rock on St. Eustatius revealed a large house that has been interpreted as having supported a roof in the shape of a Hawksbill turtle carapace and that has been called the Sea Turtle House. The possibility that this particular species had a spiritual importance to the inhabitants is supported by the discovery of an up-turned skeleton and carapace of a Hawksbill turtle in the oldest levels of occupation at the site. Turtle remains have also been found on Grenada during the last prehistoric, Suazoid period of aboriginal culture in the Lesser Antilles (ca. A.D. 1000 to A.D. 1450). In the northern Caribbean, the Lucayan peoples would have hunted marine turtles in the shallow banks of the Bahama islands.

The early European explorers and chroniclers commented on the vast numbers of sea turtles they observed while criss-crossing the Caribbean during the fifteenth and sixteenth centuries. Jamaica was described as phenomenally rich in turtles, and at one point Christopher Columbus's ships were delayed off Cuba as they passed through "a sea covered in turtles." Michele da Cuneo, who sailed with Columbus, wrote of the infinite number of huge turtles that were excellent to eat. Christopher Columbus himself during his last voyage (1502 to 1504) passed west of Jamaica and came across several small islands so completely covered with turtles that he christened them the Islas Tortugas (Turtle Islands), though today they have been renamed the Cayman Islands after the Carib term for the American crocodile.

As Europeans explored and colonized the Island Caribbean, they observed how the indigenous peoples hunted and managed turtles. In some areas, fish-hooks were made from turtle carapaces, while in others native peoples caught turtles by using the Ramora fish, which attaches itself to the turtle's carapace with its suckers. The Kuna of the San Blas Islands off the Caribbean coast of Panama used carved-wood turtle-shaped decoys to catch the animals. The sophisticated Amerindian system of turtle management was recorded by Las Casas who observed vast numbers of Green turtles on the southern shores of Cuba at the bay of Xagua (Cienfuegos). He described how the natives kept between 500 and 1,000 turtles at any one time in underwater corrals made of canes fixed into seabed.

See also: Caymen Islands; Cuba; Golden Rock (site, St. Eustatius)

References

Campbell, D. G. 1978. *The Ephemeral Islands.* London: Macmillan; Carr, A. 1967. *So Excellent A Fishe: The Classic Study of the Lives of Sea Turtles.* New York: Charles Scribner's Sons; Carr, A. 1981. Notes on the Behavioral Ecology of Sea Turtles. In K. A. Bjorndal (ed.). *Biology and Conservation of Sea Turtles,* pp. 19–26. Washington, DC: Smithsonian Institution Press; Considine, J. L., and J. L. Winberry. 1978. The Green Sea Turtle of the Cayman Islands. *Oceanus* 21 (3): 50–55; Duncan, D. D. 1943. Capturing Giant Sea Turtles in the Caribbean. *National Geographic* 84 (August): 177–190; Nietschmann, B. 1981. The Cultural Context of Sea Turtle Hunting in the Caribbean and Problems Caused by Commercial Exploitation. In K. A. Bjorndal (ed.). *Biology and Conservation of Sea Turtles.* Washington, DC: Smithsonian Institution Press; Wing, E. S., and E. J. Reitz. 1982. Prehistoric Fishing Economies of the Caribbean. *Journal of New World Archaeology* 5 (2): 13–32.

U

Underwater Archaeology

Underwater archaeology is a type of historical archaeology often combining the study of historical documents with specialized archaeological techniques. Nevertheless, underwater archaeology is also a catchall term that overlaps different types of investigation that to a greater or lesser degree involve working in water. Typically it refers to excavations carried out by scuba-wearing archaeologists who investigate sunken ships, though it can apply equally to such individuals who study the sunken remains of structures that were once on dry land. It also overlaps with what is known as wetland archaeology, the investigation of sites that are totally or partially immersed in shallow water or waterlogged areas such as lagoons and marshland. Evidence from all these different types of underwater archaeology will be dealt with here.

The Caribbean was a major crossing point between Europe and the Americas, and as such saw many losses of European ships, especially during the age of sail between the sixteenth and nineteenth centuries. For this reason, underwater archaeology in the Caribbean has focused almost exclusively on the remains of Spanish, British, French, and Dutch wood-built sailing ships. The normal sequence of events is that initial discovery of a wreck is by divers hunting for treasure, and only later, and selectively, do underwater archaeologists become involved.

Far less common, but equally underwater, are prehistoric sites that lie beneath lakes, lagoons, or the sea, items lost or deliberately placed underwater perhaps for religious reasons, and of course, more recent nineteenth- and twentieth-century shipwrecks. There are even examples of fringe archaeology beneath the waves as in the so-called remains of Atlantis off Bimini Island in the Bahamas.

The Pre-Columbian Period

Prehistoric sites or objects that for whatever reason today lie underwater represent a small but significant and growing proportion of underwater archaeological finds. These include such one-off discoveries as a ceremonial Amerindian canoe found in Stargate blue hole on Andros Island, and the chance 1990 retrieval of a unique Saladoid/Barrancoid effigy-bottle off the coast of northwest Trinidad. Submerged for around 2,000 years, this object has a zoomorphic effigy-face, and may have contained water or beer. Whether it had been lost overboard from an Amerindian seagoing canoe, or was ritually offered to the sea is unknown.

Although individual finds are important, it is the larger underwater or waterlogged sites that are having most impact on pre-Columbian Caribbean archaeology. In the late 1990s, the site of Los Buchillones on Cuba's north coast was investigated and yielded a re-markable collection of wooden artifacts, ranging from the remains of two buildings, palm-leaf thatch, carved dishes, miniature duhos, hafted stone-axes, and *zemís,* as well as stone tools and pottery. So numerous were these wooden artifacts that they doubled the number of such items known for the whole Island Caribbean.

It appears that the buildings were built on stilts over water, and that the high status of finds is suggestive of a rapid abandonment of the village for unknown reasons. Most in-triguing of all was that radiocarbon dates and the finding of a European majolica pottery fragment indicated that Los Buchillones survived into the seventeenth century, over 100 years after it was thought that the last remnants of Cuba's aboriginal inhabitants had dis-appeared. It may be that the site's location had concealed the village from the Spanish, and that Los Buchillones was the longest-surviving Taíno community on Cuba.

Also underwater, but of a quite different nature and significance, is the flooded lime-stone cavern known as the Mantanial de la Aleta in southeastern Dominican Republic (i.e., the eastern half of the island of Hispaniola). Part of a larger ceremonial site known as La Aleta, the cavern's watery conditions have preserved such normally fragile items as basketry, gourds, and an extraordinary range of carved-wood artifacts. As with Los Buchillones, this is a Taíno site, with dates ranging from A.D. 1035 to A.D. 1420; unlike the former site it appears to have been only, or mainly, a ritual and ceremonial location. The quality, diversity, and quantity of the objects that have been retrieved from this cavern sug-gest that the site had a different function from smaller watery caves such as the Cueva de Chico from whose depths have been recovered many fragments and one complete exam-ple of typically Taíno water bottles known as *potizas.*

It seems likely that La Aleta's artifacts were intended as offerings to ancestral spirits. The anoxic environment has preserved wooden items including a small duho, bowls, sev-eral hafts for holding axe-heads, a macana (war club), and fragments of a canoe paddle and crocodile figure, as well as a small bowl interpreted as being associated with the *cohoba* rit-ual. The discovery of decorated gourds engraved with typically Taíno pottery designs is unique, as was the finding of intact basketry.

Across the Caribbean, in Mexico's Yucatán Peninsula, freshwater sources are col-lapsed limestone caves known as *cenotes* into which the local Mayan peoples have ritually deposited a variety of objects. The large cenote at the city of Chichén Itzá appears to have had a mainly religious purpose. Human sacrifices, as well as objects of gold and jade, were cast into the well from a platform located on one of its sides.

Attempts to retrieve these underwater remains have been made, especially by Edward Herbert Thompson, who bought the ancient site in 1894. He spent years dredging the well, recovering large quantities of archaeological materials. Between 1960 and 1961, the

Mexican archaeologist Román Piña Chan, together with the Mexican Explorers and Divers Club (CEDAM), spent four months airlifting hundreds of artifacts to the surface. The most scientifically valuable investigation was carried out by CEDAM in association with Mexico's National Institute of Anthropology and History (INAH). This project saw the well's water level lowered, and a combination of dry-land excavation and scuba diving investigations made. Analysis of the remains indicated that the cenote had two main phases of use, ca. 750 to 1150, and ca. 1250 to 1450.

More recently, it has been discovered that the Yucatán Maya made far more extensive use of cenotes than had been realized. In the underground world of sinkholes, pools, and tunnels that lies beneath the Yucatán and extends out beneath the Caribbean seabed itself, have been found human remains and material culture placed there by the preconquest Maya. Unlike cenotes at great sites such as Chichén Itzá, it seems that rural Mayan communities also made human sacrifices to their gods and ancestors, petitioning for rain and fertility. A so-far unique discovery was of the complete skeleton of a fifty-year-old man, and another of a cache of 115 human skulls, though animal bones and pottery have also been found.

These discoveries have been made by underwater archaeologists from Mexico's INAH as part of an extensive survey prompted by the activities of an increasing number of sport divers who are attracted by the challenging conditions of this environment. As with wreck sites, uncontrolled adventure diving disturbs and sometimes destroys the archaeological context of these underwater sites and their often extraordinary remains. This technologically difficult type of archaeology is a recent development, but promises to add significant insights into the nature of Mayan social and ritual life.

The Colonial and Modern Periods

Despite these important investigations of pre-Columbian remains, underwater archaeology has traditionally focused on sites dating to the historical period of European encounters and colonization. Perhaps the most famous and sustained of these has been at Port Royal, Jamaica. This is no sunken treasure galleon, but the remains of the infamous town near present-day Kingston on Jamaica's south coast that fell into the sea after the earthquake of 1692. Much of the town still lies intact beneath the waves, and has been scavenged for objects since the disaster itself.

In 1981, the Jamaica National Heritage Trust (JNHT) joined forces with Texas A&M University and the Institute of Nautical Archaeology to scientifically investigate the site. For ten years, investigators explored the seventeenth-century remains clustered around the commercial heart of the port along Lime Street. Excavations revealed one building that had three rooms, several of which have been tentatively identified as a tavern and a cobbler's shop. Among the recovered artifacts were silver cutlery, Chinese porcelain, and pewter plates and drinking vessels, as well as the remains of children. A parallel study of historical documents associated with Port Royal revealed the identity of some of the makers and owners of these items, such as Simon Benning, a maker of pewterware.

Although the investigations at Port Royal have yielded spectacular results in objects, knowledge, and techniques, by far the greatest quantity of underwater excavations have dealt with European sailing ships of the late fifteenth to eighteenth centuries. Much effort has been expended trying to locate ships lost during Christopher Columbus's various voyages, such as the *Santa Maria,* the *Mariagalante,* the *La Gallega,* and the *Vizcaína.* Other early wreck sites that have received attention are Highborn Cay Wreck, the St. John's Bahamas Wreck in the Bahamas, and the Bahía Mujeres Wreck off Mexico.

The Bahía Mujeres Wreck is an early-sixteenth-century ship that sank off of Cancun on Mexico's Yucatán coast. Discovered in 1958, it was investigated by amateur and professional Mexican archaeologists who retrieved cannon and anchors, and who identified it as the *La Nicolesa,* which belonged to the Spanish conquistador Francisco de Montejo, the conqueror of the Yucatán. This identification, however, is disputed. The Highborn Cay Wreck, located in the Bahamas, was found in 1965, lies in six meters of water, and is covered with coral. For two years its discoverers—sports divers, not archaeologists—removed many artifacts but kept no records. Subsequent professional excavations revealed the ship to gave been an early-sixteenth-century Spanish ship that may have sunk while at anchor. The St. John's Bahamas Wreck was discovered in 1991 during an official underwater survey of an area north of Grand Bahama Island. It has been identified as a sixteenth-century Spanish ship whose wreckage is spread over more than 150 sq meters of the sea bed. Significantly, much of the internal organization of the wreck has been found intact and this has allowed for the identification of the ship's galley and stowage areas for ordnance and supplies. Measuring over 20 meters in length, the wreck also yielded the remains of numerous earthenware jars, iron spikes, crossbows, swords, and small cannon, as well as an enema syringe, helmet, and glass objects. The pottery is international, coming from Spain, Italy, and Germany, and with some probably also of Mexican Aztec origin.

The wreck of another early-sixteenth-century Spanish ship is named after the Molasses Reef in the Turks and Caicos Islands on which it foundered. The site was discovered in 1976 by treasure hunters but after many illegal activities the Turks and Caicos government called in the Institute of Nautical Archaeology at Texas A&M University. Lying in water less than six meters deep, excavations began in 1982 spread over an area of 6,000 sq meters. The Molasses wreck is unusual inasmuch as it is the earliest that has so far been exhaustively and scientifically excavated. It has yielded Spanish pottery dating to the late fifteenth and early sixteenth centuries, and a variety of ordnance, including cannon, crossbows, and swords.

In all, some ten tons of artifacts were recovered, scientifically studied, and conserved. Insights gained include the fact that some of the ship's stone ballast had probably been loaded in Lisbon, added to other ballast stones from Bristol in England. Although heavily damaged, it was possible to suggest that the ship had had at least three masts, was about nineteen meters long, and probably sank somewhere between 1510 and 1530. It may have been engaged in the trade in native Lucayans who lived on the Turks and Caicos and who were in demand as slave labor in Hispaniola (modern Haiti and the Dominican republic).

The Molasses wreck is a rare exception in the scientific attention it has received, most similar wrecks having been raided by treasure seekers. These include such famous ships as the *Nuestra Señora de Atocha* in the Florida Keys, and the *Nuestra Señora de la Concepción* and the *Nuestra Señora de Guadalupe* off the coast of Hispaniola. The *Atocha* was a Spanish vice-flagship sunk by a hurricane in the Florida Keys in September 1622. It was part of the annual fleet from the Caribbean to Spain. Located in 1985, the wreckage had been spread over a wide area by two severe storms, and gold, silver, and emeralds were recovered as well as three astrolabes. The *Atocha* had been purpose-built in Havana, Cuba, as a treasure galleon, and the shipwright's original contract has since been located in Spain. One unusual find was seeds of the *Bidens alba* plant that subsequently flowered.

The *Nuestra Señora de la Concepción* was another Spanish vice-flagship that sank in 1641. She had foundered on reefs off the north coast of Hispaniola and only 194 of the original 532 people aboard survived. The Spanish Admiral Villavivencio failed in his attempts to salvage the cargo, and four more unsuccessful attempts were made throughout the seventeenth century. In 1687 the English captain William Phips relocated the wreck and retrieved one quarter of a million pounds and a knighthood from the king. Several twentieth-century expeditions failed to find the wreck until the historian Peter Earle found the logbook of Phip's ship and located the Spanish galleon once more. Gold, silver, ceramics, glass, and an astrolabe were found, and in a sealed wooden chest, silver tableware and 1,440 congealed silver coins were found. More positive were the 1987 scientific excavations of the wreck of the *Urca de Lima,* a ship of the 1715 treasure fleet that later became the first underwater archaeological preserve of the state of Florida.

Other important underwater sites include those off Padre Island in Texas—the sunken remains of the treasure fleet that was sailing back to Spain in 1552. Although the Spanish recovered about half of the gold and silver bullion the same year, the wrecks of the *Espiritu Santo,* the *San Andres,* the *San Esteban,* and the *Santa Maria de Yciar* remained. The *Espiritu Santo* was despoiled by treasures seekers, but the *San Esteban* was professionally excavated and the remains put on permanent display at the Corpus Christi Museum of Science and History in Texas.

During the tumultuous sixteenth and seventeenth centuries, the Caribbean was an arena for the competing colonial powers of France, England, Spain, and Holland. Off the coast of the Dominican Republic has been found the *Monte Cristi* wreck, an English-built merchantman that yielded more than 2,000 clay pipes, some of which were made in Amsterdam in imitation of indigenous Amerindian types. Silver coins from Bolivia were also found, and together with many glass beads, suggests the ship may have been trading with Amerindians in North America.

On the reefs surrounding Grand Cayman Island in February 1794, nine ships of a merchant convoy of British ships and HMS *Convert* came to grief during the French Revolutionary Wars. The event became part of Cayman folklore, remembered as the Wreck of the Ten Sail. In the 1990s, a combination of archival research, underwater archaeology, and surface surveys on land mapped the disaster, and all have now become part of a cultural heritage landscape that featured in a 1994 exhibition at the Cayman Islands National Museum. Investigations off St. Ann's Bay in northern Jamaica have discovered what appears to be a ship's graveyard where boats were scuttled. One site, the so-called Reader's Point Wreck, has been professionally excavated and seems to have met its end during the

American Revolutionary War. Its original wood suggested a North American manufacture but its tropical hardwood repairs indicate a life spent plying the tropical waters of the Caribbean.

More recent wrecks also litter the Caribbean sea bed, although few of these have received the attention of the wrecks of earlier centuries. Off the coast of Puerto Rico, the *Alicante* sank in 1881, and in 1898, the *Antonio López* was sunk during the brief Spanish-American War—both have been investigated by the island's Underwater Archaeological Council. More recently, underwater archaeologists have investigated the wreck of the schooner *Geneva Kathleen,* which sank off the Cayman Islands in 1930. On Curaçao, the 1986 discovery of the *Mediator,* a British ship that sank in 1884 at the entrance to Willemstadt harbor, has led to the wreck being mapped, protected from future damage, and prepared as a dive-site for local people and tourists. Displays at the Curaçao Maritime Museum are part of a process that aims to make the *Mediator* a central feature in educating the public about diving, underwater archaeology, and the island's maritime heritage.

Underwater archaeology is a complex and multidisciplinary endeavor. Its different types variously employ the talents of specialists in prehistoric archaeology, historical archaeology, scuba diving, and associated prospecting and conservation technologies. As underwater archaeology in general is in many ways still in its infancy, it promises to add significantly to the knowledge and understanding of the underwater world of the Caribbean's many maritime pasts.

See also: Aesthetic of Brilliance; Cayman Islands; Chichén Itzá Cenote (site, Mexico); Dominican Republic; Key Marco (site, Florida, USA); La Aleta (site, Dominican Republic); Los Buchillones (site, Cuba); Maya; Molasses Reef Wreck; *Nuestra Señora de Atocha,* Wreck of; *Nuestra Señora de la Concepción,* Wreck of; *Nuestra Señora de las Maravillas,* Wreck of; Port Royal (Jamaica); Taíno (Arawak); Ten Sail, Wreck of the; Trinidad and Tobago

References
Arnold, J. B. III. 1978. *The Nautical Archeology of Padre Island: The Spanish Shipwrecks of 1554.* New York: Academic Press; Borrell, C. P. 1983. *Historia y rescate del galeon Nuestra Señora de la Concepción.* Santo Domingo, the Dominican Republic: Republica Dominicana; Coggins, C. C., and O. C. Shane III (eds.). 1984. *Cenote of Sacrifice, Maya Treasures from the Sacred Well at Chichen Itza.* Austin, TX: University of Texas Press; Coles, B., and J. Coles. 1989. *People of the Wetlands: A World Survey.* London: Thames and Hudson; Conrad, G. W., J. W. Foster, and C. D. Beeker. 2001. Organic Artifacts from the Manantial de la Aleta, Dominican Republic: Preliminary Observations and Interpretations. *Journal of Caribbean Archaeology* 2: 1–20; Delgado, J. P. 1997. *Encyclopaedia of Underwater and Maritime Archaeology.* London: British Museum Press; Gould, R. A. 2000. *Archaeology and the Social History of Ships.* Cambridge: Cambridge University Press; Hall, J. L. 1994. Spanish Coins, German Weights, Dutch Clay Pipes, and an English Ship: The 1993 Monte Cristi Shipwreck Project Interim Report. *Proceedings from the 27th Annual Conference on Historical and Underwater Archaeology, Vancouver, British Columbia.* Ann Arbor, MI; Hamilton, D. M. 1986. Port Royal Revisited. *Underwater Archaeology Proceedings from the Society for Historical Archaeology Conference 1986,* pp. 73–81; Keith, D. H. 1987. *The Molasses Reef Wreck.* Ph.D. dissertation, Texas A&M University. Ann Arbor, MI: University Microfilms; Keith, D. H., T. L. Carrell, and D.C. Lacey. 1990. The search for Columbus's caravel *Gallega* and the site of Santa María Belén. *Journal of Field Archaeology* 17, pp. 123–140; Keith, D. H., J. A. Duff, S. R. James, T. J. Oertling, and J. J. Simmons. 1984. The Molasses Reef Wreck, Turks and

Caicos Islands B.W.I.: A Preliminary Report. *International Journal of Nautical Archaeology and Underwater Exploration* 13: 45–63; Leshikar, M. E. 1993. *The 1794 "Wreck of the Ten Sail," Cayman Islands, British West Indies: A Historical Study and Archaeological Survey*. Ph.D. dissertation, Texas A&M University. Ann Arbor, MI: University Microfilms; Link, M. C. 1960. Exploring the Drowned City of Port Royal. *National Geographic Magazine* 117 (1): 151–183; Malcom, C. 1996. The St John's Bahamas Wreck: Interim Report 1: The Excavation and Artefacts, 1991–1995. *Astrolabe-Journal of the Mel Fisher Maritime Heritage Society* 9 (1); Marken, M. W. 1994. *Pottery from Spanish Shipwrecks, 1500–1800*. Gainesville, FL; Mathewson, R. D. III. 1986. *Treasure of the Atocha*. New York; Pendergast, D. M., E. Graham, J. A. Calvera, and M. J. Jardines. 2001. Houses in the Sea: Excavation and Preservation at Los Buchillones, Cuba. In B. A. Purdy (ed.). *Enduring Records: The Environmental and Cultural Heritage of Wetlands*, pp. 71–82. Oxford: Oxbow Books; Peterson, M. 1980. *The Treasure of the Concepción*. Chicago: John G. Shedd Aquarium; Purdy, B. A. (ed.). 1988. *Wet Site Archaeology*. Caldwell, NJ: The Telford Press; Saunders, N. J. n.d. *A Saladoid Effigy Bottle from Gaspare Grande Island, Trinidad*. Unpublished manuscript; Tozzer, A. M. 1957. Chichén Itzá and its Cenote of Sacrifice. *Memoirs of the Peabody Museum* 11–12. Cambridge, MA: Harvard University; Vesilind, P. J. 2003. Watery Graves of the Maya. *National Geographic* 204 (4) (October): 82–102.

V

Vespucci, Amerigo

Amerigo Vespucci (1454–1512) is universally famous yet also a somewhat shadowy figure. A respected Italian navigator and cosmographer, he was widely believed to have made four voyages to the Americas, accounts of which were published as letters that enjoyed great popularity in Europe in the wake of Columbus's discoveries in the New World.

There is scholarly debate today concerning how many voyages Vespucci actually made and how many of his newsletters are original. Some believe that he made two voyages, in 1499 to 1500, and 1501 to 1502, while others consider it more likely he journeyed to the Americas three times. Of his various popular accounts, the *Mundus Novus* (*The New World*) went to fourteen editions between 1503 and 1505. The sensationalist style of this publication has led some specialists to regard it as the work of an unknown writer referred to as the Pseudo-Vespucci. The dramatic style accounts for its popularity, with references to cannibalistic rites and flat-faced, red-skinned Amerindians who eat barbarously and offer their wives to Europeans for sex. There are cunning iguanas as large as goats and giant mice.

Vespucci knew Christopher Columbus, and the two seemed to have gotten on well together. Unlike Columbus, however, Vespucci appears to have been motivated by true scientific curiosity. Between 1500 and 1502, he appears to have written three letters to his friend Lorenzo di Pier Francesco de' Medici, in which he described his voyages to the New World, one for the Spanish and two for the Portuguese. Taken together, they represent a balanced and sober description of the Amerindians of Brazil and the Caribbean coast of Venezuela, the latter country named by Vespucci after seeing Amerindians on the offshore island of Aruba living in houses built on piles over the water (i.e., little Venice).

In measured tones, Vespucci described the incredible "newness" of the Americas, its minerals, spices, herbs, plants, and animals. He noticed fragrant trees that didn't shed their leaves, brilliantly colored birds, and giant snakes that slithered along the ground. He noticed the bright new stars and unfamiliar constellations of the southern night sky. He became fascinated with the region's human inhabitants, although he was clearly no humanitarian, taking natives by force to sell as slaves back in Spain.

Nevertheless, his interest in the Amerindians grew more insistent, and during his second voyage he stayed in a "Cannibal Village" for a month. Uniquely for the time, he did not preach, chastise, or try to engage in trade or gain commercial advantage, but simply observed and tried to understand. His account has the immediacy of the eyewitness, commenting on how the natives slept in midair (in hammocks), decorated themselves with bones and colored pebbles, and pierced their cheeks and lips. His shrewd and enquiring spirit extended to seeing Amerindian warfare as a new and unfamiliar type of conflict, motivated neither by profit nor territorial gain. He also noted the incredible variety of Amerindian languages and idioms. It is largely the measured and serious tone of these accounts that has persuaded some specialists that other sensationalist letters were not written by Vespucci.

Whatever the truth about Vespucci's voyages and letters, the Italian's name has been enshrined in the history of the world. In 1506, Martin Waldseemüller, a German draughtsman and printer, published a work called the *Cosmography* to accompany a globe and world map in which he called Columbus's New World "America." He explained that this part of the world "was discovered by Americus Vesputius . . . for which reason I do not see why anyone would rightly forbid calling it (after the discoverer Americus . . .) 'Amerige,' that is, land of Americus, or 'America.'"

See also: Columbus, Christopher; Las Casas, Bartolomé de; Oviedo y Valdés, Gonzalo Fernández de

References

Amerigo and the New World: The Life and Times of Amerigo Vespucci. 1955. New York; Gerbi, A. 1986. *Nature in the New World: From Christopher Columbus to Gonzalo Fernández de Oviedo,* pp. 35–49. Pittsburgh: University of Pittsburgh Press; Pohl, F. J. 1944. *Amerigo Vespucci, Pilot Major.* New York: Columbia University Press.

Vodoun

Vodoun, also spelled Vodun, and more widely known as voodoo, is one of several syncretistic African-Caribbean religions, the other main ones being Santería and Obeah. Vodoun, whose name derives from the word for spirit or deity in the African Fon language, developed as a mixed religion, drawing on the rituals, beliefs, and imagery of African spiritualities and Roman Catholicism. Today in the Caribbean, Vodoun is mainly known from Haiti, the western half of the island of Hispaniola.

In the late nineteenth century, Vodoun was characterized as a bizarre and evil cult in the sensationalizing book *Haiti or the Black Republic*. With its stories of cannibalism and human sacrifice, this account struck a chord in the Western imagination and later provided Hollywood with the basis for inaccurate interpretations and inventions such as zombies, nightmarish murders, and voodoo dolls. Such popular misconceptions are still widespread today.

Vodoun originated during the sixteenth century, when Europeans brought large numbers of West African peoples to the Caribbean to work as plantation slaves, cultivating cotton and tobacco, but mainly sugar. Many of these slaves belonged to the Yoruba peoples of modern Nigeria, and they brought with them elements of their indigenous African spiritual beliefs. These beliefs were part of a philosophy of life that saw the natural world as animated by powerful gods and spirits with whom humans had to converse through ritual prayers, offerings, music, and dancing. Vodoun gods are understood as multidimensional spirit beings, intimately concerned with the earthly life of humans. At this fundamental level, African beliefs shared much with the shamanistic ideas of indigenous Amerindian peoples. In its early years of development, Vodoun, like Santería and Obeah, was influenced to an unknown degree by contacts between escaped African slaves and the remnants of the indigenous Amerinidan societies with whom they initially took refuge on some islands.

When Africans first arrived in the Caribbean they were usually baptized into the Christian faith as Roman Catholics. One way of retaining their spiritual beliefs, ethnic identity, and personal dignity was to hide their religious ideas in plain view with those of their new masters. On Haiti, slaves came from many West African societies such as Fon, Ibo, Nago, and Yoruba—whose homeland lay in what was then Dahomey but is now parts of Togo and Benin. Their African beliefs mingled with elements of Christianity, thereby creating the syncretic religion known today as Vodoun. On Haiti, the colonial French rulers saw that Vodoun was being used to give strength and unity to the slaves from disparate African groups and persecuted all suspected of practicing the new religion by mutilation and burial alive. This led to the practitioners of Vodun going underground, and eventually, under the direction of Vodoun priests, to the beginnings of a revolt that lasted from 1791 to 1804 when the country finally won independence from France.

As with any religion of the oral tradition, Vodoun is a flexible set of beliefs with different groups adopting variations of ritual observance and spirit powers. At the heart of Vodoun are the spirits known as *loa,* a name meaning "mystery" in the Yoruba language. As with Santería, the omnipresent but invisible lord of creation is called Olorun, and one of his subordinates, known as Obatala, was charged with creating the world and all its inhabitants. There are many lesser spirits, which include Agwe, spirit of the sea; Erinle, spirit of the forest; Ogou Balanjo, spirit of healing; Ogun, spirit of war and iron working; Ezili, female spirit of love; and Zaka, spirit of agriculture. Particularly important is Danballah, the Great Serpent, whose prototype was the African python who represented the gods and whose hissing is the basis of the secret language of Haitian Vodoun. Aida-Wedo, the rainbow, is the wife of Danballah, and one manifestation of Ezili. She is also a serpent, whose colorful body is a decorative motif on Vodoun temples. Facilitating communication between the deities and their human devotees is Legba, the cosmic gate-keeper associated with the rising sun. Also known as Papa, he is identified with St. Peter, visualized as an old man with a walking stick, and regarded as the patron of sorcery and the "master of crossroads."

The Loa, like their Santería counterparts, the orisha, are associated with Christian saints, and the initiates of Vodoun believe that every human being has a *met tet,* or "master of the head" that corresponds to a Christian's patron saint. Vodoun believers also regard the soul of a person as having two halves—the *gros bon ange* is the "big guardian angel," and the *ti bon ange,* or "little guardian angel." It is the latter that detaches itself from the body during sleep and when a person is possessed by the loa—at which times it is prey to those who practice evil.

A distinct category of the loas is that of the *guedes,* spirits ambiguously associated with death, debauchery, graves, sexuality, and the protection of children. There exist sects of Vodoun adherents who worship only guedes, and a common image is that called Baron Samedi, which represents the spirit as a man dressed as an undertaker in tall hat and tailcoat wearing dark glasses, smoking a cigar, and drinking alcohol.

As would be expected, there are many similarities between Vodoun and Santería. In both religions, spirits are contacted during rituals with the aim of petitioning for health, luck, and food, especially at times of birth, marriage, and death. Vodoun rites seek to persuade the loa to look kindly on humans, and to protect them from ever-present evil. In return, Vodoun disciples offer animal sacrifices and other gifts. These are typically a chicken, goat, sheep, or dog, whose offering is believed to banish the loa's hunger. Often misrepresented as pointless cruelty, such sacrifices serve rather to consecrate food that is then eaten by the worshippers, and symbolically consumed by the gods, spirits, and ancestors.

There are two main types of Vodoun rites, though a host of lesser ones. Rada is a traditional African variety, which sees devotees dressed in white accompanied by rhythmic chanting that symbolizes what are called the three atmospheres of the sun—the chromosphere, photosophere, and the heart of the sun itself. The loas associated with Rada are mainly of a beneficent type. Petro was probably invented during slavery days on Haiti, and may take its name from the Spanish Vodoun priest Don Juan Felipe Pedro. It is a more violent ritual that conjures dangerous loa, and sees followers paint their faces red—possibly an influence from Haiti's remnant Amerindian population at the time the slaves arrived.

In Vodoun's magical philosophy, the symbolic homeland is the city of Guinee or Ife. While there is an Ife in Nigeria, the sacred Vodoun city is a mythical place—the location where the loa's visionary revelations first appeared to their worshippers. All aspects of life, from agriculture to Vodoun's magical art of divination are judged to have come from Guinee, whose location east of the Caribbean associates it also with the powers of the rising sun.

Vodun priests are known as *houngan* if they are male, *mambo* if female. Those who wish to become members of Vodoun are called *hounsis.* They practice their rites in a temple known as *hounfor* in whose center is the *poteau-mitan,* a pole around which the gods and spirits gather to talk to their devotees. There is also an altar decorated with images of Christian saints, candles, and jars believed to contain the spirits of the ancestors, as well as charms, flags, and other sacred paraphernalia. The hounfor is decorated with bright colorful motifs that symbolize Vodoun's loa. While some may be permanent, others are temporary, created for a single ceremony as, for example, designs made in cornmeal or flour. These designs, known as *veves,* are emblematic of the loa—such as a coffin for Baron Samedi or a serpent for Danballah. These images draw the loa to the ritual center of the hounfor. There are also evil sorcerers known as *caplatas*—those who practice what is sometimes called "left-handed Vodoun"—though houngans and mambos keep to beneficial "white" magic.

Common fears of Vodoun, magnified by gory Hollywood misrepresentations, focus on zombies—the so-called living dead who have risen from the grave and wander the land under the influence of an evil sorcerer. Yet, while most Haitians believe in zombies, only a handful have ever seen one. In reality, the zombie is more likely to be a social outcast condemned to living beyond the local community for some offense, and whose solitary life then attracts superstitious stories. Equally possible according to recent research, is that the victims of evil spells have their food or body secretly spiked with powerful hallucinogenic drugs, whose effects can lower heart rate and sometimes mimic death, from which the dead then miraculously recover—sometimes when already in the coffin. Such rare events would nevertheless make an enduring impression.

See also: Haiti; Obeah; Orisha/Shango (Trinidad); Santería; Shamanism

References
Blier, S. 1995. *African Vodun: Art, Psychology and Power.* Chicago: Chicago University Press; Cosentino D. (ed.). 1995. *Sacred Arts of Haitian Vodun.* UCLA Fowler Museum of Cultural History, Los Angeles; Davis, W. 1986. *The Serpent and the Rainbow.* New York: Simon and Schuster; Desmangles, L. G. 1992. *The Faces of the Gods: Vodou and Roman Catholicism in Haiti.* Chapel Hill: University of North Carolina Press; McAlister, E. A. 2002. *Rara: Vodou, Power, and Performance in Haiti and Its Diaspora.* Berkeley, CA: University of California Press; Métraux, A. 1959. *Voodoo in Haiti.* New York: Schocken Books; Rigaud, M. 1985. *Secrets of Voodoo.* San Francisco: City Lights Books.

W

Warao

The Warao are a Circum-Caribbean people who live mainly around the Orinoco river delta in eastern Venezuela. Archaeologically, they are probably the descendants of the Archaic age inhabitants of the region. The name Warao derives from words that mean "the canoe people," and indicates the central importance of canoes in their social, economic, and religious life.

Canoe travel, and its associated spiritual and technological aspects, was crucially important in the many migrations of South American peoples into the Island Caribbean. Today, the study of Warao society, its worldview, and philosophy of life and death, throws much light on the distinctive way of life of these earlier prehistoric voyagers. The Warao themselves consider canoe travel an ancient tradition. In 1595, Sir Walter Ralegh commented on their canoe journeys from the mainland to Trinidad.

Warao religious life centers on shamans known as *wishiratu,* who smoke tobacco to contact the spirit world in order to divine, cure and send illness, foretell the future, and guarantee the fertility of the earthly world. A special category of light shamans is believed to derive its power from the supreme Tobacco Spirit. Shamans cross from the earthly world to the celestial realm over a magical bridge of tobacco smoke to converse with powerful spirit beings. In Warao creation mythology, the great Creator Bird of Dawn made the House of Tobacco Smoke from nothing, and within it tobacco shamanism was born and bestowed consciousness and identity on all Warao.

Smoking tobacco to make spiritual journeys is paralleled by the physical journeys made to acquire the tobacco leaf. Well into the twentieth century, Warao paddled their canoes to Trinidad in order to trade hunting dogs and bird feathers for western goods. In ancient times also it is probable that such journeys were made to acquire tobacco, which grows on the island but not in the swampy lowlands of the Orinoco river delta. Crossing the open sea to Trinidad, Warao navigators encountered the cosmic serpent—Hahuba, the great Snake of Being—a huge water monster that manifests itself as long serpent-like upwellings of alluvium from the Orinoco. After crossing the Gulf of Paria, they beached their canoes and walked to the sacred mountain named after their god Na'barima, from whose flanks they obtained magic white crystals. Such journeys and

The southernmost tip of the Caribbean at Cedros in Trinidad. The Columbus Channel separates the island from mainland South America (just visible) from where the Warao sailed to Trinidad. (Courtesy Nicholas J. Saunders)

their spiritual associations provide a glimpse of a world whose origins stretch back into prehistory, possibly to Saladoid times.

The association of Warao canoe-making technology with tobacco shamanism and spirituality is indicated in their beliefs about canoes. For the Warao, trees are regarded as anthropomorphic spirit beings in ways that recall Taíno beliefs about carved-wood *zemís*. Just as the Taíno sometimes buried their dead in such zemís, so the Warao use their canoes as coffins, symbolically wrapping the deceased in a life-giving tree and linking the voyage of the spirit with those of living men.

See also: Music; Pitch Lake (site, Trinidad); Shamanism; Tobacco; Trinidad and Tobago; Zemís

References

Wilbert, J. 1972. Tobacco and Shamanistic Ecstasy Among the Warao Indians of Venezuela. In P. T. Furst (ed.). *Flesh of the Gods: The Ritual Use of Hallucinogens,* pp. 55–83. New York: Praeger; Wilbert, J. 1975. Eschatology in a Participatory Universe: Destinies of the Soul among the Warao Indians of Venezuela. In E. P. Benson (ed.). *Death and the Afterlife in Pre-Columbian America,* pp. 163–190. Washington, DC: Dumbarton Oaks; Wilbert, J. 1977. Navigators of the Winter Sun. In E. P. Benson (ed.). *The Sea in the Pre-Columbian World,* pp. 16–46. Washington, DC: Dumbarton Oaks; Wilbert, J. 1979. Geography and Telluric Lore of the Orinoco Delta. *Journal of Latin American Lore* 51 (1): 129–210; Wilbert, J. 1987. *Tobacco and Shamanism in South America.* New Haven, CT: Yale University Press; Wilbert, J. 1997. Illuminative Serpents: Tobacco Hallucinations of the Warao. *Journal of Latin American Lore* 20 (2): 317–332.

Water Island (USVI)

Water Island in the U.S. Virgin Islands has a variety of archaeological sites, ranging from prehistoric Amerindian to historical-period plantations and World War II fortifications. A detailed record and assessment of these different types of sites was undertaken in 1998 in response to the U.S. government's decision to transfer ownership of the island to the private sector.

Water Island was occupied by Danish settlers in 1672, and throughout the following eighteenth century saw several small plantations come and go, such as those belonging to Elias Baile and Jean Renaud (a free mulatto). By the early nineteenth century, a plantation known as Carolina Lyst had seventeen slave houses, and another known as La Providence had sixteen slave cabins. Perhaps because of Water Island's marginal geographic location, an unusual number of so-called free colored plantation owners existed, a fact that offers unique opportunities for historical archaeological investigations who normally excavate plantations owned by white Europeans.

Among the sites identified and investigated in 1998 were the prehistoric late Saladoid (ca. A.D. 600) and Elenan (ca. A.D. 800) remains at Elephant Bay, a shell midden yielding various dates between A.D. 500 and A.D. 1200 at Banana Bay, and several historical-period sites from the eighteenth to nineteenth centuries at Carolina Point Plantation, Ruyter's Bay, and Tamarind Tree Bay. More modern are the coastal defenses built by the U.S. government in the early 1940s. The most notable of these is Fort Segarra, which included underground bunkers, barracks, and gun emplacements as well as a dock and associated infrastructure.

References

Anderson, D. G. 2000. Archaeology in the Caribbean: The Water Island Archaeological Project. *http://www.cr.nps.gov/seac/wi/wi-report.htm*; Wild, K., and D. G. Anderson. 1992. *An Archaeological Inventory and Assessment of Cultural Resources on Water Island, U.S. Virgin Islands.* Tallahassee, FL: Southeast Archaeological Center (SEAC), National Park Service.

White-on-Red Pottery (W-O-R)

White-on-red (W-O-R) pottery takes its name from the white painting on the red slip of finely made Saladoid pottery. It is one of two types of ceramic that make up the pottery assemblage known as Cedrosan Saladoid by archaeologists—the other being zic ware, whose name comes from the zone-incised cross-hatching surface decoration. Although W-O-R has a lighter-colored paste than zic, the two share common materials, shapes, and designs, with white paint defining the former, and cross-hatching characterizing the latter.

W-O-R predominates over zic ware in the overall frequency of the two types of Cedrosan Saladoid pottery. According to Irving Rouse, it appears to derive from the preceding Ronquinan Saladoid tradition from mainland South America, and its main shape is the bell-shaped bowl to which are attached D-shape strap handles. Zoomorphic and

Typical white-on-red pottery fragments from the Saladoid Period—the first ceramics to appear in the Caribbean (Courtesy Nicholas J. Saunders)

anthropomorphic heads sometimes emerge from the rims and lugs of these vessels though their significance is not known.

W-O-R and red-painted pottery can incorporate orange and black color in their painted designs. There is also a distinctive incision where straight or curved lines outline the painted areas or themselves form areas of incised decoration. A variation of this in Puerto Rico is known as Huecan Saladoid, and features incised designs cut through the red slip in which white paint is rubbed.

See also: Cedros (site, Trinidad); Saladoid; Zic Pottery

References

Roe, P. G. 1989. A Grammatical Analysis of Cedrosan Saladoid Vessel Form Categories and Surface Decoration: Aesthetic and Technological Styles in Early Antillean Ceramics. In P. E. Siegel (ed.). *Early Ceramic Population Lifeways and Adaptive Strategies in the Caribbean,* pp. 267–382. Oxford: British Archaeological Reports International Series 506; Rouse, I. 1992. *The Tainos: Rise and Decline of the People Who Greeted Columbus,* pp. 82–89. New Haven, CT: Yale University Press.

Z

Zemís

The Taíno of Hispaniola, Puerto Rico, and Jamaica, regarded the world as animated by spiritual forces and articulated by myth. Spirits of ancestors and nature resided in every feature and phenomenon of their natural and social worlds. The worship, propitiation, and manipulation of these all-powerful, ever-present, and dangerously ambivalent spirit beings through ritual was a distinctive feature of Taíno life. In this fundamentally shamanic way of thinking about the world, spiritual powers were embodied in material culture and especially in the range of images known as *zemís*.

Zemís have been recognized as representations of formal deities, such as Yúcahu, the supreme god, or Atabey, his mother, whose image is carved onto a stone slab that is part of the ballcourt at Caguana in Puerto Rico. Anthropomorphic examples often depict grotesque human beings with male or female genitalia prominently displayed. Zoomorphic examples took the form of birds, frogs, turtles, and sometimes vegetable foods like cassava. Other types took the form of more abstract and geometric designs applied as decoration on rocks and artifacts. However, zemís were also personifications of spiritual forces and were believed to reside in trees, rocks, caves, rivers, and other features of the landscape.

In general, the term zemí has been applied to artifacts of different forms and sizes made from wood, stone, shell, pottery, cotton, gold (*guanín*), and human bones. Some were the anthropomorphic carved-wood containers in which the remains of dead chiefs were kept. Cotton zemí figures may have been representations of images seen during visions or dreams. These were sometimes elaborated with bead decoration as figurative elements on belts or took the form of a doll-like figure. The most famous example of the latter is the beaded zemí figure in the Pigorini Museum in Rome. This extraordinary object is a wooden frame covered with cotton and ingeniously decorated with glass beads and disks made from shell and seeds. The front shows a carved-wood face sewn onto the body with two mirror earrings made of Venetian glass. The rear view shows a Janus-like appearance with the back of the head depicting a zoomorphic face/mask, this time with eyes as well as earrings made from Venetian glass in the form of mirrors. This Taíno zemí is clearly a hybrid artifact incorporating Amerindian and European materials though

whether it represents a chief, shaman, or ancestor is not known. Zemí images were carved as petroglyphs on rocks and cave walls, painted on the body, and used as decorative designs on utensils, jewelry, and such elite items as the ceremonial stools known as *duhos*.

The wide but indiscriminate use of the term "zemí" often adds confusion to attempts to understand the true nature of these important objects and designs. This is illustrated by the common naming of one type of artifact as a zemí—the distinctive triangular "three-pointer stone"—an identification that embodies the idea of spirit in one easily recognized artifact yet sometimes makes it more difficult to recognize other, not-so-obvious objects as zemís. These three-pointer objects of stone or shell are common archaeological finds and may have originated in northern South America where early examples have been discovered in archaeological excavations.

It seems that the smaller examples of these artifacts appeared in the Island Caribbean during the earliest Saladoid occupation of the region and they became larger and more ornate as time went on, reaching their most sophisticated forms during the Taíno Period. This may reflect changes in the organization of the societies that produced them, with smaller ones perhaps being personal items in an egalitarian society and the larger ones designed more for public ritual characteristic of the complex societies of Taíno chiefdoms. Stone three-pointers are the only stone artifacts that were mentioned by Spanish chroniclers during the fifteenth century.

Three-pointer zemís often appear like miniature mountains in profile and sometimes this shape is an integral part of a larger figure of a god or spirit. The diagnostic shape of these artifacts has been interpreted as symbolizing mountain peaks and volcanoes, women's breasts, conical shells, and manioc shoots. The majority are undecorated and those that are incised carry designs of stylized human faces, animals, or fantastical half-human–half-animal creatures that recall the imagery experienced during shamanistic trances. A classification of four main types of three-pointers had been developed by the early twentieth century by the archaeologist Jesse Walker Fewkes: Type 1 feature realistic and stylized images of anthropomorphic and zoomorphic shape; examples of Type 2 are generally larger and carry an anthropomorphic face; Type 3 consists of anthropomorphic and zoomorphic shapes but characteristically features an upward-pointing face or mouth, and Type 4 can be shell or coral as well as stone and are simple undecorated examples.

Early Spanish sources indicate that some Taíno zemís were clearly more esteemed than others but it is not clear to what extent there was a hierarchy of such objects based either their raw materials, ownership, or imagery. It seems reasonable to suggest that while archaeologists are interested in the materiality of these objects, for the Taíno a zemí was spirit, not object.

The role of zemís in Taíno culture has similarities and differences to the role of sacred images in their ancestral South American homeland. In Amazonia it is shamans who possess magical objects, including images of stone and wood, to contact the spirit world whereas among the Taíno, it appears that every person possessed at least one zemí, with some individuals owning possibly as many as ten. It is probable that owning certain types of zemís was a privilege of the chiefs (caciques) and a marker of their elite status. It could be that as Taíno society developed in complexity, chiefs were vying for status with each other using larger and more decorative zemís as symbols of individual prestige. Alternatively, zemís were perhaps less a symbol of a chief's power than a representation of his supernatural allies to be venerated, respected, and consulted.

Whatever the truth, zemís were well-looked after, regularly supplied with food and drink and sometimes rubbed with cassava. Once a year a great ceremony took place in which the villagers dressed in their best ornaments and cotton clothing and sang songs extolling the virtues and powers of the chief's zemís. They entered the special house where the zemís were kept while the chief sat outside beating a drum. As they continued praising the spirits, the images themselves were draped with cotton clothing and offered baked cassava bread. As the festivities reached a climax, fragments of cassava bread were distributed to the heads of families who kept them for a year as a magical protection against misfortune.

Representations of gods and spirits as zemí images were used to decorate religious paraphernalia including the elite duho stools, and as stand-alone sculptural figures. They were kept in niches or on tables within their dwellings, sometimes in separate buildings, and later—perhaps to hide them from the Spanish—secreted away in caves. Spanish records indicate they could be inherited, traded, given away, or even stolen. Each zemí appears to have had a name and a biography that outlined its origin, character, and powers, often recited as a song in the musical celebrations known as *areítos*. Depending on their shape and whether or not they were representations of gods or spirits, each zemí had different powers that ranged from promoting successful childbirth to guaranteeing success in war or enhancing agricultural fertility when buried in the manioc fields known as *conucos.*

Of all the different types of zemís, those made from wood may have been preeminent due to the spiritual and medicinal importance of trees in Taíno life. Supporting this view are references to a category of hollow speaking zemís that appear to have functioned as oracles. They were regarded by the Spanish as a method for hoodwinking the gullible by ventriloquy with a shaman speaking through a tube. The close relationship between trees, wood, zemís, and Taíno spirituality is evident in a story of the Taíno of Hispaniola where it was said that wooden zemís were only made from trees occupied by the spirit of a dead chief. Such associations are explicit in an account recorded by Dr. Chanca, Columbus's physician during his second voyage. He noted that when a native passed a tree it called out to him to bring a shaman. When the shaman came he conducted certain rituals and asked the tree whether it wanted to be cut down and given a house. The tree agreed, whereupon it was felled and a zemí carved from it.

The role of wooden zemís in demonstrating the shaman's or chief's ability to link everyday life and the spirit realm is seen in the *cohoba* ceremony. By snuffing hallucinogenic cohoba powder, Taíno chiefs and shamans communed with spirits, particularly ancestors resident within trees and wooden zemís. After ritual purification by vomiting (with specially made carved-bone spatulas) cohoba was snuffed through polished wood or cane tubes from a round wooden table, an integral part of a class of anthropomorphic and zoomorphic wooden zemí figures. Columbus himself witnessed such a ritual in 1495, noting the wooden paraphernalia and the resulting intoxication of the participants.

Wooden zemís have been found throughout the Greater Antilles, in the Dominican Republic, Haiti, Cuba, and most recently in a cave in Jamaica. Here were found an anthropomorphic figure with male genitals possibly representing *Baibrama,* a deity associated with cassava cultivation and consumption, a bird with a typical cohoba-snuffing table on its back, and a small utilitarian spoon-like object with an anthropomorphic handle in the shape of a human head. Both the anthropomorphic figure and the ladle may originally have had shell and/or gold (guanín) inlays.

Zemís were a vital and integral part of Taíno spiritual and social life. Uniquely Caribbean, each possessed its own powers and symbolism depending on its material, shape, and stories attached to it by its owner. Zemí objects were associated with the cosmic powers of the universe, ancestral spirits, and the acquisition and maintenance of political power by the elite. Zemí designs bestowed supernatural power on artifacts and landscape alike. It should be remembered, however, that zemís were not only cultural objects made to contain or represent spiritual power but were also present in the everyday features of the natural world.

See also: Cohoba; Duhos; Gold; Shamanism; Taíno (Arawak); Trees, Spiritual Importance of
References
Arévalo, M. G., and L. A. Chanlatte Baik. 1976. *Las espátulas vómicas sonajeras de la cultura Taína.* Santo Domingo, the Dominican Republic: Fundación García Arevalo; de Hostos, A.

1923. Three-Pointed Stone Zemis or Idols from the West Indies: An Interpretation. *American Anthropologist* 25 (1): 56–71; Fewkes, J. W. 1891. On Zemis from Santo Domingo. *American Anthropologist* 4: 167–174; Fewkes, J. W. 1907. *The Aborigines of Port Rico and Neighboring Islands,* pp. 111–133, 197–202. Washington, DC; García Arévalo, M. 1994. Zemis en pierre, trigonolithes. In J. Kerchache (ed.). *L'art des sculpteurs taïnos: Chefs-d'oeuvre de Grandes Antilles précolombiennes,* pp. 186–221. Paris: Musée du Petit Palais; Helms, M. W. 1986. Art Styles and Interaction Spheres in Central America and the Caribbean: Polished Black Wood in the Greater Antilles, *Journal of Latin American Lore* 12 (1): 25–43; Loven, S. 1935. *The Tainan Culture of the West Indies,* pp. 598–602, 628–633. Goteborg, Sweden; McGinnis, S. 1997. Zemi Three-Pointer Stones. In F. Bercht, E. Brodsky, J. A. Farmer, and D. Taylor (eds.). *Taíno: Pre-Columbian Art and Culture from the Caribbean,* pp. 92–105. New York: The Monacelli Press; Oliver, J. R. 1997. The Taino Cosmos. In S. M. Wilson (ed.). *The Indigenous People of the Caribbean,* pp. 140–154. Gainesville, FL: University Press of Florida; Pané, Fray R. 1999. *An Account of the Antiquities of the Indians.* José Juan Arrom, ed. Durham, NC, and London: Duke University Press; Rouse, I. 1948. Zemis. In J. H. Steward (ed.). *Handbook of South American Indians 4,* pp. 535–537. Washington, DC: Smithsonian Institution; Rouse, I. 1992. *The Tainos: Rise and Decline of the People Who Greeted Columbus,* pp. 118–123. New Haven, CT: Yale University Press; Saunders, N. J., and D. Gray. 1996. Zemís, Trees, and Symbolic Landscapes: Three Taíno Carvings from Jamaica. *Antiquity* 70 (270): 801–812; Taylor, D., M. Biscione, and P. G. Roe. 1997. Epilogue: The Beaded Zemi in the Pigorini Museum. In F. Bercht, E. Brodsky, J. A. Farmer, and D. Taylor (eds.). *Taíno: Pre-Columbian Art and Culture from the Caribbean,* pp. 158–169. New York: The Monacelli Press; Vega, B. 1987. *Santos, shamanes y zemíes.* Santo Domingo, the Dominican Republic: Fundación Cultural Dominicana.

Zic Pottery

Zic pottery takes its name from the zone-incised cross-hatching that is the diagnostic feature of these ceramics. It is one of two types of pottery that make up the ceramic assemblage called Cedrosan Saladoid by archaeologists—the other being known as white-on-red (W-O-R) painted ware. Zic ware is defined by its cross-hatched decoration, and W-O-R by its white lines painted onto a red slip. Zic decoration is most often found on hemispherical bowl-shaped vessels with D-shaped handles and unpainted modeled-incised lugs. The painted designs of the W-O-R are here replaced by incised hatching and broad incised designs. Although zic ware is less frequent than W-O-R within the Cedrosan Saladoid tradition, the two types share materials and shapes and are regarded as variations on a single theme.

Irving Rouse considers that zic ware originated on the South American mainland, probably in Amazonia, where pottery with similar decoration and of the same age has been found. The first Saladoid peoples took it with them in their migrations into the Island Caribbean around 300 B.C. Zic ware may have been a special type of pottery used in ritual activities and perhaps also as trade items. It has been found at the important sites of Punta Candelero on mainland Puerto Rico and Sorcé on the offshore island of Vieques. Archaeologists regard this material as forming a subseries of Cedrosan Saladoid ceramics, designating it as Huecan Saladoid. While this pottery assemblage lacks the usual accompanying W-O-R painted ware component, its makers rubbed white or red paint into the typical zic incisions. Zic pottery disappeared around A.D. 400.

See also: Cedros (site, Trinidad); Hueca, La (Puerto Rico); Saladoid; White-on-Red Pottery (W-O-R)

References
Rodríguez, M. 1989. The Zoned Incised Crosshatch (Zic) Ware of Early Precolumbian Ceramic Age Sites in Puerto Rico and Vieques Island. In P. E. Siegel (ed.). *Early Ceramic Population Lifeways and Adaptive Strategies in the Caribbean,* pp. 249–266. Oxford: British Archaeological Reports International Series 506; Roe, P. G. 1989. A Grammatical Analysis of Cedrosan Saladoid Vessel Form Categories and Surface Decoration: Aesthetic and Technological Styles in Early Antillean Ceramics. In P. E. Siegel (ed.). *Early Ceramic Population Lifeways and Adaptive Strategies in the Caribbean,* pp. 267–382. Oxford: British Archaeological Reports International Series 506; Rouse, I. 1992. *The Tainos: Rise and Decline of the People Who Greeted Columbus,* pp. 82–89. New Haven, CT: Yale University Press.

Bibliography

This bibliography has been designed to fulfill several different purposes. First, it is a consolidation of the references that appear after each of the individual entries in the encyclopedia. Second, it offers many references that do not appear associated with individual entries. Caribbean archaeology, anthropology, and history are vast subjects with references often appearing in places that are difficult to find and access for students as well as the general reader. This bibliography has therefore been developed as a tool in its own right, to gather together in one place a comprehensive selection of important references and thereby facilitate the tracking down of items for further reading. It is hoped that this bibliography will serve as a stand-alone feature of the book, and offer a uniquely comprehensive and up-to-date list for all who wish to explore the many pasts of the Caribbean.

Aarons, G. A. 1989. The Lucayan duhos: 1828–1988. *Journal of the Bahamas Historical Society* 11, pp. 3–11.
———. 1994. Tainos of Jamaica: The Aboukir zemis. *Jamaica Journal* 25 (2), pp. 11–17.
Abrahams, R. D., and J. F. Szwed. 1983. *After Africa*. New Haven, CT: Yale University Press.
Acheson, P. 1998. *The Best of the British Virgin Islands*. Two Thousand Three Associates.
———. 1999. *The Best of St. Thomas and St. John, U.S. Virgin Islands*. Two Thousand Three Associates.
Adams, C. D. 1976. *Caribbean Flora*. Sunbury-upon-Thames: Nelson.
Addeo, S. J. Unknown. *Caribbean Journal: This Land Bonaire: Various Thoughts on Different Things from the Island of Bonaire in the Southern Caribbean Sea*. Broken Star Press.
Agorsah, E. K. 1991. Evidence and Interpretation in the Archaeology of Jamaica. *Report of the Archaeological-Anthropological Institute of the Netherlands Antilles* 9 (1), pp. 2–14.
———. 1992. Archaeology and the Maroon Heritage in Jamaica. *Jamaica Journal* 24(2):2–9.
———. 1993. Vibrations of Maroons and Marronage in Caribbean History and Archaeology. In *Proceedings of the 15th International Congress for the Study of Pre-Columbian Cultures of the Lesser Antilles, Puerto Rico 1995:* p. 401.
———. 1993. Archaeology and Resistance History in the Caribbean. *The African Archaeology Review* Vol. 11, pp. 175–196.
———. 1993. Nanny Town Excavations: Rewriting Jamaica's History. *Jamaican Geographer* (Newsletter of the Jamaican Geographical Society) 8 (1), pp. 6–8.
———. 1994 (ed). *Maroon Heritage: Archaeological, Ethnographic and Historical Perspectives*. Kingston: Canoe Press.
———. 1994. Archaeology of Maroon Settlements in Jamaica. In K. Agorsah (ed.), *Maroon Heritage: Archaeological, Ethnographic and Historical Perspectives,* pp. 163–187. Kingston: Canoe Press.
———. 1999. Ethnoarchaeological Consideration of Social Relationship and Settlement Patterning among Africans in the Caribbean Diaspora. In J. B. Haviser (ed.), *African Sites Archaeology in the Caribbean,* pp. 38–64. Princeton, NJ: Markus Wiener Publishers.
Ahee, C. B. 1992. *The Carib Community of Arima, Five Hundred Years after Columbus*. Unpublished Caribbean Studies dissertation. University of the West Indies, St. Augustine, Trinidad.
Aikhenvald, A. Y. 1999. The Arawak Language Family. In R. M. W. Dixon and A. Y. Aikhenvald (eds.), *The Amazonian Languages,* pp. 64–106. Cambridge: Cambridge University Press.

Aitken, R. 1917. Puerto Rican Burial Caves. *Proceedings of the XIX International Congress of Americanists,* pp. 224–28.

Akenson, D. H. 1997. *If the Irish Ran the World: Montserrat, 1630–1730.* McGill–Queens University Press.

Alegría, R. E. 1974. *Discovery, Conquest and Colonization of Puerto Rico 1493–1599.* San Juan, PR: Colección de Estudios Puertorriqueños.

———. 1978. *Las primeras representaciones gráficas del Indio Americano, 1493–1523.* San Juan, PR: Centro de Estudios Avanzados de Puerto Rico y El Caribe, Instituto de Cultura Puertorriqueña.

———. 1979. Apuntes para el estudio de los Caciques de Puerto Rico. *Revista del Instituto de Cultura Puertorriqueña* Vol. 85, pp. 25–41.

———. 1983. *Ball Courts and Ceremonial Plazas in the West Indies.* New Haven, CT: Yale University Publications in Anthropology No. 79.

———. 1986. *Apuntes en torno a la mitología de los Indios Taínos de las Antillas Mayores y sus orígenes Suramericanos.* San Juan, PR: Centro de Estudios Avanzados de Puerto Rico y El Caribe, Museo del Hombre Dominicano.

———. 1988. *Temas de la Historia de Puerto Rico.* San Juan: Centro de Estudios Avanzados de Puerto Rico y El Caribe.

———. 1997. An Introduction to Taíno Culture and History. In F. Bercht, E. Brodsky, J. A. Farmer, and D. Taylor (eds.), *Taíno: Pre-Columbian Art and Culture from the Caribbean,* pp. 18–33. New York: The Monacelli Press.

Alegría, R. E., H. B. Nicholson, and G. R. Willey. 1965. The Archaic Tradition in Puerto Rico. *American Antiquity* Vol. 21(2), pp. 113–121.

Alegría-Pons, J. F. 1993. *Gaga y Vudu en la Republica Dominicana.* San Juan, PR: Editiorial Chango-Prieto.

Alexis, S. 1949. *Black Liberator: The Life of Toussaint Louverture.* London: Ernest Benn.

Allaire, L. 1977. *Later Prehistory in Martinique and the Island Caribs: Problems in Ethnic Identification.* Ph.D. dissertation, Yale University.

———. 1980. On the Historicity of Carib Migrations in the Lesser Antilles. *American Antiquity* Vol. 45, pp. 238–45.

———. 1981. The Saurian Pinean Eye in Antillean Art and Mythology. *Journal of Latin American Lore* 7 (1), pp. 3–22.

———. 1984. A Reconstruction of Early Historical Island Carib Pottery. *Southeastern Archaeology* Vol. 3, No. 2, pp. 121–33.

———. 1985. The Archaeology of the Caribbean. In C. Flon (ed.), *The World Atlas of Archaeology,* pp. 370–1. Boston: C. K. Hall.

———. 1987. Some Comments on the Ethnic Identity of the Taino-Carib Frontier. In R. Auger et al. (eds.), *Ethnicity and Culture,* pp. 127–33. Calgary: Archaeological Association, University of Calgary.

———. 1991. Understanding Suazey. *Proceedings of the Thirteenth International Congress for Caribbean Archaeology, Held in Willemstadt, Curaçao, on July 24–29, 1989,* pp. 715–28.

———. 1994. *Historic Carib Site Discovered!* Winnipeg: University of Manitoba, St. Vincent Archaeological Project Newsletter.

———. 1997a. The Lesser Antilles before Columbus. In S. M. Wilson (ed.), *The Indigenous People of the Caribbean,* pp. 20–28. Gainesville: University Press of Florida.

———. 1997b. The Caribs of the Lesser Antilles. In S. M. Wilson (ed.), *The Indigenous People of the Caribbean,* pp. 177–85. Gainesville: University Press of Florida.

———. 1999. Archaeology of the Caribbean. In F. Salomon and S. B. Schwartz (eds.), *The Cambridge History of the Native Peoples of the Americas: Volume III, South America, Part 1,* pp. 668–733. Cambridge: Cambridge University Press.

———. 2003. Agricultural Societies in the Caribbean: The Lesser Antilles. In J. Sued-Badillo (ed.), *General History of the Caribbean: Volume 1. Autochthonous Societies,* pp. 195–227. Paris: UNESCO.

Allaire, L., and M. Mattioni. 1983. Boutbois et le Goudinot: Deux gisements acéramiques de la Martinique. *Proceedings of the Ninth International Congress for the Study of Pre-Columbian Cultures of the Lesser Antilles, Dominican Republic, August 2–8, 1981,* pp. 27–38.

Allen, R. M. 1991. The Folk Material Culture Related to Food Quest and Food Production in Curaçao Culture. *Proceedings of the Thirteenth International Congress for Caribbean Archaeology,* pp. 462–76.

Alleyne, M. C. 1988. *Roots of Jamaican Culture.* London: Pluto Press.

Almarales, B. 1994. *The Santa Rosa Carib Community from 1974–1993.* Unpublished Caribbean Studies dissertation. University of the West Indies, St. Augustine, Trinidad.

Alonso, E. M. 1995. *Cueva del Arriero: Un estudio arqueológico sobre comunidades aborígenes del occidente de Cuba.* Havana: Editorial Academia.

Alonso, O. M. 1950. Discovery of a Pre-Columbian Gold Figurine in Cuba. *American Antiquity* Vol. 15, No. 4, pp. 340–341.

Alvarez Nazario, M. 1977. *El influjo indígena en el español de Puerto Rico.* Río Pedras: Editorial de Arqueología y Etnología.

———. 1996. Arqueología lingüística. In *Estudios modernos dirigidos al rescate y reconstrucción del arauaco taíno.* Río Pedras: Editorial de Arqueología y Etnología.

Anderson, A. 1979. *An Account of the Bituminous Lake or Plain in the Island of Trinidad.* Philosophical Transactions of the Royal Society 79, pp. 65–70.

Anderson, C. L. G. 1971. *Life and Letters of Vasco Nuñez de Balboa, Including the Conquest and Settlement of Darien and Panama.* Westport, CT: Greenwood Press.

Anderson-Córdova, K. 1990. *Hispaniola and Puerto Rico: Indian Acculturation and Heterogeneity, 1492–1550.* Ph.D. dissertation, Yale University. Ann Arbor: University Microfilms.

Andrade, M. J. 1930. *Folk-Lore from the Dominican Republic.* Memoirs of the American Folklore Society 23. New York: American Folklore Society.

Andrews, K. 1978. *The Spanish Caribbean Trade and Plunder, 1530–1630.* New Haven, CT: Yale University Press.

Andrews, K. R. (ed.), 1959. *English Privateering Voyages to the West Indies, 1588–1595.* Hakluyt Society Publications, 2nd series, 111. Cambridge.

Annezer, J. C., D. Bégot, and J. Manlius. 1980. L'univers magico-religieux: l'example de la Guadeloupe. In J-C Bonniol (ed.), *L'histoire antillais,* pp. 459–478. Fort de France, Martinique: Dajani.

Anonymous. 1896. Jamaica wooden images in the British Museum. *Journal of the Institute of Jamaica* 2 (3), pp. 303–4.

Anonymous. 1910. *Caribbeana: Miscellaneous Papers Relating to the History, Genealogy, Topography and Antiquities of the British West Indies.* London: Mitchel, Hughes and Clarke.

Anonymous. 1922. *Guide to the Collections from the West Indies.* Indian Notes and Monographs. Museum of the American Indian, Heye Foundation. New York.

Anonymous. 1989. Student Finds 11,000 Year Old Artifact. *Trinidad Guardian,* 6 December, p. 25. Port-of-Spain.

Anonymous. 2002. New Miskito Nation Announced! *Nicaragua Network Hotline,* 29 July 2002. http://www.NicaNet@afgi.org

Antczak, A. 1999. *Late Prehistoric Economy and Society of the Islands off the Coast of Venezuela: A Contextual Interpretation of the Non-Ceramic Evidence.* Ph.D. dissertation, Institute of Archaeology, University College London.

Antczak, M. 2000. *"Idols" in Exile: Making Sense of Prehistoric Human Pottery Figurines from Dos Mosquises Island, Los Roques Archipelago, Venezuela.* Ph.D. dissertation, Institute of Archaeology, University College London.

Antczak, M., and A. Antczak. 1987. Algunas consideraciones sobre la identificación del material arquelógico de concha: El caso del *Strombus gigas* en el Archipélago de Los Roques, Venezuela. *Boletín*

Asociación Venezolana de Arqueología 4, pp. 28–37. Anthony, M. 1988. *Towns and Villages of Trinidad and Tobago.* Port of Spain: Trinidad Circle Press.

————. 1997. *Historical Dictionary of Trinidad and Tobago.* London: The Scarecrow Press.

Anthony, P. A. B. 1986. The Encounter between Christianity and Culture: The Case of the 'Kele' Ceremony in St. Lucia. In M. Kremser and K. R. Wernhart (eds.), *Research in Ethnography and Ethnohistory of St. Lucia,* pp. 103–120. Vienna: Ferdinand Berger and Söhne.

————. 1996. Changing Attitudes towards African Traditional Religion and the Implications for Afro-Caribbean Tradition in St. Lucia. In M. Kremser (ed.), *AyBoBo—African Caribbean Religions, part 1, Kulte/Cults,* pp. 69–84. Vienna: WUV-Universitätsverlag.

Arciniegas, G. 1955. *Amerigo and the New World: The Life and Times of Amerigo Vespucci.* New York.

Arens, W. 1979. *The Man Eating Myth:Anthropology and Anthropophagy:* New York: Oxford University Press.

Aretz, I. 1982. Indigenous Music of Venezuela. *The World of Music* 25 (2), pp. 22–35.

Arévalo, M. G., and L. A. Chanlatte Baik. 1976. *Las espátulas vómicas sonajeras de la cultura Taína.* Santo Domingo: Fundación García Aravalo.

Armstrong, D. V. 1978. *Archaic Shellfish Gatherers of St. Kitts, Leeward Islands: A Case Study in Subsistence and Settlement Patterns.* Unpublished M.A. thesis, UCLA.

————. 1985. An Afro-Jamaican Slave Settlement: Archaeological investigations at Drax Hall. In T. A. Singleton (ed.), *The Archaeology of Slavery and Plantation Life,* pp. 261–287. San Diego, CA: Academic Press

————. 1990. *The Old Village and the Great House: An Archaeological and Historical Examination of Drax Hall Plantation, St. Ann's Bay Jamaica.* Urbana: University of Illinois Press.

————. 1999. Archaeology and Ethnohistory of the Caribbean Plantation. In T. A. Singleton (ed.), *I, Too, Am America: Archaeological Studies of African-American Life,* pp. 173–92. Charlottesville: University Press of Virginia.

————. 2001. A Venue for Autonomy: Archaeology of a Changing Cultural Landscape, the East Community, St. John, Virgin Islands. In P. Farnsworth (ed.), *Island Lives: Historical Archaeologies of the Caribbean,* pp. 142–164. Tuscaloosa and London: The University of Alabama Press.

Armstrong, D., and K. Kelly. 2000. Settlement Patterns and the Origins of African Jamaican Society: Seville Plantation, St. Ann's Bay, Jamaica. *Ethnohistory* 47 (2), pp. 369–97.

Armstrong, I. 2001. *Robert Skeoch: Cruzan Planter.* Harris and Connor.

Arnold, J. B., III. 1978. *The Nautical Archeology of Padre Island: The Spanish Shipwrecks of 1554.* New York.

Arnoux, P. 1976. Anse Marguerite, dit "Gros Cap," Guadeloupe. *Proceedings of the Sixth International Congress for the Study of Pre-Columbian Cultures of the Lesser Antilles,* Point-à-Pitre, Guadeloupe, July 1975, pp. 21–7.

Arrivillaga Cortés, A. 1990. La música tradicional Garífuna en Guatemala. *Latin American Music Review* 11 (2), pp. 251–280.

Arrom, J. J. 1983. La lengua de los Taínos: Aportes lingüísticos al concocimiento de su cosmovisión. In *La Cultura Taína: Las culturas de América en la epoca del Descubrimiento,* pp. 53–66. Madrid: Biblioteca del V Centenario.

————. 1989. *Mitología y artes prehispanicas de las Antillas.* Revised edition. México: Siglo Veintiuno.

————. 1992. La Lengua de Los Taínos: Aportes Lingüísticos al Concocimiento de su Cosmovisión. In *Las Culturas de Américas en el Época del Descubrimiento.* Madrid: Turner.

————. 1992. Fray Ramón Pané, Discoverer of the Taíno People. In R. Jara and N. Spadaccini (eds.), *Amerindian Images and the Legacy of Columbus,* pp. 266–90. Minneapolis: University of Minnesota Press.

————. 1997. The Creation Myths of the Taíno. In F. Bercht, E. Brodsky, J. A. Farmer, and D. Taylor (eds.), *Taíno: Pre-Columbian Art and Culture from the Caribbean,* pp. 68–79. New York: The Monacelli Press.

Arrom, J. J., and M. García-Arévalo. 1986. *Cimmarón.* Série Monográfica 18. Santo Domingo: Fundación García-Arévalo.

————. 1988. *El murciélago y la lechuza en la cultura Taína.* Serie Monográfica 24. Santo Domingo: Fundación García Arévalo.

Arroyo, M., L. Blanco and E. Wagner (eds.). 2000. *El Arte Prehispanico de Venezuela.* Caracas: Editiorial Ex Libris.

Arroyo Gómez, A. 1991. *Bibliografía del folklore de Puerto Rico.* San Juan, PR: Instituto de Cultura Puertorriqueña.

Arthur, C. 2002. *Haiti in Focus: A Guide to the People, Politics and Culture.* Interlink Publishing Group.

Arthur, D., et al. 1996. *Our Country, the Turks and Caicos Islands.* London: Macmillan.

Artschwager, E., and E. W. Brandes. 1958. *Sugar Cane: Origin, Classification Characteristics, and Description of Representative Clones.* U.S. Department of Agriculture Handbook 122. Washington, DC: Government Printing Office.

Ashburn, P. M. 1947. *The Ranks of Death: A Medical History of the Conquest of America.* New York: Coward-McCann.

Assee, S. 1972. When the Pitch Lake Swallowed up the Chaimas. *Trinidad Guardian,* July 31: Port of Spain, Trinidad.

Atiles, J. G., and E. Ortega. 2001. Un Sitio Llamado el Manantial de la Aleta. *Boletin del Museo del Homebre Dominicano* 30, pp. 33–54.

Attema, Y. 1976. *St. Eustatius: A Short History of the Island and Its Monuments.* De Walburg Pers Zutphen. Holland.

Austerlitz, P. 1977. *Merengue: Dominican Music and Dominican Identity.* Philadelphia, PA: Temple University Press.

Avery, G. 1997. *Pots as Packaging: The Spanish Olive Jar and Andalusian Transatlantic Commercial Activity, 16th–18th Centuries.* Ph.D. dissertation, University of Florida.

Ayensu, E. S. 1981. *Medicinal Plants of the West Indies.* Algonac, MI: Reference Publications Inc.

Bachiller y Morales, A. 1883. *Cuba primitiva: origen, lenguas, tradiciones e historia de los indios de las Antillas Mayores y las Lucayas.* (2nd ed.). Havana: Libreria de Miguel de Villa.

Bacon, P. R. 1978. *Flora and Fauna of the Caribbean: An Introduction to the Ecology of the West Indies.* Port of Spain: Key Caribbean.

Baer, R. H. 2002. *Anomaly 27 and the S.S. Copenhagen Shipwreck Site: A Study in Underwater Archaeology and Maritime History.* Unpublished M.A. thesis, School of Archaeological Studies, University of Leicester.

Baker, B. J., and G. J. Armelagos. 1988. The Origin and Antiquity of Syphillis: Palaeopathological Diagnosis and Interpretation. *Current Anthropology* 29 (5), pp. 703–37.

Baksh-Soodeen, R. 1986. Amerindian Toponyms of Trinidad: Linguistic Legacy of Past Amerindian Occupation. Paper Presented at Sixth Biennal Conference of the Society for Caribbean Linguistics and the American Dialect Society, August 27–30, 1986. University of the West Indies, St. Augustine, Trinidad.

Balderston, D., M. Gonzalez and A. M. Lopez. 2000. *Encyclopedia of Contemporary Latin American and Caribbean Cultures.* (3 vols). London: Routledge.

Balf, T. 2003. *The Darkest Jungle: The True Story of the Darien Expedition and America's Ill-Fated Race to Connect the Seas.* Crown Publishing.

Baluntansky, K., and M-A Sourieau. 1998. *Caribbean Creolization: Reflections on the Cultural Dynamics of Language, Literature and Identity.* Gainesville, FL: University Press of Florida.

Banbury, R. T. 1895. *Jamaica Superstitions, or the Obeah Book.* Kingston: de Souza.

Barbotin, M. Les sites archéologiques de Marie-Galante (Guadeloupe). *Proceedings of the Third International Congress for the Study of Pre-Columbian Cultures of the Lesser Antilles, Grenada 1969,* pp. 27–44. Grenada.

————. 1987. *Archéologie Antillaise: Arawaks et Caraïbes.* Pointe-à-Pitre: Parc Nationale Guadeloupe.

Barka, N. F. 1988. *Archaeology of the Jewish Synagogue Honen Dalim, St. Eustatius, Netherlands Antilles.* St. Eustatius Archaeological Research Series No. 4. Department of Anthropology, College of William and Mary, Williamsburg, VA.

————. 1993. *Archaeological Survey of Sites and Buildings, St. Maarten, Netherlands Antilles, 1*. St. Maarten Archaeological Research Series No. 3. Department of Anthropology, College of William and Mary, Williamsburg, VA.

————. 1996. Citizens of St. Eustatius 1781: A Historical and Archaeological Study. In R. Paquette and S. Engerman (eds.), *The Lesser Antilles in the Age of European Expansion,* pp. 223–238. Gainesville: University of Florida Press.

————. 1996. *Archaeology of the Dutch Elite: The Country Estate of Johannes de Graff at Concordia, St. Eustatius, Netherlands Antilles.* St. Eustatius Archaeological Research Series No. 9. Department of Anthropology, College of William and Mary, Williamsburg, VA.

Barker, D., and S. Balfour. 1988. Afro-Caribbean Agriculture: A Jamaican Maroon Community in Transition. *The Geographical Journal* Vol. 154 (2), pp. 98–208.

Barnes, A. C. 1974. *The Sugar Cane.* New York: John Wiley.

Barr, K. W. 1968. *An Introduction to the Amerinidan Pre-History of Trinidad and Tobago.* Port of Spain: Trinidad and Tobago Historical Society Publication 1045.

Barrera Rubio, A. 1985. Littoral-Marine Economy at Tulum, Quintana Roo, Mexico. In A. F. Chase and P. M. Rice (eds.), *The Lowland Maya Postclassic,* pp. 50–61. Austin: University of Texas Press.

Barrett, L. 1974. *Soul-Force: African Heritage in Afro-American Religion.* New York: Anchor.

————. 1976. *The Sun and the Drum: African Roots in Jamaican Folk Tradition.* London: Heinemann.

————. 1977. *The Rastafarians: The Dreadlocks of Jamaica.* Boston: Beacon Press.

————. 1988. *Rastafarians: Sounds of Cultural Dissonance.* Boston: Beacon Press.

Barton, G. T. 1953. *The Prehistory of Barbados.* Barbados: Advocate Co. Ltd.

Bascom, W. 1952. Two Forms of Afro-Cuban Divination. *Proceedings of the Twenty-fourth Conference of Americanists,* pp. 196–199.

————. The Focus of Cuban Santeria. *Southwestern Journal of Anthropology* 6 (1), pp. 64–68.

Bass, G. F. (ed.). 1988. *Ships and Shipwrecks of the Americas.* London: Thames and Hudson.

Basso, E. B. 1977. *Carib-Speaking Indians: Culture, Society and Language.* Tucson, AZ: University of Arizona Press.

————. 1985. *A Musical View of the Universe.* Philadelphia, PA: University of Pennsylvania Press.

Bateman, R. 1990. Africans and Indians: A Comparative Study of the Black Carib and Black Seminole. *Ethnohistory* 37 (1), pp. 1–24.

Bather, F. A., and T. Sheppard (eds.). 1934. Directory of Museums in the West Indies. In *Directory of Museums in Ceylon, British Malaya, Hong Kong, Sarawak, British North Borneo, Fiji, The West Indies, British Guiana,* pp. 27–67. London: The Museums Association.

Bay Islands. http://www.bayislandsonline.com

Beard, J. S. 1949. *The Natural Vegetation of the Windward and Leeward Islands.* Oxford: Clarendon.

Beaudry, M. C. 1988. *Documentary Archaeology in the New World.* Cambridge: Cambridge University Press.

Beckles, H McD. 1990. *A History of Barbados: From Amerindian Settlement to Nation State.* Cambridge: Cambridge University Press.

————. 1992. Kalinago (Carib) Resistance to European Colonisation of the Caribbean. *Caribbean Quarterly* Vol. 38 (2&3), pp. 1–14.

Beckwith, M. W. 1929. *Black Roadways: A Study of Jamaican Folk Life.* Chapel Hill: University of North Carolina Press.

Bedini, S. A. (ed.). 1992. *The Christopher Columbus Encyclopedia.* 2 vols. New York: Simon and Schuster.

Beeker, C. D., G. W. Conrad, and J. W. Foster. 2002. Taíno Use of Flooded Caverns in the East National Park Region, Dominican Republic. *Journal of Caribbean Archaeology* 3, pp. 1–26.

Behague, G. H. (ed.). 1994. *Music and Black Ethnicity: The Caribbean and South America.* New Brunswick: Transaction Publishers.

Bell, H. H. 1970 [1889]. *Obeah, Witchcraft and the West Indies.* Westport: Negro Universities Press.

Bennett, J. P. 1989. *An Arawak-English Dictionary with an English Word-List.* Archaeology and Anthropology 6 (1–2).

Benson, E. P. 1987. Bats in South American Iconography. *Andean Past* 1, pp. 165–90.

———. 1991. The Chthonic Canine. *Latin American Indian Literatures Journal* Vol. 7 (1), pp. 95–107.

———. 1997. *Birds and Beasts of Ancient Latin America.* Gainesville: University Press of Florida.

Benzoni, G. 1857. *History of the New World.* London: Hakluyt Society.

Bercht, F., E. Brodsky, J. A. Farmer, and D. Taylor (eds.). 1997. *Taíno: Pre-Columbian Art and Culture from the Caribbean.* New York: The Monacelli Press.

Bergad, L. W., F. García Iglesias, and M. Carman Barcia. 1995. *The Cuban Slave Market 1790–1880.* Cambridge: Cambridge University Press.

Berman, M. J. 1992. Fuel Wood Selection and the Lucayan-Taino Landscape: A Preliminary View. In W. H. Eshbaugh (ed.), *Proceedings of the Fourth Symposium on the Natural History of the Bahamas,* pp. 1–12. San Salvador (Bahamas): Bahamian Field Station Ltd.

Berman, M. J., and P. L. Grivecki. 1995. The Colonization of the Bahamian Archipelago. *World Archaeology* Vol. 26, pp. 423–41.

Berman, M. J., and D. M. Pearsall. 2000. Plants, People, and Culture in the Prehistoric Central Bahamas: A View from the Three Dog Site, an Early Lucayan Settlement on San Salvador Island, Bahamas. *Latin American Antiquity* Vol. 11, pp. 219–39.

Berman, M. J., A. K. Sievert and T. R. Whyte. 1999. Form and Function of Bipolar Lithic Artifacts from the Three Dog Site, San Salvador, Bahamas. *Latin American Antiquity* Vol. 10 (4), pp. 415–32.

Bermudez, A. A. 1967. Notas para la Historia del Espiritismo in Cuba. *Etnologia y Folklore* 4, pp. 5–22.

Berrian, B. F. 2000. *Awakening Spaces: French Caribbean Popular Song, Music, and Culture.* Chicago: University of Chicago Press.

Besson, G. 1989. *Folklore and Legends of Trinidad and Tobago.* Port- of-Spain: Paria Publishing.

Besson, G., and B. Brereton (eds.). 1992. *The Book of Trinidad.* Port-of-Spain, Trinidad: Paria Publishing.

Besson, J. 1995. The Creolization of African-American Slave Kinship in Jamaican Free Village and Maroon Communities. In S. Palmie (ed.), *Slave Cultures and the Cultures of Slavery,* pp. 195–202. Knoxville: The University of Tennessee Press.

———. 1997. Caribbean Common Tenures and Capitalism: The Accompong Maroons of Jamaica. *Plantation Society in the Americas* 4 (2–3), pp. 201–232.

Bilby, K. 1980. Jamaica's Maroons at the Crossroads: Losing Touch with Tradition. *Caribbean Review* 9 (4), pp. 18–21.

———. 1981. The Kromanti Dance of the Windward Maroons of Jamaica. *Nieuwe West Indische Gids* 55 (1&2), pp. 52–101.

———. 1981. *Music of the Maroons of Jamaica.* New York: Ethnic Folkways Records.

———. 1982. Three Resistance Movements in Jamaica: the Maroons, Garveyism, and the Rastafarians. *Journal of the Afro-American Historical and Genealogical Society* 3 (1), pp. 33–39.

———. 1984. Two Sister Pikni: A Historical Tradition of Dual Ethnogenesis in Eastern Jamaica. *Caribbean Quarterly* 30 (3–4), pp. 10–25.

———. 1988. The Caribbean as a Musical Area. In S. Mintz and R. Price (eds.), *Caribbean Contours,* pp. 181–218. Baltimore: The Johns Hopkins University Press.

———. 1994. Maroon Culture as a Distinct Variant of Jamaican Culture. In E. K. Agorsah (ed.), *Maroon Heritage,* pp. 72–85. Kingston: Canoe Press.

———. 1997. Swearing by the Past, Swearing to the Future: Sacred Oaths, Alliances, and Treaties among the Guianese and Jamaican Maroons. *Ethnohistory* 44 (4), pp. 655–679.

Biondi, J., and B. Bell. 2002. *Insight Pocket Guide Cayman Islands.* Insight Guides.

Birge, W. G. 1900. *In Old Rousseau, Reminiscences of Life as I Found It in the Island of Dominica and among the Carib Indians.* New York: Isaac H. Blanchard.

Bishop, J. (ed.). 1999. *Hosay Trinidad.* Documentary Educational Resources.

Bisnauth, D. 1989. *History of Religions in the Caribbean.* Kingston: Kingston Publishers Ltd.

Blake, F. 1995. *The Trinidad and Tobago Steel Pan: History and Evolution.* Madrid.

Blier, S. 1995. *African Vodun: Art, Psychology and Power.* Chicago: Chicago University Press.

BM. 2001. http://www.bobmarley.com

BMF. 2001. http://www.bobmarley_foundation.com

Bobrow, J. D. Jinkins, J. Bowrow, and M. E. Atwood. 1985. *St. Vincent and the Grenadines.* W. W. Norton.

Boerstra, E. H. J. 1976. Burying the Dead in Pre-Columbian Aruba. *Proceedings of the Sixth International Congress for the Study of Pre-Columbian Cultures of the Lesser Antilles, Point-à-Pitre, Guadeloupe, July 1975,* pp. 125–33.

————. 1985. A Limestone Human Figure from Tanki Leendert, Aruba, Netherlands Antilles. *Proceedings of the Tenth International Congress for the Study of the Pre-Columbian Cultures of the Lesser Antilles, Martinique 1983,* pp. 409–20.

Boggs, V. W. (ed.). 1992. *Salsiology.* New York: Excelsior Music Publishing Company.

Boldero, E. 2003. *'Skin Deep': How and to What Extent Has the Physical Decay of Curaçao's Monuments Had an Impact in Its Society?* Unpublished B.Sc. dissertation, Department of Anthropology, University College London.

Bond, J. 1971. *Birds of the West Indies.* Boston: Houghton Mifflin.

Bonner, T. 1974. The Blue Mountain Expedition. *Jamaica Journal* 8 (2&3), pp. 46–50.

Boomert, A. 1982a. Our Amerindian Heritage. *Naturalist Magazine,* 4 (4), pp. 26–61: Woodbrook, Trinidad.

————. 1982b. The Rock Drawings of Caurita. *Naturalist Magazine,* 4 (6), pp. 38–44: Woodbrook, Trinidad.

————. 1983. The Saladoid Occupation of Wonotobo Falls, Western Suriname. *Proceedings of the Ninth International Congress for the Study of Pre-Columbian Cultures of the Lesser Antilles,* pp. 97–120. Montreal.

————. 1984a. The Arawak Indians of Trinidad and coastal Guiana, ca. 1500–1650. *Journal of Caribbean History,* 19 (2), pp. 123–188.

————. 1984b. Aspects of Pitch Lake.; The Pitch Lake in History.; The Pitch Lake in Amerindian Mythology.; The Pitch Lake in Archaeology. *The Naturalist Magazine* Vol. 5 (11), pp. 11–47.

————. 1985. The Guayabitoid and Mayoid Series: Amerindian Culture History in Trinidad during Late Prehistoric and Protohistoric Times. *Proceedings of the Tenth International Congress for the Study of the Pre-Columbian Cultures of the Lesser Antilles, Martinique 1983,* pp. 93–148.

————. 1986. The Cayo Complex of St. Vincent: Ethnohistorical and Archaeological Aspects of the Island-Carib Problem. *Antropológica* 66, pp. 3–68.

————. 1987a. Gifts of the Amazons: 'Greenstone' pendants and beads as items of ceremonial exchange in Amazonia. *Antropologia* 67, pp. 33–54.

————. 1987b. Notes on Barbados Prehistory. *Journal Barbados Museum Historical Society* 38 (1), pp. 8–43.

————. 1992. Arawaks and Caribs. In S. A. Bedini (ed.), *The Christopher Columbus Encyclopaedia,* 1, pp. 351–353. New York: Simon and Schuster.

————. 1995. Island Carib Archaeology. In N. L. Whitehead (ed.), *Wolves from the Sea: Readings in the Anthropology of the Native Caribbean,* pp. 23–36. Leiden: KITLV Press.

————. 1996. *The Prehistoric Sites of Tobago: A Catalogue and Evaluation.* Alkmaar (Netherlands): Privately published.

————. 2000. *Trinidad, Tobago and the Lower Orinoco Interaction Sphere: An Archaeological/Ethnohistorical Study.* Alkmaar (Netherlands): Privately Published.

————. 2001. Raptorial Birds as Icons of Shamanism in the Prehistoric Caribbean and Amazonia. In W. H. Metz, B. L. van Beek and H. Steegstra (eds.), *Patina: Essays Presented to Jay Jordan Butler on the Occasion of his 80th birthday,* pp. 99–123. Groningen: Groningen State University.

————. 2003. Agricultural Societies in the Continental Caribbean. In J. Sued-Badillo (ed.), *General History of the Caribbean: Volume 1. Autochthonous Societies,* pp. 134–194. Paris: UNESCO.

Boomert, A., and P. O'B. Harris. 1984a. The Pitch Lake in Amerindian Mythology. *Naturalist Magazine,* 5, (11), pp. 29–31: Woodbrook, Trinidad.

————. 1984b. The Pitch Lake in Archaeology. *Naturalist Magazine,* 5, (11), pp. 32–47: Woodbrook, Trinidad.

————. 1988. *An Inventory of the Archaeological Sites in Trinidad and Tobago: Report 3, A Classification in Terms of Cultural Resource Management.* Department of History, University of the West Indies, St. Augustine, Trinidad, pp. 25. (mimeograph).

Bordes, P-G-L. 1982. [1876/1883]. *The History of the Island of Trinidad under the Spanish Government.* (Transl. J. A. Bain and A. S. Mavrogordata). 2 vols. Port-of-Spain: Paria Publishing Co. Ltd.

Borrell, P. 1983. *Historia y rescate del galeon Nuestra Señora de la Concepción.* Santo Domingo.

Boucher, P. B. 1992. *Cannibal Encounters: Europeans and Island Caribs 1492–1763.* Baltimore: Johns Hopkins Press.

Bourne, E. G. 1906. Columbus, Ramón Pané and the Beginnings of American Anthropology. *Proceedings of the Antiquarian Society* 17, pp. 310–348.

Boxer, C. R. 1965. *The Dutch Seaborne Empire, 1680–1800.* London: Hutchinson.

Boyrie Moya, E. de. 1971. Tres flautas-ocarinas de manufactura alfarea de los indígenas de la isla de Santo Domingo. *Revista dominicana de arqueología y antropología* 1 (1), pp. 13–17.

Branch, C. W. 1907. Aboriginal Antiquities in Saint Kitts and Nevis. *American Anthropologist* 9 (2), pp. 315–33.

Brandon, G. 1991. *Light from the Forest: How Santeria Cures Through Plants.* New York: Blue Unity Press.

————. 1993. *Santeria from Africa to the New World.* Bloomington: Indiana University Press.

Brathwaite, K. 1981. *Folk Culture of the Slaves in Jamaica.* London: New Beacon Books.

————. 1994. Nanny, Palmares and the Caribbean Maroon Connexion. In E. K. Agorsah (ed.), *Maroon Heritage: Archaeological, Ethnographic and Historical Perspectives,* pp. 119–138. Kingston: Canoe Press.

Brenda, C., and P. Colville. 1997. *Anguilla: Tranquil Isle of the Caribbean.* London: Macmillan.

Brereton, B. 1981. *A History of Modern Trinidad and Tobago 1783–1962.* London: Heinemann International.

————. 1996. *An Introduction to the History of Trinidad and Tobago.* Oxford: Heinemann.

Breton, P. R. 1665. *La Dictionnaire Caraïbe-Française.* Auxerre: Gilles Bouquet.

————. 1978 [1647]. *Relations de l'île de la Guadeloupe.* Bibliothèque d'histoire antillaise 3. Basse-Terre: Société d'histoire de la Guadeloupe.

Brett, W. H. 1880. *Legends and Myths of the Aboriginal Indians of British Guiana.* London: William Wells Gardner.

Brewer, D. M., and S. Hammersten. 1988. *Archaeological Overview and Assessment, Virgin Islands National Park, St. John, U.S. Virgin Islands.* Southeast Archaeolgical Center, National Park Service, Tallahassee, FL.

Briggs, C. L. 1993. Personal Sentiments and Polyphonic Voices in Warao Women's Ritual Wailing: Music and Poetics in a Critical and Collective Discourse. *American Anthropologist* 95 (4), pp. 929–957.

Briggs, P. S. 1989. *Art, Death and the Social Order: The Mortuary Arts of Pre-Conquest Central Panama.* British Archaeological Reports International Series 550. Oxford.

Brill, R. H., I. L. Barnes, S. S. C. Tong, E. C. Joel, and M. J. Murtaugh. 1987. Laboratory Studies of Some European Artifacts Excavated on San Salvador Island. In D. T. Grace (ed.), *Proceedings of the First San Salvador Conference, Columbus and His World,* pp. 247–92. Fort Lauderdale, FL: CCFL Bahamian Field Station.

Brooks, W. C. 1888. On the Lucayan Indians. *National Academy of Science Memoirs* Vol. 4, pp. 215–33.

Brown, D. H. 1996. Toward an Ethnoaesthetics of Santería Ritual Arts: The Practice of Altar-Making and Gift Exchange. In A. Lindsay (ed.), *Santería Aesthetics in Contemporary Latin American Art.* Washington, DC: Smithsonian Institution Press.

Brown, I. Z. 1999. *Culture and Customs of the Dominican Republic.* Westport, CT: Greenwood Publishing Group.

Brown, K. M. *Mama Lola.* 1991. Berkeley: University of California Press.

————. 1996. Art and Resistance: Haiti's Political Murals. *African Arts* 29 (2), pp. 46–57.

Brown, M. J. 1996. *An Archaeological Study of Social Class as Reflected in a British Colonial Tavern Site in Port Royal, Jamaica.* Unpublished M.A. thesis, Department of Anthropology, University of Texas at San Antonio.

Brown, R. C. 1994. *Florida's First People: 12,000 Years of Human History.* Sarasota, FL: Pineapple Press.

Brown, S., M. Morris and G. Rohlehr (ed). 1989. *Voiceprint: An Anthology of Oral and Related Poetry from the Caribbean.* Harlow: Longman.

Browne, C. A. 1933. The Origins of Sugar Manufacture in America. *Journal of Chemical Education* 10, pp. 323–30, 421–7.

Brugman, F. H. Unknown. *The Monuments of Saba: The Island of Saba, a Caribbean Example.* Walburg Instituut.

Bruhns, K. O. 1994. *Ancient South America.* Cambridge: Cambridge University Press.

Brunt, M. A., and J. E. Davies (eds.). 1994. *The Cayman Islands: Natural History and Biogeography.* Dordrecht: Kluwer.

Budinoff, L. 1991. An Osteological Analysis of Human Burials Recovered from Maisabel, an Early Ceramic Site Located on the North Coast of Puerto Rico. *Proceedings of the Twelfth International Congress for Caribbean Archaeology, Cayenne, French Guiana, 1987,* pp. 45–51.

Buisseret, D. J. 1966. Port Royal 1655–1725. *The Jamaican Historical Review* 6, pp. 21–8.

————. 1980. *Historic Architecture of the Caribbean.* London: Heinemann.

Bullbrook, J. A. 1953. *On the Excavation of a Shell Mound at Palo Seco, Trinidad, B.W.I.* Yale University Publications in Anthropology No. 50. New Haven.

Bullen, A. K. 1970. Case Study of an Amerindian Burial with Grave Goods from Grande Anse, St Lucia. *Proceedings of the Third International Congress for the Study of Pre-Columbian Cultures of the Lesser Antilles, Grenada 1969* pp. 45–60. Grenada.

Bullen, R. P. 1962. *Ceramic Periods of St. Thomas and St. Johns Islands, Virgin Islands.* American Studies 4. Orlando: William L. Bryant Foundation.

————. 1964. *The Archaeology of Grenada, West Indies.* Contributions of the Florida State Museum, Social Sciences 11. Gainesville, FL.

————. 1965. Archaeological Chronology of Grenada. *American Antiquity* 31 (2), pp. 237–41.

————. 1968. Some Arawak Ceramic Variations between Grenada, Barbados, St. Lucia and Eastern Trinidad. *Proceedings of the Second International Congress for the Study of Pre-Columbian Cultures in the Lesser Antilles, Barbados,* pp. 81–86. Barbados.

————. 1970. The Archaeology of Grenada, West Indies, and the Spread of Ceramic People in the Antilles. *Proceedings of the Third International Congress for the Study of Pre-Columbian Cultures of the Lesser Antilles, Grenada 1969,* pp. 147–152. Grenada.

————. 1973. Krum Bay, a Preceramic Workshop on St Thomas. *Proceedings of the Fourth International Congress for the Study of Pre-Columbian Cultures of the Lesser Antilles, St. Lucia 1971,* pp. 10–114.

Bullen, R. P., and A. K. Bullen, 1968. Barbados Archaeology 1966. *Proceedings of the Second International Congress for the Study of Pre-Columbian Cultures of the Lesser Antilles, Barbados,* pp. 134–144. Barbados.

————. 1970. The Lavoutte Site, St Lucia: A Carib Ceremonial Center. *Proceedings of the Third International Congress for the Study of Pre-Columbian Cultures of the Lesser Antilles, Grenada 1969,* pp. 61–86. Grenada.

————. 1972. *Archaeological Investigations on St. Vincent and the Grenadines, West Indies.* William L. Bryant Foundation, American Studies Report 8. Orlando.

————. 1973. The Giraudy Site, Beane Field, St Lucia. *Proceedings of the Fourth International Congress for the Study of the Pre-Columbian Cultures of the Lesser Antilles, St Lucia 1971,* pp. 199–214.

Bullen, R., A. K. Bullen and E. Kirby, 1973. Dating the Troumassée Decorated Cylinder: A Horizon Style. *Proceedings of the Fourth International Congress for the Study of the Pre-Columbian Cultures of the Lesser Antilles, St Lucia 1971,* pp. 197–198.

Burg, B. 1984. *Sodomy and the Pirate Tradition: English Sea Rovers in the Seventeenth-Century Caribbean.* New York: New York University Press.

Burton, R. D. E. 1997. *Afro-Creole Power, Opposition and Play in the Caribbean.* Ithaca, NY: Cornell University Press.

Bush, B. 1990. *Slave Women in Caribbean Society.* Bloomington: Indiana University Press.

Bush, M. B., et al. 1989. A 6,000-year History of Amazonian Maize Cultivation. *Nature* 340, pp. 303–5.

Bushnell, G. H. S. 1955. Current Research: Tobago. *American Antiquity* 21 (2), pp. 208–9.

Butcher, J. 1989. Peter Minshall: Trinidad Carnival and the Carnivalesque. *International Review of African American Art* 8 (3): 39–48.

Butt, A. J. 1956. Ritual Blowing: Taling as a Causation and Cure of Illness among the Akawaio. *Timehri* 35, pp. 37–52.

Buxton, L., J. Trevor, and A. Julien. 1938. Skeletal Remains from the Virgin Islands. *Man* Vol. 38, pp. 49–51.

Cabrera, L. 1988. *Los Animales en el folklore y la magía de Cuba.* Miami, FL: Universal.

Cadallo, A., and H. Pitts. 1992. Trinidad Folklore. In G. Besson and B. Brereton, *The Book of Trinidad,* pp. 274–90. Port of Spain: Paria Publishing.

Caesar, M., and P Lundberg. 1991. The Calabash Boom Site, St. John, USVI: Preliminary Report. *Proceedings of the Twelfth International Congress for Caribbean Archaeology, French Guyana, 1987,* pp. 203–215.

Calderon, F. L. 1976. Preliminary Report on the Indian Cemetary "El Atajadizo," Dominican Republic. *Proceedings of the Sixth International Congress for the Study of Pre-Columbian Cultures of the Lesser Antilles, Point-à-Pitre, Guadeloupe, July 1975,* pp. 295–303.

Callaghan, R. T. 1991. Passages to the Greater Antilles: An Analysis of Watercraft and the Marine Environment. *Proceedings of the Fourteenth Congress of the International Association for Caribbean Archaeology,* pp. 64–72. Barbados.

Campbell, D. G. 1978. *The Ephemeral Islands.* London: Macmillan.

Campbell, H. 1980. Rastafari: Culture of Resistance. *Race and Class* 22 (1) pp. 1–22.

———. 1985. *Rasta and Resistance: From Marcus Garvey to Walter Rodney.* London: Hansib Publishing Ltd.

Campbell, M. C. 1990. *The Maroons of Jamaica 1655–1796.* Trenton, NJ: Africa World Press Inc.

———. 1993. *Back to Africa: George Moss and the Maroons: From Nova Scotia to Sierra Leone.* Trenton, NJ: Africa World Press.

Cardoso, G. 1983. *Negro Slavery in the Sugar Plantations of Veracruz And Pernambuco, 1559–1680.* Washington, DC: University Press of America.

Carlson, L. A. 1993. *Strings of Command: Manufacture and Utilization of Shell Beads Among the Taino Indians of the West Indies.* Unpublished M.A. thesis, University of Florida, Gainesville.

Carmichael, E. (ed.). 1985. *The Hidden Peoples of the Amazon.* London: British Museum Press.

Carmichael, G. 1961. *The History of the West Indian Islands of Trinidad and Tobago 1498–1900.* London.

Carneiro, R. 1978. The Knowledge and Use of Rain Forest Trees by the Kuikuru Indians of Central Brazil. In R. Ford (ed.), *The Nature and Status of Ethnobotany,* pp. 210–216. Ann Arbor: Museum of Anthropology, University of Michigan Anthropological Papers 67.

———. 1983. The Cultivation of Manioc among the Kuikuru of the Upper Xingú. In R. B. Hames and W. T. Vickers (eds.), *Adaptive Responses of Native Amazonians,* pp. 65–111. London: Academic Press.

Caro Alvarez, J. A. 1977. *Cémies y trigonolitos.* Santo Domingo: Museo del Hombre Dominicano.

———. 1977. *La Cohoba.* Santo Domingo: Museo del Hombre Dominicano.

Carr, A. 1967. *So Excellent A Fishe: The Classic Study of the Lives of Sea Turtles.* New York: Charles Scribner's Sons.

————. 1981. Notes on the Behavioral Ecology of Sea Turtles. In K. A. Bjorndal (ed.), *Biology and Conservation of Sea Turtles,* pp. 19–26. Washington, DC: Smithsonian Institution Press.

Carr, A. T. 1989. *A Rada Community in Trinidad.* Port of Spain: Paria Publishing.

Carr, R., and S. Riley. 1982. An Effigy Ceramic Bottle from Green Turtle Cay, Abaco. *Florida Anthropologist* Vol. 35, pp. 200–2.

Carroll, P. J. 1997. Mandinga: The Evolution of a Mexican Runaway Slave Community, 1735–1827. *Comparative Studies in Society and History* 19, pp. 488–505.

————. 1991. *Blacks in Colonial Veracruz.* Austin: University of Texas Press.

Carstarphen, D. 2000. *The Conch Book.* Pen and Ink Press.

Carstensen, B. 1993. *Betty's Hope: An Antiguan Sugar Plantation.* St. John's, Antigua: Betty's Hope Trust.

Cashmore, E. 1979. *Rastaman: The Rastafarian Movement in England.* London: G. Allen and Unwin.

Cassá, R. 1977. *Los Tainos de la Española.* Santo Domingo: Universidad Autónoma de Santo Domingo.

Castellanos, R. 1981. La Plaza de Chacuey, un instrumento astronómico megalítico. *Boletín del Museo del Hombre Dominicano* Vol. 16, pp. 31–40.

Catz, R. 1992. Christopher Columbus: Columbus in Portugal. In S. A. Bedini (ed.). *The Christopher Columbus Encyclopedia* Vol. 1, pp. 175–87. New York: Simon and Schuster.

Centro de Estudios Avanzados de Puerto Rico y El Caribe. 1987. *Exposicion de Esculturas de los Indios Tainos.* San Juan, PR: Centro de estudios avanzados de Puerto Rico y El Caribe.

Chamberlain, R. S. 1948. *The Conquest and Colonization of Yucatan, 1517–1550.* Washington, DC: Carnegie Institution of Washington Publication 582.

Chamoiseau, P., and L. Coverdale. 1997. *Creole Folktales.* New Press.

Chanca, D. A. 1932. *Letter to the city of Sevilla.* London: Hakluyt Society.

Chanlatte Baik, L. A. 1976. *La hueca y sorcé (Vieques, Puerto Rico): Nuevo esquema para los procesos culturales de la arqueología antillana.* Santo Domingo: Fundación García Arévalo.

————. 1981. *La Hueca y Sorcé (Vieques, Puerto Rico): Primeras migraciones agroalfereras Antillanas—Nuevo esquema para los procesos culturales de la arqueología Antillana.* Santo Domingo.

————. 1983. *Catálogo arqueología de Vieques: Exposición del 13 del Marzo al 22 de Abril de 1983.* Río Pedras: Museo de Antropología, Historia y Arte, Universidad de Puerto Rico.

————. 1985. *Arqueología de Guayanilla y Vieques.* Rio Pedras, Puerto Rico: Centro de Investigaciones Arqueológicas, Universidad de Puerto Rico.

————. 2003. Agricultural Societies in the Caribbean: The Greater Antilles and the Bahamas. In J. Sued-Badillo (ed.), *General History of the Caribbean: Volume 1. Autochthonous Societies,* pp. 228–258. Paris: UNESCO.

Chanlatte Baik, L. A., and Y. M. Narganes Storde. 1989. La Nueva Arqueología de Puerto Rico (su Proyección en las Antillas). *Museo del Hombre Dominicano Boletín* Vol. 22, pp. 9–49.

Chapman, W. 1991. Slave Villages in the Danish West Indies: Changes of the Late 18th and Early 19th centuries. In T. Carter and B. Herman (eds.), *Perspectives in Vernacular Architecture Vol. IV,* pp. 108–20. Columbia: University of Missouri Press.

Chauharjasingh, Archibald S. 1982. *Lopinot in History.* Port of Spain (Trinidad): Columbus Publishers.

————. 1994. Chevron Beads Found in Trinidad. *Gayap,* Anniversary Issue. San Fernando, Trinidad.

Chaunu, H. and P. 1955–9. *Seville et l'Atlantique 1504–1650.* 8 vols. Paris.

Chaunu, P. 1964. La Légende Noire Antihispanique. *Revue de Psychologie des Peuples,* pp. 188–223.

Cheng, P. G., and G.-K. Pang. 2000. *Grenada.* Benchmark Books.

Chevannes, B. 1994. *Rastafari: Roots and Ideology.* Syracuse, NY: Syracuse University Press.

————. 1998. *Rastafari and Other African-Caribbean Worldviews.* Rutgers University Press.

Chiarelli, B. 1987. La Isabela. (Special issue). *International Journal of Anthropology* 2 (3):195–253.

Clark, P. 1994. *Black Paradise: The Rastafarian Movement.* San Bernadino: Borgo Press.

Clendinnen, I. 1978. *Ambivalent Conquests: Maya and Spaniards in Yucatan, 1517–1570.* Cambridge: Cambridge University Press.

Clerc, E. 1968. Sites Précolombiens de la côte Nord-Est Grande Terra de la Guadeloupe. *Proceedings of the Second International Congress for the Study of Pre-Columbian Cultures of the Lesser Antilles,* pp. 47–60. Barbados.

————. 1970. Recherches archéologiques en Guadeloupe. *Parallèles* Vol. 36/7, pp. 68–97.

————. 1973. Les trois-pointes des sites précolombiens de la côtes nord-est de la grande terre de la Guadeloupe. *Proceedings of the Fourth International Congress for the Study of the Pre-Columbian Cultures of the Lesser Antilles,* St Lucia 1971, pp. 199–214.

Clifford, S. A. 1993. *An Analysis of the Port Royal Shipwreck and Its Role in the Maritime History of Seventeenth-Century Port Royal, Jamaica.* Unpublished M.A. thesis, Department of Anthropology, Texas A&M University, College Station.

Coe, S. D., and M. D. Coe. 1996. *The True History of Chocolate.* London: Thames and Hudson.

Coe, W. R. 1957. A Distinctive Artifact Common to Haiti and Central America. *American Antiquity,* Vol. 22, pp. 280–22.

Coggins, C. C. 2001. A Soft Economy: Perishable Artifacts Offered to the Well of Sacrifice, Chichén Itzá. In B. A. Purdey (ed.), *Enduring Records: The Environmental and Cultural Heritage of Wetlands,* pp. 83–91. Oxford: Oxbow.

Coggins, C. C., and O. C. Shane III (eds.). 1984. *Cenote of Sacrifice, Maya Treasures from the Sacred Well at Chichen Itza.* Austin: University of Texas Press.

Coles, B., and J. 1989. *People of the Wetlands: A World Survey.* London: Thames and Hudson.

Columbus, C. 1969. *The Four Voyages of Christopher Columbus.* Harmondsworth: Penguin.

————. 1988. *Select Documents Illustrating the Four Voyages of Columbus.* (Transl. C. Jane). New York: Dover.

Conley, T. 1992. De Bry's Las Casas. In R. Jara and N. Spadaccini (eds.), *Amerindian Images and the Legacy of Columbus,* pp. 103–131. Minneapolis: University of Minnesota Press.

Conrad, G. W., J. W. Foster, and C. D. Beeker. 2001. Organic Artifacts from the Manantial de la Aleta, Dominican Republic: Preliminary Observations and Interpretations. *Journal of Caribbean Archaeology* 2, pp. 1–20.

Conrad, G., J. Foster, C. Beeker, L. Uhls, M. Brauner, M. Veloz Maggiolo, and E. Ortega. 1997. Images of Conquest. *Archaeology* July/August, pp. 60–1.

Considine, J. L., and J. L. Winberry. 1978. The Green Sea Turtle of the Cayman Islands. *Oceanus* 21 (3), pp. 50–55.

Conzemius, E. 1923. On the Aborigenes of the Bay Islands. *Atti de XXII Congfesso Internazionale degli Americanisti* Vol. 2.

————. 1932. *Ethnographic Survey of the Miskito and Sumu Indians of Honduras and Nicaragua.* Smithsonian Institution, Bureau of American Ethnology Bulletin 106. Washington, DC.

Cook, N. D. 1993. Disease and Depopulation of Hispaniola, 1492–1518. *Colonial Latin American Review* 2: 213–45.

————. 1998. *Born to Die: Disease and New World Conquest, 1492–1650.* Cambridge: Cambridge University Press.

Cook, N. D., and W. G. Lovell (eds.), 1992. *"Secret Judgements of God": Old World Disease in Colonial Spanish America.* Norman: University of Oklahoma Press.

Cook, S. F., and W. Borah. 1971. The Aboriginal Population of Hispaniola. In S. F. Cook and W. Borah (eds.), *Essays in Population History, Vol. 1: Mexico and the Caribbean,* pp. 376–410. Berkeley: University of California Press.

Coopersmith, J. M. 1949. *Music and Musicians of the Dominican Republic.* Washington, DC: Pan American Union.

Copney, C. 1999. *Jamaican Culture and International Folklore, Supersititions, Beliefs, Dreams, Proverbs and Remedies.* Ivy House Publishing Group.

Coppa, A., A. Cucina, B. Chiarelli, F. L. Calderon, and D. Mancinelli. 1995. Dental Anthropology and Paleodemography of the Precolumbian Populations of Hispaniola from the Third Millennium B.C. to the Spanish Contact. *Human Evolution* Vol. 10 (2), pp. 153–67.

Coppens, W. (ed.). 1980–1988. *Los Aborígenes de Venezuela*. 3 vols. Caracas: Fundación La Salle de Ciencias Naturales.

Cornelius, S., and J. Amira. 1992. *The Music of Santería: Traditional Rhythms of the Batá Drums*. Crown Point (ID): White Cliffs Media.

Corruccini, R. S., A. C. Aufderheide, J. S. Handler and L. E. Wittmers Jr. 1987. Patterning of Skeletal Lead Content in Barbados Slaves. *Archaeometry* Vol. 29, pp. 233–9.

Corruccini, R. S., E. Brandon, and J. Handler. 1989. Inferring Fertility from Relative Mortality in Historically Controlled Cemetery Remains from Barbados. *American Antiquity* Vol. 54, pp. 609–14.

Corruccini, R. S., J. S. Handler, R. J. Mutaw, and F. W. Lange. 1982. Osteology of a Slave Burial Population from Barbados, West Indies. *American Journal of Physical Anthropology* Vol. 59, pp. 443–59.

Corzani, J. 1994. West Indian Mythology and Its Literary Illustrations. *Research in African Literatures* Vol. 25 (2), pp. 13–22.

Cosculluela, J. A. 1946. Prehistoric Cultures of Cuba. *American Antiquity* Vol. 12, No. 1, pp. 10–18.

Cosentino, D. (ed.). 1995. *Sacred Arts of Haitian Vodun*. UCLA Fowler Museum of Cultural History, Los Angeles.

Cotter, C. S. 1964. The Jamaica of Columbus. *Jamaican Historical Review* Vol. 3 (16), pp. 252–9.

Courlander, H. 1942. Musical Instruments of Cuba. *Musical Quarterly* 28 (2), pp. 227–240.

———. 1976. *A Treasury of Afro-American Folklore*. New York: Crown.

Courtaud, P., A. Delpuech, and T. Romon. 1999. Archaeological Investigations at Colonial Cemeteries on Guadeloupe: African Slave Burial Sites or Not? In J. B. Haviser (ed.), *African Sites Archaeology in the Caribbean,* pp. 277–90. Princeton, NJ: Markus Wiener Publishers.

Couture, P. 1997. *Saint Martin, Saint Barts*. Globe Pequot Press.

Cowley, J. 1996. *Carnival, Canboulay and Calypso: Traditions in the Making*. Cambridge: Cambridge University Press.

Craine, E. R., and R. C. Reindorp (trans. and eds.), 1979. *The Codex Pérez and the Book of Chilam Balam of Maní*. Norman: University of Oklahoma Press.

Craton, M. 1978. *Searching for the Invisible Man: Slaves and Plantation Life in Jamaica*. Cambridge, MA: Harvard University Press.

———. 1982. *Testing the Chains: Resistance to Slavery in the British West Indies*. Ithaca, NY: Cornell University Press.

———. 1986. From Caribs to Black Caribs: The Amerindian Roots of Servile Resistance in the Caribbean. In G. Y. Okihiri (ed.), *In Resistance: Studies in African, Caribbean, and Afro- American History,* pp. 96–116. Amherst.

Craton, M., and D. G. Saunders. 1991. *Islanders in the Stream: A History of the Bahamian People. Volume One: From Aboriginal Times to the End of Slavery*. Athens: University of Georgia Press.

Crock, J. G., and R. N. Bartone. 1998. Archaeology of Trants, Montserrat. Part 4. Flaked Stone and Stone Bead Industries. *Annals of the Carnegie Museum* 67 (3), pp. 197–224.

Crock, J. G., J. B. Peterson and N. Douglas. 1994. Preceramic Anguilla: A View from Whitehead's Bluff Site. *Proceedings of the Fifteenth Congress of the International Association for Caribbean Archaeology.*: San Juan, PR: Centro de Estudios Avanzados de Puerto Rico y el Caribe.

Crocker, J. C. 1985. *Vital Souls: Bororo Cosmology, Natural Symbolism, and Shamanism*. Tucson: University of Arizona Press.

Crosby, A. W. 1972. *The Columbian Exchange: Biological and Cultural Consequences of 1492*. Westport, CT: Greenwood Press.

———. 1986. *Biological Imperialism: The Biological Expansion of Europe, 900–1900*. Cambridge: Cambridge University Press.

Cruxent, J. M., and I. Rouse. 1969. Early Man in the West Indies. *Scientific American* 221 (5), pp. 42–52.

———. 1982. *Arqueología Cronológica de Venezuela*. Caracas: Ernesto Armitano.

Cummins, A. 1997. European Views of the Aboriginal Population. In S. M. Wilson (ed.), *The Indigenous People of the Caribbean,* pp. 46–55. Gainesville: University Press of Florida.

Cundall, F. 1894. The Story of the Life of Columbus and the Discovery of Jamaica, *Journal of the Institute of Jamaica* 2, pp. 1–79.

Curaçao Tourist Board. 2001. *Curaçao: The Official Island Guide.* Willemstadt: Curaçao Tourist Board.

Curet, A. L. 1996. Ideology, Chiefly Power, and Material Culture: An Example from the Greater Antilles. *Latin American Antiquity* 7 (2), pp. 114–131.

————. 1992. House Structure and Cultural Change in the Caribbean: Three Case Studies from Puerto Rico. *Latin American Antiquity* 3, pp. 160–174.

————. 1997. Technological Changes in Prehistoric Ceramics from Eastern Puerto Rico: An Exploratory Study. *Journal of Archaeological Science* Vol. 24, pp. 497–504.

————. 2002. The Chief Is Dead, Long Live . . . Who? Descent and Succession in the Protohistoric Chiefdoms of the Caribbean. *Ethnohistory* 49 (2), pp. 259–80.

Curet, A. L., and J. R. Oliver. 1998. Mortuary Practices, Social Development, and Ideology in Precolumbian Puerto Rico. *Latin American Antiquity* Vol. 9, No. 3, pp. 217–239.

Curtain, P. D. 1998. *The Rise and Fall of the Plantation Complex.* Cambridge: Cambridge University Press.

Curtin, P. 1969. *The Atlantic Slave Trade: A Census.* Madison: University of Wisconsin Press.

Cushing, F. H. 1897. Exploration of Ancient Key Dwellers' Remains on the Gulf Coast of Florida. *Proceedings of the American Philosophical Society* 25 (153), pp. 329–448.

Cusick, J. G. 1989. *Change in Pottery as a Reflection of Social Change: A Study of Taíno Pottery Before and After Contact at the Site of En Bas Saline, Haiti.* Unpublished M.A. thesis, University of Florida, Gainesville.

Dacal Moure, R. 1978. *Artefactos de Concha en las Communidades Aborigenes Cubanas.* Havana: Universidad de la Habana.

Dacal Moure, R., and M. Rivero de la Calle. 1996. *Art and Archaeology of Pre-Columbian Cuba.* Pittsburgh, PA: University of Pittsburgh Press.

Daggett, R. E. 1980. The Trade Process and Implications of Trade in the Bahamas. *Florida Anthropologist* 33 (3), pp. 143–51.

Dampier, W. 1697. *A New Voyage Round the World.* London.

Dance, C. D. 1881. *Chapters from a Guianese Log-Book. or, the Folk-Lore and Scenes of Sea-Coast and River Life in British Guiana.* Georgetown: Royal Gazette.

Dance, D. C. 1985. *Folklore from Contemporary Jamaicans.* Knoxville: University of Tennessee Press.

D'Anghiera, P. M. 1970 [1912]. *De Orbe Novo: The Eight Decades of Peter Martyr D'Anghera.* New York (NY): Burt Franklin.

Davenport, F. 1917–37. *European Treaties Bearing on the History of the United States and Its Dependencies to 1648,* Vol. 1, No. 9, pp. 84–100. Berkeley: University of California Press.

Davidson, W. V. 1974. *Historical Geography of the Bay Islands, Honduras: Anglo-Hispanic Conflict in the Western Caribbean.* Southern University Press.

Davies, J. 1665. *The History of the Charriby Islands.* London.

Davis, D. 2003. Archaeological Reconnaissance of Anegda, British Virgin Islands. *Journal of Caribbean Archaeology* 4, pp. 1–11.

Davis, D. 1982. Archaic Settlement and Resource Exploitation in the Lesser Antilles: Preliminary Information from Antigua. *Caribbean Journal of Science* Vol. 17, pp. 107–122.

————. 1988. Biogeography and Human Subsistence: Examples from the West Indies. *Archaeology in Eastern North America* 16, pp. 177–186.

————. 1993. Archaic Blade Production on Antigua, West Indies. *American Antiquity* Vol. 58, pp. 688–697.

————. 1994. Revolutionary Archaeology in Cuba. *Journal of Archaeological Method and Theory* Vol. 3 (3), pp. 159–88.

————. 2000. *Jolly Beach and the Preceramic Occupation of Antigua, West Indies.* Yale University Publications in Anthropology 84. New Haven, CT: Yale University Press.

Davis, D. D., and R. C. Goodwin. 1990. Island Carib Origins: Evidence and Non-Evidence. *American Antiquity* Vol. 54, pp. 37–48.

Davis, M. E. 1972. The Social Organization of a Musical Event: The Fiesta De Cruz in San Juan, Puerto Rico. *Ethnomusicology* 16 (1), pp. 38–62.

————. 1994. "Bi-Musicality" in the Cultural Configurations of the Caribbean. *Black Music Research Journal* 14 (2), pp. 145–160.

Davis, S., and P. Simon. 1977. *Reggae Bloodlines: In Search of the Music and Culture of Jamaica.* London: Heineman Educational.

Deagan, K. 1978. The Material Assemblage of 16th-Century Spanish Florida. *Historical Archaeology* 12, pp. 25–50.

————. 1987. *Artifacts of the Spanish Colonies of Florida and the Caribbean, 1500–1800, Vol. 1. Ceramics, Glassware, and Beads.* Washington, DC: Smithsonian Institution Press.

————. 1987. Columbus's Lost Colony. *National Geographic* 172 (5), pp. 672–5.

————. 1987. Initial Encounters: Arawak Responses to European Contact at the En Bas Saline Site, Haiti. *Proceedings, First San Salvador Conference: Columbus and His World,* pp. 341–59. San Salvador Island, Bahamas.

————. 1988. The Archaeology of the Spanish Contact Period in the Caribbean. *Journal of World Prehistory* 2 (2), pp. 187–225.

————. 1989. The Search for La Navidad, Columbus's 1492 Settlement. In J. T. Milanich and S. Millbrath (eds.), *First Encounters.* Gainesville: University Press of Florida.

————. 1992. La Isabela, Foothold in the New World. *National Geographic* 181 (1): 40–53.

————. 1993. Kelbey's Ridge 2, A 14th Century Taino Settlement on Saba, Netherlands Antilles. *Analecta Praehistorica Leidensia* Vol. 26, pp. 164–81.

————. 1995. *Puerto Real: The Archaeology of a Sixteenth-Century Spanish Town in Hispaniola.* Gainesville: University of Florida Press.

————. 2002. *Artifacts of the Spanish Colonies, Vol. 2: Portable Possessions.* Washington, DC: Smithsonian Institution Press.

Deagan, K. A., and J. M. Cruxent. 2002. *Columbus's Outpost among the Taínos: Spain and America at La Isabela, 1493–1498.* New Haven, CT: Yale University Press.

————. 2002. *Archaeology at La Isabela: America's First European Town.* New Haven, CT: Yale University Press.

DeBoer, W. R., and D. W. Lathrap. 1979. The Making and Breaking of Shipibo-Conibo Ceramics. In C. Kramer (ed.), *Ethnoarchaeology: Implications of Ethnography for Archaeology,* pp. 102–38. New York: Columbia University Press.

de Booy, T. 1912. Lucayan Remains on the Caicos Islands. *American Anthropologist* 14 (1), pp. 81–105.

————. 1913. Lucayan Artifacts from the Bahamas. *American Anthropologist* 15, pp. 1–7.

————. Pottery from Certain Caves in Eastern Santo Domingo, West Indies. *American Anthropologist* 17, pp. 69–97.

————. 1917. Certain Archaeological Investigations in Trinidad, West Indies. *American Anthropologist,* 19 (4), pp. 471–486.

————. 1919. *Archaeology of the Virgin Islands.* Indian Notes and Monographs 1(1). New York: Museum of the American Indian, Heye Foundation.

de Bry, T. 1976. *Discovering the New World.* Ed. M. Alexander. New York: Harper and Row.

DeCorse, C. 1991. West African Archaeology and the Atlantic Slave Trade. *Slavery and Abolition* Vol. 12, pp. 92–6

Deerr, N. 1949. *The History of Sugar.* Vol. 1. London: Chapman and Hall.

———. 1950. *The History of Sugar.* Vol. 2. London: Chapman and Hall.

deFrance, S. D. 1989. Saladoid and Ostionoid Subsistence Adaptations: Zooarchaeological Data from a Coastal Occupation on Puerto Rico. In P. E. Siegel (ed.), *Early Ceramic Population Lifeways and Adaptive Strategies in the Caribbean,* pp. 57–77. Oxford: British Archaeological Reports International Series 506.

———. 1990. Zooarchaeological Investigations of an Early Ceramic Age Frontier Community in the Caribbean: The Maisabel Site, Puerto Rico. *Antropológica* Vol. 73–4, pp. 3–180.

de Hostos, A. 1923. Anthropomorphic Carvings from the Greater Antilles. *American Anthropologist* 25 (4), pp. 525–8.

———. 1923. Three-Pointed Stone Zemis or Idols from the West Indies: An Interpretation. *American Anthropologist* 25 (1), pp. 56–71.

———. 1923. Anthropomorphic Carvings from the Greater Antilles. *American Anthropologist* 25 (4), pp. 525–58.

———. 1926. Antillean Stone Collars: Some Suggestions of Interpretive Value. *Journal of the Royal Anthropological Institute* 56, pp. 135–42.

———. 1951. The "Duho" and Other Wooden Objects from the West Indies. *Anthropological Papers: Papers Based Principally on Studies of the Prehistoric Archaeology and Ethnology of the Greater Antilles,* pp. 77–84. San Juan: Office of the Historian, Government of Puerto Rico.

Deive, C. E. 1983. El chamanismo Taíno. In A. G. Pantel (ed.), *La Cultura Taína: Seminario sobre la situación de investigación de la cultura Taína,* pp. 81–8. Madrid: Biblioteca del V Centenario.

———. 1989. *Los guerrilleros negros.* Santo Domingo: Fundación Cultural Dominicano.

Delawarde, J.-P. 1983. *La sorcellerie à la Martinique et dans les voisines: ses positions et ses réactions dans ses rapports avec le culte chrétien ambiant.* Paris.

Delgado, J. P. 1997. *Encyclopaedia of Underwater and Maritime Archaeology.* London: British Museum Press.

de Light, D., and P. Thomas. 1998. *The Rough Guide to Trinidad and Tobago.* London: Rough Guides.

Demorizi, E. R. 1980. *Lugares y monumentos históricos de Santo Domingo.* Santo Domingo: Editora Taller.

de Verteuil, Alex. 1999. Spirit of the Americas. *Caribbean Beat* (BWIA International Airways Magazine), No. 40, November/December pp. 40–47.

de Verteuil, Alex and N. J. Saunders. 1998. *The First Trinidadians.* Television Documentary. Port of Spain (Trinidad): Pearl and Dean (Caribbean) Ltd.

De Vorsey, L., and J. Parker (eds.). 1985. *In the Wake of Columbus: Islands and Controversy.* Detroit: Wayne State University Press.

Delle, J. A. 1998. *An Archaeology of Social Space: Analyzing Coffee Plantations in Jamaica's Blue Mountains.* New York: Plenum Press.

Delpuech, A. 2001. Historical Archaeology in the French West Indies: Recent Research in Guadeloupe. In P. Farnsworth (ed.), *Island Lives: Historical Archaeologies of the Caribbean,* pp. 21–59. Tuscaloosa and London: The University of Alabama Press.

Delpuech, A., C. L. Hofman, and M. L. P. Hoogland. 1999. Excavations at the Site of Anse a la Gourde, Guadeloupe: Organization, History, and Environmental Setting. *Proceedings of the Eighteenth International Congress for Caribbean Archaeology,* pp. 156–161.

Denevan, W. (ed.), 1976. *The Native Population of the Americas in 1492.* Madison: University of Wisconsin Press.

———. 2001. *Cultivated Landscapes of Amazonia and the Andes.* Oxford: Oxford University Press.

Deren, M. 1953. *Divine Horsemen: The Living Gods of Haiti.* London: Thames and Hudson.

Descola, P. 1994. *In the Society of Nature.* Cambridge: Cambridge University Press.

Desmangles, L. G. 1992. *The Faces of the Gods: Vodou and Roman Catholicism in Haiti.* University of North Carolina Press.

Dessalles, P., E. Forster (ed.) and R. Forster (ed.). 1996. *Sugar and Slavery, Family and Race: The Letters and Diary of Pierre Dessalles, Planter in Martinique, 1808–1856.* Baltimore: Johns Hopkins University Press.

Dethlefson, E. 1982. The Historic Archaeology of St. Eustatius. *Journal of New World Archaeology* Vol. 5 (2), pp. 73–86.

Devaux, R. 1976. Petroglyphs Recently Discovered at Stonefield, St Lucia. *Proceedings of the Sixth International Congress for the Study of the Pre-Columbian Cultures of the Lesser Antilles, Guadeloupe, 1975.*

Dick, K. C. 1977. Aboriginal and Early Spanish Names of Some Caribbean, Circum-Caribbean Islands and Cays. *Journal of the Virgin Islands Archaeological Society* Vol. 4, pp. 17–41.

Dixon, R. M. W., and A. Y. Aikhenvald (eds.). 1999. *The Amazonian Languages.* Cambridge: Cambridge University Press.

Dobbin, J. D. 1986. *The Jombee Dance of Montserrat: A Study of Trance Ritual in the West Indies.* Ohio State University Press.

Dodds, D. J. 1994. *The Ecological and Social Sustainability of Miskito Subsistence in the Río Plátano Biosphere Reserve, Honduras: the Cultural Ecology of Swidden Horticulturalists in a Protected Area.* Ph.D. dissertation UCLA. Ann Arbor, MI: University Microfilms.

Dominguez, L. 1978. *Arqueología colonial Cubana: dos estudios.* Havana: Editorial de Ciencias Sociales.

Donachie, M. 2001. *Household Ceramics at Port Royal, Jamaica, 1655–1692: The Building 4/5 Assemblage.* Unpublished Ph.D. dissertation, Department of Anthropology, Texas A&M University, College Station.

Donahue, J., D. R. Watters and S. Millspaugh. 1990. Thin Section Petrography of Northern Lesser Antilles Ceramics. *Geoarchaeology* Vol. 5, pp. 229–54.

Donkin, R. A. 1998. *Beyond Price, Pearls and Pearl-Fishing to the Age of Discoveries.* Philadelphia: Transactions of the American Philosophical Society.

Donovan, S. K., and T. A. Jackson (eds.). 1994. *Caribbean Geology: An Introduction.* Kingston, Jamaica: University of the West Indies Press.

Doran, E. B. 1953. *A Physical and Cultural Geography of the Cayman Islands.* Ph.D. dissertation, University of California, Berkeley.

Dor-Ner, Z. 1991. *Columbus and the Age of Discovery.* London: HarperCollins.

Douglas, N. 1990. The Fountain: An Amerindian Ceremonial Cavern on Anguilla, Its Petroglyphs and Other Finds, Related to Surface Archaeology of Anguilla's Major Beach Sites. *Proceedings of the Eleventh Congress of the International Association for Caribbean Archaeology,* pp. 141–152.

———. 1991. Recent Amerindian Finds on Anguilla. *Proceedings of the Thirteenth International Congress for Caribbean Archaeology, Held at Willemstadt, Curaçao, on July 24–29, 1989,* pp. 576–88. Willemstadt.

Drake, Sir F. 1963. *The World Encompassed, by Sir Francis Drake, Being His Next Voyage to That to Nombre de Dios.* London: Hakluyt Society.

Drewett, L. 2000. Tortola Material Culture 1: Pottery. In P. Drewett (ed.), *Prehistoric Settlements in the Caribbean: Fieldwork in Barbados, Tortola, and the Cayman Islands,* pp. 127–132. London: Archetype Publications.

Drewett, P. L. 1987. Archaeological Survey of Barbados. *Journal of the Barbados Museum,* No. 38, pp. 44–80.

———. 1991. *Prehistoric Barbados.* London: Institute of Archaeology and Archetype Publications.

———. 2000. *Prehistoric Settlements in the Caribbean: Fieldwork in Barbados, Tortola, and the Cayman Islands.* London: Archetype Publications.

———. 2002/2003. Feasting at the Ball Game: The Belmont Project, Tortola, British Virgin Islands. *Archaeology International* 6, pp. 56–9.

Drewett, P., and B. Bates. 2000. Settlement Archaeology on Tortola, British Virgin Islands. In P. Drewett (ed.), *Prehistoric Settlements in the Caribbean: Fieldwork in Barbados, Tortola, and the Cayman Islands,* pp. 113–125. London: Archetype Publications.

Drewett, P., and J. Oliver. 1997/98. Prehistoric Settlement in the Caribbean. *Archaeology International* 1, pp. 43–6.

Drewett, P., S. J. Scudder and I. R. Quitmyer. 2000. Unoccupied Islands? The Cayman Islands. In P. Drewett (ed.), *Prehistoric Settlements in the Caribbean: Fieldwork in Barbados, Tortola, and the Cayman Islands,* pp. 5–16. London: Archetype Publications.

Dubelaar, C. N. 1986. *South American and Caribbean Petroglyphs.* Dordrecht, Holland: Foris Publications.

————. 1995. *The Petroglyphs of the Lesser Antilles, the Virgin Islands and Trinidad.* Amsterdam: Foundation for Scientific Research in the Caribbean Region.

Duerden, J. E. 1895. Discovery of Aboriginal Remains in Jamaica [Letter to the editor]. *Nature* 52 (1338), pp. 173–174.

————. 1897. Aboriginal Indian Remains in Jamaica. *Journal of the Institute of Jamaica* 2 (4), pp. 1–52.

Duncan, D. D. 1943. Capturing Giant Sea Turtles in the Caribbean. *National Geographic* 84 (August), pp. 177–90.

Dunham, K. 1946. *Journey to Accompong.* Connecticut: Negro Universities Press.

Dunn, O., and J. E. Kelley (eds.), 1989. *The Diario of Christopher Columbus's First Voyage to America, Abstracted by Fray Bartolomé de Las Casas.* Norman: University of Oklahoma Press.

Dunn, R. S. 1972. *Sugar and Slaves: The Rise of the Planter Class in the English West Indies 1624–1713.* Chapel Hill: University of North Carolina Press.

Dyde, B. 1993. *Antigua and Barbuda: The Heart of the Caribbean.* Hunter Publishing.

————. 2002. *St Kitts: Cradle of the Caribbean.* London: Macmillan.

Earle, P. 1980. *The Treasure of the Concepción: The Wreck of the Almiranta.* New York: Viking Press.

————. 1981. *The Sack of Panamá: Sir Henry Morgan's Adventures on the Spanish Main.* New York: Viking Press.

Eastman, R., and M. Warner-Lewis. 2000. Forms of African Spirituality in Trinidad and Tobago. In J. K. Olopuna (ed.), *African Spirituality,* pp. 403–15.

Ebanks, S. O. 1983. *Caymam Emerges: A Human History of Long Ago Cayman.* Georgetown: Northwester Company.

Eckholm, Gordon. 1961. Puerto Rican Stone Collars as Ballgame Belts. In S. K. Lothrop (ed.), *Essays in Pre-Columbian Art and Archaeology,* pp. 356–71. Cambridge, MA: Harvard University Press.

Edwards, G., and J. Mason. 1985. *Black Gods-Orisha Studies in the New World.* New York: Yoruba Theological Ministry.

Elder, J. 1988. *African Survivals in Trinidad and Tobago.* London: Karia Press.

Elia, R. 1992. The Ethics of Collaboration: Archaeologists and the Whydah Project. *Historical Archaeology* 26 (4), pp. 105–117.

Eliade, M. 1974. *Shamanism: Archaic Techniques of Ecstasy.* Princeton, NJ: Princeton University Press.

Elliott, J. H. 1992. *The Old World and the New 1492–1650.* Cambridge: Canto.

Emmer, P. C. 1999. *General History of the Caribbean: Volume II, New societies: The Caribbean in the Long Sixteenth Century.* UNESCO: London.

Equinao, O. 1999. *The Life of Olaudah Equiano.* New York: Dover.

Espenshade, C. T. 2000. Reconstructing Household Vessel Assemblages and Site Duration at an Early Ostionoid Site from South-Central Puerto Rico. *Journal of Caribbean Archaeology* Vol. 1, pp. 1–22.

Etherington, M., and V. Richards. 2003. *The Antigua and Barbuda Companion.* Interlink Publishing Group.

Eubanks, T. H. 1992. *Sugar, Slavery and Emancipation: The Industrial Archaeology of the West Indian Island of Tobago.* Unpublished Ph.D. dissertation, University of Florida, Gainesville, FL.

Ewen, C. R. 1991. *From Spaniard to Creole: The Archaeology of Cultural Formation at Puerto Real, Haiti.* Tuscaloosa and London: The University of Alabama Press.

————. 2001. Historical Archaeology in the Colonial Spanish Caribbean. In P. Farnsworth (ed.), *Island Lives: Historical Archaeologies of the Caribbean,* pp. 3–20. Tuscaloosa and London: The University of Alabama Press.

Farnsworth, P. 1994. Archaeological Excavations at Promised Land Plantation, New Providence. *Journal of the Bahamas Historical Society* Vol. 16 (1), pp. 21–9.

————. 1996. The Influence of Trade on Bahamian Slave Culture. *Historical Archaeology* Vol. 30 (4), pp. 1–23.

————. Brutality or Benevolence in Plantation Archaeology. *International Journal of Historical Archaeology* 4 (2), pp. 145–58.

———— (ed.). 2001a. *Island Lives: Historical Archaeologies of the Caribbean.* Tuscaloosa and London: The University of Alabama Press.

————. 2001b. "Negroe Houses Built of Stone Besides Others Watl'd + Plaistered": The Creation of a Bahamian Tradition. In P. Farnsworth (ed.), *Island Lives: Historical Archaeologies of the Caribbean,* pp. 234–71. Tuscaloosa and London: The University of Alabama Press.

Febles Dueñas, J. 1988. *Manual para el estudio de la piedra tallada de los aborigenes de Cuba.* Havana: Editorial Academia, Academia de Ciencias de Cuba.

Ferbel, P. J. 1995. *The Politics of Taíno Indian Heritage in the Post-Quincentennial Dominican Republic: When a Canoe Means More than a Water Trough.* Unpublished Ph.D. dissertation. University of Minnesota, Minneapolis.

————. 2002. Not Everyone Who Speaks Spanish Is from Spain: Taíno Survival in the 21st Century Dominican Republic. *KACIKE: The Journal of Caribbean Amerindian History and Anthropology.* http://www.kacike.org/FerbelEnglish.html

Fergus, H. A. 1994. *Montserrat, A History of a Caribbean Colony.* London: MacMillan.

Fermor, P. L. 1950. *The Traveller's Tree: A Journey through the Caribbean Islands.* London: John Murray.

Fernandez, R., S. Mendez Mendez and G. Cueto. 1998. *Puerto Rico Past and Present.* Westport, CT: Greenwood Publishing Group.

Fernández-Armesto, F. 1991. *Columbus.* Oxford: Oxford University Press.

Fernandez, M. A. 1945. *Exploraciones arqueologicas en la Isla Cozumel, Quintana Roo.* Annals of the Institution of Anthropology and History Vol. 1, pp. 107–120.

Fernández-Méndez, E. 1972. *Art and Mythology of the Taíno Indians of the Greater Antilles.* San Juan: Ediciones El Cemí.

Fewkes, J. W. 1891. On Zemis from Santo Domingo. *American Anthropologist* 4, pp. 167–74.

————. 1904. Porto Rican Stone Collars and Tripointed Idols. In *Smithsonian Miscellaneous Collection* 47, pp. 161–86. Washington, DC: Smithsonian Institution.

————. 1904. Prehistoric Culture of Cuba. *American Anthropologist* 6 (5), pp. 585–98.

————. 1907. *The Aborigenes of Porto Rico and Neighbouring Islands.* Twenty-fifth Annual report of the Bureau of American Ethnology, pp. 3–296. Washington, DC: Smithsonian Institution Press.

————. 1913. Porto-Rican Elbow Stones in the Heye Museum, with Discussion of Similar Objects Elsewhere. *American Anthropologist* 15 (3), pp. 435–59.

————. 1914a. Prehistoric Objects from a Shell Heap at Erin Bay, Trinidad. *American Anthropologist* Vol. 16 (2), pp. 200–220.

————. 1914b. Relations of Aboriginal Culture and Environment in the Lesser Antilles. *Bulletin of the American Geographical Society* Vol. 46 (5), pp. 662–678.

————. 1915. Prehistoric Culture Centers in the West Indies. *Journal of the Washington Academy of Sciences* Vol. 5, pp. 436–443.

————. 1919. A Wooden Object from Santo Domingo. *Man* 19 (10), pp. 145–9.

————. 1922. *A Prehistoric Island Culture Area of America.* Thirty-Fourth Annual report of the Bureau of American Ethnology (1912–1913), pp. 35–281. Washington D.C.: Smithsonian Institution Press.

Ffrench, R. *A Guide to the Birds of Trinidad and Tobago.* London: Christopher Helm.

Fick, C. 1990. *The Making of Haiti: the Saint-Domingue Revolution from Below.* Knoxville: University of Tennessee Press.

Figuerado, A. E. 1978. Prehistoric Ethnoarchaeology of the Virgin Islands. *Proceedings of the Seventh International Congress for the Study of Pre-Columbian Cultures of the Lesser Antilles,* pp. 39–46. Montreal: Centre de Recherches Caraïbes, Université de Montréal.

————. 1978. The Virgin Islands as an Historical Frontier between the Tainos and the Caribs. *Revista/Review Interamericana* Vol. 8 (3), pp. 393–99.

Figueredo, A. E., and S. D. Glazier. 1978. A Revised Aboriginal Ethnohistory of Trinidad. *Proceedings of the Seventh International Congress for the Study of Pre-Columbian Cultures of the Lesser Antilles,* pp. 259–262. Centre de recherches Caraïbes, Université de Montréal, Montréal.

Flower, W. H. 1895. On Recently Discovered Remains of the Aboriginal Inhabitants of Jamaica. *Nature* 52 (1355), pp. 607–608.

Floyd, T. 1973. *The Columbus Dynasty in the Caribbean, 1492–1526.* Albuquerque: University of New Mexico Press.

Fodor. 1997. *Fodor's 98 Cancun, Cozumel, Yucatan Peninsula.* Fodor Travel Publication.

————. 2001. *Fodor's 2002 US and British Virgin Islands.* Fodor Travel Publications.

Foehr, S. 2000. *Jamaican Warriors: Reggae, Roots and Culture.* London: Sanctuary Publishing Ltd.

Fonk, H. 1999. *Curaçao: Architectural Style.* Willemstadt: Curaçao Style Foundation.

Forte, M. C. 1999. *From Smoke Ceremonies to Cyberspace, Globalized Indigeneity, Multi-Sited Research, and the Internet.* Paper presented at the 25th Annual Meeting of the Canadian Anthropology Society, Université Laval, Québec.

————. 2001a. *The Relationship of the Caribs of Arima with the Caribs of Dominica, 1992–1997.* http://www.centrelink.org/fntt/Dominica.html

————. 2001b. *The Carib Resurgence from 1973 to the Present.* http://www.centrelink.org/fntt/Resurgence.html

————. 2001c. *"Our Amerindian Ancestors": The State, the Nation, and the revaluing of indigeneity in Trinidad and Tobago.* Paper presented at the Fourth Biennial Conference of the Australian Association for Caribbean Studies, Australian National University, Canberra, 8–10 February.

————. 2001e. *A Brief Account of the Colonial History of Arima's Carib Community.* http://www.centrelink.org/fntt/History.html

————. 2001f. *The Relationship of the Caribs of Arima with the Tainos of Puerto Rico and the USA.* http://www.centrelink.org/fntt/History.html

————. 2001g. *Re-engineering Indigeneity: Cultural Brokerage, the Political Economy of Tradition and the Santa Rosa Carib Community of Arima, Trinidad and Tobago.* Unpublished Ph.D. dissertation, University of Adelaide.

Foster, B. 1986. *Heart Drum: Spirit Possession in the Garifuna Communities of Belize.* Benque Viejo del Carmen, Belize: Cubola.

Foster, J. W., and C. D. Beeker. 1997. The Conquest of a Sinkhole: Initial Archaeological Investigations at El Manantial de la Aleta, East National Park, Dominican Republic. *Underwater Archaeology* pp. 27–32.

Fox, G. L. 1999. The Kaolin Clay Tobacco Pipe Collection from Port Royal, Jamaica. In P. Davey (ed.), *The Archaeology of the Clay Tobacco Pipe.* Oxford, British Archaeological Reports International Series 809.

Franco, J. L. 1979. The Slave Trade in the Caribbean and Latin America. *Unesco Courier* 1979, pp. 88–100.

Freidel, D., and J. A. Sabloff. 1984. *Cozumel: Late Maya Settlement Patterns.* Orlando: Academic Press.

Friede, J., and B. Keen (eds.), 1971. *Bartolomé de las Casas in History: Toward an Understanding of the Man and His Work.* Illinois: DeKalb.

Funari, P. P. A., M. Hall, and S. Jones (eds.). 1999. *Historical Archaeology, back from the Edge.* London: Routledge.

Furst, Peter T. 1976. "Tobacco: Proper Food for the Gods." Chapter 2 in Peter T. Furst, *Hallucinogens and Culture,* San Francisco: Chandler and Sharp Publishers.

Fuson, R. E. 1987. *The Log of Christopher Columbus.* Camden, NJ: International Marine Publishing.

Gage, T. 1956 [1648]. *Travels in the New World.* Norman: University of Oklahoma Press.

Galloway, J. 1989. *The Sugar Cane Industry.* Cambridge: Cambridge University Press.

García Arévalo, M. 1978. La Arqueología Indo-Hispana en Santo Domingo. In E. Wagner and A. Zucchi (eds.), *Unidad y Variedad: Ensayos Antropológicos en Homenaje a Jose M. Cruxent,* pp. 77–127. Caracas: Instituto Venezolano de Investigaciones Científicas.

————. 1979. *El arte Taino.* Santo Domingo: Fundación Garcia-Arévalo.

————. 1986. *El Maniel de Jose Leta: Evidencias Arqueológicas de un posible asentimiento comarrón en el región sud-oriental de la isla de Santo Domingo.* Cimarrón Serie Monografica No. 18. Santo Domingo: Fundación Garcia-Arevalo.

————. 1988. El murciélago en el arte y mitología taína. In *El murciélago y la lechuza en la cultura taína,* pp. 29–53. Santo Domingo: Fundación García Arévalo.

————. 1988. Indigenismo, arqueología e identidad nacional. Santo Domingo: Museo del Hombre Dominicano and Fundación García Arévalo.

————. 1989. *Los signos en el arte taíno.* Serie Monográfica 25. Santo Domingo: Fundación García Arévalo

————. 1994. Zemis en pierre, trigonolithes. In J. Kerchache (ed.), *L'art des sculpteurs taïnos: Chefs-d'oeuvre de Grandes Antilles précolombiennes,* pp. 186–221. Paris: Musée du Petit Palais.

García Arévalo, M., and L. Chanlatte Baik. 1978. *Las Espátulas Vómicas Sonajeras de la Cultura Taína.* Museo del Hombre Dominicano and Fundación García Arévalo, Santo Domingo.

García-Goyco, O. 1984. *Influencias mayas y aztecas en los taínos de las Antillas Mayores.* San Juan, PR: Ediciones Xibalbay.

Gartley, R. T. 1979. Afro-Cruzan Pottery: A New Style of Colonial Earthenware from St. Croix. *Journal of the Virgin Islands Archaeological Society* 8, pp. 47–61.

Gaspar, D. B. 1985. *Bondmen and Rebels: A Study of Master-Slave Relations in Antigua.* Baltimore: Johns Hopkins University Press.

————. 1988. Slavery, Amelioration, and Sunday Markets in Antigua, 1823–1831. *Slavery and Abolition* 9, pp. 1–28.

————. Antigua Slaves and Their Struggle to Survive. In H. J. Viola and C. Margolis (eds.), *Seeds of Change: A Quincentennial Commemoration,* pp. 130–7. Washington, DC: Smithsonian Institution Press.

Geggus, D. 1983. *Slave Resistance Studies and the Saint Domingue Revolt: Some Preliminary Considerations.* Miami: Florida International University.

————. 1987. The Enigma of Jamaica in the 1790's: New Light on the Causes of Slave Rebellions. *William and Mary Quarterly* 44(2):274–299.

Gerace, K. 1982. Three Loyalist Plantations on San Salvador Island, Bahamas. *Florida Anthropologist* Vol. 35 (4), pp. 216–22.

Gerbi, A. 1985. *Nature in the New World: From Christopher Columbus to Gonzalo Fernandez de Oviedo.* (Transl. J. Moyle). Pittsburgh: University of Pittsburgh Press.

Gibson, C. (ed.), 1971. *The Black Legend: Anti-Spanish Attitudes in the Old World and the New.* New York.

Gill, F. (ed.). 1978. *Zoogeography of the Caribbean.* Philadelphia: Academy of Natural Science.

Gill, T. 1931. *Tropical Forests of the Caribbean.* Baltimore: Read-Taylor.

Gilliland, M. 1989. *Key Marco's Buried Treasure: Archaeology and Adventure in the Nineteenth Century.* Gainesville, FL: University Press of Florida.

————. 1989. *The Material Culture of Key Marco, Florida.* Gainesville, FL: University Press of Florida.

Glazier, S. D. 1978. Theoretical Approaches to the Study of Trinidad's Prehistory. *Journal of the Virgin Islands Archaeological Society* Vol. 5, pp. 32–35.

————. 1978. Trade and Warfare in Protohistoric Trinidad. *Proceedings of the Seventh International Congress for the Study of Pre-Columbian Cultures of the Lesser Antilles,* pp. 279–282. Centre de Recherches Caraïbes, Université de Montréal, Montréal.

————. 1980. A Note on Shamanism in the Lesser Antilles. *Proceedings of the Eighth International Congress for the Study of the Pre-Columbian Cultures of the Lesser Antilles, St Kitts 1979,* pp. 447–55.

————. 1980. Aboriginal Trinidad in the Sixteenth Century. *The Florida Anthropologist* Vol. 33, pp. 152–9.

————. 1980. Aboriginal Trinidad in the Sixteenth Century. *The Florida Anthropologist* Vol. 33, pp. 152–9.

————. 1982. The St. Joseph and Mayo Collections from Trinidad, West Indies. *The Florida Anthropologist* Vol. 35 (4), pp. 208–215.

————. 1991. Impressions of Aboriginal Technology: The Case of the Aboriginal Canoe. *Proceedings of the Thirteenth International Congress for Caribbean Archaeology, Held at Willemstad, Curaçao, on July 24–29, 1989,* pp. 149–61. Willemstad.

————. 1991. *Marchin' the Pilgrims Home: A Study of the Spiritual Baptists in Trinidad.* Salem, WI: Sheffield.

———— (ed.). 2001 *Encyclopedia of African and African-American Religions.* New York: Routledge.

Goeje, C. H. de. 1939. Nouvel examen des langues des Antilles. *Journal de la Société des Américanistes* Vol. 31, pp. 1.120.

Goggin, J. M. 1939. An Anthropological Reconnaissance of Andros Island, Bahamas. *American Antiquity* Vol. 5, pp. 21–6.

————. 1968. *Spanish Majolica in the New World: Types of the Sixteenth to the Eighteenth Centuries.* Yale University Publications in Anthropology 72. New Haven, CT: Yale University Press.

González, J. 1969. *The Development of Christianity in the Caribbean.* Grand Rapids: William B. Eerdmans.

González, N. L. 1959. The West Indian Characteristics of the Black Carib. *Southwestern Journal of Anthropology* Vol. 15, pp. 300–307.

————. 1988. *Sojourners of the Caribbean: Ethnogenesis and Ethnohistory of the Garifuna.* Urbana: University of Illinois Press.

————. 1997. The Garifuna of Central America. In Samuel M. Wilson (ed.), *The Indigenous People of the Caribbean,* pp. 197–205. Gainesville: University Press of Florida.

González Colón, J. 1984. *Tibes: Un centro ceremonial indígena.* M.A. thesis, Centro de Avanzados de Puerto Rico y El Caribe, San Juan, PR.

González-Whippler, M. 1982. *The Santeria Experience.* Englewood Cliffs, NJ: Prentice Hall.

Goodwin, C. M. 1982. Archaeology on the Galways Plantation. *Florida Anthropologist* 35 (4), pp. 251–8.

————. 1994. Betty's Hope Windmill: An Unexpected Problem. *Historical Archaeology* 28 (1), pp. 99–110.

Goodwin, R. 1975. *Villa Taina de Boqueron: Excavation and Analysis of an Early Taino Site in Puerto Rico.* San Juan, PR: Interamerican University Press.

————. 1978. The Lesser Antilles Archaic: New data from St. Kitts. *Journal of the Virgin Islands Archaeological Society* Vol. 5, pp. 6–16.

————. 1979. *The Prehistoric Cultural Ecology of St. Kitts, West Indies: A Case Study in Island Archaeology.* Ph.D. dissertation, Arizona State University.

Goslinga, C. 1971. *The Dutch in the Caribbean and on the Wild Coast 1580–1680.* Gainesville: University of Florida Press.

————. 1979. *A Short History of the Netherlands Antilles and Surinam.* The Hague: M. Nijhoff.

Gosner, P. 1987. *Caribbean Georgian: The Great and Small Houses of the West Indies.* Washington, DC: Three Continents Press.

Gotelipe-Miller, S. 1990. *Pewter and Pewterers from Port Royal, Jamaica Flatware before 1692.* Unpublished M.A. thesis, Department of Anthropology, Texas A&M University, College Station.

Gottlieb, K. L. 2000. *The Mother of Us All: A History of Queen Nanny, Leader of the Windward Jamaica Maroons.* Africa World Press.

Goucher, C. 1990. John Reeder's Foundry: A Study of 18th century African-Caribbean Technology. *Jamaica Journal* 23 (1), pp. 39–43.

————. 1993. African Metallurgy in the New World. *African Archaeological Review* 11, pp. 197–215.

————. 2001. African-Caribbean Metal Technology: Forging Cultural Survivals in the Atlantic World. In J. Haviser (ed.), *African Sites Archaeology in the Caribbean,* pp. 143–156. Princeton, NJ: Markus Wiener.

Goucher, C., A. Chauharjasingh and K. Agorsah. 1996. *Site Report on the Fort King George Blacksmith Shop.* Manuscript, Tobago Museum, Tobago.

Gould, R. A. 2000. *Archaeology and the Social History of Ships.* Cambridge: Cambridge University Press.

Goveia, E. V. 1965. *Slave Society in the British Leeward Islands at the End of the Eighteenth Century.* New Haven, CT: Yale University Press.

Granberry, J. 1956. The Cultural Position of the Bahamas in Caribbean Archaeology. *American Antiquity* Vol. 22, pp. 128–34.

———. 1957. An Anthropological Reconnaissance of Bimini, Bahamas. *American Antiquity* Vol. 22, pp. 378–81.

———. 1979–81. Spanish Slave Trade in the Bahamas, 1509–1530: An Aspect of the Caribbean Pearl Industry. 3 parts. *Journal of the Bahamas Historical Society* 1, 2 and 3.

———. 1980. A Brief History of Bahamian Archaeology. *Florida Anthropologist* 33, 83–93.

———. 1991. Lucayan Toponyms. *Journal of the Bahamas Historical Society* Vol. 13 (1), pp. 3–12.

Gregoire, C., and N. Kanem. 1989. The Caribs of Dominica: Land Rights and Ethnic Consciousness. *Cultural Survival Quarterly* 13 (3), pp. 52–5.

Grissim, J. 1980. *The Lost Treasure of Concepción.* New York: William Morrow & Co.

Groot, S. W. de. 1985. A Comparison Between the History of Maroon Communities in Surinam and Jamaica. *Slavery and Abolition* 6(3), pp. 173–184.

Gross, J. M. 1975. The Archaeology of Anegada Island. *Journal of the Virgin Islands Archaeological Society* 2, pp. 12–16.

Guano, E. 1994. Revival Zion: An Afro-Christian Religion in Jamaica. *Anthropos* 89, pp. 519–542.

Guarch, J. M. 1973. *Ensayo de Reconstrucción Etno-histórica del Taíno de Cuba.* Serie Arqueologica 4. Havana: Instituto de Arqueología, Academia de Ciencias de Cuba.

———. 1978. *El Taíno de Cuba: Ensayo de reconstrucción etno-histórica.* Academia de Ciencias de Cuba, Instituto de Ciencias Sociales, Havana.

———. 1988. Sitio arqueológico El Chorro de Maíta. *Revista Cubana de Ciencias Sociales* 17 (6), pp. 162–83.

———. 2003. The First Caribbean People: Part 1, The Palaeoindians in Cuba and the Circum-Caribbean. In J. Sued-Badillo (ed.), *General History of the Caribbean: Volume 1. Autochthonous Societies,* pp. 93–118. Paris: UNESCO.

Guérout, M., and M. Guillaume. 1992. Prospections sous-marines à Tobago sur le sitge de la bataille franco-hollandaise du 3 mars 1677. *Caribena* 2, pp. 181–199.

Guerra, F. 1978. The dispute over syphilis: Europe versus America. *Clio Médica* 13: 39–62.

Guerra, F. 1985. La epidemia americana de influenza en 1493. *Revista de Indias* 45, pp. 325–47.

Guerrero, J. G. 1981. Dos Plazas Indígenas y el Poblado de Cotubanamá, Parque Nacional del Este. *Boletín del Museo del Hombre Dominicano* 16, pp. 13–30.

Guggisberg, C. A. W. 1972. *Crocodiles.* London.

Guglin, T. 1974. *The Spiritual Baptist Church of Barbados: A Description of an Afro-Christian Religion.* Unpublished manuscript, University of the West Indies, Cave Hill, Barbados.

Guibault, J. 1993. *Musical Traditions of St. Lucia, West Indies: Dances and Songs from a Caribbean Island.* Smithsonian/Folkways Recordings SF 40416. Washington, DC

Guitar, L. 1998. *Cultural Genesis: Relationships among Indians, Africans, and Spaniards in Rural Hispaniola, First Half of the Sixteenth Century.* Ann Arbor, MI: University Microfilms.

———. 2000. Criollos: The Birth of a Dynamic New Indo-Afro-European People and Culture on Hispaniola. *KACIKE: The Journal of Caribbean Amerindian History and Anthropology.* http://www.kacike.org/GuitarEnglish.html

———. 2002. Documenting the Myth of Taíni Extinction. *KACIKE: The Journal of Caribbean Amerindian History and Anthropology.* http://www.kacike.org/GuitarEnglish.html

Gullick, C. J. M. R. 1976. The Black Caribs in St. Vincent: The Carib War and Its Aftermath. *Actes du XLIIe Congrès des américanistes* vi, pp. 451–65. Paris.

————. 1976. *Exiled from St. Vincent: The Development of Black Carib Culture in Central America Up To 1945.* Malta: Progress Press.

————. 1978. Black Carib Origins and Early Society. In J. Benoist and F-M. Mayer (eds.), *Proceedings of the Seventh International Congress for the Study of the Pre-Columbian Culture of the Lesser Antilles,* pp. 283–90. Montreal.

————. 1985. *Myths of a Minority: The Changing Traditions of the Vicentian Caribs.* Assen.

Gurney, J. J. 1840. *A Winter in the West Indies.* London: John Murray.

Haag, W. G. 1970. Stone Artifacts in the Lesser Antilles. *Proceedings of the Third International Congress for the Study of the Pre-Columbian Cultures of the Lesser Antilles, Grenada, 1969,* pp. 129–38.

Haberfield, C. V., and C. Knight (eds.). 1997. *Fodor's Pocket Aruba.* Fodor Travel Publications.

Hackenberger, S. 1991a. An Abstract of Archaeological Investigations by the Barbados Museum 1986. *Proceedings of the Twelfth Congress of the International Association for Caribbean Archaeology,* pp. 163–174.

Hackenberger, S. 1991b. Archaeological Test Excavation of Buccament Valley Rockshelter, St. Vincent: Preceramic Stone Tools in the Windward Islands, and the Early Peopling of the Eastern Caribbean. *Proceedings of the Thirteenth Congress of the International Association for Caribbean Archaeology,* pp. 86–91.

Hagedorn, K. J. 2001. *Divine Utterances: The Performance of Afro-Cuban Santeria.* Washington, DC: Smithsonian Institution Press.

Hall, J. L. 1992. A Brief History of Underwater Salvage in the Dominican Republic. In D. Keith and T. Carrell (eds.), *Underwater Archaeology Proceedings from the Society for Historical Archaeology Conference,* pp. 35–40. Tucson, AZ: Society for Historical Archaeology.

————. 1994. Spanish Coins, German Weights, Dutch Clay Pipes, and an English Ship: The 1993 Monte Cristi Shipwreck Project Interim Report. *Proceedings from the 27th Annual Conference on Historical and Underwater Archaeology, Vancouver, British Columbia.* Ann Arbor, MI.

Hall, N. A. T. 1992. *Slave Society in the Danish West Indies: St. Thomas, St. John, and St. Croix.* Kingston: Canoe Press.

Hamilton, C. A. 1985. *Some Belief Systems and Practices in St. Kitts.* Cave Hill: University of the West Indies.

Hamilton, D. M. 1986. Port Royal Revisited. *Underwater Archaeology Proceedings from the Society for Historical Archaeology Conference 1986,* pp. 73–81.

————. 1991. A Decade of Excavations at Port Royal, Jamaica. *Underwater Archaeology Proceedings from the Society for Historical Archaeology Conference, Richmond, Virginia, 1991,* pp. 90–94.

————. 2001. *The Port Royal Project: Archaeological Excavations.* http://nautarch.tamu.ed/portroyal/arch-hist.htm

Hamilton, D. M., and R. Woodward. 1984. A Sunken 17th-Century City: Port Royal, Jamaica. *Archaeology* 37 (1), pp. 38–45.

Hammond, N. 1972a. Classic Maya Music. Part 1: Maya Drums. *Archaeology* 25 (2), pp. 125–131.

————. 1972b. Classic Maya Music. Part 2: Rattles, Shakers, Raspers, Wind and String Instruments. *Archaeology* 25 (3), pp. 222–228.

Handler, J. S. 1963. Pottery Making in Rural Barbados. Southwestern *Journal of Anthropology* Vol. 19, pp. 314–34.

————. 1972. An Archaeological Investigation of the Domestic Life of Plantation Slaves in Barbados. *Journal of the Barbados Museum and Historical Society* 34, 64–72.

————. 1997. An African-Type Healer/Diviner and His Grave Goods: A Burial from a Plantation Slave Cemetery in Barbados. *International Journal of Historical Archaeology* 1 (2), pp. 91–130.

Handler, J., and R. Corrucini. 1983. Plantation Slave Life in Barbados: A Physical Anthropological Analysis. *Journal of Interdisciplinary History* Vol. 14, pp. 65–90.

Handler, J., and F. W. Lange. 1978. *Plantation Slavery in Barbados: An Archaeological and Historical Investigation.* Cambridge, MA: Harvard University Press.

Handler, J., F. W. Lange and C. Orser. 1979. Carnelian Beads in Necklaces from a Slave Cemetery in Barbados, West Indies. *Ornament* 4 (2), pp. 15–18.

Hanke, L. 1952. *Bartolomé de las Casas, historian: An Essay in Spanish Historiography.* Gainesville: University of Florida Press.

Hardy, J. D., Jr. 1983. Tobago: The Forgotten Island. *Naturalist Magazine* 4 (7), pp. 8–50.

Haring, C. H. 1910. *The Buccaneers in the West Indies in the XVIIth Century.* London: Methuen.

Harlow, V. T. 1924. *Colonising Expeditions to the West Indies and Guiana, 1623–1667.* London: Hakluyt Society.

Harrington, M. R. 1921. *Cuba before Columbus.* 2 vols. Indian Notes and Monographs, Museum of the American Indian, Heye Foundation, New York.

———. 1924. A West Indian Gem Centre. *Indian Notes and Monographs* Vol. 1 (4), pp. 184–9.

———. 1951. The Idol of the Cave. *Natural History* 60 (7), pp. 312–17, 335.

Harris, D. 1965. *Plants, Animals and Man in the Outer Leeward Islands, West Indies.* Berkeley: University of California Press.

Harris, P. O. B. 1971. *Banwari Trace: Preliminary Report on a Pre-ceramic Site in Trinidad, West Indies.* Trinidad and Tobago Historical Society (South Section). Pointe-a-Pierre.

———. 1973. Preliminary Report on Banwari Trace, A Preceramic Site in Trinidad. *Proceedings of the Fourth International Congress for the Study of Pre-Columbian Cultures of the Lesser Antilles, St. Lucia 1971,* pp. 115–125.

———. 1980. Caribbean Spearthrowers and Threepointers: Further Data and Considerations. Archaeology and Anthropology: *Journal of the Walter Roth Museum of Anthropology* 3 (2), pp. 113–118.

———. 1980. Excavation Report: Lovers Retreat Period IV, Tobago. *Proceedings of the Eighth International Congress for the Study of the Pre-Columbian Cultures of the Lesser Antilles, St Kitts 1979,* pp. 524–552. Anthropological Research Papers 22, Arizona State University, Tempe.

Harris, P. O'B, and E. Reyes. 1990. Supervivencias Amerindias en Trinidad y Tobago. In *Pueblos y Politicas en el Caribe Amerindio.* Instituto Indigenista Interamericano, Fundación García Arévalo, pp. 55–64: Mexico D.F.

Haslip Viera, G. (ed.). 2001. *Taino Revival: Critical Perspectives on Puerto Rican Identity and Cultural Politics.* Princeton, NJ: Markus Weiner Publishers.

Hatt, G. 1924. Archaeology of the Virgin Islands. *Proceedings of the Twenty-First International Congress of Americanists,* pt. 1, pp. 29–42. The Hague.

———. 1932. *Notes on the Archaeology of Santo Domingo.* Copenhagen: Saertyrk af Geografisk Tidsskrift 35.

———. 1941. Had West Indian Rock Carvings a Religious Significance ? *Ethnografisk Raekke* (National Museum Skriften) Vol. 1, pp. 165–202.

Hauser, M., and D. V. Armstrong. 1999. Embedded Identities: Piecing Together Relationships through Compositional Analysis of Low-Fired Eathenwares. In J. B. Haviser (ed.), *African Sites Archaeology in the Caribbean,* pp. 65–93. Princeton, NJ: Markus Wiener.

Hausman, G. 1997. *The Kebra Negast: The Book of Rastafarian Wisdom and Faith From Ethiopia and Jamaica.* New York: St. Martin's Press.

Hausman, G., and K. Rodrigues. 1996. *African-American Alphabet: A Celebration of African-American and West Indian Culture, Custom, Myth and Symbol.* New York: St. Martin's Press.

Haviser, J. B. 1985. *An Archaeological Survey of Saba, Netherlands Antilles: Pahse 1 report.* Report of the Institute of Archaeology and Anthropology of the Netherlands Antilles 3.

———. 1987. *Amerindian Cultural Geography on Curaçao.* Natuurwetenschappelijke Studiekring voor Suriname en de Nederlandse Antillen, No. 120. Amsterdam.

———. 1988. *An Archaeological Survey of St. Martin / St. Maarten.* Reports of the Archaeological-Anthropological Institute of the Netherlands Antilles 7, Curaçao.

————. 1989. A Comparison of Amerindian Insular Adaptive Strategies on Curaçao. In P. Siegel (ed.), *Early Ceramic Population Lifeways and Adaptive Strategies in the Caribbean,* pp. 3–28. British Archaeological Reports International Series 506. Oxford.

————. 1990. Perforated Prehistoric Ornaments of Curaçao and Bonaire, Netherlands Antilles. *Journal of the Society of Bead Research* Vol. 2.

————. 1991a. *The First Bonaireans.* Archaeological-Anthropological Institute of the Netherlands Antilles. Curaçao.

————. 1991b. Preliminary Results of Test Excavations at the Hope Estate Site (SM-026), St. Martin. *Proceedings of the International Congress for Caribbean Archaeology* Vol. 13, pp. 647–66.

————. 1995a. *In Search of St. Martin's Ancient Peoples: prehistoric Archaeology.* July Tree Books, St. Martin.

————. 1995b. Towards Romanticized Amerindian Identities Among Caribbean Peoples: A Case Study from Bonaire, Netherlands Antilles. In N. L. Whitehead (ed.), *Wolves from the Sea,* pp. 157–70. Leiden: KITLV Press.

———— (ed.). 1999. *African Sites Archaeology in the Caribbean.* Princeton, NJ: Markus Wiener.

————. 1999. Identifying a Post-Emancipation (1863–1940) African-Curaçaoan Material Culture Assemblage. In J. B. Haviser (ed.), *African Sites Archaeology in the Carribean,* pp. 221–275. Princeton, NJ: Markus Wiener.

————. 2001b. Historical Archaeology in the Netherlands Antilles and Aruba. In P. Farnsworth (ed.), *Island Lives: Historical Archaeologies of the Caribbean,* pp. 60–81. Tuscaloosa and London: The University of Alabama Press.

Haviser, J., and N. Simmons-Brito. 1995. Excavations at the Zuurzak Site: A Possible 17th-Century Dutch Slave Camp on Curaçao, Netherlands Antilles. *Proceedings of the Fifteenth International Congress for Caribbean Archaeology,* pp. 71–82.

Hayne, T., A. Whitaker and C. Vincer. 2001. *Cayman Islands.* Bradt Travel Guides.

Hearn, L. 1890. *Two Years in the French West Indies.* New York: Harper and Brothers.

Heath, B. J. 1988. *Afro-Caribbean Ware: A Study of Ethnicity on St. Eustatius.* Unpublished Ph.D. dissertation, Department of American Civilization, University of Pennsylvania, Philadelphia.

————. 1991. Pots of Earth: Forms and Functions of Afro-Caribbean Ceramics. *Florida Journal of Anthropology* 7 (16), pp. 33–49.

————. 1991. Afro-Caribbean Ware on St. Eustatius: A Preliminary Typology. *Proceedings of the Thirteenth International Congress for Caribbean Archaeology,* pp. 338–43.

Hedrick, B. C., and J. E. Stephens. 1977. *It's a Natural Fact: Obeah in the Bahamas.* Museum of Anthropology Miscellaneous Series no. 39. Greeley: University of Northern Colorado Museum of Anthropology.

Heekeren, H. R. van. 1963. Prehistoric Research on the Islands of Curaçao, Aruba and Bonaire in 1960. *Nieuwe West-Indische Gids* 43, pp. 1–25.

Helms, M. W. 1971. *Asang: Adaptations to Culture Contact in a Miskito Community:* Gainesville: University of Florida Press.

————. 1977. Iguanas and Crocodilians in Tropical American Mythology and Iconography with Special Reference to Panama. *Journal of Latin American Lore* 3, pp. 51–132.

————. 1984. The Indians of the Caribbean and Circum-Caribbean at the End of the 15th Century. In L. Bethell (ed.), *The Cambridge History of Latin America* Vol. 1, pp. 37–57. Cambridge: Cambridge University Press.

————. 1986. Art Styles and Interaction Spheres in Central America and the Caribbean: Polished Black Wood in the Greater Antilles. *Journal of Latin American Lore* 12 (1), pp. 25–43.

————. 1988. *Ulysses's Sail.* Princeton, NJ: Princeton University Press.

————. 1993. Cosmological Chromatics: Color-Related Symbolism in the Ceramic Art of Ancient Panama. In M. M. Graham (ed.), *Reinterpreting Prehistory of Central America,* pp. 209–252. Niwot: University Press of Colorado.

Henige, D. 1992. To Read Is to Misread, to Write Is to Miswrite: Las Casas as Transcriber. In R. Jara and N. Spadaccini (eds.), *Amerindian Images and the Legacy of Columbus,* pp. 198–229. Minneapolis: University of Minnesota Press.

Henry, F. 1957. African Powers in Trinidad: The Shango Cult. *Anthropological Quarterly* 30 (2), pp. 45–59.

Hernández Aquino, L. 1993. *Diccionario de voces indígenas de Puerto Rico.* 3rd ed. San Juan: Editorial Cultural.

Herrera Fritot, R. 1940. Un nuevo dujo taíno en las colleciones del Museo Antropológico Montané, de la Universidad de La Habana: Descripción y estudio comparativo. *Revista de Arqueología* 1 (4), pp. 26–31.

Herrera Fritot, R., and C. L. Youmans. 1946. *La Caleta: Joya arqueológica antillana: Exploración y estudio de un rico yacimiento indígena dominicano y comparación d elos ejemplares con los de Cuba y otros lugares.* Havana.

Herrera Porras, T. 1978. *Cuna Cosmology.* (Transl. Anita McAndrews). Washington DC: Three Continents Press.

Herskovits, M. J. 1937. African Gods and Catholic Saints. *American Anthropologist* 39, pp. 639–643.

Herskovits, M. J., and F. S. Herskovits. 1936. *Suriname Folk-Lore.* New York: Columbia University Press.

———. 1947. *Trinidad Village.* New York: Alfred A. Knopf.

Hesse, R. C., and K. Orr Hesse. 1977. The Conch Industry in the Turks and Caicos Islands. *Underwar Naturalist* Vol. 10, pp. 4–9.

Hester, E. N. 1999. *Pelican Guide to the Bahamas 2000.* Pelican Publishing.

Heuman, G. (ed.). 1982. *Out of the House of Bondage: Runaways, Resistance and Maroonage in Africa and the New World.* London: Frank Cass.

Highfield, A. R. 1995. *St. Croix 1493: An Encounter of Two Worlds.* St. Thomas: Virgin Islands Humanities Council.

Higman, B. W. 1974. A Report on Excavations of Montpelier and Roehampton. *Jamaica Journal* 8 (2 & 3), pp. 40–5.

———. 1976. *Slave Population and Economy in Jamaica, 1807–1834.* Cambridge: Cambridge University Press.

———. 1984. *Slave Population of the British Caribbean, 1807–1834.* Baltimore: Johns Hopkins University Press.

———. 1986. Plantation Maps as Sources for the Study of West Indian Ethnohistory. *Ethnohistory: A Researcher's Guide* Vol. 35, pp. 107–36.

———. 1987. The Spatial Economy of Jamaican Sugar Plantations: Cartographic Evidence from the 18th and 19th Centuries. *Journal of Historical Geography* 13 (1), pp. 17–39.

———. 1988. *Jamaica Surveyed.* Kingston: Institute of Jamaica.

Hill, D. 1977. *The Impact of Migration on the Metropolitan and Folk Society of Carriacou, Grenada.* Anthropological Papers of the American Museum of Natural History 54, pt.2.

Hill, D. R. 1993. *Calypso Calaloo: Early Carnival Music in Trinidad.* Gainesville: University Press of Florida.

Hill Harris, M. 1988. The Ceramics of Tobago and Barbados: A Report on Studies in Progress. In N. J. Saunders and O. de Montmollin (eds.), *Recent Studies in Pre-Columbian Archaeology,* pp. 245–73. Oxford: British Archaeological Reports International Series 421.

Hinds, R., and M. H. Harris. 1995. Pottery from Mustique. *Proceedings of the Fifteenth International Congress for Caribbean Archaeology, Puerto Rico,* pp. 459–70.

Hinds, R., B. Jardine, and K. Watson. 2000. A Preliminary Report on a Saladoid Site at Spring Barden, Barbados. *Journal of the Barbados Museum and Historical Society* Vol. XLVI, pp. 77–92.

Hodges, W. H. 1983. *The search for La Navidad: Further Inquiry.* Unpublishd manuscript, Musée de Guahabá, Limbé.

Hoffman, C. A., Jr. 1967. *Bahama Prehistory: Cultural Adaptation to an Island Environment.* Ph.D. dissertation, University of Arizona. Ann Arbor: University Microfilms.

———. 1970. The Palmetto Grove Site on San Salvador, Bahamas. *Contributions of the Florida State Museum, Social Sciences* Vol. 16, pp. 1–26.

————. 1973. Archaeological Investigations on St. Kitts. *Caribbean Journal of Science,* Vol. 13 (3–4), pp. 237–50.

————. 1973. Petroglyphs of Crooked Island, Bahamas. *Proceedings of the Fourth International Congress for the Study of Pre-Columbian Cultures of the Lesser Antilles,* pp. 9–12. Castries, St. Lucia.

————. 1987. Archaeological Investigations at the Long Bay Site, San Salvador, Bahamas. In D. T. Grace (ed.), *Proceedings of the First San Salvador Conference, Columbus and his world,* pp. 237–245. Fort Lauderdale, FL: CCFL Bahamian Field Station.

————. 1987. The Long Bay Site, San Salvador. *American Archaeology* Vol. 6, pp. 97–102.

Hoffman, P. E. 1980. *The Spanish Crown and the Defence of the Caribbean, 1535–1585: Precedent, Patrimonialism, and Royal Parsimony.* Baton Rouge: Louisiana State University Press.

Hofman, C. L. 1992. *In Search of the Native Population of Pre-Columbian Saba (400–1450 Ad), Part 1. Pottery Styles and Their Interpretations.* Unpublished Ph.D. dissertation, University of Leiden.

Hofman, C. L., A. Delpuech and M. L. P. Hoogland. 1999. Excavations at the Site of Anse a la Gourde, Guadeloupe: Stratigraphy, Ceramic Chronology and Structures. *Proceedings of the Eighteenth International Congress for Caribbean Archaeology,* pp. 162–172.

Hofman, C. L., and M. L. P. Hoogland. 1991. Ceramic Developments on Saba, N. A. (350–1450 AD). *Proceedings of the Fourteenth Congress of the International Association for Caribbean Archaeology.* Barbados.

———— (eds.). 1999. *Archaeological Investigations on St. Martin (Lesser Antilles).* Archaeological Studies Leiden University 4. Leiden, Netherlands.

Honychurch, L. 1975. *The Dominica Story: A History of the Island.* Roseau, Dominica.

————. 1983. *The Cabrits and Prince Rupert's Bay.* Roseau: Dominica Institute.

————. 1992. *Dominica: Isle of Adventure.* London: Macmillian

————. 1997. Crossroads in the Caribbean: A Site of Encounter and Exchange on Dominica. *World Archaeology* Vol. 28 (3), pp. 291–304.

————. 2002. The Leap at Sauteurs: The Lost Cosmology of Indigenous Grenada. http://www.uwichill.edu.bb/bnccde/grenada/conference

Hoogland, M. L. P. 1996. *In Search of the Native Population of pre-Columbian Saba. Part Two. Settlements in Their Natural and Social Settings.* Unpublished Ph.D. dissertation, University of Leiden.

Hoogland, M. L. P., and C. L. Hofman. 1993. Kelbey's Ridge 2, A 14th century Taino settlement on Saba, Netherlands Antilles. *Analecta Praehistorica Leidensia* 26, pp. 163–181.

Horner, D. 1990. *The Treasure Galleons.* Port Salerno: Florida Classics Press.

Horowitz, M. 1971. *Peoples and Cultures of the Caribbean.* New York: Natural History Press.

Horton, M. 1979. *A Preliminary Report of the Archaeological Project of Operation Drake.* London.

Hosein, F. E. M. 1976. *Hyarima and the Saints: A Miracle Play and Pageant of Santa Rosa.* Marabella, Trinidad: John S. Mowlah-Baksh.

Houk, J. T. 1995. *Spirits, Blood, and Drums: The Orisha Religion of Trinidad.* Temple University Press.

Howard, R. 2002. *Black Seminoles in the Bahamas.* Gainesville: University Press of Florida.

Howard, R. A. (ed.). 1989. *Flora of the Lesser Antilles.* Arnold Arboretum, MA: Jamaica Plain.

Howard, R. R. 1956. The Archaeology of Jamaica: A Preliminary Survey. *American Antiquity* Vol. 22 (1), pp. 45–59.

Howson, J. 1990. Social Relations and Material Culture: A Critique of the Archaeology of Plantation Slavery. *Historical Archaeology* Vol. 24 (4), pp. 78–91.

————. 1995. *Colonial Goods and the Plantation Village: Consumption and the Internal Economy in Montserrat from Slavery to Freedom.* Ph.D. dissertation. New York University, New York. Ann Arbor: University Microfilms.

Hugh-Jones, C. 1988. *From the Milk River: Spatial and Temporal Processes in Northwest Amazonia.* Cambridge: Cambridge University Press.

Hugh-Jones, S. 1979. *The Palm and the Pleiades: Initiation and Cosmology in Northwest Amazonia.* Cambridge: Cambridge University Press.

————. 1985. The Maloca: A World in a House. In E. Carmichael (ed.), *The Hidden Peoples of the Amazon,* pp. 77–93. London: British Museum Press.

————. 1995. Inside-Out and Back-to-Front: The Androgynous House in Northwest Amazonia. In J. Carsten and S. Hugh-Jones (eds.), *About the House—Levi-Strauss and beyond,* pp. 226–52. Cambridge: Cambridge University Press.

Hughes, G. 1750. *The Natural History of Barbados in Ten Books.* London.

Hulme, P. 1988. Chiefdoms of the Caribbean. *Critiques of Anthropology* 8, pp. 105–118.

————. 1992. *Colonial Encounters: Europe and the Native Caribbean 1492–1797.* London: Routledge.

————. 2000. *Remnants of Conquest: The Island Caribs and Their Visitors, 1877–1998.* Oxford: Oxford University Press.

Hulme, P., and N. L. Whitehead. 1992. *Wild Majesty: Encounters with Caribs from Columbus to the Present Day.* Oxford: Clarendon Press.

Humboldt, A. von. 1856. *The Island of Cuba.* New York.

Hume, N. I. 1968. A Collection of Glass from Port Royal, Jamaica, with Some Observations on the Site, Its History and Archaeology. *Historical Archaeology* Vol. 2, pp. 5–34.

Humfrey, M. 1975. *Sea Shells of the West Indies.* London: Collins.

Humphrey, C. 2000. *Honduras: Including the Bay Islands and Copan.* Moon Handbooks. Avalon Travel Publishing

Hunt, G., and P. Drewett. 2000. Tortola Material Culture II: Stone and Shell Artefacts. In P. Drewett (ed.), *Prehistoric Settlements in the Caribbean: Fieldwork in Barbados, Tortola, and the Cayman Islands.* London: Archetype Publications.

Im Thurn, E. 1882. Notes on West Indian stone-implements. *Timehri* 1, pp. 257–71.

————. 1884. Notes on West Indian Stone-Implements; and Other Indian Relics. *Timehri* 3, pp. 104–37.

Inniss, L. 1985. *Vestiges of an African Past in Barbadian Culture.* Unpublished manuscript, University of the West Indies, Cave Hill, Barbados.

Jahn, B., and T. Weber, 1998. *Reggae Island: Jamaican Music in the Digital Age.* New York: Da Capo Press.

James, C. L. R. 1994. *The Black Jacobins.* London: Allison and Busby.

James, J., J. Millet and A. Alarcon. 1998. *El Vodu en Cuba.* Santiago de Cuba: Editiorial Oriente.

Jane, C. W. E. 1982. *Shirley Heights: The Story of the Redcoats in Antigua.* Nelson's Dockyard National Park Foundation, English Harbour. Antigua.

Jesse, C. 1966. *St. Lucia: The Romance of Its Place Names.* St. Lucia Miscellany, Vol. 1. Castries, St. Lucia: St. Lucia Archaeological and Historical Society.

————. 1968. *The Amerindians in St. Lucia (Iouanalao).* Castries: St Lucia Archaeological and Historical Society.

————. 1973. Petroglyph and Rock-Cut Basins at Dauphin, St Lucia. *Proceedings of the Fourth International Congress for the Study of the Pre-Columbian Cultures of the Lesser Antilles, St Lucia 1971,* pp. 33–4.

————. 1973. The Caribs in St Lucia after A.D. 1605. *Proceedings of the Fourth International Congress for the Study of the Pre-Columbian Cultures of the Lesser Antilles, St Lucia 1971,* pp. 90–93.

Jiménez Lambertus, A. 1978. Representación Simbólica de la Tortuga Mítica en el Arte Cerámico Taíno. *Boletín del Museo del Hombre Dominicano* 11, pp. 63–76.

JNHT. 2001. Jamaica National Heritage Trust website. http://www.jnht.com

Johnson, K. 1997. *The Fragrance of Gold: Trinidad in the Age of Discovery.* School of Continuing Studies, University of the West Indies, St. Augustine, Trinidad.

Johnson, T. 1988. *Biodiversity and Conservation in the Caribbean.* ICPB Monographs 1. Cambridge, MA: International Council for Bird Preservation.

Jones, A. R. 1985. Dietary Change and Human Population at Indian Creek, Antigua. *American Antiquity* Vol. 50, No. 3, pp. 518–36.

Jones, D. J., and C. L. Johnson. 1951. *Report on Historic Sites of St. Croix, Virgin Islands of the United States. Part 2, Salt River Bay Area.* San Juan, PR: San Juan National Historic Site.

Jordan, P. B. 1986. *Herbal Medicine and Home Remedies: A Potpourri in Bahamian Culture.* Nassau: Guardian Printing Press.

Josselin de Jong, J. P. B. 1918. *The Praecolumbian and Early Postcolumbian Aboriginal Population of Aruba, Curaçao and Bonaire.* Internationales Archiv für Ethnographie 24 (3), pp. 51–114.

————. 1920. *The Praecolumbian and Early Postcolumbian Aboriginal Population of Aruba, Curaçao and Bonaire.* Internationales Archiv für Ethnographie 25, pp. 1–26.

Joyce, T. A. 1907. Prehistoric Antiquities from the Antilles, in the British Museum. *Journal of the Royal Anthropological Institute of Great Britain and Ireland,* 37, pp. 402–419.

————. 1916. *Central American and West Indian Archaeology.* London.

Judge, J., and J. L. Stanfield. 1986. The Islands of Landfall. *National Geographic* 170 (5), pp. 564–605.

Kalafou, A. n.d. *Obeah: Afro-Caribbean Shamanism.*

Kameneff, L., and J. Merlin. 1981. Archaeological Research at Crown Point, Tobago. *Caribena* 4, pp. 109–36.

Kane, R. E., et al. 1989. Emerald and Gold Treasures of the Spanish Galleon Nuestra Señora Atocha. *Gems and Gemology* 25 (4).

Karcheski, W., Jr. 1990. *Arms and Armour of the Conquistador, 1492–1600.* Gainesville: Florida Museum of Natural History.

Karsten, R. 1964. *Studies in the Religion of the South-American Indians East of the Andes. Commentationes Humanarum Litterarum* 29 (1). Helsinki: Societas Scientiarum Fennica.

Keegan, W. F. 1982. Lucayan Cave Burials from the Bahamas. *Journal of New World Archaeology* Vol. 5, pp. 57–65.

————. 1984. Pattern and Process in *Strombus gigas* Tool Replication. *Journal of New World Archaeology* Vol. 6 (2), pp. 15–24.

————. 1985. *Dynamic Horticulturalists: Population Expansion in the Prehistoric Bahamas.* Unpublished Ph.D. dissertation. Ann Arbor, MI: University Microfilms.

————. 1986. The Ecology of Lucayan Fishing Practices. *American Antiquity* Vol. 51, No. 4, pp. 816–25.

————. 1987. Diffusion of Maize from South America: The Antillean Connection Reconstructed. In W. F. Keegan (ed.), *Emergent Horticultural Economies of the Eastern Woodlands,* pp. 329–44. Center for Archaeological Investigations Occasional Papers 7. Carbondale: Southern Illinois University Press.

————. 1989. Creating the Guanahatabey (Ciboney): The Modern Genesis of an Extinct Culture. *Antiquity* Vol. 63, No. 239, pp. 373–379.

————. 1989. Transition from a Terrestial to a Marine Economy: A New View of the Crab/Shell Dichotomy. In P. E. Siegel (ed.), *Early Ceramic Population Lifeways and Adaptive Strategies in the Caribbean,* pp. 119–128. Oxford: British Archaeological Reports International Series 506.

————. 1992. *The People Who Discovered Columbus: The Prehistory of the Bahamas.* Gainesville: University Press of Florida.

————. (comp.). 1993. *Archaeology at Pearls, Grenada: The 1990 Field Season.* Miscellaneous Project Report 47, Department of Anthropology, Florida Museum of Natural History, University of Florida, Gainesville.

————. 1994. West Indian Archaeology. 1. Overview and Foragers. *Journal of Archaeological Research* 2 (3), pp. 255–284.

————. 1995. Modeling Dispersal in the Prehistoric West Indies. *World Archaeology* 26, pp. 400–20.

————. 1996. West Indian Archaeology. 2. After Columbus. *Journal of Archaeological Research* 4 (4), pp. 265–294.

————. 1997. *Bahamian Archaeology: Life in the Bahamas and Turks and Caicos Before Columbus.* Nassau: Media Publishing.

Keegan, W. F., and A. Cody. 1989. *Progress Report on the Archaeological Excavation at the Site of Pearls, Grenada, August 1989.* Miscellaneous Project Report No. 44, Florida Museum of Natural History, Gainesville, FL.

Keegan, W. F., and J. M. Diamond. 1986. Colonization of Islands by Humans: A Biogeographical Perspective. *Advances in Archaeological Method and Theory* Vol. 19, pp. 49–92.

Keegan, W. F., and M. D. Maclachlan. 1989. The Evolution of Avunculocal Chiefdoms: A Reconstruction of Taíno Kinship and Politics. *American Anthropologist* 91 (3), pp. 613–630.

Keegan, W. F., M. D. Maclachlan, and B. Byrne. 1998. Social Foundations of Taino *Caciques*. In E. Redmond (ed.), *Chiefdoms and Chieftaincy in the Americas,* pp. 217–44. Gainesville: University Press of Florida.

Keegan, W. F., and S. W. Mitchell. 1986. Possible Allochthonous Lucayan Arawak Distributions, Bahamas Islands. *Journal of Field Archaeology* Vol. 13, pp. 255–8.

Keeler, M. 1981. *Sir Francis Drake's West Indian Voyage, 1585–86.* London: Hakluyt Society.

Keen, B. 1992. Black Legend. In S. A. Bedini (ed.), *The Christopher Columbus Encyclopedia,* pp. 69–71. London: Macmillan.

Keith, D. H. 1987. *The Molasses Reef Wreck.* Ph.D. dissertation, Texas A&M University. Ann Arbor, MI: University Microfilms.

Keith, D. H., J. A. Duff, S. R. James, T. J. Oertling, and J. J. Simmons. 1984. The Molasses Reef Wreck, Turks and Caicos Islands B.W.I.: A Preliminary Report. *International Journal of Nautical Archaeology and Underwater Exploration* Vol. 13, pp. 45–63.

Keith, D. H., Carrell, T. L., and D. C. Lacey. 1990. The Search for Columbus' Caravel Gallega and the Site of Santa María Belén. *Journal of Field Archaeology* 17, pp. 123–40.

Keith, D. H., and J. J. Simmons. 1985. Analysis of Hull Remains, Ballast and Artifact Distribution of a 16th-Century Shipwreck, Molasses Reef, British West Indies. *Journal of Field Archaeology* Vol. 12, pp. 411–24.

Keith, R. G. 1971. Encomienda, Hacienda, and Corregimiento in Spanish America: A Structural Analysis. *Hispanic American Historical Review* 51, pp. 431–46.

Kelly, K. G. 2002. African Disapora Archaeology in Guadeloupe, French West Indies. *Antiquity* Vol. 76, No. 292, pp. 333–4.

Kelso, W. 1984. *Kingsmill Plantations, 1619–1800.* Orlando, FL: Academic Press.

Kerchache, J. (ed.). 1994. *L'art des sculpteurs taínos: Chefs d'oeuvres des Grandes Antilles précolombiennes.* Paris: Musée du Petit Palais.

Kerns, V. 1983. *Women and the Ancestors: Black Carib Kinship and Ritual.* Urbana: University of Illinois Press.

Kicza, J. E. 1997. Native American, African and Hispanic Communities During the Middle Period in the Colonial Americas. *Historical Archaeology* 31, pp. 9–18.

King, S. 1998. International Reggae, Democratic Socialism, and the Secularization of the rastafarian Movement, 1972–1980. *Popular Music and Society* 22 (3), pp. 39–64.

Kiple, K. F., and K. O. Ornelas. 1996. After the Encounter: Disease and Demographics in the Lesser Antilles. In R. L. Paquette and S. L. Engerman (eds.), *The Lesser Antilles in the Age of European Expansion,* pp. 50–67. Gainesville: University Press of Florida.

Kirby, E. 1976. A Newly Found Petroglyphic Rock on St Vincent. *Proceedings of the Sixth International Congress for the Study of Pre-Columbian Cultures of the Lesser Antilles, Point-à-Pitre, Guadeloupe, July 1975.*

———. 1977. *Pre-Columbian Monuments in Stone.* (2nd ed.). The St. Vincent Archaeological and Historical Society 1969. Kingstown, St. Vincent: Reliance Press Ltd.

Kirby, E., and C. I. Martin. 1986. *The Rise and Fall of the Black Caribs.* 2nd ed. Kingstown, St. Vincent.

Kirchoff, P. 1948. The Caribbean Lowland Tribes: The Mosquito, Sumo, Paya, and Jicaque. In J. H. Steward (ed.), *Handbook of South American Indians 4,* pp. 219–230. Washington, DC: Smithsonian Institution.

Knapp, J. 1993. Elizabthan Tobacco. In S. Greenblatt (ed.), *New World Encounters,* pp. 272–312. Berkeley: University of California Press.

Kopytoff, B. K. 1976a Jamaican Maroon Political Organization: The Effects of the Treaties. *Social and Economic Studies* Vol. 25(2), pp. 87–105.

―――――. 1976b. The Development of Jamaican Maroon Ethnicity. *Caribbean Quarterly* Vol. 22 (2–3), pp. 33–50.

―――――. 1979. Colonial Treaty as Sacred Charter of the Jamaican Maroons. *Ethnohistory* Vol. 26 (1), pp. 45–64.

―――――. 1987. Religious Change among the Jamaican Maroons: The Ascendance of the Christian God within a Traditional Cosmology. *Journal of Social History* Vol. 20 (3), pp. 463–484.

Kozlowski, J. K. 1974. *Preceramic Cultures in the Caribbean.* Zeszyty Naukowe, Uniwerstytetu Jagiellonskiego, 386, Prace Archeologiczne, Zezyt 20. Krakow.

Kozuch, L. 1993. *Sharks and Shark Products in Prehistoric South Florida.* Monograph of the Institute of Archaeology and Palaeoenvironmental Studies. University of Florida, Gainesville, FL.

Kremser, M. (ed.). 1990. *Ay Bo Bo: African Caribbean Religions.* Second International Conference of the Society for Caribbean Research. Vienna: WUV Universitat.

―――――. 2001. African-Derived Religions in Barbados. In S. D. Glazier (ed.), *Encyclopedia of African and African-American Religions,* pp. 41–43. New York: Routledge.

Kremser, M., and K. R. Wernhart (eds.). 1986. *Research in Ethnography and Ethnohistory of St. Lucia: A Preliminary Report.* Horn: F. Berger and Shone.

Krieger, H. W. 1929. *Archaeological and Historical Investigations in Samaná, Dominican Republic.* United States National Museum Bulletin 147. Washington, DC: Smithsonian Institution.

―――――. 1931. *Aboriginal Indian Pottery of the Dominican Republic.* United States National Museum Bulletin 156. Washington, DC: Smithsonian Institution.

―――――. 1937. The Bahama Islands and Their Prehistoric Population. In *Explorations and Fieldwork of the Smithsonian Institution in 1936,* pp. 93–8. Washington, DC: Smithsonian Institution Press.

―――――. 1938. Archaeology of the Virgin Islands. In *Explorations and Fieldwork of the Smithsonian Institution in 1937,* pp. 95–102. Washington, DC: Smithsonian Institution Press.

Kunz, G. F., and C. H. Stevenson. [1908] 1993. *The Book of the Pearl.* New York: Dover.

Kusche, L. 1995. *The Bermuda Triangle Solved.* Prometheus Books.

Labat, J.-B. 1970. *The Memoirs of Pere Labat, 1693–1705.* (transl. J. Eaden). London: Frank Cass.

Lafleaur, G., S. Branson, and G. Turner. 1993. *Amerindians, Africans, Americans: Three Papers in Caribbean History.* Department of History: University of the West Indies, Mona, Jamaica.

Laguerre, M. 1988. *Afro-Caribbean Folk Medicine.* Bergin and Garvey.

―――――. 1989. *Voodoo and Politics in Haiti.* New York: St. Martin's Press.

Laird, N. 1992. Shango Worship in Trinidad. In G. Besson and B. Brereton, *The Book of Trinidad,* pp. 368–74. Port of Spain: Paria Publishing.

Lake, O. 1998. Religion, Patriarchy, and the Status of Rastafarian Women. In P. B. Clarke (ed.), *New Trends and Developments in African Religions,* pp. 141–58. Westport, CT: Greenwood Press.

―――――. 1998. *Rastafari Women: Subordination in the Midst of Liberation Theology.* Durham: Carolina Academic Press.

Landers, J. 1990. African Presence in the Early Colonization of the Caribbean and Southeastern Borderlands. In D. H. Thomas (ed.), *Columbian Consequences,* 2, pp. 315–28. Washington, DC: Smithsonian Institution Press.

Landman-Bouges, J. 1977. Rastafarian Food Habits. *Cajanus* 9 (4) pp. 228–234.

Lane, K. E. 1999. *Blood and Silver: A History of Piracy in the Caribbean and Central America.* Oxford: Signal Books.

La Rosa Corzo, G. 1991. La Cueva de la Cachimba: Estudio Arqueólogico de un Refugio de Cimarrones. *Estudios Arqueólogicos* 1989, pp. 57–84.

―――――. 1995. *Costumbres funerarias de los aborigenes de Cuba.* Havana: Editorial Academia.

Las Casas, B. de. 1992. *A Short Account of the Destruction of the Indies.* Harmondsworth: Penguin.

―――――. 1971. *Bartolomé de Las Casas: History of the Indies.* Ed. and transl. A. M. Collard. New York: Harper and Row.

Laurence, K. M. 1975. Continuity and Change in Trinidadian Toponyms. *Nieuwe West-Indische Gids* Vol. 50, pp. 123–142.

Lawaetz, E. J. 1991. *St. Croix: 500 Years Pre-Columbus to 1990.* Herning, Denmark: Pout Kristensen.

Layng, A. 1983. *The Carib Reserve: Identity and Security in the West Indies.* Washington, DC

——. 1985. The Caribs of Dominica. *Ethnic Groups* 6 (2–3), pp. 209–21.

Lehmann, Henri. 1951. Un "duho" de la civilization taíno au Musée de l'Homme. *Journal de la Société des Américanistes* 40, pp. 153–61.

Lellouch, D. 2000. *Nevis: Queen of the Caribbean.* Hummingbird Productions.

Leshikar, M. E. 1993. *The 1794 "Wreck of the Ten Sail," Cayman Islands, British West Indies: A Historical Study and Archaeological Survey.* Ph.D. dissertation, Texas A&M University. Ann Arbor, MI: University Microfilms.

——. 1997. Underwater Cultural Resource Management: A New Concept in the Cayman Islands. *Underwater Archaeology,* pp. 33–7.

——. 1997. Wreck of the Ten Sail. In J. P. Delgado (ed.), *Encyclopaedia of Underwater and Maritime Archaeology,* p. 416. London: British Museum Press.

Levenson, Jay A. (ed.). 1991. *Circa 1492: Art in the Age of Exploration.* Washington, DC: National Gallery of Art, and New Haven: Yale University Press.

Lewin, O. 1968. Jamaican Folk Music. *Caribbean Quarterly* 14 (1–2), pp. 49–56.

Lewis, S. (ed.). 1989. Contemporary Art of Trinidad and Tobago. *International Review of African American Art* 8: 8–64.

Lewis, W. 1997. *Soul Rebels: The Rastafari.* Illinois: Waveland Press.

Linares, O. F. 1977. *Ecology and the Arts in Panama: On the Development of Social Rank and Symbolism in the Central Provinces.* Washington, DC: Dumbarton Oaks.

Lindsay, A. (ed.). 1996. *Santería Aesthetics in Conemporary Latin American Art.* Washington, DC: Smithsonian Institution Press.

Link, M. C. 1960. Exploring the Drowned City of Port Royal. *National Geographic Magazine* 117 (1), pp. 151–83.

Lippold, L. K. 1991. Animal Resource Utilization by Saladoid Peoples at Pearls. *Proceedings of the Thirteenth Congress of the International Association for Caribbean Archaeology,* pp. 264–8. Curaçao.

Littlewood, R. 1993. *Pathology and Identity: The Work of Mother Earth in Trinidad.* Cambridge: Cambridge University Press.

Littman, S. L., and W. F. Keegan. 1991. A Shell Bread Manufacturing Centre on Grand Turk, T.C.I. *Proceedings of the Fourteenth International Congress for Caribbean Archaeology, Barbados,* pp. 147–56.

Lockhart, J. 1969. Encomienda and Hacienda: The Evolution of the Great Estate in the Spanish Indies. *Hispanic American Historical Review* 49, pp. 411–429.

Long, E. 1774. *The History of Jamaica.* 3 vols. London.

Longuefosse, J-L. 1995. *100 Plantes Médicinales de la Caraibe.* Trinité, Martinique: Gondwana Editions.

López-Baralt, M. 1985. *El mito taíno: raíz y proyección en la Amazonia continental.* (Revised edition). Río Piedras: Ediciones Huracan.

López Cruz, F. 1967. *La Música Folklórica de Puerto Rico.* Sharon, CT: Troutman Press.

Lothrop, S. K. 1923. Stone Yokes from Mexico and Central America. *Man* 23 (58), pp. 97–8.

——. 1924. *Tulum: An Archaeological Study of the East Coast of Yucatan.* Carnegie Institution Washington Publication 335. Washington, DC.

——. 1952. Metals from the Cenote of Sacrifice, Chichén Itzá, Yucatán. *Memoirs of the Peabody Museum, Harvard University* X (1). Cambridge, MA.

Lovell, W. G. 1992. "Heavy Shadows and Black Night": Disease and Depopulation in Colonial Spanish America. In K. W. Butzer (ed), *The Americas before and after 1492: Current Geographical Research. Annals of the American Association of Geographers* 82 (3), pp. 426–443.

Lovén, S. 1935. *Origins of the Tainan Culture, West Indies.* Göteborg: Elanders.

Lucrece, A. (ed.). 1989. *Civilisations Precolombiennes de la Caraibe: Actes du colloque du Marin.* Saint Joseph, Martinique: Presses Universitaires Creoles.

Luis, W. 2000. *Culture and Customs of Cuba.* Greenwood Publishing Group.

Lum, K. A. 1999. *Praising His Name in the Dance: Spirit-Possession in the Spiritual Baptist Faith and Orisha Work in Trinidad, West Indies.* Amsterdam: Harwood.

Lundberg, E. R. 1985. Interpreting the Cultural Associations of Aceramic Deposits in the Virgin Islands. *Journal of Field Archaeology* Vol. 12, pp. 201–212.

———. 1989. *Preceramic Procurement Patterns at Krum Bay, Virgin Islands.* Ph.D. dissertation, University of Illinois, Urbana.

———. 1991. Interrelationships among Preceramic Complexes of Puerto Rico and the Virgin Islands. *Proceedings of the Thirteenth International Congress for Caribbean Archaeology, Willemstadt, Curaçao, July 24–29, 1989,* pp. 73–85.

Lyon, E. 1985. *The Search for the Atocha.* Port Salerno: Florida Classic Press.

———. 1989. *The Search for the Mother Lode of the Atocha.* Port Salerno: Florida Classics Press.

———. 1990. *The Enterprise of Florida.* Gainesville: University Press of Florida.

MacInnes, C. M. 1926. *The Early English Tobacco Trade.* London: Keegan Paul, Thubner.

Magaña, C. S. 1999. Crillo Pottery from San Juan de Puerto Rico. In J. B. Haviser (ed.), *African Sites Archaeology in the Caribbean,* pp. 131–43. Princeton, NJ: Markus Wiener Publishers,

Magaña, E., and F. Jara. 1982. The Carib Sky. *Journal de la Société des Américanistes* 68, pp. 105–32.

Malcom, C. 1996. The St John's Bahamas Wreck: Interim Report 1: The Excavation and Artefacts, 1991–5. *Astrolabe-Journal of the Mel Fisher Maritime Heritage Society* 9 (1).

Manuel, P. 1990. *Essays on Cuban Music: Cuban and North American Perspectives.* Lanham, MD: University Press of America.

Manuel, P., K. Bilby and R. Largey. 1995. *Caribbean Currents: Caribbean Music from Rumba to Reggae.* Philadelphia, PA: Temple University Press.

Mann, C. J. 1986. Composition and Origin of Material in Pre-Columbian Pottery, San Salvador Island, Bahamas. *Geoarchaeology* Vol. 1, pp. 183–94.

Marken, M. 1994. *Pottery from Spanish shipwrecks, 1500–1800.* Gainesville: University Press of Florida.

Marley, D. F. 1994. *Pirates and Privateers of the Americas.* Santa Barbara, CA: ABC-ClIO.

Marshall, B. 1973. The Black Caribs: Native Resistance to British Penetration into the Windward Side of St. Vincent 1763–1773. *Caribbean Quarterly* 19, pp. 4–19.

Martí, S. 1968. *Instrumentos Musicales Precortesianos.* México, D.F.: Instituto Nacional de Antropología.

Martin, R. 1999. Ceremonial Offerings and Religious Practices among Taíno Indians: An Archaeological Invesigation of Gourd Use in Taíno Culture. http://www.iusb.edu/~journal/1999/Paper11

Martínez Arango, F. 1991. Hallazgo en Cuba de un nuevo duho aborigen de las Antillas. *Boletín del Museo del Hombre Dominicano* 18 (24), pp. 15–26.

Martin-Kaye, P. H. A. 1959. *Geology of the Leeward and British Virgin Islands.* Castries (St. Lucia): The Voice Publishing Co.

Martyr D'Anghera, P. 1970. *De Orbe Novo: The Eight Decades of Peter Martyr D'Anghera.* Transl. F. A. MacNutt. New York: Burt Franklin.

Marvel, J., and R. H. Power. 1991. The Quest for Where America Began: The Case for Grand Turk. *American History Illustrated* Vol. 25 (6), pp. 48–69.

Marx, J. 1991. *Pirates and Privateers of the Caribbean.* Melbourne, FL: R. E. Krieger Publishing Co.

Marx, R. F. 1967. *Pirate Port: The Story of the Sunken City of Port Royal.* Cleveland: World.

———. 1968. Divers of Port Royal. *Jamaica Journal* Vol. 2 (1), pp. 15–33.

———. 1968. *Treasure Fleets of the Spanish Main.* New York: World Publishing Co.

————. 1973. *Port Royal Rediscovered*. New York: Doubleday.

Mason, J. A. 1941. A Large Archaeological Site at Capá, Utuado, with Notes on Other Porto Rico Sites Visited in 1914–15. *Scientific Survey of Porto Rico and the Virgin Islands* 18 (2), pp. 209–72.

Mason, O. T. 1877. Jadeite Celts from Turks and Caicos Islands, Also Two Low Wooden Stools. *American Naturalist* Vol. 11, p. 626.

Maynard, C. J. 1890. Some Inscriptions Found in Hartford Cave, Rum Cay, Bahamas. *Contributions to Science* Vol. 1, pp. 167–71.

————. 1893. Traces of the Lucayan Indian in the Bahamas. *Contributions to Science,* Vol. 2, pp. 23–34.

Mason, J. A. 1917. Excavation of a New Archaeological Site in Porto Rico. *Proceedings of the XX Congress of Americanists,* pp. 220–3. Washington, DC

————. 1941. *A Large Archaeological Site at Capá, Utuado, with Notes on Other Puerto Rican Sites Visited in 1914–15.* Scientific Survey of Puerto Rico and the Virgin Islands, Vol 18 (2). New York: New York Academy of Sciences.

Mason, M. A. 2002. *Living Santeria: Rituals and Experiences in an Afro-Cuban Religion.* Washington, DC: Smithsonian Institution Press.

Mason, O. T. 1877. *The Latimer Collection of Antiquities from Porto Rico in the National Museum at Washington, DC from the Smithsonian Report for 1876.* Washington, DC: Government Printing Office.

————. 1885. *The Guesde Collection of Antiquities in Pointe-à-Pître, Guadeloupe, West Indies, from the Smithsonian Report for 1884,* pp. 731–837. Washington, DC: Government Printing Office.

Mason, P. 1998. *Bacchanal!: The Carnival Culture of Trinidad.* Philadelphia, PA: Temple University Press.

Massé, R. 1966. Fishing Rites and Recipes in a Martiniquan Village. *Caribbean Studies* 6 (1), pp. 3–24.

Matheson, L. 1985. *The Folklore of St. Christopher's Island.* Basseterre: Creole Graphics.

Matthiesson, P. 1975. *Far Tortuga.* New York: Random House.

Mathewson, R. D. 1972a. History from the Earth: Archaeological Excavations at Old King's House. *Jamaica Journal* 6, pp. 3–11.

————. 1972b. Jamaican Ceramics: An Introduction to 18th-Century Folk Pottery in West African Tradition. *Jamaica Journal* 6, pp. 54–6.

————. 1983. *Archaeological Treasure: The Search for the "Nuestra Señora de Atocha."* Woodstock, VT: Seafarers Heritage Library.

————. 1986. *Treasure of the "Atocha": Sixteen Dramatic Years in Search of the Historic Shipwreck.* New York: Dutton.

Matibag, E. 1996. *Afro-Cuban Religious Experience: Cultural Reflections in Narrative.* Gainesville: University of Florida Press.

Mattioni, M. 1982. *Salvage Excavations at the Fond-Brulé Site, Martinique, Final Report.* University of Manitoba Anthropology Papers 27. Winnipeg: University of Manitoba.

Mattioni, M., and R. P. Bullen. 1974. Precolumbian Dogs in the Lesser and Greater Antilles. *Proceedings of the Fifth International Congress for Caribbean Archaeology,* Antigua 1973, pp. 162–165.

Mattioni, M., and M. Nicholas. 1972. *Art Precolombien de la Martinique.* Musée Departmental de la Martinique, Moure.

Mauldin, C. S. (ed.). 1995. *Fodor's 96: The Bahamas.* Fodor Travel Publications.

Mayes, P. 1972. *Port Royal Jamaica, Excavations 1969–1970.* Kingston: Jamaica National trust Commission.

Mayes, P., and P. A. Mayes. 1972. Port Royal, Jamaica: The Archaeological Problems and Potential. *International Journal of Nautical Archaeology and Underwater Exploration* 1, pp. 97–112.

McAlister, E. A. 2002. *Rara: Vodou, Power, and Performance in Haiti and Its Diaspora.* Berkeley: University of California Press.

McCartney, T. 1976. *Ten, Ten The Bible Ten: Obeah in the Bahamas.* Nassau: Timpaul Publishing Company.

McDaniel, L. 1998. *The Big Drum Ritual of Carriacou.* Gainesville: University Press of Florida.

McEwan, B. G. 1986. Domestic Adaptation at Puerto Real, Haiti. *Historical Archaeology* 20 (1), pp. 44–9.

McFarlane, M. 1977. *Cudjoe the Maroon*. London: Allison and Busby.

McGinnis, S. 1997. Zemi Three-Pointer Stones. In F. Bercht, E. Brodsky, J. A. Farmer, and D. Taylor (eds.). *Taíno: Pre-Columbian Art and Culture from the Caribbean,* pp. 92–105. New York: The Monacelli Press.

————. 1997. *Ideographic Expression in the Precolumbian Caribbean.* Unpublished Ph.D. dissertation, University of Texas, Austin.

McKusick, Marshall. 1960. *Distribution of Ceramic Styles in the Lesser Antilles, West Indies.* Ph.D. Dissertation. Yale University, New Haven, CT.

————. *Aboriginal Canoes in the West Indies.* Yale University Publications in Anthropology 63. New Haven, CT: Yale University Press.

Medina, J. T. 1988. *The Discovery of the Amazon.* New York: Dover.

Meggers, B. J., and C. Evans. 1978. Lowland South America and the Antilles. In J. D. Jennings (ed.), *Ancient South Americans,* pp. 287–336. San Francisco: W. H. Freeman.

Merrill, G. C. 1958. *The Historical Geography of St. Kitts and Nevis, The West Indies.* Mexico City: Instituto Panamericano de Geografía e Historia.

Mester, A. M. 1990. *The Pearl Divers of Los Frailes: Archaeological and Ethnohistorical Explorations of Sumptuary Good Trade and Cosmology in the North and Central Andes.* Ph.D. dissertation, University of Illinois at Urbana-Champaign. Ann Arbor: University Microfilms.

Métraux, Alfred. 1959. *Voodoo in Haiti.* New York: Schocken Books.

Meylan, A. 1981. Behavioral Ecology of the West Caribbean Green Turtle (*Chelonia mydas*) in the Internesting Habitat. In K. A. Bjorndal (ed.), *Biology and Conservation of Sea Turtles,* pp. 67–80. Washington, DC: Smithsonian Institution Press.

Michelin. 2001. *Michelin Green Sightseeing Guide to Guadeloupe and Martinique.* French and European Publishing.

Milanich, J. T. 1994. *Archaeology of Precolumbian Florida.* Gainesville: University Press of Florida.

————. 1998. *Florida Indians from Ancient Times to the Present.* Gainesville: University Press of Florida.

————. *Laboring in the Fields of the Lord: Spanish Missions and Southeastern Indians.* Washington, DC: Smithsonian Institution Press.

Milanich, J. T., and C. H. Fairbanks. 1980. *Florida Archaeology.* New York: Academic Press.

Milanich, J. T., and C. Hudson. 1993. *Hernando de Soto and the Florida Indians.* Gainesville: University Press of Florida.

Milanich, J. T., and S. Milbrath (edsa). 1989. *First Encounters: Spanish Explorations in the Caribbean and the United States, 1492–1570.* Gainesville: University Press of Florida.

Milbrath, S. 1991. Representations of Caribbean and Latin American Indians in Sixteenth-century European Art. *Archiv für Volkerkunde* 45, pp. 1–38.

Miller, A. G. 1977. The Maya and the Sea: Trade and Cult at Tancah and Tulum. In E. P. Benson (ed.), *The Sea in the Pre-Columbian World,* pp. 97–225. Washington D.C.: Dumbarton Oaks.

————. 1982. *On the Edge of the Sea: Mural Painting at Tancah-Tulum, Quintana Roo, Mexico.* Washington D.C.: Dumbarton Oaks.

Mintz, S. 1974. *Caribbean Transformations.* Baltimore: Johns Hopkins University Press.

————. 1986. *Sweetness and Power: The Place of Sugar in Modern History.* Harmondsworth: Penguin.

————. 1991. Pleasure, Profit, and Satiation. In H. J. Viola and C. Margolis (eds.), *Seeds of Change: Five Hundred Years since Columbus,* pp. 112–129. Washington, DC: Smithsonian Institution Press.

Mintz, S., and R. Price. 1976. *An Anthropological Approach to the Afro-American Past: A Caribbean Perspective.* Philadelphia, PA: Institute for the Study of Human Issues.

Mira Caballos, E. 1997. *El Indio Antillano: Repartimiento, encomienda y esclavitud (1492–1542).* Seville: Muñoz Moya Editor.

Molander, A. 1983. A New Approach to the Columbus Landfall. *Terrae Incognitae* 15, pp. 113–149.

Moldes, R. 1975. *Música folklórica cubana*. Miami, FL: Ediciones Universal.

Momsen, J. (ed.). 1993. *Women and Change in the Caribbean*. Bloomington: Indiana University Press.

Montás, O, P. J. Borrell and F. Moya Pons. 1983. *Arte taíno*. Santo Domingo: Banco Central de la República Dominicana.

Montbrun, C. Unknown. *Les Petites Antilles avant Christophe Colomb: vie quotidienne des Indiens de la Guade-loupe*. Karthala.

Moodie-Kublalsingh, S. 1994. *The Cocoa Panyols of Trinidad: An Oral Record*. London: British Academic Press.

Moore, C. 1982. Investigation of Preceramic Sites on Ile à Vache, Haiti. *Florida Anthropologist* 35 (4), pp. 186–199.

Moore, D. 1997. Nuestra Señora de la Concepción. In J. P. Delgado (ed.), *Encyclopedia of Underwater and Maritime Archaeology*, pp. 299–300. London: British Museum Press.

Morales Padron, F. 1962. *Jamaica Espanola*. Escuela de Estudios Hispano-Americanos, Pub. 67, Seville.

Morbán Laucer, F. 1988. El murciélago: sus representaciones en el arte rupestre y la mitología precolom-bina. *Boletín del Museo del Hombre Dominicano* XV (21), pp. 37–57.

Morbán, L., and A. Fernando. 1970. *Pintura rupestre y petroglífos de la Provincia de Azua*. Santo Domingo: Fundación García Arévalo.

Mordecai, M., and P. Mordecai. 2000. *Culture and Customs of Jamaica*. Westport, CT: Greenwood Publishing Group.

Morgan, G. S., and C. A. Woods. 1986. Extinction and the Zoogeography of West Indian Land Mammals. *Biological Journal of the Linnean Society* Vol. 28, pp. 167–203.

Morris, E. L. 2000. A Caribbean Feasibility—the Nevis Heritage Project. *Antiquity* Vol. 74, pp. 267–8.

Morris, P. A. 1973. *A Field Guide to Shells of the Atlantic and Gulf Coasts and the West Indies*. Boston, Mass.: Houghton Mifflin.

Morrish, I. 1982. *Obeah, Christ and Rastaman: Jamaica and Its Religions*. Cambridge, MA: James Clarke Press.

Morrison, S. E. 1940. The Route of Columbus along the North Coast of Haiti and the Site of La Navidad. *Transactions of the American Philosophical Society* 31 (4), pp. 239–85.

———. 1942. *Admiral of the Ocean Sea: A Life of Christopher Columbus*. Boston: Little, Brown.

Morse, Birgit Faber. 1989. Saladoid Remains and Adaptive Strategies in St. Croix, Virgin Islands. In Peter E. Siegel (ed.), *Early Ceramic Population Lifeways and Adaptive Strategies in the Caribbean*, pp. 29–42. Oxford: British Archaeological Reports International Series 506.

———. 1990. The Pre-Columbian Ball and Dance Court at Salt River, St. Croix. *FOLK: Journal of the Danish Ethnographical Society* 32, pp. 45–60.

———. 1997. The Salt River Site, St. Croix, at the Time of the Encounter. In Samuel M. Wilson (ed.), *The Indigenous People of the Caribbean*, pp. 36–45. Gainesville: University Press of Florida.

Moscoso, F. 1981. *The Development of Tribal Society in the Caribbean*. Ph.D. dissertation, State University of New York at Binghamton.

———. 1999. *Sociedad y Economía de los Taínos*. Río Piedras, PR: Editorial Edil.

Mowat, L. 1989. *Cassava and Chicha: Bread and Beer of the Amazonian Indians*. Princes Risborough: Shire Publications.

Moya Pons, F. 1992. The Politics of Forced Indian Labour in La Española. *Antiquity* 66 (250): 130–9.

———. 1995. *The Dominican Republic: A National History*. New Rochelle, NY: Hispaniola Books.

Muckelroy, K. 1978. *Maritime Archaeology*. Cambridge: Cambridge University Press.

——— (ed.). 1980. *Archaeology Under Water*. Cambridge: Cambridge University Press.

Mulroy, K. 1993. Ethnogenesis and Ethnohistory of the Seminole Maroons. *Journal of World History* 4 (2), pp. 287–305.

———. 1993. *Freedom on the Border: The Seminole Maroons in Florida, the Indian Territory, Coahuila, and Texas*. Lubbock: Texas Tech University Press.

Mulvaney, R. M. 1990. *Rastafari and Reggae: A Dictionary and Sourcebook*. Westport, CT: Greenwood Press.

Murphy, J. M. 1993. *Santeria: African Spirits in America.* Boston: Beacon Press.

Murphy, R. 1989. Betty's Hope Old North Mill excavated. *Antigua Historical and Archaeological Society Newsletter* 27 (1), p. 5.

—————. 1993. The Importance of Betty's Hope in a Caribbean Historical Perspective. *Antigua Historical and Archaeological Society Newsletter* 42, p. 5.

Murray, J. A. 1991. *The Islands and the Sea: Five Centuries of Nature Writing from the Caribbean.* Oxford: Oxford University Press.

Murrell, N. S., W. D. Spencer and A. A. McFarlane (eds.). 1998. *Chanting Down Babylon: The Rastafari Reader.* Kingston: Ian Randle Ltd.

Myers, R. 1984. Island Carib Cannibalism. *Nieuwe West-Indische Gids* 58, pp. 147–84.

Nader, H. 1992a. Christopher Columbus: Columbus in Spain. In S. A. Bedini (ed.). *The Christopher Columbus Encyclopedia* Vol. 1, pp. 187–98. New York: Simon and Schuster.

—————. 1992b. Christopher Columbus: Early Maritime Experience. In S. A. Bedini (ed.). *The Christopher Columbus Encyclopedia* Vol. 1, pp. 167–74. New York: Simon and Schuster.

—————. 1992c. Christopher Columbus: The Final Years, Illness, and Death. In S. A. Bedini (ed.). *The Christopher Columbus Encyclopedia* Vol. 1, pp. 198–204. New York: Simon and Schuster.

Narganes Storde, Y. M. 1991. Secuencia cronológica de dos sitios arqueólogicos de Puerto Rico (Sorcé, Vieques y Tecla, Guayanilla). *Proceedings of the Thirteenth International Congress for Caribbean Archaeology Held at Willemstadt, Curaçao, on July 24–29, 1989,* pp. 628–46. Willemstadt.

National Gallery of Jamaica. 1994. *Arawak Vibrations: Homage to the Jamaican Taino.* Kingston: National Gallery of Jamaica and Jamaica National Heritage Trust.

Nettleford, R. 1978. Heritage Tourism and the Myth of Paradise. *Caribbean Review* XVI (3 and 4), pp. 9–12.

Newman, M. T. 1976. Aboriginal New World Epidemiology and Medical Care, and the Impact of Old World Disease Imports. *American Journal of Physical Anthropology* 45, pp. 667–72.

Newsom, L. A. 1993. *Plant Use by Saladoid and Taíno People of the Caribbean.* Ph.D. dissertation, Department of Anthropology, University of Florida. Ann Arbor: University Microfilms.

Newsom, L. A., and K. Deagan. 1994. *Zea Mays* in the West Indies: The Archaeological and Early Historical Record. In S. Johannessen and C. Hastorf (eds.), *Corn and Culture in the New World,* pp. 203–17. Boulder, CO: Westview Press.

Newson, L. 1976. *Aboriginal and Spanish Colonial Trinidad.* New York: Academic Press.

Nicholls, D. 1985. *Haiti in Caribbean Context: Ethnicity, Economy and Revolt.* London: MacMillan.

Nicholson, D. V. 1976. Pre-Columbian Seafaring Capabilities in the Lesser Antilles. *Proceedings of International Congress for the Study of Pre-Columbian Cultures of the Lesser Antilles,* 6: 98–105. Gainesville, FL.

—————. 1979. The Dating of West Indian Historic Sites by the Analysis of Ceramic Sherds. *Journal of the Virgin Islands Archaeological Society* 7, pp. 52–74.

—————. 1983. *English Harbour, Antigua: An Historical and Archaeological Sketch.* Antigua Archaeological and Historical Society. St. John's, Antigua.

—————. 1983. *The Story of the Arawaks in Antigua and Barbuda.* Antigua: Antigua Archaeological Society and Linden Press.

—————. 1984. *Folk Pottery and Emancipation in Antigua and Barbuda.* Antigua Archaeological and Historical Society. St. John's, Antigua.

—————. 1994. *Heritage Landmarks, Antigua and Barbuda.* St. John's, Antigua: Museum of Antigua and Barbuda.

—————. 1995. The Archaeology of Antigua and Barbuda. Heritage Publications. St. John's, Antigua: Museum of Antigua and Barbuda.

—————. 1995. Mud and Blood: Artifacts from Dredging and the Naval Hospital, English Harbour, Antigua. *Proceedings of the Fifteenth Congress of the International Association for Caribbean Archaeology 1993,* p. 45.: San Juan, PR: Centro de Estudios Avanzados de Puerto Rico y el Caribe.

Nietschmann, B. 1972. Hunting and Fishing Focus among the Miskito Indians, Eastern Nicaragua. *Human Ecology* 1 (1), pp. 41–67.

———. 1973. *Between Land and Water: The Subsistence Ecology of the Miskito Indians, Eastern Nicaragua.* New York: Seminar Press.

———. 1981. The Cultural Context of Sea Turtle Hunting in the Caribbean and Problems Caused by Commercial Exploitation. In K. A. Bjorndal (ed.), *Biology and Conservation of Sea Turtles.* Washington, DC: Smithsonian Institution Press.

Nordenskiöld, E. 1925. *An Historical and Ethnological Survey of the Cuna Indians.* Comparative Ethnological Studies 10, Göteborg Museum, Göteborg.

———. 1929. The Relationship between Art, Religion, and Magic among the Cuna and Choco Indians. *Journal de la Société des Américanistes* 21, pp. 141–158.

Nowell, C. E. 1945. The Treaty of Tordesillas and the Diplomatic Background of American History. In *Greater America: Essays in Honour of Herbert E. Bolton.* Berkeley: University of California Press.

Núñez Jiménez, A. 1985. *Arte rupestre de Cuba.* Editorial Jaca Book Spa. (Italy).

Nunley, J. W. 1988. Masquerade Mix-up in Trinidad Carnival: Live Once, Die Forever. In J. W. Nunley and J. Bettleheim (eds.), *Caribbean Festival Arts: Each and Every Bit of Difference,* pp. 85–116. Seattle: University of Washington Press.

Nunley, J. W., and J. Bettleheim (eds.). 1988. *Caribbean Festival Arts: Each and Every Bit of Difference.* Seattle: University of Washington Press.

Nurse, K. 1999. Globalization and Trinidad Carnival: Diaspora, Hybridity, and Identity in Global Culture. *Cultural Studies* 13: 661–90.

O'Brien-Rothe, L. 1976. Music in a Maya Cosmos. *The World of Music* 18 (3), pp. 35–42.

———. 1982. Marimbas of Guatemala: The African Connection. *The World of Music* 25 (2), pp. 99–104.

Ohm, C. C. 1995. *Landscapes and Plantations on Tobago: A Regional Perspective.* Unpublished Ph.D. dissertation, Department of Anthropology, University of Florida, Gainesville.

———. 1997. Settlement Patterning on the British Caribbean Island of Tobago. *Historical Archaeology* Vol. 3 (2), pp. 93–106.

Ohm, C. C., and T. H. Eubanks 1994. The Tobago Archaeological Program: Developing a Comprehensive Historic Preservation Programm for Tobago. *Public Archaeology Review* Vol. 2 (2), pp. 14–19.

Oliver, J. R. 1989. *The Archaeological, Linguistic and Ethnological Evidence for the Expansion of Arawakan into Northwestern Venezuela and Northeastern Colombia.* Ph.D. dissertation, University of Illinois at Urbana-Champaign. Ann Arbor: University Microfilms.

———. 1997. The Taino Cosmos. In Samuel M. Wilson (ed.), *The Indigenous People of the Caribbean,* pp. 140–154. Gainesville: University Press of Florida.

———. 1997. Dabajuroid Archaeology, Settlements and House Structures: An Overview from Mainland Western Venezuela. In A. H. Versteeg and S. Rostain (eds.), *The Archaeology of Aruba: The Tanki Flip Site,* pp. 363–429. Publications of the Archaeological Museum of Aruba 8.

———. 1998. *El Centro ceremonial de Caguana, Puerto Rico. Simbolismo iconográfico, cosmovisión y el poderió caciquil taíno de Borinquén.* Oxford: British Archaeological Reports International Series 727, Archaeopress.

———. 1999. The "La Hueca Problem" in Puerto Rico and the Caribbean: Old Problems, New Perspectives, Possible Solutions. In C. L. Hofman and M. L. P. Hoogland (eds.), 1999. *Archaeological Investigations on St. Martin (Lesser Antilles),* pp. 253–97. Archaeological Studies Leiden University 4. Leiden, Netherlands.

———. 2000. Gold Symbolism among Caribbean Chiefdoms: Of Feathers, *Çibas,* and *Guanín* Power among Taíno Elites. In Colin McEwan (ed.), *Pre-Columbian Gold: Technology, Style and Iconography,* pp. 196–219. London: British Museum Press.

———. 2002. *The Proto-Taíno Monumental Cemís of Caguana: A Political-Religious "Manifesto."* Unpublished manuscript.

Olmos, M. F., and L. Paravisini-Gebert (ed). 1997. *Sacred Possessions: Vodou, Santeria, Obeah, and the Caribbean.* New Brunswick, NJ: Rutgers University Press.

Olsen, D. A. 1978–9. Musical Instruments of the Native Peoples of the Orinoco Delta, the Caribbean, and Beyond. *Revista/Review Interamericana* 7 (Winter), pp. 588–94.

———. 1996. *Music of the Warao of Venezuela: Song People of the Rain Forest.* Gainesville: University Press of Florida.

———. 2002. *Music of El Dorado: The Ethnomusicology of Ancient South American Cultures.* Gainesville: University Press of Florida.

Olsen, D. A., and D. E. Sheehy (eds.). 2000. *The Garland Handbook of Latin American Music.* New York: Garland Publishing.

Olsen, F. 1974. *On the Trail of the Arawaks.* Norman: University of Oklahoma Press.

Olwig, K. F. 1990. Cultural Identity and Material Culture: Afro-Caribbean Pottery. *Folk* 32, pp. 5–22.

———. 1993. *Global Culture, Island Identity: Continuity and Change in the Afro-Caribbean Community of Nevis.* Chur (Switzerland): Harwood Academic Publishers.

———. 1995. *Small Islands Large Questions: Society, Culture and Resistance in the Post-Emancipation Caribbean:* London: Frank Cass.

Orser, C. E. 1988. The Archaeological Analysis of Plantation Society: Replacing Status and Caste with Economics and Power. *American Antiquity* Vol. 53 (4), pp. 735–51.

Ortega, E. 1982. *Arqueología colonial en Santo Domingo.* Santo Domingo: Fundación Ortega-Alvarez.

Ortega, E., and J. Guerrero. 1988. *La Isabela y la arqueología en la ruta de Colón.* San Pedro de Macorís: Universidad Central de Este.

Ortega, E., M. Velos Maggiolo. 1973. El Caimito: un antiguo complejo ceramista de las Antillas Mayores. *Proceedings of the Sixth International Congress for the Study of Pre-Columbian Cultures of the Lesser Antilles,* 286–82.

Oriz, F. 1959. *Los Bailes y el Teatro de los Negros en el Folklore de Cuba, La Habana.* Havana: Editorial Letras Cubanas.

Osgood, C. 1942. *The Ciboney Culture of Cayo Redondo, Cuba.* Yale University Publications in Anthropology 25. New Haven, CT: Yale University Press.

Osgood, C., and G. D. Howard, 1943. *An Archaeological Survey of Venezuela.* Yale University Publications in Anthropology. No. 27, pp. 1–153.

Ostapkowicz, Joanna M. 1997. To Be Seated with "Great Courtesy and Veneration": Contextual Aspects of the Taíno Duho. In Fatima Bercht, E. Brodsky, J. A. Farmer, and D. Taylor (eds.). *Taíno: Pre-Columbian Art and Culture from the Caribbean,* pp. 56–67. New York: The Monacelli Press.

———. 1998. *Taíno Wooden Sculpture: Duhos, Rulership and the Visual Arts in the 12th–16th Century Caribbean.* Unpublished Ph.D. dissertation, School of World Art Studies, University of East Anglia.

Ottley, C. R. 1979. *Folk Beliefs; Folk Customs; and Folk Characters Found in Trinidad and Tobago.* Diego Martin: Crusoe Publishers.

Oviedo, G. F de. 1959. *The Natural History of the West Indies.* Chapel Hill: University of North Carolina Press.

———. 1979. *Sumario de la natural historia de las Indias.* México: Fondo De Cultura Economica.

Owens, J. 1979. *Dread: The Rastafarians of Jamaica.* London: Heinemann Press.

Pacini Hernández, D. 1995. *Bachata: A Social History of a Dominican Popular Music.* Philadelphia, PA: Temple University Press.

Pagden, A. 1982. *The Fall of Natural Man: The American Indian and the Origins of Comparative Ethnology.* Cambridge: Cambridge University Press.

Palmer, C. 1976. *Slaves of the White God: Blacks in Mexico, 1570–1650.* Cambridge, MA: Harvard University Press.

———. 1981. *Human Cargoes: The British Slave Trade to Spanish America, 1700–1739.* Urbana: University of Illinois Press.

Palmie, S. (ed.). 1995. *Slave Cultures and the Cultures of Slavery.* Knoxville: University of Tennessee Press.

Pané, Fray Ramón. 1999. *An Account of the Antiquities of the Indians.* Ed. José Juan Arrom. Durham, NC, and London: Duke University Press.

Panet, J.-P. and L. Hart. 1990. *Honduras and the Bay Islands.* Passport Press.

Pantel, G. A. 1976. Excavations at the Pre-Ceramic Cerrillo Site, Puerto Rico. *Proceedings of the Sixth International Congress for the Study of Pre-Columbian Cultures of the Lesser Antilles, Pointe-à-Pitre, Guadeloupe, July 6–12, 1975,* pp. 269–71.

———. 1988. *Precolumbian Flaked Stone Assemblages in the West Indies.* Ph.D. dissertation, University of Tennessee, Knoxville. Ann Arbor: University Microfilms.

———. 2003. The First Caribbean People: Part 2, The Archaics. In J. Sued-Badillo (ed.), *General History of the Caribbean: Volume 1. Autochthonous Societies,* pp. 118–133. Paris: UNESCO.

Paquette, R., and S. Engerman (eds.). 1996. *The Lesser Antilles in the Age of European Expansion.* Gainesville: University of Florida Press.

Parker, J. 1983. The Columbus Landfall problem: A Historical Perspective. *Terrae Incognitae* 15, pp. 1–28.

Parry, J. H. 1966. *The Spanish Seaborne Empire.* New York: Alfred A. Knopf.

Parsons, E. C. 1918. *Folk-Tales of Andros Island, Bahamas.* New York: American Folklore Society.

———. 1943. *Folklore of the Antilles, French and English.* New York: American Folklore Society.

Patterson, O. 1964. Ras Tafari: The Cult of Outcasts. *New Society* (1), pp. 15–17.

Patterson, T. 1991. Early Colonial Encounters and Identities in the Caribbean: A Review of Some Recent Works and Their Implications. *Dialectical Anthropology* 16: 1–13.

Pattullo, P. 1996. *Last Resorts: The Cost of Tourism in the Caribbean.* London: Cassell.

Pawson, M., and D. J. Buisseret, 1975. *Port Royal Jamaica.* Oxford: Clarendon Press.

Peguero Guzmán, L. A. 2001. La Plazas Ceremoniales como Espacio Ritual de la Culturas Prehistóricas del Caribe: Su Posible Vinculación a Otros Contextos Culturales. *Boletín del Museo del Hombre Dominicano* 29, pp. 29–62.

Pendergast, D. M., E. Graham, J. A. Calvera R., and M. J. Jardines. 2001. Houses in the Sea: Excavation and Preservation at Los Buchillones, Cuba. In B. A. Purdy (ed.), *Enduring Records: The Environmental and Cultural Heritage of Wetlands,* pp. 71–82. Oxford: Oxbow Books.

Pendergast, D. M. 1982. The 19th Century Sugar Mill at Indian Church, Belize. *Journal of the Society for Industrial Archaeology* Vol. 8 (1), pp. 57–66.

Pérez y Mena, A. I. 1991. *Speaking with the Dead: Development of Afro-Latin Religion among Puerto Ricans in the United States: A Study into the Interpenetration of Civilizations in the New World.* New York: AMS Press.

Pérotin-Dumon, A. 1999. French, English and Dutch in the Lesser Antilles: From Privateering to Planting, c. 1550–c.1650. In P. C. Emmer (ed.). *General History of the Caribbean: Volume II, New Societies: The Caribbean in the Long Sixteenth Century,* pp. 114–158. UNESCO: London.

Petersen, J. B. 1996. Archaeology of Trants, Montserrat, Pt. 3, Chronological and Settlement Data. *Annals of the Carnegie Museum* 65 (4), pp. 323–61.

Petersen, J. B., and D. R. Watters. 1991. Amerindian Ceramic Remains from Fountain Cavern, Anguilla, West Indies. *Annals of the Carnegie Museum* 60, pp. 321–57.

Peterson, M. 1974. Exploration of a 16th-Century Bahamian Shipwreck. *Nautical Geographic Society Research Reports: 1967 Projects,* pp. 231–242.

———. 1975. *The Funnel of Gold.* Boston: Little Brown.

———. 1980. *The Treasure of the Concepción.* Chicago.

Petitjean Roget, H. 1975. *Contribution à l'étude de la préhistoire des Petites Antilles.* Fort-de-France, Martinique: Ecole Pratique des Hautes Etudes.

———. 1978a. *L'art des Arawak et des Caraibes de Petites Antilles. Analise de la décoration des céramiques.* Guyana: Les cahiers du Ceraq. Centre d'Etudes Régionales Antilles-Guyane, No. 35.

————. 1978b. Note sur un vase Arawak trouvé à la Martinique. *Proceedings of the Seventh International Congress for the Study of Pre-Columbian Cultures of the Lesser Antilles,* pp. 99–115. Montreal: Centre de Recherches Caraïbes, Université de Montréal.

————. 1978c. Reconnaissance archéologique à l'île de la Dominique. *Proceedings of the Seventh International Congress for the Study of Pre-Columbian Cultures of the Lesser Antilles,* pp. 81–97. Montreal: Centre de Recherches Caraïbes, Université de Montréal.

————. 1993. Les Pierres à Trois Pointes des Antilles: Essai d'Interpretation. *Espace Caraïbe* No. 1, pp. 7–26.

Petitjean Roget, J. 1963. The Caribs as Seen through the Dictionary of Reverend Father Breton. *Proceedings of the First International Congress for the Study of Pre-Columbian Cultures of the Lesser Antilles,* pp. 43–68.

————. 1970. Archaeology in Martinique. *Parallèles* Vol. 36–7, pp. 48–67.

Phillips, W. D., and C. R. Phillips. 1992. *The Worlds of Christopher Columbus.* Cambridge: Cambridge University Press.

Picart, L. 1995. The Trelawny Maroons and Sir John Wentworth: The Struggle to Maintain Their Culture 1796–1800. *Collections of the Royal Nova Scotia Historical Society* Vol. 44, pp. 165–187.

Piña Chán, R. 1968. Exploración del Cenote Sagrado de Chichén Itzá: 1967–68. *Boletín del Instituto Nacional de Antropología e Historia* 32, pp. 1–3.

Pinart, A. L. 1894. Puerto Rico. In G. Mallory (ed.), *Picture-Writing of the American Indians: Extract from the Tenth Annual Report of the Bureau of Ethnology,* pp. 136–7. Washington, DC: Government Printing Office.

Pino, M. 1970. *La dieta y el ajuar aborigenes en el sitio Mejías, Mayarí, Cuba.* Serie Antropológica 4. Departamento de Antropología, Academia de Ciencias de Cuba, Havana.

Pitts, W. F., Jr. 1993. *The Old Ship of Zion: The Afro-Baptist Ritual in the African Diaspora.* Oxford: Oxford University Press.

Poey, A. 1853. *Cuban Antiquities.* Transactions of the American Ethnological Society III, part 1. New York.

Pohl, F. J. 1944. *Amerigo Vespucci, Pilot Major.* New York.

Polk, P. A. 1993. African Religion and Christianity in Grenada. *Caribbean Quarterly* 39 (3–4), pp. 74–81.

————. 1997. *Haitian Vodou Flags.* Jackson: University Press of Mississippi.

Pollak-Eltz, A. 1993. The Shango Cult and Other African Rituals in Trinidad, Grenada, and Cariiacou and Their Possible Influences on the Spiritual Baptist Faith. *Caribbean Quarterly* 39 (3–4), pp. 12–25.

Pons Alegría, M. 1980. The Use of Masks, Spectacles and Eye-Pieces among the Antillean Aborigines. *Proceedings of the Eighth International Congress for the Study of the Pre-Columbian Cultures of the Lesser Antilles,* pp. 578–92.

Porro, A. 1994. Social Organization and Political Power in the Amazonian Floodplain: The Ethnohistorical Sources. In A. C. Roosevelt (ed.), *Amazonian Indians: From Prehistory to the Present,* pp. 79–94. Tucson: University of Arizona Press.

Posnansky, M. 1983. Towards and Archaeology of the Black Diaspora. *Proceedings of the Ninth International Congress for the Study of Pre-Columbian Cultures of the Lesser Antilles, Santo Domingo 1981,* pp. 443–50.

Potash, C. (ed.). 1997. *Reggae, Rasta, Revolution: Jamaican Music from Ska to Dub.* New York: Schirmer Books/Prentice Hall.

PRDCL. 2001. Port Royal Development Company Ltd. The Port Royal Project. http://www.portroyal-jamaica.com

Prebble, J. 2002. *The Darien Disaster.* London: Pimlico.

Preston Blier, S. 1995. *African Vodun.* Chicago: University of Chicago Press.

Price, R. 1976. *The Guiana Maroons: A Historical and Bibliographical Introduction.* Baltimore: Johns Hopkins University Press.

————. 1996. *Maroon Societies: Rebel Slave Communities in the Americas.* Baltimore and London: The John Hopkins University Press.

Price, R., and S. Price. 1980. *Afro-American Arts of the Surinam Rain Forest*. Los Angeles: University of California Press.

———. 1990. *Maroon Arts*. Boston: Beacon Press.

———. 1992. *Equatoria*. New York: Routledge.

Priddy, A. 1975. The 17th and 18th Century Settlement Pattern of Port Royal. *Jamaica Journal* 9 (2 and 3), 8–10.

Proskouriakoff, T. 1974. Jades from the Cenote of Sacrifice, Chichén Itzá, Yucatán. *Memoirs of the Peabody Museum, Harvard University* X: 2. Cambridge, MA.

Pulis, J. W. (ed.). 1999. *Religion, Diaspora, and Cultural Identity: A Reader in the Anglophone Caribbean*. Amsterdam: Gordon and Breach.

Puls, H. 1999. *Textiles of the Kuna Indians*. Princes Risborough: Shire.

Pulsipher, L. M. 1977. *The Cultural Landscape of Montserrat, West Indies, in the 17th Century: Early Environmental Consequences of British Colonial Development*. Unpublished Ph.D. dissertation, Southern Illinois University, Carbondale.

———. 1991. Galways Plantation, Montserrat. In H. J. Viola and C. Margolis (eds.), *Seeds of Change: A Quincentennial Commemoration*, pp. 139–59. Washington, DC: Smithsonian Institution Press.

———. 1993. Changing Roles in the Life Cycles of Women in Traditional West Indian Houseyards. In J. Momsen (ed.), *Women and Change in the Caribbean*, pp. 50–64. Bloomington: Indiana University Press.

Pulsipher, L. M., and C. M. Goodwin. 1982. *Galways Plantation, Montserrat West Indies, 1981 Field Report*. Department of Geography, University of Tennessee, Knoxville.

———. 1982. A Sugar-Boiling House at Galways: An Irish Sugar Plantation in Montserrat, West Indies. *Post-Medieval Archaeology* 16, pp. 21–7.

———. 1999. Here Where the Old Time People Be: Reconstructing the Landscapes of Slavery and Post-slavery Era in Montserrat, West Indies. In J. B. Haviser (ed.), *African Sites Archaeology in the Caribbean*, pp. 9–37. Princeton, NJ: Markus Wiener Publishers,

———. 2001. "Getting the Essence of It": Galways Plantation, Montserrat, West Indies. In P. Farnsworth (ed.), *Island Lives: Historical Archaeologies of the Caribbean*, pp. 165–203. Tuscaloosa and London: The University of Alabama Press.

Purdy, B. A. 1981. *Florida's Prehistoric Stone Technology*. Gainesville, FL: University Press of Florida.

——— (ed.). 1988. *Wet Site Archaeology*. Caldwell, NJ: The Telford Press.

———. 1991. *The Art and Archaeology of Florida's Wetlands*. Boca Raton, FL: CRC Press.

———. 1996. *Indian Art of Ancient Florida*. Gainesville, FL: University Press of Florida.

Quintana M, H. J. 1995. Música aborigen en los cronistas de Indias. *Revista Montalbán* 8, pp. 157–175.

Rainey, F. G. 1940. *Porto Rican Archaeology*. Scientific Survey of Porto Rico and the Virgin Islands, Vol. XVIII, Part 1. New York: New York Academy of Sciences.

Ramón y Rivera, L. F. 1969. *La Música Folklórica de Venezuela*. Caracas: Monte Ávila Editores.

———. 1971. *La Música Afrovenezolana*. Caracas: Universidad Central de Venezuela.

Randall, J. E. 1983. *Caribbean Reef Fishes*. New Jersey: T. F. H. Publications Inc.

Rashford, J. 1985. The Cotton Tree and the Spiritual Realm in Jamaica, *Jamaica Journal* 18(1), pp. 49–57.

Rat, J. N. 1897. The Carib Language, as Now Spoken in Dominica, West Indies. *Journal of the Anthropological Institute* 27, pp. 293–315.

Ratekin, M. 1954. The Early Sugar Industry in Española. *Hispanic American Historical Review* 34, pp. 1–19.

Rediker, M. 1987. *Between the Devil and the Deep Blue Sea: Merchant Seamen, Pirates, and the Anglo-American Maritime World, 1700–1750*. Cambridge: Cambridge University Press.

Regis, L. 1999. *The Political Calypso: True Opposition in Trinidad and Tobago 1962–1987*. Gainesville, FL: University Press of Florida.

Reichel-Dolmatoff, G. 1971. *Amazonian Cosmos*. Chicago: Chicago University Press.

———. Cosmology as Ecological Analysis: A View from the Rainforest. *Man* (N.S.) II (3), pp. 307–18.

————. 1978. Desana Animal Categories, Food Restrictions and the Concept of Color Energies. *Journal of Latin American Lore* 4 (2), pp. 243–91.

————. 1979. Desana Shamans' Rock Crystals and the Hexagonal Universe. *Journal of Latin American Lore* 5 (1), pp. 117–28.

————. 1981. Things of Beauty Replete with Meaning: Metals and Crystals in Colombian Indian Cosmology. In *Sweat of the Sun Tears of the Moon: Gold and Emerald treasures in Colombia,* pp. 17–33. Los Angeles, CA: Terra Magazine Publications/Natural History Museum Alliance of Los Angeles County.

Reina, R. E., and K. M. Kensinger (eds.). 1991. *The Gift of Birds: Featherwork of Native South American Peoples.* Philadelphia: University Museum of Archaeology and Anthropology, University of Pennsylvania.

Reitz, E. J. 1990. Early Spanish Subsistence at Puerto Real, Hispaniola. *Proceedings of the Eleventh Congress of the International Association for Caribbean Archaeology,* pp. 442–7. San Juan, PR: Fundación de Arqueologia e História de Puerto Rico.

————. 1994. Archaeology of Trants, Montserrat, Part 2, Vertebrate Fauna. *Annals of Carnegie Museum* 63 (4), pp. 297–317.

Reyes, E. (ed.). 1978. *The Carib Community.* The Santa Rosa Carib Community, Arima.

Richardson, B. 1983. *Caribbean Migrants: Environment and Survival on St. Kitts and Nevis.* Knoxville: University of Tennessee Press.

Rigaud, Milo. 1985. *Secrets of Voodoo.* San Francisco: City Lights Books.

Riggio, M. C. 1998. Resistance and Identity: Carnival in Trinidad and Tobago *TDR* 42 (3): 7–23.

Righter, E. 1995. *A Critical Look at Prehistoric Site Distribution in the US Virgin Islands: 1995.* Paper presented at the Sixteenth International Congress for Caribbean Archaeology, Guadeloupe.

Ringenberg, R. 1978. *Rastafarianism, an Expanding Jamaican Cult.* Jamaica: Jamaica Theological Seminary.

Rivera-Pagán, L. N. 2003. Freedom and Servitude: Indigenous Slavery and the Spanish Conquest of the Caribbean. In J. Sued-Badillo (ed.), *General History of the Caribbean: Volume 1. Autochthonous Societies,* pp. 316–362. Paris: UNESCO.

Rivière, P. 1987. Of Women, Men and Manioc. *Etnologista Studier* Vol 38, pp. 178–201.

————. 1998. *Christopher Columbus.* Stroud: Sutton.

Robertson, C. (ed.), 1992. *Musical Repercussions of 1492: Exploration, Encounter, and Identities.* Washington, DC: Smithsonian Institution Press.

Robicsek, Rancis. 1978. *The Smoking Gods: Tobacco in Maya Art, History, and Religion.* Norman: University of Oklahoma Press.

Robinson, L. S., E. R. Lundberg, and J. B. Walker, 1983. *Archaeological Data Recovery at El Bronce, Puerto Rico: Final Report, Phases 1 and 2.* Christiansted: St. Croix Archaeological Services.

Robiou-Lamarche, S. 1983. Del Mito al Tiempo Sagrado. Un Posible Calendario Agrícola-Ceremonial Taíno. *Boletín del Museo del Hombre Dominicano* 18, pp. 117–140.

————. 1984. Astronomy in Taíno Mythology. *Archaeoastronomy* 7 (1–4), pp. 110–15.

————. 1994. *Encuentro con la Mitología Taína.* San Juan, PR: Editorial Punto y Coma.

Rodman, S., and C. Cleaver. 1992. *Spirits of the Night: The Vaudun Gods of Haiti.* Dallas: Spring Publications.

Rodríguez, M. 1989. The Zoned Incised Crosshatch (Zic) Ware of Early Precolumbian Ceramic Age Sites in Puerto Rico and Vieques Island. In Peter E. Siegel (ed.), *Early Ceramic Population Lifeways and Adaptive Strategies in the Caribbean,* pp. 249–266. Oxford: British Archaeological Reports I.S. 506.

————. 1991. Arqueología de Punta Candelero, Puerto Rico. *Proceedings of the Thirteenth International Congress for Caribbean Archaeology Held at Willemstadt, Curaçao, on July 24–29, 1989,* pp. 605–27. Willemstadt.

————. 1991. Early Trade Networks in the Caribbean. *Proceedings of the Fourteenth International Congress for Caribbean Archaeology,* 306–14.

————. 1997. Religious Beliefs of the Saladoid People. In Samuel M. Wilson (ed.), *The Indigenous People of the Caribbean,* pp. 80–87. Gainesville: University Press of Florida.

Rodríguez, M., and V. Rivera. 1991. Puerto Rico and the Caribbean Pre-Saladoid 'Crosshatch Connection'. *Proceedings of the Twelfth International Congress for Caribbean Archaeology,* pp. 45–51.

Roe, P. G. 1982. *The Cosmic Zygote: Cosmology in the Amazon Basin.* New Brunswick, NJ: Rutgers University Press.

————. 1985. A Preliminary Report on the 1980 and 1982 Field Seasons at Hacienda Grande (12PSj7–5): Overview of Site History, Mapping, and Excavations. *Proceedings of the Tenth International Congress for the Study of the Pre-Columbian Cultures of the Lesser Antilles,* pp. 151–80. Montréal.

————. 1989. A Grammatical Analysis of Cedrosian Saladoid Vessel Form Categories and Surface Decoration: Aesthetic and Technical Styles in Early Antillean Ceramics. In Peter E. Siegel (ed.), *Early Ceramic Population Lifeways and Adaptive Strategies in the Caribbean,* pp. 267–382. Oxford: British Archaeological Reports I.S. 506.

————. 1991a. The Best Enemy Is a Killed, Drilled, and Decorative Enemy: Human Corporeal Art (Frontal Bone Pectorals, Belt Ornaments, Carbed Humeri, and Pierced Teeth) in Pre-Columbian Puerto Rico. *Proceedings of the Thirteenth International Congress for Caribbean Archaeology, Willemstadt, Curaçao,* pp. 854–873. Curaçao: Archaeological-Anthropological Institute of the Netherlands Antilles.

————. 1991b. The Petroglyphs of Maisabel: A Study in Methodology. *Comptes Rendus des Communications du Douzième Congrès International d'Archeologie de la Caraïbe, Cayenne, Guyane Française,* pp. 317–370. Martinique: Association Internationale d'Archeologie de la Caraïbe.

————. 1993. Cross-Media Isomorphisms in Taíno Ceramocs and Petroglyphs from Puerto Rico. *Proceedings of the Fourteenth Congress of the International Association for Caribbean Archaeology,* pp. 637–671. Barbados.

————. 1995a. Eternal Companions: Amerindian Dogs from Tierra Firma to the Antilles. In Ricardo Alegría and Miguel Rodríguez (eds.), *Actas del XV Congreso Internacional de Arqueología del Caribe, San Juan, Puerto Rico 1993,* pp. 155–172. San Juan: Centro de Estudios Avanzados de Puerto Rico y el Caribe, Fundación Puertorriqueña de las Humanidades and Universidad del Turabo.

————. 1995b. *Myth-Material Cultural Semiotics: Prehistoric and Ethnographic Guiana-Antilles.* Paper presented at the 94th Annual Meeting of the American Anthropological Association, Washington, DC.

————. 1997. Just Wasting Away: Taíno Shamanism and Concepts of Fertility. In F. Bercht, E. Brodsky, J. A. Farmer, and D. Taylor (eds.), *Taíno: Pre-Columbian Art and Culture from the Caribbean,* pp. 124–157. New York: The Monacelli Press.

————. n.d. *The Domesticated Jaguar: The Symbolism of South Amerindian Dogs from a Lowland Perspective.* Unpublished manuscript.

Roe, P. G., A. G. Pantel, and M. B. Hamilton. 1990. Monserrate Restudied: The 1978 Centro Field Season at Luquillo Beach: Excavation Overview, Lithics and Physical Anthropological Remains. *Proceedings of the Congress of the International Association for Caribbean Archaeology* Vol. 11, pp. 338–69.

Romero, A., S. Chilbert and M. G. Eisenhart. 1999. Cubagua's Pearl-Oyster Beds: The First Depletion of a Natural Resource Caused by Europeans in the American Continent. *Journal of Political Ecology* Vol. 6, pp. 57–77.

Romoli, K. 1953. *Balboa of Darien: Discoverer of the Pacific.* New York

Roosevelt, A. C. 1980. *Parmana: Prehistoric Maize and Manioc Subsistence along the Amazon and Orinoco.* London: Academic Press.

Rosario, R. del. 1976. *Breve enciclopédia de la cultura puertorriqueña.* San Juan, PR: Editorial Cordillera.

Rose, R. 1982. The Pigeon Creek Site, San Salvador, Bahamas. *Florida Anthropologist* Vol. 35, pp. 129–45.

————. 1987. Lucayan Lifeways at the Time of Columbus. In D. T. Grace (ed.), *Proceedings of the First San Salvador Conference, Columbus and His World,* pp. 321–39. Fort Lauderdale, FL: CCFL Bahamian Field Station.

Rosemain, J. Unknown. *La musique dans la société antillaise: 1635–1902, Martinique, Guadeloupe.* L'Hamattan.

Rosenburg, J. C. 1979. *El Gaga—religion y sociedad de un culto de Santo Domingo.* Santo Domingo: Universidad Autonoma de Santo Domingo.

Roth, H. L. 1887. The Aborigines of Hispaniola. *Journal of the Royal Anthropological Institute,* 16, pp. 247–286.

Roth, W. E. 1970. *An Inquiry into the Animism and Folk-lore of the Guiana Indians.* New York: Johnson Reprint.

———. 1924. *An Introductory Study of the Arts, Crafts and Customs of the Guiana Indians.* 38th Annual Report of the Bureau of American Ethnology. Washington, DC: Smithsonian Institution.

Rouse, I. B. 1939. *Prehistory in Haiti: A Study in Method.* Yale University Publications in Anthropology No. 21. New Haven, CT.

———. 1940. Some Evidence Concerning the Origins of West Indian Pottery-Making. *American Anthropologist,* 42, pp. 49–80.

———. 1942. *Archaeology of the Maniabón Hills, Cuba.* New Haven, CT: Yale University Publications in Anthropology No.26. New Haven, CT.

———. 1947. Prehistory of Trinidad in Relation to Adjacent Areas. *MAN,* (o.s.) 47 (103), pp. 93–98.

———. 1948a. The Ciboney. In J. H. Steward (ed.), *Handbook of South American Indians 4,* pp. 497–503. Washington D.C.: Smithsonian Institution.

———. 1948b. The Arawak. In J. H. Steward (ed.), *Handbook of South American Indians 4,* pp. 507–546. Washington D.C.: Smithsonian Institution.

———. 1948c. The Carib. In J. H. Steward (ed.), *Handbook of South American Indians 4,* pp. 547–566. Washington D.C.: Smithsonian Institution.

———. 1951. Areas and Periods of Culture in the Greater Antilles. *Southwestern Journal of Anthropology,* 7, pp. 248–265.

———. 1953a. The Circum-Caribbean Theory, An Archaeological Test. *American Anthropologist,* 55, pp. 188–200.

———. 1953b. Appendix B: Indian Sites in Trinidad. In John A. Bullbrook, *On the Excavation of a Shell Mound at Palo Seco, Trinidad, B.W.I.,* pp. 94–111. New Haven, CT: Yale University Publications in Anthropology 50.

———. 1960. *The Entry of Man into the West Indies.* New Haven, CT: Yale University Publications in Anthropology 61.

———. 1961. The Bailey Collection of Stone Artifacts from Puerto Rico. In S. K. Lothrop et al. (ed.), *Essays in Pre-Columbian Art and Archaeology,* pp. 342–55. Cambridge, MA: Harvard University Press.

———. 1964. Prehistory of the West Indies. *Science,* 144, pp. 499–514.

———. 1974. The Indian Creek Excavations. *Proceedings of the Fifth International Congress for the Study of Pre-Columbian Cultures of the Lesser Antilles, Antigua, July 22–28, 1973,* pp. 166–176.

———. 1976. The Saladoid Sequence on Antigua and Its Aftermath. *Proceedings of the Sixth International Congress for the Study of Pre-Columbian Cultures of the Lesser Antilles, Pointe-à-Pitre, Guadeloupe, July 6–12, 1975,* pp. 35–41.

———. 1977. Pattern and Process in West Indian Archaeology. *World Archaeology* 9, pp. 1–11.

———. 1978. The La Gruta Sequence and Its Implications. In E. Wagner and A. Zucchi (eds.), *Unidad y Variedad: Ensayos anthrópologicos en homenaje a José M. Cruxent,* pp. 203–29. Caracas: Ediciones s A-IVIC.

———. 1982. Ceramic and Religious Development in the Greater Antilles. *Journal of New World Archaeology* Vol. 5, No. 2, pp. 45–55.

———. 1986. *Migrations in Prehistory.* New Haven, CT: Yale University Press.

———. 1992. *The Tainos: Rise and Decline of the People who Greeted Columbus.* New Haven, CT: Yale University Press.

Rouse, I., and R. E. Alegría. 1978. Radiocarbon Dates from the West Indies. *Revista / Review Interamericana,* 8 (3), pp. 495–499.

————. 1990. *Excavations at Maria de la Cruz Cave and Hacienda Grande Village site, Loiza, Puerto Rico.* New Haven, CT: Yale University Publications in Anthropology, No. 80.

Rouse, I., and L. Allaire. 1978. Caribbean. In R. E. Taylor and C. W. Meighan (eds.), *Chronologies in New World Archaeology,* pp. 431–481. New York: Academic Press.

Rouse, I., L. Allaire and A. Boomert. 1985. Eastern Venezuela, the Guianas, and the West Indies. Manuscript prepared for unpublished volume, C. Meighan (comp.), *Chronologies in South American Archaeology.* Department of Anthropology, Yale University, New Haven, CT.

Rouse, I., and J. J. Arrom. 1991. The Taínos: Principal Inhabitants of Columbus's Indies. In J. A. Levinson (ed.), *Circa 1492: Art in the Age of Exploration,* pp. 509–13. New Haven, CT: Yale University Press.

Rouse, Irving B., and J. M. Cruxent, 1963. *Venezuelan Archaeology.* New Haven, CT: Yale University Press.

Rouse, I., J. Cruxent and A. C. Roosevelt. 1976. Ronquin Revisited. *Proceedings of the Sixth International Congress for the Study of Pre-Columbian Cultures of the Lesser Antilles, Point-à-Pitre, Guadeloupe, July 1975,* pp. 117–122.

Rouse, Irving and B. F. Morse. 1999. *Excavations at the Indian Creek Site, Antigua, West Indies.* New Haven, CT: Yale University Publications in Anthropology, No. 82.

Rout, L. B., Jr. 1976. *The African Experience in Spanish America, 1502 to the Present Day.* Cambridge: Cambridge University Press.

Rowe, M. 1980. The Women in Rastafari. *Caribbean Quarterly* 26 (4), pp. 13–21.

Rubin, V., and A. Tudin (eds.). 1977. *Comparative Perspectives on Slavery in New World Plantation Societies.* New York: New York Academy of Sciences.

Rudder, D. 1990. *Kaiso, Calypso Music: David Rudder in Conversation with John LaRose.* London: New Beacon Press.

Ruggles, C. L. N, and N. J. Saunders. 1993. The Study of Cultural Astronomy, in C. L. N. Ruggles and N. J. Saunders (eds.), *Astronomies and Cultures,* pp. 1–31. Niwot, CO: University Press of Colorado.

Russell, A. D. 1926. Stone Collars and Elbow Stones. *Man* 20 (142), pp. 213–16.

Sabloff, J. A. 1977. Old Myths, New Myths: The Role of Sea Traders in the Development of Ancient Maya Civilization. In E. P. Benson (ed.), *The Sea in the Pre-Columbian World,* pp. 67–88. Washington D.C.: Dumbarton Oaks.

Sabloff, J. A., and W. L. Rathje (eds.), 1975. *A Study of Changing Pre-Columbian Commercial Systems: The 1972–1973 Seasons at Cozumel, Mexico.* Monograph 3 of the Peabody Museum of Archaeology and Ethnology. Cambridge, MA.

Sankeralli, B. (ed.). 1995. *At the Crossroads: African Caribbean Religion and Christianity.* Trinidad and Tobago: Caribbean Conference of Churches.

Sale, Kirkpatrick. 1992. *The Conquest of Paradise.* London: Papermac/Macmillan.

Salewicz, C., and A. Boot. 2001. *Reggae Explosion: The Story of Jamaican Music.* London: Virgin Publishing.

Salgado, R. M. 1974. *The Role of the Puerto Rican Spiritist in Helping Puerto Ricans with Problems of Family Relations.* Unpublished Ph.D. dissertation, Columbia University.

Salkey, A. 1998. *Caribbean Folk Tales and Legends.* Bogle L'Ouverture Press.

Sánchez, J. P. 1989. The Spanish Black Legend: Origins of Anti-Hispanic Stereotypes. *Encounters, A Quincentennial Review* (Winter), pp. 16–22.

Sanoja, M. 1989. From Foraging to Food Production in Northeastern Venezuela and the Caribbean. In D. R. Harris and G. C. Hillman (eds.), *Foraging and Farming: The Evolution of Plant Exploitation,* pp. 523–37. London: Unwin Hyman.

————. 1994. Central America, the Caribbean, the North of South America and the Amazon: The Way of Life of the Ancient Hunters. In S. J. Laet (ed.), *History of Humanity* Vol. 1: *Prehistory and the Beginnings of Civilization.* London: UNESCO/Routledge.

Sauer, C. O. 1950. Cultivated Plants of South and Central America. In J. H. Steward (ed.), *Handbook of South American Indians* 6, pp. 487–543. Smithsonian Institution, Bureau of American Ethnology Bulletin 143. Washington, DC: Government Printing Office.

————. 1969. *The Early Spanish Main*. Berkeley: University of California Press.

Saunders, N. J. 1988. *Chatoyer:* Anthropological reflections on archaeological mirrors. In N. J. Saunders and O. de Montmollin (eds.), *Recent Studies in Pre-Columbian Archaeology* 1, pp. 1–40. Oxford: British Archaeological Reports International Series 421.

————. 1998. Stealers of Light, Traders in Brilliance: Amerindian Metaphysics in the Mirror of Conquest. *RES:Anthropology and Aesthetics* 33, pp. 225–252.

————. 1999. Biographies of brilliance: pearls, transformations of matter and being, c. AD 1492. *World Archaeology* 32 (2), pp. 243–257.

————. 2002. The Colours of Light: Materiality and Chromatic Cultures of the Americas, In A. Jones and G. MacGregor (eds.), *Colouring the Past: The Significance of Archaeological Research*. Oxford: Berg Publishers.

————. 2004a. "Catching the Light": Technologies of Power and Enchantment in Pre-Columbian Goldworking. In J. Quilter and J. W. Hoopes (eds.), *Gold and Power: In Ancient Costa Rica, Panama, and Colombia*. Washington D.C.: Dumbarton Oaks.

————. 2004b. The Cosmic Earth: Materiality and Mineralogy in the Americas. In N. Boivin and M. A. Owoc (eds.), *Soil, Stones and Symbols: Cultural Perceptions of the Mineral World*. London: UCL Press.

————. n.d. *A Saladoid Effigy Bottle from Gaspare Grande Island, Trinidad*. Unpublished manuscript.

Saunders, Nicholas J., and Dorrick Gray. 1996. *Zemís,* Trees and Symbolic Landscapes: Three Taíno Carvings from Jamaica. *Antiquity* 70 (270), pp. 801–812.

Scarborough, Vernon L., and David R. Wilcox (eds.), 1991. *The Mesoamerican Ballgame*. Tucson: The University of Arizona Press.

Scott, J. F. 1985. *The Art of the Taino from the Dominican Republic*. Gainesville: University of Florida.

Schele, L., and D. Friedel. 1990. *A Forest of Kings: The Untold Story of the Ancient Maya*. New York: William Morrow.

Schomburk, R. H. 1832. Remarks on Anegada. *The Journal of the Royal Geographical Society* 2, pp. 152–170.

Schuler, M. 1979. Myalism and the African Religious Tradition in Jamaica, in M. E. Graham *and* F. W. Knight (ed.), *Africa and the Caribbean: the Legacies of a link*. Baltimore, MD: Johns Hopkins University Press.

Schultes, R. E. 1972. An Overview of Hallucinogens in the Western Hemisphere. In P. T. Furst (ed.), *Flesh of the Gods: The Ritual Use of Hallucinogens,* pp. 3–54. New York: Praeger.

Schultes, R. E., and A. Hofmann. 1980. *Plants of the Gods: Origins of Hallucinogenic Use*. London: Hutchinson.

Schwartz, A., and R. W. Henderson. 1991. *Amphibians and Reptiles of the West Indies*. Gainesville: University Press of Florida.

Schwartz, A., and R. Thomas. 1975. *A Checklist of West Indian Amphibians and Reptiles*. Carnegie Museum of Natural History Special Publication 1. Washington, DC:

Schwartz, M. 1997. *A History of Dogs in the Early Americas*. New Haven: Yale University Press.

Seaga, E. 1969. Revival Cults in Jamaica. *Jamaica Journal* 3 (2), pp. 1–12.

Sears, W. H., and S. D. Sullivan, 1978. Bahamas Prehistory, *American Antiquity,* 43 (1), pp. 3–25.

Sereno, R. 1948. Obeah: Magic and Social Structure in the Lesser Antilles. *Psychiatry* 11 (1), pp. 15–31.

Sharer, R. J. 1994. *The Ancient Maya*. 5th ed. Stanford, CA: Stanford University Press.

Shephard, C. Y. 1932. *The Cacao Industry of Trinidad*. Port-of-Spain, Trinidad.

Sheridan, R. B. 1985. The Maroons of Jamaica, 1730–1830: Livelihood, Demography, and Health. *Slavery and Abolition* Vol. 6(3), pp. 152–172.

Sherlock, P., and H. Bennett. 1998 *The Story of the Jamaican People*. Kingston: Ian Randle Publishers.

Sherzer, J. 1983. *Kuna Ways of Speaking: An Ethnographic Perspective*. Austin: University of Texas Press.

Siegel, P. E. (ed.). 1989. *Early Ceramic Population Lifeways and Adaptive Strategies in the Caribbean*. Oxford: British Archaeological Reports International Series 506.

————. 1989. Site Structure, Demography, and Social Complexity in the Early Ceramic Age of the Caribbean. In P. E. Siegel (ed.), *Early Ceramic Population Lifeways and Adaptive Strategies in the Caribbean,* pp. 193–245. Oxford: British Archaeological Reports International Series 506.

————. 1991. On the Antillean Connection for the Introduction of Cultigens in Eastern North America. *Current Anthropology* Vol. 14, pp. 315–37.

————. 1991. Migration Research in Saladoid Archaeology: A Review. *Florida Anthropologist* 44 (1), pp. 79–91.

————. 1999. Contested Places and Places of Contest: The Evolution of Social Power and Ceremonial Space in Prehistoric Puerto Rico. *Latin American Antiquity* Vol. 10 (3), pp. 209–38.

Siegel, Peter E., and Kenneth P. Severin. 1993. The First Documented Prehistoric Gold-Copper Alloy Artefact from the West Indies. *Journal of Field Archaeology* Vol. 20, pp. 67–79.

Simpson, G. 1955. Political Cultism in West Kingston, Jamaica. *Social and Economic Studies* 4 (1) pp. 133–149.

————. 1985. Religion and Justice: Some Reflections on the Rastafari Movement. *Phylon* 46 (4) pp. 286–291.

Simpson, G. E. 1965. *The Shango Cult in Trinidad.* San Juan: University of Puerto Rico.

————. 1970. *Religious Cults of the Caribbean: Trinidad, Jamaica, and Haiti.* San Juan, PR: Institute of Caribbean Studies.

————. 1973. The Kele (Chango) Cult in St. Lucia: Research Commentaries 3. *Caribbean Studies* 13 (3), pp. 110–116.

————. 1978. *Black Religions in the New World.* New York: Columbia University Press.

Singer, M., and R. Garcia. 1987. Becoming a Puerto Rican Espiritista: Life History of a Female Healer. In C. S. McClain (ed.), *Women as Healers,* pp. 157–185. New Brunswick, NJ: Rutgers University Press.

Singleton, T. A. 1985. *The Archaeology of Slavery and Plantation Life.* New York: Academic Press.

————. 2001. Slavery and Spatial Dialectics on Cuban Coffee Plantations. *World Archaeology* 33 (1), pp. 98–114.

Skinner, A. 1925. Archaeological Specimen from St. Croix, Virgin Islands. *Museum of the American Indian, Heye Foundation, Indian Notes* Vol. 2, pp. 109–15.

Sloane, H. 1707. *A Voyage to the Islands Madera, Barbados, Nieves, S. Christophes and Jamaica with the Natural History of the Herbs and Trees, Four-Footed Beasts, Fishes, Birds, Insects, Reptiles, Etc. of the Last of Those Islands.* London.

Smith, M. T., and M. E. Good. 1982. *Early Sixteenth Century Beads in the Spanish Colonial Trade.* Cottonlandia Museum Publications, Greenwood, MI.

Smith, R. C. 1985. The Search for the Caravels of Columbus. *Oceanus* 28 (1), pp. 73–7.

————. 1985. The Caymanian Catboat: A West Indian Maritime Legacy. *World Archaeology* 16 (3), pp. 329–36.

————. 1997. Nuestra Señora de Atocha. In J. P. Delgado (ed.), *Encyclopedia of Underwater and Maritime Archaeology,* pp. 298–9. London: British Museum Press.

————. 2000. *The Maritime Heritage of the Cayman Islands.* Gainesville: University Press of Florida.

Smith, R. C., and D. H. Keith. 1986. The Archaeology of Ships of Discovery. *Archaeology* 39 (2), pp. 30–35.

Smith, R. C., D. H. Keith, and D. C. Lakey. 1985. The Highborn Cay Wreck: Further Exploration of a Sixteenth Century Bahamian Shipwreck. *International Journal of Nautical Archaeology and Underwater Exploration* 14, pp. 63–72.

Smith, V. T. C. 1992. *Fire and Brimstone: The Story of the Brimstone Hill Fortress, St. Kitts, West Indies, 1690–1853.* Basseterre: Brimstone Hill Fortress National Park Society.

SRCC, 1998. *We, The Carib Community of Trinidad and Tobago.* http://www.members.tripod.com/~SRCC1CaribCommunity/weone.htm.

Stahl, A. A. 1889. *Los indios borinqueños: Estudios etnográficos.* San Juan: Imprenta y Librería de Acosta.

Stannard, D. E. 1992. *American Holocaust. Columbus and the Conquest of the New World.* Oxford: Oxford University Press.

Stienstra, P. 1988. The Economic History of Gold Mining on Aruba, Netherlands West Indies, 1824–1920. In L. J. van der Steen (ed.), *Studies in Honour of Dr. Pieter Wagenaar Hummelinck,* pp. 227–54. Natuuretenschappelijk Studiekring voor Suriname and de Nederlandse Antillen No. 123. Utrecht: Koninklijke van de Gaarde.

Stephens, J. L. 1843. *Incidents of Travel in Yucatan.* 2 vols. New York: Harper and Brothers.

Stern, Theodore. 1949. *The Rubber-Ball Games of the Americas.* Monographs of the American Ethnological Society, No. 17, New York.

Stevens-Arroyo, Antonio M. 1988. *Cave of the Jagua: The Mythological World of the Taínos.* Albuquerque: University of New Mexico Press.

Stokes, A. V., and W. F. Keegan. 1996. A Reconnaissance for Prehistoric Archaeological Sites on Grand Cayman. *Caribbean Journal of Science* Vol. 32 (4), pp. 425–30.

Stout, D. B. 1948. The Cuna. In J. H. Steward (ed.), *Handbook of South American Indians* 4, pp. 257–69. Washington, DC: Smithsonian Institution.

Stoutamire, F. 1974. *Report of the Cinnamon Bay Site, St. John's, US Virgin Islands.* Tallahassee: Southeast Archaeological Center.

Stuempfle, S. 1995. *The Steelband Movement: The Forging of a National Art in Trinidad and Tobago.* Philadelphia: University of Pennsylvania Press.

Sturtevant, W. C. 1961. Taino Agriculture. In 'The Evolution of Horticultural Systems in Native South America: Causes and Consequences—A Symposium. *Anthropologica* Supplement 2, pp. 69–73.

Sued-Badillo, J. 1978. *Los Caribes: Realidad o Fábula.* Rio Pedras, Puerto Rico: Editorial Antillana.

———. 1985. La cacicas indoantillanas. *Revista del Instituto de Cultura Puertorriqueña* Vol. 87, pp. 17–26.

———. 1992. Facing up to Caribbean History. *American Antiquity* 57 (4), pp. 599–607.

———. 1995. The Island Caribs: New Approaches to the Question of Ethnicity in the Early Colonial Caribbean. In N. Whitehead (ed.), *Wolves form the Sea,* pp. 62–98. Leiden: KITLV Press.

——— (ed.). 2003a. *General History of the Caribbean: Volume 1. Autochthonous Societies.* Paris: UNESCO.

———. 2003b. The Indigenous Societies at the Time of Conquest. In J. Sued-Badillo (ed.), *General History of the Caribbean: Volume 1. Autochthonous Societies,* pp. 259–291. Paris: UNESCO.

Sullivan, L. E. 1988. *Icanchu's drum.* London: Macmillan.

Sullivan, S. D. 1981. *Prehistoric Patterns of Exploitation and Colonization in the Turks and Caicos Islands.* Ph.D. dissertation, University of Illinois, Urbana.

Suro, D. 1966. Of Artists and Owls: Taíno Sculpture. *Américas* 18 (3), pp. 21–8.

Sutton, L. 1990. *Seashells of the Caribbean.* London: Macmillan Caribbean, London.

Sutty, L. 1976. Further Excavations at Chatham Midden, Union Island, The Grenadines. *Proceedings of the Sixth International Congress for the Study of the Pre-Columbian Cultures of the Lesser Antilles, Guadeloupe 1975,* pp. 54–65.

———. 1976. Archaeological Excavations at Miss Pierre, Union Island, The Grenadines. *Proceedings of the Sixth International Congress for the Study of the Pre-Columbian Cultures of the Lesser Antilles, Guadeloupe 1975,* pp. 66–75.

———. 1978. A Study of Shells and Shell Objects from Six Precolumbian Sites in the Grenadines of St. Vincent and the Grenadines. *Proceedings of the Seventh International Congress for the Study of the Pre-Columbian Cultures of the Lesser Antilles, Caracas 1977,* pp. 195–210.

———. 1980. A Further Study of the Troumassée Cylinder and Its Place in Arawak Society. *Proceedings of the Eighth International Congress for the Study of the Pre-Columbian Cultures of the Lesser Antilles, St Kitts 1979,* pp. 567–77.

———. 1983. Liason Arawak-Caliviny-Carib between Grenada and St. Vincent, Lesser Antilles. *Proceedings of the Ninth International Congress for the Study of the Pre-Columbian Cultures of the Lesser Antilles, Santo Domingo 1981,* pp. 145–153.

————. 1985. An Early Ceramic Effigy Bottle from Chatham Pasture, Union Island in the Grenadines. *Proceedings of the Tenth International Congress for the Study of the Pre-Columbian Cultures of the Lesser Antilles, Martinique 1983,* pp. 401–7.

————. 1990. A Listing of Amerindian Settlements on the Island of Carriacou in the Southern Grenadines and a Report on the Most Important of These: Grand Bay. *Proceedings of the Eleventh International Congress for Caribbean Archaeology, Puerto Rico 1985,* pp. 242–59.

————. 1991. A Preliminary Inventory and Short Essay on Cermaic and Stone Artifacts from Recent Excavations on Grenada and in the Southern Grenadines. *Proceedings of the Twelfth International Congress for Caribbean Archaeology, Cayenne 1987,* pp. 73–85.

————. 1991. The Use of Genital Sheaths by Insular Prehistoric Cultures: A Unique Case of Ampullaria Genital Sheath from Carriacou, Southern Grenadines. *Proceedings of the Fourteenth International Congress for Caribbean Archaeology, Barbados,* pp. 338–47.

Swanton, J. R. 1979. *The Indians of the Southeastern United States.* Washington, DC: Smithsonian Institution Press.

Tabio, E. E., and E. Rey. 1979. *Prehistoria de Cuba.* 2nd ed. Editorial de Ciencias de Cuba, Havana.

Tanna, L. 1984. *Jamaican Folk Tales and Oral Histories.* Jamaica 21 Anthology Series 1. Kingston: Institute of Jamaica Publications.

Tavares, J. 1978. *Cultura y arte precolombino de Caribe.* Santo Domingo: Museo del Hombre Dominicano.

Taviani, P. E. 1985. *Christopher Columbus: The Grand Design.* London: Orbis.

————. 1987. Why We Are Favourable for the Watling–San Salvador Landfall. In D. T. Grace (ed.), *Proceedings of the First San Salvador Conference, Columbus and his world,* pp. 197–228. Fort Lauderdale, FL: CCFL Bahamian Field Station.

————. 1992. Christopher Columbus: Birth and Origins. In S. A. Bedini (ed.). *The Christopher Columbus Encyclopedia* Vol. 1, pp. 161–63. New York: Simon and Schuster.

Taylor, D., M. Biscione and P. G. Roe, 1997. Epilogue: The Beaded Zemi in the Pigorini Museum. In F. Bercht, E. Brodsky, J. A. Farmer, and D. Taylor (eds.). *Taíno: Pre-Columbian Art and Culture from the Caribbean,* pp. 158–69. New York: The Monacelli Press.

Taylor, D. M. 1938. *The Caribs of Dominica.* Bureau of American Ethnology Bulletin 119, Anthropological Papers 3, Washington, DC.

————. 1946. Notes on the Star Lore of the Caribbees. *American Anthropologist* Vol. 48, pp. 215–22.

————. 1951. *The Black Caribs of British Honduras.* New York: Viking Fund Publications in Anthropology No 17.

————. 1952. Tales and Legends of the Dominica Caribs. *Journal of American Folklore* Vol. 65, p. 269.

————. 1954. Diachronic Note on the Carib Contribution to Island Carib. *International Journal of American Linguistics* 20, pp. 28–33.

————. 1977. *Languages of the West Indies.* Baltimore: Johns Hopkins University Press.

Taylor, D., and I. Rouse. 1955. Linguistic and Archaeological Time Depth in the West Indies. *International Journal of American Linguistics* Vol. 21 (2), pp. 105–15.

Taylor, J. 1991. *Trinidad and Tobago: An Introduction and Guide.* London: Macmillan.

Taylor, R. V. 1986. Archaeological Events in in Barbados. *Journal Barbados Historical Society* 37 (4), pp. 337–42.

Thomas, H. 1997. *The Slave Trade: The History of the Atlantic Slave Trade 1440–1870.* London: Picador.

Thomas, R. P. 1968. The Sugar Colonies of the Old Empire: Profit or Loss for Great Britain? *Economic History Review* 21 (1), pp. 30–45.

Thompson, D., and A. Figueroa de Thompson. 1991. *Music and Dance in Puerto Rico from the Age of Columbus to Modern Times: An Annotated Bibliography.* Metuchen, NJ: Scarecrow Press.

Thompson, R. F. 1983. *Flash of the Spirit: African and Afro-American Art and Philosophy.* New York: Random House.

Thornton, D. 1992. *The Probate Inventories of Port Royal, Jamaica.* Unpublished M.A. thesis, Department of Anthropology, Texas A&M University, College Station.

Thornton, R. 1987. *American Indian Holocaust and Survival: A Population History Since 1492.* Norman: University of Oklahoma Press.

Throckmorton, P. 1969. *Shipwrecks and Archaeology.* Boston: Little, Brown.

Thrower, N. J. (ed.). 1984. *Sir Francis Drake and the Famous Voyage, 1577–1580: Essays Commemorating the Quadricentennial of Drake's Circumnavigation of the World.* Berkeley: University of California Press.

Todd, L. 1990. *Pidgins and Creoles.* London: Routledge.

Tozzer, A. M. 1957. *Chichen Itza and Its Cenote of Sacrifice.* Memoirs of the Peabody Museum, Harvard University 11–12. Cambridge, MA.

Tomich, D. W. 1990. *Slavery in the Circuit of Sugar: Martinique and the World Economy, 1830–1848.* Baltimore: Johns Hopkins University Press.

Trincado, F., N. María, and J. Ulloa H. 1996. La communidades meillacoides del littoral sudoriental de Cuba. *El Caribe Arqueológico* 1, pp. 74–82.

Trotman, D. 1976. The Yoruba and Orisha Worhsip in Trinidad and British Guinea 1838–1870. *African Studies Review* 19 (2).

Tuelon, A. 1973. Nanny-Maroon Chieftainess. *Caribbean Quarterly* 19(4):20–27.

Turner, G. 1993. An Archaeological Record of Plantation Life in the Bahamas. In G. Lafleaur, S. Branson and G. Turners (eds.), *Amerindians, Africans, Americans: Three Papers in Caribbean History,* pp. 107–25. Department of History, University of the West Indies, Mona Jamaica.

Valcárcel, R., J. C. Agüero H, E. Guarch R, and R. Pedroso. 1996. La ornamentación incisa en la cerámica aborigen del centro-norte de Holguín, Cuba. *El Caribe Arqueológico* 1, pp. 46–58.

Valdés, P. G. 1948. The Ethnology of the Ciboney. In J. H. Steward (ed.), *Handbook of South American Indians 4,* pp. 503–5. Washington D.C.: Smithsonian Institution.

van De Berg, W. R. 1998. Rastafari Perceptions of Self and Symbolism. In P. B. Clarke (ed.), *New Trends and Developments in African Religions,* pp. 159–75. Westport, CT: Greenwood Press.

van der Bor, W. 1981. *Island Adrift: The Social Organization of a Small Caribbean Community: The Case of St. Eustatius.* The Hague: Smits Drukkers.

van Gijn, A. L. 1993. Flint Exploitation on Long Island, Antigua, West Indies. *Analecta Praehistoria Leidensia* Vol. 26, pp. 183–97.

van Velzen, T., and W. van Wetering. 1988. *The Great Father and the Danger: Religious Cults, Material Forces, and Collective Fantasies in the World of Surinamese Maroons.* Dordrecht: Foris Publications.

Vargas, I. 1976. La Gruta, un Nuevo Sitio Ronquinoide en Orinoco Medio. *Proceedings of the Sixth International Congress for the Study of Pre-Columbian Cultures of the Lesser Antilles, Point-à-Pitre, Guadeloupe, July 1975,* pp. 123–4.

Varner, J. G., and J. J. Varner. 1983. *Dogs of the Conquest.* Norman: University of Oklahoma Press.

Vázquez de Espinosa, A. 1942. *Compendium and description of the West Indies.* Washington, DC: Smithsonian Institute Miscellaneous Collections 102.

Vega, B. 1976. Comparison of Newly Found Cave Drawings in Santo Domingo with Petroglyphs and Pictographs in the Caribbean Region. *Comptes Rendus des Communications du Sixième Congrès d'études des Civilizations Précolombiennes des Petites Antilles,* pp. 200–12. Pointe-à-Pître, Guadeloupe.

———. 1979. *Los metales y los aborígenes de la Hispaniola.* Santo Domingo: Ediciones del Museo del Hombre Dominicano.

———. 1980. *Los cacicazgos de La Hispaniola.* Santo Domingo: Museo del Hombre Dominicano.

———. 1987. *Santos, shamanes y zemíes.* Santo Domingo: Fundación Cultural Dominicana.

———. 1996. *Las Frutas de los Taínos.* Santo Domingo: Amigo del Hogar.

Vega, M. M. 2000. *The Altar of My Soul: The Living Traditions of Santeria.* New York: Ballantine Books.

Veloz Maggiolo, M. 1971. El rito de la cohoba entre los aborigenes antillanos. *Revista dominicana de arqueología y antropología* 29 (1–2), pp. 201–16.

———. 1971/2. Localizan enterramiento Meso-Indio en Trinidad. *Revista Dominicana de Arqueologia e Antropologia* 2/3, pp. 300–302.

———. 1972. *Arqueologia Prehistorica de Santo Domingo.* New York: McGraw Hill Far Eastern Publishers.

———. 1993. *La Isla de Santo Domingo Antes de Colón.* Santo Domingo: Edición del Banco Central de la República Dominicana.

———. 1997. The Daily Life of the Taíno People. In F. Bercht, E. Brodsky, J. A. Farmer, and D. Taylor (eds.), *Taíno: Pre-Columbian Art and Culture from the Caribbean,* pp. 34–45. New York: The Monacelli Press.

Veloz Maggiolo, M., and E. Ortega. 1973. *El precerámico de Santo Domingo. Nuevos lugares y su posible relación con otros puntos del area Antilliana.* Museo del Hombre Dominicano.

Veloz Maggiolo, M., E. Ortega and A. Caba Fuentes, 1981. *Los modos de vida Meillacoides y sus posibles orígenes: Un estudio interpretativo.* Santo Domingo: Museo del Hombre Dominicano.

Veloz Maggiolo, M., E. Ortega and P. Pina P. 1974. *El Caimito: Un antiguo complejo ceramista de las Antillas Mayores.* Museo del Hombre Dominicano, Serie Monográfica 30. Santo Domingo: Ediciones Fundación García Arévalo.

Veloz Maggiolo, M., E. Ortega, M. Sanoja, and I. Vargas. 1976. Preliminary Report on Archaeological Investigations at El Atajadizo, Dominican Republic. *Proceedings of the Sixth International Congress for the Study of Pre-Columbian Cultures of the Lesser Antilles, Point-à-Pitre, Guadeloupe, July 1975,* pp. 283–94.

Veloz Maggiolo, M., I. Vargas, M. Sanoja and F. Luna Calderón. 1976. *Arqueología de Yuma (Dominican Republic).* Santo Domingo: Taller.

Verano, J. W., and D. H. Ubelaker, 1991. Health and Disease in the Pre-Columbian World. In H. J. Viola and C. Margolis (eds.), *Seeds of Change: A Quincentennial Commemoration,* pp. 209–223. Washington, DC: Smithsonian Institution Press.

Verin, P. M. 1961. Les Caraibes a Sainte-Lucie depuis les contacts coloniaux. *Nieuwe West-Indische Gids* Vol. 41 (2), pp. 66–82.

———. 1968. Carib Culture in Colonial Times. *Proceedings of the Second International Congress for the Study of Pre-Columbian Cultures of the Lesser Antilles, St. Ann's Garrison, Barbados,* pp. 115–20.

Versteeg, A. H. 1989. The Internal Organization of a Pioneer Settlement in the Lesser Antilles. In Peter E. Siegel (ed.), *Early Ceramic Population Lifeways and Adaptive Strategies in the Caribbean,* pp. 171–192. Oxford: British Archaeological Reports International Series 506.

———. 1993. Settlement Patterns within the Dabajuroid Santa Cruz site (Aruba). *Proceedings of the Fifteenth Congress of the International Association for Caribbean Archaeology,* pp. 1–6. San Juan, PR: Centro de Estudios Avanzados de Puerto Rico y el Caribe.

———. 1997. Pre-Columbian Houses at the Santa Cruz site. In L. Alofs, H. E. Coomans, and W. Rutgers (eds.), *Arubans Akkoord,* pp. 89–101. Bloemendaal: Stichting Libri Antillani.

———. 1999. *Archaeological Records from the Southern and Eastern Caribbean Area. How Different and How Similar Are They?* Paper presented at the eighteenth International Congress for Caribbean Archaeology, Nassau, Bahamas, 1997.

Versteeg, A., and S. Rostain (eds.). 1997. *The Archaeology of Aruba: The Tanki Flip Site.* Aruba/Amsterdam: Publications of the Archaeological Museum of Aruba 8.

Versteeg, A., and A. C. Ruiz. 1995. *Reconstructing Brasilwood Island: The Archaeology and Landscape of Indian Aruba.* Publications of the Archaeology Museum of Aruba No.6. Oranjestadt: Aruba.

Versteeg, A., and K. Schinkel (eds.). 1992. *The Archaeology of St. Eustatius: The Golden Rock site.* Amsterdam: St. Eustatius Historical Foundation.

Versteeg, A., J. Tacoma and P. van den Velde. 1990. *Archaeological Investigations on Aruba: The Malmok Cemetery.* Publication of the Foundation for Scientific Research in the Caribbean Region, No. 126.

Vescelius, G. S. 1952. *The Cultural Chronology of St. Croix.* Unpublished Senior Honor thesis. Department of Anthropology, Yale University, New Haven.

———. 1980. A Cultural Taxonomy for West Indian Archaeology. *Journal of the Virgin Islands Archaeological Society* 10, pp. 38–41.

Vescelius, G. S., and L. S. Robinson. 1979. *Exotic Items in Archaeological Collections from St. Croix: Prehistoric Imports and Their Implications.* Manuscript on file, Department of Anthropology, Peabody Museum, Yale University, New Haven.

Vesilind, P. J. 2003. Watery Graves of the Maya. *National Geographic* 204 (4) (October), pp. 82–102.

Viola, H. J., and C. Margolis (eds.). 1991. *Seeds of Change: A Quincentennial Commemoration.* Washington, DC: Smithsonian Institution Press.

Vivanco, J. 1946. *El Lenguaje de los indios de Cuba.* Editorial Publicación Americana, Havana.

Voeks, R. A. 1997. *Saced Leaves of Candomble: African Magic, Medicine, and Religion in Brazil.* Austin: University of Texas Press.

Wafer, L. 1933. *A New Voyage and Description of the Isthmus of America.* London: The Hakluyt Society.

Wagner, E., and C. Schubert. 1972. Pre-Hispanic Workshops of Serpentine Artifacts, Venezuelan Andes and Possible Raw Material Source. *Science* 175, pp. 888–90.

Walker, D. J. R. 1992. *Columbus and the Golden World of the Island Arawaks.* Kingston: Ian Randle Publishers Ltd.

Walker, J. 1981. Use-Wear Analysis of Caribbean Flaked Stone Tools. *Proceedings of the Ninth International Congress for the Study of Pre-Columbian Cultures of the Lesser Antilles,* pp. 239–48.

———. 1985. A Preliminary Report on the Lithic and Osteological Remains from the 1980, 1981, 1982 Field Seasons at Hacienda Grande. *Proceedings of the Tenth International Congress for the Study of Pre-Columbian Cultures of the Lesser Antilles,* pp. 181–224.

Walker, J. B. 1993. *Stone Collars, Elbow Stones and Three-Pointers, and the Nature of Taino Ritual and Myth.* Ph.D. dissertation, Washington State University. Ann Arbor: University Microfilms.

———. 1997. Taíno Stone Collars, Elbow Stones, and Three-Pointers. In F. Bercht, E. Brodsky, J. A. Farmer, and D. Taylor (eds.). *Taíno: Pre-Columbian Art and Culture from the Caribbean,* pp. 80–91. New York: The Monacelli Press.

Ward, J. R. 1990 Jamaica's Maroons. *Slavery and Abolition* 11(3): 399–403.

Warner, G. F. (ed.). 1967 [1899]. *The Voyage of Robert Dudley . . . to the West Indies, 1594–1595.* London: Hakluyt Society.

Warner-Lewis, M. 1972–3. *Africans in 19th-Century Trinidad.* The African Association of the West Indies, Bulletin Nos. 5–6.

———. 1991. *Guinea's Other Suns: The African Dynamic in Trinidad Culture.* Dover: The Majority Press.

———. 1996. *Trinidad Yoruba: From Mother Tongue to Memory.* Tuscaloosa: University of Alabama Press.

Wassén, S. H. 1938. Original Documents from the Cuna Indians of San Blas, Panama. *Etnologiska Studier* 6, pp. 1–178.

———. 1964. Some General Viewpoints in the Study of Native Drugs Especially from the West Indies and South America. *Ethnos* 29 (1–2), pp. 97–120.

———. 1967. Anthropological Survey of the Use of South American Snuffs. In D. H. Efron et al. (eds.), *Ethnopharmacologic Search for Psychoactive Drugs,* pp. 233–89. Washington, DC: US Government Printing Office. Public Health Service Publication 1645.

Watson, G. L. 1991. *Jamaican Sayings: With Notes on Folklore, Aesthetics, and Social Control.* Gainesville: University Press of Florida.

Watson, S. 2002. *The Archaeology of Rastafari.* Unpublished M.A. thesis, School of Archaeological Studies, University of Leicester.

Waters, A. M. 1985. *Race, Class, and Political Symbols: Rastafari and Reggae in Jamaican Politics.* New Brunswick, NJ: Transaction Books.

Watters, D. R. 1980. Observations on the Historic Sites and Archaeology of Barbuda. *Archaeology and Anthropology* 3 (2), pp. 125–54.

————. 1980. *Transect Surveying and Prehistoric Site Locations on Barbuda and Montserrat, Leeward Islands, West Indies.* Unpublished Ph.D. dissertation, University of Pittsburgh.

————. 1987. Excavations at the Harney Site Slave Cemetery, Montserrat, West Indies. *Annals of the Carnegie Museum* 56 (18), pp. 289–318.

————. 1994. Mortuary Patterns at the Harney Site Slave Cemetery, Montserrat in Caribbean Perspective. *Historical Archaeology* 28 (3), pp. 56–73.

————. 1994. Archaeology of Trants, Montserrat. *Annals of Carnegie Museum* 63 (3), pp. 215–37.

————. 1997. Historical Documentation and Archaeological Investigation of Codrington Castle, Barbuda. *Annals of the Carnegie Museum* 66 (3), pp. 229–88.

————. 1997. Maritime Trade in the Prehistoric Eastern Caribbean. In S. M. Wilson (ed.), *The Indigenous Peoples of the Caribbean,* pp. 88–99. Gainesville: University of Florida Press.

————. 2001. Historical Archaeology inn the British Caribbean. In P. Farnsworth (ed.), *Island Lives: Historical Archaeologies of the Caribbean,* pp. 82–102. Tuscaloosa and London: University of Alabama Press.

Watters, D. R., and D. V. Nicholson. 1982. Highland House, Barbuda: An 18th-Century Retreat. *Florida Anthropologist* Vol. 35 (4), pp. 223–42.

Watters, D. R., E. J. Reitz, D. W. Steadman and G. K. Pregill. 1984. Vertebrates from Archaeological Sites on Barbuda, West Indies. *Annals of the Carnegie Museum,* Vol. 3, No. 3, pp. 383–412.

Watters, D. R., and R. Scaglion. 1994. Beads and Pendants from Trants, Montserrat: Implications for the Pre-historic Lapidary Industry of the Caribbean. *Annals of the Carnegie Museum,* Vol. 63, pp. 215–237.

Watts, D. 1987. *The West Indies: Patterns of Development, Culture and Environmental Change Since 1492.* Cambridge: Cambridge University Press.

Weaver, D. 1994. Ecotourism in the Caribbean Basin. In E. Cater and G. Lowman (eds.), *Ecotourism: A Sustainable Option?* pp. 213–223. Chichester: John Wiley.

Wedenoja, W. 1978. *Religion and Adaptation in Rural Jamaica.* Unpublished Ph.D. dissertation, University of California.

Weeks, J. M., P. J. Ferbel, and V. R. Zabala. 1996. Rock Art at Corral de los Indios de Chacuey, Dominican Republic. *Latin American Indian Literatures Journal* Vol. 12 (1), pp. 88–97.

Weik, T. 1997. The Archaeology of Maroon Societies in the Americas: Resistance, Cultural Continuity, and Transformation in the African Disapora. *Historical Archaeology* Vol. 31 (2), pp. 81–92.

Wheeler, M. M. 1988. *Montserrat West Indies, a Chronological History.* Plymouth, Montserrat: Montserrat National Trust.

White, E. 1973. The Maroon Warriors of Jamaica and Their Successful Resistance to Enslavement. *Pan-African Journal* Vol. 6(3), pp. 297–312.

Whitehead, N. L. 1984. Carib Cannibalism: The Historical Evidence. *Journal Societe des Americanistes* Vol. 70, pp. 69–87.

————. 1988. *Lords of the Tiger Spirit: A History of the Caribs in Colonial Venezuela and Guyana 1498–1820.* Dordrecht: Foris Publications.

————. 1990. Carib Ethnic Soldiering in Venezuela, the Guianas, and the Antilles 1492–1820. *Ethnohistory* 37, pp. 357–85.

————. 1990. The Mazaruni Pectoral: A Golden Artifact Discovered in Guyana and the Historical Sources Concerning Native Metallurgy in the Caribbean, Orinoco and Northern Amazonia. *Archaeology and Anthropology* Vol. 7, pp. 19–38.

———— (ed.). 1995. *Wolves from the Sea: Readings in the Anthropology of the Native Caribbean.* Leiden: KITLV Press.

————. 1997. The Discoverie as Ethnological Text. In *Sir Walter Ralegh, The Discoverie of the Large, Rich and Bewtiful Empyre of Guiana*, pp. 60–116. Transcribed, annotated and introduced by Neil L. Whitehead. Manchester: Manchester University Press.

————. 1999a. The Crises and Transformations of Invaded Societies: The Caribbean (1492–1580). In F. Salomon and S. B. Schwartz (eds.), *The Cambridge History of the Native Peoples of the Americas: Volume III, South America, Part 1*, pp. 864–903. Cambridge: Cambridge University Press.

————. 1999b. Native Peoples Confront Colonial Regimes in Northeastern South America (c. 1500–1900). In F. Salomon and S. B. Schwartz (eds.), *The Cambridge History of the Native Peoples of the Americas: Volume III, South America, Part 2*, pp. 382–442. Cambridge: Cambridge University Press.

————. 1999c. Native Society and the European Occupation of the Caribbean Islands and Coastal Tierra Firme, 1492–1650. In P. C. Emmer (ed.), *General History of the Caribbean: Volume II, New Societies: The Caribbean in the Long Sixteenth Century*, pp. 180–200. London: UNESCO.

Whitney, M. L., D. Hussey, and R. Marley. 1994. *Bob Marley: Reggae King of the World*. Pomegranate.

Whylie, M., and M. Warner-Lewis. 1994. Characteristics of Maroon Music from Jamaica and Suriname. In E. K. Agorsah (ed.), *Maroon Heritage: Archaeological, Ethnographic and Historical Perspectives*, pp. 139–148. Kingston: Canoe Press.

Widmer, R. E. 1988. *The Evolution of the Calusa: A Nonagricultural Chiefdom on the Southwest Florida Coast*. Tuscaloosa: University of Alabama Press.

Wignall, S. 1982. *In Search of Spanish Treasure*. Newton Abbot: David and Charles.

Wilbert, Johannes. 1970. *Folk Literature of the Warao Indians: Narrative Material and Motif Content*. Latin American Studies 15, Latin American Center, University of California, Los Angeles.

————. 1972. Tobacco and Shamanistic Ecstasy among the Warao Indians of Venezuela. In P. T. Furst (ed.), *Flesh of the Gods: The Ritual Use of Hallucinogens*, pp. 55–83, New York: Praeger.

————. 1975. Eschatology in a Participatory Universe: Destinies of the Soul among the Warao Indians of Venezuela. In E. P. Benson (ed.), *Death and the Afterlife in Pre-Columbian America*, pp. 163–190. Washington, DC: Dumbarton Oaks.

————. 1977. Navigators of the Winter Sun. In E. P. Benson (ed.), *The Sea in the Pre-Columbian World*, pp. 16–46. Washington, DC: Dumbarton Oaks.

————. 1979. Geography and Telluric Lore of the Orinoco Delta. *Journal of Latin American Lore* 51 (1), pp. 129–210.

————. 1981. Warao Cosmology and Yekuana Round House Symbolism. *Journal of Latin American Lore* Vol. 7, pp. 37–72.

————. 1985. The House of the Swallow-Tailed Kite: Warao Myth and the Art of Thinking in Images. In G. Urton (ed.), *Animal Myths and Metaphors in South America*, pp. 145–182. Salt Lake City: University of Utah Press.

————. 1987. *Tobacco and Shamanism in South America*. New Haven, CT: Yale University Press.

————. 1997. Illuminative Serpents: Tobacco Hallucinations of the Warao. *Journal of latin American Lore* Vol. 20 (2), pp. 317–332.

Wilkie, L. A. 1997. Secret and Sacred: Contextualising the Artifacts of African-American Magic and Religion. *Historical Archaeology* 31 (4), pp. 81–106.

————. 2001. Evidence of African Continuities in the Material Culture of Clifton Plantation, Bahamas. In J. Haviser (ed.), *African Sites Archaeology in the Caribbean*, pp. 264–276. Princeton, NJ: Markus Wiener.

————. 2001. Communicative Bridges Linking Actors through Time: Archaeology and the Construction of Emancipatory Narratives at a Bahamian Plantation. *Journal of Social Archaeology* Vol. 1 (2), pp. 225–43.

Wilkie, L. A., and P. Farnsworth. 1995. Archaeological Excavations on Crooked Island. *Journal of the Bahamas Historical Society* 17, pp. 34–6.

Wilkie, L. A., and P. Farnsworth. 1997. Daily Life on a Loyalist Plantation: Results of the 1996 Excavations at Clifton Plantation. *Journal of the Bahamas Historical Society* Vol. 19, pp. 2–18.

Wilkinson, A. 1989. *Big Sugar.* New York: Alfred A Knopf.

Willard, T. A. 1926. *The city of the Sacred Well.* New York: The Century Co.

Willey, G R. 1971. The Caribbean Cultural Tradition in Trinidad and the West Indies. In G. R. Willey, *An Introduction to American Archaeology,* Vol. 2, South America, pp. 380–94. Englewood Cliffs, NJ: Prentice-Hall.

———. 1982. *Archaeology of the Florida Gulf Coast.* Gainesville, FL: Smithsonian Miscellaneous Collections Vol. 113.

Williams, D. 1985. *Ancient Guyana.* Georgetown (Guyana): Ministry of Education, Social Development and Culture.

Williams, J. J. 1932. *Voodoos and Obeahs: Phases of West India Witchcraft.* New York: Dial Press Inc.

———. 1934. *Psychic Phenomena of Jamaica.* New York: The Dial Press.

Williams, K. M. 1981. *The Rastafarians.* London: Ward, Lock Educational.

Williams, M. W. 1986. Sub-surface Patterning at Sixteenth-Century Spanish Puerto Real, Haiti. *Journal of Field Archaeology* 13 (3), pp. 283–96.

Wilson, S. M. 1986. *The Conquest of the Caribbean Chiefdoms: Sociopolitical Change on Prehispanic Hispaniola.* Ph.D. dissertation, University of Chicago. Ann Arbor, MI: University Microfilms.

———. 1989. The Prehistoric Settlement Pattern of Nevis, West Indies. *Journal of Field Archaeology* Vol. 16, pp. 427–50.

———. 1990. *Hispaniola: Caribbean Chiefdoms in the Age of Columbus.* Tuscaloosa: University of Alabama Press.

———. 1994. The Cultural Mosaic of the Indigenous Caribbean in Europe and America. In W. Bray (ed.), *The Meeting of Two Worlds: Europe and the Americas 1492–1650,* pp. 37–66. London: The British Academy.

——— (ed.). 1997. *The Indigenous People of the Caribbean.* Gainesville: University Press of Florida.

———. 1997. The Taíno Social and Political Order. In F. Bercht, E. Brodsky, J. A. Farmer, and D. Taylor (eds.), *Taíno: Pre-Columbian Art and Culture from the Caribbean,* pp. 46–55. New York: The Monacelli Press.

———. 1999. *The Prehistory of Nevis.* Gainesville: University Press of Florida.

Wilson, S. M., H. B. Iceland and T. R. Hester. 1998. Preceramic Connections between Yucatan and the Caribbean. *Latin American Antiquity* 9 (4), pp. 342–52.

Wilson, S. 1994. *Cuba: The Land, the History, the People, the Culture.* Running Press.

Wing, E. S. 1962. *Succession of Mammalian Faunas on Trinidad, West Indies.* Ann Arbor. Unpublished Ph.D. dissertation.

———. 1969. Vertebrate remains excavated from San Salvador Island, Bahamas. *Journal of Caribbean Science* Vol. 9 (1–2), pp. 25–9.

———. 1989. Human Exploitation of Animal Resources in the Caribbean. In C. A. Woods (ed.), *Biogeography of the West Indies: Past, Present and Future,* pp. 137–52. Gainseville: Sandhill Crane.

———. 1989. Evidences for the Impact of Traditional Spanish Animal Uses in Parts of the New World. In J. Clutton-Brock (ed.), *The Walking Larder,* pp. 72–9. London: Unwin Hyman.

———. 1990. Animal Remains from the Hacienda Grande Site, Puerto Rico. Appendix, In I. Rouse and R. E. Alegría, *Excavations at Maria de la Cruz Cave and Hacienda Grande Village site, Loiza, Puerto Rico.* New Haven, CT: Yale University Publications in Anthropology, No. 80.

———. 1995. Rice Rats and Saladoid People as Seen at Hope Estate. *Proceedings of the Fifteenth International Congress for the Study of Pre-Columbian Cultures of the Lesser Antilles,* pp. 219–232.

———. 1995. Land Crab Remains in Caribbean Sites. *Proceedings of the Sixteenth International Congress for Caribbean Archaeology,* Part 1, pp. 105–112.

————. 2000. Economy and Subsistence 1: Animal Remains from Sites on Barbados and Tortola. In P. Drewett (ed.), *Prehistoric Settlements in the Caribbean: Fieldwork in Barbados, Tortola, and the Cayman Islands,* pp. 147–154. London: Archetype Publications.

Wing, E. S., S. deFrance, and L. Kozuch. 1995. *Faunal Remains from the Tutu Archaeological Village, St. Thomas, USVI.* Manuscript on file at the Division for Archaeology and Historic Preservation.

Wing, E. S., C. A. Hofman, and C. E. Ray. 1968. Vetebrate Remains from Indian Sites on Antigua. *Caribbean Journal of Science* 8 (3&4), pp. 129–39.

Wing, E. S., and E. J. Reitz 1982. Prehistoric Fishing Economies of the Caribbean. *Journal of New World Archaeology* Vol. 5, No. 2, pp. 13–32.

Wing, E. S., and S. J. Scudder. 1980. Use of Animals by the Prehistoric Inhabitants on St. Kitts, West Indies. *Proceedings of the Eighth International Congress for the Study of the Pre- Columbian Cultures of the Lesser Antilles,* pp. 237–45. Tempe, AZ.

Winslow, J. H. 1991. Far North by Far West: Columbus's First Landfalls in the Bahamas and the North Coast of Cuba. *HRD News* 2 (5&6), pp. 1–10

Winter, J. H. 1991. Petroglyphs of the Bahamas. *Proceedings of the Fourteenth International Congress for Caribbean Archaeology, Barbados,* pp. 672–80.

Winter, J., and D. M. Pearsall. 1991. A Wooden Mortar of the Lucayans. *Proceedings of the Fourteenth International Congress for Caribbean Archaeology, Barbados,* pp. 586–90.

Wise, K. S. 1934–8. *Historical Sketches of Trinidad and Tobago.* 4 vols. Port of Spain: Trinidad Historical Society.

Wood, P. 1975. *The Caribbean.* New York: Time-Life.

Woods, C. A. (ed.). 1989. *Biogeography of the West Indies.* Gainesville, FL: Sandhill Crane Press.

Wright, I. (ed.). 1929. *Spanish Documents Concerning English Voyages to the Caribbean, 1527–1568.* London: Hakluyt Society.

Wright, M. L. 1994. Accompong Maroons of Jamaica. In E. K. Agorsah (ed.), *Maroon Heritage,* pp. 64–71. Kingston: Canoe Press.

Yentsch, A. E., and M. C. Beaudry. 1992. *The Art and Mystery of Historical Archaeology: Essays in Honor of James Deetz.* Boca Raton, FL: CRC Press.

Young, T. 1847. *Narrative of a Residence on the Mosquito Shore: With an Account of Truxillo, and the Adjacent Islands of Bonacca and Roatan; and a Vocabulary of the Mosquitan Language.* London.

Zahedieh, N. 1986. Trade, Plunder, and Economic Development in Early English Jamaica, 1655–89. *Economic History Review* 4 (2), pp. 205–22.

Zane, W. W. 1999. *Journeys to the Spiritual Lands: A Natural History of a West Indian Religion.* Oxford: Oxford University Press.

Zavala, S. 1935. *La encomienda indiana.* Madrid: Imprenta helénica.

Zink, D. 1990. *The Stones of Atlantis.* New York: Prentice Hall.

Zucchi, A. 1972. New Data on the Antiquity of Polychrome Painting from Venezuela. *American Antiquity* 37, pp. 439–46.

Index

Abeng (Maroon cow-horn), 1, 176

Accompong, 1–2, 145, 175, 176

Account of the Antiquities of the Indians, An (Father Ramón Pané), 216–217

Act of Union (England and Scotland, 1707), 93

Adornos, 28, 95, 98, 116, 117, 127, 137, 154, 173, 220, 222, 227, 236, 239, 250, 252, 257, 259, 267, 287, 301

Aesthetic of brilliance, 2–3, 61, 108, 114–115, 166, 218

Afro-Cruzan (pottery), 135, 257, 259–260

Agouti, 3, 45

Agriculture

    Amerindian (South America), 236

    Carib, 45

    Taíno, 271–272

Aguado, Juan de, 156

Agüeybana (Taíno chief), 3, 228, 275

Aguilar, Gerónimo de, 183, 184

Ah Canul (Maya ruler), 184

Ajoupa (Amerindian long-house, Trinidad), 244, 294

Ake (Battle of, in Mexico), 184

Aklis (site, St. Croix), 257

Alicante, wreck of, 308

Almiranta (Spanish treasure galleon). *See Nuestra Señora de la Concepción,* wreck of

Alphen (shipwreck site, Curaçao), 132

Aluku (Maroons), 177

Amazons, 3–6

America, naming of, 312

Amethyst, 137, 189, 240, 253, 257

Amiens, Treaty of (1802), 290

Anacaona (Taíno chief/queen), 5, 6–7, 29, 75, 128, 273

Anadel people, 18

Ancestor worship, 47, 105, 118, 190, 191, 192, 210, 239, 241, 247, 279

Andros Island, 303

Anegada (BVI), 7

Anguilla, 7–9

Animals

    agouti, 3, 45

    crocodiles, 83–84

    dogs, 37, 58, 95–96, 110, 134, 159, 214, 250, 252, 277, 317

    jaguar, 49, 81, 96, 222, 250, 277, 294

    manatee, 141

Anse à la Gourde (site, Guadeloupe), 120–121

Anse de la Petite Chapelle (site, Guadeloupe), 121

Anse des Pères (site, St. Martin), 9

Anse du Vieux-Fort (site, Guadeloupe), 121

Anse Sainte-Marguerite (site, Guadeloupe), 121

Anse Trabaud (site, Martinique), 179

Anthropophagy. *See* Cannibalism

Antigua, 10–12

Antonio López, wreck of, 308

Anvil bird, 135

Antriol (Mestizo village, Bonaire), 34

Arauquinoid (pottery), 12–13, 125, 166

Archaic Period, 10, 13–16, 24–25, 89, 96–97, 147, 150, 252, 264

Areíto, 16, 28, 79, 128, 191, 323

Armstrong Pond (site, Turks and Caicos), 300

Aruba, 17–18, 91

Ashanti, 207

Asphalt, 222, 293. *See also* Pitch Lake

Astrolabe, 307

Astronomy, 24, 48, 58, 78, 182, 185(ill.), 273(ill.), 273, 281, 287

Atabey (Taíno deity), 267, 276, 321

Atajadizo, 18–19

Ávila, Pedro de, 22

Aztecs, 37, 60, 256

Babylon, Rastafarian concept of, 234

Bahía Mujeres wreck, 306

Baibrama (Taíno deity), 217, 324

Bajans. *See* Barbados

Balboa, Vasco Núñez de, 21–22, 86, 92

Balenbouche Estate (site, St. Lucia), 134, 262

Ballast, ship's, 188, 306

Ball-game, 22–24, 105, 108, 227–228, 241, 257, 275, 300

Balliceaux Island, 113

Banana Bay (site, Water Island, USVI), 319

Bananas, 101

Bani culture (Cuba), 84

Banwari Trace (site, Trinidad), 13, 24, 211, 292

Barasana (Amazonian tribe), 58

Barbados, 25–27, 62

Barquisimeto (Venezuela, 212

Barracuda, 80

Barrancas (site, Venezuela), 27

Barrancoid, 27–28, 120, 131, 159, 179, 216, 240, 292

Barrera-Mordán/Casimira (site, Hispaniola), 14

Basse-Terre (Guadeloupe), 120

Baskets and basketry, 64, 98, 153, 244, 304

Batey. *See* Ball-Game

Bats, Amerindian symbolism of, 153–154, 222, 239, 252, 266, 277

Bayamanaco (Taíno mythic figure), 279

Beer (Amerindian), 58, 161, 216

Behechio (Taíno chief), 6, 16, 28–29, 75, 115, 128

Belén River (Veragua, Panama), 78

Bell, Henry Hesketh, 41–42, 50, 98

Belmont (site, Tortola, BVI), 287

Benning, Simon (pewter-maker, Port Royal, Jamaica), 224–225, 305

Bequia (St. Vincent and the Grenadines), 57(ill.)

Berrio, Antonio de, 231

Betty's Hope (site, Antigua), 10, 29–31, 134

Big Drum Dance (Grenada), 118

Birds and bird symbolism, 8(ill.), 31–32, 91, 98, 138, 227, 249–250, 278, 317, 324

Bitumen. *See* Asphalt; Pitch Lake

Black Caribs. *See* Garifuna

Black Legend, 32–33

Blackbeard's Castle (St. Thomas, USVI), 265

Bligh, Captain, 266

Blue Mountains (Jamaica), 175, 197

Bluefields (Nicaragua), 188

Bobadilla, Francisco de, 76

Body decoration, 12

Bois Neuf (site, Haiti), 15

Bonaire, 13, 33–34, 91

Bonampak (Maya murals at), 192

Bones, human (Amerindian use of/myths concerning), 48–49, 74, 94, 121, 220, 240–241, 250, 277–278, 321

Bontour (pottery, Trinidad), 12–13

Book of Prophecies (Christopher Columbus), 76

Boreas, HMS (captained by Horatio Nelson), 198

Bounty (British ship), 266

Bourbon (sugar species), 268

Boutbois culture (Martinique), 13, 179, 211

Brass, 115, 173, 219

Breadfruit, 266

Breath, human (symbolism of for Amerindians), 191

Breton, Father Raymond, 34–35, 49, 98, 120, 161

Brewers Bay (site, Tortola, BVI), 287

Bry, Theodore de, 32

Buccaneers, 223

Bullbrook, John, 62

Bullen, Ripley, 117, 220

Burials
    as indicator of ethnicity/religion, 134, 155, 200–201
    inhumation, 34, 62, 120–121
    urn, 34, 282

Bush magic. *See* Obeah

Cabrits (fortress, Dominica), 132

Cacao
    Amerindian use of, 37, 81
    plantations, 37–38, 65–66

Cádiz (Spain), 74, 76

Caguana/Capá (site, Puerto Rico), 24, 38–40, 228, 321

Caille Brûlee (site, Haiti), 158

Caimito, El, 40, 127

Calabashes, 45–46, 191

Caliviny Polychrome (pottery, Barbados), 63, 130

Calypso (Trinidad), 54, 193–194

Calypso Monarch (Trinidad), 53

Cambridge, Thomas, 167

Canary Islands, 70, 75, 268

Canboulay (Trinidad), 52, 53, 296

Cancun (Mexico), 306

Cane Garden Bay (site, Tortola, BVI), 287

Cannabis, 146, 232, 234

Cannibalism, 4(ill.), 5, 47, 48–49, 121

Cannon, 26, 93, 188, 198, 202, 204, 243, 258, 266, 283, 306

Canoe people. *See* Warao

Canoes, 46, 97(ill.), 214, 236, 281, 290, 298, 303, 317
    as coffins, 289, 318

Caona (pure gold), 114–115

Caonabo (Taíno chief), 23, 41, 74, 119, 158

Cantyman (Amerindian chief, Trinidad), 231

Cap Haïtien (Haiti), 157

Cape Verde Islands, 286

Capuchin monks (Trinidad), 186, 293

Caquetio, 33

Caracoli (crescent-shaped gold objects), 46

Caraibe Point (St. Lucia), 264

Caraipé (pottery temper), 61, 186

Carbet (Carib men's house), 46

Carib Leap (Grenada), 118

Carib Queen (Trinidad), 51, 242

Carib Snake (cassava squeezing container), 58

Carib Stone (petroglyph site, Trinidad), 46, 293(ill.)

Carib Street (San Fernando, Trinidad), 293

Carib Territory/Waitukubuli Karifuna Community (Dominica), 41–44, 50

Carib War (1930, Dominica), 42, 50, 98, 147

Carib/Taíno identities (created by Spanish) 48–49

Caribbean Organization of Indigenous Peoples, 51

Caribs, 34–35, 44–52, 142, 292
    arts and crafts, 43, 45–46
    canoes, 43, 44, 46
    language, 35, 43, 45, 161
    mythology, 41, 47–48
    name, 45
    raiding of Taíno Islands, 46, 48, 142, 228, 276
    relations with South America, 45
    religion, 47–48, 153
    Santa Rosa Carib Community (Trinidad), 241–245
    shamans, 250
    society, 46–47
    subsistence, 45

Carinepagotos (Amerindian tribe, Trinidad), 231, 292–293

Carnelian, 137, 189, 253, 257

Carnival (Trinidad), 52–55

Carriacou Island, 117

Carrier (pottery, Haiti), 128

Carolina Lyst (plantation, Water Island, USVI), 319

Carolina Point Plantation (Water Island, USVI), 319

Cartwright Cave (site, Long Island, Bahamas), 106

Casimiroid, 14, 40, 55–56, 84, 99, 128

Cassarip, 57–58, 221

Cassava, 35, 48, 51, 56–59, 100, 112, 217, 221, 240, 242, 276
   and Amerindian identity, 242
   griddles 19, 25, 45, 58, 62, 80, 91, 117, 127, 130, 137, 179, 187, 215, 222, 236, 240, 252, 257, 267, 287, 298, 300

Catherwood, Frederick, 81, 298

Cauixí (pottery temper), 12

Caves, Amerindian significance and use of, 38, 63, 84, 100, 106, 117, 122, 150, 153–154, 278, 281, 300, 304, 323

Cayabo (Taíno province, Hispaniola), 124

Cayman Islands, 59–61
   National Museum, 283, 307

Cayo (pottery), 45, 50, 61–62, 266

Cayo Hondo (site, Puerto Rico), 14

Cayo Redondo (site, Cuba), 14, 56, 84

CEDAM. See Mexican Explorers and Divers Club

Cedros (site, Trinidad), 62, 239, 292, 318(ill.)

Ceiba tree, 146, 229, 289

Cerillo (site, Puerto Rico), 14

Chagras (Amerindian fields), 56

Chaima (Amerindian tribe, Trinidad), 31, 222, 294

Champoton (Mexico), 184

Chanca, Dr., 74, 155, 324

Chancery Lane (site, Barbados), 25, 62–63

Chango (Santería deity), 247

Charles Town (Jamaica), 175

Chican Ostionoid (Taíno), 18

Chicha (Amerindian beverage), 58

Chichén Itzá (site, Mexico), 63–64, 183(ill.), 185(ill.), 304

Chilam Balam, The Books of (Maya, Yucatán, Mexico), 185

China, 69, 72

Chinese porcelain (Ming), 203, 224, 305

Chiriqui (Panama), 78

Chocolate. See Cacao

Cholera, 94

Chorro de Maíta (site, Cuba), 84

Christian influence (on indigenous peoples), 281

Christophe, Henri, 288

Christophe Plain (African-Caribbean pottery, Hispaniola), 226

Cibao (Hispaniola), 74, 119, 186

Çibas (Taíno polished stone jewelry), 273

Ciboney/Guanahatabey relationship, 15, 84, 122–123

Cimarrón. See Maroons

Cinnamon Bay (site, St. John, USVI), 259

Cipangu, 72

Ciudad Marta (Hispaniola), 155

Clarence, Duke of, 11

Clay pipes, 131, 200–201, 287, 307

Cleaver Woods National Park (Trinidad), 244, 294

Cleveland, USS, 87

Clifton Plantation, 65

Coastal trade (Maya, Yucatán, Mexico), 182–183. See also Tancah, Tulum, Maya

Coca (narcotic), 215

Cocal (site, Trinidad), 292

Cochrane, Admiral, 198

Cockpit Country (Jamaica), 176

Cocoa Panyols, 38, 65–66, 194, 294

Coconut shells, 248

Coconut Walk Estate (site, Nevis), 134, 261

Codrington, Sir Christopher, 10, 29

Coffee (plantations), 121, 262

Cohoba, 32, 66–67, 79, 105, 153, 217, 250, 277–279, 285, 324

Coins, 93, 100, 154, 188, 202, 203–204, 307

Colors (Amerindian ideas about/use of), 2, 26, 31, 65, 87, 88, 114–115, 119, 177, 212, 219, 249–250, 273–275, 298, 311
   Rastafarian, 234–235
   Santería, 246–247

Columbus, Bartolomé, 6, 16, 28–29, 74–75, 125

Columbus, Christopher, 67–79
   accusations of nepotism against, 156
   Book of Prophecies, 76
   early voyages, 68
   first voyage, 70–73
   second voyage, 74–75
   third voyage, 75–76
   fourth voyage, 76–78, 182–183
   and King João II of Portugal, 68, 73
   life of, 67–70
   meets Amerindians(ill.),70
   postmortem travels, 69–70
   Queen Isabella, 68, 75
   and Santa Fe Capitulations, 69

Columbus, Diego, 74

Columbus, Fernando, 217

Columbus Channel, 27, 216, 292, 318(ill.)

Communitarian Nation of Moskitia, 188

Comogre (Amerindian chief), 22, 86

Concepción de la Vega (Spanish settlement, Hispaniola), 74–75

Conch, 79–80, 131, 142, 147, 191, 252

Coñori (Amazon queen), 5

Conucos (Taíno fields), 56, 272, 324

Convert, HMS (sunk on Grand Cayman), 283, 307

Coral
   Amerindian use of, 25, 241, 252, 282
   European use of, 121

Coral Bay–Longford phase pottery (St. Croix), 257

Coralie (site, Turks and Caicos), 80, 300

Córdoba, Hernández de, 183

Coromantee (African tribe), 175

Coroso culture (Puerto Rico), 150, 211, 227

Corozal culture, 12, 172, 212

Corpse, human (drying of), 282

Corrales de los Indios (site, Dominican Republic), 23, 41

Cortés, Hernán, 76, 81, 85, 184

Costa Rica, 78

Cotton, 6, 16, 29, 34, 45–46, 64, 75, 81, 87, 113, 121, 321

Coulève, 242. *See also* Carib Snake

Courian, 14, 40, 55, 128

Cousteau, Jacques, 203

Cowrie shells, 1, 134, 200, 248

Cozumel, 80–82, 182

Crabs, blue land, 171

Creator Bird of Dawn (Warao), 317

Creole (sugar species), 268

Creole/creolization, 82, 122, 135, 161, 180, 229

Criollo pottery, 135, 229

Crocodile, 60, 83–84, 218, 304

Cropover festival (Barbados), 26

Cuba, 55, 56, 84–89

Cubagua Island (Venezuela), 13, 169, 173, 219

Cudjoe (Maroon leader), 1, 175

Cueva (Amerindian tribe), 86

Cueva de Chico (Taíno cave site, Dominican Republic), 154, 304

Cuevas culture (Dominican Republic), 99, 127, 212–213, 227

Cumberland, Earl of, 229

Cuna, 86–89, 92, 285, 302

Curaçao, 89–90, 132

Curiapan (site, Trinidad), 231

Cushing, Frank Hamilton, 149

Dabajuroid, 17, 34, 89, 91–92, 125, 160, 172, 173, 282

Dabeiba (Amerindian chief), 22, 107

Dahomey, 207, 209, 313

Dame Lorraine (Carnival figure), 52

Danballah (serpent deity of Vodoun religion), 313

Dangriga (Belize), 50, 113

Darién (Panama), 21–22, 83, 92–93, 213

Delhi, HMS (used against the Dominican Caribs), 42

Deminán Caracaracol (Taíno mythic being), 278–279

Dessalines, Jean-Jacques, 129, 288

Diablesse, La (folklore figure, Trinidad), 295

Diamant (site, Martinique), 179

Discovery Day (Trinidad), 73(ill.)

Disease, 33, 93–95, 156

Diving God, Temple of (Tulum, Mexico), 182, 299

Djiné (African families, St. Lucia), 263

Dogs

    Amerindian, 58, 95–96, 250, 277, 317

    European, 96, 110, 134, 214

    sacrifice/burial of, 37, 159, 252

Dominica, 35, 96–99

Dos Mosquises Island (Los Roques Islands, Venezuela), 166

Drake, Sir Francis, 83, 101

Drake Manuscript, 101

Drax, William, 101, 146

Drax Hall (site, Jamaica), 101–104, 133, 146

Dreadlocks, Rastafarian significance of, 234–235

Drum (Taíno), 191

Dudley, Sir Robert, 104, 221, 293

Duhos, 6, 23, 29, 75, 104–106, 115, 128, 153, 165, 250, 267, 273, 289–290

Duppies (ghosts), 146, 207

Earth People (sect, Trinidad), 295

Earthquake (1692, Port Royal, Jamaica), 223

East Caicos Island, 300

Eels, 45

Egg Island, 159

Ek Chuah (Maya deity), 37

El Bronce (site, Puerto Rico), 23, 108, 227

El Dorado, 5, 92, 107–108, 114, 231–232

Elephant Bay (site, Water Island, USVI), 319

El Porvenir (site, Dominican Republic), 14, 40, 55, 128, 301

Eleggua (Santería deity), 247

Elenan pottery (Saladoid), 108–109, 213, 227, 287, 319

Emeralds, 202, 203, 204

Enciso, Martín Fernández de, 21, 83, 92

Encomienda, 109–110, 164, 293

Erin (site, Trinidad), 27, 79, 216

Espíritu Santo, wreck of, 307

Esquivel, Juan de, 162, 199

Ethiopia, 232–233

Exchange (between Europeans and Amerindians), 2, 45–46, 72–73, 75, 104, 119, 129, 158, 160, 166, 173, 219, 274

Fancy (St. Vincent and the Grenadines), 266

Fedon, Julian, 118

Fewkes, Jesse Walker, 323

Field Museum of Natural History (Chicago), 63

Figurines, ceramic, 166–167, 267

Fish (European interest in), 214

Fisherman's Feast (St. Lucia), 263

Fishing (Amerindian techniques of), 58, 80, 102(ill.), 281

Florida (USA), 149

Flower Societies (St. Lucia), 263

Flutes (Amerindian), 191

Fon (African society), 313

Fontein (Amerindian village, Bonaire), 34

Fool's gold, 232

Fort Charlotte (St. Lucia), 262

Fort Charlotte (St. Vincent and the Grenadines), 266

Fort Christian (St. Thomas, USVI), 265

Fort Cromwell (Jamaica). *See* Port Royal

Fort Derrière (St. Lucia), 263

Fort Oranje/Oranjestad (St. Eustatius), 258

Fort Rodney (St. Lucia), 263

Fort Segarra (Water Island, USVI), 319

Fort St. Andrews (Darién, Panama), 93

Fountain Cavern (site, Anguilla), 8

Frederick, Jacob, 43

French Guiana, 177

Friendship Complex (pottery, Tobago), 167

Frog symbolism, 17, 91, 117, 257, 277

Funche Cave (site, Cuba), 14

Gaga (African-Caribbean religion, Dominican Republic), 100

Gaito (site, Curaçao), 89

Galway, David, 111

Galways Plantation, 111–112, 190

Gang Gang Sara (folklore figure, Tobago), 295

Ganja. See Cannabis

Garay, Francisco de, 199

Garifuna (Black Caribs), 50, 112–114, 161, 187, 266

Garvey, Marcus, 232, 234

Gaspar Grande Island (Trinidad), 216, 292

Geneva Kathleen, wreck of, 308

Genoa, 67–69

Gire-Gire (site, Margarita Island, Venezuela), 173

Glass

    beads, 2, 17, 45, 61, 72, 100, 119, 134, 158, 160, 173, 189, 200–201, 203, 219, 266, 274, 307, 321

    powder, 208

Gli Gli (Carib canoe), 43

Gold, 18, 22, 46, 63, 64, 72, 74, 87, 92, 104, 114–115, 124, 125, 202, 213, 232, 259, 304

    mining, 101, 129, 156, 164, 225, 254, 300

    Amerindian names/titles referring to, 41, 115, 119

    See also El Dorado; Fool's gold

Golden Grove (site and pottery complex, Tobago), 167, 292

Golden Rock (site, St. Eustatius), 9, 115–116, 258, 301

Gonâve, Ile de (Ganabara), 6, 105, 128, 273

Gotomeer (site, Bonaire), 13, 33

Gourds, 154, 278

Grand Turk Island, 80, 159, 168, 169, 300

Grande-Terre (Guadeloupe), 120–121

Granny Nanny (Maroon leader, Jamaica), 175–176

Graves, European, 287

Great Courland Bay (site, Tobago), 292

Great Inagua Island, 116–117

Grenada, 117–119

Grenville, Sir Richard, 157

Grijalva, Juan de, 81, 85, 183, 298

Guabancex (Lady of the Hurricane Winds, Taíno deity), 125, 217, 277, 289

Guacanagarí (Taíno chief), 70(ill.), 72–74, 119–120, 128, 157–158

Guadeloupe, 48, 74, 113, 120–122

Guadeloupe, Virgin of, 121

Guanahaní Island, 72, 159

Guanahaní Landfall Park (San Salvador Island), 169(ill.)

Guanahatabey, 84, 122–124

    relationship with Ciboney, 15

Guanín, 41, 46, 105, 107, 114, 119, 273, 324. *See also* Aesthetic of brilliance; Gold

Guarionex (Taíno chief), 39, 74–75, 99, 124–125, 217

Guatavita, Lake (Colombia), 107

Guayabel (pottery style), 19

Guayabita (pottery, Venezuela), 12

Guayabitoid (pottery), 125

Guayabo Blanco (site and culture, Cuba), 56, 84

Guayacán tree, 289

Guayaguare (site, Trinidad), 186

Guayahona (Taíno mythical hero), 4, 115, 179, 217, 278–279

Guaymi (Amerindian tribe), 78

Guerrero, Gonzalo de, 183

Gulf of Paria, 75, 317

Gulf of Uraba, 86, 92

Habitation Murat (site, Guadeloupe), 121, 134

Hacienda Grande (site, Puerto Rico), 40, 95, 99, 127–128, 227

Haiti, 113, 128–130, 269, 312–315

Hallucinogens, 32, 66–67, 79, 105, 114, 127, 137, 153, 214, 217, 250, 252, 267, 277, 315, 324

Hammock, 275

Harrison's Cave (Barbados), 26

Havana (Cuba), 85

Hawkins, John, 157, 254

Hawksbill turtle, 116, 149, 258, 301

Herbalists, 209. *See also* Hallucinogens; Shamanism

Heywoods (site, Barbados), 25, 130

Highborn Cay Wreck, 306

Higuanamá (Taíno chief), 99

Higüey (Taíno chiefdom), 153, 162

    massacre, 3

Hillcrest (site, Barbados), 130

Hispaniola, 55, 72–73, 99, 109, 119, 225

Histoire Naturelle des Indes. See Drake Manuscript

Historical archaeology, 30, 65, 93, 101, 103–104, 131–137, 198, 224–227, 287

Honduras, 78, 113, 187

Honduras, Cape, 76, 182

Hood, Admiral, 198

Hope Estate (site, St. Martin), 137–138, 252

Horticulture. *See* Agriculture

Hounfor (Vodoun temple), 314–315

Hoyo del Muerto (site, Cuba), 14

Hueca, La (Puerto Rico), 127, 137, 138–139, 220, 227, 320, 325

Hummingbirds, 31, 114, 222, 249, 294

Hutia, 45, 95, 168, 218, 287

Hyarima (Amerindian chief, Trinidad), 243, 294

Iberogun (Cuna hero figure), 88

Ibo (African society), 313

Icacos (site, Trinidad), 125

Igneri, 141

Incense burners, 63, 81, 141, 239, 252, 267

Indian Creek (site, Antigua), 9, 10, 109, 141–142

Indian Walk (Trinidad), 293

Indian Warner, 142–143

Indigenous peoples of the Caribbean (associations of), 44, 51

Indigo, 29, 121

Influenza, 94

Institute of Nautical Archaeology (Texas A&M University, USA), 188, 223, 305
Isla de Mujeres (Mexico), 81, 182
Itzam Cab Ain (Maya god), 83
Itzamná (Maya god), 83
Ix Chel (Maya goddess), 81, 182, 184, 299

Jack o'lantern, 261
Jade, 37, 63, 64, 81, 137, 281, 304
Jaguar imagery, 49, 81, 96, 222, 250, 277, 294
Jalousie Plantation/tourist resort (St. Lucia), 264
Jamaica, 78, 101, 145–147, 213, 232–234
Jamaica National Heritage Trust (JNHT), 218, 223, 305
Jatibonicu Taíno Tribal Nation of Boriken (Puerto Rico), 160, 229, 279–280
Jerusalem, 76, 182
Jewelry (Amerindian), 9, 17, 22, 31, 34, 46, 64, 72, 87, 99, 104, 107, 115, 116, 127, 137, 138, 142, 150, 189, 201, 212, 227, 240, 241, 253, 257, 273
    European, 100, 154, 202–204
Jewish culture and places, 26, 70, 146, 234, 258, 261
JNHT. See Jamaica National Heritage Trust
João II, King of Portugal, 68, 73, 286
Jolly Beach (site, Antigua), 14, 147
Jolly John, 42–43, 98, 147–148
Jose Maria Cave (Dominican Republic), 100
Jumbie dancers, 190
Jumbies, 261

Kalinago/Kalina, 45, 46, 112, 149, 161, 293
Kalipuna, 46, 50, 112, 241
Karinya, 161
Kebra Negast (Rastafarian holy book), 234
Kenepa (site, Curaçao), 90, 132
Key Marco (site, Florida, USA), 149–150
Koriabo (pottery, Guiana), 61, 186
Krum Bay (site, St. Thomas), 14, 150–151, 211, 264
Kwéyòl (Patois language. St. Lucia), 263
Kwinti (Maroons), 177

La Aleta (site, Dominican Republic), 99, 153–154, 304
La Brea. See Pitch Lake
La Caleta (site, Dominican Republic), 127
La Española. See Hispaniola
La Gouffre (site, Guadeloupe) 121
La Isabela (site, Dominican Republic), 74, 99–100, 154–157
La Navidad/En Bas Saline (site, Haiti), 73, 74, 99, 119, 128, 132–133, 154, 157–158, 172
La Patana (site, Cuba), 84
La Providence (site, Water Island, USVI), 319
La Sorcé (site, Vieques, Puerto Rico), 27, 95, 108, 127,138,158–159, 325
La Soufrière Volcano (St. Vincent and the Grenadines), 266
Lac Bay (site, Bonaire) 33
Lagun (site, Bonaire), 13, 33
Laguna de Limones (site, Cuba), 84
Lake Maracaibo (Venezuela), 91

Landa, Fray Diego de, 63, 182
Landfall, Columbus's first, 70(ill.), 72, 159–160
Languages, 17, 18, 35, 45, 82, 149, 160–162, 180, 177–178, 234, 263
Las Casas, Bartolomé de, 32, 85, 96, 110, 122, 153, 157, 162–165, 199, 217, 275, 302
Las Tortugas (Islands), 83, 302. See also Cayman Islands
Layou (site, St. Vincent), 46, 266
Leclerc, General, 288
L'escalier Tete Chien (Snake's Staircase, Dominica), 41
L'Espérance pottery (Martinique), 179
León, Juan Ponce de, 228, 229, 300
Levisa Rock Shelter (site, Cuba), 84
Light (Amerindian philosophy of), 2, 115
Little River culture (Jamaica), 187
Loa (spirits in Vodoun religion), 313–314
Long-distance trade, 28
Lopinot Estate (Trinidad), 38, 66
Los Barrancos (site, Venezuela), 27
Los Buchillones (site, Cuba), 84, 165–166, 304
Los Roques Islands (Venezuela), 166–167
Louquo (Carib hero), 47
Lovers' Retreat (site, Tobago), 167–168, 292
Lucayans, 79, 116, 129, 169, 168–170, 172, 174, 189, 215, 219, 300, 306

Mabiatué (Taíno chief), 217
Macana. See War club
Macapaima (pottery), 12
Macro-Dabajuroid. See Dabajuroid
Madeira, 75, 268
Madrid Codex (Maya), 281
Magens Bay culture, 297
Maima (Taíno site, Jamaica), 199
Maisabel (site, Puerto Rico), 23, 108, 171–172, 227
Maize, 12, 91, 172–173, 176, 212
Malaria, 94
Majolica pottery, 2, 100, 132, 154, 166, 226, 304
Maloccas (Amerindian houses), 116, 282
Mama Dglo (folklore figure, Trinidad), 295
Mamora Bay culture (Antigua), 10, 142
Maniabón Hills (Cuba), 84
Manioc, 17, 45, 47–48, 56–59, 173, 272. See also Cassava
Manoa (Golden City of), 232
Manos and metates, 172
Maravilla (Spanish treasure galleon). See Nuestra Señora de las Maravillas, wreck of
Marcasite. See Fool's gold
Margarita Island (Venezuela), 75, 173–174, 293
Margarite, Pedro de, 156
Marigot (Saint Martin), 253
Marley, Bob, 146, 193, 235
Maroon War, First, 175
Maroons, 1–2, 174–179, 188, 197, 255
    art, 177
Martinique, 76, 179–181
Martyr, Peter, 83, 181, 199, 217, 275

Marx, Robert (treasure diver), 204
Mas' camps (Carnival, Trinidad), 53–54, 296
Matapi (Cassava squeezing container), 58
Matawi (Maroons), 177
Matinino. *See* Martinique
Maya, 37, 63–64, 80–82, 182–186, 280–281
Maya (Putun), 81
Maya Caste War, 185
Mayapan (Yucatán, Mexico), 81, 298
Mayo (site, Trinidad), 293
Mayobanex (Taíno chief), 75, 99, 125, 217
Mayoid (pottery), 186
Mazuelo, Pedro de, 199
Mediator (shipwreck, Curaçao), 90, 132, 308
Meillacan (pottery), 117, 145, 186–187, 213, 215, 226
Mérida (Mexico), 184
Mermaids (Tobago), 295
Mestizos, 34, 85
Metalworking, 135, 154
Metamorphosis in Amerindian thought, 277
Mexican Explorers and Divers Club (CEDAM), 63–64, 305
Middle Caicos Island, 23, 95
Milan, 181
Milford (site, Tobago), 211, 292
Mill Reef culture (Antigua), 10, 142
Mirrors, 2, 173, 219, 321
Miskito, 187–188
Mission Indians/villages (Trinidad), 186, 241, 244, 293–294
Mola (traditional Cuna blouse), 87–88
Molasses, 268
Molasses Reef wreck, 188–189, 306
Monte Cristi, wreck of, 100, 307
Montego Bay (pottery style, Jamaica), 218
Montejo, Francisco de, 184, 306
Montserrat, 111–112, 189–190
Moon, Amerindian beliefs about, 58, 78
Moore Town (Jamaica), 175
Morel (site, Guadeloupe), 120
Morgan, Henry, 145
Morne des Sauteurs (Grenada), 118
Mother (Earth) goddess figures, 47, 88, 277, 295
Mother-of-pearl, 9, 127, 137, 240, 253
Mount Concordia, Treaty of (1648), 253
Mount Irvine (site, Tobago), 292
Muisca tribe (Colombia), 107
Music, 190–195
    Amerindian, 16, 79, 88
    historical and recent, 66

Nago (African society), 313
Nanny. *See* Granny Nanny
Nanny Town (site, Jamaica), 176, 197
Napoleon, 121, 288
Narcotics. *See* Hallucinogens
Narváez, Pánfilo de, 162
National Institute of Anthropology and History (INAH, Mexico), 64, 305

Natural History of the Indies (by Gonzalo Fernández de Oviedo y Valdés), 214
Ndyuka (Maroons), 177
Nelson's Dockyard (Antigua), 11(ill.), 133(ill.), 198
Nepoios (Amerindian tribe, Trinidad), 231
Nevis, 134
New Seville (site, Jamaica), 132, 145, 181, 199–200
Newton Plantation (Barbados), 200–201
Nicaragua, 187
Nicolesa, La (wreck of, Cancun, Mexico), 306
Nigeria, 313
Nijmegan, Peace of (1678), 17
Niña (Columbus's ship), 70, 73
Niño, Pedro Alonso, 219
Nombre de Dios (Panama), 101
Nord Saliña (Mestizo village, Bonaire), 34
Norman Estate (site, St. Martin), 14, 201–202
Nuestra Señora de Atocha, wreck of, 202–203, 306–307
Nuestra Señora de Guadeloupe, wreck of, 307
Nuestra Señora de la Concepción, wreck of, 203–204, 306
Nuestra Señora de las Maravillas, wreck of, 204–205
Nueva Cadiz (site, Margarita Island, Venezuela), 174

Obatala (Santería and Vodoun deity), 247, 313
Obeah, 134, 135, 146, 192, 200, 207–209, 251, 255, 261, 285
Obsidian, 81
Ocarina, 12
Ocelot (symbolism), 222, 294
Ocumaroid (pottery tradition), 33
Ogun (god of African-Caribbean religions), 210, 247, 313
Ojeda, Alonso de, 17, 41, 89, 173
Olocupinele (Cuna deity), 88
Olorun (Santería and Vodoun deity), 313
Oracles, 81
Orellana, Francisco de, 5
Orinoco River valley, 12–13, 27, 56, 62, 76, 104, 172, 186, 211, 212, 231, 236, 240, 292, 317
Orisha/Shango (Trinidad), 118, 135, 207, 209–211, 251, 294–295
Oropuche Lagoon (Trinidad), 24, 292
Ortoire (site, Trinidad), 13, 211
Ortoiroid, 13, 25, 150, 179, 211–212, 227, 260, 264, 292
Oshun (Santería deity), 247
Osoid, 172, 212
Ostiones (site and culture, Dominican Republic), 99, 127, 213, 271
Ostionoid, 80, 99, 108, 116, 145, 186, 212–213, 227, 271, 287
Otaheite (sugar species), 268
Ovando, Nicolás de, 6, 29, 76, 109, 128, 225
Oviedo y Valdés, Gonzalo Fernández de, 92, 191, 213–214, 289
Owia (St. Vincent and the Grenadines), 266
Oysters (pearl bearing), 218

Painted Cave (site, Cuba), 14

Paleopathology, 94, 220
Palmetto pottery, 116, 168, 213, 215–216
Palo Seco (site, Trinidad), 27, 216, 292
Palos (Spain), 69, 70
Pan (music, Trinidad). *See* Steel band
Panama, 78
Panama Canal, 86
Pané, Father Ramón, 74, 124, 216–218
Panther Man, 150
Papiamento, 18
Paquemar pottery (Martinique), 179
Paradise Park (site, Jamaica), 218
Paramaka (Maroons), 177
Parang (music, Trinidad), 66, 194, 294
Paraquita Bay (site, Tortola, BVI), 287
Paris, Treaty of (1763), 98, 263
Patterson, William, 93
Paya (Amerindians), 187
Peabody Museum (Harvard University), 63
Peace Cave (Jamaica), 175
Pearl diving, 219
Pearl Island. *See* Cubagua Island
Pearls (gems), 79, 169, 173, 218–220
Pearls (site, Grenada), 117, 220–221
Pelée, Mount (volcano, Martinique), 179
Pelican Man, 149
Pepper pot, 135, 168, 186, 221
Petite Martinique Island, 117
Petroglyphs and pictographs, 23, 39, 46, 84, 89, 100, 120, 153, 241, 257, 259, 260, 266, 300
Petticoat inspectors (Guadeloupe), 122
Pewter, 224–5, 305
Philipsburg (Sint Maarten), 253
Phips, William, 203, 307
Picture writing (Cuna), 88
Pidgin languages, 82, 161
Pigorini Museum, Rome, 321
Pilgrimage (Maya), 182, 281, 299
Piña Chan, Román, 63, 305
Pinta (Columbus's ship), 70, 72, 73, 188
Pinzón, Martín Alonso, 69, 72, 219
Pirates, 145
Pitch Lake (site, Trinidad), 31, 221–223, 231
Pizarro, Francisco de, 21, 184
Plantation archaeology, 133, 134. *See also individual sites*
Plazas, 39, 141, 153, 171, 191, 218, 300. *See also* Ball-game
Pliny (Roman author), 218
Plymouth Pottery Complex (Tobago), 167, 292
Poor whites, 26
Pope Alexander VI, 286
Port Royal (Jamaica), 133, 145, 223–225, 305
Ports of trade, 28, 138, 159, 189
Portuguese, 25
Preceramic/aceramic, distinction between, 15
Price, Richards and Sally, 177
Prince's Town (Trinidad). *See* Savana Grande

Privateers, 223
Proselyte (shipwreck site, St. Martin), 132
Prosperity (site, St. Croix), 257
Prosperity phase pottery (St. Croix), 257
Puerto Plata (Hispaniola), 157
Puerto Real (site, Haiti), 129, 132, 225–227
Puerto Rico, 227–230
Punta (pottery, Dominican Republic), 18
Punta Candelero (site, Puerto Rico), 158, 325
Putun Maya (Mexico), 182, 281, 298
Puuc (pottery, Yucatán, Mexico), 81

Quao (Maroon chief, Jamaica), 175
Quartz, 116, 189, 191, 232, 240, 258
Queen Conch *(Strombus gigas),* 7, 9, 17, 63, 79, 89, 130, 142, 166, 201, 218, 252, 281, 282. *See also* Conch
Queen Elizabeth I, 5, 219, 231, 284
Queen Elizabeth II, 60

Rada (African-Caribbean religion, Trinidad), 209–210
Ralegh, Sir Walter, 5, 108, 221, 231–232, 293, 317
Ramora fish, 302
Rancho Peludo (pottery), 91
Ras Tafari. *See* Selassie, Haile
Rastafarianism, 146, 161, 193, 232–236
Rattles, 191
Reader's Point Wreck (Jamaica), 307–308
Redondan 14, 56, 84, 187
Redware (pottery style), 213, 218
Reggae, 146, 193
Rendezvous Bay (site, Anguilla) 8
Richmond (site, St. Croix), 257
Rincon (Amerindian village, Bonaire), 34
Roatán Island (Honduras), 113, 266
Rodney, Admiral, 198, 258
Roldán, Francisco, 75, 76, 125, 156, 157
Ronquín (site, Orinoco River valley, Venezuela), 236
Ronquinan (culture, Venezuela), 62, 236–237, 239, 319
Rosa, Santa (Arima, Trinidad), 50, 242, 243(ill.)
Rouse, Irving, 62, 319, 325
Rubber, 64, 214
Rum, used to pay slaves, 254
Rumba, 193

Saba, 132
Sacrifice, animal, 247, 314
Saints, Christian (relationship with African-Caribbean religions), 85, 121, 192, 242–243, 245–247, 295, 313–314
Saladoid, 62, 115–116, 127, 131, 137, 141–142, 171, 179, 216, 220, 221–222, 227, 236, 239–240, 257, 264–265
Salsa, 85
Salt and salt pans, 168, 215, 253, 301
Salt Cay (Turks and Caicos), 301
Salt Pond Hill (site, Great Inagua Island, Bahamas), 117

Salt River (site, St. Croix), 23, 108, 240–241
Salybia (Carib settlement, Dominica), 41, 42(ill.), 44, 59, 147
Samana Cay, 169
San Blas Islands (Panama), 86, 285
San Esteban, wreck of, 307
San Felipe del Morro (fortress, San Juan, Puerto Rico), 229
San Gervasio (site, Cozumel, Mexico), 81, 182
San Hironimo (site, Curaçao), 90, 132
San Juan (Puerto Rico), 229
San Salvador Island, 72, 159, 300
Sandy Bay (St. Vincent and the Grenadines), 266
Sandy Ground (site, Anguilla), 8
Sandy Point (site, Tobago), 292
Santa Cruz (site, Aruba), 17
Santa Fe Capitulations, 69. *See also* Columbus, Christopher
Santa Maria (Columbus's ship), 70, 72, 99, 119, 157–158
Santa María de la Antigua del Darién, 21, 92
Santa Rosa Carib Community (Arima, Trinidad), 50, 241–245, 294
Santería, 85, 245–248, 251, 255
Santiago (Spanish galleon), 60
Santiago de Cuba, 85
Santo Domingo (Hispaniola), 156–157, 199, 214
Saracas (Grenadian festivals), 118
Saramaka (Maroons), 177
Savana Grande (Trinidad), 293
Savanne Suazey (site, Grenada), 267
Savaneta (Trinidad), 293
Scottish Settlers (in Panama), 92–93
Sea Turtle House. *See* Golden Rock
Seboruco (site, Cuba), 14
Selassie, Haile, 146, 232, 234–235. *See also* Rastafarianism
Seminoles and Seminole Maroons (Florida, USA), 176
Serpentine, 137
Serpent's Mouth, 75
Seville (Spain), 70, 76, 162
Sexuality (Amerindian symbolism about), 58, 114, 221, 276, 278
    diseases associated with, 94, 137, 289
Shamanism, 31–32, 47, 66–67, 88, 104–105, 190–191, 207, 222, 248–251, 279, 284–286, 317–318
Shango. *See* Orisha/Shango
Shango Baptists. *See* Spiritual Baptists
Shark, 80, 167
Shell artifacts/ornaments, 34, 56, 63, 79, 91, 120, 130, 137, 138, 142, 147, 168, 202, 241, 252, 253, 267, 282, 300
Shell middens, 79, 149, 150, 173, 179, 211, 216, 226, 227, 252, 264, 267, 292, 319
Shipwrecks, 202–205, 283–284, 306. *See also individual ships*
Shirley Heights (site, Antigua), 11(ill.), 132
Shouters. *See* Spiritual Baptists
Silk-cotton tree. *See* Ceiba tree
Silver (ingots), 202, 204
Silver Sands (site, Barbados), 95, 251–252
Sint Maarten/Saint-Martin, 252–253

Ska, 193
Skulls, human (cache of 115), 305
Slave villages, 30, 132, 200, 255
Slavery, 65, 112, 145, 169, 225–226, 253–256
    archaeological legacy of, 255
    See also Historical archaeology
Smallpox, 94
Smith Sloop Point (site, Great Inagua Island, Bahamas), 117
Smoke ceremony (Arima, Trinidad), 243
Snake imagery, 41, 58, 313, 317
Son (Cuban music), 193
Sorcery. *See* Obeah, Orisha/Shango, Santería, Shamanism
Soucouyan(t) (evil spirit), 261, 295
Spanish-American War, 85
Spanish Town (Jamaica), 146
Spatula. *See* Vomiting spatula
Spiritual Baptist Church (Barbados), 26, 118
St. Ann's Bay (Jamaica), 78, 101, 145, 199
St. Croix (USVI), 48, 135, 256–258
St. Eustatius, 115–116, 135, 258–259
St. John (USVI), 259–260
St. John Oropuche (site, Trinidad), 13
St. John's Bahamas wreck, 306
St. Kitts and Nevis, 260–262, 285
St. Lucia, 262–264
St. Thomas (USVI), 264–265
St. Ursula (and 11,000 martyred virgins), 257, 259, 265
St. Vincent and the Grenadines, 46, 112–113, 265–267
Stann Creek (Belize), 50, 113
Star Gate Blue Hole (Andros Island), 303
Steel band (music, Trinidad), 54, 194, 296
Stephens, John Lloyd, 81, 298
Suazey/Suazoid, 25, 117, 120, 130, 131, 179, 252, 265–266, 267–268
Sugar/sugar plantations, 26, 30, 85, 111–112, 121, 129, 134, 180, 189, 226, 254, 261, 268–270
Sumo (Amerindians), 187
Suriname, 177
Sweetwater (site, Jamaica). *See* Paradise Park
Syphilis, 94

Taboos, 45
Tagua-Tagua plant, 114
Taíno (Arawak), 84, 271–280
    arts and crafts, 272–274
    ball-game, 275
    cosmogony, 278
    as first slaves, 224
    heritage (in modern times), 279–280
    language, 160
    population decline, 33, 279
    religion and mythology, 39, 67, 153, 276–280
    shamans, 250, 279
    social/political organization, 274–276
    spiritual life, 217
    subsistence, 271–272

Taíno (Arawak) *(continued)*
  trade and exchange, 273–274
  temple floor preserved on St. John, USVI, 259
  warfare, 275–276
Tancah (site, Mexico), 81, 182, 280–281
Tanki Flip (site, Aruba), 17, 172, 282–283
Tapioca, 58
Tattoo, 87–88
Taylor, Douglas, 35, 43, 161
Tegramond (Carib chief), 261
Ten Sail, wreck of, 60, 283–284, 307
Thatch, palm, 304
Thompson, Edward Herbert, 63, 304
Tibes (site, Puerto Rico), 23, 108, 227, 229
Tipiti (Cassava squeezing implement), 242. *See also* Carib
      Snake
Tivitivas (Amerindian tribe, Venezuela), 232. *See also* Warao
Tobago beach(ill.), 291
Tobacco, 10, 29, 31, 45, 47, 65, 67, 85, 88, 201, 214, 222,
      249, 261, 284–286, 278–279, 317–318
Tobacco spittle (in Taíno mythology), 279
Toltecs, 64
Tordesillas, Treaty of, 286
Tortola (BVI), 286–288
Tourism, 136, 253
Toussaint L'Ouverture, 129, 288
Trants (site, Montserrat), 189
Trees, spiritual importance of, 16, 61, 67, 105, 146, 207,
      217, 278, 288–290, 324
Trelawney Town (Jamaica), 175
Trepanning, 94
Triana, Rodrigo de, 72
Trinidad and Tobago, 75, 65–66, 104, 125, 216, 231, 239,
      269(ill.), 290–297, 303–304, 317
  cacao plantations in, 37–38, 65–66
  folklore of, 295
Troumassoid, 25, 120, 130, 131, 179, 265, 297–298
Trova (music, Cuba), 193
Trumpets (Conch-shell), 191, 287
Tuberculosis, 94
Tulum (site, Mexico), 81, 182, 298–300
Tumbaga, 64, 108. *See also* Aesthetic of brilliance; Gold
Tunapuna (Trinidad), 293
Tupinamba (Amerindians, Brazil), 5
Turey (guanín), 41, 115. *See also* Aesthetic of brilliance; Gold
Turks and Caicos, 72, 215, 300–301
Turtles, 80, 83, 116, 154, 166, 218, 281, 300, 301–302
Turquoise, 189, 240
Tutu (site, St. Thomas, USVI), 265
Typhoid, 94

Ulloa, Alfonso de, 217
Underwater archaeology, 60, 63–64, 90, 99, 100, 150,
      153–154, 165, 202—205, 223, 303–309
UNESCO World Heritage Site (Havana, Cuba), 85
Union Creek (site, Great Inagua Island, Bahamas), 116

Urabá, Gulf of, 21
Urca de Lima, wreck of, 307

Valencia culture (Venezuela), 166
Valladolid (Spain), 69
Vega Real (Hispaniola), 124
Velázquez, Diego de, 85, 162
Venetian glass, 321
Venezuela (naming of), 17, 311
Venus (planet, Amerinidan significance of), 182, 281, 299
Versailles, Treaty of (1783), 118
Vespucci, Amerigo, 17, 89, 169, 311–312
Vignier III (site, Haiti), 55, 128
Virgin Islands National Park, 259
Vivé (site, Martinique), 179
Vodoun, 129, 251, 255, 285, 312–315
Volcanic ash, preserves Amerindian site, 179
Volcanoes, 323
Vomiting spatula (Taíno), 153, 287, 324
Vulture, South American king, 31–32

Wafer, Lionell, 88, 92
Waldseemüller, Martin, 312
Wanapa (site, Bonaire), 33
Warao, 96, 191, 232, 249, 285, 289, 317–318
War club, 153, 304
Warner, Thomas, 189
Wasp Star (Maya), 281, 299
Water Island (USVI), 319
Watlings Island, 72, 159
Wax, 81
West Indian Crown Conch, 79
West Indian Top Shell *(Cittarium pica)*, 9, 137, 166
Whim Estate (site, St. Croix), 134, 257
White Marl (pottery/culture, Jamaica), 145, 187
White Marl Museum (Jamaica), 146
White-on-red pottery (W-O-R), 9, 62, 99, 109, 127, 137,
      141, 216, 227, 236, 239, 252, 257, 319–320(ill.)
Williams, Pastor Granville, 26
Willoughby, Lord, 142
Women
  Amerindian views/myths about, 179–180, 274, 278
  European views about/relations with, 3–5, 125, 129,
      132, 226
  See also Amazons
Wood
  Amerindian use of and beliefs about, 46, 64, 88, 99,
      104–106, 149–150, 153, 165, 222, 229, 304
  See also Duhos; Trees, spiritual importance of
Woodpeckers, 31, 278
Worldview (Amerindian), 2, 47–48, 88, 114–115, 190, 239,
      249, 276, 288–290. *See also* Shamanism
World War II sites, 90, 319
Wylly, William, 65

Xagua, Bay of (Cuba), 302

Xaraguá (Taíno Kingdom, Hispaniola), 6–7, 16, 28, 75, 105, 128, 289

Yabbas (African-Caribbean pottery), 103, 134
Yambou (site, St. Vincent), 46, 266
Yams, 176
Yankee Town (site, Turks and Caicos), 301
Yao (Amerindian tribe, Trinidad), 231
Yaya (Taíno creator deity), 277–278
Yellow Caribs, 113, 266
Yoruba, 85, 118, 209, 210, 245, 263, 294–295, 313
Yuca. *See* Cassava
Yúcahu (Taíno deity), 8, 59, 217, 276, 321

Zambos, 34
Zemís, 32, 39, 46, 66, 79, 105, 120, 138, 141, 142, 165, 187, 217, 227, 229, 239, 241, 250, 259, 267, 276, 285, 287, 289, 304, 318, 321–325
  fertility associations of, 323
  three-pointers, 322–323(ill.)
  typology, 323
Zic pottery, 9, 62, 99, 115–116, 127, 137, 141, 227, 239, 252, 325–326
Zion (Rastafarian concept of), 234
Zombies, 315
Zouk (music, Martinique), 129, 180, 193
Zuurzak (site, Curaçao), 90

About the Author

Dr. Nicholas J. Saunders is Reader in material culture, Department of Anthropology at University College London. He was educated at the universities of Sheffield, Cambridge, and Southampton and has worked in Mexico, Argentina, Peru, and the Caribbean. He has specialized in the art and symbolism of native Amerindian societies and the archaeology and anthropology of the contact period. He is the author of numerous books and articles on the anthropology of South America and the Caribbean.